SAT®
Premier 2017
with 5 Practice Tests

MAY   2016

SAT®
Premier 2017
with 5 Practice Tests

PUBLISHING

New York

This publication is designed to provide accurate and authoritative information in regard to the subject matter covered. It is sold with the understanding that the publisher is not engaged in rendering legal, accounting, or other professional service. If legal advice or other expert assistance is required, the services of a competent professional should be sought.

© 2016 by Kaplan, Inc.

Published by Kaplan Publishing, a division of Kaplan, Inc.
750 Third Avenue
New York, NY 10017

Printed in the United States of America

10 9 8 7 6 5 4 3 2 1

ISBN-13: 978-1-5062-0228-0

Kaplan Publishing books are available at special quantity discounts to use for sales promotions, employee premiums, or educational purposes. For more information or to purchase books, please call the Simon & Schuster Special Sales Department at 866-506-1949.

Table of Contents

Introduction to the SAT ix

Test-Taking Strategies xiv

Common Testing Myths xvi

How to Use This Book xviii

Digital Resources xxi

PART ONE: MATH

UNIT ONE: MATH INTRODUCTION

CHAPTER 1: Prerequisite Skills & Calculator Usage 5

UNIT TWO: HEART OF ALGEBRA

CHAPTER 2: The Kaplan Method for Math & Linear Equations 19

CHAPTER 3: Systems of Equations 47

CHAPTER 4: Linear Inequalities and Systems of Inequalities 67

UNIT THREE: PROBLEM SOLVING & DATA ANALYSIS

CHAPTER 5: Rates, Ratios, Proportions, and Percentages 85

CHAPTER 6: Scatterplots 117

CHAPTER 7: Two-way Tables, Statistics, and Probability 143

UNIT FOUR: PASSPORT TO ADVANCED MATH

CHAPTER 8: Exponents, Radicals, Polynomials, and Rational Expressions and Equations 177

CHAPTER 9: Functions 207

CHAPTER 10: Quadratic Equations 233

UNIT FIVE: ADDITIONAL TOPICS IN MATH

CHAPTER 11: Geometry 263

CHAPTER 12: Imaginary Numbers and Trigonometry 301

PART TWO: EVIDENCE-BASED READING AND WRITING

UNIT SIX: READING

CHAPTER 13: The Kaplan Method for Reading Comprehension and Reading Test Passage Types 331

CHAPTER 14: Synthesis Questions and the Kaplan Method for Infographics 351

CHAPTER 15: Global and Command of Evidence Questions 369

CHAPTER 16: Connections and Vocab-in-Context Questions 385

CHAPTER 17: Rhetoric 401

CHAPTER 18: Detail and Inference Questions 417

UNIT SEVEN: EXPRESSION OF IDEAS

CHAPTER 19: The Kaplan Methods for Writing & Language and Infographics 435

CHAPTER 20: Organization 455

CHAPTER 21: Development 473

CHAPTER 22: Effective Language Use 491

UNIT EIGHT: STANDARD ENGLISH CONVENTIONS

CHAPTER 23: Sentence Structure 515

CHAPTER 24: Conventions of Usage 535

CHAPTER 25: Conventions of Punctuation 557

PART THREE: THE ESSAY

UNIT NINE: THE ESSAY

CHAPTER 26: The Kaplan Method for the SAT Essay 581

CHAPTER 27: Reading, Analyzing, and Writing the SAT Essay 601

PART FOUR: REVIEW

Putting It All Together 625

PART FIVE: PRACTICE TESTS

Diagnostic Test 639

Diagnostic Test Answers & Explanations 687

Practice Test 1 721

Practice Test 1 Answers & Explanations 771

PART SIX: ANSWERS & EXPLANATIONS 807

CHAPTER 21: Components of the Essay ....

CHAPTER 22: Constructing Your Essay ....

PART THREE: THE ESSAY

UNIT NINE: THE ESSAY

CHAPTER 23: The Applied Method of the SAT Essay ....

CHAPTER 24: Practice, Analysis, and Writing the SAT Essay ....

PART FOUR: REVIEW

Review of all Lessons ....

PART FIVE: PRACTICE TESTS

Diagnostic Test ....

Diagnostic Test Answers & Explanations ....

Practice Test 1 ....

Practice Test 1 Answers & Explanations ....

PART SIX: ANSWERS & EXPLANATIONS

Introduction to the SAT

The first step to achieving SAT success is to learn about the structure of the test and why it's so important for your future. The SAT, like any standardized test, is predictable. The more comfortable you are with the test structure, the more confidently you will approach each question type, thus maximizing your score.

SAT STRUCTURE

The SAT is 3 hours long, or 3 hours and 50 minutes long if you choose to complete the optional Essay Test. It is made up of mostly multiple-choice questions that test two subject areas: Math and Evidence-Based Reading and Writing. The latter is broken into a Reading Test and a Writing & Language Test.

Test	Allotted Time (min.)	Question Count
Reading	65	52
Writing & Language	35	44
Math	80	58
Essay (optional)	50	1
Total	180 OR 230 (w/ essay)	154 OR 155 (w/ essay)

SAT SCORING

SAT scoring can be pretty complex. You will receive one score ranging from 200 to 800 for Evidence-Based Reading and Writing and another for Math. Your overall SAT score will range from 400 to 1600 and is calculated by adding these two scores together. You will receive a separate score for the Essay Test, if you choose to take it.

In addition to your overall scores, you will receive subscores that provide a deeper analysis of your SAT performance. The SAT also gives you a percentile ranking, which allows you to compare your scores with those of other high school students who took the test. For example, a student with a percentile of 63 has earned a score better than 63 percent of test takers.

WHERE AND WHEN TO TAKE THE SAT

The SAT is offered every year on multiple Saturday test dates. Typically, exams are offered in October, November, December, January, March, May, and June. You can take the SAT multiple times. Some states offer special administrations of the SAT on different dates. Sunday tests are available by request for students requiring religious or other exemptions. The SAT is administered at high schools around the country that serve as testing centers. Your high school may or may not be a testing center. Check www.collegeboard.org for a list of testing centers near you. Note that you must register for the SAT approximately one month in advance to avoid paying a late fee. Some SAT test dates also offer SAT Subject Tests. You may not take both the SAT and the Subject Tests in a single sitting.

THE SAT MATH TEST

The SAT Math Test is broken down into a calculator section and a no-calculator section. Questions across the sections consist of multiple-choice, student-produced response (Grid-in), and more comprehensive multi-part question sets.

	Calculator Section	No-Calculator Section	Total
Duration (minutes)	55	25	80
Multiple-choice	30	15	45
Grid-in	8	5	13
Total Questions	38	20	58

The SAT Math Test is divided into four content areas: Heart of Algebra, Problem Solving and Data Analysis, Passport to Advanced Math, and Additional Topics in Math.

SAT Math Test Content Area Distribution	
Heart of Algebra (19 questions)	Analyzing and fluently solving equations and systems of equations; creating expressions, equations, and inequalities to represent relationships between quantities and to solve problems; rearranging and interpreting formulas
Problem Solving and Data Analysis (17 questions)	Creating and analyzing relationships using ratios, proportions, percentages, and units; describing relationships shown graphically; summarizing qualitative and quantitative data

SAT Math Test Content Area Distribution	
Passport to Advanced Math (16 questions)	Rewriting expressions using their structure; creating, analyzing, and fluently solving quadratic and higher-order equations; purposefully manipulating polynomials to solve problems
Additional Topics in Math (6 questions)	Making area and volume calculations in context; investigating lines, angles, triangles, and circles using theorems; and working with trigonometric functions

A few math questions might look like something you'd expect to see on a science or history test. These "crossover" questions are designed to test your ability to use math in real-world scenarios. There are a total of 18 "crossover" questions that will contribute to subscores that span multiple tests. Nine of the questions will contribute to the Analysis in Science subscore, and nine will contribute to the Analysis in History/Social Studies subscore.

THE SAT READING TEST

The SAT Reading Test will focus on your comprehension and reasoning skills when presented with challenging extended prose passages taken from a variety of content areas.

SAT Reading Test Overview	
Timing	65 minutes
Questions	52 passage-based multiple-choice questions
Passages	4 single passages and 1 set of paired passages
Passage Length	500–750 words per passage or passage set

Passages will draw from U.S. and World Literature, History/Social Studies, and Science. One set of History/Social Studies or Science passages will be paired. History/Social Studies and Science passages can also be accompanied by graphical representations of data such as charts, graphs, tables, and so on.

Reading Test Passage Types	
U.S. and World Literature	1 passage with 10 questions
History/Social Studies	2 passages or 1 passage and 1 paired-passage set with 10–11 questions each
Science	2 passages or 1 passage and 1 paired-passage set with 10–11 questions each

The multiple-choice questions for each passage will be arranged in order from the more general to the more specific so that you can actively engage with the entire passage before answering questions about details.

Skills Tested by Reading Test Questions	
Information and Ideas	Close reading, citing textual evidence, determining central ideas and themes
Summarizing	Understanding relationships, interpreting words and phrases in context
Rhetoric	Analyzing word choice, assessing overall text structure, assessing part-whole relationships, analyzing point of view, determining purpose, analyzing arguments
Synthesis	Analyzing multiple texts, analyzing quantitative information

THE SAT WRITING & LANGUAGE TEST

The SAT Writing & Language Test will focus on your ability to revise and edit text from a range of content areas.

SAT Writing & Language Test Overview	
Timing	35 minutes
Questions	44 passage-based multiple-choice questions
Passages	4 single passages with 11 questions each
Passage Length	400–450 words per passage

The SAT Writing & Language Test will contain four single passages, one from each of the following subject areas: Careers, Humanities, History/Social Studies, and Science.

Writing & Language Passage Types	
Careers	Hot topics in "major fields of work" such as information technology and health care
Humanities	Texts about literature, art, history, music, and philosophy pertaining to human culture

Writing & Language Passage Types	
History/Social Studies	Discussion of historical or social sciences topics such as anthropology, communication studies, economics, education, human geography, law, linguistics, political science, psychology, and sociology
Science	Exploration of concepts, findings, and discoveries in the natural sciences including Earth science, biology, chemistry, and physics

Passages will also vary in the "type" of text. A passage can be an argument, an informative or explanatory text, or a nonfiction narrative.

Writing & Language Passage Text Type Distribution	
Argument	1–2 passages
Informative/Explanatory Text	1–2 passages
Nonfiction Narrative	1 passage

Some passages and/or questions will refer to one or more informational graphics that represent data. Questions associated with these graphical representations will ask you to revise and edit the passage based on the data presented in the graphic.

The most prevalent question format on the SAT Writing & Language Test will ask you to choose the best of three alternatives to an underlined portion of the passage or to decide that the current version is the best option. You will be asked to improve the development, organization, and diction in the passages to ensure they conform to conventional standards of English grammar, usage, and style.

Skills Tested by Writing & Language Test Questions	
Expression of Ideas (24 questions)	Development, organization, and effective language use
Standard English Conventions (20 questions)	Sentence structure, conventions of usage, and conventions of punctuation

THE SAT ESSAY TEST (OPTIONAL)

The SAT Essay Test will assess your college and career readiness by testing your abilities to read and analyze a high-quality source document and write a coherent analysis of the source supported with critical reasoning and evidence from the given text.

The SAT Essay Test features an argumentative source text of 650–750 words aimed toward a large audience. Passages will examine ideas, debates, and shifts in the arts and sciences as well as civic, cultural, and political life. Rather than having a simple for/against structure, these passages will be nuanced and will relate views on complex subjects. These passages will also be logical in their structure and reasoning.

It is important to note that prior knowledge is not required.

The SAT Essay Test prompt will ask you to explain how the presented passage's author builds an argument to convince an audience. In writing your essay, you may analyze elements such as the author's use of evidence, reasoning, style, and persuasion; you will not be limited to those elements listed, however.

Rather than writing about whether you agree or disagree with the presented argument, you will write an essay in which you analyze how the author makes an argument.

The SAT Essay Test will be broken down into three categories for scoring: Reading, Analysis, and Writing. Each of these elements will be scored on a scale of 1 to 4 by two graders, for a total score of 2 to 8 for each category.

TEST-TAKING STRATEGIES

You have already learned about the overall structure of the SAT as well as the structure of the three tests it entails: Reading, Writing & Language, and Math. The strategies outlined in this section can be applied to any of these tests.

The SAT is different from the tests you are used to taking in school. The good news is that you can use the SAT's particular structure to your advantage.

For example, on a test given in school, you probably go through the questions in order. You spend more time on the harder questions than on the easier ones because harder questions are usually worth more points. You probably often show your work because your teacher tells you that how you approach a question is as important as getting the correct answer.

This approach is not optimal for the SAT. On the SAT, you benefit from moving around within a section if you come across tough questions, because the harder questions are worth the same number of points as the easier questions. It doesn't matter how you arrive at the correct answer—only that you bubble in the correct answer choice.

STRATEGY #1: TRIAGING THE TEST

You do not need to complete questions on the SAT in order. Every student has different strengths and should attack the test with those strengths in mind. Your main objective on the SAT should be to score as many points as you can. While approaching questions out of order may seem counter-intuitive, it is a surefire way to achieve your best score.

Just remember, you can skip around within each section, but you cannot work on a section other than the one you've been instructed to work on.

To triage the test effectively, do the following:

- First, work through all the easy questions that you can do quickly. Skip questions that are hard or time-consuming.

- For the Reading and Writing & Language Tests, start with the passage you find most manageable and work toward the one you find most challenging. You do not need to go in order.

- Second, work through the questions that are doable but time-consuming.

- Third, work through the hard questions.

- If you run out of time, pick a Letter of the Day for remaining questions.

A Letter of the Day is an answer choice letter (A, B, C, or D) that you choose before Test Day to select for questions you guess on.

STRATEGY #2: ELIMINATION

Even though there is no wrong-answer penalty on the SAT, elimination is still a crucial strategy. If you can determine that one or more answer choices are definitely incorrect, you can increase your chances of getting the correct answer by paring the selection down.

To eliminate answer choices, do the following:

- Read each answer choice.

- Cross out the answer choices that are incorrect.

- Remember: There is no wrong-answer penalty, so take your best guess.

STRATEGY #3: GUESSING

Each multiple-choice question on the SAT has four answer choices and no wrong-answer penalty. That means if you have no idea how to approach a question, you have a 25 percent chance of randomly choosing the correct answer. Even though there's a 75 percent chance of selecting the incorrect answer, you won't lose any points for doing so. The worst that can happen on the SAT is that you'll earn zero points on a question, which means you should always at least take a guess, even when you have no idea what to do.

When guessing on a question, do the following:

- Always try to strategically eliminate answer choices before guessing.
- If you run out of time, or have no idea what a question is asking, pick a Letter of the Day.

COMMON TESTING MYTHS

Since its inception, the SAT has gone through various revisions, but it has always been an integral part of the college admissions process. As a result of its significance and the changes it has undergone, a number of rumors and myths have circulated about the exam. In this section, we'll dispel some of the most common ones. As always, you can find the most up-to-date information about the SAT at the College Board website (https://www.collegeboard.org).

Myth: **There is a wrong-answer penalty on the SAT to discourage guessing.**

Fact: While this statement was true a few years ago, it is no longer true. Older versions of the SAT had a wrong-answer penalty so that students who guessed on questions would not have an advantage over students who left questions blank. This penalty has been removed; make sure you never leave an SAT question blank!

Myth: **Answer choice C is most likely to be the correct answer.**

Fact: This rumor has roots in human psychology. Apparently, when people such as high school teachers, for example, design an exam, they have a slight bias toward answer choice C when assigning correct answers. While humans do write SAT questions, a computer randomizes the distribution of correct choices; statistically, therefore, each answer choice is equally likely to be the correct answer.

Myth: **The SAT is just like another test in school.**

Fact: While the SAT covers some of the same content as your high school math, literature, and English classes, it also presents concepts in ways that are fundamentally different. While you might be able to solve a math problem in a number of different ways on an algebra test, the SAT places a heavy emphasis on working through questions as quickly and efficiently as possible.

Myth: **You have to get all the questions correct to get a perfect score.**

Fact: Many students have reported missing several questions on the SAT and being pleasantly surprised to receive perfect scores. Their experience is not atypical: Usually, you can miss a few questions and still get a coveted perfect score. The makers of the SAT use a technique called scaling to ensure that an SAT score conveys the same information from year to year, so you might be able to miss a couple more questions on a slightly harder SAT exam and miss fewer questions on an easier SAT exam and get the same scores. Keep a positive attitude throughout the SAT, and in many cases, your scores will pleasantly surprise you.

Myth: **You can't prepare for the SAT.**

Fact: You've already proven this myth false by buying this book. While the SAT is designed to fairly test students regardless of preparation, you can gain a huge advantage by familiarizing yourself with the structure and content of the exam. By working through the questions and practice tests available to you, you'll ensure that nothing on the SAT catches you by surprise and that you do everything you can to maximize your score. Your Kaplan resources help you structure this practice in the most efficient way possible, and provide you with helpful strategies and tips as well.

HOW TO USE THIS BOOK

WELCOME TO KAPLAN!

Congratulations on taking this important step in your college admissions process! By studying with Kaplan, you'll maximize your score on the SAT, a major factor in your overall college application.

Our experience shows that the greatest SAT score increases result from active engagement in the preparation process. Kaplan will give you direction, focus your preparation, and teach you the specific skills and effective test-taking strategies you need to know for the SAT. We will help you achieve your top performance on Test Day, but your effort is crucial. The more you invest in preparing for the SAT, the greater your chances of achieving your target score and getting into your top-choice college.

Are you registered for the SAT? Kaplan cannot register you for the official SAT. If you have not already registered for the upcoming SAT, talk to your high school guidance counselor or visit the College Board's website at www.collegeboard.org to register online and for information on registration deadlines, test sites, accommodations for students with disabilities, and fees.

PRACTICE TESTS

Kaplan's practice tests are just like the actual SAT. By taking a practice exam you will prepare yourself for the actual Test Day experience. One diagnostic test and a second practice test are included in this book. There are three additional practice tests in your online companion. See the Digital Resources section to learn how to access your online practice tests. You can score your tests by hand using the score conversion tables in this book, or log into the online companion for easy online scoring.

EXTRA PRACTICE

You need to reinforce what you learn in each chapter by consistently practicing the Kaplan Methods and Strategies. Each chapter contains additional practice problems that reinforce the concepts explained in that chapter. These questions are great practice for the real SAT. Answers & Explanations are provided in the back of the book.

SMARTPOINTS

Each chapter contains a breakdown of SmartPoints. By studying the information released by the College Board, Kaplan has been able to determine how often certain topics are likely to show up on the SAT, and therefore how many points these topics are worth on Test Day. If you master a given topic, you can expect to earn the corresponding number of SmartPoints on Test Day. The breakdown of SmartPoints for Math, Reading, and Writing & Language are summarized in the following tables. You can also see how these topics align to chapters in this book.

Math			
SmartPoint Category	**# of Points**	**Sub-Categories**	**SAT Chapter**
Linear Equations	110	Linear Equations, Graphs, Word Problems	Ch. 2
Systems of Linear Equations	50	Systems of Equations, Word Problems, Intersecting Graphs	Ch. 3
Inequalities	40	Inequalities, 1-D Graphs of Inequalities, 2-D Graphs of Inequalities	Ch. 4
Rates, Ratios, Proportions, and Percentages	80	Rates, Ratios, Proportions, Measurement/ Units, and Percents	Ch. 5
Scatterplots	40	Scatterplots, Lines of Best Fit, Modeling Data	Ch. 6
Statistics and Probability	50	Descriptive Statistics, Probability, TwoWay Tables, Graphical Organizers	Ch. 7
Exponents	80	Exponents, Radicals, Rational Expressions/ Equations, and Polynomial Operations	Ch. 8
Functions	50	Functions and Graphs of Functions	Ch. 9

Quadratics	40	Quadratic Equations, Modeling Data, Parabolas, Systems of Mixed Equations	Ch. 10
Geometry	40	Lines, Angles, Triangles, Similarity, Congruence, Proofs, Circles, 3D Shapes	Ch. 11
Imaginary Numbers	10	Imaginary Numbers	Ch. 12
Trigonometry	10	Trigonometry	Ch. 12
TOTAL	**600**		

Reading			
SmartPoint Category	**# of Points**	**Sub-Categories**	**SAT Chapter(s)**
Command of Evidence	60		Ch. 15
Vocab-in-Context	60		Ch. 16
Rhetoric	50	Analyzing Word Choice, Overall Text Structure, Part-Whole Text Structure, Point of View, Purpose, Claims & Counterclaims, Reasoning, and Evidence	Ch. 17
Inference	35	Determining Implicit Meanings, Using Analogical Reasoning	Ch. 18
Synthesis—Analyzing Quantitative Information	35		Ch. 14
Synthesis—Paired Passages	25		Ch. 14
Global	10	Determining Central Ideas & Themes, Summarizing	Ch. 15
Detail	15	Determining Explicit Meanings	Ch. 18
Connections	10	Understanding Relationships	Ch. 16
TOTAL	**300**		

Writing & Language			
SmartPoint Category	# of Points	Sub-Categories	SAT Chapter(s)
Effective Language Use	60	Precision, Concision, Style & Tone, Syntax	Ch. 22
Sentence Formation	60	Sentence Boundaries, Subordination & Coordination, Parallel Structure, Modifier Placement	Ch. 23
Organization	50	Logical Sequence; Introductions, Conclusions, and Transitions	Ch. 20
Usage	40	Pronouns, Possessive Determiners, Pronoun-Antecedent Agreement, Subject-Verb Agreement, Noun Agreement, Frequently Confused Words, Logical Comparison, Conventional Expression (Idioms), Shifts in Construction	Ch. 24
Development	40	Proposition, Support, Focus	Ch. 21
Punctuation	40	End-of-Sentence Punctuation, Within-Sentence Punctuation, Possessive Nouns & Pronouns, Items in a Series, Nonrestrictive & Parenthetical Elements, Unnecessary Punctuation	Ch. 25
Quantitative	10		Ch. 19
TOTAL	300		

DIGITAL RESOURCES

Register Your Online Companion

To access your online companion:

1. Go to kaptest.com/booksonline.

2. Follow the on-screen instructions. Have this book available.

Join a Live Online Event

Kaplan's SAT Live Online sessions are interactive, instructor-led prep lessons that you can participate in from anywhere you have Internet access.

SAT Live Online sessions are held in our state-of-the-art visual classroom: Actual lessons in real time, just like a physical classroom experience. Interact with your teacher using chat, whiteboards, and polling. Just like courses at Kaplan centers, SAT Live Online sessions are led by top Kaplan instructors.

To register for an SAT Live Online event:

1. Once you've signed in to your student home page, open your syllabus.

2. In the Syllabus window, go to the Live Online Registration menu option.

3. Click on the link. A separate window will appear with registration instructions.

SAT Live Online events are scheduled to take place throughout the year. Please check the registration page with dates and times.

SAT PRACTICE TESTS

Your SAT online companion includes three additional full-length practice tests. We recommend you complete these practice tests as you make your way through the content of this book. After completing each practice test, you'll receive a detailed online score report. Use this summary to help you focus and review the content areas that comprise your greatest areas of improvement.

SAT Videos and Quizzes

Your SAT online companion includes a variety of videos and quizzes. The following icons indicate what is available for you online.

 Video: a short instructional video from Kaplan SAT experts

 Quiz: a series of test-like questions to practice for Test Day

I'M OVERWHELMED. WHERE DO I START?

No matter what, read Introduction to the SAT. Then, take the Diagnostic Test provided in this book to identify the SmartPoint categories that you need to address in order to get the most points on Test Day. Then, use this table to help you prioritize and find the right practice in your book.

Math SmartPoint Category (# of SmartPoints)	Chapter
Linear Equations (110)	Chapter 2
Rates, Ratios, Proportions, and Percentages (80)	Chapter 5
Exponents (80)	Chapter 8
Systems of Linear Equations (50)	Chapter 3
Statistics & Probability (50)	Chapter 7
Functions (50)	Chapter 9
Inequalities (40)	Chapter 4
Quadratics (40)	Chapter 10
Geometry (40)	Chapter 11
Trigonometry (10)	Chapter 12
Imaginary Numbers (10)	Chapter 12

Reading SmartPoint Category (# of SmartPoints)	Chapter
Synthesis (60)	Chapter 14
Vocab-in-Context (60)	Chapter 16
Citing Textual Evidence (60)	Chapter 15
Rhetoric (50)	Chapter 17
Inferences (35)	Chapter 18
Detail (15)	Chapter 18
Global (10)	Chapter 15
Connections (10)	Chapter 16

Writing & Language SmartPoint Categories (# of SmartPoints)	Chapter
Effective Language Use (60)	Chapter 22
Sentence Formation (60)	Chapter 23
Organization (50)	Chapter 20
Punctuation (40)	Chapter 25
Development (40)	Chapter 21
Usage (40)	Chapter 24
Quantitative (10)	Chapter 19

PART ONE

Math

Math Introduction

BY THE END OF THIS UNIT, YOU WILL BE ABLE TO:

1. Identify the arithmetic and algebra concepts needed to get the most out of this book

2. Determine which calculators are best to use on the SAT

3. Develop best practices for effective use of your calculator

Math

PREREQUISITE SKILLS & CALCULATOR USAGE

Chapter 1

Even More

Math Foundations

Key

 Book Assignment

 Online Video Assignment

 Online Quiz Assignment

CHAPTER 1

Prerequisite Skills & Calculator Usage

CHAPTER OBJECTIVES

By the end of this chapter, you will be able to:

- Identify skills necessary to obtain the full benefits of the math section of this book and to hone skills not fully developed

- Use efficiency tips to boost your Test Day speed

- Distinguish between questions that need a calculator and questions in which manual calculations are more efficient

- Utilize strategies that can help when you don't know how to start a question

- Identify how expert test takers use their calculators in a balanced way

COURSE PREREQUISITES

This course focuses on the skills that are tested on the SAT. It assumes a working knowledge of arithmetic, algebra, and geometry. Before you dive into the subsequent chapters where you'll try test-like questions, there are a number of concepts—ranging from basic arithmetic to geometry—that you should master. The following sections contain a brief review of these concepts.

Algebra and Arithmetic

- Order of operations is one of the most fundamental of all arithmetic rules. A well-known mnemonic device for remembering this order is PEMDAS: Please Excuse My Dear Aunt Sally. This translates to Parentheses, Exponents, Multiplication/Division, Addition/Subtraction. Note: Multiplication and division have the same priority, as do addition and subtraction. Perform multiplication and division from left to right (even if it means division before multiplication) and treat addition and subtraction the same way.

$$(14 - 4 \div 2)^2 - 3 + (2 - 1)$$
$$= (14 - 2)^2 - 3 + 1$$
$$= 12^2 - 3 + 1$$
$$= 144 - 3 + 1$$
$$= 142$$

- Three basic properties of number (and variable) manipulation—commutative, associative, and distributive—will assist you with algebra on Test Day. These properties are outlined next.

1) Commutative: Numbers can swap places and still provide the same mathematical result. This is valid only for addition and multiplication.

$$a + b = b + a \rightarrow 3 + 4 = 4 + 3$$
$$a \times b = b \times a \rightarrow 3 \times 4 = 4 \times 3$$

BUT: $3 - 4 \neq 4 - 3$ and $3 \div 4 \neq 4 \div 3$

2) Associative: Different number groupings will provide the same mathematical result. This is valid only for addition and multiplication.

$$(a + b) + c = a + (b + c) \rightarrow (4 + 5) + 6 = 4 + (5 + 6)$$
$$(a \times b) \times c = a \times (b \times c) \rightarrow (4 \times 5) \times 6 = 4 \times (5 \times 6)$$

BUT: $(4 - 5) - 6 \neq 4 - (5 - 6)$ and $(4 \div 5) \div 6 \neq 4 \div (5 \div 6)$

3) Distributive: A number that is multiplied by the sum or difference of two other numbers can be rewritten as the first number multiplied by the two others individually. This does *not* work with division.

$$a(b + c) = ab + ac \rightarrow 6(x + 3) = 6x + 6(3) = 6x + 18$$
$$a(b - c) = ab - ac \rightarrow 3(y - 2) = 3y + 3(-2) = 3y - 6$$

BUT: $12 \div (6 + 2) \neq 12 \div 6 + 12 \div 2$

✳ Note: When subtracting an expression in parentheses, such as in $4 - (x + 3)$, distribute the negative sign outside the parentheses first: $4 + (-x - 3) \rightarrow 1 - x$. Be particularly careful with these, as negative signs are easily lost in calculations.

- Make sure you can correctly manipulate negative numbers and that you understand the additive inverse property: Subtracting a positive number is the same as adding its negative. Likewise, subtracting a negative number is the same as adding its positive.

$$r - s = r + (-s) \rightarrow 22 - 15 = 22 + (-15) = 7$$
$$r - (-s) = r + s \rightarrow 22 - (-15) = 22 + 15 = 37$$

- You should be comfortable manipulating both proper and improper fractions. To add and subtract fractions, first find a common denominator, then add the numerators together. Multiplication is straightforward: Multiply the numerators together, then repeat for the denominators. Cancel when possible to simplify the answer. Dividing by a fraction is the same as multiplying by its reciprocal. Once you've rewritten a division problem as multiplication, follow the rules for fraction multiplication to simplify.

addition/subtraction: $\dfrac{2}{3} + \dfrac{5}{4} \rightarrow \left(\dfrac{2}{3} \times \dfrac{4}{4}\right) + \left(\dfrac{5}{4} \times \dfrac{3}{3}\right) = \dfrac{8}{12} + \dfrac{15}{12} = \dfrac{23}{12}$

multiplication: $\dfrac{5}{8} \times \dfrac{8}{3} = \dfrac{5}{\cancel{8}} \times \dfrac{\cancel{8}^{1}}{3} = \dfrac{5 \times 1}{1 \times 3} = \dfrac{5}{3}$

division: $\dfrac{3}{4} \div \dfrac{3}{2} = \dfrac{\cancel{3}^{1}}{\cancel{4}_{2}} \times \dfrac{\cancel{2}^{1}}{\cancel{3}_{1}} = \dfrac{1 \times 1}{2 \times 1} = \dfrac{1}{2}$

- Know what absolute value is: the distance a number is from 0 on a number line. Because absolute value is a distance, it is always positive or 0. Absolute value can *never* be negative.

$$|-17| = 17, |21| = 21, |0| = 0$$

- Follow properties of equality: Whatever you do to one side of an equation, you must do to the other. For instance, if you multiply one side by 3, you must multiply the other side by 3 as well.

- The ability to solve straightforward, one-variable equations is critical on the SAT. Here's an example:

$$\frac{4x}{5} - 2 = 10$$
$$\frac{4x}{5} = 12$$
$$\frac{5}{4} \times \frac{4x}{5} = 12 \times \frac{5}{4}$$
$$x = 15$$

Note: $\dfrac{4x}{5}$ is the same as $\dfrac{4}{5}x$. You could see either form on the SAT.

- You should be able to extract numbers (and infer their relevance) from word problems like this one:

Annabel bought six pairs of shoes during a sale at her favorite boutique. If this purchase tripled the number of pairs of shoes she had before she went shopping, how many pairs of shoes did Annabel own before she visited the sale?

Solution: Let p represent the number of pairs of shoes Annabel had before the sale. She adds six pairs ($+ 6$) to this value, which is equal to triple her original shoe pair count ($= 3p$). Your equation should read $p + 6 = 3p$. Solving for p reveals $p = 3$, so Annabel had three pairs of shoes before she went shopping at the sale.

- You will encounter irrational numbers, such as common radicals and π, on Test Day. You can carry an irrational number through your calculations as you would a variable (e.g., $4 \times \sqrt{2} = 4\sqrt{2}$).

Only convert to a decimal when you have finished any intermediate steps and when the question asks you to provide an *approximate* value.

For Extra Efficiency

You might be a math whiz, but unless you're Isaac Newton (the inventor of calculus), you can likely benefit from knowing a few extra things that will boost your speed on Test Day.

- Don't abuse your calculator by using it to determine something as simple as $15 \div 3$ (we've seen it many times). Besides, what if you're in the middle of the no-calculator section? Save time on Test Day by reviewing multiplication tables. At a bare minimum, work up through the 10s. If you know them through 12 or 15, that's even better!

- You can save a few seconds of number crunching by memorizing perfect squares. Knowing perfect squares through 10 is a good start; go for 15 or even 20 if you can.

- The ability to recognize a few simple fractions masquerading in decimal or percent form will save you time on Test Day, as you won't have to turn to your calculator to convert them. Memorize the content of the following table.

Fraction	Decimal	Percent
$\frac{1}{10}$	0.1	10%
$\frac{1}{5}$	0.2	20%
$\frac{1}{4}$	0.25	25%
$\frac{1}{3}$	$0.333\overline{3}$	$33.3\overline{3}\%$
$\frac{1}{2}$	0.5	50%
$\frac{3}{4}$	0.75	75%

Tip: If you need the decimal (or percent) form of a multiple of one of the fractions shown in the table, such as $\frac{2}{5}$, just take the fraction with the corresponding denominator ($\frac{1}{5}$ in this case), convert to a decimal (0.2), and multiply by the numerator of the desired fraction to get its decimal equivalent: $\frac{2}{5} = \frac{1}{5} \times 2 = 0.2 \times 2 = 0.4 = 40\%$.

- Many students assume that every math problem encountered can be solved with a proportion. Proportions are not appropriate for every question. Know when to use them and when not to; review chapter 5 for more information. You must be able to recognize the type of question you have *and* use the right math tools to solve it.

Graphing

- Basic two-dimensional graphing is performed on a coordinate plane. There are two axes, *x* and *y*, that meet at a central point called the origin. Each axis has both positive and negative values that extend outward from the origin at evenly spaced intervals. The axes divide the space into four sections called quadrants, which are labeled I, II, III, and IV. Quadrant I is always the upper-right section, and the rest follow counterclockwise.

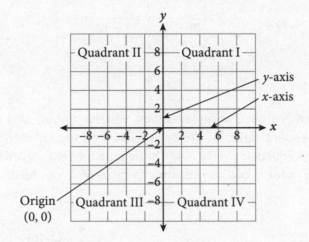

- To plot points on the coordinate plane, you need their coordinates. The *x*-coordinate is where the point falls along the *x*-axis, and the *y*-coordinate is where the point falls along the *y*-axis. The two coordinates together make an ordered pair written as (*x*, *y*). When writing ordered pairs, the *x*-coordinate is always listed first (think alphabetical order). Four points are plotted in the following figure as examples.

Math

- When two points are vertically or horizontally aligned, calculating the distance between them is easy. For a horizontal distance, only the *x*-value changes; for a vertical distance, only the *y*-value changes. Take the positive difference of the *x*-coordinates (or *y*-coordinates) to determine the distance. Two examples are presented here.

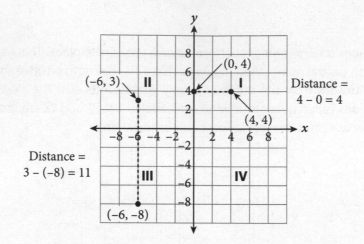

- Two-variable equations have an independent variable (input) and a dependent variable (output). The dependent variable (often *y*), depends on the independent variable (often *x*). For example, in the equation $y = 3x + 4$, *x* is the independent variable; any *y*-value depends on what you plug in for *x*. You can construct a table of values for the equation, which can then be plotted.

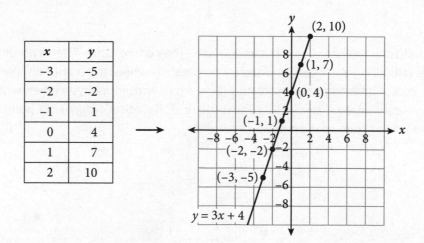

- You may be asked to infer relationships from graphs. In the first of the following graphs, the two variables are time and population. Clearly the year does not depend on how many people live in the town; rather, the population increases over time and thus depends on the year. In the second graph, you can infer that plant height depends on the amount of rain; thus, rainfall is the independent variable. Note that the independent variable for the second graph is the vertical axis; this can happen with certain nonstandard graphs. On the standard coordinate plane, however, the independent variable is always plotted on the horizontal axis.

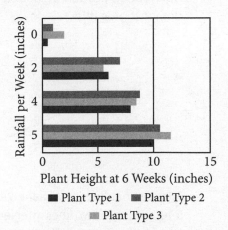

- When two straight lines are graphed simultaneously, one of three possible scenarios will occur:

1) The lines will not intersect at all (no solution).

2) The lines will intersect at one point (one solution).

3) The lines will lie on top of each other (infinitely many solutions).

Geometry

- Adjacent angles can be added to find the measure of a larger angle. The following diagram demonstrates this.

- Two distinct lines in a plane will either intersect at one point or extend indefinitely without intersecting. If two lines intersect at a right angle (90°), they are perpendicular and are denoted with ⊥. If the lines never intersect, they are parallel and are denoted with ∥.

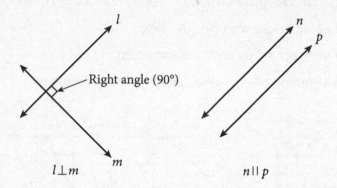

- Perimeter and area are basic properties that all two-dimensional shapes have. The perimeter of a polygon can easily be calculated by adding the lengths of all its sides. Area is the amount of two-dimensional space a shape occupies. The most common shapes for which you'll need these two properties on Test Day are triangles, parallelograms, and circles.

- The area (A) of a triangle is given by $A = \frac{1}{2}bh$, where b is the base of the triangle and h is its height. The base and height are always perpendicular. Any side of a triangle can be used as the base; just make sure you use its corresponding height (the longest perpendicular line you can draw within the triangle). You can use a right triangle's two legs as the base and height, but in non-right triangles, if the height is not given, you'll need to draw it in (from the vertex of the angle opposite the base down to the base itself at a right angle) and compute it.

- Parallelograms are quadrilaterals with two pairs of parallel sides. Rectangles and squares are subsets of parallelograms. You can find the area of a parallelogram using $A = bh$. As with triangles, you can use any side of a parallelogram as the base; in addition, the height is still perpendicular to the base. Use the side perpendicular to the base as the height for a rectangle or square; for any other parallelogram, the height (or enough information to find it) will be given.

- A circle's perimeter is known as its circumference (*C*) and is found using $C = 2\pi r$, where *r* is the radius (distance from the center of the circle to its edge). Area is given by $A = \pi r^2$. The strange symbol is the lowercase Greek letter pi (*π*, pronounced "pie"), which is approximately 3.14. As mentioned in the algebra section, you should carry *π* throughout your calculations without rounding unless instructed otherwise.

- A shape is said to have symmetry when it can be split by a line (called an *axis of symmetry*) into two identical parts. Consider folding a shape along a line: If all sides and vertices align once the shape is folded in half, the shape is symmetrical about that line. Some shapes have no axis of symmetry, some have one, some have multiple axes, and still others can have infinite axes of symmetry (e.g., a circle).

Sample axis of symmetry   Not an axis of symmetry

Sample shapes with corresponding axes of symmetry

- Congruence is simply a geometry term that means identical. Angles, lines, and shapes can be congruent. Congruence is indicated by using hash marks: Everything with the same number of hash marks is congruent.

Equilateral triangle: Isosceles triangle:
3 congruent sides,   2 congruent sides,
3 congruent angles   2 congruent angles

- Similarity between shapes indicates that they have identical angles and proportional sides. Think of taking a shape and stretching or shrinking each side by the same ratio. The resulting shape will have the same angles as the original. While the sides will not be identical, they will be proportional.

Multiply each side by 2

If you're comfortable with these concepts, read on for tips on calculator use.

CALCULATORS AND THE SAT

Educators and parents believe that calculators serve a role in mathematics, but they are concerned that students rely too heavily on calculators. They believe this dependence weakens students' overall ability to think mathematically. Therefore, the SAT has a policy on calculator use to promote the idea that students need to be able to analyze and solve math problems both with and without a calculator. One math section will allow you to use a calculator, while the other will require you to solve problems without technology. The makers of the SAT walked 12 miles uphill in the snow to school, so why should you have things any easier? Think of this chapter as your personal pair of snow boots that can make that uphill walk a little more comfortable for you.

Many students never stop to ask whether using a calculator is the most efficient way to solve a problem. This chapter will show you how the strongest test takers use their calculators strategically; that is, they carefully evaluate when to use the calculator and when to skip it in favor of a more streamlined approach. As you will see, even though you can use a calculator, sometimes it's more beneficial to save your energy by approaching a question more strategically. Work smarter, not harder.

WHICH CALCULATOR SHOULD YOU USE?

The SAT allows four-function, scientific, and graphing calculators. No matter which calculator you choose, start practicing with it now. You don't want to waste valuable time on Test Day looking for the exponent button or figuring out how to correctly graph equations. Due to the wide range of mathematics topics you'll encounter on Test Day, **we recommend using a graphing calculator**, such as the TI-83/84. If you don't already own one, see if you can borrow one from your school's math department or a local library.

A graphing calculator's capabilities extend well beyond what you'll need for the test, so don't worry about memorizing every function. The next few pages will cover which calculator functions you'll want to know how to use for the SAT. If you're not already familiar with your graphing calculator, you'll want to get the user manual; you can find this on the Internet by searching for your calculator's model number. Identify the calculator functions necessary to answer various SAT math questions, then write down the directions for each to make a handy study sheet.

WHEN SHOULD YOU USE A CALCULATOR?

Some SAT question types are designed based on the idea that students will do some or all of the work using a calculator. As a master test taker, you want to know what to look for so you can identify when calculator use is advantageous. Questions involving statistics, determining roots of complicated quadratic equations, and other topics are generally designed with calculator use in mind.

Other questions aren't intentionally designed to involve calculator use. Solving some with a calculator can save you time and energy, but you'll waste both if you go for the calculator on others. You will have to decide which method is best when you encounter the following topics:

- Long division and other extensive calculations
- Graphing quadratics
- Simplifying radicals and calculating roots
- Plane and coordinate geometry

Practicing long computations by hand and with the calculator will not only boost your focus and mental math prowess, but it will also help you determine whether it's faster to do the work by hand or reach for the calculator. If you tend to make quick work of long division and multiple-digit multiplication by hand, you can still use the calculator afterward to check your work.

Graphing quadratic equations is a big reason most of you got that fancy calculator in the first place; it makes answering these questions a snap! This is definitely an area where you need to have an in-depth knowledge of your calculator's functions. The key to making these questions easy with the calculator is being meticulous when entering the equation.

Another stressful area for students is radicals, especially when the answer choices are written as decimals. Those two elements are big red flags that trigger a reach for the calculator. Beware: Not all graphing calculators have a built-in radical simplification function, so consider familiarizing yourself with this process.

Geometry can be a gray area for students when it comes to calculator use. Consider working by hand when dealing with angles and lines, specifically when filling in information on complementary, supplementary, and congruent angles. You should be able to work fluidly through those questions without using your calculator.

> ✔ **Expert Tip**
>
> If you choose to use trigonometric functions to get to the answer on triangle questions, make sure you have your calculator set to degrees or radians as necessitated by the question.

Your calculator will come in handy when you need to work with formulas (volume, distance, arc length, etc.) and want to check your work. Because the SAT uses π instead of 3.14…, there is no need to enter the decimal form into your calculator.

TO USE OR NOT TO USE?

A calculator is a double-edged sword on the SAT: Using one can be an asset for verifying work if you struggle when doing math by hand, but turning to it for the simplest computations will cost you time that you could devote to more complex questions. Practice solving questions with and without a calculator to get a sense of your personal style as well as strengths and weaknesses. Think critically about when a calculator saves you time and when mental math is faster. Use the exercises in this book to practice your calculations so that by the time Test Day arrives, you'll be in the habit of using your calculator as effectively as possible!

Heart of Algebra

BY THE END OF THIS UNIT, YOU WILL BE ABLE TO:

1. Apply the Kaplan Method for Math to math questions on the SAT

2. Solve linear equations and inequalities

3. Graph linear equations and inequalities

4. Solve systems of linear equations and inequalities

5. Translate word problems into math

The Kaplan Method for Math & Linear Equations

CHAPTER OBJECTIVES

By the end of this chapter, you will be able to:

1. Apply the Kaplan Method for Math to Heart of Algebra questions

2. Recognize, simplify, and solve linear equations efficiently

3. Translate complex word problems into equations

4. Interpret the most commonly tested types of linear graphs

SMARTPOINTS

Point Value	SmartPoint Category
Point Builder	Kaplan Method for Math
110 Points	Linear Equations

Math

THE KAPLAN METHOD FOR MATH & LINEAR EQUATIONS

Chapter 2

Homework

Extra Practice: #1-20

Even More

The Kaplan Method for Math

Translating English to Math

Math Quiz 1

Key

 Book Assignment

 Online Video Assignment

 Online Quiz Assignment

THE KAPLAN METHOD FOR MATH

Because the SAT is a standardized test, students who approach each question in a consistent way will be rewarded on Test Day. Applying the same basic steps to every math question—whether it asks you about geometry, algebra, or even trigonometry—will help you avoid minor mistakes as well as tempting wrong answer choices.

Use the Kaplan Method for Math for every math question on the SAT. Its steps are applicable to every situation and reflect the best test-taking practices.

The Kaplan Method for Math has three steps:

>   Step 1: Read the question, identifying and organizing important information as you go
>
>   Step 2: Choose the best strategy to answer the question
>
>   Step 3: Check that you answered the *right* question

Let's examine each of these steps in more detail.

Step 1: Read the question, identifying and organizing important information as you go

This means:

- **What information am I given?** Take a few seconds to jot down the information you are given and try to group similar items together.

- **Separate the question from the context.** Word problems may include information that is unnecessary to solve the question. Feel free to discard any unnecessary information.

- **How are the answer choices different?** Reading answer choices carefully can help you spot the most efficient way to solve a multiple-choice math question. If the answer choices are decimals, then painstakingly rewriting your final answer as a simplified fraction is a waste of time; you can just use your calculator instead.

- **Should I label or draw a diagram?** If the question describes a shape or figure but doesn't provide one, sketch a diagram so you can see the shape or figure and add notes to it. If a figure is provided, take a few seconds to label it with information from the question.

> ✔ **Expert Tip**
>
> Don't assume you understand a question as soon as you see it. Many students see an equation and immediately begin solving. Solving math questions without carefully reading can take you down the wrong path on Test Day.

Step 2: Choose the best strategy to answer the question

- **Look for patterns.** Every SAT math question can be solved in a variety of ways, but not all strategies are created equally. To finish all of the questions, you'll need to solve questions as *efficiently* as possible. If you find yourself about to do time-consuming math, take a moment to look for time-saving shortcuts.

- **Pick numbers or use straightforward math.** While you can always solve an SAT math question with what you've learned in school, doing so won't always be the fastest way. On questions that describe relationships between numbers (such as percentages) but don't actually use numbers, you can often save time on Test Day by using techniques such as Picking Numbers instead of straightforward math.

> ✔ **Expert Tip**
>
> The SAT won't give you any extra points for solving a question the hard way.

Step 3: Check that you answered the *right* question

- When you get the final answer, **resist the urge to immediately bubble in the answer**. Take a moment to:

  - Review the question stem

  - Check units of measurement

  - Double-check your work

- The SAT will often ask you for quantities such as $x + 1$ or the product of x and y. **Be careful on these questions!** They often include tempting answer choices that correspond to the values of x or y individually. There's no partial credit on the SAT, so take a moment at the end of every question to make sure you're answering the right question.

LINEAR EQUATIONS

Linear equations and linear graphs are some of the most common elements on the SAT Math Test. They can be used to model relationships and changes such as those concerning time, temperature, or population.

The graphs of these equations are as important as the equations themselves. The graphs you will see most are either linear or lines of best fit. A sample graph is shown:

When working with a graph like this, you may not know anything about magnetization or cobalt ferrite, but you do see a graph with a straight line on it. That straight line is your clue that you're dealing with a linear equation.

Being able to work with, understand, and interpret linear equations will make up a substantial part of your Math score. In this chapter, we will explore all of those scenarios so you'll be ready to tackle linear equations in whatever form you encounter them on the test.

Many students inadvertently switch on "math autopilot" when solving linear equations, automatically running through the same set of steps on every equation without looking for the best way to solve the question. On the SAT, however, every second counts. You will want to use the *most* efficient strategy for solving questions. Take a look at the following example:

1. $$\frac{4 + z - (3 + 2z)}{6} = \frac{-z - 3(5 - 2)}{7}$$

What is the value of z in the equation above?

A) -61

B) $-\dfrac{61}{27}$

C) $\dfrac{61}{27}$

D) 61

The following table shows Kaplan's strategic thinking on the left, along with suggested math scratchwork on the right. Keeping your notes organized is critical for success on the SAT, so start practicing now setting up well-organized scratchwork.

Strategic Thinking	Math Scratchwork
Step 1: Read the question, identifying and organizing important information as you go This question is straightforward: You're given an equation and need to solve for z.	
Step 2: Choose the best strategy to answer the question Straightforward algebra will work well here. Combine like terms on both sides of the equation first, being mindful of negative signs. Once you've combined, cross-multiply to eliminate the fractions, and then isolate z.	$$\frac{4 + z - (3 + 2z)}{6} = \frac{-z - 3(5 - 2)}{7}$$ $$\frac{1 - z}{6} = \frac{-z - 9}{7}$$ $$7 - 7z = -6z - 54$$ $$-z = -61$$ $$z = 61$$
Step 3: Check that you answered the *right* question You've determined that z is equal to 61; therefore, (D) is correct.	$$z = 61$$

You could have approached a question like this in many ways, but remember, the goal is to get the correct answer quickly. The faster you solve algebraic equations, the more time you'll be able to devote to challenging questions, setting you up to earn more points on Test Day.

✔ **Remember**

As you practice, always ask yourself: "Is there a faster way to solve this question?" Use the Answers and Explanations at the back of this book to check!

When solving an equation, always keep in mind the fundamental principles of equality: Because both sides of an equation are equal, you need to do the same thing to both sides so that equality is preserved. Try solving another linear equation for extra practice:

2. $3y + 2(y - 2) = -25$

What value of y satisfies the equation above?

A) $-\dfrac{29}{5}$

B) $-\dfrac{21}{5}$

C) $\dfrac{21}{5}$

D) $\dfrac{29}{5}$

Work through the Kaplan Method for Math step-by-step to solve this question. The following table shows Kaplan's strategic thinking on the left, along with suggested math scratchwork on the right.

Strategic Thinking	Math Scratchwork
Step 1: Read the question, identifying and organizing important information as you go	
This looks similar to the first question: It's asking you to find the value of y.	$3y + 2(y - 2) = -25$
Step 2: Choose the best strategy to answer the question	
Straightforward algebra is the fastest route to the answer. Start by distributing the 2. Continue by collecting like terms until you isolate y.	$3y + 2y - 4 = -25$ $5y - 4 = -25$ $5y = -21$ $y = -\dfrac{21}{5}$
Step 3: Check that you answered the _right_ question	
You found y, so you're done! Choice (B) is correct.	

Notice that none of the answer choices are integers. The SAT may challenge you by designing questions so that the answer is in a form you do not expect. If you arrive at an answer in an unusual form, don't be alarmed. Fractions and decimals are often correct on the SAT.

Math

Looking carefully at how the SAT uses fractions and decimals can guide your strategy in solving linear equations. The presence of fractions in the answer choices likely means you'll need to rely on techniques for combining and simplifying fractions to get to the right answer. Seeing decimals in the answer choices, on the other hand, likely indicates that you can rely on your calculator and save time on Test Day.

Try to determine the best strategy for solving the next question.

3. $3(y - 8) + 3(6x + 2) = 24 + 3y$

Which approximate value of x satisfies the equation above?

A) 0.80

B) 1.33

C) 2.33

D) The value cannot be determined from the given information.

Work through the Kaplan Method for Math step-by-step to solve this question. The following table shows Kaplan's strategic thinking on the left, along with suggested math scratchwork on the right.

Strategic Thinking	Math Scratchwork
Step 1: Read the question, identifying and organizing important information as you go	
The question is asking you to solve for a variable. Note that there are two variables present.	$3(y - 8) + 3(6x + 2)$ $= 24 + 3y$
Step 2: Choose the best strategy to answer the question	
Before blindly choosing D because there are two variables and only one equation, determine whether the y terms can be eliminated. Divide both sides by 3, and then combine like terms. You'll see that the y terms cancel, leaving one equation with one variable. Isolate x. The presence of decimals in the answer choices means your calculator will be a great asset here. Don't worry about reducing the fraction; just punch it into your calculator to find its decimal equivalent.	$y - 8 + 6x + 2 = 8 + y$ $-8 + 6x + 2 = 8$ $-6 + 6x = 8$ $6x = 14$ $x = \dfrac{14}{6}$
Step 3: Check that you answered the *right* question	
Double-check the question stem. You've found the value of x, which is 2.33, making (C) correct.	$x = 2.33$

Notice in the previous question that careful use of your calculator can eliminate the need to complete time-consuming tasks by hand. Be conscious of the format of the answer choices—decimal answers are a great clue that you can use your calculator.

> ✔ **Note**
>
> Many graphing calculators have a built-in function that will let you input and solve algebraic equations like the previous one. Consider learning how to use it before Test Day by reading the instruction manual or searching online.

Math

LINEAR WORD PROBLEMS (REAL-WORLD SCENARIOS)

Another way linear equations can be made to look complicated is for them to be disguised in "real-world" word problems, where it's up to you to extract and solve an equation. When you're solving these problems, you may run into trouble translating English into math. The following table shows some of the most common phrases and mathematical equivalents you're likely to see on the SAT.

Word Problems Translation Table	
English	**Math**
equals, is, equivalent to, was, will be, has, costs, adds up to, the same as, as much as	$=$
times, of, multiplied by, product of, twice, double, by	$\times$
divided by, per, out of, each, ratio	$\div$
plus, added to, and, sum, combined, total, increased by	$+$
minus, subtracted from, smaller than, less than, fewer, decreased by, difference between	$-$
a number, how much, how many, what	x, n, etc.

Linear word problems are made more difficult by complex phrasing and extraneous information. Don't get frustrated—word problems can be broken down in predictable ways. To stay organized on Test Day, use the **Kaplan Strategy for Translating English into Math:**

- Define any variables, choosing letters that make sense.

- Break sentences into short phrases.

- Translate each phrase into a mathematical expression.

- Put the expressions together to form an equation.

Let's apply this to a straightforward example: Colin's age is three less than twice Jim's age.

- **Define any variables, choosing letters that make sense:** We'll choose *C* for Colin's age and *J* for Jim's age.

- **Break sentences into short phrases:** The information about Colin and the information about Jim seem like separate phrases.

- **Translate each phrase into a mathematical expression:** Colin's age $= C$; 3 less than twice Jim's age $= 2J - 3$.

- **Put the expressions together to form an equation:** Combine the results to get $C = 2J - 3$.

This strategy fits into the larger framework of the Kaplan Method for Math: When you get to **Step 2: Choose the best strategy to answer the question** and are trying to solve a word problem as efficiently as possible, switch over to this strategy to move forward quickly.

The Kaplan Strategy for Translating English into Math works every time. Apply it here to a test-like example:

4. Malia and Omar want to find the shortest route from their school to a local burger hangout. The length of Route A is 1.5 times the length of Route B and $\frac{3}{4}$ the length of Route C. If Route C is 3 kilometers long, then Route A is how many kilometers longer than Route B?

   A) 0.75

   B) 1.5

   C) 2

   D) 2.25

Work through the Kaplan Method for Math step-by-step to solve this question. The following table shows Kaplan's strategic thinking on the left, along with suggested math scratchwork on the right.

Strategic Thinking	Math Scratchwork
Step 1: Read the question, identifying and organizing important information as you go The question is asking you to solve for the difference between the lengths of Routes A and B.	C is 3 km A is $\frac{3}{4}$ of C and 1.5 times B
Step 2: Choose the best strategy to answer the question This looks like a word problem, so go through each step of the Kaplan Strategy for Translating English into Math. Use the route labels for your variables. Note each comparison of the routes in your scratchwork, and then translate them into math. Work carefully through the algebra to find the lengths of routes A and B.	$A = \frac{3}{4} \times C$ $\quad = \frac{3}{4} \times 3 = \frac{9}{4}$ $\quad = 2.25$ $A = 1.5B$ $2.25 = 1.5B$ $1.5 = B$
Step 3: Check that you answered the *right* question One more step to go. Subtract the length of Route B from the length of Route A to yield (A) as your match.	$A - B = 2.25 - 1.5$ $\quad = 0.75$

LINEAR GRAPHS

Working with equations algebraically is only half the battle. The SAT will also expect you to work with graphs of linear equations, which means using lines in slope-intercept form and point-slope form.

One of the most important quantities you'll be working with when graphing a linear equation is the slope. Slope is given by the following equation: $m = \dfrac{y_2 - y_1}{x_2 - x_1}$, where (x_1, y_1) and (x_2, y_2) are coordinates of points on the line. To remember this, think: slope $= \dfrac{\text{rise}}{\text{run}}$.

One of the most common forms of a linear equation is *slope-intercept form*, which is used to describe the graph of a straight line. The formula is quickly recognizable: $y = mx + b$. The variables y and x represent the coordinates of a point on the graph through which the line passes, while m tells us what the slope of the line is and b represents the point at which the line intersects the y-axis.

Remember: A line with a positive slope runs up and to the right ("uphill"), and a line with a negative slope runs down and to the right ("downhill"). In the following figure, lines n and l have positive and negative slopes, respectively.

Occasionally, you will encounter a line with a slope of 0—meaning it does not rise or fall from left to right. These lines are easy to spot because they are horizontal and are parallel to the x-axis (line k in the figure shown). Lines that are parallel to the y-axis, such as line m in the figure, have slopes that are "undefined." The lines themselves exist, but their slopes cannot be calculated numerically.

The slope of a graph can also tell you valuable information about the rate of change of numbers and variables associated with the line. A positive slope signifies an increase in a variable, while a negative slope indicates a decrease. *Large* numerical values for slope indicate rapid changes, while *small* numerical values point to more gradual changes. Imagine that the balance in your checking account is B, and that it changes with the number of days that go by, D. Think about how each of the following models would impact your life.

$$B = 100D + 75$$
$$B = 0.25D + 75$$
$$B = -100D + 75$$
$$B = -0.25D + 75$$

The first equation probably looks pretty good. The second equation isn't as great. An extra quarter a day isn't going to do much for you. The third equation would quickly drive you into bankruptcy, while the fourth equation might be cause for concern after a while.

The y-intercept, on the other hand, is often less significant, typically representing the initial condition in a model—that is, where the model begins. In the checking account example, the beginning balance was $75 in all four models. Notice, the y-intercept didn't change at all.

Look at the following question to see how the SAT might test your ability to match a linear equation with its graph.

5. Line A passes through the coordinate points $(-\frac{2}{5}, 0)$ and $(0, 1)$. Which of the following lines will line A never intersect?

A)

B)

C)

D)

Approach this question by using the Kaplan Method for Math. Try to ask yourself similar questions as you work through questions like this on Test Day.

Strategic Thinking	Math Scratchwork
Step 1: Read the question, identifying and organizing important information as you go This question is asking you to determine which line will never intersect the one that contains the two points provided in the question stem.	
Step 2: Choose the best strategy to answer the question Using your calculator will take too long, so use the slope formula and your critical thinking skills instead. Start by finding the slope of the line in the question stem. Because the slope is positive, you can eliminate C and D, which both contain lines with negative slopes. Two lines that never intersect are parallel and therefore have the same slope, so determine which of the remaining answer choices also has a slope of $\frac{5}{2}$. There is no need to calculate the slopes; simply counting units on the graphs will suffice.	$-\frac{2}{5}, 0$, $(0, 1)$ $m = \dfrac{y_2 - y_1}{x_2 - x_1}$ $= \dfrac{1 - 0}{0 - -\frac{2}{5}} = \dfrac{1}{\frac{2}{5}} = \dfrac{5}{2}$ $m_{Choice\,A} = \dfrac{2}{5}$ $m_{Choice\,B} = \dfrac{5}{2}$
Step 3: Check that you answered the *right* question Only (B) contains a line that will not intersect the one described in the question stem. Notice you didn't have to do any additional work, such as finding *y*-intercepts. Only do as much as you need to—this saves time on Test Day.	

Some questions are a little more challenging. They're usually similar in structure to the "checking account" equation described earlier, but they can involve more complicated scenarios. This next question requires you to choose the best model for a given "real-world" situation. See if you can match the graph to an appropriate model. Watch out: It's a science "crossover" question, so you'll need to be particularly careful to separate the question from the context.

Snowy Tree Cricket Temperature Prediction

6. Snowy tree crickets have long been used to determine the ambient air temperature. The correlation between ambient air temperature and their chirp frequency is highly consistent. The graph shows the correlation between ambient air temperature, t, in degrees Fahrenheit and the number of chirps, c, per minute that a snowy tree cricket makes at that temperature. Based on the graph, which of the following best represents this scenario?

A) $c = 4t - 160$

B) $c = \dfrac{1}{4}t - 160$

C) $c = \dfrac{1}{2}t - 40$

D) $c = 4t + 160$

Although you may enjoy learning about science with your math, you don't need to waste time digesting extraneous information. The following table shows the strategic thinking that can help you solve this question.

Strategic Thinking	Math Scratchwork
Step 1: Read the question, identifying and organizing important information as you go Only the last two sentences of the question stem describe the graph and your task. Focus on these two sentences.	
Step 2: Choose the best strategy to answer the question Graphing the equations in the answer choices on your calculator would be time-consuming; in addition, the y-intercept of the line is not visible, thereby introducing another hurdle. Opt for examining the answer choices closely instead. Pick a couple points on the line to determine the slope. You'll find it equals 4, so eliminate B and C. Now, read the axis labels carefully. The horizontal axis begins at 40 (not 0), and the line is trending downward, so the y-intercept (when $x = 0$) must be well below 0 on the vertical axis. Eliminate D.	$(40, 0)$ and $(65, 100)$ $m = \dfrac{100 - 0}{65 - 40} = \dfrac{100}{25} = 4$
Step 3: Check that you answered the *right* question Choice (A) is the only option remaining. You're done! Note that you didn't have to calculate b to find the correct answer, so you saved some time.	

While scatterplots will be described in more detail in subsequent chapters, this next question shows that the principles covered here for graphing linear equations can be equally applied to the line of best fit on a scatterplot. See what you can conclude from the slope and y-intercept of the equation of the line of best fit. Note that this question is an example of a very complex word problem—don't be intimidated! If you can tackle this problem, you'll be able to handle the most difficult SAT word problems.

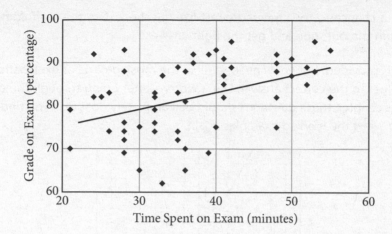

7. A physics professor presented the scatterplot above to his first-year students. What is the significance of the slope of the line of best fit?

    A) The slope represents the rate at which time spent on an exam increases based on a student's exam performance.

    B) The slope represents the average grade on the exam.

    C) The slope represents the rate at which a student's exam grade increases based on time spent on the exam.

    D) The slope has no significance.

Use the Kaplan Method for Math to make short work of this question. The following table shows the strategic thinking that can help you solve complex questions like this one.

Strategic Thinking
Step 1: Read the question, identifying and organizing important information as you go
You must determine the significance of the slope of the line of best fit on the scatterplot.
Step 2: Choose the best strategy to answer the question
Look for answer choices you can easily eliminate based on what you know about lines. A line's slope is a rate, so you can eliminate B and D. Examine A and C next. According to the graph, time spent on the exam is the independent variable (because it is graphed on the horizontal axis), and the exam grade is the dependent variable. Pick the answer choice that reflects this.
Step 3: Check that you answered the _right_ question
You've determined the significance of the slope of the line of best fit. The correct answer is (C).

Notice that even complicated-looking questions involving linear graphs often boil down to the same basic concepts of slope and _y_-intercept. Master those ideas and you'll be able to handle any linear graph you'll see on the SAT.

Now you'll have a chance to try a few more test-like questions. Use the scaffolding as needed to guide you through the question and get the right answer.

Some guidance is provided, but you'll need to fill in the missing parts of explanations or the step-by-step math to get to the correct answer. Don't worry—after going through the examples at the beginning of this chapter, these questions should be completely doable. If you find yourself struggling, however, review the worked examples again.

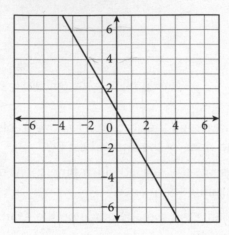

8. The line $y = -\dfrac{7x}{4} + \dfrac{1}{2}$ is shown in the graph. If the line is shifted down 2 units and then reflected over the *x*-axis, which of the following graphs represents the new line?

A)

C)

B)

D)
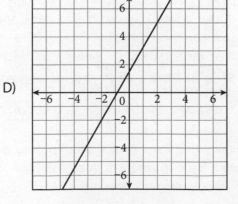

The following table can help you structure your thinking as you go about solving this problem. Kaplan's strategic thinking is provided, as are bits of structured scratchwork. If you're not sure how to approach a question like this, start at the top and work your way down.

Strategic Thinking	Math Scratchwork
Step 1: Read the question, identifying and organizing important information as you go You're asked for the graph that corresponds to the described changes made to $y = -\dfrac{7x}{4} + \dfrac{1}{2}$.	
Step 2: Choose the best strategy to answer the question While you could apply the transformations to the entire line, picking a test point will be faster. For example, draw a dot at $(-2, 4)$ on the original line and apply the changes to that point. Cross off any choices that don't pass through the new point. You might need to pick more than one point if your initial choice doesn't eliminate all of the incorrect answer choices.	
Step 3: Check that you answered the *right* question Did you get (D)? If so, you're correct! Beware of C—it results from a reflection over the wrong axis.	

Here's another test-like example to try.

9. Three years ago, Madison High School started charging an admission fee for basketball games to raise money for new bleachers. The initial price was $2 per person; the school raised the price of admission to $2.50 this year. Assuming this trend continues, which of the following equations can be used to describe the cost of admission, c, y years after the school began charging for admission to games?

A) $c = 6y + 2$

B) $c = \dfrac{y}{6} + 2.5$

C) $c = \dfrac{y}{6} + 2$

D) $c = \dfrac{y}{2} + 2$

The following table can help you structure your thinking as you go about solving this problem. The Kaplan strategic thinking is provided, as are bits of structured scratchwork. If you're not sure how to approach a question like this, start at the top and work your way down.

Strategic Thinking	Math Scratchwork
Step 1: Read the question, identifying and organizing important information as you go You need to identify the equation that correctly relates cost to years after the admission charge implementation.	
Step 2: Choose the best strategy to answer the question Look carefully; you're implicitly given two sets of coordinates. You can use these to find a key piece of a linear equation and eliminate two answer choices. The school started charging admission at a certain point in time; the price at this point is the y-intercept. Use this to pick the correct answer.	$(\underline{}, \underline{})$ $(\underline{}, \underline{})$ $m = \dfrac{\underline{}}{\underline{}} = \underline{}$ eliminate $\underline{}$ and $\underline{}$ $b = \underline{}$
Step 3: Check that you answered the _right_ question Did you come up with (C)? If so, great job! You're correct.	$\underline{}$

✔ **Note**

Because the question says "three years ago," it may be tempting to use (–3, 2) and (0, 2.5) as your coordinates. Before you do this, think about what that means: This translates to the first admission charge being $2.50, as it's impossible to have a negative year. Choice B is a trap waiting for students who attempt this route!

Now that you've seen the variety of ways in which the SAT can test you on linear equations, try the following three questions to check your understanding. Give yourself 3.5 minutes to answer the questions. Make sure you use the Kaplan Method for Math on every question. Remember, you'll need to emphasize speed and efficiency in addition to simply getting the correct answer.

10. If the line $y = -5x + 8$ is shifted down 3 units and left 2 units, what is the slope of the new line?

    A) -5

    B) 0

    C) 3

    D) 5

11. If $\frac{3}{4}y = 6 - \frac{1}{3}c$, then what is the value of $2c + \frac{9}{2}y$?

12. If m is a constant between 0 and $\frac{1}{2}$ (exclusive), which of the following could be the graph of $x - y = m(2x + y)$?

A)

B)

C)

D)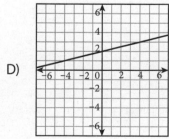

Answers and Explanations for this chapter begin on page 809.

EXTRA PRACTICE

The calculator icon means you are permitted to use a calculator to solve a question. It does not mean that you *should* use it, however.

1. If $2x + 5 = 11$, what is the value of $2x - 5$?

    A) -11

    B) -6

    C) 1

    D) 11

Number of Lightbulbs

2. A hardware store sells lightbulbs in different quantities. The graph shows the cost of various quantities. According to the graph, what is the cost of a single lightbulb?

    A) $0.56

    B) $1.80

    C) $2.50

    D) $3.60

3. A local restaurant is hosting a dance-a-thon for charity. Each couple must dance a minimum of three hours before earning any money for the charity. After the first three hours, couples earn $50 per half-hour of continuous dancing. Which expression represents the total amount earned by a couple that dances h hours, assuming they dance at least three hours?

    A) $25h$

    B) $100h$

    C) $50(h - 3)$

    D) $100h - 300$

Price of One Pound	Projected Number of Pounds Sold
$1.20	15,000
$1.40	12,500
$1.60	10,000
$1.80	7,500
$2.00	5,000
$2.20	2,500

4. Which of the following equations best describes the linear relationship shown in the table, where g represents the number of pounds of grain sold and d represents the price in dollars of one pound of grain?

A) $g = 1.2d + 12,500$

B) $g = 12,500d + 15,000$

C) $g = -12,500d + 17,500$

D) $g = -12,500d + 30,000$

$$2\left(x - \frac{5}{2}\right) = c\left(\frac{4}{5}x - 2\right)$$

5. If the equation above has infinitely many solutions and c is a constant, what is the value of c?

A) -2

B) $-\dfrac{4}{5}$

C) $\dfrac{5}{4}$

D) $\dfrac{5}{2}$

6. If a is a rational number where $a > 1$, which of the following could be the graph of $y = ay + ax + x + 1$?

A)

B)

C)

D)

7. What value of n satisfies the equation $\frac{7}{8}(n - 6) = \frac{21}{2}$?

**Expected Property Values
2014-2028**

Box Airmail

9. A realtor is studying the graph above, which shows the expected value of properties in her area over the next 24 years. If t represents the number of years after 2014, in what year should the increase in property values start to slow down?

A) 2008

B) 2018

C) 2022

D) 2030

8. A freight airline charges a flat fee to airmail a box, plus an additional charge for each pound the box weighs. The graph above shows the relationship between the weight of the box and the total cost to airmail it. Based on the graph, how much would it cost in dollars to airmail a 40-pound box?

Number of Songs Purchased

10. The graph above shows the cost of joining and buying music from a music subscription service. What does the y-intercept of the line most likely represent?

A) The cost per song

B) The cost to join the service

C) The cost of buying 20 songs

D) The cost of 20 subscriptions to the service

11. Andrew works at a travel agency. He gets paid $120 for a day's work, plus a bonus of $25 for each cruise he books. Which of the following equations represents the relationship between one day of Andrew's pay, d, and the number of cruises he books, c?

A) $c = 25d + 120$

B) $c = 120d + 25$

C) $d = 25c + 120$

D) $d = 120c + 25$

12. Which value of x makes the equation $\frac{8}{5}\left(x + \frac{33}{12}\right) = 6$ true?

A) 7.25

B) 8.75

C) 12.75

D) 13.25

13. Henry just set up direct deposit from his employer to his checking account. The equation $y = 360x - 126.13$ represents the balance in Henry's account if he deposits his weekly paycheck for x weeks. Based on this equation, which of the following statements is true?

A) Henry earns $126.13 per week.

B) Henry made an initial deposit of $126.13.

C) Before setting up the direct deposit, Henry had overdrawn his account.

D) When Henry set up the direct deposit, he already had $360 in his account.

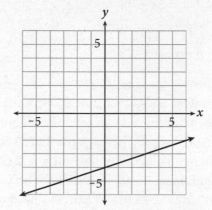

14. The graph shown represents which of the following equations?

A) $y = -3x + 4$

B) $y = -\frac{1}{3}x + 4$

C) $y = \frac{1}{3}x - 4$

D) $y = 3x - 4$

Math

Minutes Charging	10	15	30
Percent Charged	34	41.5	64

15. Jose is using his laptop and wants to recharge it before the battery completely runs out. He recorded the battery charge for the first 30 minutes after he plugged it in to get an idea of when it would be completely charged. The table above shows the results. Which linear function represents the percent battery charge on Jose's laptop x minutes after he plugged it in?

A) $f(x) = 1.5x + 19$

B) $f(x) = 2x + 14$

C) $f(x) = 2.5x + 9$

D) $f(x) = 10x + 34$

16. A laser tag arena sells two types of memberships. One package costs $325 for one year of membership with an unlimited number of visits. The second package has a $125 enrollment fee, includes five free visits, and costs an additional $8 per visit after the first five. How many visits would a person need to use for each type of membership to cost the same amount over a one-year period?

A) 20

B) 25

C) 30

D) 40

17. Which of the following equations has no solution?

A) $\frac{3}{8}(x-2) = \frac{8}{3}(x+2)$

B) $-\frac{3}{2}(2x-8) = 3x-12$

C) $4\left(\frac{3}{4}x + 5\right) = 3x + 20$

D) $6\left(\frac{2}{3}x + 5\right) = 4x + 5$

18. Vera is on her school's track and field team. In a practice long-jump competition against her teammates, she gets 5 points for landing over the closer line and 10 points for landing over the farther line. She gets a total of 7 jumps and lands x times over the farther line and the rest of the times over the closer line. Which of the following functions represents Vera's total score?

A) $f(x) = 10x$

B) $f(x) = 5x + 35$

C) $f(x) = 10x + 5$

D) $f(x) = 70 - 5x$

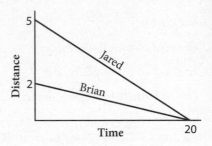

19. Brian and Jared live in the same apartment complex and they both bike to and from work every day. The figure above shows a typical commute home for each of them. Based on the figure, which of the following statements is true?

A) It takes Brian longer to bike home because his work is farther away.

B) It takes Jared longer to bike home because his work is farther away.

C) Jared and Brian arrive home at the same time, so they must bike at about the same rate.

D) Jared bikes a longer distance than Brian in the same amount of time, so Jared must bike at a faster rate.

20. When graphing a linear equation that is written in the form $y = mx + b$, the variable m represents the slope of the line and b represents the y-intercept. Assuming that $b > 0$, which of the following best describes how reversing the sign of b would affect the graph?

A) The new line will be shifted down b units.

B) The new line will be shifted down $b \times 2$ units.

C) The new line will be a perfect reflection across the x-axis.

D) The new line will be a perfect reflection across the y-axis.

Systems of Equations

CHAPTER OBJECTIVES

By the end of this chapter, you will be able to:

1. Distinguish between independent and dependent equations

2. Solve two-variable systems of linear equations

3. Determine the most efficient way to solve systems of equations

4. Translate word problems into multiple equations

SMARTPOINTS

Point Value	SmartPoint Category
50 Points	Systems of Linear Equations

Math

SYSTEMS OF EQUATIONS

Chapter 3

Homework

Extra Practice: #1-12

Key

 Book Assignment

Online Video Assignment

 Online Quiz Assignment

SYSTEMS OF EQUATIONS

The linear equations detailed in the previous chapter are well suited for modeling a variety of scenarios and for solving for a single variable in terms of another that is clearly defined (e.g., what is the cost of a data plan if you consume 4 GB of data in a month). However, sometimes you will be given a set of multiple equations with multiple variables that are interdependent. For example, suppose a $50/month cell phone plan includes $0.05 text messages and $0.40 voice calls, with a cap of 1,000 combined text messages and voice calls.

This scenario can be represented by the following system of equations:

$$\$0.05t + \$0.40v = \$50$$
$$t + v = 1{,}000$$

Solving such a system would enable you to determine the maximum number of text messages and voice calls you could make under this plan, while optimizing total usage. To solve systems of equations, you'll need to rely on a different set of tools that builds on the algebra you're already familiar with. The following question shows an example of such a system in the context of a test-like question.

1. If $28x - 5y = 36$ and $15x + 5y + 18 = 68$, what is the value of x?

A) 1

B) 2

C) 3

D) 4

You might be tempted to switch on math autopilot at this point and employ substitution, solving the first equation for y in terms of x:

$$y = \frac{1}{5}(-36 + 28x)$$

You could plug the resulting expression back into the other equation and eventually solve for x, but remember, the SAT tests your ability to solve math problems in the most efficient way. The following table contains some strategic thinking designed to help you find the most efficient way to solve this problem on Test Day, along with some suggested scratchwork.

Strategic Thinking	Math Scratchwork
Step 1: Read the question, identifying and organizing important information as you go This question is straightforward: You're being asked to solve for x.	
Step 2: Choose the best strategy to answer the question None of the coefficients in either equation is 1, so combination will be faster than substitution. Begin by writing the second equation in the same form as the first. The coefficients of the y terms are equal in magnitude but opposite in sign, so add the equations. Once the y terms are eliminated, solve for x.	$28x - 5y = 36$ $15x + 5y + 18 = 68$ $28x - 5y = 36$ $+\ \ 15x + 5y = 50$ $\overline{43x = 86}$ $x = 2$
Step 3: Check that you answered the *right* question You've solved for x, the requested quantity. You can confidently select (B).	$x = 2$

> ✔ **Note**
>
> Explanations for each simplifying step are not always included in this chapter. If you get stuck, review the information on simplifying and solving equations in chapter 2.

INDEPENDENT VERSUS DEPENDENT EQUATIONS

Generally, when you are given a system involving n variables, you need n *independent* equations to arrive at fixed values for these variables. Thus, if you have a system of two variables, you need two independent equations to solve for each of the variables. Three variables would require three independent equations, and so on.

Systems of equations are extremely useful in modeling and simulation. Complex mathematical problems such as weather forecasting or crowd control predictions often require 10 or more equations to be simultaneously solved for multiple variables. Fortunately, you won't encounter anything this daunting on Test Day.

Before we outline the process for solving two-variable systems of equations, let's clarify one of the key requirements. Earlier, it was stated that you need two independent equations to solve for two variables, but what exactly is an independent equation? Consider the equation $4x + 2y = 8$. You could use properties of equality to transform this equation in a number of different ways. For example, you could multiply both sides by 2, resulting in the equation $8x + 4y = 16$.

While it seems as though we've just created an additional equation, this is misleading, as the second equation has the same core variables and relationships as the first equation. This is termed a dependent equation, and two dependent equations cannot be used to solve for two variables. Look what happens when we try to use substitution. Start by isolating y in the original equation; the result is $y = 4 - 2x$.

Substituting that into the second equation, notice what happens:

$$8x + 4(4 - 2x) = 16$$
$$8x + 16 - 8x = 16$$
$$16 = 16$$

Although 16 does in fact equal 16, this doesn't bring us any closer to solving for either of the variables. In fact, if you arrive at a result like this when solving a system of equations, then the two equations are *dependent*. In this case, the system has infinitely many solutions because you could choose any number of possible values for x and y.

> ✔ **Note**
>
> When two equations are dependent, one equation can be obtained by algebraically manipulating the other equation. Graphically, dependent equations both describe the same line in the coordinate plane and therefore have the same slope and the same y-intercept.

At other times, you'll encounter equations that are fundamentally incompatible with each other. For example, if you have the two equations $4x + 2y = 8$ and $4x + 2y = 9$, it should be obvious that there are no values for x and y that will satisfy both equations at the same time. Doing so would violate fundamental laws of math. In this case, you would have a system of equations that has no solution. These two equations define parallel lines, which by definition never intersect.

Knowing how many solutions a system of equations has will tell you how graphing them in the same coordinate plane should look. Remember, the solution of a system of equations consists of the point or points where their graphs intersect.

If your system has...	...then it will graph as:	Reasoning
no solution	two parallel lines	Parallel lines never intersect.
one solution	two lines intersecting at a single point	Two straight lines have only one intersection.
infinitely many solutions	a single line (one line directly on top of the other)	One equation is a manipulation of the other—their graphs are the same line.

Because you could encounter any of these three situations on Test Day, make sure you are familiar with all of them.

Let's examine a sample problem to investigate the requirements for solving a system of equations:

$$\begin{cases} 5x - 3y = 10 \\ 6y = kx - 42 \end{cases}$$

2. In the system of linear equations above, k represents a constant. If the system of equations has no solution, what is the value of $2k$?

   A) $\dfrac{5}{2}$

   B) 5

   C) 10

   D) 20

Work through the Kaplan Method for Math step-by-step to solve this question. The following table shows Kaplan's strategic thinking on the left, along with suggested math scratchwork on the right.

Strategic Thinking	Math Scratchwork
Step 1: Read the question, identifying and organizing important information as you go You are looking for the value of $2k$, given the condition that the system of equations has no solution (which means the lines are parallel).	
Step 2: Choose the best strategy to answer the question If the two variables have identical coefficients in both equations, they should be equal to different constants. (This means they have the same slope but different y-intercepts.) Start by manipulating the second equation so that it is in the same format as the first. After manipulating the second equation, divide it by 2 to yield a -3 coefficient for y to match the coefficient of y in the first equation. Now, $\dfrac{k}{2}$ must equal 5, the coefficient of x in the first equation. Solve for k.	$5x - 3y = 10$ $6y = kx - 42$ $-kx + 6y = -42$ $kx - 6y = 42$ $\dfrac{k}{2}x - 3y = 21$ $\dfrac{k}{2} = 5$ $k = 10$
Step 3: Check that you answered the _right_ question Be careful: You're asked for $2k$, not k. Multiply both sides by 2 to get $2k = 20$, which is (D).	$2k = 20$

SOLVING SYSTEMS OF EQUATIONS: COMBINATION & SUBSTITUTION

Now that you understand the requirements that must be satisfied to solve a system of equations, let's look at some methods for solving these systems effectively. The two main methods for solving a system of linear equations are substitution and combination (sometimes referred to as *elimination by addition*).

Substitution is the most straightforward method for solving systems, and it can be applied in every situation. Unfortunately, it is often the longest and most time-consuming route for solving systems of equations as well. To use substitution, solve the simpler of the two equations for one variable, and then substitute the result into the other equation. You could use substitution to answer the following question, but you'll see that there's a quicker way: combination.

Combination involves adding the two equations together to eliminate a variable. Often, one or both of the equations must be multiplied by a constant before they are added together. Combination is often the best technique to use to solve a system of equations as it is usually faster than substitution.

Unfortunately, even though most students prefer substitution, problems on the SAT are often designed to be quickly solved with combination. To really boost your score on Test Day, practice combination as much as you can on Practice Tests and in homework problems so that it becomes second nature.

3. If $\frac{1}{4}x + 2y = \frac{11}{4}$ and $-6y - x = 7$, what is half of y?

Work through the Kaplan Method for Math step-by-step to solve this question. The following table shows Kaplan's strategic thinking on the left, along with suggested math scratchwork on the right.

Strategic Thinking	Math Scratchwork
Step 1: Read the question, identifying and organizing important information as you go Read carefully: You need to find *half* of y.	
Step 2: Choose the best strategy to answer the question Resist the urge to automatically use substitution. The presence of fractions in the question stem tells you that you should use combination (because substitution will be very messy). Multiply the first equation by 4 to clear the fractions, reorder the second equation so that x comes first, and then add the equations together and solve for y.	$\frac{1}{4}x + 2y = \frac{11}{4}$ $-6y - x = 7$ $4\left(\frac{1}{4}x + 2y = \frac{11}{4}\right) \rightarrow$ $x + 8y = 11$ $+ \quad -x - 6y = 7$ $\overline{\qquad 2y = 18}$ $y = 9$
Step 3: Check that you answered the *right* question Don't stop yet: You need to find half of y. Grid in 9/2 or 4.5, and you're done.	$\frac{y}{2} = \frac{9}{2} = 4.5$

Combination can also be used when the test makers ask you for a strange quantity, as in the following problem:

4. If $7c - 2b = 15$ and $3b - 6c = 2$, what is the value of $b + c$?

   A) -27

   B) -3

   C) 8

   D) 17

Work through the Kaplan Method for Math step-by-step to solve this question. The following table shows Kaplan's strategic thinking on the left, along with suggested math scratchwork on the right.

Strategic Thinking	Math Scratchwork
Step 1: Read the question, identifying and organizing important information as you go You are being asked to find the value of $b + c$. The question stem provides two equations involving b and c.	$7c - 2b = 15$ $3b - 6c = 2$
Step 2: Choose the best strategy to answer the question The fact that you're solving for $b + c$ suggests that there's a short-cut that will save time on Test Day. Add the equations together to yield $b + c$ equal to a constant. Before you add, don't forget to write the variable terms in the same order for each equation.	$\begin{array}{r} -2b + 7c = 15 \\ +\quad 3b - 6c = 2 \\ \hline b + c = 17 \end{array}$
Step 3: Check that you answered the *right* question Choice (D) correctly reflects the sum of b and c.	$b + c = 17$

That was much easier and faster than substitution. With substitution, you could spend more than two minutes solving a question like this. However, a bit of analysis and combination gets the job done in much less time.

TRANSLATING WORD PROBLEMS INTO MULTIPLE EQUATIONS

While solving systems of equations can be relatively straightforward once you get the hang of it, sometimes you'll encounter a complex word problem and need to translate it into a system of equations and then solve. It sounds a lot scarier than it actually is. Remember to use the Kaplan Strategy for Translating English into Math to set up your equations, and then solve using either substitution or combination.

 Note

The Kaplan Strategy for Translating English into Math can be found in chapter 2.

Let's take a look at an example:

5. At a certain toy store, tiny stuffed pandas cost \$3.50 and giant stuffed pandas cost \$14. If the store sold 29 panda toys and made \$217 in revenue in one week, how many tiny stuffed pandas and giant stuffed pandas were sold?

    A) 18 tiny stuffed pandas, 11 giant stuffed pandas

    B) 11 tiny stuffed pandas, 18 giant stuffed pandas

    C) 12 tiny stuffed pandas, 17 giant stuffed pandas

    D) 18 tiny stuffed pandas, 13 giant stuffed pandas

Work through the Kaplan Method for Math to solve this question step-by-step. The following table shows Kaplan's strategic thinking on the left, along with suggested math scratchwork on the right.

Strategic Thinking	Math Scratchwork
Step 1: Read the question, identifying and organizing important information as you go	
You need to find the number of tiny stuffed pandas and giant stuffed pandas sold.	tiny: $3.50 each giant: $14 each 29 total sold $217 in revenue
Step 2: Choose the best strategy to answer the question	
This is a word problem, so use the Kaplan Strategy for Translating English into Math. Because both toys are pandas, p is likely to be a confusing choice for a variable. Instead, use t for tiny and g for giant.	$t = $ tiny $g = $ giant
Break off each piece of relevant information into a separate phrase. Translating each phrase into a math expression will create the components of a system of equations.	tiny: $3.50 $\rightarrow 3.5t$ giant: $14 $\rightarrow 14g$ 29 total sold $\rightarrow\ = 29$ $217 in revenue $\rightarrow\ = 217$
After piecing together the system of equations, use combination to quickly eliminate g. Multiply the first equation by -14 before combining with the second. Solve for t. Choices B and C have different values for t, so eliminate them. Plug 18 into the first equation for t, and then solve for g.	$t + g = 29$ $3.5t + 14g = 217$ $\quad\ -14t - 14g = -406$ $+\quad 3.5t + 14g = 217$ $\overline{\qquad\quad -10.5t = -189}$ $\qquad\qquad\ t = 18$ $t + g = 29$ $18 + g = 29$ $\qquad g = 11$
Step 3: Check that you answered the *right* question	
The only answer choice that contains both quantities you found is (A).	$t = 18,\ g = 11$

Math

Watch out for B, a trap answer designed to catch students who switched the variables, possibly due to choosing an ambiguous letter such as *p*. Choosing descriptive variable names might sound silly, but in the high-stakes environment of the SAT, you must do everything you can to avoid careless errors and subsequent lost points.

> ✔ **Note**
>
> Always choose variable names that make sense to you. Countless students struggle on multi-part problems due to disorganized notes. Don't let that happen to you. Move beyond *x* and *y* when selecting variable names.

Other questions of this type will simply ask you to choose from a series of answer choices that describes the system of equations—they won't actually ask you to calculate a solution! These questions can be great time-savers. Consider the following example:

6. A state college has separate fee rates for resident students and nonresident students. Resident students are charged $421 per semester, and nonresident students are charged $879 per semester. The college's sophomore class of 1,980 students paid a total of $1,170,210 in fees for the most recent semester. Which of the following systems of equations represents the number of resident (r) and nonresident (n) sophomores and the amount of fees the two groups paid?

    A) $r + n = 1{,}170{,}210;\ 421r + 879n = 1{,}980$

    B) $r + n = 1{,}980;\ 879r + 421n = 1{,}170{,}210$

    C) $r + n = 1{,}980;\ 421r + 879n = 1{,}170{,}210$

    D) $r + n = 1{,}170{,}210;\ 879r + 421n = 1{,}980$

Work through the Kaplan Method for Math to solve this question step-by-step. The following table shows Kaplan's strategic thinking on the left, along with suggested math scratchwork on the right.

Strategic Thinking	Math Scratchwork
Step 1: Read the question, identifying and organizing important information as you go You're asked for the system of equations that represents the given situation.	
Step 2: Choose the best strategy to answer the question This question is wordy, so use the Kaplan Strategy for Translating English into Math. The first step (assigning variables) has been done for you, so you can go right to breaking up the question stem into smaller pieces. Convert these into math, and then assemble your equations.	$r =$ resident $n =$ nonresident r: \$421 in fees n: \$879 in fees 1,980 students \$1,170,210 collected r: \$421 → $421r$ n: \$879 → $879n$ $$r + n = 1{,}980$$ $$421r + 879n = 1{,}170{,}210$$
Step 3: Check that you answered the *right* question Choice (C) is the only answer choice that contains both equations you built.	

Be careful! Choice B is close but switches the fee structure, drastically overcharging the in-state students! Always pay close attention to the differences between answer choices to avoid traps on Test Day.

Now you'll have a chance to try a few more test-like questions. Use the scaffolding as needed to guide you through the question and get the right answer.

Some guidance is provided, but you'll need to fill in the missing parts of explanations or the step-by-step math to get to the correct answer. Don't worry—after going through the examples at the beginning of this chapter, these questions should be completely doable. If you find yourself struggling, however, review the worked examples again.

7. A bead shop sells wooden beads for $0.20 each and crystal beads for $0.50 each. If a jewelry artist buys 127 beads total and pays $41 for them, how much more did she spend on crystal beads than wooden beads?

   A) $11

   B) $15

   C) $23

   D) $26

The following table can help you structure your thinking as you go about solving this problem. Kaplan's strategic thinking is provided, as are bits of structured scratchwork. If you're not sure how to approach a question like this, start at the top and work your way down.

Strategic Thinking	Math Scratchwork
Step 1: Read the question, identifying and organizing important information as you go You're asked how much more the jewelry artist spent on crystal beads than on wooden beads.	
Step 2: Choose the best strategy to answer the question Use the Kaplan Strategy for Translating English into Math. Variables are easy to pick for this question. Think about what letters the words start with.	wooden: _____ crystal: _____ _____ per wooden _____ per crystal _____ total bought _____ spent
Separate each numerical piece into its own phrase, then convert to math.	_____ per wooden → _____ _____ per crystal → _____ _____ total bought → _____ _____ spent → _____
Assemble a system of equations, then solve. You can use either substitution or combination to solve for the quantity of each bead type. Remember to think critically about which approach would be faster in this situation.	_____ + _____ = _____ _____ + _____ = _____ _____ = _____ _____ = _____
Determine how much the jewelry artist spent on each type of bead, then take the difference.	$_____ on wooden $_____ on crystal _____ − _____ = _____
Step 3: Check that you answered the *right* question If you came up with (A), you're absolutely correct.	_____

8. If $y = -x - 15$ and $\dfrac{5y}{2} - 37 = -\dfrac{x}{2}$, then what is the value of $2x + 6y$?

Larger numbers don't make this question any different; just be careful with the arithmetic. Again, the following table can help you structure your thinking as you go about solving this problem. Kaplan's strategic thinking is provided, as are bits of structured scratchwork. If you're not sure how to approach a question like this, start at the top and work your way down.

Strategic Thinking	Math Scratchwork
Step 1: Read the question, identifying and organizing important information as you go You're asked to find the value of $2x + 6y$.	
Step 2: Choose the best strategy to answer the question Start by rearranging the equations so that they're in the same general format. Because you're asked for an expression, look for a shortcut. Don't bother trying to solve for either x or y individually.	$y = -x - 15$ $\dfrac{5y}{2} - 37 = -\dfrac{x}{2}$ _____ + _____ = _____ _____ + _____ = _____
A good strategy: Clear the fractions from the second equation so you can use combination. Once the fractions are gone, confirm that adding the second equation to the first will yield the expression you need.	_____ (_____ + _____ = _____) _____ + _____ = _____ + _____ + _____ = _____ _____ + _____ = _____
Step 3: Check that you answered the *right* question If your answer is 59, you're correct!	_____

Now that you've seen the variety of ways in which the SAT can test you on systems of linear equations, try the following questions to check your understanding. Give yourself 4.5 minutes to tackle the following three questions.

$$6x + 3y = 18$$

$$qx - \frac{y}{3} = -2$$

9. In the system of linear equations above, q is a constant. If the system has infinitely many solutions, what is the value of q?

   A) -9

   B) $-\dfrac{2}{3}$

   C) $\dfrac{2}{3}$

   D) 9

10. If $12x + 15y = 249$ and $5x + 13y = 124$, then what is the value of $\dfrac{y}{x}$?

11. A pizzeria's top-selling pizzas are The Works and The Hawaiian. The Works sells for $17, and The Hawaiian sells for $13. Ingredient costs for The Works are $450 per week, and ingredient costs for The Hawaiian are $310 per week. Assuming the pizzeria sells an equal number of both pizzas in one week, at what point will profits for one pizza overtake the other?

   A)   After selling 35 pizzas each, The Hawaiian profits will overtake The Works profits.

   B)   After selling 145 pizzas each, The Hawaiian profits will overtake The Works profits.

   C)   After selling 35 pizzas each, The Works profits will overtake The Hawaiian profits.

   D)   After selling 145 pizzas each, The Works profits will overtake The Hawaiian profits.

Answers and Explanations for this chapter begin on page 815.

Math

EXTRA PRACTICE

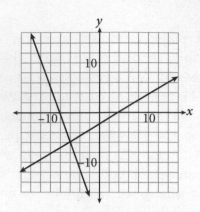

1. If (A, B) is the solution to the system of equations shown above, and A and B are integers, then what is the value of $A + B$?

   A) -12

   B) -6

   C) 0

   D) 6

$$\begin{cases} 4x + 3y = 14 - y \\ x - 5y = 2 \end{cases}$$

2. If (x, y) is a solution to the system of equations above, then what is the value of $x - y$?

   A) $\dfrac{1}{4}$

   B) 1

   C) 3

   D) 18

3. Charlie starts to solve a system of linear equations graphically. He puts both equations into slope-intercept form and notices that the lines have the same slope. Based on this information only, which of the following statements is true?

   A)   The system could have no solution, one solution, or infinitely many solutions.

   B)   The system has no solution because two equations with the same slope never intersect.

   C)   The system has either no solution or infinitely many solutions, depending on the y-intercepts.

   D)   The system has infinitely many solutions because two equations with the same slope represent the same line.

$$\begin{cases} hx - 4y = -10 \\ kx + 3y = -15 \end{cases}$$

4. If the graphs of the lines in the system of equations above intersect at $(-3, 1)$, what is the value of $\dfrac{k}{h}$?

   A) $\dfrac{3}{2}$

   B) 2

   C) 3

   D) 6

5. A sofa costs $50 less than three times the cost of a chair. If the sofa and chair together cost $650, how much more does the sofa cost than the chair?

A) $175

B) $225

C) $300

D) $475

$$\begin{cases} \dfrac{1}{2}x - \dfrac{2}{3}y = 7 \\ ax - 8y = -1 \end{cases}$$

6. If the system of linear equations above has no solution, and a is a constant, then what is the value of a?

A) -2

B) $-\dfrac{1}{2}$

C) 2

D) 6

7. A party store has 54 packs of plates in stock. The packs are either sets of 8 or sets of 12. If the store has 496 total plates in stock, how many plates would a customer buy if he or she buys all of the packs of 12 that the store has in stock?

A) 16

B) 38

C) 192

D) 304

$$\begin{cases} 3x - 9y = -6 \\ \dfrac{1}{2}x - \dfrac{3}{2}y = c \end{cases}$$

8. If the system of linear equations above has infinitely many solutions, and c is a constant, what is the value of c?

A) -6

B) -3

C) -2

D) -1

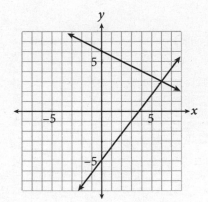

9. What is the y-coordinate of the solution to the system shown above?

A) -5

B) 3

C) 5

D) 6

10. If $2x - 3y = 14$ and $5x + 3y = 21$, then what is the value of x?

A) -1

B) 0

C) $\dfrac{7}{3}$

D) 5

Math

11. At a certain movie theater, there are 16 rows and each row has either 20 or 24 seats. If the total number of seats in all 16 rows is 348, how many rows have 24 seats?

A) 7

B) 9

C) 11

D) 13

Equation 1	
x	y
−2	6
0	4
2	2
4	0

Equation 2	
x	y
−8	−8
−4	−7
0	−6
4	−5

12. The tables above represent data points for two linear equations. If the two equations form a system, what is the x-coordinate of the solution to that system?

Linear Inequalities and Systems of Inequalities

CHAPTER OBJECTIVES

By the end of this chapter, you will be able to:

1. Identify the key differences between solving inequalities and equations
2. Efficiently solve systems of inequalities

SMARTPOINTS

Point Value	SmartPoint Category
40 Points	Inequalities

Math

LINEAR INEQUALITIES & SYSTEMS OF INEQUALITIES

Chapter 4

Homework

Extra Practice: #1-13

Key

 Book Assignment

 Online Video Assignment

 Online Quiz Assignment

RULES FOR SOLVING INEQUALITIES

There's more to algebra than just equations, and inequalities will show up rather frequently on the SAT. Fortunately, many of the same strategies that apply to solving equations also apply to inequalities. There are a few key exceptions to keep in mind, but don't worry—these will be explained throughout this chapter.

First, the language used to describe inequalities tends to be more complex than the language used to describe equations. You "solve" an equation for *x*, but with an inequality, you might be asked to "describe all possible values of *x*" or provide an answer that "includes the entire set of solutions for *x*." This difference in wording exists because an equation describes a specific value of a variable, whereas an inequality describes a range of values. Regardless of the language, your task is the same: Isolate *x* on one side.

> ✔ **Note**
>
> If the variable ends up on the right-hand side of the symbol when you solve an inequality, be careful when matching it to an answer choice. For instance, $3 > x$ can be rewritten as $x < 3$. Notice that the small end of the symbol stays pointed at *x*.

The following question tests your basic inequality-solving skills.

1. A bowling alley charges a flat \$6.50 fee for shoe and ball rental plus \$3.75 per game and 6.325% sales tax. If each person in a group of seven people has \$20 to spend on a bowling outing, which inequality represents the maximum number of shoe and ball rentals (*r*) and games (*g*) that can be purchased by the group?

    A) $1.06325(6.5r + 3.75g) \leq 140$

    B) $1.06325(6.5r + 3.75g) \leq 20$

    C) $1.06325\left(\dfrac{6.5}{r} + \dfrac{3.75}{g}\right) \leq 140$

    D) $0.06325(6.5r + 3.75g) \leq 20$

Work through the Kaplan Method for Math step-by-step to solve this question. The following table shows Kaplan's strategic thinking on the left, along with suggested math scratchwork on the right.

Strategic Thinking	Math Scratchwork
Step 1: Read the question, identifying and organizing important information as you go The question asks for an inequality that represents the situation described.	

Strategic Thinking	Math Scratchwork
Step 2: Choose the best strategy to answer the question Use the Kaplan Strategy for Translating English into Math. The variables are already defined, so you only need to correctly piece them together with the given numbers. The question states that a shoe and ball rental costs $6.50 and that a game costs $3.75. Combine these with the correct variables, remembering to incorporate sales tax. Be careful when writing the right side of the inequality; the question asks for an inequality that represents the entire group, not just one person.	$r \rightarrow$ rentals, $6.5r$ $g \rightarrow$ games, $3.75g$ including tax: 1.06325 total $\$: 7 \times 20 = 140$ $1.06325(6.5r + 3.75g) \leq 140$
Step 3: Check that you answered the *right* question Choice (A) contains the inequality you derived.	

Notice B is a trap answer. If you write the inequality to reflect the cost for just one person, you'll be led right to it.

> ✔ **Note**
>
> Choice D is a trap waiting for students who improperly incorporate the sales tax component. Using 0.06325 calculates the amount spent on sales tax, not the total amount spent on the bowling outing.

Inequalities can also be presented graphically in one or two dimensions. In one dimension, inequalities are graphed on a number line with a shaded region. For example, $x > 1$ could be graphed like this:

Notice the open dot at $x = 1$, indicating that 1 is not a solution to the inequality. This is called a **strict** inequality. By contrast, the graph of $x \leq 0$ looks like this:

Notice the closed dot, indicating that 0 should be included in the solution set for the inequality.

> ✔ **Note**
>
> To help remember which way to shade, read the $<$ symbol as "less than," which tells you to shade to the left of the dot. Note the Ls: *L*ess than means shade *L*eft.

In two dimensions, things get a bit more complicated. While linear equations graph as simple lines, inequalities graph as lines called **boundary lines** with shaded regions known as **half planes**. Solid lines involve inequalities that have $\leq$ or $\geq$ because the line itself is included in the solution set. Dashed lines involve strict inequalities that have $>$ or $<$ because, in these cases, the line itself is not included in the solution set. The shaded region represents all points that make up the solution set for the inequality.

SOLVING SYSTEMS OF INEQUALITIES

Multiple inequalities can be combined to create a system of inequalities. This system can involve multiple variables, or it can be used to provide more detailed bounds for a range of solutions for a single variable. You'll get to try both in questions shortly.

Systems of inequalities can also be presented graphically with multiple boundary lines and multiple shaded regions. Follow the same rules for graphing single inequalities, but keep in mind that the solution set is the region where the shading overlaps. Shading in different directions (e.g., parallel lines slanted up for one inequality and down for the other) makes the overlap easier to see. This is illustrated in an upcoming question.

2. Which of the following graphs represents the solution set for $5x - 10y > 6$?

A)

C)

B)

D)

Work through the Kaplan Method for Math step-by-step to solve this question. The following table shows Kaplan's strategic thinking on the left, along with suggested math scratchwork on the right.

Strategic Thinking	Math Scratchwork
Step 1: Read the question, identifying and organizing important information as you go The question is asking for the graph that matches the inequality given.	
Step 2: Choose the best strategy to answer the question It's risky to eliminate choices now, as the inequality is not in slope-intercept form. Rearrange the inequality so that it's in this form, remembering to flip the inequality symbol in the final step because you're dividing by -10. The inequality in slope-intercept form indicates a negative y-intercept, so you can eliminate A and D. The "less than" symbol indicates that the shading should be below the dashed line, meaning (C) must be correct. Alternatively, you can plug a point (such as the origin) into the inequality. When plugged into the inequality, you'll see that the origin should not be in the solution set because 0 is not greater than $0 + \dfrac{3}{5}$. This means (C) is correct.	$5x - 10y > 6$ $-10y > -5x + 6$ $\dfrac{-10y}{-10} > \dfrac{-5x}{-10} + \dfrac{6}{-10}$ $y < \dfrac{1}{2}x - \dfrac{3}{5}$
Step 3: Check that you answered the _right_ question Choice (C) matches the inequality.	

3. If $\frac{1}{2}x + \frac{2}{3}y \leq 1$ and $\frac{1}{2}x + \frac{1}{3}y \leq \frac{2}{3}$ form a system of inequalities, what is one possible value of $x + y$?

Work through the Kaplan Method for Math step-by-step to solve this question. The following table shows Kaplan's strategic thinking on the left, along with suggested math scratchwork on the right.

Strategic Thinking	Math Scratchwork
Step 1: Read the question, identifying and organizing important information as you go The question asks for a possible value of $x + y$.	
Step 2: Choose the best strategy to answer the question The question asks for an unusual quantity, $x + y$, so look for a shortcut. Examine the coefficients of the variables. If you write one equation under the other, you'll see that the coefficients of the x terms sum to 1, as do the coefficients of the y terms. You can add the inequalities together (because they have the same symbol) and get $x + y$ on one side.	$\frac{1}{2}x + \frac{1}{3}y \leq \frac{2}{3}$ $+ \ \frac{1}{2}x + \frac{2}{3}y \leq 1$ ——————— $x + y \leq \frac{5}{3}$
Step 3: Check that you answered the _right_ question This is a grid-in question, so pick a number between 0 and $\frac{5}{3}$, inclusive, such as 0, 1, or $\frac{5}{3}$.	$0 \leq x + y \leq \frac{5}{3}$

> ✔ **Note**
>
> You can add two inequalities ONLY if they have the same symbol.

4. If $12x - 4y > 8$ and $\frac{2}{3}x + 6y \geq 14$ form a system of inequalities, which of the following graphs shows the solution set for the system?

A)

C)

B)

D)

Work through the Kaplan Method for Math step-by-step to solve this question. The following table shows Kaplan's strategic thinking on the left, along with suggested math scratchwork on the right.

Strategic Thinking	Math Scratchwork
Step 1: Read the question, identifying and organizing important information as you go You need to identify the graph that shows the solution to the system of inequalities.	
Step 2: Choose the best strategy to answer the question Start by rewriting each inequality in slope-intercept form. Once finished, determine what the correct graphs will look like. The boundary line for $y < 3x - 2$ should be a dashed line, and the boundary line for $y \geq -\dfrac{1}{9}x + \dfrac{7}{3}$ should be a solid line. You can eliminate C based on this. The half-plane below $y < 3x - 2$ should be shaded, and the half-plane above $y \geq -\dfrac{1}{9}x + \dfrac{7}{3}$ should be shaded; of the remaining choices, only (B) satisfies this requirement.	$12x - 4y > 8$ $-4y > -12x + 8$ $\dfrac{-4y}{-4} > \dfrac{-12x}{-4} + \dfrac{8}{-4}$ $y < 3x - 2$ $\dfrac{2}{3}x + 6y \geq 14$ $6y \geq -\dfrac{2}{3}x + 14$ $\dfrac{6y}{6} \geq \dfrac{1}{6} \times \left(-\dfrac{2}{3}x\right) + \dfrac{14}{6}$ $y \geq -\dfrac{1}{9}x + \dfrac{7}{3}$
Step 3: Check that you answered the _right_ question Choice (B) correctly depicts the solution to the system. You can check your answer by plugging a point from (B)'s solution set, such as (4, 4), into both inequalities given in the question and verifying that each results in a true statement.	

Now you'll have a chance to try a test-like problem in a scaffolded way. We've provided some guidance, but you'll need to fill in the missing parts of the explanation or the step-by-step math to get to the correct answer. Don't worry—after going through the worked examples at the beginning of this section, this problem should be completely doable.

5. A network of hotels across the United States normally charges $180 for an overnight stay at any of its properties. This network also offers a deal for longer trips: A traveler who purchases a hotel discount card for $720 will pay only $120 per night at any of the network's properties for the duration of the traveler's trip. Which of the following inequalities represents the number of nights n a traveler must stay in any combination of the network's hotels during a trip in order to make the discount card a better deal?

A) $n > 12$

B) $n < 12$

C) $n > 9$

D) $n < 9$

Use the following scaffolding as your map through the question. If you aren't sure where to start, fill in the blanks in the table as you work from top to bottom.

Strategic Thinking	Math Scratchwork
Step 1: Read the question, identifying and organizing important information as you go You need to identify the inequality that gives the number of nights a traveler must stay during a trip in order to make the discount card a better deal.	
Step 2: Choose the best strategy to answer the question Use the Kaplan Strategy for Translating English into Math. You're told n is the number of overnight stays. The cost of travel with the card is $720 + 120n$. Without the card, a traveler would pay $180n$. Combine these expressions in an inequality and solve for n. Keep in mind that a "better deal" means the total cost is *less*.	_____ < _____ _____ < _____ _____ < _____
Step 3: Check that you answered the *right* question If you got (A), you're right!	_____

Now that you've seen the variety of ways in which the SAT can test you on linear inequalities, try the following questions to check your understanding. Give yourself 2 minutes to tackle these two questions.

6. If $-3 < \frac{4}{3}h + \frac{1}{6} < 1$, then what is one possible value of $12h - 4$?

7. Sarah and Zena are head sales associates at a dance apparel shop. In addition to their annual raises, the two will be eligible for holiday bonuses if their dance tops and pants sales meet the following criteria in December: Between the two of them, the girls must sell an average of 75 items each, and their combined generated revenue must be at least $6,000. Each top costs $35, and each pair of pants costs $60. If Sarah sells t_S tops and p_S pairs of pants and Zena sells t_Z tops and p_Z pairs of pants, which of the following systems of inequalities correctly depicts the minimum quantities the two must sell to earn a holiday bonus?

A) $t_S + p_S + t_Z + p_Z \geq 75$
$35(t_S + t_Z) + 60(p_S + p_Z) \geq 3,000$

B) $t_S + p_S + t_Z + p_Z \geq 150$
$90(t_S + p_S + t_Z + p_Z) \geq 6,000$

C) $t_S + p_S + t_Z + p_Z \geq 150$
$35(t_S + t_Z) + 60(p_S + p_Z) \geq 6,000$

D) $t_S + p_S + t_Z + p_Z \geq 150$
$35(t_S + p_S) + 60(t_Z + p_Z) \geq 6,000$

Answers and Explanations for this chapter begin on page 820.

EXTRA PRACTICE

$$\frac{1}{5}(7 - 3b) > 2$$

1. Which of the following gives all values of b that satisfy the inequality above?

   A) $b < -1$

   B) $b > -1$

   C) $b < 1$

   D) $b > 1$

2. If $n - 3 > 8$ and $n + 1 < 14$, then which of the following could be a value for n?

   A) 11

   B) 12

   C) 13

   D) 14

$$15 - x \;\boxed{}\; 9$$

3. The number line above shows the solution to the inequality. Which of the following symbols would make the statement true?

   A) <

   B) >

   C) ≤

   D) ≥

Electric Company	Price (cents per kWh)
Company A	15.2
Company B	17.4
Company C	16.5
Company D	14.8

4. A kilowatt-hour is a unit of measure for consumable energy. A kilowatt-hour, written kWh, is equivalent to using 1,000 watts of power in 1 hour. The table above shows the per-kWh rates charged by several electric companies in New England. According to the United States Energy Information Administration, an average household in New England uses between 530 and 730 kWh of energy per month. Which inequality represents how much less in energy costs a household would pay per month if it uses Company D as its energy supplier, than if it uses Company B?

   A) $x \leq 0.026$

   B) $0.148 \leq x \leq 0.174$

   C) $13.78 \leq x \leq 18.98$

   D) $29.60 \leq x \leq 34.80$

5. A shipping company employee is in charge of packing cargo containers for shipment. He knows a certain cargo container can hold a maximum of 50 microwaves or a maximum of 15 refrigerators. Each microwave takes up 6 cubic feet of space, and each refrigerator takes up 20 cubic feet. The cargo container can hold a maximum of 300 cubic feet. The employee is trying to figure out how to pack a container containing both microwaves and refrigerators. Which of the following systems of inequalities can the employee use to determine how many of each item (microwaves, m, and refrigerators, r) he can pack into one cargo container?

A) $\begin{cases} m \leq 6 \\ r \leq 20 \\ 50m + 15r \leq 300 \end{cases}$

B) $\begin{cases} m \leq 50 \\ r \leq 15 \\ m + r \leq 300 \end{cases}$

C) $\begin{cases} m \leq 50 \\ r \leq 15 \\ 6m + 20r \leq 300 \end{cases}$

D) $\begin{cases} m \leq 50 \\ r \leq 15 \\ 50m + 15r \leq 300 \end{cases}$

6. If $-\dfrac{2}{5} < 3k - 4 < \dfrac{6}{7}$, then which of the following is not a possible value for $-6k + 8$?

A) $-\dfrac{5}{7}$

B) $\dfrac{1}{7}$

C) $\dfrac{1}{3}$

D) $\dfrac{4}{3}$

$$\begin{cases} y \leq \dfrac{2}{3}x + 1 \\ 2x - 3y \leq 12 \end{cases}$$

7. Which of the following best describes the solution set for the system of inequalities above?

A) The system has no solution.

B) The solution set consists of a single point.

C) The solution set consists of all real numbers.

D) The solution set consists of all points that lie between the boundary lines.

8. Marco is paid $80 per day plus $15 per hour for overtime. If he works five days per week and wants to make a minimum of $520 this week, what is the fewest number of hours of overtime he must work?

9. Which of the following represents the solution to the inequality $2(4x - 1) > 5x + 13$?

   A)

   B)

   C)

   D)

10. Which of the following best describes the graphical solution to the inequality $y < -2x + 3$?

    A) A dashed boundary line that rises from left to right, with shading in the half-plane below the boundary line

    B) A dashed boundary line that falls from left to right, with shading in the half-plane below the boundary line

    C) A dashed boundary line that falls from left to right, with shading in the half-plane above the boundary line

    D) A solid boundary line that falls from left to right, with shading in the half-plane below the boundary line

11. The figure above shows the solution set for the system $\begin{cases} y < \dfrac{3}{5}x - 2 \\ y \leq -\dfrac{4}{3}x + 5 \end{cases}$. Which of the following is not a solution to this system?

    A) $(-1, -4)$

    B) $(1, -1)$

    C) $(4, -1)$

    D) $(6, -3)$

$$\begin{cases} y < 2x - 3 \\ y \boxed{?} mx + 3 \end{cases}$$

12. Which value of m and which symbol result in the system of inequalities shown above as having no solution?

    A) $m = -2; >$

    B) $m = -\dfrac{1}{2}; <$

    C) $m = 2; >$

    D) $m = 2; <$

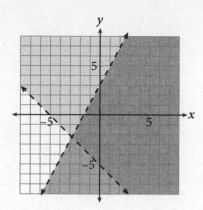

13. The figure above shows the solution for
the system of inequalities $\begin{cases} y > -x - 5 \\ y < 2x + 3 \end{cases}$.
Suppose (a, b) is a solution to the system.

If $a = 0$, what is the greatest possible integer
value of b?

Problem Solving & Data Analysis

BY THE END OF THIS UNIT, YOU WILL BE ABLE TO:

1. Apply the Kaplan Method for Multi-Part Math Questions

2. Use rates, ratios, proportions, and percentages

3. Interpret and extract information from scatterplots and two-way tables

4. Analyze simple and complex data sets using descriptive statistics

CHAPTER 5

Rates, Ratios, Proportions, and Percentages

 ## CHAPTER OBJECTIVES

By the end of this chapter, you will be able to:

1. Use the Kaplan Method for Multi-Part Math Questions to answer Problem Solving and Data Analysis questions effectively

2. Solve multi-part question sets involving rates, ratios, and proportions

3. Use appropriate formulas to find percentages and single or multiple percent changes

SMARTPOINTS

Point Value	SmartPoint Category
Point Builder	Kaplan Method for Multi-Part Math Questions
80 Points	Rates, Ratios, Proportions & Percentages

Math

RATES, RATIOS, PROPORTIONS, AND PERCENTAGES

Chapter 5

Homework

Extra Practice: #1-20

Even More

The Kaplan Method for
Multi-Part Math

Math Quiz 2

Key

  Book Assignment

  Online Video Assignment

  Online Quiz Assignment

The new SAT contains multiple-choice and grid-in questions, as well as multi-part math question sets. These question sets have multiple parts that are based on the same scenario and may require more analysis and planning than a typical multiple-choice question. To help you answer these questions effectively, use the Kaplan Method for Multi-Part Math Questions.

KAPLAN METHOD FOR MULTI-PART MATH QUESTIONS

Step 1: Read the first question in the set, looking for clues

Step 2: Identify and organize the information you need

Step 3: Based on what you know, plan your steps to navigate the first question

Step 4: Solve, step-by-step, checking units as you go

Step 5: Did I answer the *right* question?

Step 6: Repeat for remaining questions, incorporating results from the previous question if possible

The next few pages will walk you through each step in more detail.

Step 1: Read the first question in the set, looking for clues

- **Focus all your energy here** instead of diluting it over the whole set of questions; solving a multi-part question in pieces is far simpler than trying to solve all the questions in the set at once. Further, you may be able to use the results from earlier parts to solve subsequent ones. Don't even consider the later parts of the question set until you've solved the first part.

- **Watch for hints** about what information you'll actually need to use to answer the questions. Underlining key quantities is often helpful to separate what's important from extraneous information.

Step 2: Identify and organize the information you need

If you think this sounds like the Kaplan Method for Math, you're absolutely correct. You'll use some of those same skills. The difference: A multi-part math question is just more involved with multiple pieces.

- **What information am I given?** Jot down key notes, and group related quantities to develop your strategy.

- **What am I solving for?** This is your target. As you work your way through subsequent steps, keep your target at the front of your mind. This will help you avoid unnecessary work (and subsequent time loss). You'll sometimes need to tackle these problems from both ends, so always keep your goal in mind.

> ✔ **Expert Tip**
>
> Many students freeze when they encounter a problem with multiple steps and seemingly massive amounts of information. Don't worry! Take each piece one at a time, and you won't be intimidated.

Step 3: Based on what you know, plan your steps to navigate the first question

- **What pieces am I missing?** Many students become frustrated when faced with a roadblock such as missing information, but it's an easy fix. Sometimes you'll need to do an intermediate calculation to reveal the missing piece or pieces of the puzzle.

Step 4: Solve, step-by-step, checking units as you go

- **Work quickly but carefully**, just as you've done on other SAT math questions.

Step 5: Did I answer the *right* question?

- As is the case with the Kaplan Method for Math, **make sure your final answer is the requested answer**.
- Review the first question in the set.
- Double-check your units and your work.

Step 6: Repeat for remaining questions, incorporating results from the previous question if possible

- Now take your results from the first question and think critically about whether they fit into the subsequent questions in the set. Previous results won't always be applicable, but when they are, they often lead to huge time savings. But be careful—don't round results from the first question in your calculations for the second question—only the final answer should be rounded.

When you've finished, congratulate yourself for persevering through such a challenging task. A multi-part math question is likely to be one of the toughest on the SAT. If you can ace these questions, you'll be poised for a great score on Test Day. Don't worry if the Kaplan Method seems complicated; we'll walk through an example shortly.

> ✔ **Expert Tip**
>
> Because these question sets take substantially more time, consider saving multi-part math questions for last.

RATES, MEASUREMENT, AND UNIT CONVERSIONS

By now, you've become adept at using algebra to answer many SAT math questions, which is great, because you'll need those algebra skills to answer questions involving rates. You're likely already familiar with many different rates—kilometers per hour, meters per second, and even miles per gallon are all considered rates.

A fundamental equation related to rates is "Distance = rate × time" (a.k.a. the DIRT equation— **D**istance **I**s **R**ate × **T**ime). If you have two of the three components of the equation, you can easily find the third. An upcoming multi-part math example demonstrates this nicely.

You'll notice units of measurement are important for rate questions (and others that require a unit conversion) and, therefore, also an opportunity to fall for trap answers if you're not careful. How can you avoid this? Use the factor-label method (also known as dimensional analysis). The factor-label method is a simple yet powerful way to ensure you're doing your calculations correctly and getting an answer with the requested units.

For example, suppose you're asked to find the number of cups there are in two gallons. First, identify your starting quantity's units (gallons) and then identify the end quantity's units (cups). The next step is to piece together a path of relationships that will convert gallons into cups, canceling out units as you go. Keep in mind that you will often have multiple stepping stones between your starting and ending quantities, so don't panic if you can't get directly from gallons to cups.

The test makers won't expect you to know English measurements by heart. Instead, they'll provide conversion factors when needed. For example, a gallon is the same as 4 quarts, every quart contains 2 pints, and a pint equals 2 cups. And there you have it! Your map from gallons to cups is complete. The last step is to put it together as a giant multiplication problem. Each relationship, called a conversion factor, is written as a fraction. The basic rules of fraction multiplication apply, so you can cancel a unit that appears in both the numerator and denominator.

> ✔ Note
>
> The SAT will not require you to memorize conversions for conventional units. If the test asks you to convert miles into inches, for example, you will be provided with enough conversion factors to solve the problem.

Follow along as we convert from gallons to quarts to pints to cups using the factor-label method:

$$2 \text{ gallons} \times \frac{4 \text{ quarts}}{1 \text{ gallon}} \times \frac{2 \text{ pints}}{1 \text{ quart}} \times \frac{2 \text{ cups}}{1 \text{ pint}} = (2 \times 4 \times 2 \times 2) \text{ cups} = 32 \text{ cups}$$

The DIRT equation is actually a variation of this process. Suppose you travel at 60 mph for 5 hours. You would calculate the distance traveled using the equation $d = rt = \frac{60 \text{ mi}}{1 \text{ h}} \times 5 \text{ h} = 300$ miles.

The units for hours cancel out, leaving only miles, which is precisely what you're looking for, a distance. This built-in check is a great way to ensure your path to the answer is correct. If your units are off, check your steps for mistakes along the way. The SAT will never ask you for a quantity such as miles[4] or gallons[3], so if you end up with funky units like that, you've made an error somewhere in your work.

> ✔ Note
>
> When using the factor-label method, don't be afraid to flip fractions and rates to make the units cancel out as needed.

The following question demonstrates the factor-label method in a test-like question.

1. Quinn wants to rent a self-storage unit for her college dorm room furniture for the summer. She estimates that she will need 700 cubic feet of storage space, but the self-storage provider measures its units in cubic meters. If 1 meter is approximately 3.28 feet, about how many cubic meters of space will Quinn need?

    A)   19.84

    B)   25.93

    C)   65.07

    D)   213.41

Work through the Kaplan Method for Math to solve this question step-by-step. The following table shows Kaplan's strategic thinking on the left, along with suggested math scratchwork on the right.

Strategic Thinking	Math Scratchwork
Step 1: Read the question, identifying and organizing important information as you go You need to determine how many cubic meters of space Quinn needs for her belongings.	700 ft^3 space needed $= ? \text{ m}^3$
Step 2: Choose the best strategy to answer the question The factor-label method will be the quickest path to the correct answer. You're starting in cubic feet and need to convert to cubic meters. You know that 1 m = 3.28 ft, but be careful: 1 m^3 is not the same as 3.28 ft^3! Consider each feet-to-meters conversion separately.	starting qty: 700 ft^3 end qty: $? \text{ m}^3$ $\dfrac{700 \text{ ft}^3}{1} \times \dfrac{1 \text{ m}}{3.28 \text{ ft}} \times \dfrac{1 \text{ m}}{3.28 \text{ ft}} \times \dfrac{1 \text{ m}}{3.28 \text{ ft}}$ $= \dfrac{700}{(3.28)^3} \text{ m} \sim 19.84 \text{ m}^3$
Step 3: Check that you answered the *right* question You've correctly converted cubic feet to cubic meters to get the correct answer, which is (A).	19.84 m^3

 Note

The conversion from feet to meters is not the same as the conversion from cubic feet to cubic meters (or square feet to square meters). Trap answers will often use incorrect conversion factors. Be particularly careful when dealing with area or volume conversions that have multiple dimensions.

Next, you'll walk through a test-like multi-part question that involves rates. Follow along with the Kaplan Method and think about how knowledge of rates and conversion factors is used to get to the answer.

Remember, even though these questions have multiple parts, you'll rely on the same math skills you'd use in a simple multiple-choice question to solve each part. If you find that there are missing pieces or missing quantities, use techniques such as the factor-label method to bridge the gap. Also keep in mind that you may be able to use the answer from one part as a shortcut to answering the next part. If you do, don't round until the final answer, especially on grid-in questions.

Questions 2 and 3 refer to the following information.

Dismantling fraud rings, intercepting enemy communications, and protecting national infrastructure are just a few tasks for which Special Agents in the FBI's Cyber Division utilize state-of-the-art computers and other technology. The New Haven field office recently seized a hard drive with 2.43 terabytes (TB) of encrypted information during a raid on an infrastructure-hacking operations base, which agents believe contains information on a planned attack.

2. The cyber team's decryption software can decrypt 4.5 MB per second. How many hours will it take to decrypt the entire hard drive? (One TB is equal to 10^6 megabytes (MB).)

3. Newly gathered intelligence indicates a high likelihood of an infrastructure attack occurring before the hard drive is fully decrypted. Consequently, the New York and Boston field offices have been asked to divert resources to the decryption task. New York's decryption software is 40% faster than New Haven's, but Boston's is 20% slower than New Haven's. By how many hours will the decryption time be reduced with the three cyber teams working together? Round your answer to the nearest hour.

Work through the Kaplan Method for Multi-Part Math Questions step-by-step to solve this set of questions. The following table shows Kaplan's strategic thinking on the left, along with suggested math scratchwork on the right.

Strategic Thinking	Math Scratchwork
Step 1: Read the first question in the set, looking for clues You're told the size of the seized hard drive and the speed at which it will be decrypted.	2.43 TB drive 4.5 MB/s decryption
Step 2: Identify and organize the information you need The first part of the question set asks for the time required to decrypt the hard drive. The given rate will help you determine this amount.	hours to decrypt: ?
Step 3: Based on what you know, plan your steps to navigate the first question The hard drive's capacity is in TB, but the rate is in MB/s (and you're asked for time in hours), so the DIRT equation requires a couple of extra calculations before you can use it. The factor-label method will be faster. Map your conversion steps.	starting qty: 2.43 TB desired qty: ? h TB $\rightarrow$ MB $\rightarrow$ s $\rightarrow$ min $\rightarrow$ h
Step 4: Solve, step-by-step, checking units as you go Plug in the appropriate conversion factors. When properly set up, all units except hours will cancel, and you'll have the time needed for the decryption.	$2.43 \text{ TB} \times \dfrac{10^6 \text{ MB}}{1 \text{ TB}} \times \dfrac{1 \text{ s}}{4.5 \text{ MB}} \times \dfrac{1 \text{ min}}{60 \text{ s}}$ $\times \dfrac{1 \text{ h}}{60 \text{ min}} = 150 \text{ h}$
Step 5: Did I answer the *right* question? It will take 150 hours to fully decrypt the hard drive.	

✔ **Note**

You might be given extra information on questions like these. If you don't need it to get to the answer, then don't worry about it.

Now on to Step 6: Repeat for remaining questions in the set. Kaplan's strategic thinking is on the left, along with suggested math scratchwork on the right.

Strategic Thinking	Math Scratchwork
Step 1: Read the second question in the set, looking for clues This part of the question set provides a relative description of New York and Boston's decryption software speeds.	NY: 40% faster than NH B: 20% slower than NH
Step 2: Identify and organize the information you need You need to determine the reduction in decryption time (in hours) if all three systems work together.	new decryption time: ? difference between old and new times: ?
Step 3: Based on what you know, plan your steps to navigate the second question You must calculate the decryption speeds of the New York and Boston systems; you can't simply use the given percents to directly get the final answer. With the speeds in hand, you can find the total rate and the adjusted decryption time.	% → MB/s TB → MB → s → min → h
Step 4: Solve, step-by-step, checking units as you go Use the given percents to determine the speeds of the New York and Boston systems, being mindful when picking which decimal to plug in for what percent. Apply the factor-label method to calculate the required decryption time with all three systems working, and then find the difference in times.	NY: $1.4 \times 4.5 = 6.3$ MB/s B: $0.8 \times 4.5 = 3.6$ MB/s total rate $= 4.5 + 6.3 + 3.6$ $\qquad\qquad = 14.4$ MB/s $2.43 \text{ TB} \times \dfrac{10^6 \text{MB}}{1 \text{ TB}} \times \dfrac{1 \text{ s}}{14.4 \text{ MB}} \times \dfrac{1 \text{ min}}{60 \text{ s}}$ $\times \dfrac{1 \text{ h}}{60 \text{ min}} = 46.875$ h $150 - 46.875 = 103.125$
Step 5: Did I answer the *right* question? Round per the question stem's instructions, and you're done.	103

RATIOS AND PROPORTIONS

Ratios and proportions are quite common in everyday life. Whether it's making a double batch of meatballs or calculating the odds of winning the lottery, you'll find that ratios and proportions are invaluable in myriad situations.

A ratio is a comparison of one quantity to another. When writing ratios, you can compare part of a group to another part of that group, or you can compare a part of the group to the whole group. Suppose you have a bowl of apples and oranges. You can write ratios that compare apples to oranges (part to part), apples to total fruit (part to whole), and oranges to total fruit (part to whole).

You can also combine ratios. If you have two ratios, $a:b$ and $b:c$, you can derive $a:c$ by finding a common multiple of the b terms. Take a look at the following table to see this in action.

a	:	b	:	c
3	:	4		
		3	:	5
9	:	12		
		12	:	20
9	:			20

What's a common multiple of the b terms? The number 12 is a good choice because it's the least common multiple of 3 and 4 which will reduce the need to simplify later. Where do you go from there? Multiply each ratio by the factor (use 3 for $a:b$ and 4 for $b:c$) that will get you to $b = 12$.

The ratio $a:c$ equals 9:20. Notice we didn't merely say $a:c$ is 3:5; this would be incorrect on Test Day (and likely a wrong-answer trap!).

A proportion is simply two ratios set equal to each other. Proportions are an efficient way to solve certain problems, but you must exercise caution when setting them up. Watching the units of each piece of the proportion will help you with this. Sometimes the SAT will ask you to determine whether certain proportions are equivalent—check this by cross-multiplying. You'll get results that are much easier to compare.

$$\text{If } \frac{a}{b} = \frac{c}{d}, \text{ then: } ad = bc, \frac{a}{c} = \frac{b}{d}, \frac{d}{b} = \frac{c}{a}, \frac{b}{a} = \frac{d}{c}, \text{ BUT } \frac{a}{d} \neq \frac{c}{b}$$

Each derived ratio shown except the last one is simply a manipulation of the first, so all except the last are correct. You can verify this via cross-multiplication ($ad = bc$).

Alternatively, pick numerical values for *a*, *b*, *c*, and *d*; then simplify and confirm the two sides of the equation are equal. For example, take the two equivalent fractions $\frac{2}{3}$ and $\frac{6}{9}$ ($a = 2$, $b = 3$, $c = 6$, $d = 9$).

Cross-multiplication gives $2 \times 9 = 3 \times 6$, which is a true statement. Dividing *a* and *b* by *c* and *d* gives $\frac{2}{6} = \frac{3}{9}$, also true, and so on. However, attempting to equate $\frac{a}{d}\left(\frac{2}{9}\right)$ and $\frac{b}{c}\left(\frac{3}{6}\right)$ will not work.

Let's take a look at a test-like question that involves ratios:

4. Neil is preparing two cans of paint for a client. The first is 25 parts red paint and 60 parts blue paint; the second is 30 parts yellow paint, 70 parts blue paint, and 15 parts white paint. The client has also asked Neil to prepare a third can containing only white and red paint per the ratios of the first two cans. What ratio of white to red paint should Neil use for the third can?

    A) 35:18

    B) 18:35

    C) 5:3

    D) 3:5

Work through the Kaplan Method for Math step-by-step to solve this question. The following table shows Kaplan's strategic thinking on the left, along with suggested math scratchwork on the right.

Strategic Thinking	Math Scratchwork
Step 1: Read the question, identifying and organizing important information as you go You're asked for the ratio of white to red paint in the third can. Two ratios are given.	R:B = 25:60 Y:B:W = 30:70:15
Step 2: Choose the best strategy to answer the question The ratio terms are rather large, so reduce the first ratio with a common factor, and then repeat with the second ratio. To combine two ratios, they must share a common term. Both ratios contain blue paint, but the blue paint terms aren't identical. Find a common multiple of 12 and 14. Once you've found one, merge the two ratios to directly compare white and red paint.	R:B = 25:60 → 5:12 Y:B:W = 30:70:15 → 6:14:3 common multiple of 12 & 14: 84 R:B = (5:12) × 7 = 35:84 Y:B:W = (6:14:3) × 6 = 36:84:18 R:B:Y:W = 35:84:36:18 R:W = 35:18
Step 3: Check that you answered the *right* question The question asks for the ratio of white paint to red paint, so flip your ratio, and you're done. Choice (B) is correct.	W:R = 18:35

> ✔ **Note**
>
> Beware of trap answers that contain incorrect ratios. Always confirm that you've found the ratio requested.

PERCENTAGES

Percentages aren't just for test grades; you'll find them frequently throughout life—discount pricing in stores, income tax brackets, and stock price trackers all use percents in some form. It's critical that you know how to use them correctly, especially on Test Day.

Suppose you have a bag containing 10 blue marbles and 15 pink marbles, and you're asked what percent of the marbles are pink. You can determine this easily by using the formula $\text{Percent} = \frac{\text{part}}{\text{whole}} \times 100\%$.

Plug 15 in for the part and $10 + 15 (= 25)$ for the whole to get $\frac{15}{25} \times 100\% = 60\%$ pink marbles.

Another easy way to solve many percent problems is to use the following statement: (blank) percent of (blank) is (blank). Translating from English into math, you obtain (blank)% × (blank) = (blank). As you saw with the DIRT equation in the rates section, knowledge of any two quantities will unlock the third.

> ✔ **Note**
>
> The percent formula requires the percent component to be in decimal form. Remember to move the decimal point appropriately before using this formula.

You might also be asked to determine the **percent change** in a given situation. Fortunately, you can find this easily using a variant of the percent formula:

$$\text{Percent increase or decrease} = \frac{\text{amount of increase or decrease}}{\text{original amount}} \times 100\%$$

Sometimes more than one change will occur. Be especially careful here, as it can be tempting to take a "shortcut" by just adding two percent changes together (which will almost always lead to an incorrect answer). Instead you'll need to find the total amount of the increase or decrease and calculate accordingly. We'll demonstrate this in an upcoming problem.

The following is a test-like question involving percentages.

5. Some people like to dilute 100% juice drinks with water to lessen the flavor intensity and reduce caloric intake. Kristina, a personal trainer, is preparing several blends of varying juice concentrations to see which ratio her fitness club's clients prefer. She plans to make 240 ounces each of 80% juice, 60% juice, 50% juice, 40% juice, and 20% juice blends. If the 100% juice Kristina plans to buy comes in 32-ounce bottles and partial bottles cannot be bought, how many bottles will Kristina need to make her blends?

   A)   8

   B)   18

   C)   19

   D)   60

Work through the Kaplan Method for Math step-by-step to solve this question. The following table shows Kaplan's strategic thinking on the left, along with suggested math scratchwork on the right.

Strategic Thinking	Math Scratchwork
Step 1: Read the question, identifying and organizing important information as you go You're asked how many bottles of 100% juice Kristina needs to buy to make her five blends. You're given the percent juice content of each.	five blends: 80%, 60%, 50%, 40%, 20% juice
Step 2: Choose the best strategy to answer the question Although this looks like calculator busywork, there's a faster (but less obvious) route to the answer. Notice that each percentage is a multiple of 10. Therefore, all you need to do is find 10% of 240 and multiply by the appropriate number to get the ounces of juice in each blend.	$0.1 \times 240\,oz = 24\,oz$ $\times\,2: 20\% = 48\,oz\,juice$ $\times\,4: 40\% = 96\,oz\,juice$ $\times\,5: 50\% = 120\,oz\,juice$ $\times\,6: 60\% = 144\,oz\,juice$ $\times\,8: 80\% = 192\,oz\,juice$ sum: 600 oz. $\dfrac{600}{32} = 18.75 \rightarrow 19$
Step 3: Check that you answered the *right* question You've found the number of juice bottles required; the correct answer is (C).	19

An example of a multi-part question that tests your percentage expertise follows on the next page.

Questions 6 and 7 refer to the following information.

Projected Undergraduate Costs at the University of California

2014-15	2015-16	2016-17	2017-18	2018-19	2019-20
$12,192	$12,804	$13,446	$14,118	$14,820	$15,564

Source: regents.universityofcalifornia.edu

Over the last decade, colleges have come under fire for significant tuition and fee increases. In 2014, the University of California approved a series of tuition and fee increases over the course of five years. The table above summarizes the total cost per undergraduate per year through the 2019-20 academic year.

6. If fees account for 8.75% of one year's total expenses, what is the average fee increase per academic year? Round your answer to the nearest dollar.

7. Suppose the University of California system wants to extend these increases through the 2022-23 academic year. Assuming the average yearly increase for this extension remains the same as it was from 2014-15 through 2019-20, by what percentage will total tuition and fees have increased at the end of the 2022-23 academic year since their implementation? Round your answer to the nearest whole percent.

Work through the Kaplan Method for Multi-Part Math Questions step-by-step to solve this question. The following table shows Kaplan's strategic thinking on the left, along with suggested math scratchwork on the right.

Strategic Thinking	Math Scratchwork
Step 1: Read the first question in the set, looking for clues You are given a table with total costs for several academic years. The first question in the set states that fees account for 8.75% of one year's expenses.	
Step 2: Identify and organize the information you need This question asks for the portion of the total cost increase that is comprised of fees.	*fees (in $): ?*
Step 3: Based on what you know, plan your steps to navigate the first question Find the total cost increase in dollars and the average annual increase. From there, determine the portion of the increase that fees make up. The percent given in the first question indicates you should use the three-part percent formula.	*8.75% is fees* *(blank)% of (blank) is (blank)*

Math

Strategic Thinking	Math Scratchwork
Step 4: Solve, step-by-step, checking units as you go Instead of finding each year-to-year increase, find the total increase from 2014-15 through 2019-20. Once there, determine the average increase for each year. Use the three-part percent formula to find the fee portion of the average increase.	$\$15{,}564 - \$12{,}192 = \$3{,}372$ $avg = \dfrac{\$3372}{5}$ $\quad = \$674.40$ $0.0875 \times \$674.40 = \$59.01$
Step 5: Did I answer the *right* question? You found the average fee increase per year. Once you round appropriately, the first question is complete.	59

✔ **Note**

By finding the total increase instead of each individual increase, you saved yourself a substantial amount of time.

The first part of the question set is finished! Now on to Step 6: Repeat for the other questions in the set.

The following table shows Kaplan's strategic thinking is on the left, along with suggested math scratchwork on the right.

Strategic Thinking	Math Scratchwork
Step 1: Read the second question in the set, looking for clues There's a proposal to extend the tuition/fee hikes through 2022-23.	
Step 2: Identify and organize the information you need The second part of the question set asks for the percent increase in total tuition/fee cost between 2014-15 and 2022-23.	% increase: ?
Step 3: Based on what you know, plan your steps to navigate the second question You know the average yearly increase from the first question. Use this to determine what the cost for the 2022-23 year will be, and then calculate the total increase. Use this result to calculate the percent increase.	2014-15 thru 2019-20: $3,372 avg. yearly incr.: $674.40
Step 4: Solve, step-by-step, checking units as you go Extending the increases past 2019-20 means increases for 2020-21, 2021-22, and 2022-23, which is 3 years total. Multiply the average yearly increase by 3 to determine the additional increase. Add this to the increase you found in the first question to find the total increase from 2014-15 through 2022-23.	$674.40 × 3 = $2,023.20 $2,023.20 + $3,372 = $5,395.20
To calculate the percent change, divide the total increase by the original cost from 2014-15, and multiply the result by 100.	$\dfrac{\$5,395.20}{\$12,192} \times 100 = 44.252\%$
Step 5: Did I answer the *right* question? Round the percent change per the instructions, and you're done.	44

Practice

Now you'll have a chance to try a few test-like problems in a scaffolded way. We've provided some guidance, but you'll need to fill in the missing parts of explanations or the step-by-step math to get to the correct answer. Don't worry—after going through the worked examples at the beginning of this section, these problems should be completely doable.

8. Ramp meters are often used in and around metropolitan areas to reduce freeway congestion during AM and PM rush hours. Depending on freeway volume, ramp meters in Milwaukee allow one car onto the freeway every 5-9 seconds. Assuming a constant ramp car queue, between the hours of 3:30 PM and 6:30 PM, how many more cars can move through a ramp meter with a 5-second interval than one with an 8-second interval?

   A) 270

   B) 320

   C) 810

   D) 960

The following table can help you structure your thinking as you go about solving this problem. Kaplan's strategic thinking is provided, as are bits of structured scratchwork. If you're not sure how to approach a question like this, start at the top and work your way down.

Strategic Thinking	Math Scratchwork
Step 1: Read the question, identifying and organizing important information as you go You must determine how many more cars pass through a ramp meter with a 5-second interval.	
Step 2: Choose the best strategy to answer the question One car every 5 (or 8) seconds is a rate, so turn to the DIRT equation. Be careful here; you need to manipulate the given form of the rate before you can use it. The 3:30 PM to 6:30 PM window translates to 3 hours, which is your time. Your rate, however, involves seconds, so you'll need to convert time to seconds. Finding d will give you the number of cars; do this for both intervals. Watch your units! Almost finished. Subtract the 8-second car count from the 5-second car count to find the difference.	5-second interval: $r_5 = 1$ car per 5 s = ____ cars/s 8-second interval: $r_8 = 1$ car per 8 s = ____ cars/s $3\,\text{h} \times$ ____ $\times$ ____ = ____ s 5 seconds $d_5 =$ ____ $\times$ ____ $d_5 =$ ____ 8 seconds $d_8 =$ ____ $\times$ ____ $d_8 =$ ____ ———— − ———— = ————

Strategic Thinking	Math Scratchwork
Step 3: Check that you answered the *right* question If your answer is (C), you're correct!	 ____

> ✔ **Expert Tip**
>
> Sometimes distance or time units won't look like those you're used to (e.g., miles, minutes, etc.). Don't let this deter you. If you have a rate, you can use the DIRT equation.

Here's another test-like example to try using this method:

Murray's Annual Income Tax Liability

Federal (up to $9,225)	Federal ($9,226-$37,450)	Federal ($37,451-$90,750)	State (flat rate)
10%	15%	25%	4.5%

9. Murray has an annual salary of $75,400. He contributes 20% of his pre-tax income to his 401(k), and he pays $150 per month for health insurance (pre-tax, deducted after 401(k)). The table above summarizes Murray's tax liability; all taxes are calculated based on Murray's adjusted gross income (pay remaining after 401(k) and insurance payments). He must pay 10% on the first $9,225 in income, 15% on any income between $9,226 and $37,450, 25% on income between $37,451 and $90,750, and a 4.5% state-tax on all of his adjusted gross income. All taxes are deducted simultaneously. What is Murray's biweekly take-home pay after all deductions have been made?

A) $1,537.98

B) $1,586.79

C) $1,699.78

D) $1,748.57

The following table can help you structure your thinking as you go about solving this problem. Kaplan's strategic thinking is provided, as are bits of structured scratchwork. If you're not sure how to approach a question like this, start at the top and work your way down.

Strategic Thinking	Math Scratchwork

Step 1: Read the question, identifying and organizing important information as you go
 	
 You need to find Murray's income after deductions. You have information about each deduction, as well as the order in which they're taken.
	start ($_____) – _____ 401(k)
	       – _____ insurance
	       – taxes
	       = take-home pay

Step 2: Choose the best strategy to answer the question The table provides tax information for annual income, so don't convert to biweekly yet. Follow the order you extracted in Step 1 to calculate each deduction first. To find the amount Murray deducts before taxes, use the three-part percent formula to find his 401(k) contribution, then subtract his health insurance cost. The question states that all taxes are deducted simultaneously; that is, don't deduct state tax and then take federal tax on what's left and vice versa. Use the quantity left after the insurance deduction for all tax calculations, and then subtract Murray's total tax liability from the remaining quantity post-insurance. The question asks for Murray's biweekly take-home pay. Divide by the number of pay periods in one year to get the final answer.	401(k): _____ × _____ = $ _____ annually insurance: $ _____ × _____ = $ _____ annually $ _____ – $ _____ – $ _____ = $ _____ annual pre-tax taxes: state _____ × _____ = _____ M. owes $ _____ for state fed 10% bracket _____ × _____ = _____ M. owes $ _____ for 10% bracket fed 15% bracket _____ × _____ = _____ M. owes $ _____ for 15% bracket fed 25% bracket _____ × _____ = _____ M. owes $ _____ for 25% bracket total tax: $ _____ take-home: $ _____ – $ _____ = $ _____ annually $ \dfrac{_____}{wks}$ = $ _____ biweekly
Step 3: Check that you answered the *right* question If you chose (D), you're right.	_____

Now try your hand at a multi-part question.

Questions 10 and 11 refer to the following information.

Shuang has a set of square ceramic plates she'd like to glaze. She wants to create evenly spaced concentric squares on the plates with gray and black glaze as shown in the diagram above. The squares' edges are each 0.5 inches apart.

10. What fraction of one plate will Shuang cover with gray glaze?

11. Shuang also plans to glaze smaller square plates with the same type of pattern as the plate in the figure. The smaller plates' squares are the same size and distance apart as those of the larger plates. If a small plate has four concentric squares, by how many times is the fraction of a small plate that Shuang will cover with black glaze greater than that of a large plate?

The following table can help you structure your thinking as you go about solving this problem. Kaplan's strategic thinking is provided, as are bits of structured scratchwork. If you're not sure how to approach a question like this, start at the top and work your way down.

Strategic Thinking	Math Scratchwork
Step 1: Read the first question in the set, looking for clues You're given a picture of one of Shuang's plates and told that she will use two colors to create the design.	
Step 2: Identify and organize the information you need You need to find the fraction of the plate that will be gray.	gray/total: ?
Step 3: Based on what you know, plan your steps to navigate the first question You might think this problem is unsolvable, but it asks for a relative quantity, not an absolute quantity. You'll need to pick a value for the area of one square and calculate the others based on the one you chose. Label the squares to help keep your calculations clear.	 1 2 3 4 5 6 7 8
Step 4: Solve, step-by-step, checking units as you go Pick a small, manageable number for this value. Remember how far apart the square edges are; this will help you find the side lengths and areas of the other squares. Also keep in mind you'll need to account for the fact that each square outside the first is not actually a full square. To find the ratio of gray glaze to total glaze, divide the gray glaze area by the total glaze area.	sq. 1 = ____ in.^{2} sq. 2 = ____^{2} − ____ = ____ in.^{2} sq. 3 = ____^{2} − ____ = ____ in.^{2} sq. 4 = ____^{2} − ____ = ____ in.^{2} sq. 5 = ____^{2} − ____ = ____ in.^{2} sq. 6 = ____^{2} − ____ = ____ in.^{2} sq. 7 = ____^{2} − ____ = ____ in.^{2} sq. 8 = ____^{2} − ____ = ____ in.^{2} gray: ____ + ____ + ____ + ____ = ____ in.^{2} black: ____ + ____ + ____ + ____ = ____ in.^{2} gray/total = _____
Step 5: Did I answer the *right* question? If you got 7/16, great job! You're correct.	_____

Fantastic! Now repeat for the other question in the set. Once again, Kaplan's strategic thinking is provided, as are bits of structured scratchwork. If you're not sure how to approach the second part, start at the top and work your way down.

Strategic Thinking	Math Scratchwork
Step 1: Read the second question in the set, looking for clues You're told a smaller plate has four concentric squares with edges 0.5 inches apart as in a larger plate.	4 squares in a small plate
Step 2: Identify and organize the information you need You'll need to find the fraction of black glaze on one small plate and one large plate.	sm. black: ? lg. black: ?
Step 3: Based on what you know, plan your steps to navigate the second question You'll need to find the black fraction of the two plates. Fortunately, the black fraction for the larger plate is easy to find because you found its gray counterpart in the previous question.	large black = 1 − _____ = _____
Step 4: Solve, step-by-step, checking units as you go Good news! To find the black fraction for the small plate, you already did most of the work in the previous question. Just use the same numbers.	square 1 (gray) = ____ in.^{2} square 2 (black) = ____ in.^{2} square 3 (gray) = ____ in.^{2} square 4 (black) = ____ in.^{2} small gray: ____ + ____ = ____ in.^{2} small black: ____ + ____ = ____ in.^{2} small black vs. large black: ____ ÷ ____ = ____ × ____ = ____
Step 5: Did I answer the *right* question? Did you get 10/9? If so, congrats! You're correct.	———

Now that you've seen the variety of ways in which the SAT can test you on ratios, rates, proportions, and percentages, try the following questions to check your understanding. Give yourself 5 minutes to answer the following four questions. Make sure you use the Kaplan Method for Math as often as you can (as well as the Kaplan Method for Multi-Part Math Questions when necessary). Remember, you want to emphasize speed and efficiency in addition to simply getting the correct answer.

12. Grocery stores often differ in how they price fruit; some charge by weight, and others charge per piece. FoodCo sells bananas for $0.60 a pound, Bob's charges $0.29 per banana, Acme charges $1.50 for a two-pound banana bunch, and Stu's offers a special: buying three pounds of bananas at $0.65 per pound gets you a fourth pound free. If one banana weighs $\frac{1}{3}$ lb, which of the following correctly lists the four grocers in order of decreasing cost per banana (assuming all purchases are made in 4-lb increments)?

A) Bob's, Acme, FoodCo, Stu's

B) Bob's, FoodCo, Acme, Stu's

C) Stu's, FoodCo, Acme, Bob's

D) Stu's, Acme, FoodCo, Bob's

13. The owner of an aerial adventure park wants to construct a zipline for kids who aren't tall enough to ride the regular zipline, which starts at a platform in a tree 10 meters above the ground and is 26 meters in length. The desired platform height for the new zipline is 3 meters. If the owner wants the kids' zipline length and platform height to be proportional to those of the regular zipline, what will be the difference in length of the two ziplines?

Questions 14 and 15 refer to the following information.

Gas stations in the United States sell gasoline by the gallon, whereas those in Great Britain sell it by the liter. Mark is assembling a budget for a trip to Great Britain. He plans to drive from London to Edinburgh and back with various excursions along the way; he estimates his total mileage to be 960 miles. The Great Britain pound (GBP) to U.S. dollar (USD) exchange rate is currently 1:1.52, and 1 gallon (gal) is approximately 3.785 liters (L).

14. If Mark rents a car that averages 40 miles per gallon throughout the trip and estimates an average gas cost of 1.20 GBP per liter, how much money (in USD) should Mark budget for fuel? Round your answer to the nearest dollar.

15. The rental car company Mark is using has a special offer: For an extra 30 GBP, Mark can lock in a subsidized fuel cost of 0.75 GBP per liter for the duration of his trip. How much, in USD, would Mark save with this offer? Round your answer to the nearest dollar.

Answers and Explanations for this chapter begin on page 824.

EXTRA PRACTICE

 You may use your calculator for all questions in this section.

1. At all trials and hearings, a court reporter types every word spoken during the proceedings so that there is a written record of what transpired. Because they must type every word, the average court reporter must be able to type at a minimum rate of 3.75 words per second in order to be certified. Suppose a trial transcript contains 25 pages with an average of 675 words per page. Assuming the court reporter typed the transcript at the minimum rate, how long was she actively typing?

   A) 1 hour, 15 minutes

   B) 1 hour, 45 minutes

   C) 2 hours, 30 minutes

   D) 3 hours

2. In 1912, the original candidates for United States President were Woodrow Wilson and William H. Taft. Because of party disagreements, former President Theodore Roosevelt also decided to run and ended up splitting the vote with his fellow Republican and incumbent, Taft. In a certain state, the ratio of the popular vote of Taft to Roosevelt to Wilson was approximately 35:41:63. If approximately 208,500 votes were cast in that state for the three candidates altogether, how many were cast for Taft?

   A) 15,000

   B) 45,000

   C) 52,500

   D) 69,500

3. Political canvassers polled voters in two locations on whether they viewed a particular candidate for governor favorably. At the first location, they asked 125 people and of those, 22.4% responded favorably. At the second location, 37.5% of 272 people responded favorably. What percent of all the people surveyed responded favorably?

   A) 25.7%

   B) 30.0%

   C) 31.5%

   D) 32.7%

4. At 350°F, an oven can cook approximately 3 pounds of turkey per hour. At 450°F, it can cook approximately 4.5 pounds per hour. How many more ounces of turkey can the oven cook at 450° than at 350° in 10 minutes? (1 pound = 16 ounces)

   A) 4

   B) 6

   C) 8

   D) 12

5. A company specializes in converting people's VHS movies and DVDs to digital formats, which, once converted, are approximately 4.5 gigabytes in size. Once converted, the company uploads the videos to a secure cloud drive, where the customers can retrieve their files. The company uploads the videos every day, from closing time at 5:00 PM until 9:00 PM. Their internet service provider has an upload speed of 12 megabytes per second. What is the maximum number of videos the company can upload each evening?
(1 gigabyte = 1,024 megabytes)

A)   2

B)   37

C)   242

D)   682

6. A museum is building a scale model of Sue, the largest *Tyrannosaurus rex* skeleton ever found. Sue was 13 feet tall and 40 feet long, and her skull had a length of 5 feet. If the length of the museum's scale model skull is 3 feet, 1.5 inches, what is the difference between the scale model's length and its height?

A)   8 feet, 1.5 inches

B)   16 feet, 10.5 inches

C)   22 feet, 6.5 inches

D)   27 feet, 4 inches

Questions 7 and 8 refer to the following information.

Mia is planning to work as a hostess at a restaurant. Two restaurants in her area have offered her jobs, both of which utilize "tip share," which means that the hostess gets a portion of all tips left by all customers. Restaurant A has a tip share for hostesses of 7%, while Restaurant B has a tip share of only 4%.

7. Mia does some research and finds that, on average, restaurants in her area bring in approximately $1,100 in tips for the evening shift. Based on this information, how much more in dollars would Mia make in tips at Restaurant A than at Restaurant B if she worked 5 evenings a week for 4 weeks?

8. Upon further research, Mia discovers that Restaurant B is making some improvements to become a more upscale establishment, which will result in an increase in meal prices and, consequently, should also increase tips. Assuming both restaurants originally brought in the average tips given in the previous question, what percent increase would Restaurant B need to experience in tips in order for Mia to make the same amount of money in one evening at both restaurants from the hostess tip share? Assume that Restaurant B doesn't increase its tip share percentage. Enter your answer as a whole number and ignore the percent sign.

9. While reviewing for exams, a teacher knows that the number of topics he can cover is directly proportional to the length of time he has to review. If he can cover 9 topics in a single 45-minute period, how many topics can he cover in a 1-hour period?

   A) 5

   B) 7

   C) 10

   D) 12

10. Weight is dependent on the gravitational force exerted on an object. In other words, in space, you would weigh nothing because there is no gravity. Likewise, because the moon's gravitational pull is less than Earth's, objects weigh less on the moon. In general, 1 pound on Earth is equal to approximately 0.166 pounds on the moon. If a man weighs 29 pounds on the moon, about how much, in pounds, does he weigh on Earth?

    A) 21

    B) 48

    C) 175

    D) 196

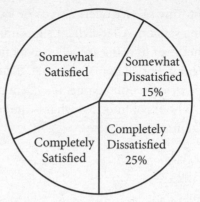

11. A company conducts a customer satisfaction survey. The results are summarized in the pie graph. If 240 customers responded to the survey, how many customers were either completely or somewhat satisfied?

    A) 60

    B) 96

    C) 144

    D) 204

12. When medical tests are conducted, there is always the possibility that the test will return a false positive or a false negative. A false positive means the test shows that a patient has the condition being studied, when the patient actually does not; a false negative indicates that a patient does not have the condition, when the patient actually does. Suppose a certain medical test has a false positive rate of 6 out of 3,500. How many people were tested during a period when 27 false positives came back?

    A) 14,000

    B) 15,750

    C) 17,500

    D) 21,000

13. A tutoring service offers a free one-hour tutoring session. After a client signs up, the next 10 hours of tutoring are billed at a rate of $30 per hour. For all hours after that, the client receives a discounted rate. If a client pays $664 for 25 hours of tutoring, what is the service's discounted hourly rate?

A) $24.50

B) $25.54

C) $26.00

D) $26.56

14. In a week, a light bulb factory produces 12,500 light bulbs. The ratio of light emitting diodes (LED bulbs) to compact fluorescent lamps (CFL bulbs) is 2:3. Of the LED bulbs produced, 3% were defective. How many LED bulbs were not defective?

A) 150

B) 2,425

C) 4,850

D) 7,275

15. In 1950, scientists estimated a certain animal population in a particular geographical area to be 6,400. In 2000, the population had risen to 7,200. If this animal population experiences the same percent increase over the next 50 years, what will the approximate population be?

A) 8,000

B) 8,100

C) 8,400

D) 8,600

16. On average, Betsy reads 1 page of her book every 1.5 minutes. Her book has 116 pages. Raymond starts a 94-page book on Saturday morning at 8:30 AM and reads straight through until he finishes it at 11:38 AM. How many more minutes does it take Raymond to read his book than Betsy to read hers?

17. An emergency room doctor prescribes a certain pain medication to be delivered through an IV drip. She prescribes 800 mL of the medication to be delivered over the course of 8 hours. The IV delivers 1 mL of medication over the course of 30 drips. How many drips per minute are needed to deliver the prescribed dosage?

18. A power company divides the geographic regions it serves into grids. The company is able to allocate the power it generates based on the usage and needs of a particular grid. Certain grids use more power at certain times of the day, so companies often shift power around to different grids at various times. On any given day, the company makes several changes in the power allocation to Grid 1. First, it increases the power by 20%. Then, it decreases it by 10%. Finally, it increases it by 30%. What is the net percent increase in this grid's power allocation? Round to the nearest whole percent and ignore the percent sign when entering your answer.

Math

Questions 19 and 20 refer to the following information.

Every Saturday morning, three friends meet for breakfast at 9:00 AM. Andrea walks, Kellan bikes, and Joelle drives.

19. Last Saturday, all three friends were exactly on time. Andrea left her house at 8:30 AM and walked at a rate of 3 miles per hour. Kellan left his house at 8:15 AM and biked at a rate of 14 mph. Joelle left her house at 8:45 AM and drove an average speed of 35 miles per hour. How many miles from the restaurant does the person who traveled the farthest live?

20. Kellan lives 12 miles away from Andrea. On a different Saturday, Kellan biked at a rate of 15 miles per hour to Andrea's house. The two then walked to the restaurant at a rate of 2.5 miles per hour, and they arrived five minutes early. What time did Kellan leave his house? Enter your answer as three digits and ignore the colon. For example, if your answer is 5:30 AM, enter 530.

CHAPTER 6

Scatterplots

 ## CHAPTER OBJECTIVES

By the end of this chapter, you will be able to:

1. Decide whether a linear, quadratic, or exponential model describes the data presented in a scatterplot

2. Use an equation for a line of best fit to describe trends between variables in a scatterplot

3. Use a line of best fit to determine an average rate of change and to extrapolate values from given data

SMARTPOINTS

Point Value	SmartPoint Category
40 Points	Scatterplots

Math

SCATTERPLOTS

Chapter 6

Homework

Extra Practice: #1-20

Key

 Book Assignment

 Online Video Assignment

 Online Quiz Assignment

SCATTERPLOT BASICS

Some students tend to associate scatterplots with nasty-looking statistical analyses and consequently become nervous when they hear they'll likely encounter a few scatterplots on Test Day. However, these seemingly difficult plots are usually straightforward—if you know what to look for. We'll go over the foundational concepts of scatterplots, growth and decay examples, and modeling with scatterplots over the next several pages.

First, let's look at the anatomy of a scatterplot.

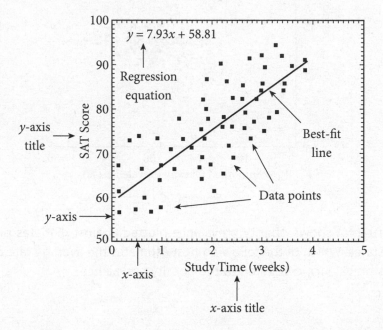

- You're already familiar with the **x- and y-axes**, but something that might be new is their **units**. Most scatterplots that use real data have units on the axes; these are important when trying to draw conclusions and inferences based on data (more on this later).

- The **domain** of a set of data points is the set of inputs, which corresponds to the x-values of the data points when plotted on a graph. The set of values that make up the **range** corresponds to the y-values.

- The **line of best fit** is drawn through the **data points** to describe the relationship between the two variables as an equation. This line does not need to go through most or all data points, but it should accurately reflect the trend shown by the data with about half the points above the line and half below. As in "plain" equations, x is the independent variable, and y is the dependent variable.

- The **equation of the line of best fit** (also called the **regression equation**) is the equation that describes the line of best fit algebraically. On Test Day, you'll most likely encounter this equation as linear, quadratic, or exponential, though it can also be other types of equations.

Prepare

An outlier is defined as a data point that does not follow the same overall trend as the other data points.

Below is a test-like question that involves a scatterplot.

Source: CDC

1. The scatterplot shows obesity prevalence plotted against diabetes prevalence in the United States. Which of the following best estimates the average rate of change in the diabetes prevalence compared to the obesity prevalence?

    A) 0.25

    B) 0.87

    C) 1.5

    D) 4

Work through the Kaplan Method for Math step-by-step to solve this question. The following table shows Kaplan's strategic thinking on the left, along with suggested math scratchwork on the right.

Strategic Thinking	Math Scratchwork
Step 1: Read the question, identifying and organizing important information as you go You need to determine the average rate of change in diabetes prevalence vs. obesity prevalence. An infographic is provided.	
Step 2: Choose the best strategy to answer the question Examine the infographic. Look for units, labels, variables, and trends. Obesity prevalence is plotted along the *x*-axis, and diabetes prevalence along the *y*-axis. As the former increases, so does the latter. A rate of change corresponds to the slope of the line of best fit, so estimate a pair of points and find the slope between them.	$(16, 9)$ and $(44, 16)$ $m = \dfrac{y_2 - y_1}{x_2 - x_1} = \dfrac{16 - 9}{44 - 16} = \dfrac{7}{28} = \dfrac{1}{4}$ slope $= 0.25$
Step 3: Check that you answered the *right* question You found the rate of change, also known as the slope. The correct answer is (A).	

Remember that you don't need to understand fully what "diabetes prevalence" is to correctly answer this question. As long as you can interpret and use a scatterplot, you'll be in good shape.

> ✔ **Note**
>
> Make a note of the scales along the axes. Misreading them is an easy way to fall for a trap answer.

GROWTH AND DECAY

The real world is full of examples of growth and decay, and you're bound to see some examples on Test Day. The two most common types are linear and exponential. Following is the model for a linear equation:

$$y = kx + x_0$$

If this equation looks familiar, it would be for good reason: It's a linear equation in slope-intercept form with different variables standing in for the ones you've seen in the past. You should be able to match each piece to a quantity in the slope-intercept form of an equation. Take a look at the following table for a translation of the new components.

Linear Growth/ Decay Variable	What It Represents	Slope-Intercept Counterpart
x_0	y-intercept or initial quantity in a word problem	b
k	rate of change, slope	m

Recognizing that the previous equation, which might look weird at first glance, is really something you've seen before, will go a long way on Test Day.

> ✔ **Note**
>
> You might also see this expressed in function notation. We've included several homework problems in this format for you to try. For an overview of functions, see chapter 9.

A more complex model is the exponential equation:

$$y = x_0(1 + r)^x$$

You'll notice most of the terms, such as y, x_0 (pronounced "x-naught"), and x are in both linear and exponential equations, which makes exponential equations a bit easier to understand. The new variable, r, is the rate of change, akin to k in a linear equation. Also note that x is now an exponent.

What happens if you have a negative exponential rate of change?

Suppose $r = -\dfrac{3}{4}$ and $x_0 = 100$. Substituting these values into the exponential model gives $y = 100\left(1 - \dfrac{3}{4}\right)^x = 100\left(\dfrac{1}{4}\right)^x$. Use exponent rules to distribute the x, which yields $y = 100 \times \dfrac{1^x}{4^x}$. Because 1^x will always be 1, you can drop it and move 100 to the numerator to give the final equation, $y = \dfrac{100}{4^x}$. This can also be written as $y = 100 \times 0.25^x$, so be ready for both fraction and decimal forms. Here's an easy way to remember whether you have exponential growth or decay: If r is positive, you're looking at growth; if r is negative, decay is occurring. An r of 0 will give you 1^x, which drops out and leaves y equal to a constant (and therefore a horizontal line instead of an exponential curve).

Another key difference to note: The rate of change in linear growth and decay is constant, but it is variable for exponential growth or decay. Graphically, linear growth/decay is a straight line, whereas exponential growth/decay has a curve. This will often help you identify which is occurring in a given situation.

Now let's look at a test-like question that involves growth. It's up to you to figure out whether it is linear or exponential.

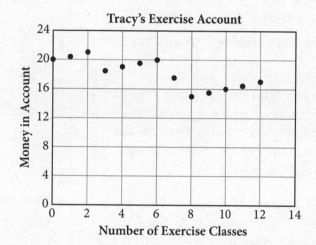

2. Tracy recently joined a workout group in which each member commits to attending three exercise classes per week. To increase accountability, each member sets aside $20 in an account. If a member misses a class, that individual will lose $2.50, which is then equally distributed among the members who attended that class. After missing three classes, Tracy vows to hold herself more accountable and not miss any more. The scatterplot above shows Tracy's account balance over time. Assuming exactly one person is absent from any given class and no one else has joined or left the group since its inception, which of the following equations could represent Tracy's account balance after she resolves not to miss any further classes?

A) $y = 20(1.5)^x$

B) $y = x^{1.5} + 11$

C) $y = 0.5x + 11$

D) $y = 0.5x + 20$

Work through the Kaplan Method for Math step-by-step to solve this question. The following table shows Kaplan's strategic thinking on the left, along with suggested math scratchwork on the right.

Strategic Thinking	Math Scratchwork
Step 1: Read the question, identifying and organizing important information as you go You need to determine which equation correctly represents Tracy's account balance after her second missed class, assuming she does not miss any after that. You're given some information about the account's behavior.	$20 @ start present: $+x$ no-show: $-\$2.50$
Step 2: Choose the best strategy to answer the question Find the relevant data points on the scatterplot. The last class Tracy missed corresponds to the third (and final) decrease on the scatterplot. You need the equation that represents Tracy's account balance after that class, so you can disregard her attendance prior to that. Because the no-show count and group size do not change, you can assume Tracy's account balance will increase at a constant rate, indicating a linear equation. You can therefore eliminate A and B. To determine which of the remaining answer choices is correct, draw a line of best fit through the appropriate points. The y-intercept is 11, meaning (C) must be correct.	**Tracy's Exercise Account** **Tracy's Exercise Account**
Step 3: Check that you answered the *right* question Only choice (C) contains a linear equation with the correct y-intercept.	$y = 0.5x + 11$

Nice job! Let's continue our exploration of scatterplots with a section on modeling.

SCATTERPLOT MODELING

As you've seen, the SAT can ask a variety of questions related to scatterplots. In addition, you might be asked to do some more advanced tasks, such as drawing conclusions and making predictions. This task sounds daunting, but it's not as challenging as you might think.

Look at the following graphs for a preview of the types of models you might see.

Linear   Quadratic   Exponential

A **linear model** will always increase (when its slope is positive) or always decrease (when its slope is negative) at a constant rate, making it easy to spot.

A **quadratic model** is U-shaped and the trend of the data changes from decreasing to increasing, or vice versa. The graph of a quadratic equation takes the shape of a parabola, which has either a minimum or a maximum called the vertex (although it is sometimes not shown on the graph). A parabola opens upward when the coefficient of the x^2 term is positive, and it opens downward when the coefficient of the x^2 term is negative.

An **exponential model** typically starts with a gradual rate of change, which increases significantly over time. Unlike a quadratic model, the trend of the data does not change direction, and the graph does not have a vertex.

Using a Graphing Calculator to Model Data

There are times when using a graphing calculator on Test Day can speed things up considerably; deriving an equation that fits a data set is one of those times. These equations are called **regression equations** and can take several shapes depending on the data's behavior. The **correlation coefficient**, *r*, indicates how well a regression equation fits the data; the closer *r* is to 1 for an increasing equation (or −1 for a decreasing equation), the better the fit. To find the equation for the line of best fit and the correlation coefficient, follow the steps on the next page (for a TI-83/84 calculator).

Step 1: Press the [STAT] button. Choose [EDIT], then enter your data for [L₁] and [L₂].

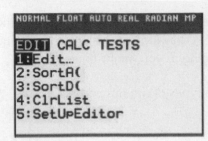

Step 2: Press the [STAT] button again and scroll to [CALC]. Select [4] for a linear regression, [5] for quadratic, or [0] for exponential and press the [ENTER] button. Make sure [L₁] and [L₂] are listed beside [XList] and [YList], respectively.

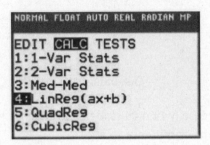

Step 3: Scroll down to [Calculate], then press the [ENTER] button. The variable values are listed, as is the correlation coefficient. If *r* is not close to 1/−1, try another regression type.

Note: If *r* is not displayed, go to the [CATALOG] menu (press [2nd] then [0]), scroll to the Ds, then select [DiagnosticOn].

✔ **Note**

If you have a calculator other than the TI-83/84, make sure you read its manual prior to Test Day so you're familiar with how to use this function.

Below is a test-like example that asks you to extrapolate data from a scatterplot.

3.   Inhabitants of colder climates are often concerned about frostbite in the winter months and use the wind chill factor to gauge how much time they can safely spend outside. Wind chill reflects the temperature that one feels when outside based on the actual temperature and the wind speed. Wind chill was first introduced in 1939, and the formula was revised in 2001. If the outside temperature is 0°F, what is the approximate wind chill at 40 mph based on the 2001 formula, and what wind speed would produce the same wind chill using the 1939 formula?

A)   −30°F, 10 mph

B)   −30°F, 15 mph

C)   −50°F, 15 mph

D)   −50°F, 40 mph

Work through the Kaplan Method for Math step-by-step to solve this question. The following table shows Kaplan's strategic thinking on the left, along with suggested math scratchwork on the right.

Strategic Thinking	Math Scratchwork
Step 1: Read the question, identifying and organizing important information as you go You are asked to identify a wind chill value and a wind speed. Although the question stem is lengthy, most of the information is irrelevant. Pay attention to both the title and axis labels on the scatterplot when solving.	

Strategic Thinking	Math Scratchwork
Step 2: Choose the best strategy to answer the question Use the trend of the 2001 formula data to draw a line that extends to 40 mph. Next, draw a vertical line from 40 mph on the *x*-axis to intersect the data extension that you drew, and then draw a horizontal line from that intersection to the *y*-axis to estimate the wind chill factor, which is approximately −30°F. You can eliminate C and D based on this finding. The second part asks for the temperature that would yield the same wind chill (−30°F) using the 1939 formula. The horizontal line that you drew for the first part crosses right through a point on the 1939 curve. Draw another line down to the *x*-axis from that point to find that the wind speed is approximately 15 mph.	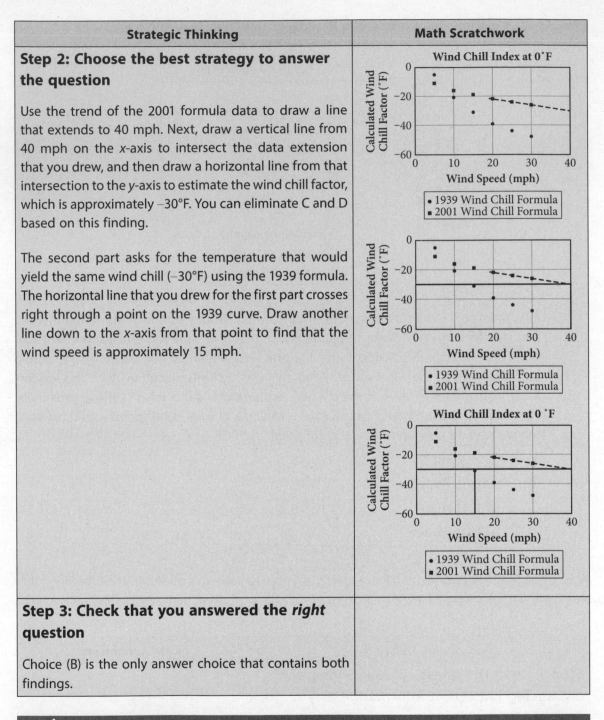
Step 3: Check that you answered the *right* question Choice (B) is the only answer choice that contains both findings.	

✔ **Note**

Watch the axis labels. Don't assume each grid-line always represents one unit.

Now you'll have a chance to try a couple test-like problems in a scaffolded way. We've provided some guidance, but you'll need to fill in the missing parts of explanations or the step-by-step math in order to get to the correct answer. Don't worry—after going through the worked examples at the beginning of this section, these problems should be completely doable.

4. Which of the following plots could be modeled by the equation $y = 3^x + 4$?

A)

C)

B)

D)

Math

This question is different from the previous ones, but don't worry. The following table can help you structure your thinking as you go about solving this problem. Kaplan's strategic thinking is provided, as are bits of structured scratchwork. If you're not sure how to approach a question like this, start at the top and work your way down.

Strategic Thinking	Math Scratchwork
Step 1: Read the question, identifying and organizing important information as you go You need to match the given equation to the correct plot.	
Step 2: Choose the best strategy to answer the question The x in the exponent position indicates that you have a certain type of graph; there are two choices you can eliminate based on this. To choose between the remaining graphs, plug in a manageable value for x, and see what y is at that point. Determine which graph contains this point.	*need a(n) _____ graph;* *eliminate _____* *when x = _____, y = _____* *_____ matches*
Step 3: Check that you answered the *right* question If you chose (C), you'd be correct!	*_____*

> ✔ **Note**
>
> Remember that 3^x is very different from $3x$ and x^3.

Coming up next, you'll get a chance to try a multi-part question involving a scatterplot.

Questions 5 and 6 refer to the following information.

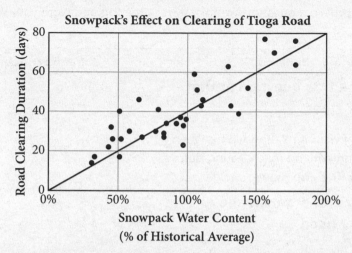

(Data source: www.nps.gov/yose/planyourvisit/tiogaopen.htm)

Tioga (pronounced tie-OH-ga) Road is a mountain pass that crosses the Sierra Nevada through northern Yosemite National Park. Due to its high elevation and the unpredictability of Sierra weather in the winter and early spring, the road is closed from about November through late May. This time period can change depending on the quantity and nature of the season's snowfall, as well as unforeseen obstacles like fallen trees and/or rocks. The scatterplot above compares the snowpack water content on April 1 (for years 1981-2014) as a percent of the historical average to the time it takes the National Park Service to fully clear the road and open it to traffic.

5. For every 5% increase in snowpack water content, how many more days does it take the National Park Service to clear Tioga Road?

6. Assuming no unforeseen obstacles or machinery issues, if the road's snowpack water content on April 1 is 248% of the historical average, how many days will it take to fully clear Tioga Road?

The following tables can help you structure your thinking as you go about solving this more involved question set. Kaplan's strategic thinking is provided, as are bits of structured scratchwork. If you're not sure how to approach a question like this, start at the top and work your way down.

Strategic Thinking	Math Scratchwork
Step 1: Read the first question in the set, looking for clues The infographic shows the relationship between snowpack water content and road clearing duration. A line of best fit is also drawn.	
Step 2: Identify and organize the information you need You are asked to find how much the road clearing time increases with each 5% increase in snowpack water content.	
Step 3: Based on what you know, plan your steps to navigate the first question You need a rate, which means you need to find the slope of the line of best fit. Pick a pair of points to use (look for places where the line passes through a grid-line intersection to minimize error). Read the axes carefully when writing the coordinates!	$(\underline{\quad}, \underline{\quad})$ $(\underline{\quad}, \underline{\quad})$
Step 4: Solve, step-by-step, checking units as you go Use the slope formula to determine the change in clearing time per 1% increase in snowpack water content.	$m = \dfrac{y_2 - y_1}{x_2 - x_1} = \underline{\qquad} = \underline{\qquad}$ $= \underline{\qquad}$
Step 5: Did I answer the *right* question? Be careful; you're not done yet! The slope represents the clearing duration increase for a 1% increase in snowpack water content. Multiply m by 5 to get the requested change. If you got 2, you'd be correct!	$\underline{\quad} \times \underline{\quad} = \underline{\quad}$

Great job! Repeat this for the second question in the set. Kaplan's strategic thinking is on the left, and bits of scratchwork guidance are on the right.

Strategic Thinking	Math Scratchwork
Step 1: Read the second question in the set, looking for clues Not a whole lot of new information, just a bit on the snowpack water content during a particularly snowy winter.	
Step 2: Identify and organize the information you need This question asks for the road clearing duration if snowpack water content is 248% of the historical average. The slope you found in the previous question could be useful here.	$m = \rule{1cm}{0.4pt}$
Step 3: Based on what you know, plan your steps to navigate the second question 248% snowpack water content is not on the graph, and you can easily make an error if you try to extend the line of best fit to estimate at 248%. You can use the slope to write the equation of the line and extrapolate from there.	$y = mx + b$
Step 4: Solve, step-by-step, checking units as you go Determine where the line of best fit intersects the y-axis to identify the value of b. Once there, plug 248 into the equation for the line of best fit, and then solve for y.	$eqn:\ \rule{1.5cm}{0.4pt} = \rule{1.5cm}{0.4pt} + \rule{1.5cm}{0.4pt}$ $x = 248:$ $\rule{1.5cm}{0.4pt} = \rule{1.5cm}{0.4pt} \times \rule{1.5cm}{0.4pt} + \rule{1.5cm}{0.4pt}$ $\rule{1.5cm}{0.4pt} = \rule{1.5cm}{0.4pt} + \rule{1.5cm}{0.4pt} = \rule{1.5cm}{0.4pt}$
Step 5: Did I answer the *right* question? You needed to find the number of days to clear Tioga Road at 248% snowpack water content. Did you get 99.2? If so, you'd be right!	$\rule{1.5cm}{0.4pt}$

Nicely done! Now test what you've learned by taking a brief quiz.

Now that you've seen the variety of ways in which the SAT can test you on scatterplots, try the following questions to check your understanding. Give yourself 4 minutes to tackle the following three questions. Make sure you use the Kaplan Method for Math as often as you can. Remember, you want to emphasize speed and efficiency in addition to simply getting the correct answer.

7. The graph above shows the percent of school age children in the United States who received immunizations for various illnesses between 1996 and 2012. What was the average rate of increase in the percent of children immunized over the given time period?

    A)   5%

    B)   10%

    C)   25%

    D)   70%

8. A marketing team is conducting a study on the use of smartphones. In a certain metropolitan area, there were 1.6 million smartphone users at the end of 2014. The marketing team predicts that the number of smartphone users will increase by 35% each year. If y represents the number of smartphone users in this metropolitan area after x years, then which of the following equations best models the number of smartphone users in this area over time?

    A) $y = 1,600,000(1.35)^x$

    B) $y = 1,600,000(35)^x$

    C) $y = 35x + 1,600,000$

    D) $y = 1.35x + 1,600,000$

9. A microbiologist is comparing the growth rates of two different yeast strains. She indirectly measures the number of yeast cells by recording the optical density (OD600) of each strain every ten hours. The measurements are presented in the graph above. Based on the data, which of the following is NOT a true statement?

    A)   Strain 1 had a higher OD600 reading than Strain 2 throughout the monitored period.

    B)   The growth rate of Strain 2 was less than the growth rate of Strain 1 until hour 50, at which point Strain 1's growth rate became the lesser one.

    C)   Between hours 50 and 70, Strain 2's OD600 reading increased by approximately 0.03 every hour.

    D)   The growth rate of Strain 1 was greater than the growth rate of Strain 2 throughout the monitored period.

Answers and Explanations for this chapter begin on page 831.

EXTRA PRACTICE

 You may use your calculator for all questions in this section.

1. Which of the following is best modeled using a linear regression equation, $y = ax + b$, where $a < 0$?

A)

B)

C)

D)

2. Adriana used the data from a scatterplot she found on the U.S. Census Bureau's website to determine a regression model showing the relationship between the population in the area where she lived and the number of years, x, after she was born. The result was an exponential growth equation of the form $y = x_0(1 + r)^x$. Which of the following does x_0 most likely represent in the equation?

A) The population in the year that she was born

B) The rate of change of the population over time

C) The maximum population reached during her lifetime

D) The number of years after her birth when the population reached its maximum

Math

Seatbelt Use in England (1983-2009)

Percent Front Seat Belt Usage

Years After Seatbelt Law Enacted

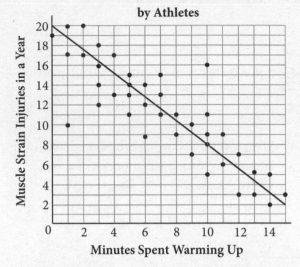

Minor Muscle Strains Sustained by Athletes

Muscle Strain Injuries in a Year

Minutes Spent Warming Up

3. In 1983, the British Parliament enacted a mandatory seat belt law. The scatterplot above shows data collected each year after the law was enacted regarding the percent of drivers and front seat passengers who wore seat belts. Which of the following equations best represents the trend of the data shown in the figure?

    A) $y = 0.4x + 25$

    B) $y = 1.8x + 15$

    C) $y = 2.1x + 35$

    D) $y = 2.6x + 25$

4. The scatterplot above shows the number of minor muscle strain injuries sustained in a year by athletes, plotted against their self-reported amount of time spent stretching and doing other "warm up" activities before engaging in rigorous physical activity. Which of the following best estimates the average rate of change in the number of injuries compared with the number of minutes spent warming up?

    A) -1.2

    B) -0.8

    C) 2

    D) 20

5. The Federal Reserve controls certain interest rates in the United States. Investors often try to speculate as to whether the Federal Reserve will raise or lower rates and by how much. Suppose a company conducts extensive interviews with financial analysts, and as a result, predicts that "the Fed" will increase rates by an average of 0.25 percentage points every six months for the foreseeable future. Which type of equation could be used to model the predicted interest rates over the next several years, assuming no other significant changes?

A) A linear equation

B) A quadratic equation

C) A polynomial equation

D) An exponential equation

6. A physics class is doing an experiment in order to write a function that models the height of a new super bouncy ball after each time that it bounces off the parking lot. The ball is thrown from the roof of the gym straight down to the parking lot pavement. The ball bounces to a height of 80 feet. The ball is allowed to bounce again, without anyone touching it, this time reaching a maximum height of 40 feet. It bounces again, reaching a height of 20 feet, and continues until it eventually stops bouncing. Which of the following functions could be used to model the height (H) of the ball after each time that it hits the pavement (b), until the ball stops bouncing?

A) $H(b) = \dfrac{80}{2^b}$

B) $H(b) = \dfrac{80}{2^{b-1}}$

C) $H(b) = 80 - 2b$

D) $H(b) = 80 - 2(b - 1)$

Questions 7 and 8 refer to the following information.

Most chickens reach maturity and begin laying eggs at around 20 weeks of age. From this point forward, however, as the chicken ages, its egg production decreases. A farmer was given a flock of 100 chickens (all of which are the same age) and asked to measure daily egg output for the entire flock at random intervals starting at maturity until the chickens were 70 weeks old. The data is recorded in the scatterplot below and the line of best fit has been drawn.

7. How many times did the farmer's data differ by at least 5 eggs from the number of eggs predicted by the line of best fit?

8. Based on the line of best fit, what is the predicted number of eggs that will be produced by the flock when it is 36 weeks past maturity?

9. If a scatterplot shows a strong positive linear correlation, then which of the following best describes the trend of the data points?

    A) Points in a perfectly straight line that rises from left to right

    B) Points in a perfectly straight line that falls from left to right

    C) Points that fit fairly close to a straight line that rises from left to right

    D) Points that fit fairly close to a straight line that falls from left to right

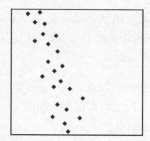

10. Which of the following is the best estimate for the slope of the line that best fits the data shown in the figure above? (Assume that the black bordered area is a square and that the scale of measurement is the same on every side.)

    A) -3

    B) $-\dfrac{1}{3}$

    C) $\dfrac{1}{3}$

    D) 3

11. Which of the equations best models the data shown above?

    A) $y = 0.5x - 1$

    B) $y = 0.5x + 1$

    C) $y = 1.5x + 1$

    D) $y = 1.5x - 1$

12. Suppose a scatterplot shows a weak negative linear correlation. Which of the following statements is true?

    A) The slope of the line of best fit will be a number less than -1.

    B) The slope of the line of best fit will be a number between -1 and 0.

    C) The data points will follow, but not closely, the line of best fit, which has a negative slope.

    D) The data points will be closely gathered around the line of best fit, which has a negative slope.

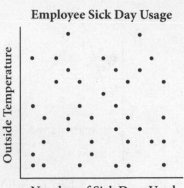

Employee Sick Day Usage

Outside Temperature

Number of Sick Days Used

13. The Human Resources department of a company tracks employee sick day usage to see if there are patterns. One of the HR representatives decides to check employee sick day usage against outside temperature. He compiles the information for the employees' sick day usage and temperature in the scatterplot above. Which of the following conclusions can he draw based on this data?

A) There is no relationship between the number of sick days used by employees in general and outside temperature.

B) There is no relationship between the number of sick days used by this company's employees and outside temperature.

C) No conclusions can be drawn about the number of sick days used by this company's employees and outside temperature.

D) There is a relationship between, but not causation by, the number of sick days used by this company's employees and outside temperature.

14. Scientists plotted data for two animal populations on a scatterplot: Population A, which they graphed along the x-axis, and Population B, which they graphed along the y-axis. The data showed a strong negative correlation. Which of the following statements is justified?

A) The rise in Population A caused the decline in Population B.

B) The decline in Population B caused the rise in Population A.

C) Because the correlation is negative, there cannot be causation between the two populations.

D) The rise in Population A is correlated to the decline in Population B, but causation is unknown.

15. If a scatterplot shows data points in the first quadrant of a coordinate plane that decrease very quickly at first, and then continue to decrease but at a much slower rate, then which of the following functions is the best model for the data?

A) $f(x) = ax^2 + bx + c$, where $a > 0$

B) $f(x) = ax^2 + bx + c$, where $a < 0$

C) $f(x) = a(1 + r)^x$, where $r > 0$

D) $f(x) = a(1 + r)^x$, where $r < 0$

16. When a baby is born, it has a small stomach and therefore only needs small amounts of breast milk or formula at a time. As the baby gets older, it needs more calories to grow, so it starts consuming more milk. At about 6 months, babies are able to eat solid foods and will get some of their calories from that. Accordingly, the child's need for milk starts to decrease, until it is no longer even necessary, which occurs at about one year of age. If data is collected on a typical infant's milk intake over the first year and plotted on a scatterplot, what kind of model would most likely match the data?

A) Positive linear

B) Negative linear

C) Positive quadratic

D) Negative quadratic

17. Genji is compiling data relating snowfall to temperature where he lives. He records his data points in the form (temperature in degrees Fahrenheit, snowfall in inches). He plots the data on a scatterplot and draws a line of best fit, which indicates a strong negative correlation. He then remembers that his temperature gauge reads 10 degrees colder than it actually is. This means all of his data points are correct for the amount of snowfall, but the temperature readings are all lower than they should be. To correct the problem, he adds 10 degrees to all of his temperature readings and re-plots the data. What does this mean for his data?

A) The data is no longer necessarily correlated.

B) There is no change in the strength of correlation.

C) The rate of change for the line of best fit is less now.

D) The rate of change for the line of best fit is greater now.

18. The maximum value of the data shown in the scatterplot above occurs at $x = 25$. If the data is modeled using a quadratic regression and the correlation coefficient is 1.0 (the fit is exact), then what is the y-value when $x = 35$?

A) 10

B) 15

C) 22

D) 27

Math

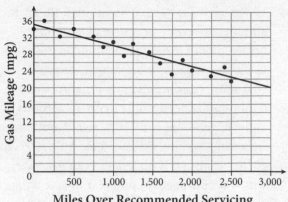

Miles Over Recommended Servicing

19. What is the *y*-value of the data point that has the highest percent error from the mean of the data shown in the scatterplot above?

20. Research suggests that for any given make and model of car, the more miles the car is driven over the recommended miles between servicing, the worse gas mileage the car gets. Suppose a car dealership compiles data on a specific make and model of car and creates the scatterplot shown above. They then use the equation $y = -\dfrac{1}{200}x + 35$ to model the data. Based on the information, how many miles per gallon could be expected if this particular car is driven 3,400 miles over the recommended miles between servicing?

CHAPTER 7

Two-way Tables, Statistics, and Probability

CHAPTER OBJECTIVES

By the end of this chapter, you will be able to:

1. Use two-way tables to summarize data and calculate basic probabilities

2. Make inferences about population parameters based on sample data

3. Evaluate scenarios and reports to make inferences, justify conclusions, and determine appropriateness of data collection methods

4. Use statistics to investigate measures of center of data and analyze shape, center, and spread

SMARTPOINTS

Point Value	SmartPoint Category
50 Points	Statistics and Probability

Math

TWO-WAY TABLES, STATISTICS, AND PROBABILITY

Chapter 7

Homework

Extra Practice: #1-20

Even More

Math Quiz 3

Key

 Book Assignment

 Online Video Assignment

 Online Quiz Assignment

TWO-WAY TABLES AND CHARTS/GRAPHS

Data can be represented in a multitude of ways. In this chapter, we'll focus on a numerical approach (two-way table) and a pictorial one (chart or graph).

A two-way table is a table that contains data on two variables. This type of table can be used to make comparisons and determine whether relationships exist between the variables. You might see this data referred to as bivariate (two-variable) data.

If you're worried about having to learn a new topic, you need not be. You've likely encountered two-way tables in the past and just not known their formal name—if you've ever generated a spreadsheet, two-way tables should look familiar. Take a look at the following example that contains data on several antique book stores' sales to see what we mean.

	Bob's Books	Nalia's Novels	Tumiko's Tomes	Vladimir's Volumes	Total
Monday	14	7	15	12	48
Tuesday	8	13	15	13	49
Wednesday	10	13	12	14	49
Thursday	8	15	14	10	47
Friday	13	7	10	9	39
Total	53	55	66	58	232

Two-way tables contain a wealth of information: You can quickly determine how many books Nalia's Novels sold on Friday just by finding the appropriate cell in the table. You can also find quantities that are not explicitly written. For instance, you can determine numerous ratios: total books sold on Wednesday to total books sold on Thursday, Tumiko's Monday sales to Tumiko's total sales, and so on. You can also calculate percentages and probabilities.

> **Note**
>
> Although two-way tables are generally easy to follow, they're also easy to misinterpret when you're in a rush. Take time to ensure that you've extracted the correct information for a given question.

Ratios and the like aside, you could be asked to make a prediction based on given data; that is, you'll need to extrapolate data to derive an answer. For instance, let's say the community in which these four shops are located has an annual antique appreciation week, and Nalia anticipates that her antique book sales will increase by 40% from the week for which the data is shown in the table. She sold 55 books that week, and 40% of 55 is 22. This means that if Nalia's prediction is true, she can expect to sell 55 + 22 = 77 books during antique appreciation week.

In addition to two-way tables, the SAT can also ask questions about charts and graphs, whether about the data itself or a prediction based on the data. Take a look at the next few pages for sample questions involving two-way tables, charts, and graphs.

Use the table introduced at the beginning of this section to answer the following question.

1. Which of the four shops made the greatest fraction of its total sales on Tuesday?

   A) Bob's Books

   B) Nalia's Novels

   C) Tumiko's Tomes

   D) Vladimir's Volumes

Work through the Kaplan Method for Math step-by-step to solve this question. The following table shows Kaplan's strategic thinking on the left, along with suggested math scratchwork on the right.

Strategic Thinking	Math Scratchwork
Step 1: Read the question, identifying and organizing important information as you go Understanding what's being asked is the trickiest part of this question. You *do not* want the shop that sold the most books on Tuesday. Rather, you are looking for the shop whose Tuesday sales, as a fraction of the shop's total sales, were the greatest.	$need\ \dfrac{Tuesday}{Total}$
Step 2: Choose the best strategy to answer the question Only two rows matter for this question: the Tuesday row and the Total row (*not* the Total column). Divide each shop's Tuesday sales by its total sales. The shop with the largest result is the correct answer. Because the fractions involve less manageable numbers, using a calculator to simplify the arithmetic is reasonable here. Nalia's Tuesday sales as a fraction of her total sales were the highest of the four shops.	$B: \dfrac{8}{53} \approx 0.1509$ $N: \dfrac{13}{55} \approx 0.2364$ $T: \dfrac{15}{66} \approx 0.2273$ $V: \dfrac{13}{58} \approx 0.2241$
Step 3: Check that you answered the *right* question You've identified the shop that had the highest fraction of its sales on Tuesday, so you're done. Choice (B) is correct.	

> ✔ **Expert Tip**
>
> If you're adept at quantitative comparison of fractions, you can omit the decimal conversion calculations (and save some time).

The following question requires the table used for question 1.

2. What fraction of all the books sold on Monday, Wednesday, and Friday were sold at Tumiko's Tomes and Vladimir's Volumes?

    A) $\frac{9}{29}$

    B) $\frac{11}{32}$

    C) $\frac{9}{17}$

    D) $\frac{18}{31}$

Work through the Kaplan Method for Math step-by-step to solve this question. The following table shows Kaplan's strategic thinking on the left, along with suggested math scratchwork on the right.

Strategic Thinking	Math Scratchwork
Step 1: Read the question, identifying and organizing important information as you go You need to find how many books Tumiko and Vladimir sold on Monday, Wednesday, and Friday as a fraction of the total number of books all four shops sold on those days.	
Step 2: Choose the best strategy to answer the question Use the Monday, Wednesday, and Friday rows and the Tumiko, Vladimir, and Total columns (*not* the Total row). Add the number of books Tumiko and Vladimir sold on these three days, and then repeat the process with the total number of books all four shops sold on these days. Combine these values into a fraction.	Mon + Wed + Fri for T & V: (15 + 12) + (12 + 14) + (10 + 9) = 72 Mon + Wed + Fri total: 48 + 49 + 39 = 136 $\frac{72}{136}$
Step 3: Check that you answered the *right* question You'll need to simplify the fraction. The GCF of 72 and 136 is 8, so the most simplified form of the fraction is $\frac{9}{17}$. Select (C) and you're done.	$\frac{72}{136} = \frac{9}{17}$

STATISTICS AND PROBABILITY

While there are entire high school and college courses devoted to the study of statistics, the SAT will (fortunately) only test you on a few basic statistical concepts. If you aren't a statistics fan, now is a great time to rethink your position: Statistics is a part of almost every major in college and can be used in a variety of careers. Using an example from high school, let's take a look at the sort of concepts the SAT expects you to be familiar with.

Suppose you took five tests in a world history class and earned scores of 85, 92, 85, 80, and 96. Descriptions of six fundamental statistics figures you can find for this data set follow:

- **Mean (also called average):** The sum of the values divided by the number of values. For your history class, the mean of your test scores is $\dfrac{85 + 92 + 85 + 80 + 96}{5} = \dfrac{438}{5} = 87.6$. At most schools, that's a B or B+.

- **Median:** The value that is in the middle of the set *when the values are arranged in ascending order*. The test scores in ascending order are 80, 85, 85, 92, and 96, making the median 85. Be careful: The SAT could give you a set of numbers that is not in order. Make sure you properly arrange them before determining the median.

- **Mode:** The value that occurs most frequently. The score that appears more than any other is 85 (twice vs. once), so it is the mode. If more than one value appears the most often, that's okay: A set of data can have multiple modes.

- **Range:** The difference between the highest and lowest values. From finding the median, you know the highest and lowest scores are 96 and 80, respectively; so the range is $96 - 80 = 16$.

- **Standard deviation:** A measure of how far a typical data point is from the mean. A low standard deviation means most values in the set are fairly close to the mean; a high standard deviation means there is much more spread in the data set. On the SAT, **you will need to know what standard deviation is and what it tells you about a set of data, but you won't have to calculate it.**

- **Margin of error:** A description of the maximum expected difference between a true value for a data pool (e.g., mean) and a random sampling from the data pool. A lower margin of error is achieved by increasing the size of the data pool. **As with standard deviation, you will need to know what a margin of error is on the SAT, but you won't be asked to calculate one.**

Mean, median, and mode are referred to as measures of central tendency because they can be used to represent a typical value in the data set. Range, standard deviation, and margin of error are measures of spread because they show how much the data in a set vary.

> ✔ **Note**
>
> To find the median of a data set that contains an even number of terms, arrange the terms in ascending order, then find the average of the two middle terms.

On Test Day, you might also be asked to analyze the shape of data. The shape of a data set can be either symmetric (also referred to as a *normal* distribution) or skewed (asymmetric). Many data sets have a head, where many data points are clustered in one area, and tails, where the number of data points slowly decreases to 0. Examining the tails will help you describe the shape of a data set. A data set is skewed in the direction of its longer tail.

Symmetric

The data are evenly spread out.
mean ≈ median

Skewed to the Left **Skewed to the Right**

The tail is longer on the left. The tail is longer on the right.
mean < median mean > median

> ✔ **Expert Tip**
>
> When you have a group of evenly spaced terms (e.g., 2, 4, 6, 8, 10, 12), the mean and median will be identical. With this data set, the mean is
>
> $$\frac{2 + 4 + 6 + 8 + 10 + 12}{6} = \frac{42}{6} = 7, \text{ and}$$
>
> the median is $\frac{6 + 8}{2} = \frac{14}{2} = 7$. In
>
> addition, you can find the mean of a group of evenly spaced terms by taking the mean of the highest and lowest:
>
> $$\frac{12 + 2}{2} = \frac{14}{2} = 7.$$

It is possible to determine the mean of a data set from a bar graph (also called a histogram). Suppose a teacher made a bar graph, such as the one shown here, of student performance on a recent test.

To find the mean test score, first determine the sum of the scores and then divide by the number of scores. From the graph, 3 students scored 60, 9 scored 65, 11 scored 70, and so on. Add these values to find the sum of the scores; then divide by the total number of scores.

$$\frac{3(60) + 9(65) + 11(70) + 13(75) + 18(80) + 15(85) + 12(90) + 8(95) + 2(100)}{3 + 9 + 11 + 13 + 18 + 15 + 12 + 8 + 2} = \frac{7,265}{91} = 79.8$$

The mean score on this test was 79.8.

A concept closely linked to statistics is probability. **Probability** is a fraction or decimal comparing the number of desired outcomes to the number of total possible outcomes. The formula is:

$$\text{Probability} = \frac{\text{\# desired outcomes}}{\text{\# total possible outcomes}}$$

For instance, if you have a full deck of playing cards and want to know the probability of drawing an ace, you would compute $\frac{\text{\# aces}}{\text{\# cards}} = \frac{4}{52} = \frac{1}{13} \approx 0.077$. To find the probability that an event will *not* happen, subtract the probability that the event will happen from 1. In the ace example, this would be:

$$1 - \frac{\text{\# aces}}{\text{\# cards}} = 1 - \frac{4}{52} = \frac{48}{52} = \frac{12}{13} \approx 0.923$$

You can also find the probability for a series of events. If you're asked for the probability of drawing an ace without replacement (the card does not go back in the deck) followed by a red nine, multiply the probability of the first event by that of the second:

$$\frac{\text{\# aces}}{\text{\# cards}} \times \frac{\text{\# red nines}}{\text{\# cards} - 1} = \frac{4}{52} \times \frac{2}{51} = \frac{8}{2,652} \approx 0.003$$

> ✔ **Note**
>
> "With replacement" means the item chosen, in this case a card, is returned to the original group (here, the deck). The number of possible outcomes in the denominator will stay constant. "Without replacement" indicates the item is not returned; the number of possible outcomes will change to reflect the new possible outcome count.

Using a two-way table, you can find the probability that a randomly selected data value (be it a person, object, etc.) will fit a certain profile. In addition, you might be asked to calculate a conditional probability. Conditional probability questions are easy to spot, as the word *given* is often present.

The following is a two-way table summarizing a survey on water preference.

	Bottled	Carbonated	Tap	Total
Female	325	267	295	887
Male	304	210	289	803
Total	629	477	584	1,690

If asked for the probability of randomly selecting a female who prefers bottled water from all the participants of the original survey for a follow-up survey, you would calculate it using the same general formula as before: $\dfrac{\text{\# female, bottled}}{\text{\# total}} = \dfrac{325}{1,690} = \dfrac{5}{26} \approx 0.192$.

If asked for the probability of randomly selecting a female for the follow-up survey, given that the chosen participant prefers bottled water, the setup is a little different. The clause starting with "given" indicates the number of possible outcomes is the total participants who prefer bottled water, which is 629, not the grand total of 1,690. The calculation is now $\dfrac{\text{\# female, bottled}}{\text{\# total, bottled}} = \dfrac{325}{629} \approx 0.517$.

Conversely, if you need to find the probability of selecting someone who prefers bottled water for the follow-up survey, given that the chosen participant is female, the new number of possible outcomes is the female participant total (887). The calculation becomes $\dfrac{\text{\# bottled}}{\text{\# total, females}} = \dfrac{325}{887} \approx 0.366$.

Take a look at the next few pages for some test-like questions involving two-way tables and probability.

Math

Questions 3 and 4 refer to the following information.

The table below summarizes the results of a survey about favorite video game genres for a group of high school students. Assume that every student had a favorite video game genre and that each student could only select one favorite.

	Freshmen	Sophomores	Juniors	Seniors	Total
First-person shooters	144	122	134	115	515
Strategy games	126	140	152	148	566
Role-playing games	120	117	153	148	538
Indie games	110	114	63	98	385
Total	500	493	502	509	2004

3. The research group that conducted the survey wants to select one sophomore and one senior at random for a follow-up survey. What is the probability that both students selected will prefer a type of video game other than strategy games?

A) $\dfrac{140}{493} + \dfrac{148}{509}$

B) $\dfrac{140}{493} \times \dfrac{148}{509}$

C) $\dfrac{353}{493} + \dfrac{361}{509}$

D) $\dfrac{353}{493} \times \dfrac{361}{509}$

There's no scratchwork for this question, but Kaplan's strategic thinking is provided in the table on the next page. Follow along as we reason through the question to get the correct answer.

Strategic Thinking
Step 1: Read the question, identifying and organizing important information as you go
You need to determine the probability that a sophomore and a senior selected at random will both prefer a video game genre other than strategy games.
Step 2: Choose the best strategy to answer the question
The answer choices are unsimplified expressions, which means that you don't need to find the actual probability—you just need to set up the correct expression.   The word "both" in the question stem signals that you need to find the probability that one event AND another will both happen. To find the probability that more than one event will occur, multiply the individual probabilities together. This means that A and C, which feature addition rather than multiplication, are incorrect.   You can determine which of the remaining answer choices is correct without any number crunching. Of the 493 sophomores, 140 prefer strategy games. Choice B contains the probability $\frac{140}{493}$, which means it's incorrect—you want the probability of picking students who *don't* prefer strategy games.
Step 3: Check that you answered the *right* question
By process of elimination, you know that (D) must be correct.

4. The research group that conducted the survey wishes to see if there is a connection between the time a student spends playing video games and that student's grade point average (GPA). The school at which the initial survey was conducted was in Dallas, Texas; the group decides to include three additional Dallas high schools in the follow-up study. Data produced from the follow-up study showed a moderately strong negative correlation between time spent playing video games and GPA. Based on these findings, which of the following is a valid conclusion?

    A) There is an association between the amount of time a high school student in Dallas spends playing video games and his/her GPA.

    B) There is an association between the amount of time a high school student anywhere in Texas spends playing video games and his/her GPA.

    C) An increase in the amount of time a high school student in Dallas spends playing video games causes a decrease in his/her GPA.

    D) An increase in the amount of time a high school student anywhere in Texas spends playing video games causes a decrease in his/her GPA.

There's no scratchwork for this question, but Kaplan's strategic thinking is provided in the table. Follow along as we reason through the question to get the correct answer.

Strategic Thinking
Step 1: Read the question, identifying and organizing important information as you go
You're asked to identify the valid conclusion (in other words, the true statement).
Step 2: Choose the best strategy to answer the question
Carefully examine each answer choice. You're told that there is a moderately strong correlation between time spent playing video games and GPA. However, because the study involved students in Dallas only, no conclusions about the entire Texas high school population can be drawn. Eliminate B and D. To determine which of the two remaining answer choices is correct, carefully read each choice and compare it to the question stem. Although there is a correlation between time spent playing video games and GPA, the study did not conclude that one causes the other. Eliminate C.
Step 3: Check that you answered the *right* question
Choice (A) matches your analysis.

✔ Expert Tip

Look for key details—such as the study's population, location, and any results derived—in questions like this one. These details will help you quickly solve for the correct answer.

On the next few pages, we'll work through another multi-part question set involving the concepts you've learned in this chapter. Remember to answer the questions one step at a time, and follow the Kaplan Method for Multi-Part Math Questions.

Questions 5 and 6 refer to the following information.

Attendance at Museum X:
Age Distribution

The pie graph above shows the age distribution of visitors to Museum X in 2014. Visitors aged 0-9 years get into Museum X for free, visitors aged 50 and older pay $5 for admission, and everyone else pays $10.

5. If 553 people aged 20 years and older visited Museum X in 2014, then approximately how many people visited Museum X in 2014 ?

6. Based on the pie graph and the result from the previous question, how much revenue did Museum X collect from tickets sold to people aged 40 and older in 2014 ?

Work through the Kaplan Method for Multi-Part Math Questions step-by-step to solve this question (for a review of this Method, see chapter 5). The following table shows Kaplan's strategic thinking on the left, along with suggested math scratchwork on the right.

Strategic Thinking	Math Scratchwork
Step 1: Read the first question in the set, looking for clues The infographic shows the age distribution of visitors to Museum X in 2014. From the accompanying text you also learn the ticket prices based on age.	0–9: free 10–49: $10 50+: $5
Step 2: Identify and organize the information you need You're asked to find the total number of visitors to Museum X in 2014, given that 553 of the visitors were aged 20 and up.	need total # attendees

Strategic Thinking	Math Scratchwork
Step 3: Based on what you know, plan your steps to navigate the first question You know the *number* of visitors aged 20 and up. If you find the accompanying percent, you can figure out the total using the three-part percent formula you learned previously.	_____ % of total is 553
Step 4: Solve, step-by-step, checking units as you go You could add the percentages for the 20-29, 30-39, 40-49, and 50+ categories, but there's a faster route. Look at the sections of the pie graph for the two groups that are *not* 20 or older: 0-9 and 10-19. Those two groups represent 5% and 16% of the total, respectively. Subtract these values from 100% to find what percent of visitors were aged 20 and up. To find the total number of visitors, plug what you know into the three-part percent formula.	% not aged 20+: 5% + 16% = 21% % aged 20+: 100% − 21% = 79% total × 0.79 = 553 $total = \dfrac{553}{0.79} = 700$
Step 5: Did I answer the *right* question? The question asks for the total number of visitors in 2014, which is 700.	

The first question is complete. Now on to Step 6: Repeat for the second question in the set. Kaplan's strategic thinking is on the left, along with suggested math scratchwork on the right.

Strategic Thinking	Math Scratchwork
Step 1: Read the second question in the set, looking for clues From the previous question, you know the total number of visitors in 2014; nothing new is given in this question.	700 total attendees
Step 2: Identify and organize the information you need This question asks for the revenue from tickets sold to people aged 40 and older. The total number of visitors, which you learned in the previous question, will help calculate this figure.	$ from aged 40+: ?

Strategic Thinking	Math Scratchwork
Step 3: Based on what you know, plan your steps to navigate the second question Because you already know the total number of visitors, you can calculate the number of visitors aged 40-49 and 50+ using the percentages given in the pie graph.	*find # of 40–49, 50+*
Step 4: Solve, step-by-step, checking units as you go Calculate the number of attendees in the 40-49 and 50+ age groups by taking 25% of 700 and 8% of 700, respectively. The 40-49 group paid \$10 per ticket, and the 50+ group paid \$5 per ticket. Use these facts to determine the revenue generated from these groups.	*# aged 40–49: 700 × 0.25 = 175* *# aged 50+: 700 × 0.08 = 56* *175 ppl paid \$10/ticket* *56 ppl paid \$5/ticket* *175 × \$10 = \$1,750* *56 × \$5 = \$280* *\$1,750 + \$280 = \$2,030*
Step 5: Did I answer the *right* question? \$2,030 was collected from the 40-49 and 50+ age groups; grid in 2030.	

> ✔ **Note**
>
> It's easy to misread questions like #6 and use a part of the infographic other than the one you need. Take time to ensure that you know what you need to find.

WORD PROBLEMS

You're already well versed in deciphering SAT word problems, but word problems involving probability sometimes require you to use different skills. You'll need to use your analytical abilities to develop inferences and predictions, draw and justify logical conclusions, and evaluate the appropriateness of data collection techniques. Sometimes you'll need to consult a provided two-way table as you did for some earlier questions, and in other cases you'll just study the question stem to gather pertinent information. Perhaps the best part of these questions is the fact that they often require little or no actual mathematical calculation!

Here is a test-like question.

7. A local softball league has male and female members. If m is the average age of the males, f is the average age of the females, a is the overall average age, and 65 percent of the league's members are male, then which one of the following statements must be true about m, f, and a ?

A) If $m < f$, then $a > \dfrac{m + f}{2}$.

B) If $m > f$, then $a < \dfrac{m + f}{2}$.

C) If $m < f$, then $a < \dfrac{m + f}{2}$.

D) $a = \dfrac{m + f}{2}$

There's no scratchwork for this question, but Kaplan's strategic thinking is provided in the table. Follow along as we reason through the question to get the correct answer.

Strategic Thinking
Step 1: Read the question, identifying and organizing important information as you go
The question asks you to identify the statement that is true. You're told that 65% of the league's members are male, and you're given the definition of three variables: m, f, and a.
Step 2: Choose the best strategy to answer the question
Don't panic over the limited amount of information. Examine the answer choices to see if you can spot any useful patterns. Each answer choice makes a comparison between a (the overall average age) and $\frac{m+f}{2}$. If the male and female member counts were equal, then the overall average age would simply be the average of the male and female average ages, or $\frac{m+f}{2}$. However, because there are more males than females in the group, the overall average must be closer to the average male age than to the average female age. You don't know which of m or f is greater, so use a number line to visualize this information. There are two ways to do so: The first assumes that $m < f$; the second assumes that $m > f$.   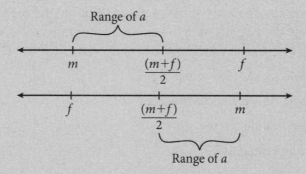   The only choice consistent with the visualization is (C): Based on the top number line, when m is less than f, the value of a is less than the average age of both groups.
Step 3: Check that you answered the *right* question
Choice (C) matches your analysis.

✔ **Note**

For questions like this, think about what information is given or not given, the conclusion(s) you can draw from either, and answers you can eliminate based on those conclusion(s).

Now you'll have a chance to try a few more test-like problems in a scaffolded way. We've provided some guidance, but you'll need to fill in the missing parts of explanations or the step-by-step math in order to get to the correct answer. Don't worry—after going through the worked examples at the beginning of this section, these problems should be completely doable.

8. A history professor observes that the scores of a recent 20-question multiple choice exam are normally distributed as shown in the histogram above. However, she later discovers that 25% of the results were omitted from the distribution. Of the omitted scores, 80% are greater than what the professor thought the mean was; the rest are less. Assuming all new data points fit in the current histogram range, which of the following is most likely to occur upon adding the new scores to the data?

A) The data will be skewed to the right.

B) The data will be skewed to the left.

C) The median will decrease.

D) The range will decrease.

The following table can help you structure your thinking as you go about solving this more involved problem. Kaplan's strategic thinking is provided, as are bits of structured scratchwork. If you're not sure how to approach a question like this, start at the top and work your way down.

Strategic Thinking	Math Scratchwork
Step 1: Read the question, identifying and organizing important information as you go You need to determine the effect of adding extra data points, most of which are above the mean, to what was previously a normal (symmetric) distribution.	

Strategic Thinking	Math Scratchwork
Step 2: Choose the best strategy to answer the question The question states that most of the new scores are above the mean. Draw a rough sketch of what the new distribution will look like. The choices mention skew, median, and range. Think about the effect the additions to the data set will have on each of these.	post-addition: direction of skew: _____ median shift: _____ range shift: _____
Step 3: Check that you answered the *right* question If you chose (B), congrats! You're correct.	_____

Now try a multi-part question set.

Questions 9 and 10 refer to the following information.

	1	2	3	4	5	Total
Worker Placement	5	17	24	10	5	61
Bidding	3	12	28	8	3	54
Area Control	3	10	30	14	2	59

A small boutique sells board games online. The boutique specializes in worker placement, bidding, and area control board games. Any customer who purchases a game is invited to rate the game on a scale of 1 to 5. A rating of 1 or 2 is considered "bad," a rating of 3 is considered "average," and a rating of 4 or 5 is considered "good." The table above shows the distribution of average customer ratings of the board games sold by the boutique. For example, 24 of the worker placement games sold by the boutique have an average rating of 3.

9. According to the table, what percent of all the board games sold by the boutique received a rating of "bad"? Round to the nearest tenth of a percent and ignore the percent sign when entering your answer.

10. The boutique decides to stop selling 50% of the board games that received a rating of "bad" to make room for promising new stock. Assuming no significant changes in ratings in the foreseeable future, what should the difference be between the percentages of board games with a rating of "bad" before and after this change? Round to the nearest tenth of a percent and ignore the percent sign when entering your answer.

The following table can help you structure your thinking as you go about solving this more involved problem. Kaplan's strategic thinking is provided, as are bits of structured scratchwork. If you're not sure how to approach a question like this, start at the top and work your way down.

Strategic Thinking	Math Scratchwork
Step 1: Read the first question in the set, looking for clues You're provided a chart with data on the average ratings of board games sold by a boutique.	
Step 2: Identify and organize the information you need You're asked to find the percent of games that received a rating of "bad", meaning a rating of 1 or 2.	find % of games with "bad" rating
Step 3: Based on what you know, plan your steps to navigate the first question Examine the chart carefully, identifying the necessary data from each type of game. You need to determine how many games received a rating of 1 or 2. Add the figures to get the total number of games that received a rating of "bad."	worker placement 1: _____ games 2: _____ games bidding 1: _____ games 2: _____ games area control 1: _____ games 2: _____ games total: _____
Step 4: Solve, step-by-step, checking units as you go Use the values in the table to find the total number of games in these groups. Write the "bad" *part* over the *total* game count, and then convert to a percent.	_____ × 100% = _____%
Step 5: Did I answer the *right* question? If you got 28.7, you're correct!	_____

Great job! Repeat for the second question. Kaplan's strategic thinking is on the left, and bits of scratchwork guidance are on the right.

Strategic Thinking	Math Scratchwork
Step 1: Read the second question in the set, looking for clues From the previous question, you know the number (and percent) of games that received a rating of "bad."	# games with "bad" rating: _____ ; = _____ %
Step 2: Identify and organize the information you need You're asked for the difference between the percentages of games that received a "bad" rating before and after 50% of such games are removed from the store's inventory. Your answer from the previous question is key to this calculation.	"bad" % pre-removal: _____ % "bad" % post-removal: ?
Step 3: Based on what you know, plan your steps to navigate the second question You know the store wants to get rid of 50% of the games that received a "bad" rating. You already know the current number with a "bad" rating, so finding the new "bad" game count is straightforward. Once there, determine the new "bad" percentage and subtract that from the original.	_____ × old "bad" count = new "bad" count → convert to % old "bad" % − new "bad" % = answer
Step 4: Solve, step-by-step, checking units as you go After the 50% reduction in "bad" games, how many games should have a "bad" rating? Reduce the original "bad" game count by 50%. Divide your new "bad" count by the total game count. Remember that when the number of "bad" games decreases, the total count decreases by the same amount. Write your results using a couple of decimal points to minimize rounding errors. Subtract the new "bad" percent from the old "bad" percent.	_____ % × old "bad" count = new "bad" count _____ × _____ = _____ new "bad" %: _____ × 100 = _____ % old "bad" % − new "bad" %: _____ % − _____ % = _____ %
Step 5: Did I answer the *right* question? Did you get 11.9? If so, you're absolutely correct!	% change: _____

Nice work! Now test what you've learned by taking a brief quiz.

Now that you've seen the variety of ways in which the SAT can test you on two-way tables, statistics, and probability, try the following questions to check your understanding. Give yourself 5 minutes to tackle the following four questions. Make sure you use the Kaplan Method for Math (and the Kaplan Method for Multi-Part Math Questions where appropriate) as often as you can. Remember, you want to emphasize speed and efficiency in addition to simply getting the correct answer.

	Ceren	Han	Billy
Run 1	8.3	8.5	8.4
Run 2	7.7	8.0	8.0
Run 3	7.1	8.5	7.5
Run 4	6.6	7.8	9.0
Run 5	8.0	8.1	7.5
Run 6	6.6	7.5	7.2
Mean Score	7.38	8.07	7.93
Standard Deviation	0.73	0.39	0.67

11. Randolph recently completed a book of 20 deduction puzzles. The scatterplot above shows the time it took Randolph to solve a puzzle versus the number of clues it had. If a puzzle is selected at random from the book, what is the probability that it had fewer than six clues, took Randolph fewer than 100 seconds to solve, or both?

    A) 10%

    B) 15%

    C) 85%

    D) 90%

12. Ceren, Han, and Billy participated in a snowboarding competition. The scores for each of their six qualifying runs are in the table above. According to the data, which of the following is a valid conclusion?

    A) Ceren had the smallest mean score, so her performance was the least consistent.

    B) Han had the smallest standard deviation, so his performance was the most consistent.

    C) Ceren had the largest standard deviation, so her performance was the most consistent.

    D) Billy had the highest score on any one run, so his performance was the most consistent.

Questions 13 and 14 refer to the following information.

	Scarves	Pairs of Mittens	Hats	Pairs of Socks	Total
Wilhelmina	7	2	24	19	52
Emanuel	8	2	9	14	33
Jose Raul	3	4	18	10	35
Alexandra	15	1	9	9	34
Total	33	9	60	52	154

Wilhelmina, Emanuel, Jose Raul, and Alexandra are in a knitting club. The table above shows the quantity of several different items each person has knitted over the lifetime of the club.

13. The four club members plan to knit hats to sell for Spirit Week at their college. They surveyed a group of students regarding their hat pattern preferences and found that 60% of those surveyed prefer solid-colored hats, 22% prefer stripes, and 18% prefer stars. The club anticipates that 1,800 students will each buy one hat. If the ratios in the table remain constant for Spirit Week hat production, how many solid-colored hats will Wilhelmina and Alexandra be responsible for knitting?

14. The knitting club plans to embroider a small, hidden emblem on the interior of 20% of the hats they make for Spirit Week; anyone who finds this emblem on their hat will win a free scarf. The four members will split up the making of the free scarves according to the ratios in the table. For how many winning hats and scarf prizes will Emanuel and Jose Raul be responsible?

Answers and Explanations for this chapter begin on page 837.

EXTRA PRACTICE

 You may use your calculator for all questions in this section.

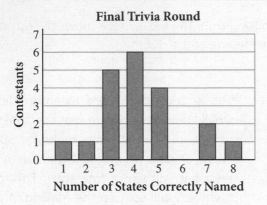

Final Trivia Round

Number of States Correctly Named

1. In the final round of a trivia competition, contestants were asked to name as many states that begin with the letter M as they could in 15 seconds. The bar graph shows the number of states the contestants were able to name. How many contestants participated in the final round of this competition?

A) 6

B) 8

C) 14

D) 20

2. An electronics manufacturer wants to know if customers would be interested in a detachable keyboard for their tablets and if so, what the most important features would be. The manufacturer partners with an electronics store to include copies of the survey with every purchase at that store for one week. Which of the following best explains why this random sample is unlikely to be a good representative sample of tablet owners' preferences for a detachable keyboard?

A) One week is likely not enough time to get a large enough sample.

B) Most people won't bother to send in the survey, which is likely to skew the results.

C) There is no way to verify whether the responders to the survey actually own a tablet.

D) The survey is biased because it was conducted through an electronics store, not the general population.

Appliance Sales

Number Sold

Distribution of Fish Breeds

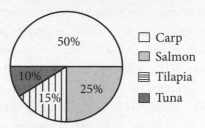

3. An appliance salesman sets a goal to sell an average of 6 appliances per day for the first two weeks of his new job. The dot plot shows the number he sold each day during the first 13 days. What is the minimum number of appliances he must sell on the 14th day in order to reach his goal?

A) 5

B) 6

C) 7

D) 8

4. Muscles, a membership-only gym, is hoping to open a new branch in a small city in Pennsylvania that currently has no fitness centers. According to their research, approximately 12,600 residents live within driving distance of the gym. Muscles sends out surveys to a sample of 300 randomly selected residents in this area (all of whom respond) and finds that 40 residents say they would visit a gym if one was located in their area. Based on past survey research, Muscles estimates that approximately 30% of these respondents would actually join the gym if they opened one in the area. Based on this information and the results of the sample survey, about how many residents should Muscles expect to join its new branch?

A)   134

B)   504

C)   1,680

D)   3,780

5. Mercury poisoning is a dangerous overload of mercury within the body. A major source of mercury poisoning is consuming fish that contain mercury. Certain fish are more prone to having higher levels of mercury than others. The pie chart shows the distribution of four breeds of fish at a hatchery. The hatchery has approximately 6,000 fish. A biologist from the Centers for Disease Control and Prevention randomly tests 5% of each breed of fish for mercury content. Her findings are shown in the following table.

Mercury Content Test Results

Breed	Number of Fish with Dangerous Mercury Levels
Carp	11
Salmon	6
Tilapia	5
Tuna	8

Based on the biologist's findings, if a single salmon is randomly selected from those that were tested, what is the probability that this particular fish would have a dangerous mercury level?

A)   0.001

B)   0.004

C)   0.02

D)   0.08

6. A Writer's Association sponsored a nation-wide convention for nonfiction writers. The association received 1,650 responses from members indicating that they were planning to attend the convention. The association sent a randomly generated follow-up email to 250 writers who were planning to attend and asked them about lunch preferences. Seventy-four said salads, 22 said pizza, 30 said pasta salad, 29 said grilled chicken, and the rest said sandwiches. Out of all of the writers planning to attend, about how many could the association expect to want sandwiches for lunch at the convention?

Questions 7 and 8 refer to the following information.

The amount of glucose, or sugar, in a person's blood is the primary indicator of diabetes. When a person fasts (doesn't eat) for eight hours prior to taking a blood sugar test, his/her glucose level should be below 100 mg/dL. A person is considered at risk for diabetes, but is not diagnosed as diabetic, when fasting glucose levels are between 100 and 125. If the level is above 125, the person is considered to have diabetes. The following table shows the ages and glucose levels of a group of diabetes study participants.

Diabetes Study Results

Age Group	<100 mg/dL	100-125 mg/dL	>125	Total
18-25	9	22	17	48
26-35	16	48	34	98
36-45	19	35	40	94
Older than 45	12	27	21	60
Total	56	132	112	300

7. According to the data, which age group had the smallest percentage of people with a healthy blood sugar level?

   A) 18-25

   B) 26-35

   C) 36-45

   D) Older than 45

8. Based on the table, if a single participant is selected at random from all the participants, what is the probability that he or she will be at risk for diabetes and be at least 36 years old?

   A) $\dfrac{7}{60}$

   B) $\dfrac{11}{25}$

   C) $\dfrac{31}{77}$

   D) $\dfrac{31}{150}$

9. Most animals give birth during a general time of year. This is because animals naturally breed so that their young will be born at the time of year when there will be an adequate food supply. The bar graph shows the number of live births of a jackrabbit native to California over the course of Year X. Based on the data, which of the following would be an appropriate conclusion?

A) In general, rabbits give birth during the spring months.

B) In general, rabbits give birth during the summer months.

C) In general, Californian jackrabbits give birth during the spring months.

D) In general, Californian jackrabbits give birth during the summer months.

Cookies Baked

	Chocolate Chip	Oatmeal Raisin	Total
With Nuts		40	
Without Nuts			104
Total			186

10. A baker makes 186 cookies. Some are chocolate chip and some are oatmeal raisin, and both kinds are made with and without nuts, as shown in the table above. Because they are more popular, the baker made $\frac{2}{3}$ of the cookies chocolate chip. If a chocolate chip cookie is chosen at random, what is the probability that it will have nuts?

A) $\frac{21}{93}$

B) $\frac{21}{62}$

C) $\frac{41}{93}$

D) $\frac{21}{41}$

11. A bottled water company conducts a survey to find out how many bottles of water people consume per day. If a representative sample of 500 people is chosen without bias from a population estimated to be 50,000, which of the following accurately describes how the mean of the sample data relates to the estimated mean of the entire population?

A) The mean of the sample data is equal to the estimated mean of the population.

B) The mean of the sample data cannot be used to estimate the mean of the much larger population.

C) The mean of the sample data should be multiplied by 100 to get the estimated mean of the population.

D) The mean of the sample data should be multiplied by 1,000 to get the estimated mean of the population.

12. A fertilizer company conducted an experimental study to determine which of five compounds is most effective relative to helping soil retain nutrients. If, after application of the compounds, the fertilizer company only tested for nitrogen and potassium, which of the following is a valid conclusion?

A) The compound that is found to be the most effective will work for all nutrients in the soil.

B) The compound that is found to be the most effective will work only for nitrogen and potassium.

C) The study is clearly biased and therefore not significant relevant to determining which compound is most effective.

D) The study will only be able to produce results concerning the effects of the compounds on nitrogen and potassium.

History Majors Declared at College X

Year	Number of History Majors
2010	225
2011	287
2012	162
2013	240
2014	s

13. The table above shows the number of history majors declared each year at a certain college from 2010 to 2014. If the median number of history majors declared for the five years was 225, what is the greatest possible value of s?

A) 161

B) 225

C) 239

D) 288

Country Music Festival Attendees

	Attendees
Entertainer A (Day 1)	1,280
Entertainer B (Day 2)	1,120
Entertainer C (Day 3)	1,600

14. Three well-known entertainers performed at a country music festival, one on each day. Tickets sold were valid for the full three-day period, and ticket holders were permitted to enter and leave as desired. The table above shows the number of people who attended each day of the festival. The host of the festival wants to know which performer was the most popular. If the host defines a performer's popularity rating as the ratio of the number of attendees on that performer's day to the combined number of attendees across all three days, then what was the most popular performer's popularity rating?

Questions 15 and 16 refer to the following information.

Numerous health studies have found that people who eat breakfast are generally healthier and weigh less than people who skip it. Although scientists are not certain as to the reason, it is generally believed that breakfast jumpstarts the metabolism and encourages a more regular consumption of calories throughout the day, instead of the calories being consumed in two big meals at lunch and dinner. The following table shows the results of a study related to this topic.

Breakfast Study Results

	Breakfast ≤1 time per week	Breakfast 2-4 times per week	Breakfast 5-7 times per week	Total
Within Healthy Weight Range	6	15	36	57
Outside Healthy Weight Range	38	27	9	74
Total	44	42	45	131

15. What percent of the participants who were outside a healthy weight range ate breakfast one or fewer times per week?

A) 29.00%

B) 51.35%

C) 56.49%

D) 86.36%

16. A large company that provides breakfast for all its employees wants to determine how many of them are likely to be within a healthy weight range, given that all the employees take advantage of the free breakfast all 5 weekdays. If the company has 3,000 employees, and assuming the participants in the study were a good representative sample, about how many of the employees are likely to be within a healthy weight range?

A) 825

B) 1,030

C) 1,900

D) 2,400

Questions 17 and 18 refer to the following information.

When people sleep, they experience various types of brain activity. Scientists have classified these types of activity into four sleep stages: 1, 2, 3, and 4 (also known as REM). Stage 3 is the only stage considered to be deep sleep. Suppose a person went to a sleep clinic to have his/her sleeping brainwaves analyzed. A technician monitored the person's brainwaves in 15-minute intervals, for 8 continuous hours, and categorized them into one of the four stages. The bar graph below shows the results of the one-night study.

8-Hour Sleep Study Results

Each bar = 15 minutes

17. Based on the graph, how many minutes did the patient spend in non-deep sleep over the course of the entire night?

18. If one 15-minute time period is chosen at random, what is the probability that the patient was in deep sleep during that time?

Math

Questions 19 and 20 refer to the following information.

As part of its market research, a company sent out a survey to see how much consumers would be willing to pay for a certain product. The survey distinguished between a store brand version of the product and a brand name version, and people participating in the survey only received questions about one of the versions. A summary of the survey results is shown in the following bar graph.

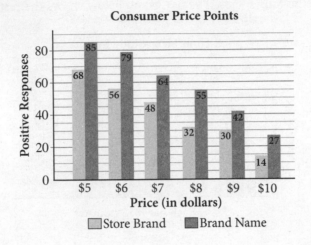

19. On average, how many more cents are consumers willing to pay for the brand name version of the product than the store brand version? Round your answer to the nearest cent.

20. If a consumer is chosen at random from all of the respondents, what is the probability that the consumer is willing to pay at least $8 for the product?

Passport to Advanced Math

BY THE END OF THIS UNIT, YOU WILL BE ABLE TO:

1. Simplify, solve, and rewrite expressions and equations involving polynomials, radicals, and exponents

2. Solve a formula for a given variable

3. Solve function questions graphically and algebraically

4. Combine multiple functions

5. Solve quadratic equations with and without a calculator

6. Connect quadratic equations to features of a parabola

Exponents, Radicals, Polynomials, and Rational Expressions and Equations

CHAPTER OBJECTIVES

By the end of this chapter, you will be able to:

1. Simplify and solve expressions and equations involving exponents and/or radicals

2. Perform arithmetic operations on polynomials

3. Simplify expressions using polynomial long division and find polynomial remainders

4. Simplify and solve rational expressions and equations

5. Solve a formula for a given variable

SMARTPOINTS

Point Value	SmartPoint Category
80 Points	Exponents

EXPONENTS, RADICALS, POLYNOMIALS, AND RATIONAL EXPRESSIONS AND EQUATIONS

Chapter 8

Homework

Extra Practice: #1-20

Even More

Math Quiz 5

Key

 Book Assignment

Online Video Assignment

 Online Quiz Assignment

INTRODUCTION TO EXPONENTS AND RADICALS

We often turn to our calculators to solve difficult radical and exponent problems, especially in math-intensive classes. However, being too calculator dependent can cost you time and points on the SAT. Further, on the SAT, many radical and exponent problems are structured in such a way that your calculator can't help you, even if it is allowed.

This chapter will review algebra and arithmetic rules that you may have learned at some point but likely haven't used in a while. This chapter will reacquaint you with the formulas and procedures you'll need to simplify even the toughest expressions and equations on the SAT. We'll start with exponents.

Questions involving exponents often look intimidating, but when you know the rules governing them, you'll see that there are plenty of shortcuts. First, it's important to understand the anatomy of a term that has an exponent. This term is comprised of two pieces: a base and an exponent (also called a power). The base is the number in larger type and is the value being multiplied by itself. The exponent, written as a superscript, shows you how many times the base is being multiplied by itself.

$$\textit{Base} \Rightarrow 3^4 \Leftarrow \textit{Exponent} \text{ is the same as } 3 \times 3 \times 3 \times 3$$

The following table lists the rules you'll need to handle any exponent question you'll see on the SAT.

Rule	Example
When multiplying two terms with the same base, add the exponents.	$a^b \times a^c = a^{(b+c)} \rightarrow 4^2 \times 4^3 = 4^{2+3} = 4^5$
When dividing two terms with the same base, subtract the exponents.	$\dfrac{a^b}{a^c} = a^{(b-c)} \rightarrow \dfrac{4^3}{4^2} = 4^{3-2} = 4$
When raising a power to another power, multiply the exponents.	$(a^b)^c = a^{(bc)} \rightarrow (4^3)^2 = 4^{3\times2} = 4^6;$ $(2x^2)^3 = 2^{1\times3} x^{2\times3} = 8x^6$
When raising a product to a power, apply the power to all factors in the product.	$(ab)^c = a^c \times b^c \rightarrow (2m)^3 = 2^3 \times m^3 = 8m^3$
Any term raised to the zero power equals 1.	$a^0 = 1 \rightarrow 4^0 = 1$
A base raised to a negative exponent can be rewritten as the reciprocal raised to the positive of the original exponent.	$a^{-b} = \dfrac{1}{a^b}; \dfrac{1}{a^{-b}} = a^b \rightarrow 4^{-2} = \dfrac{1}{4^2}; \dfrac{1}{4^{-2}} = 4^2$

✔ **Note**

Raising an expression involving addition or subtraction to a power, such as $(a + b)^2$, requires a special process called FOIL, which you'll learn about in chapter 10. You *cannot* merely distribute the exponent; this will certainly lead you to a trap answer.

Different things happen to different kinds of numbers when they are raised to powers. Compare the locations and values of the variables and numbers on the following number line to the results in the table for a summary.

Quantity	Even Exponent Result	Odd Exponent Result	Example
w	positive, absolute value increases	negative, absolute value increases	$(-5)^2 = 25; (-5)^3 = -125$
-1	always 1	always -1	n/a
x	positive, absolute value decreases	negative, absolute value decreases	$\left(-\dfrac{1}{2}\right)^2 = \dfrac{1}{4}; \left(-\dfrac{1}{2}\right)^3 = -\dfrac{1}{8}$
0	always 0	always 0	n/a
y	positive, absolute value decreases	positive, absolute value decreases	$\left(\dfrac{1}{4}\right)^2 = \dfrac{1}{16}; \left(\dfrac{1}{4}\right)^3 = \dfrac{1}{64}$
1	always 1	always 1	n/a
z	positive, absolute value increases	positive, absolute value increases	$3^2 = 9; 3^3 = 27$

Give this exponent question a try:

1. Which expression is equivalent to $2(-4j^3k^{-4})^{-3}$?

A) $\quad -\dfrac{k^{12}}{512j^9}$

B) $\quad -\dfrac{k^{12}}{32j^9}$

C) $\quad -\dfrac{j^9}{32k^{12}}$

D) $\quad -\dfrac{k^{12}}{128j^9}$

Use the Kaplan Method for Math to solve this question, working through it step-by-step. The following table shows Kaplan's strategic thinking on the left, along with suggested math scratchwork on the right.

Strategic Thinking	Math Scratchwork
Step 1: Read the question, identifying and organizing important information as you go You're asked to find the equivalent expression.	
Step 2: Choose the best strategy to answer the question Use exponent rules to quickly find the answer. Move the expression in parentheses to the denominator to make the exponent outside the parentheses positive. Then distribute the exponent to each term it contains. You're not done yet. Look for terms you can cancel, and eliminate any remaining negative exponents by appropriately moving their respective terms.	$2(-4j^3k^{-4})^{-3}$ $= \dfrac{2}{(-4j^3k^{-4})^3}$ $= \dfrac{2}{(-4)^3(j^3)^3(k^{-4})^3}$ $= \dfrac{\cancel{2}}{-\cancel{64}\,j^9k^{-12}}$ $= -\dfrac{k^{12}}{32j^9}$
Step 3: Check that you answered the *right* question Choice (B) matches the simplified expression.	

Let's try one more before moving on.

2. What is the value of $\dfrac{3^5 \times 27^3}{81^3}$?

Work through the Kaplan Method for Math step-by-step to solve this question. The following table shows Kaplan's strategic thinking on the left, along with suggested math scratchwork on the right.

Strategic Thinking	Math Scratchwork
Step 1: Read the question, identifying and organizing important information as you go You're asked to find the value of the expression presented, which means you'll need to simplify it.	
Step 2: Choose the best strategy to answer the question Simplify the expression using exponent rules. You can't combine the bases or the exponents of the expression as written. However, $27 = 3^3$ and $81 = 3^4$, so rewrite the numerator and denominator to reflect these relationships. Add the exponents of the numbers in the numerator. Once finished, subtract the exponent of the number in the denominator.	$$\frac{3^5 \times 27^3}{81^3} = \frac{3^5 \times (3^3)^3}{(3^4)^3}$$ $$= \frac{3^5 \times 3^9}{3^{12}} = \frac{3^{14}}{3^{12}} = 3^2$$
Step 3: Check that you answered the *right* question After simplification is complete, you'll get 9 as the correct answer.	9

> ✔ **Note**
>
> A calculator could probably handle numbers the size of those in the previous question, but what if the question is in the no-calculator section? Knowing exponent rules for Test Day is critical.

RADICALS

A radical can be written using a fractional exponent. You can think of addition and subtraction (and multiplication and division) as opposites; similarly, raising a number to a power and taking the root of the number are another opposite pair. Specifically, when you raise a term to the nth power, taking the nth root will return the original term. Consider for example $3^4 = 3 \times 3 \times 3 \times 3 = 81$. If you take the fourth root of 81 (that is, determine the number that can be multiplied by itself four times to get 81), you will arrive at the original term: $\sqrt[4]{81} = \sqrt[4]{3 \times 3 \times 3 \times 3} = 3$.

Radicals can be intimidating at first, but remembering the basic rules for radicals can make them much easier to tackle. The following table contains all the formulas you'll need to know to achieve "radical" success on the SAT.

Rule	Example
When a fraction is under a radical, you can rewrite it using two radicals: one containing the numerator and the other containing the denominator.	$\sqrt{\dfrac{a}{b}} = \dfrac{\sqrt{a}}{\sqrt{b}} \rightarrow \sqrt{\dfrac{4}{9}} = \dfrac{\sqrt{4}}{\sqrt{9}} = \dfrac{2}{3}$
Two factors under a single radical can be rewritten as separate radicals multiplied together.	$\sqrt{ab} = \sqrt{a} \times \sqrt{b} \rightarrow \sqrt{75} = \sqrt{25} \times \sqrt{3} = 5\sqrt{3}$
A radical can be written using a fractional exponent.	$\sqrt{a} = a^{\frac{1}{2}}, \sqrt[3]{a} = a^{\frac{1}{3}} \rightarrow \sqrt{289} = 289^{\frac{1}{2}}$
When you have a fractional exponent, the numerator is the power to which the base is raised, and the denominator is the root to be taken.	$a^{\frac{b}{c}} = \sqrt[c]{a^b} \rightarrow 5^{\frac{2}{3}} = \sqrt[3]{5^2}$
When a number is squared, the original number can be positive or negative, but the square root of a number can only be positive.	If $a^2 = 81$, then $a = \pm 9$, BUT $\sqrt{81} = 9$ only.

✔ **Note**

Note this difference: By definition, the square root of a number is positive. However, when you take the square root to solve for a variable, you get two solutions, one that is positive and one that is negative. For instance, by definition $\sqrt{4} = 2$. However, if you are solving $x^2 = 4$, x will have two solutions: $x = \pm 2$.

It is not considered proper notation to leave a radical in the denominator of a fraction. However, it's sometimes better to keep them through intermediate steps to make the math easier (and sometimes the radical is eliminated along the way). Once all manipulations are complete, the denominator can be rationalized to remove a remaining radical by multiplying both the numerator and denominator by that same radical.

1. Original Fraction	2. Rationalization	3. Intermediate Math	4. Resulting Fraction
$\dfrac{x}{\sqrt{5}}$	$\dfrac{x}{\sqrt{5}} \times \dfrac{\sqrt{5}}{\sqrt{5}}$	$\dfrac{x\sqrt{5}}{\sqrt{5 \times 5}} = \dfrac{x\sqrt{5}}{\sqrt{25}} = \dfrac{x\sqrt{5}}{5}$	$\dfrac{x\sqrt{5}}{5}$
$\dfrac{14}{\sqrt{x^2 + 2}}$	$\dfrac{14}{\sqrt{x^2 + 2}} \times \dfrac{\sqrt{x^2 + 2}}{\sqrt{x^2 + 2}}$	$\dfrac{14\sqrt{x^2 + 2}}{\sqrt{(x^2 + 2)(x^2 + 2)}} = \dfrac{14\sqrt{x^2 + 2}}{\sqrt{(x^2 + 2)^2}}$	$\dfrac{14\sqrt{x^2 + 2}}{x^2 + 2}$

Sometimes, you'll have an expression such as $2 + \sqrt{5}$ in the denominator. To rationalize this, multiply by its conjugate, which is found by negating the second term; in this case, the conjugate is $2 - \sqrt{5}$.

As a general rule of thumb, you are not likely to see a radical in the denominator of the answer choices on the SAT, so you'll need to be comfortable with rationalizing expressions that contain radicals.

> ✔ **Note**
>
> When you rationalize a denominator, you are not changing the value of the expression; you're only changing the expression's appearance. This is because the numerator and the denominator of the fraction that you multiply by are the same, which means you're simply multiplying by 1.

Ready to take on a test-like question that involves radicals? Take a look at the following:

3. Which of the following represents $\dfrac{\sqrt[6]{x^{10}y^{12}}}{\sqrt[3]{x^5y^6}}$ written in simplest form?

A) 1

B) 2

C) $x^2y^3\sqrt{x}$

D) $xy^2\sqrt[3]{x^2}$

Work through the Kaplan Method for Math step-by-step to solve this question. The following table shows Kaplan's strategic thinking on the left, along with suggested math scratchwork on the right.

Strategic Thinking	Math Scratchwork
Step 1: Read the question, identifying and organizing important information as you go You must simplify the given expression.	
Step 2: Choose the best strategy to answer the question Attempting to combine the radicals as written is incorrect and will lead you to a trap answer. Rewrite each variable with a fractional exponent instead. When simplifying fractional exponents, remember "power over root." Once you have simplified, subtract the exponents for the x terms, and then repeat for the y terms.	$\dfrac{\sqrt[6]{x^{10}y^{12}}}{\sqrt[3]{x^5y^6}} = \dfrac{x^{\frac{10}{6}}y^{\frac{12}{6}}}{x^{\frac{5}{3}}y^{\frac{6}{3}}}$ $x^{\frac{10}{6}-\frac{5}{3}}y^{\frac{12}{6}-\frac{6}{3}} = x^{\frac{10}{6}-\frac{10}{6}}y^{\frac{12}{6}-\frac{12}{6}}$ $= x^0y^0$
Step 3: Check that you answered the *right* question Any quantity raised to the zero power is equal to 1, which means (A) is correct.	$x^0y^0 = 1 \times 1 = 1$

POLYNOMIALS

By now you're used to seeing equations, exponents, and variables; another important topic you are sure to see on the SAT is polynomials. A **polynomial** is an expression comprised of variables, exponents, and coefficients, and the only operations involved are addition, subtraction, multiplication, division (by constants *only*), and non-negative integer exponents. A polynomial can have one or multiple terms. The following table contains examples of polynomial expressions and non-polynomial expressions.

Polynomial	$23x^2$	$\dfrac{x}{5} - 6$	$y^{11} - 2y^6 + \dfrac{2}{3}xy^3 - 4x^2$	47
Not a Polynomial	$\dfrac{10}{z} + 13$	$x^3 y^{-6}$	$x^{\frac{1}{2}}$	$\dfrac{4}{y-3}$

> ✔ **Note**
>
> Remember that a constant, such as 47, is considered a polynomial; this is the same as $47x^0$. Also, keep in mind that for an expression to be a polynomial, division by a constant is allowed, but division by a variable is not.

Identifying **like terms** is an important skill that will serve you well on Test Day. To simplify polynomial expressions, you combine like terms just as you did with linear expressions and equations (*x* terms with *x* terms, constants with constants). To have like terms, the types of variables present and their exponents must match. For example, $2xy$ and $-4xy$ are like terms; *x* and *y* are present in both, and their corresponding exponents are identical. However, $2x^2y$ and $3xy$ are not like terms because the exponents on *x* do not match. A few more examples follow:

Like terms	$7x$, $3x$, $5x$	3, 15, 900	xy^2, $7xy^2$, $-2xy^2$
Not like terms	3, x, x^2	$4x$, $4y$, $4z$	xy^2, x^{2y}, $2xy$

You can also **evaluate** a polynomial expression (just like any other expression) for given values in its domain. For example, suppose you're given the polynomial expression $x^3 + 5x^2 + 1$. At $x = -1$, the value of the expression is $(-1)^3 + 5(-1)^2 + 1$, which simplifies to $-1 + 5 + 1 = 5$.

A polynomial can be named based on its **degree**. For a single-variable polynomial, the degree is the highest power on the variable. For example, the degree of $3x^4 - 2x^3 + x^2 - 5x + 2$ is 4 because the highest power of *x* is 4. For a multi-variable polynomial, the degree is the highest sum of the exponents on any one term. For example, the degree of $3x^2 y^2 - 5x^2 y + x^3$ is 4 because the sum of the exponents in the term $3x^2y^2$ equals 4.

On Test Day you might be asked about the nature of the **zeros** or **roots** of a polynomial. Simply put, zeros are the *x*-intercepts of a polynomial's graph, which can be found by setting each factor of the polynomial equal to 0. For example, in the polynomial equation $y = (x + 6)(x - 2)^2$, you would have three equations: $x + 6 = 0$, $x - 2 = 0$, and $x - 2 = 0$ (because $x - 2$ is squared, that binomial appears twice in the equation). Solving for x in each yields -6, 2, and 2; we say that the equation has two zeros: -6 and 2. Zeros can have varying levels of **multiplicity**, which is the number of times that a factor appears in the polynomial equation. In the preceding example, $x + 6$ appears once in the equation, so its corresponding zero (-6) is called a **simple zero**. Because $x - 2$ appears twice in the equation, its corresponding zero (2) is called a **double zero**.

You can recognize the multiplicity of a zero from the polynomial's graph as well. Following is the graph of $y = (x + 6)(x - 2)^2$.

When a polynomial has a simple zero (multiplicity 1) or any zero with an odd multiplicity, its graph will cross the x-axis (as it does at $x = -6$ in the graph above). When a polynomial has a double zero (multiplicity 2) or any zero with an even multiplicity, it just touches the x-axis (as it does at $x = 2$ in the graph above).

Use your knowledge of polynomials to answer the following test-like question.

4. If y is a polynomial equation that has a simple zero at $x = 4$ and a triple zero at $x = -4$, which of the following could be the factored form of y?

A) $y = (x + 4)(2x - 8)^3$

B) $y = (x - 4)(3x + 12)$

C) $y = 3(x + 4)(2x - 8)$

D) $y = (2x + 8)^3(x - 4)$

There's no scratchwork for this question, but Kaplan's strategic thinking is provided in the table. Follow along as we reason through the question to get the correct answer.

Strategic Thinking
Step 1: Read the question, identifying and organizing important information as you go
You need to determine which equation could be the factored form of the equation that contains the zeros described.

Step 2: Choose the best strategy to answer the question

Adjectives such as "simple" and "triple" indicate how many times a zero's corresponding binomial is repeated in its polynomial equation. This means that you need one binomial raised to the first power and one raised to the third power. You can eliminate B and C, both of which lack the third power exponent.

The remaining answer choices each contain two binomial expressions: one with an exponent of 1 (remember, if no exponent is written, it is assumed to be 1) and one with an exponent of 3. Quick mental math reveals that both have 4 and −4 as zeros. You need the equation that has an exponent of 3 on the binomial that gives $x = -4$ and an exponent of 1 on the binomial that gives $x = 4$. Only (D) meets this requirement.

Step 3: Check that you answered the *right* question

Choice (D) is the only answer choice that satisfies the criteria in the question.

Adding and subtracting polynomials are straightforward operations, but what about multiplying and dividing them? These operations are a little tougher but (fortunately) far from impossible.

Multiplying polynomials is just like multiplying ordinary numbers except you want to pay special attention to distributing and combining like terms. Take the expression $(3x^3 + 5x)(2x^2 + x - 17)$ as an example. All you need to do is distribute each term in the first set of parentheses to each term in the second set. Distribute the $3x^3$ first, then repeat with $5x$:

$$\overset{1 \quad 2 \quad 3}{(3x^3 + 5x) \; (2x^2 + x - 17)} \qquad \overset{4 \quad 5 \quad 6}{(3x^3 + 5x) \; (2x^2 + x - 17)}$$

The following table shows the product for each step:

1	2	3
$3x^3 \cdot 2x^2 = 6x^5$	$3x^3 \cdot x = 3x^4$	$3x^3 \cdot (-17) = -51x^3$
4	**5**	**6**
$5x \cdot 2x^2 = 10x^3$	$5x \cdot x = 5x^2$	$5x \cdot (-17) = -85x$

All that's left to do now is write out the expression and combine any like terms.

$$6x^5 + 3x^4 - 51x^3 + 10x^3 + 5x^2 - 85x$$

$$= 6x^5 + 3x^4 - 41x^3 + 5x^2 - 85x$$

Although it is relatively straightforward to add, subtract, and multiply polynomials, dividing polynomial expressions requires a different, more involved process called **polynomial long division**. Polynomial long division is just like regular long division except, as the name suggests, you use polynomials in place of numbers.

Suppose you want to divide $x^3 + 3x + 7$ by $x + 4$. You can set this up as a long division problem:

$$x + 4 \overline{\smash{)}\, x^3 + 0x^2 + 3x + 7}$$

Notice that even though the dividend does not have an x^2 term, a placeholder is used to keep the terms organized. Because $0x^2$ is equal to 0, adding this placeholder term doesn't change the value of the polynomial. Start by dividing the first term of the dividend by the first term of the divisor to get x^2. Multiply the entire divisor by x^2 and subtract this product from the dividend.

$$
\begin{array}{r}
x^2 \\
x + 4 \overline{\smash{)}\, x^3 + 0x^2 + 3x + 7} \\
\underline{-(x^3 + 4x^2)} \\
-4x^2 + 3x + 7
\end{array}
$$

Continue by dividing the next term, $-4x^2$, by the first term of the divisor. Bring down leftover terms as needed. Multiply the quotient, $-4x$, by the entire divisor and then subtract.

$$
\begin{array}{r}
x^2 - 4x \\
x + 4 \overline{\smash{)}\, x^3 + 0x^2 + 3x + 7} \\
\underline{-(x^3 + 4x^2)} \\
-4x^2 + 3x + 7 \\
\underline{-(-4x^2 - 16x)} \\
19x + 7
\end{array}
$$

Finally, repeat this process with the $19x + 7$.

$$
\begin{array}{r}
x^2 - 4x + 19 \\
x + 4 \overline{)\; x^3 + 0x^2 + 3x + 7} \\
-(x^3 + 4x^2) \\
\hline
-4x^2 + 3x + 7 \\
-(-4x^2 - 16x) \\
\hline
19x + 7 \\
-(19x + 76) \\
\hline
-69
\end{array}
$$

When all is said and done, the quotient is $x^2 - 4x + 19$ with a remainder of -69; the remainder is written over the divisor in a separate term. Thus, the final answer is $x^2 - 4x + 19 - \dfrac{69}{x+4}$.

This is a topic many students tend to forget soon after it's tested in math class, so make sure you spend sufficient time brushing up on it.

> ✔ **Note**
>
> You can use polynomial long division to determine whether a binomial is a factor of a polynomial. If the remainder in the previous example had been 0, then $x + 4$ would have been a factor of the polynomial $x^3 + 3x + 7$.

Let's try a polynomial long division question.

5.   What is the remainder when $16a^2 + 3$ is divided by $4a + 2$?

   A) -7

   B) -1

   C) 1

   D) 7

Work through the Kaplan Method for Math step-by-step to solve this question. The following table shows Kaplan's strategic thinking on the left, along with suggested math scratchwork on the right.

Strategic Thinking	Math Scratchwork
Step 1: Read the question, identifying and organizing important information as you go You must find the remainder when $16a^2 + 3$ is divided by $4a + 2$.	
Step 2: Choose the best strategy to answer the question Write as a polynomial long division problem. Once it's set up, work carefully through each step until you get to the end.	$$\begin{array}{r} 4a - 2 \\ 4a + 2 \overline{)16a^2 + 0a + 3} \\ -(16a^2 + 8a) \\ \hline -8a + 3 \\ -(-8a - 4) \\ \hline 7 \end{array}$$
Step 3: Check that you answered the *right* question You get 7 for the remainder, which is (D).	

RATIONAL EXPRESSIONS

A **rational expression** is simply a ratio (or fraction) of polynomials. In other words, it is a fraction with a polynomial as the numerator and another polynomial as the denominator. The rules that govern fractions and polynomials also govern rational expressions, so if you know these well, you'll be in good shape when you encounter one on Test Day.

There are a few important tidbits to remember about rational expressions; these are summarized here. They are also true for rational equations.

- For an expression to be rational, the numerator and denominator must both be polynomials.

- Like polynomials, rational expressions are also designated certain degrees based on the term with the highest variable exponent sum. For instance, the expression $\frac{1 - 2x}{3x^2 + 3}$ has a first-degree numerator and a second-degree denominator.

- Because rational expressions by definition can have polynomial denominators, they will often be undefined for certain values. For example, the expression $\frac{x - 4}{x + 2}$ is defined for all values of

x except -2. This is because when $x = -2$, the denominator of the expression is 0, which would make the expression undefined.

- Factors in a rational expression can be cancelled when simplifying, but under no circumstances can you do the same with individual terms. Consider, for instance, the expression $\dfrac{x^2 - x - 6}{x^2 + 5x + 6}$.

  Many students will attempt to cancel the x^2, x, and 6 terms to give $\dfrac{1 - 1 - 1}{1 + 5 + 1} = \dfrac{-1}{7}$, which is *never* correct. Don't even think about trying this on Test Day.

- Like fractions, rational expressions can be proper or improper. A proper rational expression has a lower-degree numerator than denominator $\left(\text{e.g., } \dfrac{1 - x}{x^2 + 3}\right)$, and an improper one has

  a higher-degree numerator than denominator $\left(\text{e.g., } \dfrac{x^2 + 3}{1 - x}\right)$. The latter can be simplified using polynomial long division.

 Note

For those who are curious, the correct way to simplify $\dfrac{x^2 - x - 6}{x^2 + 5x + 6}$ is to factor, which you'll learn about in chapter 10. For now, know that this equals $\dfrac{(x + 2)(x - 3)}{(x + 2)(x + 3)}$. Cancel the $x + 2$ factors to get $\dfrac{x - 3}{x + 3}$.

SOLVING RATIONAL EQUATIONS

Rational equations are just like rational expressions except for one difference: They have an equal sign. They follow the same rules as rational expressions. The steps you take to solve the more friendly looking linear equations apply to rational equations as well.

When solving rational equations, beware of **extraneous solutions**—solutions derived that don't satisfy the original equation. This happens when the derived solution causes 0 in the denominator of *any* of the terms in the equation (because division by 0 is not possible). Take the equation $\dfrac{1}{x + 4} + \dfrac{1}{x - 4} = \dfrac{8}{(x + 4)(x - 4)}$, for instance. After multiplying both sides by the common denominator $(x + 4)(x - 4)$, you have $(x - 4) + (x + 4) = 8$. Solving for x yields $2x = 8$ which simplifies to $x = 4$. However, when 4 is substituted for x, you get 0 in the denominator of both the second and third terms of the equation, so 4 is an extraneous solution. Therefore, this equation is said to have no solution.

 Note

Whenever you encounter an equation with variables in a denominator or under a radical, make sure you check the solutions by plugging the values back into the original equation.

Math

6. $\dfrac{x}{x+2} + \dfrac{2}{x+6} = \dfrac{-8}{(x+2)(x+6)}$

What are the solution(s) to the equation shown above?

A) -2

B) 2

C) -2 and -6

D) No solution

Work through the Kaplan Method for Math step-by-step to solve this question. The following table shows Kaplan's strategic thinking on the left, along with suggested math scratchwork on the right.

Strategic Thinking	Math Scratchwork
Step 1: Read the question, identifying and organizing important information as you go You're asked for the solution(s) to the equation.	
Step 2: Choose the best strategy to answer the question The first order of business is to eliminate the fractions. Do this by multiplying both sides of the equation by the least common denominator for the whole equation, $(x+2)(x+6)$.	Left side: $(x+2)(x+6)\left(\dfrac{x}{x+2} + \dfrac{2}{x+6}\right)$ $= x(x+6) + 2(x+2)$ $= x^2 + 6x + 2x + 4$ $= x^2 + 8x + 4$ Right side: denominator cancels and you just get -8. Set the sides equal.
You've created a quadratic equation, so move all the terms to one side so that it is equal to 0, and then factor to solve it. Look for a pair of integers with a sum of 8 and a product of 12; the magic picks are 2 and 6. Split the two binomials into separate equations, set them equal to 0, and then solve.	$x^2 + 8x + 4 = -8$ $x^2 + 8x + 12 = 0$ $(x+2)(x+6) = 0$ $x + 2 = 0 \rightarrow x = -2$ and $x + 6 = 0 \rightarrow x = -6$
Be careful here. The question asks for the solutions, but you must plug them back into the equation (at least mentally) to make sure they're not extraneous: -2 causes $x+2$ to be 0, and -6 causes $x+6$ to be 0, so both solutions are extraneous. Therefore, the equation actually has no solution.	

Strategic Thinking	Math Scratchwork
Step 3: Check that you answered the *right* question You've solved for x and determined that both solutions are extraneous. Choice (D) is the correct answer.	

> ✔ **Note**
>
> Extraneous solutions are solutions that cause the entire expression to become undefined. Look out for zeros in denominators and negatives under square roots.

MODELING REAL-WORLD APPLICATIONS USING POLYNOMIAL, RADICAL, AND RATIONAL EQUATIONS

A typical rational equation that models a real-world scenario (and that you're likely to see on Test Day) involves rates. Recall from chapter 5 that distance is the product of rate and time ($d = rt$); this equation will serve you well when solving rational equations involving rates. In some cases, you may want to change d to W (for work), as some questions ask how long it will take to complete some kind of work or a specific task. The good news is that the math doesn't change. For example, you can calculate a combined rate by rewriting $W = rt$ as $r = \dfrac{W}{t}$ for each person (or machine) working on a job and then adding the rates together.

Here's an example: Suppose machine A can complete a job in 2 hours and machine B can do the same job in 4 hours. You want to know how long it will take to do this job if both machines work together. Their rates would be $r_A = \dfrac{W_A}{t_A} = \dfrac{1}{2}$ job per hour and $r_B = \dfrac{W_B}{t_B} = \dfrac{1}{4}$ job per hour, respectively. The combined rate would be $\dfrac{3}{4}$ job per hour, which means $t_{total} = \dfrac{W_{total}}{r_{total}} = \dfrac{1}{\frac{3}{4}} = \dfrac{4}{3}$. Thus, it will take $\dfrac{4}{3}$ hours to complete the job if A and B work together.

Ready for a real-world example? Check out the next couple of pages.

7. Johanna, Elizabeth, and Dan are preparing a chemical solution for a research project. When working alone, either Johanna or Elizabeth can prepare the solution in six minutes. Dan can prepare the solution in four minutes if he works alone. How many minutes will it take the three of them to prepare the solution if they work together?

A) $\dfrac{5}{12}$

B) $\dfrac{7}{12}$

C) $\dfrac{12}{7}$

D) $\dfrac{12}{5}$

Work through the Kaplan Method for Math step-by-step to solve this question. The following table shows Kaplan's strategic thinking on the left, along with suggested math scratchwork on the right.

Strategic Thinking	Math Scratchwork
Step 1: Read the question, identifying and organizing important information as you go You're asked how long it will take the three colleagues to prepare the solution if they work together. A rate for each colleague is given.	
Step 2: Choose the best strategy to answer the question The question asks for a total time, so start by determining individual rates. Once you've done that, add them together to find the combined rate in terms of time. There is one solution to prepare (or one job to do), so use 1 for W.	$W = rt \rightarrow r = \dfrac{W}{t}$ J: 6 min to complete $\rightarrow \dfrac{1}{6}$ completed per minute E: 6 min to complete $\rightarrow \dfrac{1}{6}$ completed per minute D: 4 min to complete $\rightarrow \dfrac{1}{4}$ completed per minute t = time working together $\dfrac{1}{6} + \dfrac{1}{6} + \dfrac{1}{4} = \dfrac{1}{t}$

Strategic Thinking	Math Scratchwork
Once you have an equation, isolate t. Start by combining the fractions on the left side (by first writing them over the same denominator), then cross-multiply to solve for t.	$\dfrac{2}{12} + \dfrac{2}{12} + \dfrac{3}{12} = \dfrac{1}{t}$ $\dfrac{7}{12} = \dfrac{1}{t}$ $7t = 12$ $t = \dfrac{12}{7}$
Step 3: Check that you answered the *right* question Working together, Johanna, Elizabeth, and Dan will need $\dfrac{12}{7}$ minutes to prepare the solution, which is (C).	

SOLVING A FORMULA OR EQUATION FOR A GIVEN VARIABLE

If you've ever taken a chemistry or physics course, you probably noticed that many real-world situations can't be represented by simple linear equations. There are frequently radicals, exponents, and fractions galore. For example, the root-mean-square velocity for particles in a gas can be described by the following equation:

$$v = \sqrt{\left(\frac{3kT}{m}\right)}$$

In this equation, v represents the root-mean-square velocity, k is the Boltzmann constant, T is the temperature in degrees Kelvin, and m is the mass of one molecule of the gas. It's a great equation if you have k, T, and m and are looking for v. However, if you're looking for a different quantity, having that unknown buried among others (and under a radical to boot) can be unnerving, but unearthing it is easier than it appears. Let's say you're given v, k, and m but need to find T. First, square both sides to eliminate the radical to yield $v^2 = \dfrac{3kT}{m}$. Next, isolate T by multiplying both sides by m and dividing by $3k$; the result is $\dfrac{mv^2}{3k} = T$.

At this point, you can plug in the values of m, v, and k to solve for T. Sometimes the SAT will have you do just that: Solve for the numerical value of a variable of interest. In other situations, you'll need to rearrange an equation so that a different variable is isolated. The same rules of algebra you've used all along apply. The difference: You're manipulating solely variables.

Now you'll have a chance to try a few more test-like questions. Some guidance is provided, but you'll need to fill in the missing parts of explanations or the step-by-step math to get to the correct answer. Don't worry—after going through the examples at the beginning of this chapter, these questions should be completely doable. If you're still struggling, review the worked examples in this chapter.

8. Special relativity is a branch of physics that deals with the relationship between space and time. The Lorentz term, a term that relates the change in time, length, and relativistic mass of a moving object, is given by the following formula:

$$\gamma = \frac{1}{\sqrt{1 - \dfrac{v^2}{c^2}}}$$

In the formula, v is the relative velocity of the object and c is the speed of light in a vacuum. Which of the following equations correctly represents the relative velocity in terms of the other variables?

A) $v = c\sqrt{\dfrac{1}{\gamma^2} - 1}$

B) $v = c\sqrt{1 - \gamma^2}$

C) $v = c\left(1 - \dfrac{1}{\gamma^2}\right)$

D) $v = c\sqrt{1 - \dfrac{1}{\gamma^2}}$

Use the scaffolding that follows as your map through the question. Strategic thinking is on the left, and bits of scratchwork are on the right. If you aren't sure where to start, fill in the blanks in the table as you work from top to bottom.

Strategic Thinking	Math Scratchwork
Step 1: Read the question, identifying and organizing important information as you go You need to identify the expression that equals relative velocity. Translation: Solve the given equation for v.	$$\gamma = \frac{1}{\sqrt{1 - \dfrac{v^2}{c^2}}}$$
Step 2: Choose the best strategy to answer the question Don't let the multiple variables intimidate you; just treat them as you would when manipulating a "friendlier" equation. Start by undoing the radical so you can get to what's underneath, and then isolate the correct variable.	_____ = _____ _____ = _____ _____ = _____ _____ = _____ _____ = _____ _____ = _____
Step 3: Check that you answered the *right* question Did you get (D)? If so, you're absolutely correct!	_____

> ✔ **Note**
>
> Don't panic over the unfamiliarity of the physics terms or symbols; just identify what you need to do (in this case, isolate v on one side of the equation).

Now try simplifying a fairly complicated-looking radical expression:

9. Given that g and h are both positive, which of the following is equivalent to the expression $\sqrt[3]{g^6h^3 - 27g^4h^3}$?

    A) $\frac{1}{3}gh\sqrt[3]{g^2 - 27}$

    B) $gh\sqrt[3]{g^3 - 27g}$

    C) $g^2h - 3gh\sqrt[3]{g}$

    D) $g^2h - 3\sqrt[3]{g}$

Use the scaffolding that follows as your map through the question. Strategic thinking is on the left, and bits of scratchwork are on the right. If you aren't sure where to start, fill in the blanks in the table as you work from top to bottom.

Strategic Thinking	Math Scratchwork
Step 1: Read the question, identifying and organizing important information as you go You need to simplify the given expression.	
Step 2: Choose the best strategy to answer the question Identifying the GCF should be your first step. Once this is complete, check to see whether any part of it can be "cube rooted" and placed outside the radical. Double check to make sure no factoring was missed, and then look for a match in the answer choices. If you can't find one, try rewriting the expression.	$GCF:\underline{\quad}$ $\sqrt[3]{\underline{\quad}(\underline{\quad} - \underline{\quad})}$ $= \underline{\quad}\sqrt[3]{\underline{\quad}(\underline{\quad} - \underline{\quad})}$ $= \underline{\quad}\sqrt[3]{\underline{\quad} - \underline{\quad}}$
Step 3: Check that you answered the *right* question If your answer is (B), congrats! You're correct.	$\underline{\quad}$

Ready to try an exponent question?

10. Human blood contains three primary cell types: red blood cells (RBC), white blood cells (WBC), and platelets. In an adult male, a single microliter (1×10^{-3} milliliters) of blood contains approximately 5.4×10^6 RBC, 7.5×10^3 WBC, and 3.5×10^5 platelets on average. What percentage of an adult male's total blood cell count is comprised of red blood cells?

    A) 1.30%

    B) 6.21%

    C) 60.79%

    D) 93.79%

Use the scaffolding that follows as your map through the question. Strategic thinking is on the left, and bits of scratchwork are on the right. If you aren't sure where to start, fill in the blanks in the table as you work from top to bottom.

Strategic Thinking	Math Scratchwork
Step 1: Read the question, identifying and organizing important information as you go You need to calculate the percent of an adult male's blood that is comprised of red blood cells.	
Step 2: Choose the best strategy to answer the question Remember that a percentage is derived from a ratio that compares a partial quantity to a total quantity. Write an equation that compares the RBC count to the total blood cell count and simplify. You can save time by using exponent rules instead of punching everything into your calculator. Note that the answer choices are fairly far apart. Compare the numerator and denominator of your simplified expression; you can estimate the resulting quantity and eliminate incorrect answers accordingly. Multiply the RBC fraction you found by 100 to convert it to a percent.	$RBC\% = \underline{\hspace{2cm}}$ $\dfrac{}{\underline{\,}+\underline{\,}+\underline{\,}}$ $= \underline{\hspace{2cm}}$ $= \underline{\hspace{2cm}}$ $= \underline{\hspace{2cm}}$ $\underline{\hspace{1.5cm}} \times 100 = \underline{\hspace{1cm}}\%$
Step 3: Check that you answered the *right* question Did you get (D)? If so, you're absolutely correct!	$\underline{\hspace{1cm}}$

✔ **Expert Tip**

You can do this question almost entirely without a calculator. Just use what you know about exponents and scientific notation.

It's time to try a question involving rational expressions.

11. A botanical garden is draining its lily pad pools for the winter using three pumps. The second pump is two times faster than the first pump, which is three times faster than the third. If the three pumps can completely drain the pools in four hours when working together, which expression could represent the portion of the draining that could be completed by the second pump in one hour?

A) $\dfrac{6}{x}$

B) $\dfrac{2}{x}$

C) $\dfrac{1}{4} - \dfrac{6}{x}$

D) $\dfrac{1}{4} - \dfrac{2}{x}$

Use the scaffolding that follows as your map through the question. Strategic thinking is on the left, and bits of scratchwork are on the right.

Strategic Thinking	Math Scratchwork
Step 1: Read the question, identifying and organizing important information as you go You need to identify the expression that could represent the portion of the draining done by the second pump in one hour.	
Step 2: Choose the best strategy to answer the question Don't assume that the terms related to the pumps are ordered 1-2-3 in the equation. Start by ordering the pumps in order of increasing drain speed. Write the pump speeds as a ratio based on the information in the question stem. Use the second pump component of the ratio to derive an expression that represents the portion of the draining it could complete in one hour.	speed: ___ < ___ < ___ ___ : ___ : ___ 2nd pump completes ___
Step 3: Check that you answered the *right* question Did you get (A)? If so, congrats! You're right.	___

Now that you've seen the variety of ways in which the SAT can test you on the topics in this chapter, try the following questions to check your understanding. Give yourself 3.5 minutes to tackle the following three questions. Make sure you use the Kaplan Method for Math as often as you can. Remember, you want to emphasize speed and efficiency in addition to simply getting the correct answer.

12. An object launched straight up into the air is said to have parabolic motion (because it goes up, reaches a maximum height, and then comes back down). The height (h) of a projectile at time t is given by the equation $h = \frac{1}{2}at^2 + v_0t + h_0$, where a is the acceleration due to gravity and v_0 and h_0 are the object's initial velocity and initial height, respectively. Which of the following equations correctly represents the object's acceleration due to gravity in terms of the other variables?

A) $a = \dfrac{h - v_0t - h_0}{t}$

B) $a = \dfrac{h - v_0t - h_0}{2t^2}$

C) $a = \dfrac{2(h - v_0t - h_0)}{t^2}$

D) $a = t\sqrt{2(h - v_0t - h_0)}$

13. Which of the following expressions is equivalent to $\dfrac{3 + \sqrt{72}}{3 - \sqrt{72}}$?

A) $\dfrac{9 + 4\sqrt{2}}{-7}$

B) $\dfrac{9 + 2\sqrt{2}}{-7}$

C) $\dfrac{9}{-7}$

D) $1 + \dfrac{4\sqrt{2}}{9}$

14. Car dealerships often require car buyers to provide a down payment (money paid up front), which is a percent of a car's price. The down payment is deducted from the purchase price, and the buyer usually takes out a loan to pay for what is left. Teri is buying a car that costs $19,560. Her monthly car payment is given by $m = \dfrac{Pr}{1 - (1 + r)^{-N}}$, where P is the initial loan balance, r is the monthly interest rate expressed as a decimal, and N is the number of payments to be made over the duration of the loan. If Teri wants to fully pay off the loan in five years at 1.5% annual interest and wishes to have a monthly payment of $200, what percent of the purchase price will she need for her down payment? Round to the nearest whole percent and ignore the percent sign when entering your answer.

Answers and Explanations for this chapter begin on page 842.

Math

EXTRA PRACTICE

1. If $-2x^2 + 5x - 8$ is multiplied by $4x - 9$, what is the coefficient of x in the resulting polynomial?

   A) -77

   B) -45

   C) -32

   D) -13

2. If $p(x)$ is a polynomial that has a simple zero at $x = -3$ and a double zero at $x = \dfrac{5}{4}$, then which of the following could be the factored form of $p(x)$?

   A) $p(x) = 2(x + 3)(5x - 4)$

   B) $p(x) = (x + 3)(5x - 4)^2$

   C) $p(x) = 2(x + 3)(4x - 5)$

   D) $p(x) = (x + 3)(4x - 5)^2$

$$v = \frac{2\pi r}{T}$$

3. Uniform circular motion is used in physics to describe the motion of an object traveling at a constant speed in a circle. The speed of the object is called tangential velocity, and it can be calculated using the formula above, where r is the radius of the circle and T is the time is takes for the object to make one complete circle, called a period. Which of the following formulas could be used to find the length of one period if you know the tangential velocity and the radius of the circle?

   A) $T = \dfrac{v}{2\pi r}$

   B) $T = \dfrac{2\pi r}{v}$

   C) $T = 2\pi r v$

   D) $T = \dfrac{1}{2\pi r v}$

$$\frac{8x}{3(x - 5)} + \frac{2x}{3x - 15} = \frac{50}{3(x - 5)}$$

4. What value(s) of x satisfy the equation above?

   A) 0

   B) 5

   C) No solution

   D) Any value such that $x \neq 5$

5. Given the equation $\dfrac{6}{x} = \dfrac{3}{k + 2}$, and the constraints $x \neq 0$ and $k \neq -2$, what is x in terms of k?

   A) $x = 2k + 4$

   B) $x = 2k + 12$

   C) $x = 2k - \dfrac{1}{4}$

   D) $x = \dfrac{1}{4}k + 12$

6. If $A = 4x^2 + 7x - 1$ and $B = -x^2 - 5x + 3$, then what is $\dfrac{3}{2}A - 2B$?

   A) $4x^2 + \dfrac{31}{2}x - \dfrac{9}{2}$

   B) $4x^2 + \dfrac{41}{2}x - \dfrac{15}{2}$

   C) $8x^2 + \dfrac{31}{2}x - \dfrac{9}{2}$

   D) $8x^2 + \dfrac{41}{2}x - \dfrac{15}{2}$

$$\frac{\sqrt[3]{x} \cdot x^{\frac{5}{2}} \cdot x}{\sqrt{x}}$$

7. If x^n is the simplified form of the expression above, what is the value of n?

8. If $\dfrac{16}{7x + 4} + A$ is equivalent to $\dfrac{49x^2}{7x + 4}$, what is A in terms of x?

A) $7x + 4$

B) $7x - 4$

C) $49x^2$

D) $49x^2 + 4$

9. Which of the following expressions is equivalent to $-x^{\frac{1}{4}}$?

A) $-\dfrac{1}{4x}$

B) $-\dfrac{1}{x^4}$

C) $-\sqrt[4]{x}$

D) $\dfrac{1}{\sqrt[4]{-x}}$

10. What is the difference when $\dfrac{3x + 7}{x - 1}$ is subtracted from $\dfrac{8x - 5}{x - 1}$?

A) $\dfrac{5x + 2}{x - 1}$

B) $\dfrac{5x + 2}{2x - 1}$

C) $\dfrac{5x - 12}{x - 1}$

D) $\dfrac{-5x + 12}{x - 1}$

11. What is the sum of the polynomials $6a^2 - 17a - 9$ and $-5a^2 + 8a - 2$?

A) $a^2 - 9a - 11$

B) $a^2 - 25a - 7$

C) $11a^2 - 9a - 11$

D) $11a^2 - 25a - 7$

$$\frac{18x^4 + 27x^3 - 36x^2}{9x^2}$$

12. Which of the following is equivalent to the expression above?

A) $2x^2 + 3x - 4$

B) $2x^2 + 3x - 6$

C) $2x^4 + 3x^3 - 4x^2$

D) $2x^6 + 3x^5 - 4x^4$

$$8 + \frac{\sqrt{2x + 29}}{3} = 9$$

13. For what value of x is the equation above true?

A) -10

B) -2

C) 19

D) No solution

$$\frac{6x^2 + 19x + 10}{2x + 5}$$

14. If $ax + b$ represents the simplified form of the expression above, then what is the value of $a + b$?

A) 2

B) 3

C) 5

D) 6

15. Which of the following expressions is equivalent to $25x^2y^4 - 1$?

A) $5(x^2y^4 - 1)$

B) $-5(xy^2 + 1)$

C) $(5xy - 1)(5xy + 1)$

D) $(5xy^2 - 1)(5xy^2 + 1)$

16. For all a and b, what is the sum of $(a - b)^2$ and $(a + b)^2$?

A) $2a^2$

B) $2a^2 - 2b^2$

C) $2a^2 + 2b^2$

D) $2a^2 + 4ab + 2b^2$

$$T = 2\pi\sqrt{\frac{L}{g}}$$

17. The formula above was created by Italian scientist Galileo Galilei in the early 1600s to demonstrate that the time it takes for a pendulum to complete a swing, called its period (T), can be found using only the length of the pendulum, L, and the force of gravity, g. He proved that the mass of the pendulum did not affect its period. Based on the equation above, which of the following equations could be used to find the length of the pendulum given its period?

A) $L = \dfrac{gT}{2\pi}$

B) $L = \dfrac{gT^2}{4\pi^2}$

C) $L = \dfrac{T^2}{4\pi^2 g}$

D) $L = \dfrac{g}{4\pi^2 T^2}$

18. Mail-order pharmacies typically use machines to count pills and dispense them into bottles, particularly pills that are prescribed on a regular basis by physicians, such as blood pressure medicine, cholesterol medicine, and diabetes medicine. Suppose a pharmacy has two pill counters that work in tandem (together). The first counter can finish separating a typical batch of blood pressure pills in 1 hour, and the second counter can finish the same batch in 40 minutes. How many minutes should it take to finish a typical batch if both pill counters work together?

A) 18

B) 24

C) 36

D) 50

19. When simplified, $8^{\frac{4}{3}}$ is what number?

$$\frac{2x^4 + 16x^3 + 34x^2 + 10x + k}{x + 4}$$

20. For what value of k, where k is a constant, will the expression above have no remainder?

CHAPTER 9

Functions

CHAPTER OBJECTIVES

By the end of this chapter, you will be able to:

1. Use function notation to answer questions containing equations, tables, and/or graphs

2. Interpret functions and functional statements that represent real-world scenarios

3. Combine functions using basic operations and compute compositions of functions

4. Determine when a function is increasing, decreasing, or constant and apply transformations to a given function or functions

SMARTPOINTS

Point Value	SmartPoint Category
50 points	Functions

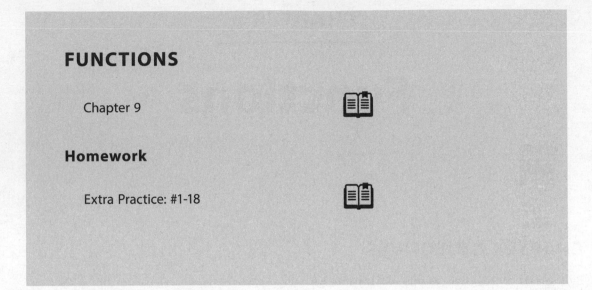

FUNCTIONS

Chapter 9

Homework

Extra Practice: #1-18

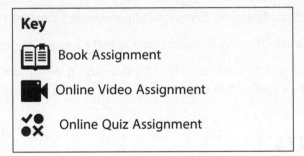

Key

Book Assignment

Online Video Assignment

Online Quiz Assignment

FUNCTIONS

Functions act as rules that transform inputs into outputs, and they differ from equations in that each input must have only one corresponding output. For example, imagine a robot: Every time you give it an apple, it promptly cuts that apple into three slices. The following table summarizes the first few inputs and their corresponding outputs.

Domain, *x*: # apples given to robot	Range, *f(x)*: # slices returned by robot
0	0
1	3
2	6
3	9

From the table you see that the output will always be triple the input, and you can express that relationship as the function $f(x) = 3x$ (read "f of x equals three x").

SAT questions, especially those involving real-world situations, might ask you to derive the equation of a function, so you'll need to be familiar with the standard forms. Following is the standard form of a linear function:

$$f(x) = kx + f(0)$$

The input, or **domain**, is the value represented by *x*. Sometimes the domain will be constrained by the question (e.g., *x* must be an integer). Other times, the domain could be defined by real-world conditions. For example, if *x* represents the time elapsed since the start of a race, the domain would need to exclude negative numbers. The output, or **range**, is what results from substituting a domain value into the function and is represented by *f(x)*. The initial amount, or **y-intercept**, is represented by *f(0)*—the value of the function at the very beginning. If you think this looks familiar, you're absolutely right. It's just a dressed-up version of the standard $y = mx + b$ equation you've already seen. Take a look at the following table for a translation:

Function Notation	What It Represents	Slope-Intercept Counterpart
f(x)	dependent variable or output	*y*
k	rate of change, slope	*m*
f(0)	*y*-intercept or initial quantity in a word problem	*b*

Math

As you might have guessed, an exponential equation has a standard function notation as well. Here we've used *g* in place of *f* for visual clarity. Know that the letter used to represent a function (*f*, *g*, *h*, etc.) is sometimes arbitrarily chosen.

$$g(x) = g(0)(1 + r)^x$$

Just as before, $g(0)$ represents the initial amount and *r* represents the growth (or decay) rate. Recognizing that function notation is a variation of something you already know will go a long way toward reducing nerves on Test Day. You should also note that graphing functions is a straightforward process: In the examples above, just replace $f(x)$ or $g(x)$ with *y* and enter into your graphing calculator.

> ✔ **Note**
>
> A quick way to determine whether an equation is a function is to conduct the vertical line test: If a vertical line passes through the graph of the equation more than once for any given value of *x*, the equation is not a function.

Below is an example of a test-like question about functions.

1. The cube of *x* subtracted from the fourth root of the sum of three and the square of the product of two and *x* is less than $f(x)$. Which of the following correctly depicts the function described?

   A) $f(x) < \sqrt[4]{3 + 4x^2} - x^3$

   B) $f(x) > x^3 - \sqrt[4]{3 + 4x^2}$

   C) $f(x) > \sqrt[4]{3 + 4x^2} - x^3$

   D) $f(x) > \sqrt[4]{3 + 2x^2} - x^3$

Because there isn't any scratchwork required for a question like this, only the column containing Kaplan's strategic thinking is included. Follow along as we reason our way through this question.

Strategic Thinking
Step 1: Read the question, identifying and organizing important information as you go
The question asks for the function that correctly describes the situation presented.
Step 2: Choose the best strategy to answer the question
This is an exercise in translating English into math, so utilize tactics from that Kaplan Strategy. Take each piece one at a time. "The cube of *x*" becomes x^3." The fourth root of the sum of three and the square of the product of two and *x*" becomes $\sqrt[4]{3 + (2x)^2}$; don't forget the parentheses around 2*x*.

Strategic Thinking
Read carefully when deciding how to combine these two pieces. "The cube of *x*" is being subtracted from "the fourth root … ," so the expression should now read $\sqrt[4]{3 + (2x)^2} - x^3$. According to the question, this entire quantity is less than *f*(*x*) (in other words, *f*(*x*) is greater than the quantity). The inequality should read $f(x) > \sqrt[4]{3 + (2x)^2} - x^3$. Simplify $(2x)^2$ as $4x^2$ and you should see a match.
Step 3: Check that you answered the *right* question
Choice (C) is the correct answer.

Once broken into simpler pieces, this function question became much easier. Read on for more information about other ways the SAT can test your knowledge of functions.

FUNCTIONS DEFINED BY TABLES AND GRAPHS

The ability to interpret the graph of a function will serve you well on Test Day. To interpret graphs of functions, you'll need to utilize the same skills you use to interpret "regular" equations on the coordinate plane, so this material shouldn't be completely foreign.

You know from the first part of this chapter that a function is merely a dressed-up equation, so translating from function to "regular" notation or vice versa is a straightforward process. Consider the following brief example.

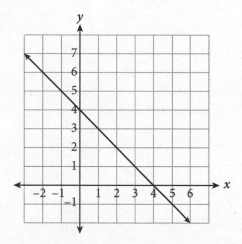

Suppose you're asked to find the value of *x* for which *f*(*x*) = 6. Because *f*(*x*) represents the output value, or range, translate this as "When does the *y* value equal 6?" To answer the question, find 6 on the *y*-axis, then trace over to the function (the line). Read the corresponding *x* value: It's −2, so when *f*(*x*) = 6, *x* must be −2.

The SAT might also present functions in the form of tables. These may or may not have an equation associated with them, but regardless, you'll need to be adept at extracting the information necessary to answer questions. Most of the time the table will have just two columns, one for the domain and another for the range.

> ✔ **Note**
>
> Remember: A value of $f(x)$ corresponds to a location along the y-axis. A value of x corresponds to a location on the x-axis.

Now let's try a test-like example.

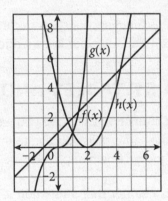

2. In the figure above, what is the value of $h(0) - 3(g(2) - f(2))$?

    A) -23

    B) -11

    C) $-\dfrac{11}{2}$

    D) $-\dfrac{3}{2}$

Work through the Kaplan Method for Math step-by-step to solve this question. The following table shows Kaplan's strategic thinking on the left, along with suggested math scratchwork on the right.

Strategic Thinking	Math Scratchwork
Step 1: Read the question, identifying and organizing important information as you go You're asked to determine the value of $h(0) - 3(g(2) - f(2))$. In other words, you need to find the y-value of function h when $x = 0$, the y-value of function g when $x = 2$, and the y-value of function f when $x = 2$. You then need to manipulate them as dictated by the given expression.	
Step 2: Choose the best strategy to answer the question Consider each value in the expression one at a time. Study the graph to determine the value of each function at the specified x-values. Plug each value into the original expression, and then follow the order of operations to simplify. Be careful as you do this, as it's easy to make careless mistakes, especially with negative signs.	 $h(0) - 3(g(2) - f(2))$ $4 - 3(8 - 3) = 4 - 3(5) = -11$
Step 3: Check that you answered the *right* question You found that the expression equals -11, which is (B).	

✔ **Note**

Watch your axis scales; just like scatterplot questions, questions involving graphs of functions often contain trap answers for students who misread the axes.

Although this question would have been much simpler if the graph had labeled the points or given you an equation to plug values into, it wouldn't have tested your knowledge of functions. Your ability to figure out what questions about functions are actually asking is key to solving them correctly on Test Day.

Try out a question in which a function is presented in the form of a table.

Day	Vote Count
3	21
4	35
5	53
6	75
7	101

3. Clara is one of five contest finalists in the running for a year's worth of college book expenses. The winner is the finalist with the highest number of votes on the contest host's website. Clara recorded her vote total each day of the contest; data for five days are in the table above. Which of the following represents Clara's vote count, v, as a function of time, t, in days?

A) $v(t) = 2t^2 + 3$

B) $v(t) = \dfrac{t^2}{2} + 3$

C) $v(t) = 2t^2 + 21$

D) $v(t) = \dfrac{t^2}{2} + 21$

Work through the Kaplan Method for Math step-by-step to solve this question. The following table shows Kaplan's strategic thinking on the left, along with suggested math scratchwork on the right.

Strategic Thinking	Math Scratchwork
Step 1: Read the question, identifying and organizing important information as you go The question is asking which function accurately depicts the relationship between time (t) and Clara's vote count (v). A table with data for selected days is given.	

Strategic Thinking	Math Scratchwork
Step 2: Choose the best strategy to answer the question Look for answer choices you can easily eliminate. From the table, you can tell that the rate of change of $v(t)$ is not constant and therefore not linear, but none of the choices are linear. However, the first table entry indicates Clara has 21 votes on day 3, and two choices have 21 as a y-intercept. The y-intercept is where $t = 0$; according to the table, $v(t) = 21$ at $t = 3$, not 0. Therefore, you can eliminate C and D. To evaluate the remaining choices, try plugging in a pair of data points. The point (4, 35) validates (A). To ensure (A) is the correct answer, you can repeat this process with B.	$v(3) = 21, v(0) \neq 21$ use $(4, 35)$ A: $35 = 2 \times 4^2 + 3$ $35 = 2 \times 16 + 3$ $35 = 32 + 3$ $35 = 35$ B: $35 = \dfrac{1}{2} \times 4^2 + 3$ $35 = \dfrac{1}{2} \times 16 + 3$ $35 = 8 + 3$ $35 \neq 11$
Step 3: Check that you answered the *right* question The only function that fits the data is (A).	

As you saw, you won't always have to plug points into each answer choice; you can often reduce your work by eliminating blatantly incorrect answers first. This is crucial for saving time on the SAT and quickly getting to the correct answer.

> ✔ **Note**
>
> When you have only one answer choice remaining, it isn't necessary to evaluate it. If you've done your math correctly up until that point, you know the remaining answer choice *has* to be correct. However, if you're at all worried that you made a mistake earlier, check the remaining answer choice to validate your math.

REAL-WORLD APPLICATION OF FUNCTIONS

Because functions are equations, you have a great deal of flexibility in working with them. For example, order of operations (PEMDAS) and the basic rules of algebra apply to functions just as they do to equations. You learned in Unit 1 that equations can represent real-world situations in convenient ways, and the same is true for functions.

For example, suppose a homeowner wants to determine the cost of installing a certain amount of carpet in her living room. In prose, this would quickly become awkward to handle, as a description would need to account for the cost per square foot, fixed installation fee, and sales tax to get the final cost. However, you can easily express this as a function.

Suppose that, in the homeowner example, carpet costs $0.86 per square foot, the installer charges a $29 installation fee, and sales tax on the total cost is 7%. Using your algebra and function knowledge, you can describe this situation in which the cost, c, is a function of square footage, f. The equation would be $c = 1.07(0.86f + 29)$. In function notation, this becomes $c(f) = 1.07(0.86f + 29)$, where $c(f)$ is shorthand for "cost as a function of square footage." The following table summarizes what each piece of the function represents in the scenario.

English	Overall cost	Square footage	Material cost	Installation fee	Sales tax
Math	c	f	$0.86f$	29	1.07

> ✔ **Note**
>
> Why does a 7% tax translate to 1.07? Using 0.07 would only provide the sales tax due. Because the function is meant to express the total cost, 1.07 is used to retain the carpet cost and installation fee while introducing the sales tax. Think of it as 100% (the original price) + the 7% sales tax on top. In decimal form, $1 + 0.07 = 1.07$.

This test-like question will test your ability to write a function.

4. Each calendar year, a certain credit card gives cardholders 5% cash back on gasoline purchases up to $1,500 and 2% cash back on any amount spent on gasoline thereafter. If $g(x)$ and $e(x)$ represent cash back earned on gasoline purchases up to $1,500 and in excess of $1,500, respectively, which of the following sets of functions could be used to determine the amount of cash back earned at each tier?

A) $g(x) = 0.05x, 0 \leq x < 1{,}500; e(x) = 0.02(x - 1{,}500), x \geq 1{,}500$

B) $g(x) = 0.05x, 0 < x \leq 1{,}500; e(x) = 0.02x, x > 1{,}500$

C) $g(x) = 0.05x, 0 \leq x \leq 1{,}500; e(x) = 0.02(x - 1{,}500), x > 1{,}500$

D) $g(x) = 0.05x, 0 \leq x \leq 1{,}500; e(x) = 0.02(1{,}500 - x), x > 1{,}500$

A word problem like this is a great time to reach for the Kaplan Strategy for Translating English into Math. The following table shows Kaplan's strategic thinking on the left, along with suggested math scratchwork on the right.

Strategic Thinking	Math Scratchwork
Step 1: Read the question, identifying and organizing important information as you go You're asked to find the functions that describe the situation given.	
Step 2: Choose the best strategy to answer the question Use the Kaplan Strategy for Translating English into Math to extract what you need. The question has already defined the variables for you. The function $g(x)$ represents cash back on gasoline purchases up to \$1,500, which the question states is 5%. Therefore, a cardholder earns $0.05x$ on this portion of gasoline purchases. Because this rate applies only to the first \$1,500, there is a restriction on the function domain: $0 \le x \le 1,500$. Eliminate A and B. The function $e(x)$ is used for cash back on gasoline purchases over \$1,500. To account for this \$1,500, you must subtract it from x. The difference is then multiplied by 0.02 to calculate the additional cash back for gasoline purchases beyond \$1,500. Like $g(x)$, $e(x)$ has a domain restriction.	$g(x) = 5\%$ on gas up to \$1,500 $g(x) = 0.05x, \ 0 \le x \le 1,500$ $e(x) = 2\%$ above \$1,500 $e(x) = 0.02(x - 1,500), \ x > 1,500$
Step 3: Check that you answered the *right* question Choice (C) is the only choice with both of the functions you built. Watch out for choice A, which lacks the correct inequality symbols in the domain restrictions.	

✔ **Note**

On Test Day it would take considerable time to write out everything in this scratchwork column verbatim; use good judgment when doing scratchwork, and abbreviate when you can. For clarity, we've included more than the average student would write.

Notice that even with a more difficult word problem, the Kaplan Strategy for Translating English into Math gets the job done. You also should have noticed how function notation can help keep your scratchwork clear and organized.

Math

MULTIPLE FUNCTIONS

There are several ways in which the SAT might ask you to juggle multiple functions simultaneously. Fortunately, the rules governing what to do are easy to understand. To start, we'll look at how to combine functions. This technique simply involves adding, subtracting, multiplying, and/or dividing the functions in play. Check out the following table for a synopsis of how to combine functions with the four basic operations (and make them look less intimidating).

When you see . . .	. . . convert it to:
$(f + g)(x)$	$f(x) + g(x)$
$(f - g)(x)$	$f(x) - g(x)$
$(fg)(x)$	$f(x) \times g(x)$
$\left(\dfrac{f}{g}\right)(x)$	$\dfrac{f(x)}{g(x)}$

You'll have a chance to solve a problem involving combined functions shortly.

A more challenging type of function question that you're likely to see is a **composition of functions** or **nested functions**. Questions involving a composition of functions require that you find an output value for one function and use the result as the input for another function to get the final solution. A composition of functions can be written as $f(g(x))$ or $(f \circ g)(x)$. The first is read as *f of g of x*, and the second, *f composed with g of x*. To answer these questions, start with the innermost parentheses and work your way out.

> ✔ **Note**
>
> You might see a composition of functions written as $(f \circ g)(x)$. Just remember that it's the same as $f(g(x))$, and solve as you would normally, working from the inside outward.

Suppose $f(x) = 8x$ and $g(x) = x + 3$. To find the value of $f(g(1))$, your steps would be as follows:

1. Determine $g(1)$, the innermost function when $x = 1$.

2. By substituting 1 for x in $g(x)$, you find that $g(1) = 1 + 3 = 4$. Now rewrite $f(g(1))$ as $f(4)$.

3. Find $f(4)$, the outer function when $x = 4$. Substituting 4 for x in function f, the final answer is $8(4) = 32$.

> ✔ **Note**
>
> Note that $f(g(x))$ does *not* equal $g(f(x))$. Not only is interchanging these incorrect, but this practice might also lead to a trap answer on Test Day.

On Test Day, you might see **piecewise functions**. A piecewise function is a function that is defined, literally, by multiple pieces. What breaks a function into pieces are different rules that govern different parts of the function's domain. Here's an example:

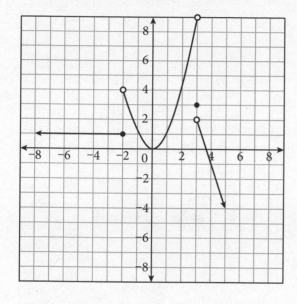

$$f(x) = \begin{cases} 1, & \text{if } x \le -2 \\ x^2, & \text{if } -2 < x < 3 \\ 3, & \text{if } x = 3 \\ -3x + 11, & \text{if } x > 3 \end{cases}$$

In the function shown, the behavior of the graph depends on the domain. Linear, quadratic, and even a single point interval make up this function. Each "rule" is written inside the open bracket in "pieces." To the right is the domain interval for which each "rule" applies. On the graph, an open dot indicates that a point is not included in the interval; a closed dot indicates one that is. Note that the different inequality signs used in the domain constraints dictate whether a dot is open or closed on the graph. For a single-point interval, an equal sign is used.

To evaluate a piecewise function, first determine to which piece of the domain the input value belongs, and then substitute the value into the corresponding rule. For example, in the function above, $f(2) = (2)^2 = 4$, because the input value 2 is between -2 and 3 (the second piece of the domain). Similarly, $f(5) = -3(5) + 11 = -4$ because the input value 5 is greater than 3 (the last piece of the domain). You can confirm these values by looking at the graph. At $x = 2$, the point on the graph is $(2, 4)$, and at $x = 5$, the point on the graph is $(5, -4)$.

Give this function question a try:

5. If $p(x) = x^2 - 4x + 8$ and $q(x) = x - 3$, what is the value of $\dfrac{q(p(5))}{p(q(5))}$?

A) 0

B) 0.4

C) 1

D) 2.5

Appearances can be deceiving. At first glance, this question looks tough, but the following table will clarify anything confusing. Kaplan's strategic thinking is on the left, along with suggested math scratchwork on the right.

Strategic Thinking	Math Scratchwork
Step 1: Read the question, identifying and organizing important information as you go You're asked for the value of $\dfrac{q(p(5))}{p(q(5))}$.	
Step 2: Choose the best strategy to answer the question The numerator and denominator look quite similar, so keep track of your calculations. Start with the numerator: Compute the innermost set of parentheses first, and then work your way outward. Repeat this process with the denominator. Once finished, combine the final values in the original expression.	$p(5) = 5^2 - 4 \times 5 + 8 = 13$ $q(13) = 13 - 3 = 10$ $q(p(5)) = 10$ $q(5) = 5 - 3 = 2$ $p(2) = 2^2 - 4 \times 2 + 8 = 4$ $p(q(5)) = 4$ $\dfrac{q(p(5))}{p(q(5))} = \dfrac{10}{4} = 2.5$
Step 3: Check that you answered the _right_ question You've correctly calculated the expression. The correct answer is (D).	

Following is another example of a real-world scenario involving functions. Recall that the notation $(f \circ g)(x)$ means that f and g are functions of x such that $f(x)$ is computed based on $g(x)$.

6. Everett works at an electronics store. His base salary is $1,000 per week, and he earns a 10% commission on any sales over his $4,000 per week goal. If Everett's commission (c) and sales in excess of $4,000 ($e$) are both functions of his overall sales (s), which of the following correctly describes Everett's total weekly pre-tax pay?

    A) $(c \circ e)(s + 1,000)$

    B) $(e \circ c)(s + 1,000)$

    C) $(e \circ c)(s) + 1,000$

    D) $(c \circ e)(s) + 1,000$

Because there isn't any scratchwork required for a question like this, only the column containing Kaplan's strategic thinking is included. Follow along as we reason our way through this question.

Strategic Thinking
Step 1: Read the question, identifying and organizing important information as you go
You need to identify the expression that correctly depicts Everett's total weekly pay.
Step 2: Choose the best strategy to answer the question
Consider each part of Everett's pay separately. To find Everett's commission, you must first determine the portion of his sales to use for the commission calculation. In other words, commission (c) depends on sales in excess of $4,000 ($e$). This means you'll have a composition of functions with c computed based on e, which translates to c of e of s, or using composition notation, $(c \circ e)(s)$.
Everett earns $1,000 regardless of sales, so this figure is independent of functions c and e. It should be added outside the composition of the functions. You can eliminate incorrect answer choices based on this information and the previous information.
Step 3: Check that you answered the right question
The only match for your function is (D).

Handling multiple functions in the same question or equation is only slightly more involved than manipulating a single function. Be sure to read particularly carefully when the question is embedded in a real-world scenario.

DESCRIBING FUNCTION BEHAVIOR AND PERFORMING TRANSFORMATIONS

When describing the graph of a function or an interval (a specific segment) of a function, the trend of the relationship between the x- and y-values while reading the graph from left to right is often important. Three terms you are sure to see in more difficult function questions are **increasing**, **decreasing**, and **constant**. Let's look at what these terms mean and how they apply to SAT questions.

- **Increasing** functions have y-values that *increase* as the corresponding x-values increase.

- **Decreasing** functions have y-values that *decrease* as the corresponding x-values increase.

- **Constant** functions have y-values that *stay the same* as the x-values increase.

The SAT can ask about function trends in a variety of ways. The most basic would be to examine a function's behavior and determine whether (and where) the function is increasing, decreasing, or constant. Tougher questions might ask you to identify the trend and then explain what it means in the context of a real-life situation presented in the question, or to identify the effect a transformation would have on the trend of a function.

A function **transformation** occurs when a change is made to the function's equation or graph. Transformations include translations (moving a graph up/down, left/right), reflections (flips about an axis or other line), and expansions/compressions (stretching or squashing horizontally or vertically). How do you know which is occurring? The following table provides some rules for guidance when altering a hypothetical function $f(x)$.

Algebraic Change	Corresponding Graphical Change	Graph	Algebraic Change	Corresponding Graphical Change	Graph
$f(x)$	N/A—original function		$f(x + a)$	$f(x)$ moves left a units	
$f(x) + a$	$f(x)$ moves up a units		$f(x - a)$	$f(x)$ moves right a units	

Algebraic Change	Corresponding Graphical Change	Graph	Algebraic Change	Corresponding Graphical Change	Graph
$f(x) - a$	$f(x)$ moves down a units		$-f(x)$	$f(x)$ reflected over the x-axis (top to bottom)	
$f(-x)$	$f(x)$ reflected over the y-axis (left to right)		$af(x)$ $(0 < a < 1)$	$f(x)$ undergoes vertical compression	
$f(ax)$ $(0 < a < 1)$	$f(x)$ undergoes horizontal expansion		$af(x)$ $(a > 1)$	$f(x)$ undergoes vertical expansion	
$f(ax)$ $(a > 1)$	$f(x)$ undergoes horizontal compression				

If you forget what a particular transformation looks like, you can always plug in a few values for x and plot the points to determine the effect on the function's graph.

✔ **Expert Tip**

Adding or subtracting inside the parentheses of a function will always cause a horizontal change (e.g., shift left/right, horizontal reflection); if the alteration is outside the parentheses, the result is a vertical change.

A function transformation question for you to try follows.

7. Given function $j(x)$, which of the following choices corresponds to a horizontal compression, a reflection about the x-axis, and an upward shift?

    A) $-j(2x) + 2$

    B) $-j(2x + 2)$

    C) $j(-2x) + 2$

    D) $-j\left(\dfrac{1}{2}x\right) + 2$

Because there isn't any scratchwork required for a question like this, only the column containing Kaplan's strategic thinking is included. Follow along as we reason our way through this question.

Strategic Thinking
Step 1: Read the question, identifying and organizing important information as you go
You must determine which function shows the transformations specified in the question stem.
Step 2: Choose the best strategy to answer the question
Remember your transformation rules. A horizontal compression results when there is a coefficient greater than 1 on the variable (for example, $f(3x)$); D doesn't contain this, so eliminate it. A reflection about the x-axis (vertical) requires a negative sign before j. Eliminate C. An upward shift (also vertical) means there must be a constant added outside the function argument parentheses. Of the remaining choices, (A) is the only function that satisfies the conditions in the question stem.
Step 3: Check that you answered the *right* question
The only matching function is (A).

Now you'll have a chance to try a couple test-like problems in a scaffolded way. We've provided some guidance, but you'll need to fill in the missing parts of explanations or the step-by-step math in order to get to the correct answer. Don't worry—after going through the worked examples at the beginning of this section, these problems should be completely doable.

8. Joan is an entomologist (a scientist who studies insects) researching possible causes of honeybee disappearance. At the start of a recent study, she estimated the number of honeybees in a 50 square mile area to be 4.23×10^8 distributed among 7,050 hives. Joan discovered that the honeybee population in this area decreases by 35% every month. Assuming the rate of disappearance remains 35% every month, approximately how many honeybees will remain after one year?

   A)   340

   B)   1,430

   C)   2,406,000

   D)   116,166,000

The following table can help you structure your thinking as you go about solving this question. Kaplan's strategic thinking is provided, as are bits of structured scratchwork. If you're not sure how to approach a question like this, start at the top and work your way down.

Strategic Thinking	Math Scratchwork
Step 1: Read the question, identifying and organizing important information as you go You need to determine the approximate number of honeybees remaining in Joan's study area after one year.	
Step 2: Choose the best strategy to answer the question You're asked about the honeybee population, so focus on information on the honeybee count and any rates of change. A reduction of 35% each month means the exact number of honeybees lost will change over time, so the best model is an exponential decay function. Add the values you know to create a function. The question wants a value, so plug in the correct duration into your function to find the number of remaining honeybees. Watch your time units.	exponential change: $y = x_0(1 + r)^x$ $p(t) =$ honeybee population $t =$ time in _____ $p(t) = ($ _____ $)(1 +$ _____ $)^t$ $p($__$) = ($ ____ $)($ ____ $) -$ $=$ ____
Step 3: Check that you answered the *right* question If you picked (C), you'd be correct.	_____

9. The graph of the function $a(x)$ is shown above. If $b(x) = \dfrac{1}{x}$, which of the following is a true statement about $(b \circ a)(x)$?

A) $(b \circ a)(x)$ is defined for all real numbers.

B) $(b \circ a)(x)$ is undefined for three real values of x.

C) $(b \circ a)(x)$ is undefined for four real values of x.

D) $(b \circ a)(x)$ is undefined for all real numbers.

The following table can help you structure your thinking as you go about solving this problem. Kaplan's strategic thinking is provided, as are bits of structured scratchwork.

Strategic Thinking	Math Scratchwork
Step 1: Read the question, identifying and organizing important information as you go You need to figure out when the composition of the functions is undefined (if it is).	
Step 2: Choose the best strategy to answer the question Think about what a composition means. The output of one function becomes the input for the other. You'll notice there's an x in the denominator of $b(x)$; think about what restriction this places on $b(x)$ and when this would make $(b \circ a)(x)$ undefined. Examine the graph of $a(x)$ to determine how many times this value occurs.	$(b \circ a)(x) \rightarrow b(a(x))$ output of _____ = input of _____ If $b(x) = \dfrac{1}{x}$, then $x \neq$ _____. $\rightarrow a(x) \neq$ _____ in $(b \circ a)(x)$ $a(x) =$ _____ at _____ places
Step 3: Check that you answered the *right* question If you got (C), you're absolutely correct!	_____

Now that you've seen the variety of ways in which the SAT can test you on functions, try the following questions to check your understanding. Give yourself 3.5 minutes to tackle the following three questions. Make sure you use the Kaplan Method for Math as often as you can. Remember, you want to emphasize speed and efficiency in addition to simply getting the correct answer.

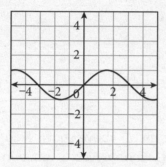

10. The graph of a trigonometric function, $h(x) = \sin x$, is shown above. Which of the following correctly depicts the transformations effected in $\dfrac{h(2x)}{3} - 4$?

A)

B)

C)

D)

11. Briana is writing a 60-page paper for a law school class; she has completed a full outline of the paper and needs to convert it to prose. She estimates that she will average 45 words per minute while typing. If one page of prose contains approximately 500 words, which of the following correctly estimates the number of prose pages, p, remaining as a function of the number of minutes, m, that Briana types?

A) $p(m) = 60 - \dfrac{9m}{100}$

B) $p(m) = \dfrac{60 - 100}{9m}$

C) $p(m) = 60 - \dfrac{100}{9m}$

D) $p(m) = \dfrac{60 - 9m}{100}$

Speed vs. Fuel Economy

12. The graph above shows a compact car's fuel economy as a function of speed. Which of the following is true?

A) The rate of increase in fuel economy below 50 mph is greater than the rate of decrease in fuel economy above 50 mph.

B) The rate of increase in fuel economy below 50 mph is equal to the rate of decrease in fuel economy above 50 mph.

C) Fuel economy peaks at 50 mph, but nothing can be said about the rates of change in fuel economy above and below 50 mph.

D) The rate of increase in fuel economy below 50 mph is less than the rate of decrease in fuel economy above 50 mph.

Answers and Explanations for this chapter begin on page 849.

EXTRA PRACTICE

1. If $k(x) = 5x + 2$, then what is the value of $k(4) - k(1)$?

   A) 15

   B) 17

   C) 19

   D) 21

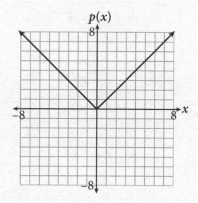

2. The figure shows the function $p(x) = |x|$. Which statement about the function is not true?

   A) $p(0) = 0$

   B) $p(-4) = 4$

   C) $p(4) = -4$

   D) The domain of $p(x)$ is all real numbers.

3. The graph above shows Carmel's distance from home over a one-hour period, during which time he first went to the library, then went to the grocery store, and then returned home. Which of the following statements could be true?

   A) The grocery store is about 5 miles from Carmel's house.

   B) Carmel traveled a total of 7 miles from the time he left home until he returned.

   C) The grocery store is 7 miles farther from Carmel's house than the library is.

   D) Carmel spent 10 minutes at the library and 15 minutes at the grocery store.

4. If the graph of a function $g(x)$ passes through the point $(5, 3)$, and $h(x)$ is defined as $h(x) = -g(x - 2) + 8$, through which point does the graph of $h(x)$ pass?

   A) $(-3, 11)$

   B) $(3, 5)$

   C) $(7, 5)$

   D) $(7, 11)$

x	$g(x)$
-6	-3
-3	-2
0	-1
3	0
6	1

x	$h(x)$
0	6
1	-4
2	2
3	0
4	-2

5. Several values for the functions $g(x)$ and $h(x)$ are shown in the tables above. What is the value of $g(h(3))$?

   A) -1

   B) 0

   C) 3

   D) 6

6. If p is a function defined over the set of all real numbers and $p(x + 2) = 3x^2 + 4x + 1$, then which of the following defines $p(x)$?

   A) $p(x) = 3x^2 - 7x + 3$

   B) $p(x) = 3x^2 - 8x + 5$

   C) $p(x) = 3x^2 + 16x + 9$

   D) $p(x) = 3x^2 + 16x + 21$

7. A company uses the function $P(x) = 150x - x^2$ to determine how much profit the company will make when it sells 150 units of a certain product that sells for x dollars per unit. How much more profit per unit will the company make if it charges $25 for the product than if it charges $20 ?

8. The customer service department of a wireless cellular provider has found that on Wednesdays, the polynomial function $C(t) = -0.0815t^4 + t^3 + 12t$ approximates the number of calls received by any given time, where t represents the number of hours that have passed since the department opened at 7 AM. Based on this function, how many calls can be expected by 5 PM ?

9. If $g(x) = -2x^2 + 7x - 3$, what is the value of $g(-2)$?

   A) -25

   B) -9

   C) -1

   D) 3

10. Which of the following does not represent the graph of a function?

A)

B)

C)

D)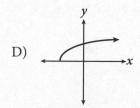

11. A biologist is studying the effect of pollution on the reproduction of a specific plant. She uses the function $n(p)$ to represent these effects, where p is the number of seeds germinated by the test group of the plant over a given period of time. Which of the following lists could represent a portion of the domain for the biologist's function?

A) $\{...-150, -100, -50, 0, 50, 100, 150...\}$

B) $\{-150, -100, -50, 0, 50, 100, 150\}$

C) $\{0, 0.25, 0.5, 0.75, 1, 1.25, 1.5...\}$

D) $\{0, 20, 40, 60, 80...\}$

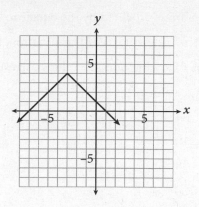

12. The graph of $f(x)$ is shown above. Which of the following represents the domain and range of the function?

A) Domain: $f(x) \geq 4$; Range: all real numbers

B) Domain: $f(x) \leq 4$; Range: all real numbers

C) Domain: all real numbers; Range: $f(x) \geq 4$

D) Domain: all real numbers; Range: $f(x) \leq 4$

13. If $g(x) = (x-2)^2 - 5$, which of the following statements is true?

A) The function $g(x)$ is increasing over the entire domain.

B) The function $g(x)$ is decreasing over the entire domain.

C) The function $g(x)$ is increasing for $x < 2$ and decreasing for $x > 2$.

D) The function $g(x)$ is decreasing for $x < 2$ and increasing for $x > 2$.

14. A function is defined by the equation $f(x) = \dfrac{x^2}{4} - 11$. For this function, which of the following domain values corresponds to a range value of 14?

A) -4

B) 10

C) 38

D) 100

$$f(x) = \begin{cases} x^2 + 1, & \text{if } x \le 0 \\ \dfrac{2x}{3} - 1, & \text{if } 0 < x \le 3 \\ 4 - x, & \text{if } x > 3 \end{cases}$$

15. For the piecewise function $f(x)$ defined above, what is the value of $f(-3)$?

A) -3

B) 7

C) 10

D) $-3, 7,$ and 10

16. Based on the figure above, what is the value of $f(-2) + g(2)$?

A) -3

B) 0

C) 3

D) 6

17. If $f(x) = 3 - x$ and $g(x) = \dfrac{x^2}{2}$, which of the following is not in the range of $f(g(x))$?

A) -3

B) 0

C) 2

D) 4

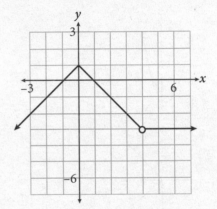

18. Which of the following piecewise functions could have been used to generate the graph above?

A) $g(x) = \begin{cases} -|x|, & \text{if } x \le 4 \\ -3, & \text{if } x > 4 \end{cases}$

B) $g(x) = \begin{cases} -|x|, & \text{if } x < 4 \\ x - 3, & \text{if } x > 4 \end{cases}$

C) $g(x) = \begin{cases} -|x| + 1, & \text{if } x < 4 \\ -3x, & \text{if } x > 4 \end{cases}$

D) $g(x) = \begin{cases} -|x| + 1, & \text{if } x < 4 \\ -3, & \text{if } x > 4 \end{cases}$

Quadratic Equations

CHAPTER OBJECTIVES

By the end of this chapter, you will be able to:

1. Solve quadratic equations via algebra, graphing, or the quadratic formula

2. Sketch the graph of a given quadratic equation

3. Identify how various components of a quadratic equation are significant to its graph or a real-world scenario

SMARTPOINTS

Point Value	SmartPoint Category
40 Points	Quadratics

Math

QUADRATIC EQUATIONS

Chapter 10

Homework

Extra Practice: #1-20

Even More

Math Quiz 4

Key

 Book Assignment

 Online Video Assignment

 Online Quiz Assignment

INTRODUCTION TO QUADRATIC EQUATIONS

A quadratic equation or expression is simply one that contains a squared variable (x^2) as the highest-order term (also called highest-powered term). In standard form, a quadratic equation is written as $ax^2 + bx + c = 0$, where a, b, and c are constants. However, quadratics can be written in a variety of other forms as well, such as these:

$$x^2 - 9 = 0 \qquad 2r^2 - 8r + 10 = 4 \qquad 2(x - 3)^2 = 8 \qquad (x - 2)(x + 3) = 6$$

 Note

At first glance, the last equation might not look quadratic, but it is; it's merely masquerading as a product of binomials. You'll learn a strategy for unveiling its x^2 term shortly.

All quadratic equations have 0, 1, or 2 real solutions. When you are asked to find the solutions of a quadratic equation, all you need to do is equate the variable to a constant. Solutions might also be called roots, x-intercepts, or zeros.

Before you can solve, however, there is a step you must always complete: **Set the equation equal to 0**. In other words, move everything to one side of the equation so that 0 is the only thing left on the other side. Once the quadratic equation is equal to 0, you can take one of three routes to determine how many solutions it has: **algebra**, **graphing**, or the **quadratic formula**. Read on for more information about these three techniques.

SOLVING QUADRATICS ALGEBRAICALLY

Using algebra is often necessary when working with quadratic equations, so getting comfortable with it is critical. We'll start with a technique that is highly useful for manipulating quadratics: FOIL. **FOIL is essential for putting a quadratic into standard form.**

 Expert Tip

If you get stuck on the algebra in a question about a quadratic equation, Picking Numbers can often help. Just remember that it might take more time than the algebraic route, so use good judgment if you're in a bind—and remember that you can always skip the question and revisit it later.

FOIL

Whenever you see a pair of binomials on the SAT, your default algebra strategy should be FOIL, which stands for **F**irst, **O**uter, **I**nner, **L**ast. This acronym helps ensure that you don't forget any terms when distributing. Multiply the first terms in each binomial together, then repeat with the outer, inner, and last terms. Then add the four products together, combining like terms as needed. Here is a generic scheme for the FOIL procedure:

$$(a + b)(c + d) = ac + ad + bc + bd$$
$$\text{(Binomial 1)(Binomial 2)} = \textbf{F}\text{irst} + \textbf{O}\text{uter} + \textbf{I}\text{nner} + \textbf{L}\text{ast}$$

It is often tempting to FOIL in your head, but this is risky: It is very easy to lose a negative sign or switch a pair of coefficients (and arrive at a trap answer). Show *all* of your work when using FOIL.

Factoring

Factoring, also known as reverse-FOILing, allows you to go from a quadratic to a product of two binomials. This is a very powerful tool; once you have a binomial pair, you're a few short algebraic steps away from finding the solution(s). The factoring process for a quadratic equation that is written in standard form ($ax^2 + bx + c$) is demonstrated in the following table:

Step	Scratchwork
Starting point: Notice a, the coefficient in front of x^2, is equal to 1, a great condition for factoring.	$x^2 + 5x + 6 = 0 \rightarrow (x \pm ?)(x \pm ?) = 0$
1. What are the factors of c? Remember to include negatives.	factors of 6: 1 & 6, −1 & −6, 2 & 3, −2 & −3
2. Which factor pair, when added, equals b, the coefficient in front of x?	$2 + 3 = 5$
3. Write as a product of binomials.	$(x + 2)(x + 3) = 0$
4. Split the product of binomials into two equations set equal to 0.	$x + 2 = 0, x + 3 = 0$
5. Solve each equation.	$x = -2, x = -3$

Factoring is easiest when a is 1, so whenever possible, try to simplify the expression so that is the case. In addition, if you see nice-looking numbers (integers, simple fractions) in the answer choices, this is a clue that factoring is possible. If you're ever not sure that you've done your factoring correctly, go ahead and FOIL to check your work. You should get the expression you started with.

> ✔ **Note**
>
> Sometimes, the two binomials factors will be identical. In this case, the quadratic equation will have only one real solution (because the two solutions are identical).

Completing the Square

For more difficult quadratics, you'll need to turn to a more advanced strategy: **completing the square**. In this process you'll create a perfect square trinomial, which has the form $(x + h)^2 = k$, where h and k are constants. This route takes some practice to master but will pay dividends when you sail through the most challenging quadratic equation questions on Test Day. The following table illustrates the procedure along with a corresponding example (even though the equation could have been factored).

Step	Scratchwork
Starting point.	$x^2 + 6x - 7 = 0$
1. Move the constant to the opposite side.	$x^2 + 6x = 7$
2. Divide b by 2, then square the quotient.	$b = 6; \left(\dfrac{b}{2}\right)^2 = \left(\dfrac{6}{2}\right)^2 = (3)^2 = 9$
3. Add the number from the previous step to both sides of the equation, then factor.	$x^2 + 6x + 9 = 7 + 9 \rightarrow (x + 3)(x + 3) = 16 \rightarrow$ $(x + 3)^2 = 16$
4. Take the square root of both sides.	$\sqrt{(x + 3)^2} = \pm\sqrt{16} \rightarrow x + 3 = \pm 4$
5. Split the product into two equations and solve each one.	$x + 3 = 4, x + 3 = -4 \rightarrow x = 1, x = -7$

A note about completing the square: a needs to be 1 to use this process. You can divide the first term by a to convert the coefficient to 1, but if you start getting strange-looking fractions, it may be easier to use the quadratic formula instead.

Grouping

Although less commonly seen than other strategies, **grouping** is useful with more challenging quadratics, especially when the leading coefficient (the value of a) is not 1. You'll need two x terms to use this route. The goal of grouping is to identify the greatest common factor (GCF) of the first two terms, repeat for the second two terms, then finally combine the two GCFs into a separate binomial. Check out the following example.

Step	Scratchwork
Starting point.	$2x^2 - 7x - 15 = 0$
1. You need to split the x term in two; the sum of the new terms' coefficients must equal b, and their product must equal ac.	$a \times c = 2 \times (-15) = -30, b = -7$ new x term coefficients: 3 and -10 $2x^2 - 10x + 3x - 15 = 0$

Step	Scratchwork
2. What's the GCF of the first pair of terms? How about the second pair of terms?	GCF of $2x^2$ and $-10x$ is $2x$ GCF of $3x$ and -15 is 3
3. Factor out the GCFs for each pair of terms.	$2x^2 - 10x + 3x - 15 = 0$ $2x(x-5) + 3(x-5) = 0$
4. Factor out the newly formed binomial and combine the GCFs into another factor.	$2x(x-5) + 3(x-5) = 0$ $(2x+3)(x-5) = 0$
5. Split into two equations and solve as usual.	$2x + 3 = 0, x - 5 = 0 \rightarrow x = -\dfrac{3}{2}, x = 5$

Straightforward Math

Sometimes you can get away with not having to FOIL or factor extensively, but you need to be able to spot patterns or trends. Don't resort to complex techniques when some easy simplification will get the job done. Equations similar to the following examples are highly likely to appear on the SAT.

No Middle Term	No Last Term	Squared Binomial
$x^2 - 9 = 0$	$x^2 - 9x = 0$	$(x - 3)^2 = 9$
$x^2 = 9$	$x(x - 9) = 0$	$(x - 3) = \pm\sqrt{9}$
$x = \pm\sqrt{9}$	$x = 0, x - 9 = 0$	$(x - 3) = \pm 3$
$x = \pm 3$	$x = 0, x = 9$	$x - 3 = 3 \rightarrow x = 6$ $x - 3 = -3 \rightarrow x = 0$

> ✔ **Expert Tip**
>
> You can also factor $x^2 - 9$ to get $(x + 3)(x - 3)$; this is called a difference of squares. Note that this only works when the terms are being subtracted.

Quadratic Formula

The quadratic formula can be used to solve any quadratic equation. However, because the math can often get complicated, use this as a last resort or when you need to find exact (e.g., not rounded, fractions, and/or radicals) solutions. If you see square roots in the answer choices, this is a clue to use the quadratic formula.

The quadratic formula that follows yields solutions to a quadratic equation that is written in standard form, $ax^2 + bx + c = 0$:

$$x = \frac{-b \pm \sqrt{b^2 - 4ac}}{2a}$$

The $\pm$ sign that follows $-b$ indicates that you will have two solutions, so remember to find both.

The expression under the radical ($b^2 - 4ac$) is called the discriminant, and its value determines the number of real solutions. If this quantity is positive, the equation has two distinct real solutions; if it is equal to 0, there is only one distinct real solution; and if it's negative, there are no real solutions.

> ✔ **Note**
>
> Being flexible and familiar with your strengths on Test Day is essential. By doing so, you can identify the path to the answer to a quadratics question that is the most efficient for you.

On the next few pages, you'll get to try applying some of these strategies to test-like SAT problems.

1. Which of the following is an equivalent form of the expression $(6 - 5x)(15x - 11)$?

   A) $-75x^2 + 35x - 66$

   B) $-75x^2 + 145x - 66$

   C) $90x^2 - 141x + 55$

   D) $90x^2 + 9x + 55$

Work through the Kaplan Method for Math step-by-step to solve this question. The following table shows Kaplan's strategic thinking on the left, along with suggested math scratchwork on the right.

Strategic Thinking	Math Scratchwork
Step 1: Read the question, identifying and organizing important information as you go You're asked to identify the quadratic expression equivalent to $(6 - 5x)(15x - 11)$.	
Step 2: Choose the best strategy to answer the question You have a product of two binomials in the question stem and quadratics written in standard form in the answer choices, so FOIL is the quickest route. Follow the standard FOIL procedure, and then simplify.	$(6-5x)(15x-11)$ $=(6)(15x)+(6)(-11)$ $\quad +(-5x)(15x)+(-5x)(-11)$ $=90x-66-75x^2+55x$ $=-75x^2+145x-66$
Step 3: Check that you answered the *right* question You correctly expanded the quadratic using FOIL and got an exact match for (B), the correct answer.	$-75x^2+145x-66$

Use the strategies you've learned in this section to simplify the rational expression that follows.

2. Which of the following is equivalent to $\dfrac{x^2 - 10x + 25}{3x^2 - 75}$?

A) $\dfrac{3(x - 5)}{(x + 5)}$

B) $\dfrac{3(x + 5)}{(x - 5)}$

C) $\dfrac{(x - 5)}{3(x + 5)}$

D) $\dfrac{(x + 5)}{3(x - 5)}$

Work through the Kaplan Method for Math step-by-step to solve this question. The following table shows Kaplan's strategic thinking on the left, along with suggested math scratchwork on the right.

Strategic Thinking	Math Scratchwork
Step 1: Read the question, identifying and organizing important information as you go You need to identify which answer choice contains an expression equivalent to the one in the question stem.	
Step 2: Choose the best strategy to answer the question There are a few x^2 terms, so you should be thinking about quadratics and factoring. Also, whenever you're given a fraction, think about ways to cancel terms. Examine the numerator first: You can use the quadratic shortcut $a^2 - 2ab + b^2 = (a - b)^2$ to rewrite it. The denominator is more involved. Factor out a 3 first, and then factor the quadratic, which is a difference of squares. Lastly, cancel any factors that the numerator and denominator share.	$\dfrac{x^2 - 10x + 25}{3x^2 - 75}$ $= \dfrac{(x - 5)(x - 5)}{3(x^2 - 25)}$ $= \dfrac{(x - 5)\cancel{(x - 5)}}{3(x + 5)\cancel{(x - 5)}}$
Step 3: Check that you answered the *right* question The expression is now in simplest form, so you're done. Choice (C) is correct.	$\dfrac{x - 5}{3(x + 5)}$

3. Which of the following is a value of x that satisfies the equation $x^2 + 2x - 5 = 0$?

A) -1

B) $1 - \sqrt{6}$

C) $1 + \sqrt{6}$

D) $-1 - \sqrt{6}$

This question is full of radicals, but don't panic. You can use the Kaplan Method for Math to efficiently tackle this kind of question on Test Day. The following table shows Kaplan's strategic thinking on the left, along with suggested math scratchwork on the right.

Strategic Thinking	Math Scratchwork
Step 1: Read the question, identifying and organizing important information as you go The question asks for a solution to the given equation.	
Step 2: Choose the best strategy to answer the question The equation is a quadratic, so you have a few potential options. Because -5 does not have factors that add up to 2, you cannot factor or group. However, because the coefficient of x^2 is 1, completing the square is doable. We'll use that method here, but you could also use the quadratic formula if you prefer.	$x^2 + 2x - 5 = 0$ $x^2 + 2x = 5$ $\left(\dfrac{b}{2}\right)^2 = \left(\dfrac{2}{2}\right)^2 = 1^2 = 1$ $x^2 + 2x + 1 = 5 + 1$ $(x + 1)^2 = 6$ $x + 1 = \pm\sqrt{6}$ $x = -1 \pm \sqrt{6}$
Step 3: Check that you answered the *right* question The question asks for one possible value of x, so you should expect to see one (but not both) of the values in the choices. Choice (D) contains one of these values.	$x = -1 + \sqrt{6}$ or $x = -1 - \sqrt{6}$

CONNECTIONS BETWEEN QUADRATICS AND PARABOLAS

A quadratic function is simply a quadratic equation set equal to y or $f(x)$ instead of 0. To solve one of these, you would follow the same procedure as before: Substitute 0 for y, or $f(x)$, then solve using one of the three methods demonstrated (algebra, graphing, quadratic formula). Consider the graphical connection: When you set y equal to 0, you're really finding the x-intercepts.

The graph of every quadratic equation (or function) is a parabola, which is a symmetric U-shaped graph that opens either up or down. To determine whether a parabola will open up or down, examine the value of a in the equation. If a is positive, the parabola will open up; if a is negative, it will open down. Take a look at the examples below to see this graphically.

Like quadratic equations, quadratic functions will have zero, one, or two real solutions, corresponding to the number of times the parabola crosses the x-axis. As you saw with previous examples, graphing is a powerful way to determine the number of solutions a quadratic function has.

There are three algebraic forms that a quadratic equation can take: standard, factored, and vertex. Each is provided in the following table along with some features that are revealed by writing the equation in that particular form.

Standard	Factored	Vertex
$y = ax^2 + bx + c$	$y = a(x - m)(x - n)$	$y = a(x - h)^2 + k$
y-intercept is c	Solutions are m and n	Vertex is (h, k)
In real-world contexts, starting quantity is c	x-intercepts are m and n	Minimum/maximum of function is k
Format used to solve via quadratic formula	Vertex is halfway between m and n	Axis of symmetry is given by $x = h$

You've already seen standard and factored forms earlier in this chapter, but vertex form might be new to you. In vertex form, a is the same as the a from standard form, and h and k are the coordinates of the **vertex** (h, k). If a quadratic function is not in vertex form, you can still find the x-coordinate of the vertex by plugging the appropriate values into the equation $h = \dfrac{-b}{2a}$, which is also the equation for the axis of symmetry (see graph that follows). Once you determine h, plug this value into the quadratic function and solve for y to determine k, the y-coordinate of the vertex.

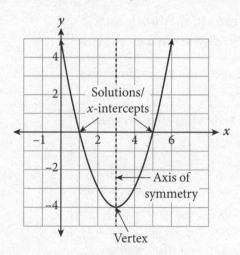

In addition to familiarity with the various forms a quadratic equation/function can take, you should have a foundational knowledge of the structure of a parabola. Some of the basic pieces you could be asked about on Test Day are shown above. You already know how to determine the solutions and the vertex, and finding the axis of symmetry is straightforward. The **equation of the axis of symmetry** of a parabola is $x = h$, where h is the x-coordinate of the vertex.

✔ **Note**

The formula for a parabola's axis of symmetry is easy to remember: It's the quadratic formula without the radical component. If the x-intercepts are rational numbers, you can also determine the axis of symmetry by finding the midpoint, the point exactly halfway between.

Take some time to explore the questions on the next several pages to test your new wealth of quadratic knowledge.

A question like this next one could arise in either the calculator or the no-calculator section. Think critically about how you'd solve it in either case.

4. What are the *x*-intercepts of the parabolic function $f(x) = 3x^2 - 2x - 8 = 0$?

    A) $\frac{1}{3}$ and -25

    B) $\frac{4}{3}$ and -2

    C) $-\frac{4}{3}$ and 2

    D) $-\frac{4}{3}$ and -2

Work through the Kaplan Method for Math step-by-step to solve this question. The following table shows Kaplan's strategic thinking on the left, along with suggested math scratchwork on the right.

Strategic Thinking	Math Scratchwork
Step 1: Read the question, identifying and organizing important information as you go You're given a quadratic equation in standard form and asked to find its *x*-intercepts.	
Step 2: Choose the best strategy to answer the question Because the coefficient of x^2 isn't 1, you can't easily factor. However, the grouping method will work. You'll need two numbers whose product is *ac* (-24) and whose sum is *b* (-2); the two magic numbers are -6 and 4. Rewrite the middle term using these numbers before you group, then factor and solve for *x*.	$f(x) = 3x^2 - 2x - 8 = 0$ $ac = 3 \times (-8) = -24$ $b = -2$ $3x^2 - 6x + 4x - 8 = 0$ $3x(x-2) + 4(x-2) = 0$ $(3x+4)(x-2) = 0$ $(3x+4) = 0$ or $(x-2) = 0$
Step 3: Check that you answered the *right* question The question asks for the *x*-intercepts of the equation, which is what you calculated. Select (C) and move on.	$x = -\frac{4}{3}$ and $x = 2$

 Note

If a question like this were in the calculator section, you could also solve it by graphing.

In one final type of quadratic-related problem, you may be asked to match a function to a graph or vice-versa. An example of this follows; unfortunately, it is not likely to appear in the calculator section of the test.

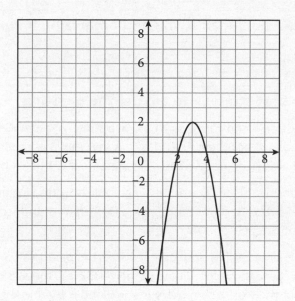

5.   If the function shown in the graph is represented by $f(x) = a(x - h)^2 + k$, which of the following statements is not true?

   A)   The value of a is negative.

   B) $f(x)$ is symmetrical across the line $y = 3$.

   C)   The function $g(x) = \dfrac{2x}{3}$ intersects $f(x)$ at its vertex.

   D)   The value of h is positive.

Because there isn't any scratchwork required for a question like this, only the column containing Kaplan's strategic thinking is included.

Strategic Thinking
Step 1: Read the question, identifying and organizing important information as you go The equation given is in vertex form. You must pick the answer choice that is *not* true.
Step 2: Choose the best strategy to answer the question Take control of this question—consider everything in a strategic order. Choices A and D contain the simplest statements, so check them first. Choice A says that *a* is negative. For parabolas that open downward, *a* will always be negative, so this statement is true. Eliminate it. Choice D says that *h* is positive. Recall that when a parabola is written in vertex form, *h* represents the *x*-coordinate of the vertex. Because the vertex is (3, 2), *h* must indeed be positive. Choice D is therefore true, so eliminate it. Of the remaining answer choices, B is simpler: It involves the parabola's axis of symmetry, which you can quickly find. Because the *x*-coordinate of the vertex is 3, the axis of symmetry is the line $x = 3$. Choice B says that the axis of symmetry is $y = 3$ and is therefore false.
Step 3: Check that you answered the *right* question Remember that you're looking for a false statement, not a true statement. Choice (B) is false, so you can select it confidently without even bothering to evaluate C.

✔ **Note**

Stay on the lookout for words such as "not" that are easily missed if you don't read the question stem carefully. This is especially true of questions testing more involved topics.

GRAPHING QUADRATIC EQUATIONS ON A CALCULATOR

At this point, you've become quite an expert at working with quadratics on paper. In this part, we'll explore how you can use your calculator to efficiently graph quadratics. Calculators can be great time-savers *when you're allowed to use them*.

Graphing

All quadratic equations can be solved by graphing, unless they happen to have imaginary solutions which are covered in chapter 12. That said, you might ask why you need to learn all the algebra techniques. There are a few reasons why graphing shouldn't be the first option you turn to:

- Remember, there's a no-calculator section on the SAT; graphing isn't an option here.
- Graphing is often slower because entering complex equations and then zooming to find points of interest can be tedious.
- It is easy to accidentally mistype when you're being timed—a misplaced parenthesis or negative sign will likely lead to a trap answer choice.

However, if you have complicated algebra ahead (e.g., fractional coefficients), decimals in the answer choices, or time-consuming obstacles to overcome, graphing can be a viable alternative to solving quadratic equations algebraically. Steps for graphing on a calculator follows:

1. Manipulate the equation so that it equals 0.

2. Substitute $y =$ for the 0.

3. Enter the equation into your calculator.

4. Trace the graph to approximate the x-intercepts (usually the answer choices will be sufficiently different to warrant an approximation over an exact value) or use your calculator's built-in capability to find the x-intercepts exactly.

Graphing on the TI-83/84

While on the home screen, press [**Y=**]. Then enter the function to be graphed. Press [**GRAPH**] and allow the function to plot. If you can't see everything or want to make sure there isn't something hiding, consider pressing [**WINDOW**] to set your own manual parameters or hitting [**ZOOM**] to quickly zoom in and out. If you want to simply investigate your graph, press [**TRACE**] and use the right and left arrow keys to move around on the graph. If you type in any x-value and press [**ENTER**], the y-value will be returned on screen.

Determining Solutions on the TI-83/84

Once you have your graph on screen, you're ready to find solutions. Press [**2ND**] [**TRACE**] to pull up the **CALC** menu, which has options for finding points of interest. Select option **2:ZERO** by highlighting and pressing [**ENTER**]. You will be taken back to the graph. Use the arrow keys to move to the left of the x-intercept (zero) that you want to calculate. Once you are just to the left of only the zero you are interested in, press [**ENTER**]—this is called the Left Bound. Next, move to the right of that zero only, careful not to go past any others, and press [**ENTER**]—this is called the Right Bound. Finally, the calculator will ask you to "Guess," so move left or right to approximate this zero, and press [**ENTER**].

Because you've already set the quadratic equation equal to zero, you know the zeros that your calculator returns will be the solutions to the overall equation.

 Note

Take the time to get comfortable with your calculator functions regardless of what calculator you have. You can find great instructions and even video demonstrations on the Internet.

Next, you'll get to try a sample test-like problem that could be solved via graphing or the quadratic formula. Choose wisely. In almost every case, graphing will be faster, but familiarize yourself with the quadratic formula approach in case you encounter a problem like this in the no-calculator section.

6. Which of the following are the real values of x that satisfy the equation $2x^2 - 5x - 2 = 0$?

A) 1 and 4

B) $-\dfrac{5}{4} + \dfrac{\sqrt{41}}{4}$ and $-\dfrac{5}{4} - \dfrac{\sqrt{41}}{4}$

C) $\dfrac{5}{4} + \dfrac{\sqrt{41}}{4}$ and $\dfrac{5}{4} - \dfrac{\sqrt{41}}{4}$

D) No real solutions

Work through the Kaplan Method for Math step-by-step to solve this question. The following table shows Kaplan's strategic thinking on the left, along with suggested math scratchwork on the right.

Strategic Thinking	Math Scratchwork
Step 1: Read the question, identifying and organizing important information as you go You need to solve the given equation for x.	
Step 2: Choose the best strategy to answer the question Attempting to factor is not wise, as the coefficients aren't factoring-friendly. Using a calculator would work, but it's likely to be messy: Two answer choices contain radicals, so you'd have to plug both solutions into the calculator and use the **[TRACE]** feature to see which ones approximately match the values you find. The quadratic formula, although a longer route, is actually the most efficient option for this question. Plug in the coefficients and the constant carefully. Labeling the equation will help keep the values of a, b, and c straight.	$\overset{a}{}\ \overset{b}{}\ \overset{c}{}$ $2x^2 - 5x - 2 = 0$ $x = \dfrac{-b \pm \sqrt{b^2 - 4ac}}{2a}$ $x = \dfrac{-(-5) \pm \sqrt{(-5)^2 - 4(2)(-2)}}{2(2)}$ $ = \dfrac{5 \pm \sqrt{25 - (-16)}}{4}$ $ = \dfrac{5 \pm \sqrt{41}}{4}$ $x = \dfrac{5}{4} \pm \dfrac{\sqrt{41}}{4}$
Step 3: Check that you answered the *right* question The question asks for the solutions to the equation, so you're finished. Your match is (C).	$\dfrac{5}{4} + \dfrac{\sqrt{41}}{4}$ and $\dfrac{5}{4} - \dfrac{\sqrt{41}}{4}$

> **✔ Note**
>
> Note that in the previous question, the quadratic formula was the most efficient approach. Be prepared to use any of the quadratic equation tools at your disposal on Test Day.

Nicely done! Take a look at another example.

7. The equation $\frac{1}{4}(4x^2 - 8x - k) = 30$ is satisfied when $x = -5$ and when $x = 7$. What is the value of $2k$?

    A)   40

    B)   20

    C)   0

    D) −20

Although this question seems more complicated than others you've seen in this chapter, if you use the Kaplan Method for Math, you'll arrive at the correct answer. The following table shows Kaplan's strategic thinking on the left, along with suggested math scratchwork on the right.

Strategic Thinking	Math Scratchwork
Step 1: Read the question, identifying and organizing important information as you go You're asked to find the value of $2k$.	
Step 2: Choose the best strategy to answer the question Notice that the equation in the question stem is not in standard form. Distributing the $\frac{1}{4}$ won't result in unmanageable fractions, so doing so won't cost you a lot of time. After distributing, set the equation equal to 0. The "normal" routes to the solutions (factoring, etc.) would be difficult to take here because of the presence of k. Instead, use the given solutions to construct and FOIL two binomials. The quadratic expressions must be equal because they share the same solutions. Set them equal to each other, and then use algebra to solve for k.	$\frac{1}{4}(4x^2 - 8x - k) = 30$ $x^2 - 2x - \frac{k}{4} = 30$ $x^2 - 2x - \frac{k}{4} - 30 = 0$ $(x - 7)(x + 5) = 0$ $x^2 - 2x - 35 = 0$ so $x^2 - 2x - \frac{k}{4} - 30 = x^2 - 2x - 35$ $-\frac{k}{4} = -5$ $-k = -20$ $k = 20$
Step 3: Check that you answered the *right* question Be careful! Many students will select B, but you're asked for the value of $2k$. Multiply the value of k by 2, and select (A).	$k = 20$ $2k = 40$

As demonstrated, even the most daunting quadratic equation questions are made more straightforward by using the Kaplan Method for Math.

Now you'll have a chance to try a few test-like problems in a scaffolded way. We've provided some guidance, but you'll need to fill in the missing parts of explanations or the step-by-step math in order to get to the correct answer. Don't worry—after going through the worked examples at the beginning of this section, these problems should be completely doable.

8. The height of a potato launched from a potato gun can be described as a function of elapsed time according to the following quadratic equation: $f(t) = -16t^2 + 224t + 240$. What is the sum of the potato's maximum height and the time it takes the potato to reach the ground?

   A) 15

   B) 240

   C) 1,024

   D) 1,039

Use the scaffolding in the table that follows as your map through the question. If you aren't sure where to start, fill in the blanks in the table as you work from top to bottom.

Strategic Thinking	Math Scratchwork
Step 1: Read the question, identifying and organizing important information as you go You're asked to find the sum of the maximum height and the time it takes the potato to hit the ground. The t^2 indicates a quadratic (and therefore a parabolic trajectory).	
Step 2: Choose the best strategy to answer the question Because a (the t^2 coefficient) is negative, this parabola opens down, which means the maximum height will be at the vertex. First, find the x-coordinate of the vertex, h, and then use it to find the maximum height.	$h = \dfrac{-b}{2a} = $ _____ $k = f(h)$ $k = 16(\_\_)^2 + 224(\_\_) + 240$ $k = $ _____
Next, find the amount of time it takes the potato to hit the ground. (Hint: Its height will be zero.) Translation: Factor!	$0 = $ _____ $0 = ($ _____ $)($ _____ $)$ $t = $ _____ , $t = $ _____
Step 3: Check that you answered the *right* question Remember, the question asks you for the sum of the potato's maximum height and the time it takes the potato to hit the ground. If you came up with (D), you're absolutely correct.	sum = _____ + _____ = _____

If you're up for a challenge, try the next question.

9. If $ab > 0$, $b^2ac < 0$, a is a constant, and b and c are distinct x-intercepts of the function $f(x)$, then $f(x)$ could equal which of the following?

   A) $f(x) = 5x^2 + 1$

   B) $f(x) = (x - \sqrt{17})(x + \sqrt{24})$

   C) $f(x) = (x - \sqrt{17})(x - \sqrt{24})$

   D) $f(x) = (x + \sqrt{17})(x + \sqrt{24})$

Use the scaffolding that follows as your map through the question. If you aren't sure where to start, fill in the blanks in the table as you work from top to bottom.

Strategic Thinking	Math Scratchwork
Step 1: Read the question, identifying and organizing important information as you go You need to select the equation that satisfies the given properties of $f(x)$.	
Step 2: Choose the best strategy to answer the question If $ab > 0$, then a and b are either both positive or both negative. In the inequality $b^2ac < 0$, b^2 will be positive regardless of the sign of b. Therefore, either a or c is positive, and the other must be negative. The x-intercepts are b and c. Since b has the same sign as a, while c has the opposite sign as a, it follows that b and c also have opposite signs. The correct answer must be a function with one negative root and one positive root. Scan the functions to find the correct one. Ignore the complicated-looking numbers; all that matters are the signs!	$ab > 0$ a and b have _____ sign $b^2ac < 0$ a and c have _____ signs b and c are roots of $f(x)$ $f(x)$ has one _____ root and one _____ root A's roots are _____ B's roots are _____ C's roots are _____ D's roots are _____
Step 3: Check that you answered the *right* question If you picked (B), then you got it!	_____

Now that you've seen the variety of ways in which the SAT can test you on quadratics, try the following questions to check your understanding. Give yourself 5 minutes to tackle the following four questions. Make sure you use the Kaplan Method for Math as often as you can. Remember, you want to emphasize speed and efficiency in addition to simply getting the correct answer.

$$4x - 12\sqrt{x} + 9 = 16$$

10. If the equation above is true, then what is the positive value of the expression $10\sqrt{x} - 15$?

A) 20

B) 25

C) 30

D) 35

11. How many times do the parabolas given by the equations $f(x) = 3(x - 4)^2 + 4$ and $g(x) = (x + 5)^2 + 2x - 135$ intersect?

A) Never

B) Once

C) Twice

D) More than twice

12. What is the positive difference between the x-intercepts of the parabola given by the equation $g(x) = -2.5x^2 + 10x - 7.5$?

13. Which equation represents the axis of symmetry for the graph of the quadratic function $f(x) = -\dfrac{11}{3}x^2 + 17x - \dfrac{43}{13}$?

A) $x = -\dfrac{102}{11}$

B) $x = -\dfrac{51}{22}$

C) $x = \dfrac{51}{22}$

D) $x = \dfrac{102}{11}$

Answers and Explanations for this chapter begin on page 854.

EXTRA PRACTICE

1. The factored form of a quadratic equation is $y = (2x + 1)(x - 5)$, and the standard form is $y = 2x^2 - 9x - 5$. Which of the following statements accurately describes the graph of y?

   A) The x-intercepts are -1 and 5, and the y-intercept is -5.

   B) The x-intercepts are $-\dfrac{1}{2}$ and 5, and the y-intercept is -5.

   C) The x-intercepts are $-\dfrac{1}{2}$ and 5, and the y-intercept is 5.

   D) The x-intercepts are 1 and -5, and the y-intercept is -5.

2. Taylor fires a toy rocket from ground level. The height of the rocket with respect to time can be represented by a quadratic function. If the toy rocket reaches a maximum height of 34 feet, 3 seconds after it was fired, which of the following functions could represent the height, h, of the rocket t seconds after it was fired?

   A) $h(t) = -16(t - 3)^2 + 34$

   B) $h(t) = -16(t + 3)^2 + 34$

   C) $h(t) = 16(t - 3)^2 + 34$

   D) $h(t) = 16(t + 3)^2 + 34$

3. If $x^2 - 7x = 30$ and $x > 0$, what is the value of $x - 5$?

   A) 5

   B) 6

   C) 10

   D) 25

4. Which of the following linear expressions divides evenly into $6x^2 + 7x - 20$?

   A) $3x - 10$

   B) $3x - 5$

   C) $3x - 4$

   D) $3x - 2$

$$\begin{cases} y = 2x \\ 2x^2 + 2y^2 = 240 \end{cases}$$

5. If (x, y) is a solution to the system of equations above, what is the value of x^2?

   A) 24

   B) 40

   C) 120

   D) 576

Math

Tyree's Punt

6. Tyree punts a football into the air. The equation $h = -16t^2 + 60t$ represents the height of the ball in feet, t seconds after it was punted. The graph of part of the equation is shown in the figure above. If Craig punts a ball higher than Tyree did, which of the following equations could be used to find the height of Craig's punt?

    A) $h = -16(t^2 - 3t)$

    B) $h = -8t(2t - 9)$

    C) $h = -4(2t - 5)^2 + 48$

    D) $h = -4(2t - 6)^2 + 52$

7. If $x = -5$ when $x^2 + 2xk + k^2 = 0$, what is the value of k?

8. If the graph of $y = ax^2 + bx + c$ passes through the points $(-2, -10)$, $(0, 2)$, and $(4, 14)$, what is the value of $a + b + c$?

9. Which of the following is equivalent to $(2a + 5b)(a - 3b)$?

    A) $2a^2 - 2ab - 15b^2$

    B) $2a^2 - ab - 15b^2$

    C) $2a^2 + 2ab - 15b^2$

    D) $2a^2 + 11ab - 15b^2$

10. Which of the following are roots of the quadratic equation $(x + 3)^2 = 49$?

    A) $x = -10, x = 4$

    B) $x = -10, x = 10$

    C) $x = -4, x = 10$

    D) $x = 3 \pm 2\sqrt{13}$

11. What information does the value of c reveal when a quadratic equation is written in the form $y = ax^2 + bx + c$, assuming $a \neq 0$, $b \neq 0$, and $c \neq 0$?

    A) The solution (zero) of the equation

    B) The location of the graph's axis of symmetry

    C) The y-intercept of the graph of the equation

    D) The maximum or minimum value of the equation

12. Which of the following could be the equation of the graph shown?

A) $y = 2x + 10$

B) $y = -x^2 + \dfrac{3}{2}x + 10$

C) $y = -(x - 2)(x + 5)$

D) $y = -(x + 2)(x - 5)$

13. Which of the following equations has the same solutions as the equation $40 - 6x = x^2$?

A) $y = (x - 6)^2 - 40$

B) $y = (x - 6)^2 + 40$

C) $y = (x + 3)^2 - 49$

D) $y = (x + 3)^2 + 49$

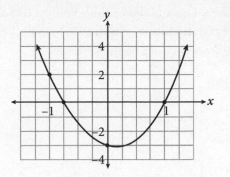

14. The following quadratic equations are all representations of the graph above. Which equation reveals the exact values of the x-intercepts of the graph?

A) $y = 4x^2 - x - 3$

B) $y = (4x + 3)(x - 1)$

C) $y = 4(x - 0.125)^2 - 3.0625$

D) $y + 3.0625 = 4(x - 0.125)^2$

15. Given the equation $y = -(2x - 4)^2 + 7$, which of the following statements is not true?

A) The vertex is $(4, 7)$.

B) The y-intercept is $(0, -9)$.

C) The parabola opens downward.

D) The graph crosses the x-axis at least one time.

16. The x-coordinates of the solutions to a system of equations are 3.5 and 6. Which of the following could be the system?

A) $\begin{cases} y = x + 3.5 \\ y = x^2 + 6 \end{cases}$

B) $\begin{cases} y = 2x - 7 \\ y = -(x - 6)^2 \end{cases}$

C) $\begin{cases} y = \dfrac{1}{2}x + 3 \\ y = -(x - 5)^2 + 7 \end{cases}$

D) $\begin{cases} y = \dfrac{1}{2}x + 7 \\ y = -(x - 6)^2 + 3.5 \end{cases}$

17. What is the positive difference between the roots of the equation $y = \dfrac{1}{3}x^2 - 2x + 3$?

Questions 18-20 refer to the following information.

The following graph shows the paths of two bottle rockets that were fired straight up at the same time. The functions $h_1(t)$ and $h_2(t)$ represent the heights in feet of the rockets t seconds after they were fired off.

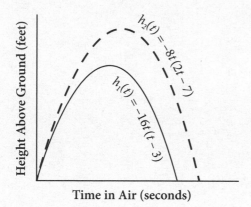

19. How many seconds longer did it take the second rocket to reach its maximum height than the first rocket?

20. When the functions are written in the form $h(t) = -16t^2 + v_0 t + h_0$, the variable quantities v_0 and h_0 represent the initial velocity in feet per second of the rocket and the initial height in feet of the rocket, respectively. How much greater was the initial velocity in feet per second of the second rocket than the first?

18. After 1 second in the air, how many feet higher was the second bottle rocket than the first?

Additional Topics in Math

BY THE END OF THIS UNIT, YOU WILL BE ABLE TO:

1. Solve geometry questions involving lines, angles, triangles, and other complex shapes

2. Use special right triangles and Pythagorean triplets to save time on Test Day

3. Solve for unknown parts of circles

4. Interpret 3-D figures and solve problems using formulas for volume

5. Solve problems involving imaginary and complex numbers

6. Interpret basic trigonometric functions and use them to solve problems involving right triangles

Geometry

CHAPTER OBJECTIVES

By the end of this chapter, you will be able to:

1. Apply the properties of lines and angles to solve geometry questions

2. Use the Pythagorean theorem, Pythagorean triplets, and special right triangles to answer questions involving triangles

3. Use concepts and theorems about congruence and similarity to solve problems about lines, angles, and triangles

4. Identify simple shapes within complex figures and use them to solve questions

5. Apply theorems about circles to find arc lengths, angle measures, chord lengths, and areas of sectors

6. Create or use an equation with two variables to solve a problem about a circle in the coordinate plane

7. Solve problems using volume formulas

SMARTPOINTS

Point Value	SmartPoint Category
40 Points	Geometry

Math

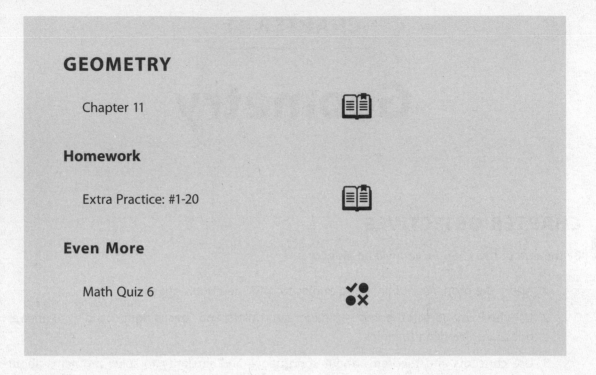

GEOMETRY

Chapter 11

Homework

Extra Practice: #1-20

Even More

Math Quiz 6

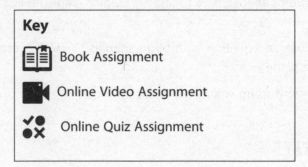

Key

Book Assignment

Online Video Assignment

Online Quiz Assignment

LINES AND ANGLES

Lines and angles are the foundation of SAT geometry. Therefore, mastering their basic rules will make solving these questions, as well as related geometry questions, easier. With the knowledge you'll gain from this chapter, you can quickly identify geometric relationships, build upon the information given in the question, and often bypass complex algebra.

Familiarity with angle types will often unlock information that is not explicitly given in a question. This makes getting to the answer much easier for even the toughest geometry questions. First, let's take a look at the types of angles you should be able to recognize.

Angle Type	Angle Measurement	Example
Acute	Less than 90°	
Right	90°	
Obtuse	Between 90° and 180°	
Straight	180°	

More often than not, you'll work with multiple angles in a single question. Therefore, it's worth noting two likely familiar terms that involve working with two or more angles: complementary and supplementary angles. Two angles are **complementary** if their measures add up to 90°; if their measures add up to 180°, the angles are **supplementary**.

 Note

Two angles need *not* be adjacent to be complementary or supplementary.

Intersecting lines create angles with special relationships you'll need to know as well. When two lines intersect, adjacent angles are supplementary, and **vertical** angles (two angles opposite a vertex) are equal, or **congruent**. Take a look at the following figure for an example.

The angles marked $a°$ and $b°$ are supplementary; therefore, $a + b = 180$. The angle marked $a°$ is vertical (and thus equal) to the one marked 60°, so $a = 60$. With this new information, you can find b: $a + b = 60 + b = 180$, so $b = 120$.

> ✔ **Note**
>
> Unless otherwise noted, figures on the SAT are drawn to scale. Be especially careful when you see "<u>Note:</u> Figure not drawn to scale."

When two parallel lines are intersected by another line (called a **transversal**), all acute angles are equal, and all obtuse angles are equal. Additionally, **corresponding angles** are angles that are in the same position but on different parallel lines/transversal intersections; they are also equal. Furthermore, **alternate interior angles** and **alternate exterior angles** are equal. Alternate interior angles are angles that are positioned between the two parallel lines on opposite sides of the transversal, whereas alternate exterior angles are positioned on the outside of the parallel lines on opposite sides of the transversal. Consider the following figure:

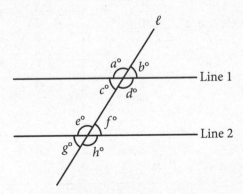

- Line 1 and Line 2 are parallel and cut by transversal ℓ.

- Angles a, d, e, and h are obtuse and equal.

- Angles b, c, f, and g are acute and equal.

- Angle pairs (b and f), (c and g), (a and e), and (d and h) are corresponding angles.

- Angle pairs (a and h) and (b and g) are alternate exterior angles.

- Angle pairs (d and e) and (c and f) are alternate interior angles.

Below is a summary of the essential theorems related to parallel lines that you'll need to know. Notice that the converse of most of these theorems is also true.

Angle Theorem	Definition
Alternate Interior Angles	• If two parallel lines are cut by a transversal, the alternate interior angles are congruent. • If two lines are cut by a transversal and the alternate interior angles are congruent, the lines are parallel.
Alternate Exterior Angles	• If two parallel lines are cut by a transversal, the alternate exterior angles are congruent. • If two lines are cut by a transversal and the alternate exterior angles are congruent, the lines are parallel.
Corresponding Angles	• If two parallel lines are cut by a transversal, the corresponding angles are congruent. • If two lines are cut by a transversal and the corresponding angles are congruent, the lines are parallel.
Vertical Angles	• If two parallel lines are cut by a transversal, the vertical angles are congruent.

✔ **Note**

Parallel lines cut by a transversal are powerful: Even if you know only one angle measure, you can get the other seven in mere seconds by knowing these rules.

TRIANGLES

Lines and angles form the basis of triangles—some of the most commonly occurring shapes on the SAT. Luckily, triangle questions usually don't involve a lot of complex algebra and are a great way to earn a few quick points on Test Day. Having a good command of triangle properties will help you recognize and solve these questions quickly. Many seemingly difficult questions will become easier once you can confidently speak the language of triangles.

All triangles follow the rules listed here, regardless of the type of triangle, so take the time now to get comfortable with these rules.

Triangle Theorem	Definition
Triangle Sum and Exterior Angle Theorems	• Interior angles add up to 180°. • An exterior angle equals the sum of the two opposite interior angles.
Isosceles Triangle Theorems	• If two sides of a triangle are congruent, the angles opposite them are congruent. • If two angles of a triangle are congruent, the sides opposite them are congruent.
Triangle Inequality Theorem	• The sum of the lengths of any two sides of a triangle must be greater than the length of the third side. • The difference of the lengths of any two sides of a triangle must be less than the length of the third side.
Side-Angle Relationship	• In a triangle, the longest side is across from the largest angle. • In a triangle, the largest angle is across from the longest side.
Mid-Segment Theorem	• A triangle mid-segment (or midline) is parallel to one side of the triangle and joins the midpoints of the other two sides. • The mid-segment's length is half the length of the side to which it is parallel.

The corresponding angles and side lengths of **congruent triangles** are equal. **Similar triangles** have the same angle measurements and proportional sides. In the figure below, $\triangle ABC$ and $\triangle DEF$ have the same angle measurements, so the side lengths can be set up as the following proportion:

$$\frac{A}{D} = \frac{B}{E} = \frac{C}{F}.$$

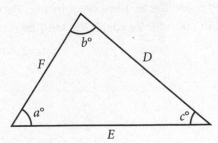

Drawing multiple heights in one triangle creates similar triangles, as shown in the diagram below. When you encounter a question like this, redrawing the similar triangles with their angles and sides in the same positions will help keep information in order.

COMPLEX FIGURES

Complex figures are also a recurring SAT geometry topic, particularly ones that involve triangles. A complex figure is not a shape such as a dodecahedron. Instead, a complex figure is usually a larger shape that is composed of multiple (familiar) shapes; these can be obvious or cleverly hidden. These figures can always be broken down into squares, rectangles, triangles, and/or circles. Although this chapter emphasizes triangles, you'll get plenty of practice with other figures over the next few questions. No matter how convoluted the figure, following the guidelines here will lead you to the correct answer on Test Day.

- Transfer information from the question stem to the figure. If a figure isn't provided, draw one!

- Break the figure into familiar shapes.

- Determine how one line segment can play multiple roles in a figure. For example, if a circle and triangle overlap correctly, the circle's radius might be the triangle's hypotenuse.

- Work from the shape with the most information to the shape with the least information.

Now use your knowledge of lines, angles, triangles, and complex figures to answer a couple of test-like questions.

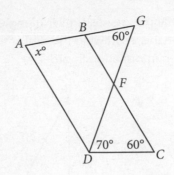

1. In the figure above, $\overline{AD}$ and $\overline{BC}$ are parallel. What is the value of x?

A) 60

B) 70

C) 80

D) 110

Work through the Kaplan Method for Math step-by-step to solve this question. The following table shows Kaplan's strategic thinking on the left, along with suggested math scratchwork on the right.

Strategic Thinking	Math Scratchwork
Step 1: Read the question, identifying and organizing important information as you go You're asked for the value of x.	
Step 2: Choose the best strategy to answer the question Look for familiar shapes within the given figure. There are three triangles present. Because $\overline{AD}$ and $\overline{BC}$ are parallel, $BFDA$ is a trapezoid. Although x might seem far removed from the known angles, you can find it. It will just take more than one step. In $\triangle FDC$, only one angle is missing, so you can solve for it and fill it in easily. Note that $\angle DFC$ and $\angle BFG$ are vertical angles, so $m\angle BFG$ is also 50°. At this point, you have two of the three angles in $\triangle BFG$, so you can solve for the third. $\angle FBG$ and $\angle BAD$ are corresponding angles (and are therefore congruent). You can now conclude that $x = 70$.	$m\angle DFC = 180° - 70° - 60° = 50°$ $m\angle BFG = m\angle DFC = 50°$ $m\angle FBG = 180° - 50° - 60° = 70°$ $m\angle BAD = x = m\angle FBG = 70°$
Step 3: Check that you answered the *right* question You're asked for x, so select (B), and you're done.	$x = 70$

Let's try another test-like question. Refer back to the properties and theorems as needed.

2. In the figure above, $\overline{ST}$ is a mid-segment of $\triangle PQR$. If $ST = 4x + 9$ and $PR = 16x + 6$, what is the length of $\overline{PR}$?

A) 0.25

B) 1.5

C) 15

D) 30

Work through the Kaplan Method for Math step-by-step to solve this question. The following table shows Kaplan's strategic thinking on the left, along with suggested math scratchwork on the right.

Strategic Thinking	Math Scratchwork
Step 1: Read the question, identifying and organizing important information as you go You must find the length of $\overline{PR}$.	
Step 2: Choose the best strategy to answer the question A triangle's mid-segment has a length that is half that of the side to which it is parallel. In other words, $ST = \frac{1}{2}PR$. You're given an expression for each segment, so plug in the expressions and solve for x.	$ST = \frac{1}{2}PR$ $4x + 9 = \frac{1}{2}(16x + 6)$ $-4x = -6$ $x = \frac{3}{2}$
The question asks for the length of $\overline{PR}$. Substitute the value you got for x back into the expression for PR and simplify.	$16 \times \frac{3}{2} + 6 = 30$
Step 3: Check that you answered the *right* question The correct choice is (D).	

Prepare

THE PYTHAGOREAN THEOREM, PYTHAGOREAN TRIPLETS, & SPECIAL RIGHT TRIANGLES

The Pythagorean theorem is one of the most fundamental equations in geometry, and it will be of great use to you on the SAT. Common Pythagorean triplets and special right triangle ratios that originate from this formula will also serve you well on Test Day.

The **Pythagorean theorem** is an important triangle topic that you are probably familiar with already. If you know the lengths of any two sides of a right triangle, you can use the Pythagorean theorem equation to find the missing side. The equation is expressed as $a^2 + b^2 = c^2$, where a and b are the shorter sides of the triangle (called legs) and c is the hypotenuse, which is always across from the right angle of the triangle.

✔ **Note**

The Pythagorean theorem can only be applied to right triangles.

Consider an example: A right triangle has a leg of length 9 and a hypotenuse of length 14. To find the missing leg, plug the known values into the Pythagorean theorem: $9^2 + b^2 = 14^2$. This simplifies to $81 + b^2 = 196$, which becomes $b^2 = 115$. Take the square root of both sides to get $b = \sqrt{115}$. Because no factors of 115 are perfect squares, $b = \sqrt{115}$ is the answer.

✔ **Note**

Wait to simplify radicals until you have your final answer. Leave answers in radical form unless a question says otherwise or the answer choices are written as decimals.

Because time is at such a premium on the SAT, time-saving strategies are invaluable, and there are two that will come in handy on triangle questions. The first is knowing common **Pythagorean triplets**, which are right triangles that happen to have integer sides. These triangles show up *very* frequently on the SAT. The two most common are 3-4-5 and 5-12-13. Multiples of these (e.g., 6-8-10 and 10-24-26) can also pop up, so watch out for them as well. The beauty of these triplets is that if you see any two sides, you can automatically fill in the third without having to resort to the time-consuming Pythagorean theorem.

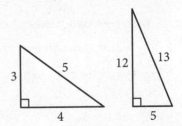

The second time-saving strategy involves recognizing **special right triangles**. Like Pythagorean triplets, special right triangles involve a ratio comparing the lengths of a right triangle's legs and hypotenuse, but with these triangles, you only need to know the length of one side in order to calculate the other two. These triangles are defined by their angles.

The ratio of the sides of a **45-45-90** triangle is $x : x : x\sqrt{2}$, where x is the length of each leg and $x\sqrt{2}$ is the length of the hypotenuse.

The ratio of the sides of a **30-60-90** triangle is $x : x\sqrt{3} : 2x$, where x is the shorter leg, $x\sqrt{3}$ is the longer leg, and $2x$ is the hypotenuse.

While the Pythagorean theorem can always be used to solve right triangle questions, it is not always the most efficient way to proceed. Further, many students make errors when simplifying radicals and exponents. The Pythagorean triplets and special right triangles allow you to save time and avoid those mistakes. Use them whenever possible!

> ✔ **Note**
>
> Although you will be given the special right triangle ratios on Test Day, you can save yourself some time by memorizing them. That way you won't have to keeping flipping back to the formula page! You should also commit Pythagorean triplets to memory to bypass the Pythagorean theorem on Test Day.

AREA OF A TRIANGLE

On Test Day, you might also be asked to find the area of a triangle or use the area of a triangle to find something else. The area of a triangle can be determined using $A = \frac{1}{2}bh$, where b is the triangle base and h is the triangle height.

When you have a right triangle, you can use the legs as the base and the height. If the triangle isn't a right triangle, you'll need to draw the height in, as demonstrated in the figure shown. Remember that the height *must* be perpendicular to the base.

A final note about triangles: You are likely to see triangle questions involving real-world situations. But don't fret: All you need to do is follow the Kaplan Strategy for Translating English into Math. Extract the geometry information you need, then solve.

Take a look at the next example for another test-like triangle question.

3. When Ted earned his driver's license, he wanted his first solo drive to be to a friend's house. Previously, Ted had always biked to his friend's house and was able to cut through the yards of neighbors and a park in order to bike there in a straight line. In his car, however, Ted had no choice but to follow the streets. As a result, he traveled 6 miles east, 6 miles south, and 2 more miles east. How much shorter, in miles, is Ted's bike route than his car route?

Work through the Kaplan Method for Math step-by-step to solve this question. The following table shows Kaplan's strategic thinking on the left, along with suggested math scratchwork on the right.

Strategic Thinking	Math Scratchwork
Step 1: Read the question, identifying and organizing important information as you go You're given the lengths of various sections of streets. If only there were some way to arrange this information visually.	
Step 2: Choose the best strategy to answer the question To translate this question into a geometry problem, draw a figure. Sketch the streets, label the distances, and add a direct line between the start and destination. Based on the diagram, Ted's car route is $6 + 6 + 2 = 14$ miles. Two triangles are now visible, but you'll notice the current information is insufficient because you don't know exactly where the dashed line intersects the vertical line.	
Drawing in extra lines reveals a third triangle, and you already know its dimensions. The new triangle has legs measuring 6 miles and 8 miles. Do you see the Pythagorean triplet? It's a 6-8-10 triangle, meaning Ted's bike route (the hypotenuse) is 10 miles.	 Car: 14 mi Bike: 10 mi
Step 3: Check that you answered the *right* question The difference is $14 - 10 = 4$ miles. Grid in 4, and you're done!	

TRIANGLE CONGRUENCE THEOREMS

Many students ask why they need to learn how to do proofs when they take geometry. Although you will likely not need them in college (unless you're a math or computer science major), there is a fundamental skill that comes with constructing proofs: the ability to construct an argument effectively for a statement or position. This skill is critical in numerous situations and fields—for criminal cases in law, research proposals in science, treatment plans in medicine, and others—so it's a powerful tool to have in your skill set.

That being said, there's no question that proofs can be unnerving. The good news: You will *not* need to construct a complete proof on the SAT. The language of certain questions might still be slightly intimidating, but it will be far more manageable than a full-blown proof.

There are several theorems that can be used to prove two triangles are congruent; these are summarized in the following table. Make sure you are comfortable with all of them—you may need to determine that two triangles are congruent in order to find a side length or an angle measure in one or both of the triangles.

Triangle Congruence Theorem	Notation	Diagram
If three sides of one triangle are congruent to the corresponding sides of another triangle, then the two triangles are congruent.	SSS (side-side-side)	
If two sides and the included angle of one triangle are congruent to the corresponding parts of another triangle, then the two triangles are congruent.	SAS (side-angle-side)	
If two angles and the non-included side of one triangle are congruent to the corresponding parts of another triangle, then the two triangles are congruent.	AAS (angle-angle-side)	
If two angles and the included side of one triangle are congruent to the corresponding parts of another triangle, then the two triangles are congruent.	ASA (angle-side-angle)	
If the hypotenuse and leg of one right triangle are congruent to the corresponding parts of another right triangle, then the two triangles are congruent.	HL (hypotenuse-leg)	
An angle or line segment is congruent to itself.	Reflexive Property	
Corresponding parts of congruent triangles are congruent.	CPCTC	

> **✔ Note**
>
> There are two bogus congruence "theorems" to watch out for: AAA and SSA. Two triangles with identical angles are always similar, but they aren't necessarily congruent. If you have two triangles with two adjacent congruent sides and a congruent angle outside them, the third side can be two different lengths. SSA is valid only with right triangles, in which case you call it HL. Never use AAA.

QUADRILATERAL THEOREMS

Quadrilaterals are four-sided figures, with interior angles that add up to 360°. You will likely not see a question solely about quadrilaterals; if a quadrilateral appears at all, it will likely contain hidden triangles. However, the properties of the quadrilateral will allow you to deduce information about the triangles present, so make sure you know the basic properties of the most common quadrilaterals.

Given the high likelihood of a Test Day geometry problem containing hidden triangles, you should familiarize yourself with the types of quadrilaterals that are most likely to have useful triangles within.

Parallelogram Theorems	Properties
Parallelogram	• Both pairs of sides are parallel. • Both pairs of sides are congruent. • Both pairs of opposite angles are congruent. • An angle is supplementary to both angles adjacent to it. • The diagonals bisect each other.
Rhombus	• It has all the properties of a parallelogram. • All four sides are congruent. • Diagonals bisect angles and are perpendicular.
Rectangle	• It has all the properties of a parallelogram. • All angles are right angles. • Diagonals are congruent.
Square	• It has all the properties of a parallelogram, rhombus, and rectangle. • All sides are congruent.

A word of caution: Do not make any assumptions about a test figure that go beyond the information provided in the question. It's tempting to assume a quadrilateral is a rectangle or other more "friendly" shape, but unless this is proven or stated in the question (or indicated in the figure), don't do it!

Math

INTRODUCTION TO CIRCLES

You already know the SAT can ask a variety of questions about lines, angles, and triangles; it can also test you on your knowledge of circles. Keep reading for a refresher on these ubiquitous shapes.

Circle Anatomy & Basic Formulas

There are a number of circle traits you should know for Test Day. The good news: Most will already be familiar to you if you've taken geometry.

- **Radius (*r*):** The distance from the center of a circle to its edge
- **Chord:** A line segment that connects two points on a circle
- **Diameter (*d*):** A chord that passes through the center of a circle. The diameter is always the longest chord a circle can have and is twice the length of the radius.
- **Circumference (*C*):** The distance around a circle; the equivalent of a polygon's perimeter. Find this using the formula $C = 2\pi r = \pi d$.
- **Area:** The space a circle takes up, just like a polygon. A circle's area is found by computing $A = \pi r^2$.
- Every circle contains 360°. You'll find out more about this fact's utility shortly.

As the formulas demonstrate, the radius is often the key to unlocking several other components of a circle. Therefore, your first step for many circle questions will be to find the radius.

Circles on the Coordinate Plane and Their Equations

When you have a circle on the coordinate plane, you can describe it with an equation. The equation of a circle in **standard form** is as follows:

$$(x - h)^2 + (y - k)^2 = r^2$$

In this equation, *r* is the radius of the circle, and *h* and *k* are the *x*- and *y*-coordinates of the circle's center, respectively: (*h*, *k*).

> ✔ **Note**
>
> A circle is one of the four conic sections, which are made by slicing a double cone with a plane. The parabola is another conic section that you read about in chapter 10. The ellipse and hyperbola (with standard forms $\frac{(x-h)^2}{a^2} + \frac{(y-k)^2}{b^2} = 1$ and $\frac{(x-h)^2}{a^2} - \frac{(y-k)^2}{b^2} = 1$, respectively) will not be tested on the SAT. Watch out for them in trap answer choices, however!

You might also see what is referred to as **general form**:

$$x^2 + y^2 + Cx + Dy + E = 0$$

At first glance, this probably doesn't resemble the equation of a circle, but the fact that you have an x^2 term and a y^2 term with coefficients of 1 is your indicator that the equation does indeed graph as a circle. To convert to standard form, complete the square for the x terms, then repeat for the y terms. Refer to chapter 10 for a review of completing the square.

> ✔ **Note**
>
> The x^2 and y^2 terms in the equation of a circle occasionally have coefficients other than 1 (but the coefficients must be equal). If this is the case, simply divide all terms in the equation by the coefficient to eliminate them.

Ready to try a circle question?

$$x^2 + 6x + y^2 - 8y = 171$$

4. The equation of a circle in the xy-plane is shown above. What is the positive difference between the x- and y-coordinates of the center of the circle?

Work through the Kaplan Method for Math step-by-step to solve this question. The following table shows Kaplan's strategic thinking on the left, along with suggested math scratchwork on the right.

Strategic Thinking	Math Scratchwork
Step 1: Read the question, identifying and organizing important information as you go You need to determine the positive difference between the x- and y-coordinates of the center of the circle.	
Step 2: Choose the best strategy to answer the question You'll need to rewrite the equation in standard form to find what you need. The coefficients of the x and y terms are even, so consider completing the square for x and y. Divide b (from the x term) by 2 and square the result. Repeat for y. Then add the resulting amounts to both sides of the equation. Factor to write the equation in standard form. The center of the circle is $(-3, 4)$; subtract -3 from 4 to get the positive difference.	$(x - h)^2 + (y - k)^2 = r^2$ $x^2 + 6x + y^2 - 8y = 171$ x term: $\dfrac{b}{2} = \dfrac{6}{2} = 3 \rightarrow 9$ y term: $\dfrac{b}{2} = \dfrac{-8}{2} = -4 \rightarrow 16$ $x^2 + 6x + 9 + y^2 - 8y + 16 = 171 + 9 + 16$ $(x + 3)^2 + (y - 4)^2 = 196$ center: $(-3, 4)$
Step 3: Check that you answered the _right_ question The positive difference between the two coordinates is 7.	$4 - (-3) = 7$

Circle Ratios: Arcs, Central Angles, & Sectors

The SAT can ask you about parts of circles as well. There are three partial components that can be made in a circle: arcs, central angles, and sectors. These circle pieces are frequently used in proportions with their whole counterparts, so the ability to set up ratios and proportions correctly is of utmost importance for these questions.

- An **arc** is part of a circle's circumference. Both chords and radii can cut a circle into arcs. The number of arcs present depends on how many chords and/or radii are present. If only two arcs are present, the smaller arc is called the **minor arc**, and the larger one is the **major arc**. If a diameter cuts the circle in half, the two formed arcs are called **semicircles**. An arc length can never be greater than the circle's circumference.

- When radii cut a circle into multiple (but not necessarily equal) pieces, the angle at the center of the circle contained by the radii is the **central angle**. Because a full circle contains 360°, a central angle measure cannot be greater than this.

- Radii splitting a circle into pieces can also create **sectors**, which are parts of the circle's area. The area of a sector cannot be greater than its circle's total area.

Here's a summary of the ratios formed by these three parts and their whole counterparts.

$$\frac{\text{arc length}}{\text{circumference}} = \frac{\text{central angle}}{360°} = \frac{\text{sector area}}{\text{circle area}}$$

Notice that all of these ratios are equal. Intuitively, this should make sense: When you slice a pizza into four equal slices, each piece should have $\frac{1}{4}$ of the cheese, sauce, crust, and toppings. If you slice a circle into four equal pieces, the same principle applies: Each piece should have $\frac{1}{4}$ of the degrees, circumference, and area.

Inscribed Angle Theorem

An angle whose vertex is on the edge of the circle is called an **inscribed angle**. As this vertex moves along the edge, the measure of the inscribed angle remains constant as long as the minor arc created (in other words, isolated or **subtended** by the chords) does not change. When the chords that create an inscribed angle subtend the same minor arc that a pair of radii do, a special relationship appears: The central angle measure is twice that of the inscribed angle.

x remains constant

Arcs Formed Between Parallel Chords

Another theorem states that two parallel chords will intercept two congruent arcs; see the following diagram for an example. The congruent arcs will be between the chords.

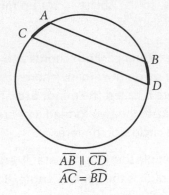

$$\overline{AB} \parallel \overline{CD}$$
$$\overset{\frown}{AC} = \overset{\frown}{BD}$$

Tangent Lines

A **tangent line** touches a circle at exactly one point and is perpendicular to a circle's radius at the point of contact. The following diagram demonstrates what this looks like.

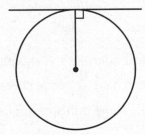

The presence of a right angle opens up the opportunity to draw otherwise hidden shapes, so pay special attention to tangents when they're mentioned. They often come up in complex figure questions.

The next question will give you a chance to see how these properties of circles can be tested on the SAT.

5. An orange with a diameter of 2 inches is sitting on a counter. If the distance from the center of the orange to the edge of the counter is 10 inches, how many inches is it between the point where the orange sits on the counter to the counter edge?

    A) $4\sqrt{6}$

    B) $3\sqrt{11}$

    C) 10

    D) $\sqrt{101}$

Work through the Kaplan Method for Math step-by-step to solve this question. The following table shows Kaplan's strategic thinking on the left, along with suggested math scratchwork on the right.

Strategic Thinking	Math Scratchwork
Step 1: Read the question, identifying and organizing important information as you go You must calculate the distance between where the orange sits and the edge of the counter.	
Step 2: Choose the best strategy to answer the question Draw a cross section of the orange on the counter; you'll see this is a circle with a tangent line. Draw in a perpendicular radius and a line from the center of the orange to the edge of the counter to reveal a right triangle. Use the Pythagorean theorem to calculate the distance requested.	$1^2 + x^2 = 10^2$ $x^2 = 99$ $x = \sqrt{99}$
Step 3: Check that you answered the *right* question Simplify the radical; (B) is correct.	$\sqrt{99} = \sqrt{9 \times 11} = 3\sqrt{11}$

INTRODUCTION TO 3-D SHAPES

Over the last several pages, you learned about two-dimensional (2-D) shapes and how to tackle SAT questions involving them. Now you'll learn how to do the same for questions containing three-dimensional (3-D) shapes, also called solids. There are several different types of solids that might appear on Test Day—rectangular solids, cubes, cylinders, prisms, spheres, cones, pyramids—so it is critical that you be familiar with them. The following is a diagram showing the basic anatomy of a 3-D shape.

A **face** (or **surface**) is a 2-D shape that acts as one of the sides of the solid. Two faces meet at a line segment called an **edge**, and three faces meet at a single point called a **vertex**.

Keep reading for more on types of 3-D shapes and questions you could be asked about them.

Volume

Volume is the amount of 3-D space occupied by a solid. This is analogous to the area of a 2-D shape like a triangle or circle. You can find the volume of many 3-D shapes by finding the area of the base and multiplying it by the height. We've highlighted the base area components of the formulas in the following table using parentheses.

Rectangular Solid	Cube	Right Cylinder
$(l \times w) \times h$	$(s \times s) \times s = s^3$	$(\pi \times r^2) \times h$

> ✔ **Note**
>
> Recall that a square is a special type of rectangle that has four equal sides. Likewise, a cube is a special type of rectangular solid whose edges (and faces) are all equal.

These three 3-D shapes are prisms. Almost all prisms on the SAT are right prisms; that is, all faces are perpendicular to those with which they share edges.

Following are some examples of less commonly seen prisms.

Triangular Prism	Hexagonal Prism	Decagonal Prism

Like the rectangular solids, cubes, and cylinders you saw earlier, these right prisms use the same general volume formula ($V = A_{\text{base}} \times h$).

> ✔ **Note**
>
> You might not be told explicitly the area of the base of a prism, in which case you'll need to rely on your two-dimensional geometry expertise to find it before calculating the volume.

More complicated 3-D shapes include the right pyramid, right cone, and sphere. The vertex of a right pyramid or right cone will always be centered above the middle of the base. Their volume formulas are similar to those of prisms, albeit with different coefficients.

> ✔ **Note**
>
> Some of these formulas might look daunting, but don't fret—you won't have to memorize them for Test Day. They'll be provided on the reference page at the beginning of each math section.

Right (Square) Pyramid	Right Cone	Sphere
$\frac{1}{3} \times (l \times w) \times h$	$\frac{1}{3} \times (\pi \times r^2) \times h$	$\frac{4}{3} \times \pi \times r^3$

> ✔ **Note**
>
> A right pyramid can have any regular polygon as its base; the square variety is the one you're most likely to see. Also note that the vertex above the base of a right pyramid or cone is not necessarily formed by an intersection of exactly three faces, as in prisms, but it is still a single point and is still called a vertex.

Surface Area

Surface area is the sum of the areas of all faces of a solid. You might liken this to determining the amount of wrapping paper needed to cover all faces of a solid.

To calculate the surface area of a solid, simply find the area of each face using your 2-D geometry skills, then add them all together.

> ✔ **Note**
>
> You won't be expected to know the surface area formulas for right pyramids, right cones, and spheres; they'll be provided if you need them. However, you could be asked to find the surface area of a prism, in which case you'll be given enough information to find the area of each surface of the solid.

You might think that finding the surface area of a solid with many sides, such as a 10-sided right octagonal prism, is a tall order. However, you can save time by noticing a vital trait: This prism has two identical octagonal faces and eight identical rectangular faces. Don't waste time finding the area of each of the 10 sides; find the area of one octagonal face and one rectangular face instead. Once complete, multiply the area of the octagonal face by 2 and the area of the rectangular face by 8, add the products together, and you're done! The same is true for other 3-D shapes such as rectangular solids (including cubes), other right prisms, and certain pyramids.

If you're ready to test your knowledge of 3-D shapes, check out the next question.

6. Desiree is making apple juice from concentrate. The cylindrical container of concentrate has a diameter of 7 centimeters and a height of 12 centimeters. To make the juice, the concentrate must be diluted with water so that the mix is 75% water and 25% concentrate. If Desiree wishes to store all of the prepared juice in one cylindrical pitcher that has a diameter of 10 centimeters, what must its minimum height in centimeters be (rounded to the nearest centimeter)?

Work through the Kaplan Method for Math step-by-step to solve this question. The following table shows Kaplan's strategic thinking on the left, along with suggested math scratchwork on the right.

Strategic Thinking	Math Scratchwork
Step 1: Read the question, identifying and organizing important information as you go You need to find the minimum height of a pitcher with a diameter of 10 centimeters that can hold the entire amount of juice after it has been properly mixed.	
Step 2: Choose the best strategy to answer the question Before finding the height of the pitcher, you'll need to determine the volume of the juice after it has been mixed with the water. Determine the volume of concentrate Desiree has, then multiply this amount by 4 (because the concentrate only makes up 25% of the new juice volume) to calculate the post-dilution volume. Use the volume formula again to find the minimum height of the juice pitcher.	$d_{conc} = 7 \rightarrow r_{conc} = 3.5$ $V_{conc} = \pi r^2 h$ $\quad = \pi \times 3.5^2 \times 12$ $\quad = 147\pi$ $V_{dil} = 4 \times 147\pi = 588\pi$ $d_{pitcher} = 10 \rightarrow r_{pitcher} = 5$ $588\pi = \pi \times 5^2 \times h$ $h = \dfrac{588\pi}{25\pi} \approx 23.52$
Step 3: Check that you answered the *right* question Round to the nearest centimeter, and you're done!	24

> ✔ **Note**
>
> Double-check your rounding on questions like this: Make sure you've rounded to the correct place *and* done so correctly.

Now you'll have a chance to try a few more test-like geometry problems in a scaffolded way. We've provided some guidance, but you'll need to fill in the missing parts of explanations or the step-by-step math in order to get to the correct answer. Don't worry—after going through the worked examples at the beginning of this section, these problems should be completely doable.

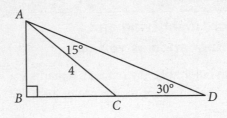

7. Given $\triangle ABC$ and $\triangle ABD$ above, what is the perimeter of $\triangle ACD$?

    A) $2\sqrt{6} - 2\sqrt{2}$

    B) $4\sqrt{3}$

    C) $4 + 2\sqrt{6} + 2\sqrt{2}$

    D) $2\sqrt{6} + 6\sqrt{2}$

Use the following scaffolding as your map through the question. Fill in the blanks in the table as you work from top to bottom.

Strategic Thinking	Math Scratchwork
Step 1: Read the question, identifying and organizing important information as you go You need to find the perimeter of $\triangle ACD$.	
Step 2: Choose the best strategy to answer the question Look for unknown values that you can derive from the information in the question stem. For instance, you can find the measure of $\angle ACD$ from the two given angles. From there you can easily determine the measures of the angles in $\triangle ABC$. Fill in the blanks on the right as you go. Notice that both $\triangle ABC$ and $\triangle ABD$ have special characteristics. Use these to determine the length of each missing side. Once again, update the figure on the right as you work. $\overline{BD}$ is the sum of $\overline{BC}$ and $\overline{CD}$. Subtract $\overline{BC}$ from $\overline{BD}$ to find $\overline{CD}$. Once you find all three sides of $\triangle ACD$, add them together to find its perimeter.	$m\angle ACD = \underline{\quad}^\circ - \underline{\quad}^\circ - \underline{\quad}^\circ$ $\qquad = \underline{\quad}^\circ$ ABC: $\underline{\quad} - \underline{\quad} - \underline{\quad}$ ABD: $\underline{\quad} - \underline{\quad} - \underline{\quad}$ $\overline{CD} = \underline{\quad} - \underline{\quad} = \underline{\quad}$ $P_{ACD} = \underline{\quad} + (\underline{\quad}) + \underline{\quad}$ $\qquad = \underline{\quad}$
Step 3: Check that you answered the *right* question If you got (C), you are correct!	_____

8. The diagram above shows a 40-foot flagpole and its shadow in relation to a nearby building that is 324 feet tall. If the flagpole's shadow is 50% longer than the flagpole itself, how far is the building from the flagpole?

The following table can help you structure your thinking as you go about solving this problem. Kaplan's strategic thinking is provided, as are bits of structured scratchwork. If you're not sure how to approach a question like this, start at the top and work your way down.

Strategic Thinking	Math Scratchwork
Step 1: Read the question, identifying and organizing important information as you go You're asked to find the distance between the building and the flagpole.	
Step 2: Choose the best strategy to answer the question You have a pair of similar triangles. Once you find the length of the flagpole's shadow using the percentage given, you can use a proportion to find the distance between the building and the flagpole. There are a couple of different ways you can write your proportion. Follow the rules for assembling a proportion (see chapter 5 for a refresher), and you'll be in good shape. Don't forget to subtract the length of the shadow from the horizontal leg of the large triangle after solving the proportion!	flagpole shadow: _____ × _____ = _____ _____ = _____ _____ = _____ _____ = _____ _____ − _____ = _____
Step 3: Check that you answered the *right* question If you got 426 feet, congrats! You're correct.	_____

Note: Figure not drawn to scale.

9. In circle P above, RS = 4 and ∠RQS measures 45°. What is the circumference of circle P?

A) 4π

B) 4π√2

C) 8π

D) 8π√2

Use the scaffolding that follows as your map through the question. Fill in the blanks in the table as you work from top to bottom.

Strategic Thinking	Math Scratchwork
Step 1: Read the question, identifying and organizing important information as you go You need to find the circumference of circle P.	
Step 2: Choose the best strategy to answer the question Pay attention to the note below the figure. The shapes are not drawn to scale, and although it looks like it, all the angles in the triangle are not 45° (they can't be because the sum wouldn't be 180°). You'll need to draw in a couple of additional lines to reveal a more useful triangle. Once done, use your knowledge of subtended arcs to determine a special property of your new triangle. The legs of your new triangle are radii of the circle, so they are congruent. Use this and the fact that RS = 4 to determine the radius and then the circumference of the circle.	[figure of circle with inscribed triangle QRS, point P, 45° angle at Q, RS = 4] △ _____ is a _____ - _____ - _____ triangle
Step 3: Check that you answered the *right* question Did you get (B)? If so, you're absolutely right!	_____

10. Brian wants to inflate several beach balls for a pool party. Each ball has a diameter of 66 centimeters, and Brian can exhale 6 liters (L) of air per full breath into a ball. Given that 1 L = 1,000 cm³, approximately how many full breaths will Brian use to fully inflate three of these beach balls?

A)   25

B)   75

C)   151

D)   201

Work through the Kaplan Method for Math step-by-step to solve this question. The following table shows Kaplan's strategic thinking on the left, along with suggested math scratchwork on the right.

Strategic Thinking	Math Scratchwork
Step 1: Read the question, identifying and organizing important information as you go You must find the number of full breaths Brian will need to inflate three beach balls. You're given some useful facts and an equation. Also note the word "approximately"; you'll eventually need to round π.	
Step 2: Choose the best strategy to answer the question Start by finding the volume of one beach ball. Take care to find the radius and avoid the trap of using the diameter in your calculations. Use the given relationship, 1 L = 1,000 cm³ = 6 full breaths, to convert to the desired units. Be careful; you're asked for the number of breaths for three beach balls, not one. Triple the number of breaths from the last calculation.	$V_{sphere} = \underline{\hspace{1cm}}$ $d = \underline{\hspace{1cm}} \rightarrow r = \underline{\hspace{1cm}}$ $V = \underline{\hspace{1cm}} \times (\ \ )^3 = \underline{\hspace{1cm}}$ cm³ $\underline{\hspace{1cm}}$ cm³ $\times \dfrac{1\,L}{1,000\ cm^3} \times \dfrac{1\,breath}{\underline{\hspace{0.5cm}}\ L}$ $= \underline{\hspace{1cm}}$ breaths $\underline{\hspace{1cm}} \times 3 = \underline{\hspace{1cm}}$ breaths
Step 3: Check that you answered the *right* question Did you get (B)? If so, you're absolutely right.	$\underline{\hspace{1cm}}$

Now that you've seen the variety of ways in which the SAT can test your geometry skills, try the following questions to check your understanding. Give yourself 5 minutes to answer the following four questions. Make sure you use the Kaplan Method for Math as often as you can. Remember, you want to emphasize speed and efficiency in addition to simply getting the correct answer.

11. During a camping trip, Aundria and Annette decide to climb a mountain using two different routes to the top. Aundria takes the hiking route that travels 5 miles south, 6 miles east, 7 miles south, and 2 miles west to the summit; Annette uses the climbing route that starts at the same point as the hiking route but goes directly from there to the summit. Assuming vertical travel distance is not considered, about how many miles in all will the two travel?

A) 32.65

B) 33.42

C) 34.00

D) 34.42

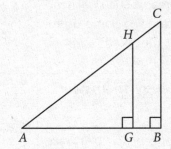

Note: Figure not drawn to scale.

12. △ABC above has an area of 150 square units. If $\overline{AB} = \overline{AH} = 20$, then what is the length of $\overline{HG}$?

A)   5

B) 12

C) 16

D) 20

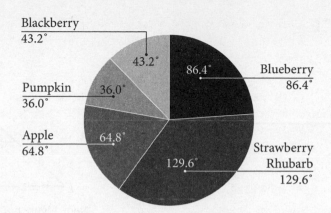

Blackberry
43.2°

Pumpkin
36.0°

Apple
64.8°

43.2°

86.4°   Blueberry
86.4°

36.0°

64.8°

129.6°   Strawberry
Rhubarb
129.6°

13. After the local Pie-Athon, John brought home several different kinds of pie in a single 10-inch diameter pie tin. The portion that each type of pie takes up in the tin is shown above. What is the area, in square inches, of the portion of leftover pie that is not strawberry rhubarb?

A) 9π

B) 16π

C) 36π

D) 64π

14. Marcus has a square sandbox measuring 24 feet across that is currently one-third full of sand from the bottom up. He purchases 96 cubic feet of sand, which, when added to the box, will completely fill it. How many inches deep is the sandbox?

A)   2

B)   3

C)   4

D)   5

Answers & Explanations for this chapter begin on page 861.

EXTRA PRACTICE

Note: Figure not drawn to scale.

1. A tourist ranch built the horse-riding trail shown in the figure. The trail takes a rider from the ranch to an old watering hole, then to a historic barn, and finally to a campsite where riders can spend the night. If a rider took a horse on a direct path from the ranch to the campsite, how much shorter, in miles, would the trip be?

   A)   6

   B)   8

   C) 17

   D) 23

2. Triangle *LOW* is shown in the figure above, where $\overline{HI}$ is the bisector of both $\overline{LO}$ and $\overline{OW}$. Given that $\overline{LW} = 30$ and $\overline{HI} = 4x - 1$, what is the value of *x*?

   A) 3.5

   B) 4

   C) 7.75

   D) 8

3. Cherie is jogging around a circular track. She started at point J and has jogged 200 yards to point G. If the radius of the track is 120 yards, what is the measure to the nearest tenth of a degree of minor angle JOG?

A) 95.5

B) 98.2

C) 102.1

D) 105.4

4. Alma pours water into a small cylindrical glass with a height of 6 inches and a diameter of 3 inches. The water fills the glass to the very top, so she decides to pour it into a bigger glass that is 8 inches tall and 4 inches in diameter. Assuming Alma doesn't spill any when she pours, how many inches high will the water reach in the bigger glass?

A) 1.5

B) 2.25

C) 3.375

D) 6.0

5. What is the area of the triangle shown in the figure?

A) $18\sqrt{3}$

B) $9 + 9\sqrt{3}$

C) $9 + 18\sqrt{3}$

D) $18 + 18\sqrt{3}$

$$x^2 + y^2 + 8x - 20y = 28$$

6. What is the diameter of the circle given by the equation above?

A) 12

B) 24

C) 28

D) 56

7. The height of the cone shown above is 16 centimeters. If the top quarter of the cone's height is cut off and discarded, what will be the volume in cubic centimeters of the remaining solid?

A) 192π

B) 576π

C) 756π

D) 768π

8. Triangle *ANT* is similar to triangle *BUG*, which are both plotted on a coordinate plane (not shown). The vertices of triangle *ANT* are $A(3, 2)$, $N(3, -1)$, and $T(-1, -1)$. Two of triangle *BUG*'s vertices are $(-8, -3)$ and $(8, -3)$. If vertex *B* is in the same quadrant of the coordinate plane as vertex *A*, what is the *y*-coordinate of vertex *B*?

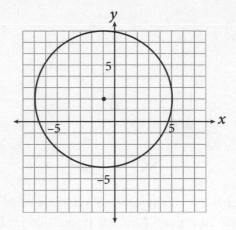

10. Which of the following represents the equation of the circle shown above?

    A) $(x - 1)^2 + (y + 2)^2 = 6$

    B) $(x + 1)^2 + (y - 2)^2 = 6$

    C) $(x - 1)^2 + (y + 2)^2 = 36$

    D) $(x + 1)^2 + (y - 2)^2 = 36$

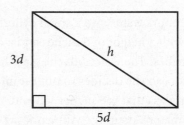

9. In the figure above, if $q = 140$, what is the value of $r - p$?

    A)   0

    B)   10

    C)   90

    D)   130

11. In the figure above, the diagonal of the rectangle has length *h*. What is the value of *h* in terms of *d*?

    A) d

    B) $4d$

    C) $\sqrt{34d}$

    D) $d\sqrt{34}$

12. If △*OLD* is similar to △*NEW*, and the ratio of the length of $\overline{OL}$ to $\overline{NE}$ is 7:4, which of the following ratios must also be equal to 7:4 ?

A) $\overline{OD}:\overline{EW}$

B) $m\angle D:m\angle W$

C) area of △*OLD* : area of △*NEW*

D) perimeter of △*OLD* : perimeter of △*NEW*

13. If the area of the shaded sector in circle *O* is 14π square units, what is the radius of the circle?

A) 6

B) 8

C) 9

D) 12

14. If the volume of the pyramid shown in the figure above can be represented by the function $V(x) = x^3 - x$, which of the following expressions represents the height?

A) x

B) $2x$

C) $x - 1$

D) $x - 3$

15. A pet store just decided to sell fish, so the manager purchased 50 of the fish tanks shown above to hold the fish. The staff need to fill the bottom two inches of each tank with sand, which comes in bags of 40 pounds. If 1 cubic inch of sand weighs about 2 ounces, how many bags of sand does the pet store need to buy? (There are 16 ounces in 1 pound.)

A) 45

B) 68

C) 84

D) 125

16. Two rectangles, *LION* and *PUMA,* are similar. Rectangle *LION* has a length of 86 units and a width of 52 units. If the perimeter of rectangle *PUMA* is 69 units, what is its width?

    A) 13

    B) 17.25

    C) 26

    D) 34.5

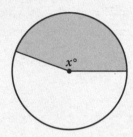

17. In the figure above, the ratio of the shaded area to the unshaded area is 4 to 5. What is the value of *x*?

    A) 135

    B) 145

    C) 160

    D) 170

18. The area of a right triangle is 35 square inches. If the longer leg is 3 inches longer than the shorter leg, what is the length of the hypotenuse in inches?

    A) 10

    B) $\dfrac{\sqrt{35}}{2}$

    C) $7\sqrt{10}$

    D) $\sqrt{149}$

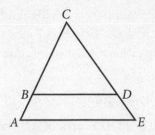

Note: Figure not drawn to scale.

19. In the figure above, $\overline{BD} \parallel \overline{AE}$ and $AB = 5$. If *BC* is three times *AB* and *CD* is 2 more than half *AC*, then what is the length of segment *DE* ?

    A) 3

    B) 4

    C) 5

    D) 6

20. A yogurt factory fills cylindrical containers 80% of the way to the top, putting 6 ounces of yogurt in each cup. The containers are 4 inches tall and 2.5 inches wide. Approximately how many cubic inches of space does one ounce of yogurt take up?

    A) 2.1

    B) 2.6

    C) 3.3

    D) 4.2

CHAPTER 12

Imaginary Numbers and Trigonometry

CHAPTER OBJECTIVES

By the end of this chapter, you will be able to:

1. Perform arithmetic operations on imaginary and complex numbers
2. Solve equations that have imaginary solutions
3. Use trigonometric ratios to calculate sides of right triangles
4. Convert between degrees and radians

SMARTPOINTS

Point Value	SmartPoint Category
10 Points	Imaginary Numbers
10 Points	Trigonometry

Math

IMAGINARY NUMBERS AND TRIGONOMETRY

Chapter 12

Homework

Extra Practice: #1-16

Key

 Book Assignment

 Online Video Assignment

 Online Quiz Assignment

INTRODUCTION TO IMAGINARY NUMBERS

Until you reached more advanced math classes like Algebra 2 and Trigonometry, you were likely taught that it is impossible to take the square root of a negative number. There is some truth to this, as the result isn't a **real number**. What you get instead is an **imaginary number**.

To take the square root of a negative number, it is necessary to use i, which is defined in math as the square root of -1. Take $\sqrt{-49}$ as an example. To simplify this expression, rewrite $\sqrt{-49}$ as $\sqrt{-1 \times 49}$, take the square root of -1 (which is by definition i), and then take the square root of 49, which is 7. The end result is $7i$.

> ✔ **Expert Tip**
>
> The simplification $i^2 = \left(\sqrt{-1}\right)^2 \rightarrow i^2 = -1$ also comes in handy when working with imaginary numbers.

> ✔ **Note**
>
> Be particularly careful when multiplying two radicals that contain negative numbers. The first step is *always* to rewrite each quantity as the square root of the product of -1 and a positive number. Take the square root of -1 and then multiply the resulting expressions. For example, if you're asked to simplify $\sqrt{-16} \times \sqrt{-25}$, you must first rewrite the expression as $i\sqrt{16} \times i\sqrt{25}$, which becomes $4i \times 5i = 20i^2 = -20$. Combining the two radicals into one and canceling the negative signs to give $\sqrt{16 \times 25}$ is incorrect and will likely lead to a trap answer.

When a number is written in the form $a + bi$, where a is the real component and b is the imaginary component (and i is $\sqrt{-1}$), it is referred to as a **complex number**. The realm of complex numbers encompasses all numbers, including those that do not have an imaginary component (such as 5, π, and $\sqrt{2}$), in which case $b = 0$, and those that do not have a real component (such as $3i$), in which case $a = 0$. When writing complex numbers, the real part is typically written first, followed by the imaginary part.

Operations on Complex Numbers

You can add, subtract, multiply, and divide complex numbers just as you do real numbers.

- To add (or subtract) complex numbers, simply add (or subtract) the real parts and then add (or subtract) the imaginary parts.

- To multiply complex numbers, treat them as binomials and use FOIL. To simplify the product, use the simplification $i^2 = -1$ and combine like terms.

- To divide complex numbers, write them in fraction form and then rationalize the denominator (just as you would a fraction with a radical in the denominator) by multiplying top and bottom by the conjugate of the complex number in the denominator.

Math

Rationalizing the Denominator of a Complex Number

In chapter 8, you learned how to use the conjugate of an expression to rationalize a denominator; you can do this with complex numbers as well. Suppose you're asked to simplify the expression $\frac{21}{3 + 5i}$. The conjugate of $3 + 5i$ is $3 - 5i$, so you would multiply the expression by $\frac{3 - 5i}{3 - 5i}$. This is the same as multiplying by 1, so you're not changing the value of the expression. The result is this:

$$\frac{21}{3 + 5i} \times \frac{3 - 5i}{3 - 5i} = \frac{21(3 - 5i)}{(3 + 5i)(3 - 5i)} = \frac{63 - 105i}{9 - 25i^2}$$

You know $i^2 = -1$, so the expression simplifies to $\frac{63 - 105i}{9 - (25)(-1)} = \frac{63 - 105i}{34}$. To separate the complex expression into its real and imaginary components, you can write each of the terms in the numerator over the denominator in separate fractions, yielding $\frac{63}{34} - \frac{105}{34}i$.

Powers of *i*

When an imaginary number is raised to a power, you can use the pattern shown below to determine what the resulting term will be. Knowing the cycles of *i* will save you time on Test Day.

When you have ...	i^1	i^2	i^3	i^4
... it becomes:	i	$\sqrt{-1} \times \sqrt{-1} = -1$	$i^2 \times i = -i$	$i^2 \times i^2 = -1 \times -1 = 1$

When you have an imaginary number with *i* raised to an exponent greater than 4, divide the exponent by 4. The remainder will dictate what the *i* component will become. For example, if you're asked to simplify $-3i^{44}$, start by dividing 44 by 4. The quotient is 11 with a remainder of 0, meaning $i^{44} = (i^4)^{11} = 1^{11}$. Therefore, the expression $-3i^{44}$ becomes -3. Take $15i^{63}$ as another example. Divide 63 by 4 to get 15 with a remainder of 3. This means that $i^{63} = (i^4)^{15} \times i^3 = 1^{15}i^3$. Because $i^3 = -i$, $15i^{63}$ becomes $-15i$.

Ready to try some test-like questions involving imaginary numbers? Check out the next few pages.

1. Which of the following is the correct simplification of the expression $(2i - 3) - (6 + 4i)$?

   A) $-9 - 2i$

   B) $-9 + 6i$

   C) $-7 - 4i$

   D) $3 + 6i$

Work through the Kaplan Method for Math step-by-step to solve this question. The following table shows Kaplan's strategic thinking on the left, along with suggested math scratchwork on the right.

Strategic Thinking	Math Scratchwork
Step 1: Read the question, identifying and organizing important information as you go You must correctly simplify the expression given.	
Step 2: Choose the best strategy to answer the question Use straightforward math to simplify. Distribute the negative sign and then combine like terms.	$(2i - 3) - (6 + 4i)$ $2i - 3 - 6 - 4i$ $-9 - 2i$
Step 3: Check that you answered the _right_ question Choice (A) contains the correct simplification.	

> ✔ **Note**
>
> Read carefully! Don't trust that both expressions in the parentheses have the real and imaginary components in the same order. Not checking the order means you risk falling for a trap answer.

2. Which of the following is equal to $(17 + 7i)(3 - 5i)$? (Note: $i = \sqrt{-1}$)

A) 16

B) 86

C) $16 - 64i$

D) $86 - 64i$

Work through the Kaplan Method for Math step-by-step to solve this question. The following table shows Kaplan's strategic thinking on the left, along with suggested math scratchwork on the right.

Strategic Thinking	Math Scratchwork
Step 1: Read the question, identifying and organizing important information as you go You need to correctly simplify the given expression.	
Step 2: Choose the best strategy to answer the question Use FOIL as you did when multiplying regular binomials in chapter 10. Be careful when multiplying the two imaginary components together; i^2 will become -1.	$(17 + 7i)(3 - 5i)$ $= (17)(3) + (17)(-5i) + (7i)(3) + (7i)(-5i)$ $= 51 - 85i + 21i - 35i^2$ $= 51 - 64i - (35)(-1)$ $= 51 - 64i + 35$ $= 86 - 64i$
Step 3: Check that you answered the *right* question Choice (D) is equal to the original expression.	

3. Which of the following is equivalent to $\dfrac{6 + \sqrt{-8}}{3 + \sqrt{-18}}$?

A) $\dfrac{10}{9}$

B) $\dfrac{8}{3}$

C) $\dfrac{2}{9} - \dfrac{4\sqrt{2}}{9}i$

D) $\dfrac{10}{9} - \dfrac{4\sqrt{2}}{9}i$

Work through the Kaplan Method for Math step-by-step to solve this question. The following table shows Kaplan's strategic thinking on the left, along with suggested math scratchwork on the right.

Strategic Thinking	Math Scratchwork
Step 1: Read the question, identifying and organizing important information as you go You need to simplify the expression.	
Step 2: Choose the best strategy to answer the question Use caution in the first couple of steps. There's a negative under the radical in the denominator, as well as under the one in the numerator. Rewrite the expression with the negatives properly removed before rationalizing the denominator. No match in the answer choices? Look for a way to simplify your expression. Separate the real and imaginary components and then reduce the fractions.	$\dfrac{6 + \sqrt{-8}}{3 + \sqrt{-18}} = \dfrac{6 + i\sqrt{8}}{3 + i\sqrt{18}}$ conjugate of denominator: $3 - i\sqrt{18}$ $\dfrac{6 + i\sqrt{8}}{3 + i\sqrt{18}} \times \dfrac{3 - i\sqrt{18}}{3 - i\sqrt{18}}$ $= \dfrac{6(3) + (6)(-i\sqrt{18}) + (i\sqrt{8})(3) + (i\sqrt{8})(-i\sqrt{18})}{3(3) + (3)(-i\sqrt{18}) + (i\sqrt{18})(3) + (i\sqrt{18})(-i\sqrt{18})}$ $= \dfrac{18 - 6i\sqrt{18} + 3i\sqrt{8} - i^2\sqrt{144}}{9 - 18i^2}$ $= \dfrac{18 - 6i\sqrt{9 \times 2} + 3i\sqrt{4 \times 2} - (-1)(12)}{9 - (18)(-1)}$ $= \dfrac{18 - 18i\sqrt{2} + 6i\sqrt{2} + 12}{9 + 18}$ $= \dfrac{30 - 12i\sqrt{2}}{27}$ $= \dfrac{30}{27} - \dfrac{12\sqrt{2}}{27}i = \dfrac{10}{9} - \dfrac{4\sqrt{2}}{9}i$
Step 3: Check that you answered the *right* question You've correctly simplified the expression. Choice (D) is correct.	

Great job persevering through that challenging question! As you saw, complex numbers follow the same rules of arithmetic that real numbers do.

Quadratic Equations That Have Imaginary Solutions

Chapter 10 showed you how to find the real solutions of a quadratic equation using a variety of techniques, including factoring, completing the square, using the quadratic formula, and graphing. This chapter will expand on that by showing you how to find imaginary solutions.

Recall that the quadratic formula is $x = \dfrac{-b \pm \sqrt{b^2 - 4ac}}{2a}$ and that the sign of the discriminant, $b^2 - 4ac$, dictates the nature of the solutions. When $b^2 - 4ac < 0$, the equation will have two imaginary solutions because you are taking the square root of a negative quantity.

Graphically, a quadratic equation has imaginary solutions when its vertex is above the x-axis and the parabola opens upward, or when its vertex is below the x-axis and the parabola opens downward. In either case, the graph does not cross the x-axis and therefore has no real solutions.

Let's try another test-like question.

4. What are the solutions to the equation $x^2 - 4x + 5 = 0$?

   A) $5, -1$

   B) $2 \pm i$

   C) $2 \pm 3i$

   D) $-2 \pm i$

Work through the Kaplan Method for Math step-by-step to solve this question. The following table shows Kaplan's strategic thinking on the left, along with suggested math scratchwork on the right.

Strategic Thinking	Math Scratchwork
Step 1: Read the question, identifying and organizing important information as you go You're asked to identify the solutions (a.k.a. the x-intercepts) of the given equation.	
Step 2: Choose the best strategy to answer the question The x^2 term indicates a quadratic equation. Attempts to factor will reveal no pair of numbers that yields a product of 5 and a sum of -4. Because the numbers are fairly small, try completing the square. Start by subtracting 5 from each side of the equation. Divide b (the coefficient of the x term) by 2, square that result, and then add it to both sides. Rewrite the left side as the square of a binomial and take the square root of both sides. Don't fret about the negative sign; this equation just has imaginary solutions. Replace $\sqrt{-1}$ with i and solve for x.	*factors of* 5: 1, 5; $-1, -5$ $$x^2 - 4x + 5 = 0$$ $$x^2 - 4x = -5$$ $$b = -4 \rightarrow \frac{-4}{2} = -2 \rightarrow (-2)^2 = 4$$ $$x^2 - 4x + 4 = -5 + 4$$ $$(x - 2)^2 = -1$$ $$x - 2 = \pm\sqrt{-1}$$ $$x = 2 \pm i$$
Step 3: Check that you answered the *right* question You've found the (imaginary) solutions to the equation, so you're done! Choice (B) is correct.	

✔ **Note**

You can also answer this question using the quadratic formula, but it might take more time, especially if a question like this is in the no-calculator section. Additionally, if it's in the calculator section, you can graph the equation to make sure the solutions really are imaginary (the graph will not touch or intersect the x-axis).

Working with Complex Numbers Using a Calculator

You can use your TI-83/84 to simplify challenging complex number expressions more quickly than you can by hand (if a question happens to be in the calculator section of the test).

Step 1: Press [**MODE**] and then scroll down to the row that starts with REAL. Highlight $a + bi$ and press [**ENTER**]. If you miss this step, you'll get an error message when you try to compute a complex expression.

```
NORMAL  SCI  ENG
FLOAT  0123456789
RADIAN  DEGREE
FUNC  PAR  POL  SEQ
CONNECTED  DOT
SEQUENTIAL  SIMUL
REAL  a+bi  re^θi
FULL  HORIZ  G-T
SET CLOCK01/01/01 12:04AM
```

Step 2: Exit the mode screen and enter the expression you wish to simplify. Press [**ENTER**] when done. If you wish to convert decimal coefficients into fractions, press [**MATH**][**ENTER**][**ENTER**].

```
√(-4)
                    2i
(4-2i)/(4+2i)
                  .6-.8i
Ans▶Frac
                3/5-4/5i
```

> ✔ **Note**
>
> If you have an expression containing a fraction with imaginary components in the numerator and/or denominator, such as $\dfrac{4 - 2i}{4 + 2i}$, you need to be very careful. Enter the expression using parentheses: $(4 - 2i)/(4 + 2i)$.

INTRODUCTION TO TRIGONOMETRY

Although the word *trigonometry* comes from Greek words meaning "triangle" and "measure," some students fear the subject enough that they believe the word came from the Greek roots *trig*, meaning "designed," and *onometry*, meaning "to give high school students nightmares." Fortunately, any SAT trig questions you encounter won't be ludicrously difficult, and investing just a little time in studying this topic will give you a slight edge over your competition.

Trigonometric Ratios

You probably remember learning the acronym SOH CAH TOA, a mnemonic device for the sine, cosine, and tangent ratios. Check out the triangle and the table beneath for a summary of the ratios and what each equals for angle *A* in triangle *CAB*.

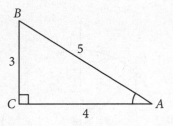

Sine (sin)	Cosine (cos)	Tangent (tan)
opposite / hypotenuse	adjacent / hypotenuse	opposite / adjacent
$\dfrac{3}{5}$	$\dfrac{4}{5}$	$\dfrac{3}{4}$

> ✔ **Note**
>
> Related note: $\tan A = \dfrac{\sin A}{\cos A}$.

> ✔ **Note**
>
> Alternate mnemonic: Some Old Hag Cracked All Her Teeth On Asparagus.

Chapter 12: Imaginary Numbers and Trigonometry **311**

The Unit Circle

Up until now, you've likely been told that the trigonometric ratios are only applicable to right triangles; however, you can expand their utility to include angles greater than 90° by using the **unit circle**. The unit circle is a circle with a radius of 1 centered around the origin in the *xy*-plane. Below is such a circle containing an example triangle.

> ✔ **Note**
>
> An angle in the unit circle always begins with its radius on the positive side of the *x*-axis. As the angle measure increases, the radius moves counterclockwise through each quadrant. If you have a negative angle, the radius starts in the same spot but moves clockwise as the absolute value of the angle measure increases.

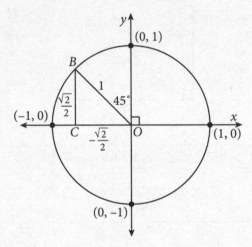

Suppose you were asked to determine sin 135° and cos 135°. Draw a radius at 135° (which is 45° past the *y*-axis in the second quadrant) and then add a vertical line from where the radius intersects the circle down to the *x*-axis. Because this radius ($\overline{OB}$) is within the unit circle, its length is 1. Triangle

OBC is a 45-45-90 triangle, so each of its legs has a length of $\frac{\sqrt{2}}{2}$. This means $\sin 135° = \dfrac{\frac{\sqrt{2}}{2}}{1} = \dfrac{\sqrt{2}}{2}$.

Note that because $\overline{OC}$ lies on the negative part of the *x*-axis, you should use $-\dfrac{\sqrt{2}}{2}$ as the "measure"

of the adjacent side. Therefore, $\cos 135° = \dfrac{-\frac{\sqrt{2}}{2}}{1} = -\dfrac{\sqrt{2}}{2}$. Notice that if you were to label point *B*

on the unit circle, its (*x*, *y*) coordinates would correspond to (cos 135°, sin 135°).

Radians

Most geometry questions present angle measures in degrees. In trigonometry, however, you will encounter a different unit: the radian. The prospect of learning a new unit shouldn't scare you, though; just remember that $180° = \pi$ radians. For instance, if you're asked to convert 90° into radians, use this relationship as a conversion factor with the factor-label method (refer to chapter 5 to brush up): $90° \times \dfrac{\pi}{180°} = \dfrac{\pi}{2}$. Note that there isn't a symbol for radians, so $\dfrac{\pi}{2}$ in trigonometry is read as "$\dfrac{\pi}{2}$ radians." This conversion works in the opposite direction as well: To convert radians to degrees, multiply by $\dfrac{180°}{\pi}$.

> ✔ **Note**
>
> Most graphing calculators have both degree and radian modes. Make sure you're in the correct mode when working on trigonometry questions!

Here is a handy unit circle diagram with common degree and radian measures (and the coordinates of the ends of their respective radii) that you're likely to see on Test Day.

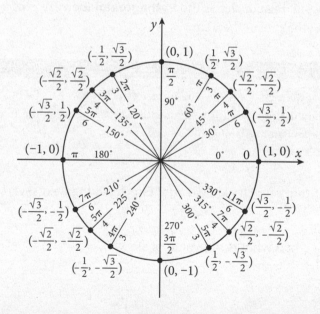

> ✔ **Note**
>
> The coordinates at a particular angle measure translate into the leg lengths of the triangle created when a vertical line is drawn from the end of the radius down (or up if you're in quadrant III or IV) to the x-axis. For example, at 60°, the horizontal leg has a length of $\dfrac{1}{2}$, and the vertical leg has a length of $\dfrac{\sqrt{3}}{2}$.

Benchmark Angles

Knowing the trig functions for the most commonly tested "benchmark" angles (multiples of 30° and 45°) will save time on Test Day. You will not be asked to evaluate trig functions for angles that require a calculator.

Other Trig Relationships

Complementary angles have a special relationship relative to sine and cosine.

- $\sin x = \cos\left(\dfrac{\pi}{2} - x\right)$ or $\sin x = \cos(90° - x)$

- $\cos x = \sin\left(\dfrac{\pi}{2} - x\right)$ or $\cos x = \sin(90° - x)$

In plain English, this translates as: The sine of an acute angle is equal to the cosine of the angle's complement and vice versa. To see some examples, look at the first quadrant of the unit circle: $\cos 30° = \sin 60°$, $\cos 45° = \sin 45°$, and $\cos 60° = \sin 30°$. Understanding how trig functions of complementary angles work can help you learn the unit circle and answer trig questions on Test Day.

Another particularly useful relationship is the **Pythagorean identity**: $\sin^2 x + \cos^2 x = 1$. (Notice that it resembles the Pythagorean theorem.)

> ✔ **Note**
>
> Note that $\sin^2 x$ is *not* the same as $\sin x^2$. The former dictates that the sine of x is squared, but the latter indicates finding the sine of x^2. The exponent is written between the trigonometric function and the variable to eliminate this ambiguity.

Ready to test your SAT trigonometry knowledge? Check out the next several pages for some test-like questions.

5. If $\tan x = \dfrac{7}{24}$, then what is the value of $\sin x$?

Work through the Kaplan Method for Math step-by-step to solve this question. The following table shows Kaplan's strategic thinking on the left, along with suggested math scratchwork on the right.

Strategic Thinking	Math Scratchwork
Step 1: Read the question, identifying and organizing important information as you go You need to find the value of sin x.	
Step 2: Choose the best strategy to answer the question If $\tan x = \dfrac{7}{24}$, then the sides that are opposite and adjacent to angle x must be 7 and 24, respectively. Draw a diagram to reflect this. Because $\sin x = \dfrac{opp}{hyp}$, you'll need to find the length of the hypotenuse using the Pythagorean theorem. Once you calculate this, plug that value into the sine ratio.	$\tan x = \dfrac{opp}{adj}$, $\sin x = \dfrac{opp}{hyp}$ *(diagram of right triangle: hyp, 7, 24, angle x)* $7^2 + 24^2 = hyp^2$ $49 + 576 = hyp^2$ $625 = hyp^2$ $25 = hyp$
Step 3: Check that you answered the *right* question The value of sin x is $\dfrac{7}{25}$. Grid in $\dfrac{7}{25}$ or .28.	$\sin x = \dfrac{7}{25}$

✔ **Expert Tip**

The triangle in this question is another Pythagorean triplet (7-24-25). Although the 7-24-25 is not as common as the 3-4-5 and 5-12-13, knowing it means you can skip a Pythagorean theorem calculation (and save a few seconds).

6. If $\cos x = \sin y$, then which of the following pairs of angle measures could not be the values of x and y?

A) $\dfrac{\pi}{4}, \dfrac{\pi}{4}$

B) $\dfrac{\pi}{6}, \dfrac{\pi}{3}$

C) $\dfrac{\pi}{8}, \dfrac{3\pi}{8}$

D) $\dfrac{\pi}{2}, \dfrac{\pi}{2}$

Work through the Kaplan Method for Math step-by-step to solve this question. The following table shows Kaplan's strategic thinking on the left, along with suggested math scratchwork on the right.

Strategic Thinking	Math Scratchwork
Step 1: Read the question, identifying and organizing important information as you go You need to determine which pair of angle measures do not satisfy the equation $\cos x = \sin y$.	
Step 2: Choose the best strategy to answer the question Complementary angles have a special relationship relative to trig values: The cosine of an acute angle is equal to the sine of the angle's complement and vice versa. The question states that $\cos x = \sin x$, and all the angles in the answer choices are acute angles, so you are looking for the pair that are *not* complementary angles. In degrees, complementary angles add up to 90, so in radians they must add up to $90° \times \dfrac{\pi}{180°} = \dfrac{\pi}{2}$. Add each pair of angles to see which one does not give the correct sum.	A: $\dfrac{\pi}{4} + \dfrac{\pi}{4} = \dfrac{2\pi}{4} = \dfrac{\pi}{2}$ B: $\dfrac{\pi}{6} + \dfrac{\pi}{3} = \dfrac{\pi}{6} + \dfrac{2\pi}{6} = \dfrac{3\pi}{6} = \dfrac{\pi}{2}$ C: $\dfrac{\pi}{8} + \dfrac{3\pi}{8} = \dfrac{4\pi}{8} = \dfrac{\pi}{2}$ (D): $\dfrac{\pi}{2} + \dfrac{\pi}{2} = \dfrac{2\pi}{2} = \pi$
Step 3: Check that you answered the *right* question The only pair of angles that are not complementary is (D).	

Now let's try a question that tests both your geometry skills and what you've learned about trig ratios. Remember, trig ratios apply to right triangles.

7. If the area of $\triangle ABC$ is 225 and $AB = 17$, then what is the value of $\cos x$?

A) $\dfrac{8}{17}$

B) $\dfrac{8}{15}$

C) $\dfrac{17}{30}$

D) $\dfrac{15}{17}$

Work through the Kaplan Method for Math step-by-step to solve this question. The following table shows Kaplan's strategic thinking on the left, along with suggested math scratchwork on the right.

Strategic Thinking	Math Scratchwork
Step 1: Read the question, identifying and organizing important information as you go You're asked to calculate the value of cos x. You're given that $AB = 17$.	
Step 2: Choose the best strategy to answer the question The area of a triangle is half the product of the base and height, so draw in a height. Label the point at which the base and height intersect D to help keep things clear.	*(triangle with vertices A, B, C; apex B; side AB labeled 17; angle x at A; dashed height BD meeting base at right angle at D; DC labeled 30)*
Use the triangle area formula to find the height; you'll find that $BD = 15$. You now have two sides of a right triangle ($\triangle ABD$), but not necessarily the two sides you need. To find the value of cos x, you need the side adjacent to x and the hypotenuse. Here, you have the opposite side (BD) and the hypotenuse (AB), so you need to find the length of the third side (AD). You might recognize $\triangle ABD$ as an 8-15-17 Pythagorean triplet, but if not, use the Pythagorean theorem.	$A = \dfrac{1}{2}bh$ $225 = \dfrac{1}{2} \times 30h$ $225 = 15h$ $h = \dfrac{225}{15} = 15 = BD$ $AD^2 + 15^2 = 17^2$ $AD^2 = 17^2 - 15^2$ $AD^2 = 289 - 225$ $AD = \sqrt{64} = 8$
Step 3: Check that you answered the *right* question The question asks for cos x. Recall that $\cos x = \dfrac{adjacent}{hypotenuse}$. Thus, $\cos x = \dfrac{AD}{AB} = \dfrac{8}{17}$, (A).	$\cos x = \dfrac{adj}{hyp} = \dfrac{8}{17}$

Now you'll have a chance to try a couple of test-like questions. Some guidance is provided, but you'll need to fill in the missing parts of explanations or the step-by-step math in order to get to the correct answer. Don't worry—after going through the examples at the beginning of this chapter, these questions should be completely doable. If you're still struggling, review the worked examples in this chapter.

Many students ask when they'd need to use imaginary numbers in the real world. One field that commonly uses them is electrical engineering, as demonstrated below. Note that electrical engineers use j to represent $\sqrt{-1}$, as i is used to represent a different quantity in their field.

8. The voltage of an alternating current circuit is given by the formula $E = I \times Z$, where E is voltage in volts, I is current in amps, and Z is impedance (a type of resistance encountered with alternating current) in ohms. If a certain circuit has a voltage of $38 + 18j$ volts and an impedance of $4 + 6j$ ohms, what is the current, in amps, that passes through the circuit? (Note: $j = \sqrt{-1}$)

    A) $\dfrac{11}{13} - 3j$

    B) $5 - 3j$

    C) $\dfrac{19}{2} + 3j$

    D) $44 + 300j$

Use the following scaffolding as your map through the question, filling in the blanks in the table as you work from top to bottom.

Strategic Thinking	Math Scratchwork
Step 1: Read the question, identifying and organizing important information as you go You're asked to calculate the current of an alternating current circuit. The question provides an equation and the values of two of the variables in it.	
Step 2: Choose the best strategy to answer the question You know the voltage and impedance, so all you need to do is plug those values into the given equation and solve for current (*I*). Once there, determine the conjugate of the denominator and use it to eliminate the imaginary component from the denominator. If your answer isn't among the choices, remember that complex numbers can be broken into their real and imaginary components. Do this with your fraction and simplify.	$E = I \times Z$ $\underline{\hspace{2cm}} = I \times \underline{\hspace{2cm}}$ $I = \underline{\hspace{2cm}} \times \underline{\hspace{2cm}}$ $I = \underline{\hspace{3cm}}$ $I = \underline{\hspace{2cm}}$ $I = \underline{\hspace{2cm}}$ $I = \underline{\hspace{1.5cm}}$ $I = \underline{\hspace{1.5cm}} - \underline{\hspace{1.5cm}} j$ $I = \underline{\hspace{1.5cm}}$
Step 3: Check that you answered the *right* question Did you get (B)? If so, you're right!	$\underline{\hspace{2cm}}$

9. If the measure, in radians, of one acute angle in a right triangle is $\frac{\pi}{3}$, what is the measure of the other acute angle?

A) $\frac{\pi}{12}$

B) $\frac{\pi}{6}$

C) $\frac{\pi}{3}$

D) $\frac{2\pi}{3}$

Use the following scaffolding as your map through the question, filling in the blanks in the table as you work from top to bottom.

Strategic Thinking	Math Scratchwork
Step 1: Read the question, identifying and organizing important information as you go You're given the measure of one acute angle in a right triangle, and you need to find the measure of the other acute angle.	right triangle one acute angle has measure $\frac{\pi}{3}$ answers in radians
Step 2: Choose the best strategy to answer the question One angle in a right triangle has a measure of 90°, so the missing acute angle must have a measure of $90° - \frac{\pi}{3}$. The answer choices are all given in radians, so convert 90° to radians and then subtract. You'll need to find a common denominator to subtract.	$90° \times \underline{\hspace{1cm}} = \underline{\hspace{1cm}}$ in radians $\underline{\hspace{1cm}} - \frac{\pi}{3} = ?$ $\underline{\hspace{1cm}} - \underline{\hspace{1cm}} = \underline{\hspace{1cm}}$
Step 3: Check that you answered the *right* question Did you get (B)? If so, you're right.	$\underline{\hspace{1cm}}$

Math

Now that you've seen the variety of ways in which the SAT can test you on imaginary numbers and trigonometry, try the following questions to check your understanding. Give yourself 4 minutes to answer the following three questions. Make sure you use the Kaplan Method for Math as often as you can. Remember, you want to emphasize speed and efficiency in addition to simply getting the correct answer.

10. When the complex number $(11 + 14i)^3$ is expanded, simplified, and written in the form $a + bi$ where a is the real component, b is the imaginary component, and $i = \sqrt{-1}$, what is the value of b?

$$(x^4 + 84x^2 + 243)(x^2 + 5x - 36) = 0$$

11. Which of the following is not a solution to the equation shown above?

A) $-9i$

B) $-\sqrt{3}i$

C) $3i$

D) $9i$

12. If $\sin x = \cos\left(\dfrac{13\pi}{6}\right)$, then which of the following could be the value of x? (Assume this question is in the no-calculator section of the test.)

A) $\dfrac{\pi}{6}$

B) $\dfrac{\pi}{4}$

C) $\dfrac{\pi}{3}$

D) $\dfrac{\pi}{2}$

Answers and Explanations for this chapter begin on page 869.

EXTRA PRACTICE

1. Which of the following is equivalent to $4i(5 - 7i)$? (Note: $i = \sqrt{-1}$)

   A) $-8i$

   B) $48i$

   C) $-28 + 20i$

   D) $28 + 20i$

2. Which of the following represents $\dfrac{1}{3 - i}$ written in the form $a + bi$? (Note: $i = \sqrt{-1}$)

   A) $\dfrac{3}{10} + \dfrac{1}{10}i$

   B) $\dfrac{1}{3} - \dfrac{1}{i}$

   C) $\dfrac{3}{8} + \dfrac{1}{8}i$

   D) $3 + i$

3. Which of the following is equivalent to $(3 + 2i)^4$? (Note: $i = \sqrt{-1}$)

   A) 97

   B) $-119 + 120i$

   C) $5 + 12i$

   D) $81 - 16i$

4. Which of the following has the same value as $i^{14} + i^{122}$? (Note: $i = \sqrt{-1}$)

   A) i^{136}

   B) $2i^2$

   C) $2i^{136}$

   D) $(1 + i)(1 - i)$

5. What are the solutions over the complex number system to the equation $x^2 + 13 = 4x$? (Note: $i = \sqrt{-1}$)

   A) $-4 \pm 3i$

   B) $2 \pm 3i$

   C) $2 \pm 6i$

   D) $4 \pm 3i$

6. Which of the following shows the product $\left(2 + \sqrt{-9}\right)\left(-1 + \sqrt{-4}\right)$ written in the form $a + bi$? (Note: $i = \sqrt{-1}$)

   A) $-8 + i$

   B) $-8 - i$

   C) $4 + i$

   D) $4 - i$

7. Which of the following is equivalent to the complex number $\dfrac{1}{4 - 2i} + (3 + i)$? (Note: $i = \sqrt{-1}$)

   A) $\dfrac{4 + i}{4 - 2i}$

   B) $\dfrac{4 - i}{4 + 2i}$

   C) $\dfrac{15 - 2i}{4 - 2i}$

   D) $\dfrac{15 + 2i}{4 + 2i}$

Math

8. The absolute value of a complex number
$a + bi$ is defined as $\sqrt{a^2 + b^2}$. What is
$|15 + 8i|$? (Note: $i = \sqrt{-1}$)

9. What is the measure in degrees of $\angle PQR$
shown above?

A) 105

B) 120

C) 135

D) 150

10. Which of the following angles has the same
trigonometric values as 450°?

A) 30°

B) 45°

C) 60°

D) 90°

11. The cosine of which of the following angles is
not equal to the cosine of the other three?

A) −120

B) −60

C) 120

D) 240

12. Based on the figure above, which of the following is true?

A) $\sin 22.6° = \dfrac{5}{12}$

B) $\sin 67.4° = \dfrac{5}{13}$

C) $\cos 22.6° = \dfrac{5}{13}$

D) $\cos 67.4° = \dfrac{5}{13}$

13. If $\sin x = \cos\left(\dfrac{\pi}{6}\right)$, then which of the following could not be the value of x?

A) $\dfrac{\pi}{3}$

B) $\dfrac{2\pi}{3}$

C) $\dfrac{5\pi}{3}$

D) $\dfrac{7\pi}{3}$

14. If the hypotenuse of the triangle shown above has length 24 units, what is the area in square units of the triangle?

   A) $72\sqrt{3}$

   B) $144\sqrt{3}$

   C) 288

   D) $288\sqrt{3}$

Note: Figure not drawn to scale.

16. If the area of the triangle shown above is 240 square inches, what is tan β?

15. The triangle shown above is a cross section of a feeding trough that is 24 inches deep and whose top is 36 inches across. If cos $x = B$, what is the value of B?

Evidence-Based Reading and Writing

UNIT SIX

Reading

BY THE END OF THIS UNIT, YOU WILL BE ABLE TO:

1. Apply the Kaplan Method for Reading Comprehension

2. Identify Reading Test question types and apply the appropriate strategies to correctly answer them

CHAPTER 13

The Kaplan Method for Reading Comprehension and Reading Test Passage Types

 ## CHAPTER OBJECTIVES

By the end of this chapter, you will be able to:

1. Identify the three types of passages on the SAT Reading Test

2. Passage Map passages using the Kaplan Method for Reading Comprehension, identifying keywords and central ideas across passage types

3. Predict an answer and find its match among the answer choices using a Passage Map

SMARTPOINTS

Point Value	SmartPoint Category
Point Builder	The Kaplan Method for Reading Comprehension
Point Builder	Passage Mapping
Point Builder	U.S. and World Literature Passages
Point Builder	History/Social Studies Passages
Point Builder	Science Passages

Reading & Writing

THE KAPLAN METHOD FOR READING COMPREHENSION & READING TEST PASSAGE TYPES

Chapter 13

Homework

Extra Practice: #1-10

Even More

The Kaplan Method for Reading Comprehension

History/Social Studies Passages

Reading Quiz 1

Key

 Book Assignment

 Online Video Assignment

 Online Quiz Assignment

OVERVIEW OF THE SAT READING TEST PASSAGE TYPES

SAT Reading Test Passage Distribution	
U.S. and World Literature	1 passage; 10–11 questions
History/Social Studies	2 passages OR 1 passage and 1 paired-passage set; 10–11 questions each
Science	2 passages OR 1 passage and 1 paired-passage set; 10–11 questions each

It is imperative that you use the Kaplan Method for Reading Comprehension for every passage on the SAT Reading Test. Doing so ensures that you spend your time efficiently and maximize your opportunity to earn points.

THE KAPLAN METHOD FOR READING COMPREHENSION

The Kaplan Method for Reading Comprehension consists of three steps:

> Step 1: Read actively
>
> Step 2: Examine the question stem
>
> Step 3: Predict and answer

Let's take a closer look at each step.

Step 1: Read actively

Active reading means:

- Ask questions and take notes *as* you read the passage. Asking questions about the passage and taking notes are integral parts of your approach to acing the SAT Reading Test.

You should ask questions such as:

- Why did the author write this word/detail/sentence/paragraph?

- Is the author taking a side? If so, what side is he or she taking?

- What are the tone and purpose of the passage?

Reading & Writing

Make sure you remember to:

- Identify the passage type.

- Take notes, circle keywords, and underline key phrases.

> ✔ **Expert Tip**
>
> Questions will range from general to specific. By using clues in the question stem to identify what the question is looking for, you will be better able to complete Step 3 of the Kaplan Method for Reading Comprehension.

Step 2: Examine the question stem

This means you should:

- Identify keywords and line references in the question stem.

- Apply question type strategies as necessary.

Step 3: Predict and answer

This means you should:

- Predict an answer before looking at the answer choices, also known as "predict before you peek."

- Select the best match.

Predicting before you peek helps you:

- Eliminate the possibility of falling into wrong answer traps.

PASSAGE MAPPING

Step 1 of the Kaplan Method for Reading Comprehension dictates that you must take notes as you read the passage. We call these notes a Passage Map because they guide you through the passage and will lead you to the correct answers.

> ✔ **On Test Day**
>
> A Passage Map should not replace the occasional underline or circle—it is important that you underline, circle, *and* take notes to create the most effective Passage Map.

Make sure you pay attention and take note of the following when you map the passage:

- The "why" or the central idea of the passage—in other words, the thesis statement

- Transitions or changes in direction in a passage's logic

- The author's opinions and other opinions the author cites

- The author's tone and purpose

While Passage Mapping may seem time-consuming at first, with practice it will become second nature by Test Day, and your overall SAT Reading Test timing will greatly improve because you'll spend less time searching the passage for answers to the questions.

> ✔ **Remember**
>
> The SAT Reading Test is an open-book test! The answer is always in the passage.

Just as the passages span different genres, your approaches will also vary from subject to subject. The approach for each type of SAT Reading Test passage will be addressed in this chapter.

Now, let's look at the specific passage types individually.

U.S. AND WORLD LITERATURE PASSAGES

There will be a single U.S. and World Literature passage on the SAT. It is different from the other passages because:

- There will be multiple characters and, therefore, multiple opinions.

- The tone will be nuanced and emotion-based, rather than informative or explanatory.

As you read a U.S. and World Literature passage, you should:

1. Identify the characters and evaluate how the author describes them

   - What do the characters want?

   - What are the characters doing?

   - What adjectives describe each character?

2. Assess the characters' opinions of each other and themselves

   - Do they like each other? Dislike each other?

   - Why does each character make a particular decision or take a particular course of action?

   - What do these decisions or actions tell you about a character?

3. Identify the themes of the story

   - What are the "turning points" in the passage?

   - Is there a moral to the story?

> ✔ **Remember**
>
> Because U.S. and World Literature passages have multiple characters with multiple opinions, remember to keep straight who said what.

Reading & Writing

Let's look at the following example of an abbreviated U.S. and World Literature passage and question set. After the mapped passage, the left column contains questions similar to those you'll see on the SAT Reading Test on Test Day. The column on the right features the strategic thinking a test expert employs when approaching the passage and questions presented. Note how a test expert can quickly condense the entire passage into a few words, and use his or her Passage Map to ask questions that build a prediction for the correct answer.

Strategic Thinking
Step 1: Read actively
Read the passage and the notes provided. Remember, a well-crafted Passage Map should summarize the central idea of each paragraph as well as important topics or themes. Your notes for U.S. and World Literature passages should focus on characters. Use your Passage Map to help you answer each question.

Questions 1-2 are based on the following passage.

The following passage is an excerpt from English novelist and poet Thomas Hardy's *Tess of the D'Urbervilles*, published in 1891.

The women—or rather girls, for they were mostly young—wore drawn cotton bonnets with great flapping curtains to keep off the sun, and
Line gloves to prevent their hands being wounded by
(5) the stubble. There was one wearing a pale pink jacket, another in a cream-coloured, tight-sleeved gown, another in a petticoat as red as the arms of a reaping-machine; and others, older in the brown-rough "wropper," or over-all—the old-established
(10) and most appropriate dress of the field-woman, which the young ones were abandoning. This morning, the eye returns involuntarily to the girl in the pink cotton jacket, she being the most flexuous and finely-drawn figure of them all. But her bonnet
(15) is pulled so far over her brow that none of her face is disclosed while she binds, though her complexion may be guessed from a stray twine or two of dark brown hair which extends below the curtain of her bonnet. Perhaps one reason why she seduces
(20) casual attention is that she never courts it, though the other women often gaze around them.

Her binding proceeds with clock-like monotony. From the sheaf last finished she draws a handful of

ears, patting their tips with her left palm to bring
(25) them even. Then, stooping low, she moves forward, gathering the corn with both hands against her knees and pushing her left gloved hand under the bundle to meet the right on the other side, holding the corn in an embrace like that of a lover. She
(30) brings the ends of the bond together and kneels on the sheaf while she ties it, beating back her skirts now and then when lifted by the breeze. A bit of her naked arm is visible between the buff leather of the gauntlet and the sleeve of her gown; and as
(35) the day wears on, its feminine smoothness becomes scarified by the stubble and bleeds.

At intervals she stands up to rest, and to retie her disarranged apron, or to pull her bonnet straight. Then one can see the oval face of a handsome
(40) young woman with deep, dark eyes and long, heavy, clinging tresses, which seem to clasp in a beseeching way anything they fall against. The cheeks are paler, the teeth more regular, the red lips thinner than is usual in a country-bred girl.

¶1: girls work in fields; one stands out

¶2: girl's system for work

¶3: girl is pretty; not usual country girl (theme)

Questions	Strategic Thinking
1. The passage is best described as A) a psychological study of a character's personality. B) a sweeping portrait of nature in autumn. C) a drab rendering of a farmland routine. D) a gradual focusing on a single individual.	**Step 2: Examine the question stem** Identify the key words and phrases in the question stem. The phrase "passage is best described as" implies that you are looking for a description of the passage as a whole. Use your Passage Map notes to find the author's central theme. **Step 3: Predict and answer** Although the passage begins with a general description of many women doing agricultural labor, the majority of the passage focuses on the features and actions of one young woman. Choice (D) is correct.
2. The activity described in lines 22-29 ("Her binding … of a lover") seems indicative of A) routine. B) memory. C) necessity. D) optimism.	**Step 2: Examine the question stem** Identify the key words and phrases in the question stem. The word "activity" and the line reference indicate you should look at your Passage Map notes surrounding those lines. **Step 3: Predict and answer** Lines 22-29 include the phrase "clock-like monotony" (line 22) and the Passage Map note says, "girl's system for work." In this context, "system" is synonymous with "routine." Choice (A) is correct.

> ✔ **Expert Tip**
>
> Some paragraphs are longer than others. If you are mapping a very long paragraph, you can write two or three short notes rather than trying to fit everything into just one long note.

HISTORY/SOCIAL STUDIES PASSAGES

The History/Social Studies portion of the SAT Reading Test will consist of either two single History/Social Studies passages or one single History/Social Studies passage and one History/Social Studies paired-passage set. History/Social Studies passages are different from other passage types because:

- The passage will have a clearly stated topic, a well-defined scope, and a specific purpose.

- There will be at least one primary source passage that uses antiquated language.

Because History/Social Studies passages can be densely written, you should:

1. Identify the topic and scope of the passage

    - You can usually find the topic and scope in the first paragraph.

2. Identify the topic sentence of each succeeding paragraph

    - What does this paragraph accomplish? Does it provide evidence to support a previous statement? Or does it introduce questions about an earlier claim?

3. Summarize the purpose of the passage

    - Some common purposes include: to inform, to refute, to promote, to explore.

> ✔ **Note**
>
> Resist the temptation to reread large portions of the passage. Your Passage Map can help you predict and answer questions correctly without having to dive completely back into the text. Doing so will save you time on Test Day!

Let's look at the following example of an abbreviated History/Social Studies passage and question set. After the mapped passage, the left column contains questions similar to those you'll see on the SAT Reading Test on Test Day. The column on the right features the strategic thinking a test expert employs when approaching the passage and questions presented. Note how a test expert can quickly condense the entire passage into a few words and use his or her Passage Map to ask questions that build a prediction for the correct answer.

Strategic Thinking

Step 1: Read actively

Read the passage and the notes provided. Remember, a well-crafted Passage Map should summarize the central idea of each paragraph as well as important topics or themes. Use your Passage Map to help you answer each question.

Questions 3-4 are based on the following passage.

The following passage is an excerpt from a speech by Canassatego, an Iroquois, as printed by Benjamin Franklin in the 1740s.

We know that you highly esteem the kind of learning taught in those colleges, and that the maintenance of our young men, while with you,
Line would be very expensive to you. We are convinced,
(5) therefore, that you mean to do us good by your proposal, and we thank you heartily. But you who are wise must know that different nations have different conceptions of things; and you will therefore not take it amiss if our ideas of this
(10) kind of education happen not to be the same with yours. We have had some experience of it: several of our young people were formerly brought up at the colleges of the northern provinces; they were instructed in all your sciences; but
(15) when they came back to us, they were bad runners; ignorant of every means of living in the woods; unable to bear either cold or hunger; knew neither how to build a cabin, take a deer, or kill an enemy; spoke our language imperfectly; were therefore
(20) neither fit for hunters, warriors, or counselors; they were totally good for nothing. We are, however, not the less obliged by your kind offer, though we decline accepting it: and to show our grateful sense of it, if the gentlemen of Virginia will send us a
(25) dozen of their sons, we will take great care of their education, instruct them in all we know, and make men of them.

¶1: Iro. thank BF for ed offer

¶1, cont.: diff groups = diff ed

¶1, cont.: decline BF's offer (purpose)

Questions	Strategic Thinking
3. In lines 6-11 ("But . . . yours"), what general idea is the author most likely conveying? A) It can be a mistake to disagree on the purpose of education. B) What constitutes a useful education for one group of people may not be useful for another group of people. C) Although grateful for the opportunity to attend college, the author wishes to pursue a more practical course of study. D) Challenging wise men on their concept of education is best done on a national basis.	**Step 2: Examine the question stem** The key phrases in this question stem are the line reference, "general idea," and "most likely conveying." **Step 3: Predict and answer** The Passage Map notes that different people have different ideas about what constitutes an appropriate and complete education. Choice (B) is correct.
4. The passage can best be described as A) an attempt to explain why the Iroquois could not accept such a generous offer. B) a desire to describe the benefits of promoting multiple points of view on a subject. C) an examination of the similarities and differences between two viable options. D) an argument that the Iroquois' concept of education was better suited to tribal needs.	**Step 2: Examine the question stem** There are no key words or phrases in this question stem; the fact that there are no specific keywords indicates this is a general question about the passage as a whole. Use the entire Passage Map to answer this question and particularly focus on the author's purpose for writing. **Step 3: Predict and answer** The purpose of the passage is decline Benjamin Franklin's education proposal by providing information about how the Iroquois' own system of education is better for their nation than Benjamin Franklin's offered system. Choice (D) is correct.

Reading & Writing

SCIENCE PASSAGES

The SAT Reading Test will contain either two single Science passages or one single Science passage and one set of paired Science passages. Science passages differ from other passage types because:

- They often contain a lot of jargon and technical terms.

- They can utilize unfamiliar terms and concepts.

While Science passages can be tricky due to unfamiliar language, you will never need to employ knowledge outside of the passage when answering questions. Use the following strategy when approaching Science passages on the SAT:

1. Locate the central idea in the first paragraph

2. Note how each paragraph relates to the central idea. Does the paragraph...

- Explain?

- Support?

- Refute?

- Summarize?

3. Don't be distracted by jargon or technical terms.

- Unfamiliar terms will generally be defined within the passage or in a footnote.

Let's look at the following example of an abbreviated Science passage and question set. After the mapped passage, the left column contains questions similar to those you'll see on the SAT Reading Test on Test Day. The column on the right features the strategic thinking a test expert employs when approaching the passage and questions presented. Note how a test expert can quickly condense the entire passage into a few words and use his or her Passage Map to ask questions that build a prediction for the correct answer.

 Remember

When you encounter more than one theory or idea, paraphrase each in as few words as possible in your Passage Map.

Reading & Writing

Strategic Thinking
Step 1: Read actively Read the passage and the notes provided. Remember, a well-crafted Passage Map should summarize the central idea of each paragraph as well as important topics or themes. Your notes for Science passages should focus on the passage's central idea and how each paragraph relates to that idea. Use your Passage Map to help you answer each question.

Questions 5-6 are based on the following passage.

This passage details the regular journey of a group of green sea turtles from their feeding to breeding grounds.

Green sea turtles, shelled reptiles that traversed the oceans eons before mammals evolved, are known for their prodigious migrations. One group
Line of green sea turtles makes a regular journey from
(5) feeding grounds near the Brazilian Coast to breeding beaches on Ascension Island, a barren, relatively predator-free island in the central equatorial Atlantic. Proverbially slow on land, these turtles cover the distance of more than 2,000 kilometers
(10) in as little as two weeks. But how is this navigation of deep, featureless ocean accomplished? The sun's movements seem to provide the turtles with a navigational aid, but this is only part of the answer.

In addition to possessing good eyesight, green
(15) turtles appear to have an excellent sense of smell. In fact, the turtles may orient themselves by detecting traces of substances released from Ascension Island itself. Because Ascension Island lies in the midst of a major west-flowing ocean current, scientists
(20) believe that chemical substances picked up from the islands would tend to flow westward toward the feeding grounds of the turtle. As a result, these substances may provide a scented chemical trail that the turtles are able to follow. A mathematical
(25) model has been used to show that a concentration of substances delivered from Ascension Island to the turtles' feeding grounds, though diluted, would probably be sufficient to be sensed by the turtles.

The turtles' eyesight, meanwhile, may help direct
(30) the turtles from their feeding grounds into the path of this chemical trail. It is an established fact that turtles are capable of distinguishing between different light densities. Turtles recognize at least four colors and are especially attuned to the color
(35) red, because it often appears in their shell coloration. Researchers believe that these turtles swim east toward the rising sun at the beginning of their migration, changing course toward Ascension Island's beaches as soon as their route intersects the
(40) scented path.

¶1: long-dist. turtle migration: how? (central idea)

¶2: use smell to navigate

¶3: use sight (swim east) & then smell (to beach)

Questions	Strategic Thinking
5. The main purpose of the last paragraph, lines 29-40, is to A) connect two partial explanations for the turtles' navigational ability. B) describe how color perception depends upon the eye's ability to recognize different light densities. C) establish that color sensitivity and shell coloration are closely linked but not explained. D) argue that color perception is the main reason that sea turtles can navigate to Ascension Island.	**Step 2: Examine the question stem** The key words and phrases in the question stem are "main purpose" and the paragraph/line reference. The Passage Map notes from the last paragraph will help you answer this question. **Step 3: Predict and answer** The Passage Map notes for the last paragraph state that the turtles' eyesight helps them find the scented path discussed in paragraph 2. Choice (A) is correct.
6. According to the passage, turtles' eyesight is especially sensitive to A) patterns of stars. B) the sun's movements. C) the color red. D) the chemical trail.	**Step 2: Examine the question stem** The key words and phrases of this question stem are "according to the passage" and "turtles' eyesight." Your Passage Map notes will help you identify which paragraph contains the information to answer this question. **Step 3: Predict and answer** The turtles' eyesight is discussed in the third paragraph. The author says that turtles are sensitive to the color red: "Turtles recognize at least four colors and are especially attuned to the color red" (lines 33-35). Choice (C) is correct.

Reading & Writing

You have seen the ways in which the SAT presents Reading passages and the way an SAT expert approaches these types of questions.

You will use the Kaplan Method for Reading Comprehension to complete this section. Part of the test-like passage has been mapped already. Your first step is to complete the Passage Map. Then, you will continue to use the Kaplan Method for Reading Comprehension and the strategies discussed in this chapter to answer the questions. Strategic thinking questions have been included to guide you—some of the answers have been filled in, but you will have to fill in the answers to others.

Use your answers to the strategic thinking questions to select the correct answer, just as you will on Test Day.

Strategic Thinking

Step 1: Read actively

The passage below is partially mapped. Read the passage and the first part of the Passage Map. Then, complete the Passage Map on your own. Remember to focus on the central ideas of each paragraph as well as the central idea of the overall passage. Use your Passage Map as a reference when you're answering questions.

Questions 7-8 are based on the following passage.

The following passage explains the forces of flight.

¶1: 4 forces of flight (central idea)

What do paper airplanes and large commercial airliners such as the Boeing 747 have in common? Plenty. Despite differences in size and weight, both *Line* must make use of the same physical forces in order (5) to fly. The flight of any airplane results from the interaction of four different forces: thrust, drag, gravity, and lift.

All of the forces acting on the airplane must balance each other in order for the plane to travel (10) along in steady horizontal flight. Thrust supplied by jet engines or propellers (or by a person's hand for a paper airplane) is the force that drives the airplane forward. The airplane cannot actually move any distance forward, however, unless the amount of (15) thrust is enough to overcome the force of drag.

¶2: #1 - thrust

¶2, cont.: #2 - drag, impact on aircraft design

Drag is the air resistance that the plane encounters in flight. Just as the name indicates, air resistance has the effect of dragging the airplane backward as it moves through the air. Jet engines are designed (20) so that the airplane has the necessary thrust to overcome air resistance. Drag can be reduced if the

airplane is streamlined—that is, constructed in such a way that air flows smoothly around it so that there is little friction at the airplane's surface.

(25)   To rise into the air, an airplane has to overcome the force of gravity, the downward pull that the Earth exerts on everything on or near its surface. The airplane accomplishes this feat with lift force, which acts in an upward direction opposite to (30) gravity. Lift is provided by the airplane's wings. The wings and wing flaps are shaped and angled so that air will flow more rapidly over them than under them. When air flows more rapidly over the wing tops, air pressure above the wings drops (35) in comparison with the air pressure below the wings. (This phenomenon is known to engineers as Bernoulli's principle.) When an airplane taxis down the runway (or when a paper airplane is released from a person's hand), the greater air pressure (40) below the wings pushes the wings upward, allowing the airplane to rise despite the pull of gravity. Once the plane is safely in the air, all four of the basic aerodynamic forces figure into the flight as well, whether it is the flight of a big jet or a paper (45) airplane.

Don't get distracted by less important details. While there is a lot going on in this passage, your additions to the Passage Map should have noted the final two forces (gravity and lift) as well as how planes take off. If you're stuck, review the example Passage Map in the Answers & Explanations for this chapter on page 874.

Questions	Strategic Thinking
7. As used in line 29, "acts" most nearly means A) behaves. B) works. C) portrays. D) pretends.	**Step 2: Examine the question stem** *What are the keywords in the question stem?* The line reference, cited word, and "most nearly means." **Step 3: Predict and answer** *Read around the cited word. What synonym can you predict to replace "acts" in this context?* "Functions" or "works." *What answer choice matches this prediction?* _____
8. Which of the following does the passage imply about drag force? A) Drag is the most important physical force needed for flight. B) Drag increases when surface friction increases. C) Drag decreases as a function of increased thrust. D) Drag reduces wind speed and direction.	**Step 2: Examine the question stem** *What are the keywords in the question stem?* "Drag force." *What parts of the passage are relevant?* Paragraph 2, which is where drag force is introduced. **Step 3: Predict and answer** *What does the second paragraph state about drag and drag force?* _____ _____ _____ *Which answer choice correctly reflects the passage's discussion of drag force?* _____

Reading & Writing

Now, try a test-like SAT Reading passage and question set on your own. Give yourself 6 minutes to read the passage and answer the questions.

Questions 9-12 are based on the following passage.

The following passage is an excerpt from Abraham Lincoln's second autobiography, published in a Pennsylvania newspaper in 1860.

I was born February 12, 1809, in Hardin County, Kentucky. My parents were both born in Virginia, of undistinguished families—second families,
Line perhaps I should say. My mother, who died in my
(5) tenth year, was of a family of the name of Hanks, some of whom now reside in Adams, and others in Macon County, Illinois. My paternal grandfather, Abraham Lincoln, emigrated from Rockingham County, Virginia, to Kentucky about 1781 or 1782,
(10) where a year or two later he was killed by the Indians, not in battle, but by stealth, when he was laboring to open a farm in the forest. His ancestors, who were Quakers, went to Virginia from Berks County, Pennsylvania. An effort to identify them with the
(15) New England family of the same name ended in nothing more definite than a similarity of Christian names in both families, such as Enoch, Levi, Mordecai, Solomon, Abraham, and the like.

My father, at the death of his father, was but
(20) six years of age, and he grew up literally without education. He removed from Kentucky to what is now Spencer County, Indiana in my eighth year. We reached our new home about the time the state came into the Union. It was a wild region,
(25) with many bears and other wild animals still in the woods. There I grew up. There were some schools, so called, but no qualification was ever required of a teacher beyond "readin', writin', and cipherin'" to the rule of three. If a straggler supposed to understand
(30) Latin happened to sojourn in the neighborhood, he was looked upon as a wizard. There was absolutely nothing to excite ambition for education. Of course, when I came of age I did not know much. Still, somehow I could read, write, and cipher to the rule

(35) of three, but that was all. I have not been to school since. The little advance I now have upon this store of education I have picked up from time to time under the pressure of necessity.

I was raised to farm work, which I continued till
(40) I was twenty-two. At twenty-one I came to Illinois, Macon County. Then I got to New Salem, at that time in Sangamon, now in Menard County, where I remained a year as a sort of clerk in a store.

Then came the Black Hawk War, and I was
(45) elected a captain of volunteers, a success which gave me more pleasure than any I have had since. I went the campaign, was elated, ran for the legislature the same year (1832), and was beaten—the only time I have ever been beaten by the people. The next and
(50) three succeeding biennial elections I was elected to the legislature. I was not a candidate afterward. During this legislative period I had studied law, and removed to Springfield to practice it. In 1846 I was once elected to the lower house of Congress.
(55) I was not a candidate for reelection. From 1849 to 1854, both inclusive, practiced law more assiduously than ever before. Always a Whig in politics; and generally on the Whig electoral tickets, making active canvasses. I was losing interest in politics
(60) when the repeal of the Missouri Compromise aroused me again. What I have done since then is pretty well known.

If any personal description of me is thought desirable, it may be said I am, in height, six feet four
(65) inches, nearly; lean in flesh, weighing on an average one hundred and eighty pounds; dark complexion, with coarse black hair and gray eyes. No other marks or brands recollected.

9. The author's stance is most similar to that of

    A) an ambitious politician campaigning for office.

    B) an education activist arguing for school reform.

    C) an accomplished storyteller spinning fanciful yarns.

    D) a common man describing his humble beginnings.

10. The author's central purpose for writing this passage is most likely to

    A) emphasize the influence his early education had on his later accomplishments.

    B) recount the important events that shaped his political philosophy.

    C) describe his life prior to his rise to national prominence.

    D) convey the idea that early hardship can strengthen an individual's character.

11. As used in line 38, "under the pressure of necessity" most nearly means

    A) when most convenient.

    B) when he needed to.

    C) whenever he could.

    D) when he was interested.

12. Based on the passage, which answer choice best describes the effect of the Black Hawk War on the author's life?

    A) It gave him an understanding of military tactics.

    B) It allowed him to escape the drudgery of working as a clerk.

    C) It launched his career into electoral politics.

    D) It informed his opinions on the necessity of the Civil War.

Answers & Explanations for this chapter begin on page 874.

EXTRA PRACTICE

Questions 1-10 are based on the following passage.

This passage is adapted from Guy de Maupassant's short story, "The False Gems," from *The Entire Original Maupassant Short Stories*.

Monsieur Lantin had met the young girl at a reception at the house of the second head of his department and had fallen head over heels in love
Line with her.
(5)   Her simple beauty had the charm of angelic modesty, and the imperceptible smile which constantly hovered about the lips seemed to be the reflection of a pure and lovely soul.

Monsieur Lantin, then chief clerk in the
(10) Department of the Interior, enjoyed a snug little salary of three thousand five hundred francs, and he proposed to this model young girl, and was accepted. He was unspeakably happy with her. She governed his household with such clever economy
(15) that they seemed to live in luxury.

He found fault with only two of her tastes: her love for the theatre and her taste for imitation jewelry.

After a time, Monsieur Lantin begged his wife to
(20) request some lady of her acquaintance to accompany her, and to bring her home after the theatre. She opposed this arrangement, at first; but, after much persuasion, finally consented, to the infinite delight of her husband.

(25)   Now, with her love for the theatre, came also the desire for ornaments. Her costumes remained as before, simple, in good taste, and always modest; but she soon began to adorn her ears with huge rhinestones, which glittered and sparkled like real
(30) diamonds. Around her neck she wore strings of false pearls, on her arms bracelets of imitation gold, and combs set with glass jewels.

Her husband frequently remonstrated with her, saying:
(35)   "My dear, as you cannot afford to buy real jewelry, you ought to appear adorned with your beauty and modesty alone, which are the rarest ornaments of your sex."

But she would smile sweetly, and say:
(40)   "Look! are they not lovely? One would swear they were real."

One evening, in winter, she had been to the opera, and returned home chilled through and through. The next morning she coughed, and
(45) eight days later she died of inflammation of the lungs.

He wept unceasingly; his heart was broken as he remembered her smile, her voice, every charm of his dead wife.

(50)   Time did not assuage his grief. Everything in his wife's room remained as it was during her lifetime; all her furniture, even her clothing, being left as it was on the day of her death. Here he was wont to seclude himself daily and think of her who had
(55) been his treasure—the joy of his existence.

But life soon became a struggle.

One morning, finding himself without a cent in his pocket, he resolved to sell something, and immediately the thought occurred to him of disposing
(60) of his wife's paste jewels, for he cherished in his heart a sort of rancor against these "deceptions," which had always irritated him in the past. The very sight of them spoiled, somewhat, the memory of his lost darling.

(65)   To the last days of her life she had continued to make purchases, bringing home new gems almost every evening, and he turned them over some time before finally deciding to sell the heavy necklace, which she seemed to prefer, and which, he thought,
(70) ought to be worth about six or seven francs; for it was of very fine workmanship, though only imitation.

He put it in his pocket, and started out in search of what seemed a reliable jeweler's shop. At length
(75) he found one, and went in, feeling a little ashamed to expose his misery, and also to offer such a worthless article for sale.

"Sir," said he to the merchant, "I would like to know what this is worth."

(80)   The man took the necklace, examined it, called his clerk, and made some remarks in an undertone; he then put the ornament back on the counter, and looked at it from a distance to judge of the effect.

        Monsieur Lantin, annoyed at all these ceremo-
(85) nies, was on the point of saying: "Oh! I know well enough it is not worth anything," when the jeweler said: "Sir, that necklace is worth from twelve to fif-teen thousand francs; but I could not buy it,unless you can tell me exactly where it came from."

(90)   The widower opened his eyes wide and re-mained gaping, not comprehending the merchant's meaning. Finally he stammered: "You say—are you sure?"

        Monsieur Lantin, beside himself with astonish-
(95) ment, took up the necklace and left the store.

1. As used in line 5, "angelic" most nearly means

    A) invisible.

    B) generous.

    C) religious.

    D) innocent.

2. The author describes Monsieur Lantin's wife early in their marriage as

    A) wealthy.

    B) artistic.

    C) frugal.

    D) flighty.

3. The passage suggests that Lantin believed the jewels to be false because

    A) they did not have enough money to buy real jewels of this size.

    B) the theatregoers all wore elaborate costume jewelry.

    C) his wife preferred costume jewelry to real jewels.

    D) Madame Lantin was too concerned with modesty to wear real jewels.

4. Which choice provides the best evidence for the answer to the previous question?

    A) Lines 16-18 ("He found fault . . . jewelry")

    B) Lines 19-24 ("After a time . . . of her husband")

    C) Lines 25-30 ("Now, with her love . . . real diamonds")

    D) Lines 33-38 ("Her husband frequently . . . your sex")

5. Lines 47-55 ("He wept . . . joy of his exist-ence") suggest that which of the following is true of Lantin?

    A) He holds a grudge due to his wife's spending.

    B) He is profoundly depressed after his wife's death.

    C) He idealized his wife and overlooked her flaws.

    D) He is resilient and will find happiness in the future.

6. Which choice provides the best evidence for the answer to the previous question?

    A) Lines 19-24 ("After a time … her husband")

    B) Lines 47-49 ("He wept unceasingly … his dead wife")

    C) Lines 65-72 ("To the last … only imitation")

    D) Lines 90-95 ("The widower opened … left the store")

7. As used in line 61, "rancor" most nearly means

    A) passion.

    B) prejudice.

    C) warning.

    D) bitterness.

8. The main purpose of lines 87-89 ("'Sir, that necklace is worth . . . where it came from'") is to

 A) offer a resolution to Lantin's crisis.

 B) foreshadow future happiness for Lantin.

 C) create a plot twist by suggesting a conflict.

 D) develop an antagonist character in the story.

9. The end of the passage suggests that which of the following was true of Madame Lantin?

 A) She was a notorious jewel thief.

 B) She accrued massive debts to purchase her jewels.

 C) She hid a substantial inheritance from her husband.

 D) She was not as virtuous as her husband believed.

10. What central theme does the excerpt communicate through Lantin's experiences?

 A) Appearances can be deceiving.

 B) People never appreciate what they have until it is gone.

 C) Beautiful things make for a rich life.

 D) A good reputation is easily damaged.

CHAPTER 14

Synthesis Questions and the Kaplan Method for Infographics

 ## CHAPTER OBJECTIVES

By the end of this chapter, you will be able to:

1. Apply the Kaplan Strategy for Paired Passages to History/Social Studies and Science paired passages and question sets

2. Synthesize, compare, and contrast information from two different but related passages

3. Use the Kaplan Method for Infographics to analyze quantitative information and infographics

4. Combine information from infographics and text to answer questions about charts and graphs

SMARTPOINTS

Point Value	SmartPoint Category
Point Builder	The Kaplan Method for Infographics
35 Points	Quantitative Synthesis
25 Points	Paired Passage Synthesis

Reading & Writing

SYNTHESIS QUESTIONS AND THE KAPLAN METHOD FOR INFOGRAPHICS

Chapter 14

Homework

Extra Practice: #1-11

Even More

The Kaplan Method for Infographics

Paired Passages

Reading Quiz 3

Key

 Book Assignment

 Online Video Assignment

 Online Quiz Assignment

SYNTHESIS QUESTIONS

There are two types of Synthesis questions on the SAT:

- Questions asking you to synthesize information from both passages of a Paired Passage set

- Questions associated with an infographic

Synthesis questions require you to analyze information from separate sources and then understand how those sources relate to each other.

Let's take a closer look at the two types of Synthesis questions.

PAIRED PASSAGES

There will be exactly one set of Paired Passages on the SAT Reading Test. These passages will be either History/Social Studies passages or Science passages.

The Kaplan Strategy for Paired Passages helps you attack each pair you face by dividing and conquering, rather than processing two different passages and 10–11 questions all at once:

- Read Passage 1, then answer its questions

- Read Passage 2, then answer its questions

- Answer questions about both passages

By reading Passage 1 and answering its questions before moving on to Passage 2, you avoid falling into wrong answer traps that reference the text of Passage 2. Furthermore, by addressing each passage individually, you will have a better sense of the central idea and purpose of each passage. This will help you answer questions that ask you to synthesize information about both passages.

> ✔ **Remember**
>
> **Even though the individual passages are shorter in a Paired Passage set, you should still map both of them. Overall, there is still too much information to remember effectively in your head. Your Passage Maps will save you time by helping you locate key details.**

Fortunately, questions in a Paired Passage set that ask about only one of the passages will be no different from questions you've seen and answered about single passages. Use the same methods and strategies you've been using to answer these questions.

Other questions in a Paired Passage set are Synthesis questions. These questions will ask you about both passages. You may be asked to identify similarities or differences between the passages or how the author of one passage may respond to a point made by the author of the other passage.

THE KAPLAN METHOD FOR INFOGRAPHICS

The SAT Reading Test will contain two passages that include infographics. One History/Social Studies passage (or Paired Passage set) and one Science passage (or Paired Passage set) will include infographics. Infographics will convey or expand on information related to the passages. Questions about infographics may ask you to read data, to draw conclusions from the data, or to combine information from the infographic and the passage text.

The Kaplan Method for Infographics consists of three steps:

> Step 1: Read the question

> Step 2: Examine the infographic

> Step 3: Predict and answer

Let's take a closer look at each step.

 Expert Tip

Expert test takers consider infographics as part of the corresponding passages, so they make sure to take notes on the infographic as part of their Passage Map.

Step 1: Read the question

Assess the question stem for information that will help you zero in on the specific parts of the infographic that apply to the question.

Step 2: Examine the infographic

Make sure to:

- Identify units of measurement, labels, and titles
- Circle parts of the infographic that relate directly to the question

✔ **Expert Tip**

For more data-heavy infographics, you should also make note of any trends in the data or relationships between variables.

Step 3: Predict and answer

Just as in Step 3 of the Kaplan Method for Reading Comprehension, do not look at the answer choices until you've used the infographic to make a prediction.

Let's look at the following example of a test-like passage and question set. After the mapped passage, the left column contains questions similar to those you'll see on the SAT Reading Test on Test Day. The column on the right features the strategic thinking a test expert employs when approaching the passage and questions presented. Pay attention to how test experts vary the approach to answer different question types.

Strategic Thinking

Step 1: Read actively

Read the paired passages and the notes provided. Remember, a well-crafted Passage Map should summarize the central idea of each paragraph as well as important topics or themes. Use your Passage Map to help you answer each question.

✔ Remember

When answering Paired Passage questions, first read and answer questions about Passage 1. Then read and answer questions about Passage 2. Finally, answer the questions about both passages.

Questions 1-3 are based on the following passages and supplementary material.

Passage 1 warns against society becoming preoccupied with the rehabilitation of criminals. Passage 2 discusses the merits of said rehabilitation.

Passage 1

Nowadays, you hear quite a bit of mealy-mouthed hogwash about diversion and rehabilitation of criminals. If we were to listen to the
Line so-called experts, we would conclude as a society
(5) that criminals are simply misunderstood, and that
the only thing that separates good, law-abiding
citizens from the worst scofflaws is an accident of
birth. These pundits can quote all sorts of statistics
and studies, but they seem to do so at the expense
(10) of one simple fact: as a society, we must uphold the
standards of right and wrong. If we lose track of this
obligation to reward the just and punish the guilty,
then it is not just the criminals who have lost their
moral compass, but society itself.

¶1: author: criminal rehab foolish; punish = moral

Passage 2

(15)   When a crime is committed in our society, we
are always quick to cast blame. The politicians
and pundits who profit from fear and anger will
be quick to promote newer and harsher penalties
nearly every time that a violent crime appears in the
(20) national news, locking up the criminals for longer
at greater expense to the taxpayers and society itself, and yet nothing changes. The root cause of the
crime has not been addressed, and in the rush to
blame, nothing has been done to prevent the next

¶1: society/ pol. want harsher punish- ments; not root cause; author: prevention better

(25) violent crime from occurring. For only a fraction
of the money it takes to lock up an offender, we
could intercede earlier on, mentoring at-risk kids
and making sure that they have the educational
opportunities that will steer them away from
(30) crime. Instead of locking up criminals forever, we
can give them the counseling and job training they
need to become productive members of society. It
is easy to blame, but changing things for the better
requires more.

Education of Inmates

Chapter 14: Synthesis Questions and the Kaplan Method for Infographics **355**

Questions	Strategic Thinking
1. The authors of both passages agree that A) the root causes of crime need to be addressed. B) society must uphold standards of right and wrong. C) it is important for society to confront the problem of crime. D) diversion and rehabilitation can help criminals become productive members of society.	**Step 2: Examine the question stem** Identify the keywords in the question stem: "authors of both passages agree." The correct answer will describe a point on which the authors of both passages agree. **Step 3: Predict and answer** Review your Passage Maps to find each author's main idea. The authors have very different purposes for writing, but both are writing about the same topic: the importance of addressing crime. Choice (C) is correct.
2. One difference between the conclusions reached in the two passages is that, unlike the author of Passage 1, the author of Passage 2 A) recommends lighter sentences for violent criminals. B) argues that increasing educational opportunities can help reduce crime. C) blames politicians instead of pundits for the increase in criminal behavior. D) believes that individuals must be held accountable for their actions.	**Step 2: Examine the question stem** The keywords in this question stem are "one difference between the conclusions" and "unlike the author of Passage 1, the author of Passage 2." The correct answer will focus on how the conclusion of Passage 2 differs from that of Passage 1. **Step 3: Predict and answer** The author of Passage 1 concludes, "we must uphold the standards of right and wrong" (lines 10-11) by punishing criminals. The author of Passage 2 concludes that addressing the root causes of crime will provide better societal outcomes. Predict that prevention efforts like education can help reduce crime. Choice (B) is correct.

Questions	Strategic Thinking
3. How would author 2 describe the graph's data about high school dropouts? A) Evidence that education could be an effective crime prevention measure B) Evidence that criminals should have longer sentences C) Evidence that there is no relationship between education and crime D) Evidence that imprisoning inmates is expensive for taxpayers	**Step 1: Read the question** Assess the question for information on what part of the infographic to focus on: the bars that represent the percentage of high school dropouts in inmate populations. The bars that represent the percentage of high school graduates can be ignored for the sake of this question. **Step 2: Examine the infographic** The unit of measurement on the *y*-axis is the percentage of the inmate population. The labels on the *x*-axis are different kinds of inmates: federal, jail, and prison. The key also provides labels for the two different categories: high school graduates and high school dropouts. The title of the graph is "Education of Inmates." **Step 3: Predict and answer** Since the graph concerns inmates and education, review what author 2 thinks about education. Use your Passage Map to find the part of the passage about prevention. Here, author 2 considers education a way to keep "at-risk kids" out of trouble (lines 27-30). Predict that author 2 would think the statistics in the graph showing numerous high school dropouts indicate greater education opportunities would help prevent crime. Choice (A) is correct.

You have seen the ways in which the SAT tests you on Synthesis in Reading passages and the way an SAT expert approaches these types of questions.

You will use the Kaplan Method for Reading Comprehension to complete this section. Part of the test-like passage has been mapped already. Your first step is to complete the Passage Map. Then, you will continue to use the Kaplan Method for Reading Comprehension and the strategies discussed in this chapter to answer the questions. Strategic thinking questions have been included to guide you—some of the answers have been filled in, but you will have to fill in the answers to others.

Use your answers to the strategic thinking questions to select the correct answer, just as you will on Test Day.

When answering Paired Passage questions, remember to first read and answer questions about Passage 1. Then read and answer questions about Passage 2. Finally, answer the questions about both passages.

Strategic Thinking

Step 1: Read actively

The paired passage set below is partially mapped. Read the first passage and its Passage Map. Then, complete the Passage Map for the second passage on your own. Remember to focus on the central ideas of each paragraph as well as the central idea of the overall passage. Use your Passage Map as a reference when you're answering questions.

Questions 4-6 are based on the following passages and supplementary material.

Passage 1 describes how scientists study stem cells and possible uses. Passage 2 discusses the potential risks of stem cell research.

Passage 1

¶1: author: SC = "miracle cure;" how SC work

Stem cells truly are science's miracle cure. These undifferentiated cells have not yet chosen what type of cell to become, and can be nudged into becom-
Line ing whatever type of cell is needed to help a sick
(5) patient. Stem cells can be used to replace damaged cells in a person who has a degenerative disease or a serious injury.

¶2: embryonic → adult SCs; help diseases; help research

Scientists obtain stem cells primarily from discarded embryos. True, they can also be obtained
(10) from the blood or organs from healthy adults, but these stem cells, while showing some usefulness, are not as adaptable as embryonic stem cells. Embryonic stem cells are incredibly helpful and can mean a revolutionary change in quality of life for patients
(15) suffering from debilitating diseases such as Parkinson's or Alzheimer's. Someday, stem cells could even eliminate the need for human test subjects in drug tests. Without the use of embryonic stem cells, though, that could take an immeasurably longer
(20) amount of time to become a reality.

With stem cell research, the benefits for living, breathing, sentient people outweigh any debate regarding the origins of the cells themselves. In this age of scientific enlightenment, we must always ask
(25) ourselves: What action can best benefit humanity? By answering, we see clearly that stem cell research must continue.

¶3: author: SC research must go on

Passage 2

We stand at an important crossroads in scientific progress. We have the capability now to improve
(30) humanity in ways never thought possible, but at what cost? At what point must progress bow before conscience? Just because we can, is it true that we should?

Stem cell research has the potential to be an
(35) enormous boon to the medical industry. The advance of diseases can be assuaged or halted completely through this remarkable new medicine. But scientists assault the dignity of life when they use embryonic stem cells for their work. By taking
(40) cells from discarded embryos, we begin treading on a slippery slope. It is all too easy to transition from using discarded embryos to creating embryos solely for the purpose of stem cell medicine.

Since stem cells can be obtained from healthy
(45) adults with no cost to life, this is the path on which we should be progressing. These stem cells, safely obtained, can have a significant positive impact on the lives of patients.

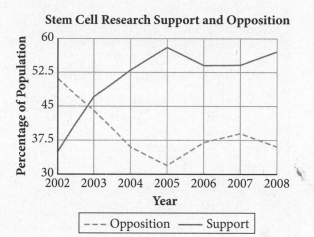

Don't get distracted by less important details. Your Passage Map for Passage 2 should note the author's views on the ethics surrounding embryonic stem cell research. If you're stuck, review the example Passage Map in the Answers & Explanations for this chapter on page 877.

Questions	Strategic Thinking
4. Which assumption do the authors of both passages share? A) Embryonic stem cells have greater potential than adult stem cells. B) The medical benefits of stem cell research outweigh any ethical concerns. C) Stem cell research could provide enormous benefits to humanity. D) The medical benefits of stem cell research must be weighed against ethical concerns.	**Step 2: Examine the question stem** *What are the keywords in this question stem?* The keywords in this question stem are "assumption" and "both passages share." The correct answer will describe an assumption both authors make. **Step 3: Predict and answer** *Although the authors have very different arguments, what can you predict they share in common about their central ideas?* The authors of both passages claim that stem cell research is potentially beneficial. *Which answer choice matches this prediction?* _____

Questions	Strategic Thinking
5. The authors of the passages disagree most strongly on which issue? A) The benefit of stem cells for treating diseases B) The value of stem cell research to medical science C) The adaptability of adult stem cells D) The ethics of using embryonic stem cells	**Step 2: Examine the question stem** *What are the keywords in this question stem?* The keywords in this question stem are "disagree most strongly." You will find the correct answer by finding the biggest difference between the two different opinions. **Step 3: Predict and answer** *What is the central idea of Passage 1?* _____ _____ *What is the central idea of Passage 2?* _____ _____ *What is the biggest difference between these central ideas?* _____ _____ *Which answer choice matches this prediction?* _____

Questions	Strategic Thinking
6. What claim about stem cell research is supported by the graph? A) Between 2003 and 2005, support for stem cell research increased more than opposition to stem cell research decreased. B) Between 2004 and 2006, support for stem cell research decreased and then increased. C) Between 2005 and 2007, opposition to stem cell research increased more than support for stem cell research decreased. D) Between 2006 and 2008, opposition to stem cell research decreased and then increased.	**Step 1: Read the question** *What are the keywords in this question stem?* The question stem does not offer any information about what part of the infographic will provide the answer. **Step 2: Examine the infographic** *What are the units of measurement, labels, or titles of the infographic? What trends do you see in the data?* _____ _____ _____ _____ **Step 3: Predict and answer** *What can you predict?* Because this question stem is general, it is difficult to make a prediction. While keeping in mind the trends on the graph, evaluate each answer choice. *Is choice A supported by the graph? How do you know?* No, because the increase of support and the decrease of opposition are equal, according to the graph. (You can determine they're equal by counting the number of boxes each line spans on the y-axis.)

Reading & Writing

Questions	Strategic Thinking
	Is choice B supported by the graph? How do you know? _____ _____ *Is choice C supported by the graph? How do you know?* _____ _____ *Is choice D supported by the graph? How do you know?* _____ _____ *What is the correct answer?* _____

Now, try a test-like SAT Reading passage on your own. Give yourself 6 minutes to read the passage and answer the questions.

Remember to first read and answer questions about Passage 1. Then read and answer questions about Passage 2. Finally, answer the questions about both passages.

Questions 7-9 are based on the following passages and supplementary material.

The following passages reflect on the Machnovschina, an anarchist peasant uprising in the Ukraine active from approximately 1917 to 1922. During their brief and turbulent history, the Makhnovshchina (also known as Makhnovists) fought against the Central Powers, the White Army, and the Red Army, their sometimes ally that eventually turned on them and defeated them. During this time period, Ukraine alternated between rule by Russia (later the Soviet Union) and brief periods of independence.

The first passage discusses the relationship between the Makhnovists and their supporters, while the second discusses the differences between the Makhnovists on the outskirts of the emerging Soviet Union and the Bolsheviks who controlled the Soviet Union.

Passage 1

Even had the Ukrainian civilians wanted to ignore the sectarianism of their time and remain neutral, they did not have that luxury—the tur-
Line moil was too absolute, the excitement and terror of
(5) revolutionary upheaval too absolutely compelling. Even for the most isolated of peasants, political impartiality was impossible. From the beginning, there was a bond among revolutionary intellectuals, civilians, and military leaders.

(10)   The causes of civil unrest compounded. Adding to the burden of uncounted years of economic and political subjugation under a quasi-feudal system[1] was the added pressure of an invading Austro-Hungarian army. Meanwhile, Russia was in a state of
(15) chaos, and the Bolsheviks[2] were rapidly consolidating power in a system that promised equality and the rule of the proletariat[3]. There was no central authority to organize them (Russia had all but given up the Ukraine to the invading Central Powers[4]),
(20) and the traditional power of the rich landlords had collapsed with the Czarist government. There was no status quo and no safe choice.

Faced with this state of affairs, many Ukrainian peasants chose to organize themselves within the
(25) Makhnovshchina. Educated in the field and trained behind the plow, they were now charged with the task of organizing and defending a new society under conditions of tremendous adversity. Although the Makhnovshchina was an anarchist, revolution-
(30) ary movement, it was one that emerged out of necessity. It was a way for peasants to join together for mutual aid, revolutionary intellectuals to explore the possibility of a society without central authority, and generals to attempt to secure the rights of the
(35) Ukrainian people to self-determination.

Passage 2

The revolutionary period in Russian history is a classic example of the conflicts between the programs of dogmatic, rigid leaders and the desires and needs of ordinary people. One of the
(40) best examples of this is the struggle between the Bolsheviks and the Makhnovshchina. Not only did the word "revolution" mean very different things to the Kremlin[5] bureaucrats and the Ukrainian partisans, but the reality of the revolution was
(45) very different as well. This fact was noted by one anonymous soldier who, beginning his career as a Kremlin guard, eventually became a member of the Makhnovist army. He noted that "conditions could not have been more different between the
(50) two camps. In the one, decisions were based on the political theories of Marx[6] and Lenin,[7] theories which were never doubted or questioned in the least. In the other, theories were even more important—debated vigorously and openly—but

Reading & Writing

Reading & Writing

(55) only after the day's work had been done and the important decisions had been made based on the needs of the community for food, freedom, and self-defense."

Although the Kremlin's approach might seem (60) like harmless intellectualism, it had disastrous con sequences that the anonymous soldier couldn't have forseen. As the Bolshevik Party gained increasing power, it began to control the official view of events with a systematic paranoia unprecedented in (65) history. If the events differed from the official view, the events themselves (and those who participated in them) were deemed the enemy.

The wartime writings of Leon Trotsky[8] are the best indication of this trend. He alternately char-(70) acterized the Makhnovists as heroes and traitors depending on the current needs of the Bolsheviks. When he required Makhnovists to fight alongside the Red Army,[9] he portrayed them as courageous heroes and valiant fighters, but when he did not, (75) they suddenly became traitors and enemies of the revolution. In 1920, as the Makhnovshchina and the Red Army united to fight against a powerful White Army[10] campaign, Trotsky wrote:

"The working class of the Ukraine can never, (80) and especially not in conditions of tremendous military danger, allow particular units sometimes to fight in our ranks and sometimes to stab us in the back.[11] Waging war against the world's exploiters, the workers' and peasants' Red Army says: 'Who is not (85) with me is against me, and whoever is with me is to remain in my ranks and not leave them till the end.'"

The Ukranian partisans, even as peasants and workmen, were painted as the servants of foreign aristocrats bent on undermining the revolution. (90) Even though Bolshevik presence had been weak in the Ukraine, Trotsky still saw fit to portray himself as the representative of "the working class of the Ukraine" and the Makhnovists as loyal to the work-ing class only to the degree that they recognized (95) Red Army authority.

[1] Serfdom had only been abolished in 1861, and many traces of it remained.
[2] The Bolsheviks were the Communist party that established the Soviet Union.
[3] Working class
[4] The Central Powers fought the Allies during World War I (which took place from 1914 to 1918). During the period in question, the Austro-Hungarian Army was occupying much of the Ukraine.
[5] The Russian capital building which, at the time, was occupied by the Bolshevik Party
[6] Karl Marx, the ideological founder of Communism
[7] Vladimir Ilyich Lenin, the leader of the Bolshevik
[8] Leon Trotsky, one of the leaders of the Bolsheviks
[9] The Bolshevik Army
[10] A conservative army opposed to the revolutionary movements in Russia
[11] The previous alliance between the Makhnovshchina and the Red Army had been broken when the Bolsheviks attacked and devas-tated the unsuspecting anarchists in a surprise attack.

Proportion of Seats in the Russian Constituent Assembly, 1918

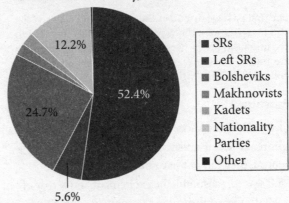

7. The author of Passage 2 would most likely characterize the Bolsheviks' promise described in Passage 1 as

A) the reason the Makhnovischina fought alongside the Red Army.

B) based on theories that had been openly debated.

C) an example of the Bolsheviks' attempt to control the official view of events.

D) inspired by Trotsky's wartime writings.

8. The authors of both passages would most likely agree that

A) the Bolshevik and Makhnovischina leaders shared many fundamental principles.

B) the Austro-Hungarian army posed the greatest threat to the Ukranian peasants.

C) the Makhnovischina were servants of foreign aristocrats.

D) the Makhnovischina was composed of peasants, intellectuals, and soldiers.

9. It can be reasonably inferred from Passage 2 and the graphic that the Bolsheviks

A) wielded political power disproportionate to their voting power.

B) must have had supporters in the Nationality Parties.

C) represented a loyal opposition to the ruling SR group.

D) allied with the Makhnovischina only when necessary to form a majority.

Answers & Explanations for this chapter begin on page 877.

EXTRA PRACTICE

The following questions provide an opportunity to practice the concepts and strategic thinking covered in this chapter. While many of the questions pertain to Synthesis, some touch on other concepts tested on the Reading Test to ensure that your practice is test-like, with a variety of question types per passage.

Questions 1-11 are based on the following passages.

Passage 1 tells the story behind the writing of the United States' national anthem. Passage 2 discusses how the prevalence, use, and value of the United States' national anthem have changed over time.

Passage 1

The story behind "The Star-Spangled Banner," America's national anthem, begins with the War of 1812. This war, which began just three decades after
Line the Revolution, was again waged between American
(5) and British forces for various reasons, including trade interference. Stakes were high: this was one of America's earliest opportunities to solidify its status as a sovereign nation equal to other world powers. Moreover, many Americans feared that the
(10) nation might forfeit its hard-earned liberty were the British to defeat them.

Britain's involvement was limited in the war's first two years due to conflict at home, where Napoleon's army had attacked. But in the summer
(15) of 1814, after the conflict with France had mostly subsided, Britain's focus turned to the American theater, which up to this point had been merely a distraction. In August of that year, the British sent an invading force that quickly defeated a smaller
(20) American force was ill-equipped and poorly trained. Later that night, the British Army invaded Washington, setting fire to several buildings, including the president's home and the Capitol. A few weeks later, on September 12th, British infantry
(25) troops tried to overtake Baltimore, but America's defenses prevailed. The next morning, Britain's navy began a heavy bombardment of Baltimore's Fort McHenry, located at the mouth of Baltimore's harbor.

(30) Some American men, including lawyer Francis Scott Key, happened to be aboard a British ship

in the harbor that same day. These men had come to peacefully request a captive friend's release—a request that, to their fortune, was granted. But
(35) the British detained them on the ship until the attack on McHenry had run its course. From this vantage point, Key and his companions witnessed Fort McHenry's bombardment: twenty-five rain-drenched hours of rockets, explosions, and gunfire.

(40) Through the night, Key waited in grim ex-pectation that the morning would reveal a white flag raised over the fort, symbolizing McHenry's surrender. But instead, by dawn's light he saw the American flag. McHenry had endured; British
(45) forces were already retreating. Moved by the sight, Key began to write, on the back of a letter he was carrying, the words that would become America's national anthem.

This event marked a turning point in America's
(50) favor; within months, the war would be over. The War of 1812 would list among the less significant wars in United States history, by many accounts. But Francis Scott Key's eloquent description of the flag—and the brave victory it represented—would
(55) become a lasting emblem of American patriotism.

Passage 2

America's National Anthem began as a poem titled "The Defence of Fort McHenry." Its melody came from the British tune, "Anacreon in Heaven." Written on September 14, 1814, and distributed
(60) shortly thereafter, the song enjoyed almost instant popularity. A Baltimore theater housed its first public performance about a month after its writing. Following this, a music shop printed the song un-der the enduring title "The Star-Spangled Banner."
(65) Over the next century, the song gained increas-

ing value in the hearts of Americans, growing especially popular during the Civil War. Around the 1890s, the military began playing the song for ceremonial uses. At the time of World War I, when
(70) patriotic music again served as a crucial ideological refuge for America's people, "The Star-Spangled Banner" began to be treated by the military as the national anthem. Also around this time, the anthem was played in its first baseball game: a Cubs
(75) versus Red Sox game in which the song surprised and moved the crowds during the seventh-inning stretch. This effect made national headlines, and, in each game to follow during that series, the anthem was played, meeting an equally enthusiastic recep-
(80) tion. This launched the tradition of the national anthem's now near-ubiquitous presence at major American sporting events.

In 1931, Congress and President Hoover passed the bill to officially designate the song as America's
(85) national anthem. It had long since distinguished itself from other patriotic songs and held special significance in American hearts, but now it would remain the nation's staple celebratory score. Today, the song is taught to children in schools, used in
(90) various ceremonies, printed in many church hymnals and community songbooks, and sung collectively at sporting events, including those featuring American participation internationally, such as World Cup Soccer or the opening ceremonies of
(95) the Olympics. The anthem's final words about those over whom the flag waves ("O'er the land of the free / and the home of the brave") remind Americans of the liberty for which the country was established and the courage of those who fought for it.

1. What is the author of Passage 1's overall purpose?

   A) Analyzing the impact of the War of 1812

   B) Describing the reasons for the War of 1812

   C) Explaining the origins of the national anthem

   D) Evaluating the legacy of the national anthem

2. The author of Passage 1 most likely includes the information in lines 6-11 ("Stakes were high . . . defeat them") in order to

   A) call attention to the reasons for going to war.

   B) emphasize the role of Francis Scott Key in defending the nation.

   C) explain the symbolism featured in the anthem.

   D) show the significance of the outcome of the war.

3. As used in line 26, "prevailed" most nearly means

   A) entrenched.

   B) floundered.

   C) persuaded.

   D) succeeded.

4. The information in paragraph 4 of Passage 1 most clearly suggests that Francis Scott Key wrote the national anthem to

   A) call public attention to the bombardment of American forces.

   B) honor the act of American fortitude that he witnessed.

   C) denounce critics of the War of 1812.

   D) inspire the defenders of Fort McHenry.

5. Which choice provides the best evidence for the answer to the previous question?

   A) Lines 40-41 ("Through the night . . . expectation")

   B) Lines 41-42 ("morning . . . the fort")

   C) Lines 44-45 ("British forces . . . retreating")

   D) Lines 45-46 ("Moved by . . . to write")

6. The author of Passage 1 would most likely agree with which of the following statements?

   A) The national anthem grew out of an incidental war but gained importance as a result of government propaganda during later wars.

   B) The national anthem captured the triumph of the United States in defending its sovereignty and might during the War of 1812.

   C) The national anthem would have gone unnoticed if it were not for its popular resonance with an American people steeped in British musical tradition.

   D) The national anthem rallied support for the defense of Fort McHenry and helped sustain American forces through the War of 1812.

7. Why does the author of Passage 2 most likely begin with lines 56-58 ("America's National Anthem . . . 'Anacreon in Heaven'")?

   A) To show that Key did not set out to write the national anthem

   B) To give credit to the influence of British tradition in American culture

   C) To highlight the poetic devices that Key used in the writing of the national anthem

   D) To demonstrate that the national anthem describes a specific event, not American patriotism

8. As used in line 81, "near-ubiquitous" most nearly means

   A) commonplace.

   B) controversial.

   C) intermittent.

   D) offensive.

9. In lines 96-97, the author quotes "The Star-Spangled Banner" primarily to

   A) demonstrate the lyrical mastery of Francis Scott Key.

   B) explain the symbolism of the American flag in the national anthem.

   C) recall the specific events of the War of 1812.

   D) show how the lyrics of the national anthem reflect American patriotism.

10. How does the information in Passage 2 most enhance the content of Passage 1?

    A) It describes the immediate popularity of the original poem.

    B) It emphasizes the patriotic nature of the national anthem.

    C) It explores the origins of the national anthem in the War of 1812.

    D) It explains how Key's words became the national anthem.

11. Which choice provides the best evidence for the answer to the previous question?

    A) Lines 59-61 ("Written . . . popularity")

    B) Lines 69-73 ("At the time . . . anthem")

    C) Lines 88-92 ("Today . . . events")

    D) Lines 95-98 ("The anthem's . . . established")

CHAPTER 15

Global and Command of Evidence Questions

 ## CHAPTER OBJECTIVES

By the end of this chapter, you will be able to:

1. Locate appropriate textual evidence to support the answer to a previous question

2. Summarize the passage or key information and ideas within the passage

3. Identify central ideas and themes of a passage to answer questions about central ideas and themes

SMARTPOINTS

Point Value	SmartPoint Category
10 Points	Global
60 Points	Command of Evidence

369

Reading & Writing

GLOBAL AND COMMAND OF EVIDENCE QUESTIONS

Chapter 15

Homework

Extra Practice: #1-11

Even More

Science Passages

Command of Evidence

Reading Quiz 2

Key

 Book Assignment

 Online Video Assignment

 Online Quiz Assignment

GLOBAL QUESTIONS

Global questions require you to both identify explicit and determine implicit central ideas or themes in a text. If you pay attention to the big picture—the author's central idea and purpose—while reading SAT Reading passages, you will be able to answer Global questions with little to no rereading of the passage. To fully understand the central ideas and themes of a passage, you must synthesize the different points the author makes with his or her thesis statement, which you should underline when Passage Mapping.

Global questions may also ask you to choose a correct summary of the passage as a whole or identify key information and ideas within the passage. When presented with this type of Global question, you can use your Passage Map, which is essentially a brief summary of what you have read.

> ✔ **On Test Day**
>
> The introductory portion at the beginning of an SAT Reading passage can be very helpful in determining the author's central ideas and themes. Make sure you take the time on Test Day to read this information—it orients you to the passage.

You can recognize Global questions because they typically do not reference line numbers or even individual paragraphs. To confidently answer Global questions, you need to not only identify the central idea or theme of the passage but also avoid choosing answers that summarize secondary or supplementary points.

Note that there is a slight difference between nonfiction and fiction passages. Science and History/Social Studies passages are nonfiction and will have a definite central idea and thesis statement; U.S. and World Literature passages are fiction and will have a central theme but no thesis statement.

> ✔ **Remember**
>
> History/Social Studies and Science passages on the SAT Reading Test are just well-written essays or article excerpts. You can normally find the thesis statement of a well-written piece at the end of the introductory paragraph.

COMMAND OF EVIDENCE QUESTIONS

A Command of Evidence question relies on your answer to the question that precedes it. These questions require you to identify the portion of the text that provides the best evidence for the conclusion you reached when selecting your answer to the previous question.

Kaplan's Strategy for Command of Evidence questions involves retracing your steps; that is, you must return to the previous question to ensure you answer the Command of Evidence question correctly.

To answer Command of Evidence questions efficiently and correctly, employ the following Kaplan Strategy:

- When you see a question asking you to choose the best evidence to support your answer to the previous question, review how you selected that answer.

- Avoid answers that provide evidence for incorrect answers to the previous question.

- The correct answer will support why the previous question's answer is correct.

> ✔ **Expert Tip**
>
> You can recognize Command of Evidence questions easily. The question stem usually reads, "Which choice provides the best evidence for the answer to the previous question?" Furthermore, the answer choices are always line numbers with parentheses containing the first and last word of the intended selection. Answer choices are listed in the order they appear in the passage.

Command of Evidence questions ask that you cite the textual evidence that best supports, disputes, strengthens, or weakens a given claim or point. Whether the argument is supported or not, the use of textual evidence is the same. The evidence can be personal stories, scientific facts, tone, writing style, and infographics. It is important to identify the appropriate aspect of the text used for Command of Evidence questions and not to make assumptions beyond what is written.

The first step to approaching a Command of Evidence question is to make sure you answered the previous question—no matter its type—correctly. If you answer the question preceding a Command of Evidence question incorrectly, you have a smaller chance of selecting the correct answer.

> ✔ **Remember**
>
> There is no wrong answer penalty on the SAT, so even if you have no idea of how to approach a question, take your best guess and move on.

Let's look at the following example of a test-like passage and question set. After the mapped passage, the left column contains questions similar to those you'll see on the SAT Reading Test on Test Day. The column on the right features the strategic thinking test experts employ when approaching the passage and questions presented. Pay attention to how test experts vary the approach to answer different question types.

Strategic Thinking
Step 1: Read actively
Read the passage and the notes provided. Remember, a well-crafted Passage Map should summarize the central idea of each paragraph as well as important topics or themes. Use your Passage Map to help you answer each question.

Questions 1-3 are based on the following passage.

The following is excerpted from Frederick Douglass's autobiographical *Narrative of the Life of Frederick Douglass, An American Slave*.

¶1: Mrs. helped FD read; Mr. thought "slaves not human"

His mistress had been severely reprimanded by her husband for helping Frederick Douglass learn to read. After all, the husband admonished, giving a

Line slave the knowledge to read was like giving the slave
(5) access to thinking he or she was human. If you give the slaves an inch, they will take the ell.

¶2: Mrs. = kind at first

My mistress was, as I have said, a kind and tender-hearted woman; and in the simplicity of her soul she commenced, when I first went to live with
(10) her, to treat me as she supposed one human being ought to treat another. In entertaining upon the duties of a slaveholder, she did not seem to perceive that I sustained to her the relation of a mere chattel, and that for her to treat me as a human being
(15) was not only wrong, but dangerously so. Slavery proved as injurious to her as it did to me. When I went there, she was a pious, warm, and tender-hearted woman. There was no sorrow or suffering for which she had not a tear. She had bread for

¶2, cont.: being a slave owner turned Mrs. hard and mean

(20) the hungry, clothes for the naked, and comfort for every mourner that came within her reach. Slavery soon proved its ability to divest her of these heavenly qualities. Under its influence, the tender heart became stone, and the lamblike disposition gave
(25) way to one of tiger-like fierceness. The first step in her downward course was in her ceasing to instruct me. She now commenced to practice her husband's precepts. She finally became even more violent in her opposition [to my learning to read] than her
(30) husband himself. She was not satisfied with simply doing as well as he had commanded; she seemed anxious to do better. Nothing seemed to make her

more angry than to see me with a newspaper. She seemed to think that here lay the danger. I have
(35) had her rush at me with a face made all up of fury, and snatch from me a newspaper, in a manner that fully revealed her apprehension. She was an apt woman; and a little experience soon demonstrated, to her satisfaction, that education and slavery were
(40) incompatible with each other.

¶3: FD no longer allowed to learn to read

From this time I was most narrowly watched. If I was in a separate room any considerable length of time, I was sure to be suspected of having a book, and was at once called to give an account of myself.
(45) All this, however, was too late. The first step had been taken. Mistress, in teaching me the alphabet, had given me the inch, and no precaution could prevent me from taking the ell.

¶4: FD got children to teach him

The plan which I adopted, and the one by which
(50) I was most successful, was that of making friends of all the white children whom I met in the street. As many of these as I could, I converted into teachers. With their kindly aid, obtained at different times and in different places, I finally succeeded in
(55) learning to read. When I was sent on errands, I always took my book with me, and by going one part of my errand quickly, I found time to get a lesson before my return. I used also to carry bread with me, enough of which was always in the house, and
(60) to which I was always welcome, for I was much better off in this regard than many of the poor white children in our neighborhood. This bread I used to bestow upon the hungry little urchins, who, in return, would give me that more valuable
(65) bread of knowledge. I am strongly tempted to give the names of two or three of those children, as a testimonial of the gratitude and affection I bear

them; but prudence forbids—not that it would injure me, but it might embarrass them; for it is al-
(70) most an unpardonable offense to teach slaves to read in this Christian country. I used to talk this matter of slavery over with them. I would sometimes say to them, I wished I could be as free as they would be when they got to be men. This used to trouble
(75) them; they would express for me the liveliest sympathy, and console me with the hope that something would occur by which I might be free.

¶4, cont.: FD hopes for change

Questions	Strategic Thinking
1. The main purpose of the passage is to A) emphasize the cruelty of slavery. B) refute the idea that education and slavery are incompatible. C) offer historical background to provide context for positions Douglass later espoused. D) describe the risks Douglass willingly took to learn to read.	**Step 2: Examine the question stem** Identify the keywords in the question stem. The phrase "main purpose" indicates that you will find the answer by using the entire Passage Map to summarize the central idea and purpose of the passage. **Step 3: Predict and answer** While the beginning of the passage discusses Douglass's relationship with his mistress, it is primarily about how Douglass learned to read despite his slave status. Choice (D) matches this prediction.
2. The statement in lines 15-16 ("Slavery proved . . . to me") suggests that A) the mistress and Douglass suffered equally from the institution of slavery. B) owning slaves destroyed the mistress's admirable human qualities. C) the mistress regretted the actions she was forced to take as a slave owner. D) Douglass pitied the mistress for the sacrifices she made.	**Step 2: Examine the question stem** Identify the keywords in the question stem: the line references and parenthetical quotation, as well as the phrase "suggests that." You can find your answer by using your Passage Map notes near lines 15-16, particularly those about the mistress, to answer the question. **Step 3: Predict and answer** In this section, the Passage Map notes about the mistress say that she was kind at first but slavery was eventually harmful to her as well because she became hard and mean. Choice (B) matches this prediction.

Reading & Writing

Questions	Strategic Thinking
3. Which choice provides the best evidence for the answer to the previous question? A) Lines 11-15 ("In entertaining . . . dangerously so") B) Lines 23-25 ("Under its . . . fierceness") C) Lines 41-44 ("If I . . . of myself") D) Lines 53-55 ("With their . . . to read")	**Step 2: Examine the question stem** This question stem indicates that you will need to choose the answer choice featuring the lines from the passage that best support your answer to the previous question. Use the Kaplan Strategy for Command of Evidence questions when you encounter this question stem. **Step 3: Predict and answer** You found the answer to the previous question—that owning slaves destroyed the mistress's admirable human qualities—by using the Passage Map notes surrounding the cited sentence in lines 15-16. The Passage Map says that the mistress became hard and mean. This is supported from line 21 through the end of the paragraph (line 40). Choice (B) is the only answer choice that falls within these lines and is therefore correct.

✔ **Note**

Remember the Kaplan Strategy for Command of Evidence questions: Review how you selected the answer to the previous question and avoid answer choices that provide evidence for incorrect answer choices to it. The correct answer will support why the previous question's answer is correct.

You have seen the ways in which the SAT tests you on Citing Textual Evidence and Global Questions in Reading passages and the way an SAT expert approaches these types of questions.

You will use the Kaplan Method for Reading Comprehension to complete this section. Part of the test-like passage has been mapped already. Your first step is to complete the Passage Map. Then, you will continue to use the Kaplan Method for Reading Comprehension and the strategies discussed in this chapter to answer the questions. Strategic thinking questions have been included to guide you—some of the answers have been filled in, but you will have to fill in the answers to others.

Use your answers to the strategic thinking questions to select the correct answer, just as you will on Test Day.

Strategic Thinking
Step 1: Read actively The passage below is partially mapped. Read the passage and the first part of the Passage Map. Then, complete the Passage Map on your own. Remember to focus on the central ideas of each paragraph as well as the central idea of the overall passage. Use your Passage Map as a reference when you're answering questions.

Questions 4-6 are based on the following passage.

The following passage explains the challenges facing a population of trees and possible solutions.

Today, oaks are plagued with problems. There is lack of regeneration in populations of certain species. Pests such as the acorn weevil and the
Line filbert worm eat away at acorns and prevent
(5) germination. By undermining the root systems of seedlings and saplings, ground squirrels, gophers, and other small mammals often prevent these young plants from reaching tree size. Severe diseases, such as sudden oak death, kill many
(10) adult oaks. Many mature oaks are having a tough time with fire suppression. In the past, with light surface fires, the oaks had been able to maintain a stronghold where other plants were not able to compete and died out. Now oaks are being toppled
(15) by trees that have a higher tolerance for shade and are not fire-resistant; earlier such trees would have been killed when Native Americans set fires.

Given all of these challenges, the "old-growth" oaks—the large old valley oaks, Garry oaks, coast
(20) live oaks, and canyon live oaks that have huge girth and large canopies—may become a thing of the past. These oaks in particular are important because there are often more terrestrial vertebrates living in mature oak stands than in seedling and
(25) sapling areas. This prevalence of animals occurs because the large crowns of such oaks provide cover and feeding sites for a large variety of wildlife.

The University of California has embarked
(30) on an ambitious and necessary research program called the Integrated Hardwood Range Management Program to explore the significant causes of oak decline and offer varied solutions. These include investigating the use of grassing
(35) regimes that are compatible with oak seedling establishment, revegetating sites with native grasses to facilitate better germination of oak seedlings, documenting insects and pathogens that attack oaks, and exploring the ways that native
(40) people managed oaks in the past. Scientists at the Pacific Northwest Research Station in Olympia, Washington, and at Redwood National Park in northern California are reintroducing the burning practices of Native Americans. When used in

¶1: oak problems: pests & disease, other trees

¶2: oaks in danger

¶3: research into problems & solutions

¶3:
various
solutions
include
Native
American
approach
of using
fire

(45) Garry oak ecosystems, fires keep Douglas firs from encroaching on the oaks and promote the growth of wildflowers that are important food plants. Further investigations about these fire practices may be essential in figuring out how to maintain (50) oaks in the western landscape today, given that the fires address many of the factors that are now causing oak decline, from how to eliminate insect pests of acorns to how to maintain an open structure in oak groves.

(55)   Ecological restoration, the traditional approach to woodland maintenance, refers to humans intervening on a very limited time scale to bring back plants and animals known to have historically existed in an area. The decline of oaks, one of the (60) most significant plants to Native Americans, shows us that humans may play an integral part in the restoration of oak areas. While animals such as jays have been recognized as crucial partners in oak well-being, human actions through the eons may (65) also have been key to the oaks' flourishing.

    Sudden oak death, for example, although of exotic origin, may be curtailed locally by thinning around coastal oaks and tan oaks and setting light surface fires, simulating ancient fire management (70) practices of Native Americans. Indigenous shrubs and trees that grow in association with oaks are hosts to the sudden oak death pathogen. By limiting the growth of these shrubs, burning that mimics earlier Native American ways may reduce (75) opportunities for disease agents to jump from other plants to oak trees. With a more open environment, it may be harder for sudden oak death to spread.

    The oak landscapes that we inherited, which still bear the marks of former Native American (80) interactions, demand a new kind of restoration that complements other forms of ecological restoration. This new kind of restoration could be called ethnobotanical restoration, defined as reestablishing the historic plant communities of (85) a given area and restoring indigenous harvesting, vegetation management, and cultivation practices (seedbearing, burning, pruning, sowing, tilling, and weeding) necessary to maintain these communities in the long term.

(90)   Thus, this kind of restoration is not only about restoring plants but also about restoring the human place within nature. Ethnobotanical restoration is viewed not as a process that can be completed but rather as a continuous interaction (95) between people and plants, as both of their fates are intertwined in a region. Using oaks (through harvesting acorns and making products from all parts of the tree) and human intervention (by thinning tree populations and lighting light fires) (100) may offer us ways to beneficially coexist while improving the long-term health and well-being of the remarkable oak.

Don't get distracted by less important details. While there is a lot going on in this passage, your additions to the Passage Map should note the views regarding human involvement in ecological restoration as well as the definitions of unfamiliar terms like "ecological restoration" and "ethnobotanical restoration." If you're stuck, review the Suggested Passage Map Notes in the Answers & Explanations for this chapter on page 881.

Questions	Strategic Thinking
4. Throughout the passage, the author emphasizes that a key element in the restoration of the oak tree is A) protecting the wildlife diversity found in the oaks' large crowns. B) preventing Douglas firs from encroaching on oak tree habitats. C) utilizing a continuous restoration process focused on human and oak interactions. D) curtailing sudden oak death by eliminating exotic pathogens.	**Step 2: Examine the question stem** *What are the keywords in the question stem?* The keywords in this question stem are "throughout the passage" and "a key element in the restoration of the oak tree." *What parts of your Passage Map are relevant?* The author begins to focus on the restoration of the oak tree in line 55. Look at your Passage Map notes from this point through the end of the passage to determine what the "key element" is. **Step 3: Predict and answer** *What can you predict?* The Passage Map notes from this point on focus on how humans can affect ecological restoration. *Which answer choice matches this prediction?* _____
5. According to the passage, an important distinction between "ecological restoration" in line 55 and "ethnobotanical restoration" in line 83 is that the latter A) recreates ecosystems that accurately reflect historical uses of an area. B) aspires to reintegrate humans into the continuous maintenance of plant communities. C) intervenes for a limited time to restore an area to an earlier condition. D) uses fire suppression more effectively to reduce risks from a variety of factors.	**Step 2: Examine the question stem** *What are the keywords in the question stem?* The keywords in this question stem are "according to the passage," which implies the answer will be directly stated in the text, as well as the two quoted phrases and the lines in which they appear. *What parts of your Passage Map are relevant?* Use your Passage Map near these lines to compare the two types of restoration. **Step 3: Predict and answer** *What is the primary difference between ecological restoration and ethnobotanical restoration?* _____ _____ _____ _____ *Which answer choice matches this prediction?* _____

Questions	Strategic Thinking
6. Which choice provides the best evidence for the answer to the previous question? A) Lines 11-14 ("In the . . . died out") B) Lines 44-47 ("When used . . . plants") C) Lines 72-76 ("By limiting . . . trees") D) Lines 90-92 ("Thus, this . . . nature")	**Step 2: Examine the question stem** *What are the keywords in the question stem?* _____ _____ _____ _____ _____ *What parts of your Passage Map are relevant?* _____ _____ _____ _____ **Step 3: Predict and answer** *What part of the passage supports your answer to the previous question?* _____ _____ _____ *Which answer choice matches this prediction?* _____

Reading & Writing

Now, try a test-like SAT Reading passage on your own. Give yourself 6 minutes to read the passage and answer the questions.

Questions 7-11 are based on the following passage.

The following passage details findings from different eras of prenatal screening and the methods and experiments those findings prompted.

Screening newborns for rare genetic diseases is a relatively new practice that began in the mid-20th century. Prior to the advent of screening,
Line biomedical researchers and health professionals
(5) were preoccupied with the most prominent causes of newborn mortality, such as diarrheal diseases, influenza, and other infectious diseases. By 1960, however, the infant mortality rate had dropped to less than three percent of live births from over
(10) ten percent fifty years earlier. The declining rate was due, in part, to the widespread use of antibiotics; the development of vaccines, particularly the Salk and Sabin polio vaccines; improved nutrition; better education; and generally improved sanitary
(15) practices. As infant mortality rates dropped, attention shifted to the etiology of rare diseases. The first major milestone in this focus shift occurred in 1962, when President Kennedy announced that the federal government would begin exploring the
(20) problem of mental disability—until then, a largely ignored issue. He created the President's Panel on Mental Retardation to lead this exploration.

During roughly the same time period, a major scientific breakthrough in the study of
(25) phenylketonuria, or PKU, was underway. In 1934, Dr. Asbjorn Folling of Norway first described the condition when he observed that some of his mentally disabled patients had phenylpyruvic acid in their urine, a finding indicative of a deficiency in
(30) the enzyme that converts phenylalanine to tyrosine, a necessary component for protein synthesis. When this transformation does not occur, phenylalanine accumulates in the blood. High levels of phenylalanine are toxic to the developing brain of
(35) an infant and cause mental retardation. At the time,

the preventive strategy was to reduce phenylalanine levels in the patient's diet. This approach had one serious drawback, though. Phenylalanine is an essential amino acid necessary for proper growth,
(40) so deficiencies in it may also lead to mental retardation.

Despite this risk, the younger siblings of children with PKU were given diets low in phenylalanine from a very early age. The results were somewhat
(45) encouraging and, in light of the beneficial evidence from this special diet, two therapeutically promising research initiatives were launched. One was to devise a source of protein free of phenylalanine. The outcome was the infant formula Lofenalac,
(50) which is still in use today. The other initiative was aimed at developing a method for detecting high phenylalanine levels before damage to the developing brain could occur.

Dr. Robert Guthrie led the second initiative,
(55) which yielded a breakthrough in the early 1960s. He developed a test to detect PKU before it became clinically symptomatic. The test consisted of a culture of *Bacillus subtilis* and B-2-thienylalanine, which inhibits the growth of the bacteria. Once a
(60) blood sample from the newborn was added to this culture, the bacteria would leach the phenyl-alanine from the blood spot, overcome the inhibition caused by the B-2-thienylalanine, and grow. Bacterial growth beyond a normal range indicated
(65) elevated levels of phenylalanine and thus the presence of PKU in the newborn.

The test was not perfect. Over the next few years, it produced quite a few false positives, and some children unnecessarily received low phenyl-
(70) alanine diets. To compound the problem, there was uncertainty about the amount of phenylalanine to cut from the diet; as a result, some healthy children developed mental disabilities because of the treat-

ment. Nevertheless, PKU screening was generally con-
(75) sidered a success, and spurred questions about whether
other diseases might be prevented through early detection. After further study, it became clear that they could.
By the late 1960s, newborn screening for rare genetic
diseases had become a permanent part of infant health
(80) care in the United States.

7. The passage most strongly suggests that prior
to the research initiatives described in lines
42-53,

A) little research had been conducted on the
causes of newborn mortality.

B) influenza research had yielded the most
effective treatments.

C) a treatment for PKU was implemented,
despite its inherent risks.

D) screening newborns for genetic diseases
was a well-established practice.

8. Which choice provides the best evidence for
the answer to the previous question?

A) Lines 1-3 ("Screening newborns . . . mid-
20th century")

B) Lines 6-7 ("such as . . . diseases")

C) Lines 31-33 ("When this . . . blood")

D) Lines 39-41 ("Phenylalanine . . . retardation")

9. This passage can best be described as

A) a brief history of biomedical research in
the 20th century.

B) a description of how an important diagnostic tool grew out of an attempt to treat
a specific disease.

C) an argument in support of genetic
screening for rare diseases.

D) an essay questioning the ethical nature of
using untested medical treatments.

10. According to the passage, which of the
following contributed to the practice of
screening newborns for rare genetic diseases?

A) Increased use of antibiotics

B) The development of Lofenalac

C) The false positives produced by Dr.
Guthrie's test

D) The success of PKU screening

11. Which choice provides the best evidence for
the answer to the previous question?

A) Lines 10-15 ("The declining . . .
practices")

B) Lines 49-50 ("The outcome . . . today")

C) Lines 67-70 ("Over the . . . diets")

D) Lines 74-77 ("Nevertheless, PKU . . .
detection")

Answers & Explanations for this chapter begin on
page 881.

EXTRA PRACTICE

The following questions provide an opportunity to practice the concepts and strategic thinking covered in this chapter. While many of the questions pertain to Citing Textual Evidence and Global questions, some touch on other concepts tested on the Reading Test to ensure that your practice is test-like, with a variety of question types per passage.

Questions 1-11 are based on the following passage and supplementary material.

This passage describes how tree farms, widely thought to offer little support to wildlife, became home to a rare species of birds.

As our environment changes over time, certain species thrive while others become rarer. One such species is the small, difficult-to-find Swainson's
Line warbler. Scientists struggle to estimate the
(5) population of this songbird because it is challenging to track. America's foremost wildlife artist, John James Audubon, attempted to describe the bird in the 1830s. Even then, it was considered uncommon. Some of the other birds studied by Audubon
(10) have already become extinct, including the ivory-billed woodpecker. Others, such as the Allen's hummingbird, the spotted owl, and the osprey, are at increased risk of extinction due to their habitats disappearing. Against all odds, the Swainson's
(15) warbler has held on by changing where it spends its summer seasons.

The Swainson's warbler has been at risk for extinction due to the specificity of its needs. During breeding season, summer, the bird traditionally
(20) spends time in the southeastern United States forests and lowlands. It then migrates to subtropical locations in the winter, seeking the dry forests of Jamaica or other evergreen forests in Mexico and Cuba. The low population has been attributed to the
(25) loss of these habitats due to the gradual conversion of hardwood forests into farmland, reservoirs, and urban or suburban areas. With numbers as low as 90,000 worldwide, the prognosis for the continued survival of the bird has been bleak.
(30) Scientists have been studying the birds across the southern United States for more than two decades, but attempts to conserve the species have fallen

short due to a lack of understanding of their true habitat needs. Scientists tried to shift the Swainson's
(35) warbler to national forests, public refuges, and private sanctuaries, but success was limited. Recently, though, researchers found that the population is increasing. Since the 1990s, Swainson's warblers have been doing what scientists attempted to do for
(40) them: the birds have created new breeding grounds for themselves by moving into industrial pine plantations that have been planted in ten different states.

Millions of acres of industrial pine forests have been planted since the 1920s. Some of these planta-
(45) tions are even located in the same areas that Swainson's warblers used to use for breeding grounds before the area's natural forests disappeared. With trees cut every 25 to 35 years, these plantations support a $200 billion industry that produces wood-
(50) based goods from housing lumber to notebook paper. The pine plantations were once thought by scientists to offer little support to any wildlife. They do not make ideal habitats due to the even spacing of planted rows and the lack of diversity in tree
(55) species. These plantations, though, happen to offer the Swainson's warbler two of the things they most require from their habitats.

When the pines at these tree farms reach about twenty feet high, they hit the one specific stage of
(60) growth that appeals to the birds. This height creates high-density undergrowth that the birds rely on for protection during their breeding season. This point of the pine development best mimics the bird's traditional habitat. Before deforestation occurred in
(65) the Southeastern United States, Swainson's warblers lived in thickets of cane or areas with dense vines and tangled undergrowth. At the pine plantations,

the habitat lasts for about seven to eight years before the trees grow too tall to provide the birds
(70) the coverage that they seek. The birds move on once the tangled undergrowth they prefer disappears.

The Swainson's warbler's secondary requirement that pine plantations can easily provide is space. A single breeding pair of the species requires between
(75) 10 and 20 acres of land. This large amount of space is one of the reasons why the species was so vulnerable to deforestation.

Today, pine plantations occupy some 40 million acres in the southern United States. Not all of these
(80) acres are usable to the birds, though. When the cutting cycles and the amount of time the trees offer the type of undergrowth desirable to the Swainson's warblers are considered, it is estimated that approximately 10 million acres of pine plantations
(85) are available to the birds at one time.

These numbers suggest that pine plantations will become the Swainson's warbler's primary habitat over time. The species owes its continued existence to its ability to adapt. While other species of war-
(90) bler have disappeared entirely due to the clearing of natural forests, the Swainson's warbler has remained flexible, shifting its behavior to ensure its own preservation.

Planted vs. Natural Pine Forests in the Southern U.S.

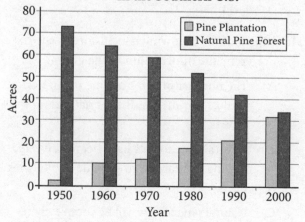

Adapted from *United States Geological Survey, Land Cover Trends Project.*

1. The central idea of the passage is primarily concerned with

   A) the impact of deforestation on endangered birds throughout North America and the Caribbean.

   B) how industrial pine plantations have affected the manufacturing of wood-based commercial goods.

   C) how the population of the Swainson's warbler is recovering despite the destruction of the bird's natural habitat.

   D) the ways in which scientists have struggled to increase populations of the Swainson's warbler.

2. The author refers to the Allen's hummingbird, spotted owl, and osprey in lines 11-12 to

   A) contrast the habitat needs of the Swainson's warbler with that of other bird species.

   B) illustrate the difficulties faced by conservationists attempting to protect threatened birds.

   C) provide examples of other birds threatened by the disappearance of their habitats.

   D) imply that more species of birds will find alternative habitats as deforestation continues.

3. Based on the information in the passage, conservation efforts to protect the Swainson's warbler have been unsuccessful because scientists have

   A) been unable to track the Swainson's warbler population.

   B) not had the resources to move the birds to new habitats.

   C) not understood the bird's habitat needs.

   D) been unable to get the birds to breed in captivity.

4. Which choice provides the best evidence for the answer to the previous question?

A) Lines 4-6 ("Scientists struggle . . . track")

B) Lines 18-21 ("During breeding . . . low-lands")

C) Lines 30-34 ("Scientists have . . . habitat needs")

D) Lines 58-60 ("When the pines . . . birds")

5. As used in line 25, "conversion" most nearly means

A) translation.

B) destruction.

C) variation.

D) transformation.

6. Based on the information in the passage, the reader can infer that

A) bird populations will continue to decrease if their natural habitats are destroyed.

B) the Swainson's warbler's population will decrease again if more pine forests are not planted.

C) the profitability of the pine forests is increased by the presence of the Swainson's warbler.

D) populations of other endangered birds would increase if they moved to private sanctuaries.

7. Which choice provides the best evidence for the answer to the previous question?

A) Lines 1-4 ("As our environment . . . warbler")

B) Lines 11-14 ("Others, such as . . . disappearing")

C) Lines 43-44 ("Millions of acres . . . 1920s")

D) Lines 51-52 ("The pine plantations . . . wildlife")

8. The primary purpose of this passage is to

A) argue that more must be done to protect endangered bird species.

B) persuade readers to learn more about how they can help protect birds.

C) summarize the ways that conservation groups have failed to protect endangered birds.

D) explain how one threatened species of bird has adapted to its disappearing habitat.

9. The migration of the Swainson's warbler to industrial pine forests is most similar to which of the following?

A) Beavers building dams using sticks and logs

B) Spiders creating cobwebs in bushes and trees

C) Aquatic animals creating artificial reefs from shipwrecks

D) Raccoons foraging for food in garbage bins

10. As used in line 62, "point" most nearly means

A) stage.

B) purpose.

C) detail.

D) level.

11. Which of the following conclusions is supported by the information in the graph?

A) The number of acres of pine plantation could soon surpass that of natural pine forests.

B) Natural pine forests have been converted to pine plantations to provide habitats for birds.

C) Natural pine forests will be completely replaced by pine plantations by the year 2050.

D) Pine plantations produce more usable lumber per acre than natural pine forests.

Connections and Vocab-in-Context Questions

CHAPTER OBJECTIVES

By the end of this chapter, you will be able to:

1. Identify and answer Connections questions that ask about explicitly stated cause-and-effect, compare-and-contrast, and sequenced relationships in a passage

2. Identify and answer Connections questions implicit cause-and-effect, compare-and-contrast, and sequenced relationships in a passage

3. Interpret words and phrases in context to answer test-like questions

SMARTPOINTS

Point Value	SmartPoint Category
10 Points	Connections
60 Points	Vocab-in-Context

Reading & Writing

CONNECTIONS & VOCAB-IN-CONTEXT QUESTIONS

Chapter 16

Homework

Extra Practice: #1-10

Even More

The Kaplan Method for Vocab-in-Context

Reading Quiz 4

Key

 Book Assignment

 Online Video Assignment

 Online Quiz Assignment

CONNECTIONS QUESTIONS

Before we jump into the specifics about inferring connections—explicit and implicit—let's look at different kinds of connections that can exist in an SAT Reading passage.

Connections questions ask about how two events, characters, or ideas are related. The three most common connection types are:

1. **Cause-and-Effect** connections require you to identify an action or condition that brings about a predictable result. You can identify cause-and-effect relationships by the keywords *caused by*, *results in*, *because*, and *therefore*.

2. **Compare-and-Contrast** connections highlight the similarities or differences between two items. Common compare-and-contrast keywords are *similar*, *different*, *despite*, and *like*.

3. **Sequential** connections describe the chronology, or order, in which the items are arranged or occur. Keywords include *first*, *second*, *following*, and *after*.

Reading & Writing

EXPLICIT CONNECTIONS QUESTIONS

Some Connections questions will ask about explicit information; the question stem will provide one part of the relationship and ask you to find the other part. In an explicit Connections question, the wording of the correct answer will be very similar to the wording of the passage.

> ✔ **Remember**
>
> Don't forget Step 2 of the Kaplan Method for Reading Comprehension: Examine the question stem.

IMPLICIT CONNECTIONS QUESTIONS

Questions about implicit connections, like those about explicit connections, ask you to identify how items are related. However, unlike explicit Connections questions, an implicit Connections question requires you to find a relationship that may not be directly stated in the passage.

When answering Implicit Connections questions, describe the relationship being tested in your own words by using keywords like *because*, *although*, and *in order to*.

> ✔ **Expert Tip**
>
> Eliminating answer choices that are clearly wrong will help you answer even the toughest Implicit Connections questions correctly.

VOCAB-IN-CONTEXT QUESTIONS

Vocab-in-Context questions require you to deduce the meaning of a word or phrase by using the context in which the word or phrase appears. You can recognize Vocab-in-Context questions because the wording of the question stem is often like this: "As used in line 7, 'clairvoyant' most nearly means . . . "

> ✔ **Expert Tip**
>
> Some Vocab-in-Context questions ask about infrequently used words that you don't know or that may not have a common meaning. Approach these questions exactly the same way you would any other Vocab-in-Context question—by using the Kaplan Strategy.

Kaplan's Strategy for Vocab-in-Context questions relies heavily on Step 3 of the Kaplan Method for Reading Comprehension: Predict and answer.

To answer Vocab-in-Context questions efficiently and correctly, employ the following Kaplan Strategy:

- Pretend the word is a blank in the sentence
- Predict what word could be substituted for the blank
- Select the answer choice that best matches your prediction

> ✔ **Real-World Application**
>
> You can use the Kaplan Strategy for Vocab-in-Context questions outside of the test preparation context. It works for texts you read for school and in your free time.

Let's look at the following example of a test-like passage and question set. After the mapped passage, the left column contains questions similar to those you'll see on SAT Reading Test on Test Day. The column on the right features the strategic thinking test experts employ when approaching the passage and questions presented. Pay attention to how test experts vary the approach to answer different question types.

> ✔ **Note**
>
> SAT passages often use primary source material, which means the language can seem antiquated to modern readers. In some instances, we have modified this language. Don't let that distract you from making a Passage Map focusing on the central ideas.

Strategic Thinking

Step 1: Read actively

Read the passage and the notes provided. Remember, a well-crafted Passage Map should summarize the central idea of each paragraph, as well as important topics or themes. Use your Passage Map to help you answer each question.

Questions 1-3 are based on the following passage.

The following passage is adapted from President Abraham Lincoln's Second Inaugural Address, delivered on March 4, 1865.

¶1: 1st vs 2nd AL inauguration address

At this second appearing to take the oath of the Presidential office there is less occasion for an extended address than there was at the first. Then,
Line a statement somewhat in detail of a course to be
(5) pursued seemed fitting and proper. Now, at the expiration of four years, during which public declarations have been constantly called forth on every point and phase of the great contest which still absorbs the attention and engrosses the energies

¶1, cont.: progress good; public knows too

(10) of the nation, little that is new would be presented. The progress of our arms, upon which all else chiefly depends, is as well known to the public as to myself, and it is, I trust, reasonably satisfactory and encouraging to all. With high hope for the future,
(15) no prediction in regard to it is ventured.

¶2: before: war about to happen but no one wanted it

On the occasion corresponding to this four years ago all thoughts were anxiously directed to an impending civil war. All dreaded it, all sought to avert it. While the inaugural address was being delivered

¶2, cont.: bad guys made war to destroy Union; good guys accepted to save it

(20) from this place, devoted altogether to *saving* the Union without war, urgent agents were in the city seeking to *destroy* it without war—seeking to dissolve the Union and divide effects by negotiation. Both parties deprecated war, but one of them would
(25) *make* war rather than let the nation survive, and the other would *accept* war rather than let it perish, and the war came.

¶3: before: most slaves in South

One-eighth of the whole population were black slaves, not distributed generally over the Union,
(30) but localized in the southern part of it. These slaves constituted a peculiar and powerful interest. All

¶3, cont.: slavery = cause of war

knew that this interest was somehow the cause of the war. To strengthen, perpetuate, and extend this interest was the object for which the insurgents
(35) would rend the Union, even by war; while the Government claimed no right to do more than to restrict the territorial enlargement of it. Neither party expected for the war the magnitude or the duration which it has already attained. Neither an-

¶3, cont.: no one knew how big or how long war would be

(40) ticipated that the cause of the conflict might cease with or even before the conflict itself should cease. Each looked for an easier triumph, and a result less fundamental and astounding.

Questions	Strategic Thinking
1. Which choice best describes the differing attitudes of the insurgents and the government toward slavery? A) The insurgents wanted to preserve slavery's reach, while the government wanted to reduce it. B) The insurgents wanted to extend slavery's reach, while the government wanted to abolish the institution. C) The insurgents wanted to extend slavery's reach, while the government wanted to limit the expansion of slavery. D) The insurgents wanted to reduce slavery's reach, while the government wanted to preserve it.	**Step 2: Examine the question stem** Identify the key words and phrases in the question stem: "differing attitudes of the insurgents and the government toward slavery." The Passage Map note "goals of both sides" indicates that the answer will be found in the third paragraph. **Step 3: Predict and answer** According to the third paragraph, the insurgents wanted "to strengthen, perpetuate, and extend" slavery (line 33) and the government wanted to "restrict the territorial enlargement" of slavery (line 37). Choice (C) matches this prediction.
2. As used in line 34, "interest" most nearly means A) involvement. B) attention. C) claim. D) return.	**Step 2: Examine the question stem** The keywords in this question stem are the cited word and "most nearly means." Use the Kaplan Strategy for Vocab-in-Context questions to answer question stems with this phrasing. **Step 3: Predict and answer** "Interest" is used three times in lines 31-34, but this question is asking about its third appearance. The context of "interest" in this sentence is related to the goals of the insurgents, who wanted to extend slavery. "Interest" could be replaced by *ownership* or *privilege*. Choice (C) matches this prediction.

Questions	Strategic Thinking
3. The result referred to in lines 42-43 ("a result . . . astounding") was most likely caused by the A) magnitude of the war. B) limitation of slavery. C) duration of the war. D) dissolution of the Union.	**Step 2: Examine the question stem** The key words and phrases in the question stem are the cited phrase and "most likely caused by." The Passage Map notes for paragraph 3 will point toward the correct answer. **Step 3: Predict and answer** The Passage Map notes for this paragraph cite slavery as the cause of the war. Choice (B) matches this prediction.

Reading & Writing

You have seen the ways in which the SAT tests you on Connections and Vocab-in-Context questions in Reading passages and the way an SAT expert approaches these types of questions.

You will use the Kaplan Method for Reading Comprehension to complete this section. Part of the test-like passage has been mapped already. Your first step is to complete the Passage Map. Then, you will continue to use the Kaplan Method for Reading Comprehension and the strategies discussed in this chapter to answer the questions. Strategic thinking questions have been included to guide you—some of the answers have been filled in, but you will have to fill in the answers to others.

Use your answers to the strategic thinking questions to select the correct answer, just as you will on Test Day.

Strategic Thinking

Step 1: Read actively

The passage below is partially mapped. Read the passage and the first part of the Passage Map. Then, complete the Passage Map on your own. Remember to focus on the central ideas of each paragraph as well as the central idea of the overall passage. Use your Passage Map as a reference when you're answering questions.

Questions 4-6 are based on the following passage.

The following passage is an excerpt from the preface of Moll Flanders *(1722) by Daniel Defoe.*

¶1: book is not fiction

The world is so taken up of late with novels and romances, that it will be hard for a private history to be taken for genuine, where the names and other
Line circumstances of the person are concealed, and on
(5) this account we must be content to leave the reader to pass his own opinion upon the ensuing sheet, and take it just as he pleases.

¶2: MF conceals name

The author is here supposed to be writing her own history, and in the very beginning of her
(10) account she gives the reasons why she thinks fit to conceal her true name, after which there is no occasion to say any more about that.

¶3: MF uses modest tone

It is true that the original of this story is put into new words, and the style of the famous lady we here
(15) speak of is a little altered; particularly she is made to tell her own tale in modester words than she told it at first, the copy which came first to hand having been written in language more like one still in Newgate than one grown penitent and humble, as
(20) she afterwards pretends to be.

The pen employed in finishing her story, and making it what you now see it to be, has had no little difficulty to put it into a dress fit to be seen, and to make it speak language fit to be read. When
(25) a woman debauched from her youth, nay, even being the offspring of debauchery and vice, comes to give an account of all her vicious practices, and even to descend to the particular occasions and circumstances by which she ran through in
(30) threescore years, an author must be hard put to wrap it up so clean as not to give room, especially for vicious readers, to turn it to his disadvantage.

¶4: MF's story is dark

All possible care, however, has been taken to give no lewd ideas, no immodest turns in the
(35) new dressing up of this story; no, not to the worst parts of her expressions. To this purpose some of the vicious part of her life, which could not be modestly told, is quite left out, and several other parts are very much shortened. What is left 'tis
(40) hoped will not offend the chastest reader or the modest hearer; and as the best use is made even of the worst story, the moral 'tis hoped will keep the

reader serious, even where the story might incline him to be otherwise. To give the history of a wicked
(45) life repented of, necessarily requires that the wicked part should be make as wicked as the real history of it will bear, to illustrate and give a beauty to the penitent part, which is certainly the best and brightest, if related with equal spirit and life.

(50) But as this work is chiefly recommended to those who know how to read it, and how to make the good uses of it which the story all along recommends to them, so it is to be hoped that such readers will be more pleased with the moral than the
(55) fable, with the application than with the relation, and with the end of the writer than with the life of the person written of.

There is in this story abundance of delightful incidents, and all of them usefully applied. There
(60) is an agreeable turn artfully given them in the relating, that naturally instructs the reader, either one way or other. The first part of her lewd life with the young gentleman at Colchester has so many happy turns given it to expose the crime,
(65) and warn all whose circumstances are adapted to it, of the ruinous end of such things, and the foolish, thoughtless, and abhorred conduct of both the parties, that it abundantly atones for all the lively description she gives of her folly and wickedness.

(70) Upon this foundation this book is recommended to the reader as a work from every part of which something may be learned, and some just and religious inference is drawn, by which the reader will have something of instruction, if he
(75) pleases to make use of it.

Don't get distracted by less important details. While there is a lot going on in this passage, your additions to the Passage Map should show that Moll Flanders did eventually change and how the author thinks the reader should respond to the story. If you're stuck, review the Suggested Passage Map Notes in the Answers & Explanations for this chapter on page 884.

Reading & Writing

Questions	Strategic Thinking
4. According to the passage, the narrator is concerned that readers may not believe the story because A) each reader is entitled to form his or her own opinion about the story. B) some parts of the story have been omitted. C) different readers will interpret the story in different ways. D) readers will assume that the story is a novel.	**Step 2: Examine the question stem** *What are the keywords in this question stem?* The keywords in this question stem are "According to the passage" and "readers may not believe the story because . . . " The answer will be found in the passage. *What parts of your Passage Map are relevant?* The Passage Map notes for the first paragraph say that the story might not seem true, which corresponds to the question stem. The answer will be in the first paragraph. **Step 3: Predict and answer** *What can you predict?* The author is concerned that the readers might not believe the story because "the world is so taken up of late with novels and romances," which may cause many readers to believe that the story is fictional (lines 1-2). *Which answer choice matches this prediction?* _____
5. Based on the passage, the narrator hopes that readers of the story will A) understand the reasons for omitting certain parts of the story. B) recognize the harm that a misguided reading might cause. C) use the moral of the story to improve their own lives. D) enjoy the story for the vividness of the characterizations.	**Step 2: Examine the question stem** *What are the keywords in this question stem?* The keywords in this question stem are the phrase "Based on the passage," which implies that the correct answer is not explicitly stated, and "narrator hopes." *What parts of the passage are relevant?* The narrator discusses his hopes for the reader in the final paragraph, where you will find the answer. **Step 3: Predict and answer** *What does the narrator specifically want the reader to take away from the story?* _____ _____ _____ _____ *Which answer choice matches this prediction?* _____

Questions	Strategic Thinking
6. As used in line 59, "usefully applied" most nearly means A) well written. B) consistent with the author's purpose. C) useful in the proper context. D) humorously recounted.	**Step 2: Examine the question stem** *What are the keywords in this question stem?* _____ _____ _____ _____ *How can you find the answer?* _____ _____ _____ _____ **Step 3: Predict and answer** *What word or phrase can you substitute for the phrase in question?* _____ _____ _____ *Which answer choice matches this prediction?* _____

Now, try a test-like SAT Reading passage on your own. Give yourself 6 minutes to read the passage and answer the questions.

Questions 7-10 are based on the following passage.

The following passage is about the role chemistry plays in archaeology.

Demonstrating that chemistry sometimes can inform history, researchers from the National Institute of Standards and Technology (NIST), Colorado College and Mount Saint Mary's University in
(5) Emmitsburg, Maryland, have shown that sensitive nondestructive evaluation (NDE) techniques can be used to determine the elemental composition of ancient coins, even coins that generally have been considered too corroded for such methods. Along
(10) the way, the researchers' analysis of coins minted in ancient Judea has both raised new questions about who ruled the area while giving insight into trading patterns and industry in the region.

Elemental and isotope analysis of the metals in
(15) ancient artifacts sometimes can pinpoint the places where the metal was mined because ores in a given region often have a unique composition. This can be combined with historical records of when mines in the area were operating to determine when the
(20) coin was likely struck. The results not only help date the coin, but also offer insight into trade and power relationships in the region.

To compare the effectiveness of various non-destructive analytical methods with destructive
(25) methods often used to determine the age and origin of ancient coins, the group studied coins minted by Kings Herod Agrippa I and Herod Agrippa II, in what is modern day Palestine and Israel, during a biblically and historically significant period.

(30) The vast numbers of a particular coin, the *prutah*, found in the archaeological record has led scholars to disagree about when they were struck and by whom. The provenance of the coin is important because it is used to establish dates for places
(35) and events in the early years of Christianity and the onset of the Jewish War (66-70 CE) against the Romans and the Diaspora that followed.

To better establish whether the coins were minted by Agrippa I (41-45 CE) or Agrippa II (after
(40) 61 CE), the team performed X-ray fluorescence and lead isotope analysis to fingerprint the ores used in the production of the coins. These NDE methods are not commonly used on corroded coins because the corrosion can affect the results—in some cases
(45) making it difficult to get a result at all. The team showed that these problems could be overcome using polarizing optics and powerful new software for X-ray fluorescence analysis, combined with careful calibration of the mass spectrometer using
(50) Standard Reference Materials from NIST.

The lead isotope analysis, performed at NIST, showed that the coins that had been attributed to Agrippa I were indeed from that era. More interestingly, however, the group found that the
(55) copper from which the coins were made most likely came from mines that scholars thought hadn't been opened until a century later.

"All the archaeological evidence has thus far suggested that the Romans had moved into Arabia
(60) in the second century CE," says Nathan Bower of Colorado College. "What this analysis shows is that the Romans may have reached the region earlier or found that these mines had already been opened. Either way, our findings suggest that the Romans
(65) had a much closer relationship with this particular region than scholars had previously thought."

To follow up on their research, the group is planning to perform more tests to determine if the mines in question may have been operating even
(70) earlier than their recent findings suggest.

Reading & Writing

7. As used in line 32, "struck" most nearly means

    A) made.

    B) hit.

    C) ignited.

    D) discovered.

8. The passage strongly suggests that the results of the lead isotope analysis on the ancient coins

    A) proved the value of an experimental method of analysis.

    B) offered a definitive analysis regarding the strength of ancient regimes.

    C) showed how the ability to mine coins affects trading practices.

    D) answered old questions and raised new ones.

9. According to the passage, the researchers chose to analyze a particular coin because

    A) it was less corroded than other coins of the same era.

    B) historians knew very little about the era during which it was minted.

    C) the metal used to mint the coin came from mines in Arabia.

    D) scholars disagreed about the origin of the coin.

10. As used in line 38, "establish" most nearly means

    A) ascertain.

    B) install.

    C) build.

    D) begin.

Answers & Explanations for this chapter begin on page 884.

Reading & Writing

EXTRA PRACTICE

The following questions provide an opportunity to practice the concepts and strategic thinking covered in this chapter. While many of the questions pertain to Connections and Vocab-in-Context questions, some touch on other concepts tested on the Reading Test to ensure that your practice is test-like, with a variety of question types per passage.

Questions 1-10 are based on the following passage.

The following passage is adapted from *Around the World in Eighty Days* by Jules Verne.

Phileas Fogg, having shut the door of his house at half-past eleven, and having put his right foot before his left five hundred and seventy-five times,
Line and his left foot before his right five hundred and
(5) seventy-six times, reached the Reform Club. He repaired at once to the dining-room and took his place at the habitual table, the cover of which had already been laid for him. A flunkey handed him an uncut Times, which he proceeded to cut with
(10) a skill which betrayed familiarity with this delicate operation. The perusal of this paper absorbed Phileas Fogg until a quarter before four, whilst the Standard, his next task, occupied him till the dinner hour. Dinner passed as breakfast had done, and
(15) Mr. Fogg re-appeared in the reading-room and sat down to the Pall Mall[1] at twenty minutes before six. Half an hour later several members of the Reform came in and drew up to the fireplace. They were Mr. Fogg's usual partners at whist:[2] Andrew Stuart,
(20) an engineer; John Sullivan and Samuel Fallentin, bankers; Thomas Flanagan, a brewer; and Gauthier Ralph, one of the Directors of the Bank of England.

"Well, Ralph," said Thomas Flanagan, "what about that robbery?"

(25) "Oh," replied Stuart, "the Bank will lose the money."

"On the contrary," broke in Ralph, "I hope we may put our hands on the robber. Skillful detectives have been sent to all the principal ports of America
(30) and the Continent, and he'll be a clever fellow if he slips through their fingers."

"But have you got the robber's description?" asked Stuart.

"In the first place, he is no robber at all,"
(35) returned Ralph, positively.

"What! a fellow who makes off with fifty-five thousand pounds, no robber?"

"No."

"Perhaps he's a manufacturer, then."

(40) "The Daily Telegraph says that he is a gentleman."

It was Phileas Fogg, whose head now emerged from behind his newspapers, who made this remark. A package of banknotes, to the value of
(45) fifty-five thousand pounds, had been taken from the principal cashier's table, that functionary being at the moment engaged in registering the receipt of three shillings and sixpence. Let it be observed that the Bank of England reposes a touching confidence
(50) in the honesty of the public. There are neither guards nor gratings to protect its treasures; gold, silver, banknotes are freely exposed, at the mercy of the first comer. A keen observer of English customs relates that, being in one of the rooms of the Bank
(55) one day, he had the curiosity to examine a gold ingot weighing some seven or eight pounds. He took it up, scrutinised it, passed it to his neighbour, he to the next man, and so on until the ingot, going from hand to hand, was transferred to the end of a
(60) dark entry; nor did it return to its place for half an hour. Meanwhile, the cashier had not so much as raised his head. But in the present instance things had not gone so smoothly. The package of notes not being found when five o'clock sounded from the
(65) ponderous clock in the "drawing office," the amount was passed to the account of profit and loss.

There were real grounds for supposing, as the Daily Telegraph said, that the thief did not belong

to a professional band. On the day of the robbery a
(70) well-dressed gentleman of polished manners, and with
a well-to-do air, had been observed going to and fro in
the paying room where the crime was committed. A
description of him was easily procured and sent to the
detectives; and some hopeful spirits, of whom Ralph
(75) was one, did not despair of his apprehension. The papers
and clubs were full of the affair, and everywhere people
were discussing the probabilities of a successful pursuit;
and the Reform Club was especially agitated, several of
its members being Bank officials.

(80)   Ralph would not concede that the work of the
detectives was likely to be in vain, for he thought that
the prize offered would greatly stimulate their zeal and
activity. But Stuart was far from sharing this confidence;
and, as they placed themselves at the whist-table, they
(85) continued to argue the matter.

    "I maintain," said Stuart, "that the chances are in
favour of the thief, who must be a shrewd fellow."

    "Well, but where can he fly to?" asked Ralph. "No
country is safe for him."

(90)   "Pshaw!"

    "Where could he go, then?"

    "Oh, I don't know that. The world is big enough."

    "It was once," said Phileas Fogg, in a low tone.

[1] Pall Mall: a street in the city of Westminster, London
[2] whist: a trick-taking card game; modern derivatives
include hearts and spades.

1. As used in line 6, "repaired" most nearly
means

  A) fixed.

  B) returned.

  C) stormed.

  D) proceeded.

2. The passage suggests that Phileas Fogg is a
man who

  A) focuses on cultural activities.

  B) lives beyond his means.

  C) enjoys routine.

  D) keeps to himself.

3. Which choice provides the best evidence for
the answer to the previous question?

  A) Lines 5-8 ("He repaired . . . for him")

  B) Lines 8-11 ("A flunkey . . . delicate operation")

  C) Lines 14-16 ("Dinner passed . . . before
six")

  D) Lines 28-31 ("Skillful detectives . . . their
fingers")

4. The passage suggests that Fogg

  A) keeps abreast of current events.

  B) is a political reformer.

  C) has strong opinions about crime.

  D) makes his living as a banker.

5. Which choice provides the best evidence for
the answer to the previous question?

  A) Lines 8-11 ("A flunkey . . . delicate operation")

  B) Lines 17-18 ("Half an hour . . . the fireplace")

  C) Lines 28-31 ("Skillful detectives . . . their
fingers")

  D) Lines 42-44 ("It was . . . this remark")

6. According to the passage, which statement
about the Bank of England is true?

  A) The public has faith in the integrity of the
Bank.

  B) The Bank has taken few precautions to
guard against theft.

  C) The Bank has a history of money being
stolen.

  D) The Bank has carefully managed public
relations.

7. As used in line 46, "functionary" most nearly means

   A) official.

   B) money.

   C) servant.

   D) criminal.

8. The passage suggests that the thief was not part of a professional crime ring because

   A) the suspect acted alone.

   B) the Bank had never been burglarized before.

   C) the suspect was described as a gentleman.

   D) the Bank carefully screened the customers.

9. The purpose of line 93 ("'It was once,' … a low tone") is to

   A) create an ominous atmosphere at the table.

   B) foreshadow Fogg's ideas about the world.

   C) illustrate Fogg's proper demeanor and social skills.

   D) introduce the conflict of the plot.

10. What is the primary purpose of the passage?

   A) To illustrate the problems with theft at the Bank of England

   B) To examine the lives of wealthy men in England

   C) To introduce Phileas Fogg and his social circle at the Reform Club

   D) To parody the social customs of the upper class

CHAPTER 17

Rhetoric

CHAPTER OBJECTIVES

By the end of this chapter, you will be able to:

1. Determine the author's purpose and point of view in a given passage

2. Determine why the author uses a certain word or phrase in a given passage

3. Evaluate both the overall and part-to-whole text structure of a given test-like passage

4. Distinguish between claims and counterclaims and evaluate the use of evidence to support the author's reasoning

SMARTPOINTS

Point Value	SmartPoint Category
50 Points	Rhetoric

Reading & Writing

RHETORIC QUESTIONS

Chapter 17

Homework

Extra Practice: #1-11

Even More

US and World Literature Passages

Reading Quiz 5

Key

 Book Assignment

 Online Video Assignment

 Online Quiz Assignment

RHETORIC QUESTIONS: ANALYZING PURPOSE

Overall, rhetoric refers to the language the author uses, especially in order to persuade or influence the reader.

Some Analyzing Purpose questions ask about the purpose of the passage as a whole. Every author has a reason for writing. To identify that reason—or purpose—ask these two questions:

- Why did the author write this passage?

- What does the author want the reader to think about this topic?

Other Analyzing Purpose questions will ask you to identify the purpose of part of a passage, usually one or more paragraphs. To answer this type of question, read around the cited portion, review your Passage Map, and ask these two questions:

- What is the function of this section?

- How does this section help achieve the author's purpose?

RHETORIC QUESTIONS: ANALYZING POINT OF VIEW

The author's point of view is closely tied to the purpose of the passage. Though some authors are neutral, most authors have an opinion, or point of view. Questions that ask you to analyze point of view require you to establish the author's perspective and how that perspective affects the content and the style of the passage. That is, you need to figure out not only what the author says, but also how the author says it. Mapping the passage will help you determine the author's point of view.

As you map a passage, ask:

- Is the author's tone positive, negative, or neutral?

- Does the author want things to change or stay the same?

- Is the author addressing supporters or opponents?

RHETORIC QUESTIONS: ANALYZING WORD CHOICE

Rhetoric questions about word choice ask about how a particular word or phrase affects your understanding of the author's purpose and point of view.

Don't confuse analyzing word choice questions with Vocab-in-Context questions, which ask about the meaning of a word or phrase. Analyzing Word Choice questions ask about the function of a word or phrase within the passage; that is, why did the author use this word or phrase?

To answer Analyzing Word Choice questions, ask what the function of the cited word or phrase is. Common functions of words or phrases include:

- Setting a mood
- Conveying an emotion
- Building to a conclusion
- Calling to action
- Stating an opinion

✔ **Remember**

Correct answers to Analyzing Word Choice questions will always be in line with the author's overall purpose.

RHETORIC QUESTIONS: ANALYZING TEXT STRUCTURE

Some Rhetoric questions will require you to analyze the structure of the passage. The SAT Reading Test will ask about two kinds of text structures:

1. **Overall text structure** refers to how the information within a passage is organized. Some common text structures are cause-and-effect, compare-and-contrast, sequence, problem-and-solution, and description.

2. **Part-whole relationships** describe how a particular part of the passage (e.g., a sentence, quotation, or paragraph) relates to the overall text. When asked about a part-whole relationship, make sure you determine what function the part plays in the passage.

✔ **Expert Tip**

Include the structure of the passage in your Passage Map. Identifying the structure of the text will make it easier to understand and analyze its content.

RHETORIC QUESTIONS: ANALYZING ARGUMENTS

Other Rhetoric questions will ask you to analyze arguments within the text for both their form and content.

Questions that ask you to analyze a text's arguments vary in scope. There are three types of Analyzing Arguments questions. You may be asked to:

1. **Analyze claims and counterclaims.** A claim is not an opinion but rather the main point or thesis of a passage the author promotes. A counterclaim is the opposite of a claim—it will negate or disagree with the thesis or central idea of the passage.

2. **Assess reasoning.** The reasoning of a passage is composed of the statements offering support for claims and counterclaims. On the SAT Reading test, you may be asked whether an author's or character's reasoning is *sound*—that is, whether the argument is valid and the reasoning for the argument is true.

3. **Analyze evidence.** Evidence can be facts, reasons, statistics, and other information the author employs to *support* a claim or counterclaim. You will have to assess how and why this evidence is used.

Let's look at the following example of a test-like passage and question set. After the mapped passage, the left column contains questions similar to those you'll see on the Reading Test on Test Day. The column on the right features the strategic thinking test experts employ when approaching the passage and questions presented. Pay attention to how test experts vary the approach to answer different question types.

Strategic Thinking

Step 1: Read actively

Read the passage and the notes provided. Remember, a well-crafted Passage Map should summarize the central idea of each paragraph as well as important topics or themes. Use your Passage Map to help you answer each question.

Questions 1-3 are based on the following passage.

This passage details the varying and changing scientific theories surrounding sunspots.

Astronomers noted more than 150 years ago that sunspots wax and wane in number in an 11-year cycle. Ever since, people have speculated that the solar
Line cycle might exert some influence on the Earth's
(5) weather. In this century, for example, scientists have linked the solar cycle to droughts in the American Midwest. Until recently, however, none of these correlations has held up under close scrutiny.

¶1: sunspot cycle & weather

One problem is that sunspots themselves are so
(10) poorly understood. Observations have revealed that the swirly smudges represent areas of intense magnetic activity where the sun's radiative energy has been blocked and that they are considerably cooler than bright regions of the sun. Scientists have not
(15) been able, however, to determine just how sunspots are created or what effect they have on the solar constant (a misnomer that refers to the sun's total radiance at any instant).

¶2: sunspots = poorly understood

The latter question, at least, now seems to have
(20) been resolved by data from the *Solar Maximum Mission* satellite, which has monitored the solar constant since 1980, the peak of the last solar cycle. As the number of sunspots decreased through 1986, the satellite recorded a gradual dimming
(25) of the sun. Over the past year, as sunspots have proliferated, the sun has brightened. The data suggest that the sun is 0.1 percent more luminous at the peak of the solar cycle, when the number of sunspots is greatest, than at its nadir, according to
(30) Richard C. Willson of the Jet Propulsion Laboratory and Hugh S. Hudson of the University of California at San Diego.

¶3: SMM = effects of spots on solar constant

The data show that sunspots do not themselves make the sun shine brighter. Quite the contrary.
(35) When a sunspot appears, it initially causes the sun to dim slightly, but then after a period of weeks or months islands of brilliance called faculas usually emerge near the sunspot and more than compensate for its dimming effect. Willson says faculas
(40) may represent regions where energy that initially was blocked beneath a sunspot has finally breached the surface.

¶4: not sunspots, but faculas that brighten

¶5: spots indirectly affect weather (QBO)

Does the subtle fluctuation in the solar constant manifest itself in the Earth's weather? Some recent (45) reports offer statistical evidence that it does, albeit rather indirectly. The link seems to be mediated by a phenomenon known as the quasi-biennial oscillation (QBO), a 180-degree shift in the direction of stratospheric winds above the Tropics that occurs (50) about every two years.

Karin Labitzke of the Free University of Berlin and Harry van Loon of the National Center for Atmospheric Research in Boulder, Colorado, were the first to uncover the QBO link. They gathered

¶6: KL & HvL found link to temp & pressure

(55) temperature and air-pressure readings from various latitudes and altitudes over the past three solar cycles. They found no correlation between the solar cycle and their data until they sorted the data into two categories: those gathered during the QBO's (60) west phase (when the stratospheric winds blow west) and those gathered during its east phase. A remarkable correlation appeared: temperatures and pressures coincident with the QBO's west phase rose and fell in accordance with the solar cycle.

¶7: BT found link b/t solar cycle & storms

(65) Building on this finding, Brian A. Tinsley of the National Science Foundation discovered a statistical correlation between the solar cycle and the position of storms in the North Atlantic. The latitude of storms during the west phase of the QBO, Tinsley (70) found, varied with the solar cycle: storms occurring toward the peak of a solar cycle traveled at latitudes about six degrees nearer the Equator than storms during the cycle's nadir.

Labitzke, van Loon, and Tinsley acknowledge

¶8: sci. can't explain links

(75) that their findings are still rather mysterious. Why does the solar cycle seem to exert more of an influence during the west phase of the QBO than it does during the east phase? How does the 0.1 percent variance in solar radiation trigger the much (80) larger changes—up to six degrees Celsius in polar regions—observed by Labitzke and van Loon? Van Loon says simply, "We can't explain it."

John A. Eddy of the National Center for Atmospheric Research, nonetheless, thinks these QBO (85) findings as well as the *Solar Maximum Mission* data "look like breakthroughs" in the search for a link

between the solar cycle and weather. With further research into how the oceans damp the effects of solar flux, for example, these findings may lead to (90) models that have some predictive value. The next few years may be particularly rich in solar flux.

¶9: break-throughs, but more research to be done

Questions	Strategic Thinking
1. The author's point of view can best be described as that of A) a meteorologist voicing optimism that the findings of recent solar research will improve weather forecasting. B) an astronomer presenting a digest of current findings to a review board of other astronomers. C) a science writer explaining the possible influence of a solar phenomenon on terrestrial weather patterns. D) a historian detailing the contributions to climate science made by the *Solar Maximum Mission*.	**Step 2: Examine the question stem** Identify the keywords in the question stem: "The author's point of view." Any Passage Map notes about the author's viewpoint will help answer this question. However, the Passage Map doesn't note any specific view or opinion the author offers. **Step 3: Predict and answer** Because the author doesn't express his or her own opinions regarding the topic, the correct answer will accurately reflect the informative style and neutral tone of the passage, as well as the passage's central idea. Choice (C) is correct.
2. The main purpose of the questions in paragraph 8 (lines 74-82) is to A) emphasize how little scientists know about the solar constant. B) explain more fully the mysterious nature of the scientists' findings. C) question the basis upon which these scientists built their hypotheses. D) express doubts about the scientists' interpretations of their findings.	**Step 2: Examine the question stem** Identify the keywords in the question stem: "main purpose of the questions" and "paragraph 8." Look at the Passage Map notes for paragraph 8 to answer this question. **Step 3: Predict and answer** The notes next to paragraph 8 say, "sci. can't explain links." The correct answer will allude to the uncertainty that surrounds Labitzke, van Loon, and Tinsley's findings. Choice (B) is correct.
3. The use of the quoted phrase "look like breakthroughs" in line 86 is primarily meant to convey the idea that A) information about the solar cycle has allowed scientists to predict changes in Earth's complex climate system. B) additional analysis of the link between the solar cycle and Earth's weather may yield useful models. C) despite the associated costs, space missions can lead to important discoveries. D) an alternative interpretation of the data may contradict the initial findings.	**Step 2: Examine the question stem** Identify the keywords in the question stem. The key words include not only the cited phrase and its line number, but also the phrase, "primarily meant to convey the idea." The correct answer will not restate the meaning of the cited phrase but its purpose within the passage. Look at the Passage Map notes surrounding "look like breakthroughs" in line 86. **Step 3: Predict and answer** The cited phrase is a quotation from an official at the National Center for Atmospheric Research. The note next to this part of the passage says that more research is required to fully comprehend any possible link between the solar cycle and weather. Choice (B) is correct.

You have seen the ways in which the SAT tests you on Rhetoric in Reading passages and the way an SAT expert approaches these types of questions.

You will use the Kaplan Method for Reading Comprehension to complete this section. Part of the test-like passage has been mapped already. Your first step is to complete the Passage Map. Then, you will continue to use the Kaplan Method for Reading Comprehension and the strategies discussed in this chapter to answer the questions. Strategic thinking questions have been included to guide you—some of the answers have been filled in, but you will have to fill in the answers to others.

Use your answers to the strategic thinking questions to select the correct answer, just as you will on Test Day.

Strategic Thinking
Step 1: Read actively The passage below is partially mapped. Read the passage and the first part of the Passage Map. Then, complete the Passage Map on your own. Remember to focus on the central ideas of each paragraph as well as the central idea of the overall passage. Use your Passage Map as a reference when you're answering questions.

Questions 4-6 are based on the following passage.

The following passage was written (on the last night of 1849) by Florence Nightingale. She was not only a pioneer in the profession of nursing but also one of the first European women to travel to Egypt (1849-1850) and keep a detailed journal of her letters and reflections of her journey.

My Dear People,

Yes, I think your imagination has hardly followed me through the place where I have been
Line spending the last night of the old year. Did you
(5) listen to it passing away and think of me? Where
do you think I heard it sigh out its soul? In the
dim unearthly colonnades of Karnak, which stood
and watched it, motionless, silent, and awful, as
they had done for thousands of years, to whom, no
(10) doubt, thousands of years seem but as a day. Would
that I could call up Karnak before your eyes for one
moment, but it "is beyond expression."

No one could trust themselves with their
imagination alone there. Gigantic shadows spring
(15) upon every side; "the dead are stirred up for thee to
meet thee at thy coming, even the chief ones of the
earth," and they look out from among the columns,

*¶1: impos-
sible to
describe
Karnak*

and you feel as terror-stricken to be there, miserable intruder, among these mighty dead, as if you
(20) had awakened the angel of the Last Day. Imagine
six columns on either side, of which the last is
almost out of sight, though they stand very near
each other, while you look up to the stars from
between them, as you would from a deep narrow
(25) gorge in the Alps, and then, passing through 160
of these, ranged in eight aisles on either side, the
end choked up with heaps of rubbish, this rubbish consisting of stones twenty and thirty feet
long, so that it looks like a mountain fallen to ruin,
(30) not a temple. How art thou fallen from heaven,
oh Lucifer, son of the morning! He did exalt his
throne above the stars of God; for I looked through
a colonnade, and under the roof saw the deep
blue sky and star shining brightly; and as you look
(35) upon these mighty ruins, a voice seems continually
saying to you, And seekest thou good things for
thyself? Seek them not, for is there ought like this
ruin? One wonders that people come back from
Egypt and live lives as they did before.

*¶2: details of
K temple ruins*

(40)   Yet Karnak by starlight is not to me painful: we had seen Luxor in the sunshine. I had expected the temples of Thebes to be solemn, but Luxor was fearful. Rows of painted columns, propylae, colossi, and—built up in the Holy Place—mud [not even huts, (45) but] unroofed enclosures chalked out, or rather mudded out, for families, with their one oven and broken earthen vessel; and, squatting on the ground among the painted hieroglyphs, creatures with large nose-rings, the children's eyes streaming with matter, on (50) which the mothers let the flies rest, because "it is good for them," without an attempt to drive them off; tattooed men on the ground, with camels feeding out of their laps, and nothing but a few doura stalks strewed for their beds;—I can-not describe the impression it (55) makes: it is as if one were steering towards the sun, the glorious Eastern sun, arrayed in its golden clouds, and were to find, on nearing it, that it were full—instead of glorified beings as one expect-ed—of a race of dwarf cannibals, stained with (60) blood and dressed in bones. The contrast could not be more terrible than the savages of the Present in the temples of the Past at Luxor.

But Karnak by starlight is peace; not peace and joy, but peace—solemn peace. You feel like (65) spirits revisiting your former world, strange and fallen to ruins; but it has done its work, and there is nothing agonizing about it. Egypt should have no sun and no day, no human beings. It should always be seen in solitude (70) and by night; one eternal night it should have, like Job's, and let the stars of the twilight be its lamps; neither let it see the dawning of the day.

Don't get distracted by less important details. While there is a lot going on in this passage, your additions to the Passage Map should continue to note how the author perceives and describes what she experienced on her trip to Egypt. If you're stuck, review the suggested Passage Map notes in the Answers & Explanations for this chapter on page 887.

Questions	Strategic Thinking
4. The statement in lines 38-39 ("One wonders . . . before") is primarily included to A) suggest that many people who visit Egypt overlook many of its important temples. B) express how profoundly Egypt has affected the author. C) emphasize how difficult it can be to understand someone else's experience. D) criticize travelers who do not experience Egypt in the same way the author did.	**Step 2: Examine the question stem** *What are the keywords in this question stem?* The keywords in this question stem are the cited statement and "primarily included to." *What parts of your Passage Map are relevant?* Looking at how the Passage Map notes surrounding the cited lines serve the passage as a whole will help you find the answer. **Step 3: Predict and answer** *What can you predict?* The Passage Map note next to the cited phrase should reveal that the author believes traveling to Egypt is a life-changing experience. *Which answer choice matches this prediction?* _____

Reading & Writing

Practice

Questions	Strategic Thinking
5. What is the most likely reason the author draws a distinction between the two cities in lines 40-41 ("Yet Karnak . . . sunshine")? A) To show that some ancient ruins have retained special relevance while others have reverted to everyday use B) To argue that Egyptian authorities should do more to protect Luxor C) To communicate how dreadful it was to find mundane activities in a place meant to hold great spiritual significance D) To demonstrate how much more difficult it is to describe Karnak than it is to describe Luxor	**Step 2: Examine the question stem** *What are the keywords in this question stem?* The keywords in this question stem are "the most likely reason," "distinction between the two cities," and the cited lines. **Step 3: Predict and answer** *What parts of your Passage Map are relevant?* Look at your Passage Map for notes about the author's contrast of the two cities. The author has a generally positive attitude toward Karnak and a generally negative attitude toward Luxor. *What purpose does providing this contrast serve in the passage as a whole?* _____ _____ *Which answer choice matches this prediction?* _____
6. Throughout the passage, the author employs which of the following techniques to convey her meaning? A) Physical descriptions interspersed with lyrical portrayals B) A series of analogies emphasizing the difference between past and present C) An extended metaphor evoking eternal truths D) Expository prose describing a journey to Egypt	**Step 2: Examine the question stem** *What are the keywords in this question stem?* The keywords in the question stem are "throughout the passage" and "techniques." The answer to the question will be found by analyzing how the author conveys her meaning rather than what that meaning is. *What parts of your Passage Map are relevant?* Your Passage Map probably will not contain the answer, but it can guide you to the more important parts of the passage. **Step 3: Predict and answer** *What are the consistencies in the author's style and tone throughout the passage?* _____ _____ *Which answer choice matches this prediction?* _____

Now, try a test-like Reading passage on your own. Give yourself 6 minutes to read the passage and answer the questions.

Questions 7-10 are based on the following passage.

This passage explores the differences in perception between humans and owls.

It's not difficult to believe that humans and animals perceive the world in different ways. As humans, sight is the sense with which we primarily in-
Line terpret the information around us, and other senses
(5) are generally subordinate. Our sense of survival is
fortunately not dependent on our acute senses, or
we would surely starve to death or be hunted into
extinction. Owls, however, are masters of their
senses, making such optimal use of their biologi-
(10) cal strengths that we, by comparison, can best be
described as wearing blindfolds and earplugs. Were
an owl to attempt to hunt with our limited senses,
it would most likely call us the lesser species, and
possibly initiate attempts to label us as endangered.

(15) As evidenced by our expression "owl-eyed," owls
are known for their acute vision and all-seeing
nature. Surprisingly, however, owls have a more
limited range of view than humans. Whereas a
human can see 180 degrees without turning his or
(20) her head, an owl can only see 110 degrees under
the same conditions. Owls have extremely well-
developed eyes, but their structure is such that they
are fixed in one position: an owl can look nowhere
but straight ahead. They are farsighted, prevented
(25) from seeing clearly anything within a few inches
of their eyes; the popular image of a cartoon owl
with reading glasses is not far removed from truth.
Despite these limitations, however, owls maximize
their advantages. Their sensitive eyes are very
(30) effective at collecting and processing light, making them efficient night hunters. They can turn
their heads almost completely around and nearly
upside down, capitalizing on this range of movement to see over their own shoulders and directly
(35) beneath themselves. They optimize their farsight-
edness to spot the minute movements of prey at

great distances. With regard to auditory efficiency,
owls, like humans, hear a limited range of audible
sounds. Within that range, however, they have
(40) acute hearing at certain frequencies, helping them
detect diminutive movements in the undergrowth.
Some nocturnal species, such as the barn owl, have
asymmetrical ear openings and disc-like facial
feathers to facilitate the channeling and interpreta-
(45) tion of sounds. They aggregate sensory information
instantaneously to produce a mental map of their
surroundings and location of possible prey.

Like owls, we use our senses to map the world
around us, but the similarities end there. We cannot
(50) understand the complex means by which the owl's
hearing and sight work concurrently to detect the
subtle shifting of snow or leaves that signals food.
The comparison itself is ludicrous, in fact, because
our means for survival are so different; humans do
(55) not live solitary lives, constantly alert to the movement of prey that determines whether we live or
die. We do not think in the same way, if thought is
even the right concept: we interpret information
using extremely different cerebral processes, and
(60) we can't know whether owls are even consciously
aware of the complex workings of their brains.
When I sit in the forest and study my environment,
my world is interpreted with language. The owl's
world is—well, it's impossible to tell, isn't it?

(65) The owl may see the same forest we see, but
he is aware of it in a completely different way. I
admire the foliage and the rustling leaves, and listen
to birdsong. He hears the soft rustle of a leaf and
knows that a chipmunk moves thirty feet off to our
(70) right, directly underneath the poplar tree. I can say
that the owl thinks about the chipmunk, but not
how, for I don't have the correct mental processes
to describe the complex interpretations of sensory
detail into impulse and action; I am governed by
(75) words instead of instinct.

7. Which of the following statements supports the author's central argument?

    A) Owls are better adapted to survive than humans because owls are masters of their senses.

    B) Owls, as opposed to humans, overcome limitations by maximizing their advantages.

    C) Humans and owls evolved in differing environments, resulting in a variety of adaptations.

    D) Human brains and owl brains share few, if any, similarities in how sensory input is interpreted.

8. The author provides support for which of the following claims about owls?

    A) Their survival is not dependent on their acute senses.

    B) They do not live solitary lives.

    C) They maximize their advantages.

    D) They have a greater range of view than humans.

9. In line 42, the author refers to the barn owl in order to

    A) contrast the barn owl's hearing to human hearing.

    B) illustrate the range of evolutionary adaptations displayed by various species.

    C) imply that feathers are uniquely suited to channeling sound.

    D) provide an example of adaptation that improves the owl's ability to locate prey.

10. The structure of the passage can best be described as a

    A) comparison between humans and other animals using specific examples to illustrate similarities and differences.

    B) discussion of the evolutionary advantages afforded by differing adaptations to various environmental stimuli.

    C) philosophical discourse on the role of language and its limitations when discussing the acquisition of knowledge.

    D) hypothetical situation presented in the context of adaptive strategies employed by various species in response to environmental stress.

Answers & Explanations for this chapter begin on page 887.

EXTRA PRACTICE

The following questions provide an opportunity to practice the concepts and strategic thinking covered in this chapter. While many of the questions pertain to Rhetoric questions, some touch on other concepts tested on the Reading Test to ensure that your practice is test-like, with a variety of question types per passage.

Questions 1-11 are based on the following passage.

The following passage explores the history and impact of public higher education in the United States.

Every year, hundreds of thousands of students graduate from U.S. public universities. Many of the largest and most elite schools in the nation fall into
Line the category of public, or state, institutions. Unlike
(5) private universities, which generally operate independently from any government influence, public higher education was established through government legislation and is sustained through state and federal involvement in various ways. A look into
(10) the history of U.S. public higher education can shed light on the changing ideals of the American story over the past century and a half.

America's earliest higher-education institutions, like Harvard, were initially developed by and for
(15) clergy, or church workers. For 17th-century Puritans in America, church leadership was of utmost importance. At that time, clergy was the main profession for which college degrees were offered. Later, during the 18th and 19th centuries, parallel-
(20) ing the onset of secular (and increasingly scientifically inclined) modern thought, the nation and government acknowledged the need for broader higher education opportunities. Philosophers and politicians alike were aware that well-educated
(25) citizens were a vital element of a functional democracy. A better-informed voting population could secure a better political future. Moreover, with aims to advance the fields of technology and agriculture through higher education, legislators anticipated
(30) potential economic improvements nationwide as well. It was in the nation's best interest to make college more accessible.

In 1862, President Lincoln signed the Morill Land-Grant Act. This was, in many ways, the force
(35) behind the public university system. The Morill Act ensured that public land would be set aside for the establishment of universities across the country. The coming decades saw a massive increase in the opening of universities in the nation. Hundreds
(40) of U.S. public universities began to operate. These schools received federal and state support, offered practical, accessible education, and sought, originally, to advance the fields of agriculture and mechanics. Soon these schools offered wide varieties
(45) of subjects and specialties. These universities would be operated by their respective states, but all would adhere to certain broad federal regulations.

At the time, the government was seeking to mend racial injustices through legislation. To this
(50) effect, a second land act was passed in 1890 in hopes of inhibiting discrimination in public universities. While at the time this did not accomplish the intended openness and diversity, it paved the way for the culture of diversity the American university
(55) system enjoys today. Many public universities are now richly diverse, with regulations in place to accept students of any race, ethnicity, or socioeconomic status. In a similar vein, women, who were once a minority in colleges, increasingly gained a
(60) strong presence in U.S. universities over the past 150 years. Women actually surpassed men in overall U.S. college attendance around the turn of the 21st century.

Since the legislation of the 19th century, public
(65) universities have undergone momentous growth. The system has evolved to address and accommodate the nuances of 20th- and 21st-century Ameri-

can culture and development. Offering in-state students some of the most affordable degree programs in higher (70) education, these schools have now graduated millions of undergraduate and graduate students. Public universities also manage the majority of the nation's government-funded academic research initiatives. Featuring some of the most competitive athletic programs in the (75) world, as well as elite scholarship and arts programs, the U.S. public universities' accomplishments seem boundless. With schools in Alaska, Hawaii, and even U.S. territories like Puerto Rico and Guam, public university impact reaches the farthest corners and populations of (80) the nation. The state school system has been formative for American culture, philosophy, economics, medicine, politics, and much more.

The eminence of the U.S. public university network stretches beyond the United States. Students travel from (85) across the globe to study at top programs. Cutting-edge schools like the University of Virginia (UVA) and University of California at Los Angeles (UCLA) receive continual international attention for their accomplishments in scholarship and research. Programs, faculty, (90) and students from these schools participate in the global conversation in significant ways, working toward a better future for the planet.

Given those early visions for a more robustly educated voting population, the enormity of the system (95) that the Morrill Act launched is remarkable. U.S. public universities have both shaped and employed many of America's greatest thinkers. Considering their timeline and their accomplishments, these schools seem to reflect the post–Civil War history of diversity, liberty, (100) creativity, and equal opportunity that in many ways distinguishes the American cultural identity.

1. In the second paragraph, the author uses the idea that educated citizens are necessary for a functioning democracy to

   A) show why an educated work force increased agricultural production.

   B) demonstrate the continued role of the clergy in American public life.

   C) explain why the government was playing a larger role in public education.

   D) emphasize the importance of technological innovation for the economy.

2. Which choice provides the best evidence for the answer to the previous question?

   A) Lines 17-18 ("At that time . . . were offered")

   B) Lines 19-23 ("Later, during . . . opportunities")

   C) Lines 26-27 ("A better-informed . . . political future")

   D) Lines 27-31 ("Moreover, with aims . . . nationwide as well")

3. The purpose of the third paragraph is to

   A) highlight an example of the government increasing access to public education.

   B) discuss initial technological advances in agriculture and mechanics.

   C) outline the effects of the Morrill Land-Grant Act on the U.S. economy.

   D) explain the relationship between federal and state control of public universities.

4. In line 42, the author's use of the word "accessible" implies that

    A) public universities would expand course offerings to encompass a range of subjects.

    B) the likelihood that people with limited means could attend a university was increasing.

    C) agriculture and mechanics would receive the most federal and state support.

    D) President Lincoln supported passage of the Morill Land-Grant Act to expand education.

5. As used in line 47, "adhere" most nearly means

    A) resist.

    B) notice.

    C) acquiesce.

    D) comply.

6. Which of the following pieces of evidence would most strengthen the author's line of reasoning throughout the passage?

    A) Information about the ways in which private and public universities differ in paragraph 1

    B) An example of how the 17th-century clergy benefited from higher education in paragraph 2

    C) Statistics showing increased enrollment numbers of minority students in paragraph 4

    D) An example of a competitive public university athletic program in paragraph 5

7. In the fourth paragraph, the author uses the fact that more women than men now attend college to

    A) contrast the advances of women's rights with racial injustice in public universities.

    B) provide an example of how the land acts initially failed to stop discrimination.

    C) show that public universities have grown increasingly diverse over time.

    D) illustrate the challenges many people still face to attend public universities.

8. Which choice provides the best evidence for the answer to the previous question?

    A) Lines 49-52 ("To this effect . . . public universities")

    B) Lines 52-55 ("While at the time . . . enjoys today")

    C) Lines 55-58 ("Many public universities . . . status")

    D) Lines 58-61 ("In a similar vein . . . 150 years")

9. As used in line 67, "nuances" most nearly means

    A) eras.

    B) categories.

    C) circumstances.

    D) variations.

10. The passage's primary purpose is to

   A) summarize the accomplishments of U.S. public universities since the 19th century.

   B) explain the historical influence of religion on the development of the university system.

   C) discuss the relationship between U.S. higher education and the cultural values of the nation.

   D) summarize the historical effect of the Morill Land-Grant Act on United States public universities.

11. The fifth paragraph supports the central idea of the passage by

   A) discussing how public university athletic programs have grown increasingly competitive.

   B) providing evidence of the success of federal legislation meant to invest in public universities.

   C) explaining that in-state tuition rates have increased enrollment in United States public universities.

   D) noting that the U.S. public university system has expanded into U.S. territories.

CHAPTER 18

Detail and Inference Questions

 ## CHAPTER OBJECTIVES

By the end of this chapter, you will be able to:

1. Identify and answer Detail questions that ask about explicit meanings within the passage

2. Identify and answer Inference questions that ask about implicit meanings within the passage

3. Identify and answer Inference questions that require analogical reasoning

SMARTPOINTS

Point Value	SmartPoint Category
15 Points	Detail
35 Points	Inference

Reading & Writing

DETAIL AND INFERENCE QUESTIONS

Chapter 18

Homework

Extra Practice: #1-11

Even More

Reading Quiz 6

Key

  Book Assignment

  Online Video Assignment

  Online Quiz Assignment

DETAIL QUESTIONS

Detail questions ask about a specific part of the passage. Because your Passage Map should note only the *location* of key details rather than the details themselves, you will have to refer to the passage to answer these questions.

You can recognize Detail questions because they normally include line references or phrasing that directs you to a particular part of the passage.

When answering Detail questions:

- Read around the cited text to understand the context.

- Predict by rephrasing the relevant section in your own words.

- Eliminate any answer choices that do not match your prediction.

Also, make sure to read answer choices carefully. Watch out for negatives such as *not* and *no* that change an otherwise correct answer choice into the opposite of what you are looking for.

 ✔ Expert Tip

Watch out for misused details—details that are in the passage but do not answer the question.

INFERENCE QUESTIONS: IMPLICIT MEANING

Implicit Meaning Inference questions ask you to find something that must be true based on the passage but is not directly stated in the passage. The answer will be in the text, but you will need to read between the lines to find it.

To answer these questions efficiently and effectively, you must not only use your Passage Map but also fully utilize Step 3 of the Kaplan Method for Reading Comprehension: Predict and answer. If you need to review the Kaplan Method for Reading Comprehension, please turn to chapter 13.

There are two types of inferences that can be derived from questions asking about implicit meanings:

1. **Narrow Inferences** refer to specific parts of the passage. To answer these questions, find the relevant details and look for clues indicating how the author connects these details. Then, make a general prediction based on how the details are connected.

These questions will use phrasing such as:

- In lines xx-xx, the author implies that . . .

- The author strongly suggests that . . .

- It can be reasonably inferred that . . .

2. **Broad Inferences** ask about what can be inferred from the passage as a whole or what the author would generally agree with. To answer these questions, consider how the author's point of view limits the range of what could be true.

These questions will use phrasing such as:

- The passage indicates that . . .
- It can be inferred from the passage . . .

> ✔ **Expert Tip**
>
> An inference is NOT an opinion. It is a conclusion drawn from facts in the passage.

INFERENCE QUESTIONS: ANALOGICAL REASONING

Analogical Reasoning Inference questions ask you to take ideas and information found in the passage and use an analogy to describe a new and parallel situation. In every Analogical Reasoning Inference question, there is a strong connection between the two ideas. Identify that relationship and describe it in a short sentence.

You can recognize Analogical Reasoning Inference questions because they normally include line references or phrasing such as "The situation described in line x is most comparable to . . ."

When answering Analogical Reasoning Inference questions:

- Go to the cited lines and read around them to understand the context.
- Identify the relationship between the characters, the information, or the ideas cited in the question stem.
- Describe the relationship through characteristics (qualities that each idea possesses) and functions (roles played by each part).
- Look for the answer choice that describes a situation that is similar to the one in the passage.

Also, make sure to read answer choices carefully. Eliminate answer choices that include only one of the parts or have the parts in reverse order.

> ✔ **Remember**
>
> The question stem will describe the situation and tell you where to look for it in the passage. Always go back to the passage and find it.

Let's look at the following example of a test-like passage and question set. After the mapped passage, the left column contains questions similar to those you'll see on the Reading Test on Test Day. The column on the right features the strategic thinking test experts employ when approaching the passage and questions presented. Pay attention to how test experts vary the approach to answer different question types.

Strategic Thinking
Step 1: Read actively
Read the passage and the notes provided. Remember, a well-crafted Passage Map should summarize the central idea of each paragraph as well as important topics or themes. Use your Passage Map to help you answer each question.

Questions 1-3 are based on the following passage.

This passage looks into the effects of and interactions between light and color and the resulting types of luminescence.

Atoms can be excited in many ways other than by absorbing a photon. The element phosphorous spontaneously combines with oxygen when
Line exposed to air. There is a transfer of energy to
(5) the phosphorous electrons during this chemical reaction, which excites them to sufficiently high energy states so that they can subsequently emit light when dropping into a lower state. This is an example of what is termed chemiluminescence, the
(10) emission of light as a result of chemical reaction.

A related effect is bioluminescence, when light is produced by chemical reactions associated with biological activity. Bioluminescence occurs in a variety of life forms and is more common in marine
(15) organisms than in terrestrial or freshwater life. Examples include certain bacteria, jellyfish, clams, fungi, worms, ants, and fireflies. There is considerable diversity in how light is produced. Most processes involve the reaction of a protein with oxygen,
(20) catalyzed by an enzyme. The protein varies from one organism to another, but all are grouped under the generic name luciferin. The enzymes are known as luciferase. Both words stem from the Latin *lucifer* meaning light-bearing. The various chemical steps
(25) leading to bioluminescence are yet to be explained in detail, but in some higher organisms the process is known to be activated by the nervous system.

The firefly is best understood. Its light organ is located near the end of the abdomen. Within it
(30) luciferin is combined with other atomic groups in a series of processes in which oxygen is converted

into carbon dioxide. The sequence culminates when the luciferin is split off from the rest, leaving it in an excited state. The excess energy is released
(35) as a photon. The peak in the emission spectrum lies between 550 and 600 nm depending on the type of luciferase. This flash produced by the simultaneous emission of many photons serves to attract mates, and females also use it to attract
(40) males of other species, which they devour.

Certain bacteria also produce light when stimulated by motion. This is why the breaking sea or a passing boat generates the greenish light seen in some bodies of water such as Phosphorescent
(45) Bay in Puerto Rico. Some fish have a symbiotic relationship with bacteria. The "flashlight fish" takes advantage of the light created by bacteria lodged beneath each eye. Certain other fish produce their own bioluminescence, which
(50) serves as identification. However, the biological advantage, if any, of bioluminescence in some other organisms such as fungi remains a mystery.

Triboluminescence is the emission of light when one hard object is sharply struck against
(55) another. This contact, when atom scrapes against atom, excites electrons and disrupts electrical bonds. Light is then created when the electrons find their way to lower states. Triboluminescence is not to be confused with the glow of small
(60) particles that may be broken off by the impact. Such "sparks" are seen as a result of their high temperature. Light given off by hot objects is known as thermoluminescence, or incandescence.

¶1: intro chemilumin

2: intro olumin, how produces ght, intro ciferin

¶3: how fireflies use biolumin

¶4: light producing bacteria in sea, advantages not known for all organisms

¶5: tribolum. vs thermolum.

¶6: ther-
molum.
used for
dating

(65) Another form of thermoluminescence is the basis for dating ancient ceramic objects. Quartz and other constituents of clay are continually irradiated by naturally occurring radioactive elements (e.g., uranium and thorium) and by cosmic rays. This produces defects in the material where electrons (70) may be trapped. Heating pottery to 500°C releases the trapped electrons, which can then migrate back to their original atoms, where on returning to an atomic orbit they then emit a photon. The intensity of thermoluminescence is therefore a measure of (75) the duration of irradiation since the time when the pottery had been previously fired.

Excitation is also possible by other means. The passage of an electrical current (electroluminescence) is one. The impact of high- (80) energy particles is another. The *aurora borealis* and its southern counterpart the *aurora australis*, arise when a stream of high-energy particles from the sun enters the Earth's upper atmosphere and literally shatters some of the molecules in the air. (85) This leaves their atoms in excited states, and the light subsequently given off is characteristic of the atoms. Although the oxygen molecule, a major constituent of our atmosphere, has no emission in the visible spectrum, the oxygen atom can emit (90) photons in either the red or green portions of the spectrum. Other atoms contribute to light at other wavelengths.

¶7: aurora
borealis

Questions	Strategic Thinking
1. The statement "the emission spectrum lies between 550 and 600 nm" in lines 35-36 most strongly suggests that the spectrum A) contains mostly ultraviolet light. B) requires special equipment to detect. C) is produced only by fireflies. D) is visible to a variety of insects.	**Step 2: Examine the question stem** The key words and phrases in this question stem are the cited phrase and "most strongly suggests." The cited lines are from paragraph 3, which your Passage Map notes details the example of the firefly. **Step 3: Predict and answer** The emission spectrum in the cited phrase refers to light produced by fireflies. This light is used to attract mates and prey. Therefore, you can infer that if insects are attracted to the spectrum, they must be able to see it. Choice (D) is correct.
2. According to the passage, "bioluminescence," line 11, is more often found A) with oxygen when exposed to the air. B) among terrestrial creatures. C) in marine life. D) in light given off by hot objects.	**Step 2: Examine the question stem** The key words and phrases in the question stem are "according to the passage," the quoted word, and its line reference. The Passage Map notes for the second paragraph, where the quoted word in the question stem ("bioluminescence") is first mentioned, will help you answer the question. **Step 3: Predict and answer** The Passage Map note for paragraph 2 says that bioluminescence is common in marine life. Choice (C) is correct.
3. Which of the following situations most closely parallels the description of the excitation caused by the impact of high-energy particles in lines 77-87? A) A bowling ball striking bowling pins B) A snowflake hitting the pavement C) A prism reflecting light D) A goalie stopping a shot	**Step 2: Examine the question stem** The key words and phrases in the question stem are "most closely parallels" and the line numbers of the cited description. The Passage Map for the last paragraph will help you answer this question. **Step 3: Predict and answer** The last paragraph is about the excitation caused by the impact of high-energy particles. According to the passage, the "stream of high-energy particles … literally shatters some of the molecules in the air" (lines 82-84). Choice (A) is correct.

You have seen the ways in which the SAT tests you on Detail and Inference questions in Reading passages and the way an SAT expert approaches these types of questions.

You will use the Kaplan Method for Reading Comprehension to complete this section. Part of the test-like passage has been mapped already. Your first step is to complete the Passage Map. Then, you will continue to use the Kaplan Method for Reading Comprehension and the strategies discussed in this chapter to answer the questions. Strategic thinking questions have been included to guide you—some of the answers have been filled in, but you will have to fill in the answers to others.

Use your answers to the strategic thinking questions to select the correct answer, just as you will on Test Day.

Strategic Thinking
Step 1: Read actively
The passage below is partially mapped. Read the passage and the first part of the Passage Map. Then, complete the Passage Map on your own. Remember to focus on the central ideas of each paragraph as well as the central idea of the overall passage. Use your Passage Map as a reference when you're answering questions.

Questions 4-6 are based on the following passage.

The following passage describes findings regarding American colonists based on archaeological explorations at Jamestown, Virginia.

¶1: artifacts show how colonists lived

Archaeological explorations at Jamestown, Virginia, have brought to light thousands of colonial period artifacts that were used by the
Line Virginia settlers from 1607 until 1699. A study of
(5) these objects, which were buried under the soil at Jamestown for decades, reveals in many ways how the English colonists lived on a small wilderness island over 300 years ago. Artifacts unearthed include building materials and handwrought
(10) hardware, kitchen utensils and fireplace accessories, furniture hardware, and many items relating to household and town industries.

¶2: clues about life

These artifacts provide valuable information concerning the everyday life and manners of the
(15) first Virginia settlers. Excavated artifacts reveal that the Jamestown colonists built their houses in the same style as those they knew in England, insofar as local materials permitted. There were differences, however, for the settlers were in a land replete with

(20) vast forests and untapped natural resources close at hand that they used to their advantage.

¶3: settlers used woodworking skills

The Virginia known to the first settlers was a carpenter's paradise, and consequently the early buildings were the work of artisans in wood. The
(25) first rude shelter, split-wood fencing, clapboard roof, puncheon floors, cupboards, benches, stools, and wood plows are all examples of skilled working with wood.

¶4: early structures primitive, focus on survival

Timber at Jamestown was plentiful, so many
(30) houses, especially in the early years, were of frame construction. During the first decade or two, house construction reflected a primitive use of materials found ready at hand, such as saplings for a sort of framing, and use of branches, leafage, bark, and
(35) animal skins. During these early years, when the settlers were having such a difficult time staying alive, mud walls, wattle-and-daub, and coarse marsh-grass thatch were used. Out of these years of improvising, construction with squatted posts,
(40) and later with studs, came into practice. There

was probably little thought of plastering walls during the first two decades. When plastering was adopted, clay, either by itself or mixed with oyster-shell lime, was first used. The early floors were of clay, and such (45) floors continued to be used in the humbler dwellings throughout the 1600s. It can be assumed that most of the dwellings, or shelters, of the early Jamestown settlers had a rough and primitive appearance.

After Jamestown had attained some degree of (50) permanency, many houses were built of brick. It is quite clear from documentary records and archaeological remains that the colonists not only made their own brick but also that the process, as well as the finished products, followed closely the (55) English method. Four brick kilns were discovered on Jamestown Island during archaeological explorations.

While some of the handwrought hardware found at Jamestown was made in the colony, most of it was imported from England. Types of building hardware (60) unearthed include an excellent assortment of nails, spikes, staples, locks, keys, hinges, pintles, shutter fasteners, bolts, hasps, latches, door knockers, door pulls, bootscrapes, gutter supports, wall anchors, and ornamental hardware. In many instances, each type (65) is represented by several varieties. It is believed that wooden hardware was used on many of the early houses.

A few glass windowpanes may have been made in the Jamestown glass factory, which (70) was built in 1608. Most of the window glass used in the colony, however, was shipped from England. Many of the early panes used were diamond-shaped pieces known as "quarrels" and were held in place by means of slotted lead (75) strips known as "cames." The window frames used in a few of the Jamestown houses were handwrought iron casements. Most of the humbler dwellings had no glass panes in the windows. The window openings were closed (80) by batten shutters, operated by hinges of wood, and fitted with wooden fastening devices.

Busy conquering a stubborn wilderness, the first Jamestown settlers had only a few things to make their homes cozy and cheerful. In (85) most cases, their worldly goods consisted of a few cooking utensils, a change of clothing, a weapon or two, and a few pieces of handmade furniture. After the early years of hardship had passed, the colonists began to acquire pos- (90) sessions for more pleasant living; by 1650 the better houses were equipped with most of the necessities of life of those times, as well as a few luxuries of comfortable living.

Don't get distracted by less important details. While there is a lot going on in this passage, your additions to the Passage Map should have noted the evolution of building practices, bricks, furniture, and glass. If you're stuck, review the example Passage Map in the Answers & Explanations for this chapter on page 890.

Reading & Writing

Questions	Strategic Thinking
4. The statement in lines 40-42 ("There was . . . decades") suggests that the Jamestown colonists A) followed London fashions. B) lacked the resources to import the raw materials from England. C) focused their energies on survival, not on decoration. D) hesitated to build more permanent homes until bricks were available.	**Step 2: Examine the question stem** The key words and phrases in this question stem are the cited statement with its corresponding line numbers and the word "suggests." **Step 3: Predict and answer** *Read around the cited lines. Why was there "little thought of plastering walls during the first two decades" (lines 41-42)?* _____ _____ _____ *Which answer choice matches this prediction?* _____
5. All of the following are true about the Jamestown colonists EXCEPT A) some of them were skilled woodworkers. B) they struggled to survive in the early decades. C) they made floors out of clay. D) they constructed most of their own hardware.	**Step 2: Examine the question stem** *What are the key words and phrases in this question stem?* _____ *What parts of your Passage Map are relevant?* _____ **Step 3: Predict and answer** *Is A mentioned in the passage? If so, where?* _____ *Is B mentioned in the passage? If so, where?* _____ *Is C mentioned in the passage? If so, where?* _____ *Is D mentioned in the passage? If so, where?* _____ *Which answer choice is not mentioned in the passage and is therefore correct?* _____

Reading & Writing

Questions	Strategic Thinking
6. The description of the Jamestown colonists' brick industry, as discussed in lines 49-56, is most comparable to A) traditional weavers making cloth with imported cotton. B) mountain climbers carrying all of their food and shelter on their expedition. C) pioneer farmers bringing seeds and agricultural techniques to new lands. D) an immigrant chef using local ingredients to make recipes from her homeland.	**Step 2: Examine the question stem** *What are the key words and phrases in this question stem?* _____ *What parts of your Passage Map are relevant?* _____ **Step 3: Predict and answer** *How do the cited lines describe the brick industry?* _____ *Which answer choice is most similar to this process?* _____

Now, try a test-like SAT Reading passage on your own. Give yourself 6 minutes to read the passage and answer the questions.

Questions 7-10 are based on the following passage.

The following passage is an excerpt from "The Murders in the Rue Morgue," a short story by Edgar Allan Poe published in 1841.

Our first meeting was at an obscure library in the Rue Montmartre, where the accident of our both being in search of the same very rare and
Line very remarkable volume, brought us into closer
(5) communion. We saw each other again and again. I was deeply interested in the little family history which he detailed to me with all that candor which a Frenchman indulges whenever mere self is the theme. I was astonished too, at the vast
(10) extent of his reading; and, above all, I felt my soul enkindled within me by the wild fervor, and the vivid freshness of his imagination. Seeking in Paris the objects I then sought, I felt that the society of such a man would be to me a treasure beyond
(15) price; and this feeling I frankly confided to him. It was at length arranged that we should live together during my stay in the city; and as my worldly circumstances were somewhat less embarrassed than his own, I was permitted to be at the expense
(20) of renting, and furnishing in a style which suited the rather fantastic gloom of our common temper, a time-eaten and grotesque mansion, long deserted through superstitions into which we did not inquire, and tottering to its fall in a retired and
(25) desolate portion of the Faubourg St. Germain.

Had the routine of our life at this place been known to the world, we should have been regarded as madmen—although, perhaps, as madmen of a harmless nature. Our seclusion was perfect. We
(30) admitted no visitors. Indeed the locality of our retirement had been carefully kept a secret from my own former associates; and it had been many years since Dupin had ceased to know or be known in Paris. We existed within ourselves alone.

(35) It was a freak of fancy in my friend (for what else shall I call it?) to be enamored of the Night for her own sake; and into this bizarrerie, as into all his others, I quietly fell; giving myself up to his wild whims with a perfect abandon. The sable divin-
(40) ity would not herself dwell with us always; but we could counterfeit her presence. At the first dawn of the morning we closed all the massy shutters of our old building; lighted a couple of tapers which, strongly perfumed, threw out only the ghastliest
(45) and feeblest of rays. By the aid of these we then busied our souls in dreams—reading, writing, or conversing, until warned by the clock of the advent of the true Darkness. Then we sallied forth into the streets, arm and arm, continuing the topics of
(50) the day, or roaming far and wide until a late hour, seeking, amid the wild lights and shadows of the populous city that infinity of mental excitement which quiet observation can afford.

At such times I could not help remarking and
(55) admiring (although from his rich ideality I had been prepared to expect it) a peculiar analytic ability in Dupin. He seemed, too, to take an eager delight in its exercise—if not exactly in its display—and did not hesitate to confess the
(60) pleasure thus derived. He boasted to me, with a low chuckling laugh, that most men, in respect to himself, wore windows in their bosoms, and was wont to follow up such assertions by direct and very startling proofs of his intimate knowledge of
(65) my own. His manner at these moments was frigid and abstract; his eyes were vacant in expression; while his voice, usually a rich tenor, rose into a treble which would have sounded petulantly but for the deliberateness and entire distinctness of the
(70) enunciation. Observing him in these moods, I often dwelt meditatively upon the old philosophy of the Bi-Part soul, and amused myself with the fancy of a double Dupin—the creative and the resolvent.

7. The statement in lines 17-19 ("my worldly . . . his own") suggests that

   A) Dupin wishes his family history were different.

   B) the narrator was more self-confident about his own wealth.

   C) Dupin was less well-off than the narrator.

   D) the narrator led an exemplary life.

8. In the third paragraph, the relationship between the narrator and Dupin most closely parallels which of the following situations?

   A) Two scientists collaborating on a research project

   B) A professor instructing a new student

   C) An art student adapting a teacher's techniques in a new way

   D) A fan dressing and acting like a pop star

9. According to the passage, the narrator and Dupin met because they

   A) lived in the Rue Montmartre.

   B) wanted to find the same book.

   C) preferred the night to the day.

   D) enjoyed solitude.

10. The narrator would most likely agree with which of the following statements?

    A) Dupin understood other people's inner thoughts in ways the narrator could not comprehend.

    B) Dupin was a humorously eccentric character given to flights of fancy.

    C) Dupin enjoyed entertaining groups of other fashionable Parisians.

    D) Dupin represented an obscure aspect of French society that the narrator wished to study.

Answers & Explanations for this chapter begin on page 890.

Reading & Writing

EXTRA PRACTICE

The following questions provide an opportunity to practice the concepts and strategic thinking covered in this chapter. While many of the questions pertain to Inference and Detail questions, some touch on other concepts tested on the Reading Test to ensure that your practice is test-like, with a variety of question types per passage.

Questions 1-11 are based on the following passages and supplementary material.

The following passages detail different aspects of the United States National Parks System.

Passage 1

In the mid- to late-nineteenth century, America legislated an idea that would come to be emulated worldwide: the National Parks System. Starting
Line with Yellowstone National Park in 1872, the
(5) United States government sparked a national and international trend of setting aside treasured spaces for preservation, protection, and public enjoyment. Since then, over 400 national parks have been established in American states and territories, and
(10) globally over a thousand parks are now protected by similar systems in their respective nations.

The United States National Park Service (NPS) is responsible for managing and protecting these parks. Set up by President Wilson in 1916, this
(15) federal organization oversees budgeting, care, advocacy, and education for the country's parks. As a piece of legislation enacted in 1933, the NPS includes landmarks of historic and scientific significance in addition to those significant for their
(20) sheer natural beauty or unique wildlife populations. There are now 84 million acres of United States national parkland (and water). Thousands of employees and millions of volunteers work with the NPS to accomplish its vast responsibilities. From
(25) national monuments and battlegrounds, to the breathtaking vistas of the Great Smoky Mountains, Alaska's Glacier Bay, and even underwater snorkeling trails in the U.S. Virgin Islands, spaces marked with awe and meaning are preserved for
(30) the enjoyment of generations to come.

Today, more than 275 million people visit America's national parks yearly. They come

prepared to be amazed; the stunning beauty, powerful history, and inspiring intricacies of nature
(35) they encounter never disappoint. And America's great idea, in which over a hundred countries now participate, enables that amazement to be spread and shared across nations and generations. The National Park System teaches and invites people
(40) worldwide to practice preservation in their daily lives by making choices to protect the earth's wonders and treasures.

Passage 2

John Muir, often called "Father of the National Park System," was America's most famous and
(45) influential naturalist. Born in 1838, he bore witness to the establishment of the first national parks and the many visions, debates, and victories of the early environmentalist movement. Muir was a man of many talents. He began his career working
(50) in carriage production but soon chose a life of exploring the nation's spectacular wilderness, traveling thousands of miles by foot and across oceans. From relative anonymity as a wayfarer, shepherd, and mill laborer, Muir would soon
(55) become a national hero whose widely read writings would drive government policy makers to action.

When Muir encountered California's Yosemite Valley and the greater Sierra Nevada mountains, he immediately recognized their worth. He saw in
(60) them not only astounding scenic beauty, but also crucial ecological significance. Over the rest of his life, he would advocate for their protection. Yet his interest would stretch far beyond the Sierras. Muir regularly traversed California's forested mountains
(65) and made a home in Yosemite Valley, but his activism and wanderlust also drew him to other

picturesque locations, such as Washington's Mount Rainier and Alaska's coast and glaciers. He published hundreds of articles documenting his travels. These invoked the
(70) wonder of the natural beauty he witnessed, channeling that marvel into the hearts of readers nationwide.

The political impact of Muir's life was immense. His publications were elemental in persuading the United States government to establish Yosemite, Sequoia,
(75) the Grand Canyon, and Mount Rainier as national parks. His relationship with Theodore Roosevelt was foundational to the environmental policies and gains made during Roosevelt's presidency; Muir's relentless advocacy for protecting the Sierras catalyzed and
(80) empowered a movement that would carry through the coming centuries. Much of this advocacy manifested itself in Muir's founding of a political activist organization called the Sierra Club. Internationally this group was one of the first of its kind, and it remains one
(85) of the nation's leading environmental organizations.

However, perhaps even greater than Muir's political accomplishments was his ideological impact. His unforgettable philosophies about the importance of nature reminded Americans that the wild was worth
(90) cherishing and saving, even at the expense of short-lived material gains for which it might be exchanged. Muir's legacy has invited and inspired billions of people worldwide to guard the global ecosystem and to go out and enjoy it all.

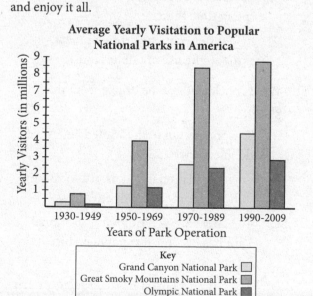

Average Yearly Visitation to Popular National Parks in America

Yearly Visitors (in millions)

Years of Park Operation

Key
Grand Canyon National Park ☐
Great Smoky Mountains National Park ☐
Olympic National Park ☐

1. As used in line 2, "emulated" most nearly means

   A) admired.

   B) feared.

   C) imitated.

   D) invented.

2. What is the most likely purpose of the second paragraph of Passage 1?

   A) To describe the impressive scale of the National Parks System

   B) To show that national parks have become popular despite early setbacks

   C) To argue that national parks are valuable because of their aesthetic value

   D) To defend the existence of national parks against critics of their economic cost

3. What can be most strongly concluded about the United States National Parks System from Passage 1?

   A) It is more popular with visitors today than it was initially.

   B) Its accomplishments have historically been controversial.

   C) It is the most popular service provided by the American government.

   D) Its ideas about conservation have been influential internationally.

4. Which choice provides the best evidence for the answer to the previous question?

   A) Lines 14-16 ("Set up . . . country's parks")

   B) Lines 22-24 ("Thousands of . . . vast responsibilities")

   C) Lines 31-32 ("Today, more than . . . yearly")

   D) Lines 35-38 ("And America's . . . and generations")

5. As used in line 66, "wanderlust" most likely means

   A) an interest in travel.

   B) an inability to concentrate.

   C) a love of diversity.

   D) a desire for the countryside.

6. What does the use of the word "channeling" in line 70 suggest about Muir's writings?

   A) They were focused on his spiritual connection with nature.

   B) They were emotionally moving to his readers.

   C) They were entertaining in a manner similar to television.

   D) They were strident and opinionated.

7. With which statement would the author of Passage 2 most likely agree?

   A) The preservation of the wilderness came at an economic cost.

   B) John Muir's contributions were largely unrecognized during his life.

   C) Many naturalists were important in creating the national parks system.

   D) The most important work John Muir did was in helping create government policy.

8. Which choice provides the best evidence for the answer to the previous question?

   A) Lines 72-76 ("His publications . . . national parks")

   B) Lines 76-81 ("His relationship . . . coming centuries")

   C) Lines 86-87 ("However . . . ideological impact")

   D) Lines 87-91 ("His unforgettable . . . exchanged")

9. How do the central ideas of the two passages primarily differ?

   A) Passage 1 describes the parks system generally, while Passage 2 focuses on its founding.

   B) Passage 1 argues that the parks system is underappreciated, while Passage 2 celebrates it as a national treasure beloved by many.

   C) Passage 1 focuses on the parks system's creation, while Passage 2 focuses on its structure.

   D) Passage 1 describes the idea of national parks, while Passage 2 focuses specifically on how the idea was applied in the United States.

10. The authors of both passages would most likely agree that the most important role of national parks is to

    A) preserve natural beauty so it can inspire visitors.

    B) allow city residents to escape polluted environments.

    C) instill a sense of patriotism in those who spend time there.

    D) help foster economic development through the use of public lands.

11. What conclusion can be drawn from the graph?

    A) The population of the United States has doubled since 1930.

    B) Olympic National Park is in a location difficult for most visitors to access.

    C) The Great Smoky Mountains National Park has become less popular since its inception.

    D) The Grand Canyon has consistently been a more popular destination than the Olympic National Park.

Expression of Ideas

BY THE END OF THIS UNIT, YOU WILL BE ABLE TO:

1. Apply the Kaplan Method for Writing & Language

2. Evaluate the effectiveness and clarity of a given passage

3. Identify proper and effective language use

4. Utilize the standard conventions of usage in written English

CHAPTER 19

The Kaplan Methods for Writing & Language and Infographics

CHAPTER OBJECTIVES

By the end of this chapter, you will be able to:

1. Distinguish among the three different Writing and Language text types

2. Identify issues in a passage and select the correct answer by applying the Kaplan Method for Writing & Language

3. Identify and analyze quantitative information and infographics

4. Synthesize information from infographics and text

SMARTPOINTS

Point Value	SmartPoint Category
Point Builder	The Kaplan Method for Writing & Language
Point Builder	The Kaplan Method for Infographics
10 Points	Quantitative

Reading & Writing

THE KAPLAN METHOD FOR WRITING & LANGUAGE & INFOGRAPHICS

Chapter 19

Homework

Extra Practice: #1-11

Even More

Writing & Language Text Types

The Kaplan Method for Writing & Language

Key

 Book Assignment

 Online Video Assignment

 Online Quiz Assignment

OVERVIEW OF THE WRITING & LANGUAGE PASSAGE TYPES

You will see four Writing & Language passages on Test Day, each of which will have 11 questions. Recognizing the text type of a Writing & Language passage helps you focus on the questions as they relate to the passage's general purpose. Knowing the overarching aim of the passage will help you answer questions more efficiently and accurately.

Writing & Language Passage Types	
1–2 Argumentative texts	Author will advocate a point, idea, or proposal
1–2 Informative/Explanatory texts	Author will explain, describe, or analyze a topic in order to impart information without necessarily advocating
1 Nonfiction Narrative text	Author will use a story-like approach to convey information or ideas

✔ **Remember**

The SAT rewards critical thinking in context. Pay attention to the text type to answer Writing & Language questions more efficiently.

Let's look at three short Writing & Language passage excerpts (without errors) and see how an SAT expert identifies the text type of each. The left column features the passage excerpt, while the right column demonstrates the strategic thinking a test expert employs when identifying Writing & Language text types.

Reading & Writing

Passages	Strategic Thinking
As if malpractice suits and unnecessary bank-ruptcies were not enough of a problem, lawyers have chosen to increase the burden that they place on society by engineering an excess of increasingly ridiculous product warnings. Why else would a box of sleeping pills be marketed with the cautionary note that consumers may experience drowsiness? Or a cup of coffee be emblazoned with a notice that "THIS PRODUCT MAY BE HOT"? Anyone with common sense will not need to be warned about these possibilities, and anyone WITHOUT common sense is prob-ably not going to be stopped from undertaking a foolish course of action by a warning label anyway. So honestly, in the long run, the only ones who benefit from these warnings are the lawyers who are paid hundreds of dollars an hour to compose them.	The phrases "ridiculous product warnings," "any-one with common sense," and "foolish course of action," in addition to the rhetorical questions in the passage, indicate that the tone of the passage is incredulous, cynical, and mocking. The author is mocking the "excess of increasingly ridiculous product warnings." The author states that "the only ones who benefit from these warnings are the lawyers who are paid hundreds of dollars an hour to compose them." The text type of this passage excerpt is therefore **Argumentative.**
It is amazing how little the structure of the American public school system has changed since its inception. Students still change classes according to bells, even though the bell system originated during the days of factories. School is still not in session during the summer, although most students will not use that time to work on farms. Although class and school sizes have varied widely and the curriculum has certainly become varied, the actual system remains sur-prisingly similar to the way it once was. Despite these idiosyncrasies, however, the American public school system continues to educate the children of this country in a fair and equitable fashion. Without the established structure, the chaotic nature of school would severely inhibit learning.	In the first sentence of the passage, the author establishes the topic of the passage. The keywords "although" and "despite" later in the passage suggest that the author is reporting on various aspects of the public school system. The text type of this passage excerpt is **Infor-mative/Explanatory.**

Passages	Strategic Thinking
I still remember the magic of walking home under the cold, brittle blue sky, watching the sun strike the glittering blanket laid down by that first snowfall. The world dripped with frosting, and everything was pure and silent. I breathed deeply, enjoying the sting of the icy air in my nostrils, and set off through the trees, listening to the muffled crunch of my footsteps and the chirps of the waking birds. Later, the cars and schoolchildren and mundane lives would turn the wonderland back into dingy slush; the hush would be interrupted by horns and shouts. Indeed for now, the sparkling, cloistered world was mine alone. I smiled, and for a moment, my mind was still.	This passage is explicitly different from the previous two passages because it is written in the first person, as evidenced by the author's use of personal pronouns such as "I." The text type of this passage is **Nonfiction Narrative**.

THE KAPLAN METHOD FOR WRITING & LANGUAGE

The Kaplan Method for Writing & Language is the method you will use to boost your score on the Writing & Language Test. By understanding what the question is looking for, how it relates to the passage, and the questions you should ask yourself on Test Day, you will maximize the number of points you earn. Use the Kaplan Method for Writing & Language for every SAT Writing & Language Test passage and question you encounter, whether practicing, completing your homework, working on a Practice Test, or taking the actual exam on Test Day.

The Kaplan Method for Writing & Language has three steps:

Step 1: Read the passage and identify the issue

- If there's an infographic, apply the Kaplan Method for Infographics

Step 2: Eliminate answer choices that do not address the issue

Step 3: Plug in the remaining answer choices and select the most correct, concise, and relevant one

✔ On Test Day

The SAT will expect you to be able to recognize errors in organization, pronouns, agreement, comparisons, development, sentence structure, modifiers, verbs, wordiness, style, tone, and syntax.

Let's take a closer look at each step.

Step 1: Read the passage and identify the issue

This means:

- Rather than reading the whole passage and then answering all of the questions, you can answer questions as you read because they are mostly embedded in the text itself.

- When you see a number, stop reading and look at the question. If you can answer it with what you've read so far, do so. If you need more information, keep reading until you have enough context to answer the question.

Step 2: Eliminate answer choices that do not address the issue

Eliminating answer choices that do not address the issue:

- Increases your odds of getting the correct answer by removing obviously incorrect answer choices

Step 3: Plug in the remaining answer choices and select the most correct, concise, and relevant one

Correct, concise, and relevant means that the answer choice you select:

- Makes sense when read with the correction
- Is as short as possible while retaining the information in the text
- Relates well to the passage overall

> **✔ Remember**
>
> There is no wrong answer penalty on the SAT. When in doubt, eliminate what you can and then guess. You won't lose points for guessing.

Answer choices should not:

- Change the intended meaning of the original sentence, paragraph, or passage
- Introduce new grammatical errors

> **✔ On Test Day**
>
> If you have to guess, eliminate answer choices that are clearly wrong and then choose the shortest one—the SAT rewards students who know how to be concise.

When you encounter a Writing & Language question, use the Kaplan Method, asking yourself a series of strategic thinking questions. By asking these strategic thinking questions, you will be able to select the correct answer choice more easily and efficiently. Pausing to ask yourself questions before answering each question may seem like it takes a lot of time, but it actually saves you time by preventing you from weighing the four answer choices against each other; it's better to ask questions that lead you directly to the correct answer than to debate which of four answers seems the least incorrect.

Let's look at the following Writing & Language passage and questions. After the passage, there are two columns. The left column contains test-like questions. The column on the right features the strategic thinking a test expert employs when approaching the passage and questions presented.

Child Expenditures

A 2005 report from the United States Department of Agriculture estimates that the cost of raising a child from birth until age seventeen is approximately $500,000. This cost includes housing, food, clothing, transportation, health care, child care, and education and does, of course, vary considerably. However, with the average cost of having and raising a child set at half a million dollars, and with additional children in the family raising that financial expenditure accordingly, it becomes clear that parenthood should not be entered into lightly. Even for families that plan for children, there may be costs for which they are unprepared. For instance, if a woman chooses to spend the first years of her child's life as a full-time mother and homemaker, she can lose career momentum and end up making a substantially lower salary than a woman with the same background who maintains consistent employment. While these factors should in no way be construed as a recommendation against having children, **1** <u>if you're planning a family, be ready.</u>

Questions	Strategic Thinking
1. A) NO CHANGE B) but think about the problems it might cause. C) they speak to the need for responsible family planning and financial preparation. D) make sure you understand what you're getting into.	**Step 1: Read the passage and identify the issue** The underlined phrase is grammatically correct. When there is no apparent grammatical issue, check style, tone, and syntax. The tone of the underlined portion is much more informal than the tone of the overall passage, as evidenced by the use of the second person ("you"). **Step 2: Eliminate answer choices that do not address the issue** Eliminate A because there is a tone issue in the underlined portion. Eliminate B and D because they still use the second person (it's implied in B with the imperative mood of the verb "think"). **Step 3: Plug in the remaining answer choices and select the most correct, concise, and relevant one** Choice (C) is correct.

THE KAPLAN METHOD FOR INFOGRAPHICS

The SAT Writing & Language Test will contain one or more passages that include infographics. Each infographic will convey or expand on information related to the passage.

The Kaplan Method for Infographics has three steps:

Step 1: Read the question

Step 2: Examine the infographic

Step 3: Predict and answer

Let's examine these steps a bit more closely.

Step 1: Read the question

Analyze the question stem for information that will help you zero in on the specific parts of the infographic that apply to the question.

Step 2: Examine the infographic

Make sure to:

- Identify units of measurement, labels, and titles
- Circle parts of the infographic that relate directly to the question

> ✔ **Expert Tip**
>
> For more data-heavy infographics, you should also make note of any trends in the data or relationships between variables.

Step 3: Predict and answer

Just as in Step 3 of the Kaplan Method for Reading Comprehension, do not look at the answer choices until you've used the infographic to make a prediction. Asking questions and taking time to assess the given information before answering the test question will increase your chances of selecting the correct answer. Infographics vary in format—there can be tables, graphs, charts, and so on—so be flexible when you ask yourself these critical-thinking questions.

When you apply the Kaplan Method for Infographics, keep in mind that infographics will either represent data described in the passage or present new data that expand on what the passage is about.

Let's look at the following Writing & Language infographic and questions. After the infographic, there are two columns. The left column contains test-like questions. The column on the right features the strategic thinking a test expert employs when approaching the infographic and questions presented.

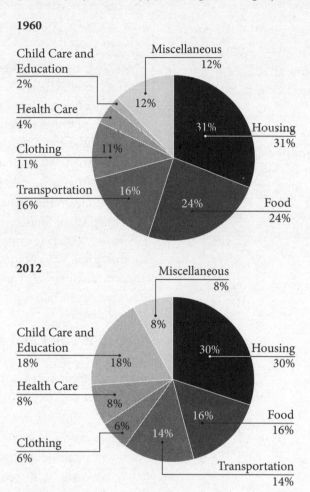

1960

Child Care and Education 2%
Health Care 4%
Clothing 11%
Transportation 16%
Miscellaneous 12%
12%
11%
16%
31%
Housing 31%
24%
Food 24%

2012

Child Care and Education 18%
Health Care 8%
Clothing 6%
Miscellaneous 8%
8%
18%
8%
6%
14%
30%
Housing 30%
16%
Food 16%
Transportation 14%

Expenditures on a Child from Birth Through Age 17: Budgetary Component Shares, 1960 versus 2012

Questions	Strategic Thinking
2. Which claim about the cost of raising children is supported by the two pie charts? A) Between 1960 and 2012, the percent of a budget spent on food increased. B) Between 1960 and 2012, the percent of a budget spent on health care decreased. C) Between 1960 and 2012, the percent of a budget spent on transportation experienced the greatest decrease. D) Between 1960 and 2012, the percent of a budget spent on child care and education experienced the greatest increase.	**Step 1: Read the question** The question is asking you to evaluate which answer choice is correct when compared to the two pie charts. **Step 2: Examine the infographic** It is unclear which parts of the infographic relate directly to the question because the question stem is very general. You'll have to look at the answer choices for guidance on what part of the infographic to examine closely. The title of the infographic is "Expenditures on a Child from Birth Through Age 17: Budgetary Component Shares, 1960 versus 2012." The labels are "1960" for one pie chart and "2012" for the other. The categories in both pie charts are Housing, Food, Transportation, Clothing, Health Care, Child Care and Education, and Miscellaneous. **Step 3: Predict and answer** Choice A claims that the percent of a budget spent on food increased from 1960 to 2012; however, it decreased from 24% to 16%. Eliminate A. Choice B claims that the percent of a budget spent on health care decreased from 1960 to 2012; however, it increased from 4% to 8%. Eliminate B. Choice C claims that the greatest cost decrease occurred in transportation. However, the percent of a budget spent on transportation decreased from 16% in 1960 to 14% in 2012, while the percent of a budget spent on food decreased from 24% in 1960 to 16% in 2012. Eliminate C. The percent of a budget spent on child care and education increased from 2% in 1960 to 18% in 2012. This is the greatest increase, as choice (D) claims. Choice (D) is correct.

You have seen the ways in which the SAT tests you on Infographics in Writing & Language passages and the way an SAT expert approaches these types of questions.

Use the Kaplan Method for Writing & Language to answer the three questions that accompany the following Writing & Language passage excerpt. Remember to look at the strategic thinking questions that have been laid out for you—some of the answers have been filled in, but you will have to complete the answers to others.

Use your answers to the strategic thinking questions to select the correct answer, just as you will on Test Day.

Questions 3–5 are based on the following passage.

Industrial Progress

Is industrial progress a mixed blessing? **3** <u>Hundred years</u> ago, this question was seldom asked. Science and industry were flooding the world with products that made life easier. But today we know that many industrial processes create pollution that can destroy our environment. Industries produce toxic waste, discharging harmful chemicals directly into lakes, rivers, and the air. One of the results of this pollution that must be managed in order to protect our ecosystems is acid rain.

Air, clouds, and rain containing acids caused by industrial pollution can have terrible effects. Acid droplets in the air can be inhaled, causing illness. From clouds, these acid droplets fall as rain. If natural chemical processes in soils do not deactivate the acids, these acids can accumulate and kill both plant and animal life. In some parts of the Northeast and Midwest, 10 percent of all lakes show dangerous acid levels. In eastern mountains in the United States, large forest tracts have disappeared at elevations where trees are regularly bathed in acid rain.

Acid rain is caused by industrial processes that release compounds of nitrogen and sulfur. **4** <u>These pollutants</u> combine with clean air, the results are nitric and sulfuric acids. The main components of acid rain **5** <u>is</u> oxides of nitrogen and sulfur dioxide, which are emitted by oil- and coal-burning power plants. To reduce acid rain, emissions from these plants, particularly sulfur dioxide, must be reduced. One way to do this is to install machines that remove sulfur dioxide from a plant's emissions. Another is to build new plants modeled on currently experimental designs that produce less sulfur dioxide.

Questions	Strategic Thinking
3. A) NO CHANGE B) A hundred years, give or take, C) One hundred years D) Hundred years or so	**Step 1: Read the passage and identify the issue** *What is the issue?* As written, the underlined portion uses the incorrect form of a number, which is an error in idiom construction. **Step 2: Eliminate answer choices that do not address the issue** *What answer choice(s) can you eliminate?* _____ _____ _____ **Step 3: Plug in the remaining answer choices and select the most correct, concise, and relevant one** *What is the correct answer?*_____
4. A) NO CHANGE B) Because these pollutants C) When these pollutants D) Where these pollutants	**Step 1: Read the passage and identify the issue** *What is the issue?* While there is nothing obviously incorrect about the underlined portion, if you keep reading the entire sentence, you'll see that it is a run-on. **Step 2: Eliminate answer choices that do not address the issue** *What answer choice(s) can you eliminate?* _____ _____ _____ **Step 3: Plug in the remaining answer choices and select the most correct, concise, and relevant one** *What is the correct answer?* _____

Questions	Strategic Thinking

5. A) NO CHANGE
   B) are
   C) was
   D) were
	Step 1: Read the passage and identify the issue
	
	What is the issue?
	
	The singular verb "is" does not agree with its subject, "the main components." You need a plural verb in the present tense.
	
	Step 2: Eliminate answer choices that do not address the issue
	
	What answer choice(s) can you eliminate?
	
	_____
	
	_____
	
	_____
	
	Step 3: Plug in the remaining answer choices and select the most correct, concise, and relevant one
	
	What is the correct answer? _____

Perform

Now, try a test-like Writing & Language passage and infographic on your own. Give yourself 5 minutes to read the passage and answer the questions.

Questions 6-13 are based on the following passage and supplementary material.

Jupiter

As the fifth planet from the Sun, and by far the most massive in our solar system at 318 times the mass of Earth, Jupiter has **6** fascinated and intrigued scientists for centuries. In fact, it was the initial discovery of this massive, gaseous planet that marked the first time astronomers considered the possibility that the movement of other planets was not centered around the Earth. More specifically, when Jupiter was first viewed from Earth by the Italian astronomer Galileo in 1610, four large moons were also spotted in orbit around this enormous planet. It was these moons, now known as the Galilean moons, that provided important evidence for Galileo's outspoken support of Copernicus's heliocentric theory of planetary **7** movement. Because these moons seemed to revolve around a planet other than Earth.

The first close look at Jupiter came in 1973, when the unmanned NASA probe *Pioneer 10* completed a successful **8** flyby, and it collected important data regarding the planet's chemical composition and interior structure. **9** After completing its mission to Jupiter, *Pioneer 10* became the first spacecraft to leave the solar system. Designated as one of the gas planets—along with Saturn, Uranus, and Neptune—Jupiter is composed of about 90 percent hydrogen and 10 percent helium

6. A) NO CHANGE
   B) fascinated
   C) intrigued, and fascinated
   D) fascinated intriguing

7. A) NO CHANGE
   B) movement. These
   C) movement. Although
   D) movement because

8. A) NO CHANGE
   B) flyby and it collected
   C) flyby, and collecting
   D) flyby and collected

9. The writer is considering deleting the underlined sentence. Should the writer do this?
   A) No, because it adds an interesting detail about the *Pioneer 10* mission.
   B) No, because it provides support for the claim that the mission was successful.
   C) Yes, because it shifts the focus of the passage from Jupiter to the *Pioneer 10* mission.
   D) Yes, because it does not include information about when *Pioneer 10* left the solar system.

and has no solid surface, only varying densities of gas. In fact, very little is known about the interior of Jupiter. When looking at a gas planet like Jupiter, it is really only possible to see the tops of the clouds making up the outermost atmosphere, and probes have been able to penetrate only about 90 miles below this layer. However, after analyzing traces of water and minerals collected from Jupiter's atmosphere, scientists believe that the planet has a core of rocky material amounting to a mass perhaps as much as 15 times that of Earth.

[10] Jupiter is like other gaseous planets. Jupiter has high-velocity winds that blow in wide bands of latitude, each moving in an alternate direction. Slight chemical and temperature changes between these bands, and the resulting chemical reactions, are probably responsible for the array of vibrant colors that dominate the planet's appearance. [11] Measurement taken by a number of probes indicate that the powerful winds moving these bands can reach speeds exceeding 400 miles per hour and likely extend thousands of miles below Jupiter's outer atmosphere.

Yet perhaps the most fascinating characteristic of this planet is the rotational speed of the entire globe of gas itself. While Earth takes 24 hours to make a full rotation, Jupiter completes a full rotation [12] in less time, an amazingly short period of time for a planet with a diameter roughly 11 times that of [13] ours. How Jupiter is able to rotate so fast is just one of many mysteries that scientists continue to explore in their efforts to understand our largest neighbor.

10. A) NO CHANGE
    B) Like other gaseous planets,
    C) Jupiter is like other gaseous planets,
    D) Jupiter, like other gaseous planets,

11. A) NO CHANGE
    B) A measurement
    C) The measurement
    D) Measurements

12. Which choice most accurately reflects the data in the table on the following page?
    A) NO CHANGE
    B) in half that time,
    C) in fewer than 10 Earth hours,
    D) in more time than all the other planets,

13. A) NO CHANGE
    B) our planet.
    C) our own.
    D) our planet's diameter.

Reading & Writing

Planets in Our Solar System				
Planet	Period of Revolution Around the Sun (1 planetary year)	Period of Rotation (1 planetary day)	Mass (kg)	Diameter (miles)
Mercury	87.96 Earth days	58.7 Earth days	3.3×10^{23}	3,031 miles
Venus	224.68 Earth days	243 Earth days	4.87×10^{24}	7,521 miles
Earth	365.26 days	24 hours	5.98×10^{24}	7,926 miles
Mars	686.98 Earth days	24.6 Earth hours	6.42×10^{23}	4,222 miles
Jupiter	11.862 Earth years	9.84 Earth hours	1.90×10^{27}	88,729 miles
Saturn	29.456 Earth years	10.2 Earth hours	5.69×10^{26}	74,600 miles
Uranus	84.07 Earth years	17.9 Earth hours	8.68×10^{25}	32,600 miles
Neptune	164.81 Earth years	19.1 Earth hours	1.02×10^{26}	30,200 miles

Answers & Explanations for this chapter begin on page 893.

EXTRA PRACTICE

Questions 1-11 are based on the following passage.

Physical Therapy Careers: Health Care in Motion

Physical therapy is a health care field that is **1** concurrently rated by the U.S. Bureau of Labor Statistics as one of today's best career choices. Featuring considerable variety in work environments, patient relationships, and job activity levels, the work of a physical therapist has the potential to be both highly motivating and satisfying. **2** And current projections indicate that this particular field of physical therapy should grow significantly over the next decade and continue to be one of the more flexible—not to mention enjoyable and fun—jobs in health care.

3 A license is required to practice as a physical therapist, even in a foreign country. After completing a bachelor's degree (and specific science-related prerequisites), students must obtain a Doctor of Physical Therapy (DPT) degree. This program typically lasts three years. All graduates of DPT programs must then pass the National Physical Therapy Examination. After the exam, they must complete any additional requirements for licensure in the state in which they intend to practice. Once licensed by the state, physical therapists (PTs) are equipped to begin their careers.

1. A) NO CHANGE
   B) consistently
   C) unusually
   D) finally

2. A) NO CHANGE
   B) And current projections indicate that the field should grow significantly over the next several years and the next decade and remain one of the more flexible—not to mention enjoyable—jobs in health care.
   C) Current projections and predictions by the Bureau of Labor indicate that the field should grow significantly over the next decade and remain one of the more flexible and even enjoyable—jobs in the health care industry.
   D) Current projections indicate that the field should grow significantly over the next decade and remain one of the more flexible and enjoyable jobs in health care.

3. Which choice most effectively establishes the main topic of the second paragraph?
   A) NO CHANGE
   B) Those pursuing careers in physical therapy must undergo the appropriate education and licensure processes.
   C) Requirements vary from state to state to practice physical therapy, just as they do for physicians and physicians' assistants.
   D) Physical therapists must pass a national exam that covers a wide range of material.

4 PTs work with a broad range of patients in a wide variety of settings such as hospitals or private clinics. Some clientele, for example, are elderly or ill. Other patients include athletes ranging from elite professionals and college sports stars to middle school sports players.

5 **6** And some kinds of PTs have personal, long-term patient relationships, while others focus on research or testing most of the time and occasionally interact with patients only minimally.

4. A) NO CHANGE

B) PTs work with a broad range of patients, in a wide variety of settings some work in hospitals, while others work in private clinics.

C) PTs work with a broad range of patients; in a wide variety of settings. Some work in hospitals; others in private clinics.

D) PTs work with a broad range of patients: the variety of settings, includes hospitals and private clinics.

5. At this point, the writer is considering adding a sentence to support the main topic of the paragraph. Which choice best supports the main topic of paragraph 3?

A) PTs must demonstrate their willingness to spend long hours on the job.

B) Still others include people who have been injured at work.

C) The clientele pay for their physical therapy services according to their ability, so some PTs earn more than others.

D) No special license is required to work with patients who are professional athletes, but some states may require additional courses to work with students.

6. A) NO CHANGE

B) Some PTs have personal, long-term patient relationships, while others, who focus on research or testing, have minimal interaction with patients.

C) Some PTs have personal, long-term patient relationships; others interact with patients only minimal and focus on research or testing.

D) And some kinds of PTs have personal, long-term patient relationships. Others focus on research or testing and interact with patients only minimally.

[1] **7** A physical therapist primarily works with patients who have suffered motion loss from illness or injury. The goal is to restore mobility while managing and limiting pain. [2] **8** This job often involves long-term planning, creatively personalized application, and patience, in addition to highly refined medical knowledge. [3] In many cases, physical therapists invite and rely on patients to participate actively in their own recovery. [4] This interpersonal and **9** collaborative aspect of physical therapy is often essential to the medical work itself. [5] For example, recovering athletes must often commit to long-term conditioning programs before returning to their sports. [6] Surgery or medication alone isn't always enough to restore full mobility; many PT patients must relearn their muscle use and work hard to increase flexibility. [7] PTs determine the course of action and coach their patients through the steps to recovery. **10**

7. A) NO CHANGE
   B) A physical therapist primarily works with patients. They have suffered motion loss from illness or injury. And the therapist's goal is to restore mobility. While managing and limiting pain.
   C) A physical therapist, whose goal is to restore mobility and manage pain primarily works with patients who have suffered motion loss or illness or injury.
   D) A physical therapist primarily works with patients who have suffered motion loss from illness or injury to restore mobility while managing and limiting pain.

8. A) NO CHANGE
   B) This job often involves long-term planning, creatively personalized application, and highly refined medical knowledge.
   C) This job often involves long-term planning, creative personalized application and patience, in addition to highly refined medical knowledge.
   D) This job often involves long-term planning, creatively personal application and patience, as well as highly refined medical knowledge.

9. A) NO CHANGE
   B) concentrated
   C) planned
   D) consolidated

10. To make this paragraph most logical, sentence 2 should be placed
    A) before sentence 1.
    B) after sentence 3.
    C) after sentence 5.
    D) after sentence 7.

[1] The horizon for employment rates in physical therapy is exceptionally bright. [2] The Bureau of Labor Statistics predicts that the coming decade will see a 36% growth in PT jobs. [3] This means that there should be a need for over 70,000 new PTs nationwide. [4] Physical therapist assistants (PTAs) will also be needed. [5] For those willing to commit the time and effort to become experts in physical therapy, the possibilities and quality of the PT work environment are among the most desirable in health care, and considering projected employment rates, such a career seems to be an especially prudent choice. **11**

11. Which sentence should be removed in order to improve the focus of this paragraph?

A) Sentence 1

B) Sentence 2

C) Sentence 3

D) Sentence 4

Organization

CHAPTER OBJECTIVES

By the end of this chapter, you will be able to:

1. Organize a text's information and ideas into the most logical order

2. Evaluate whether transition words, phrases, or sentences are used effectively to introduce, conclude, or connect information and ideas, and revise the text to improve these transitions when necessary

SMARTPOINTS

Point Value	SmartPoint Category
50 Points	Organization

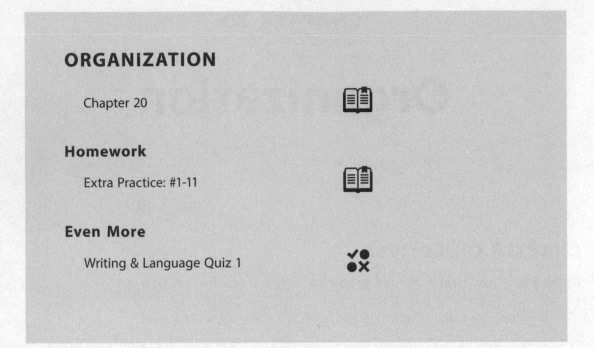

ORGANIZATION

Chapter 20

Homework

Extra Practice: #1-11

Even More

Writing & Language Quiz 1

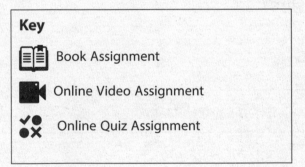

Key

Book Assignment

Online Video Assignment

Online Quiz Assignment

Reading & Writing

ORGANIZATION

Organization questions require you to assess the logic and coherence of a Writing & Language passage. These questions differ in scope; you might be asked to organize the writing at the level of the sentence, the paragraph, or even the entire passage.

There are two kinds of Organization questions:

1. Logical Sequence

- These questions ask you to reorder the sentences in a paragraph or paragraphs in a passage to ensure that information and ideas are logically conveyed.

- When rearranging sentences or paragraphs, begin by determining which sentence or paragraph most logically introduces the paragraph or the passage, respectively.

2. Introductions, Conclusions, and Transitions

- These questions task you with improving the beginning or ending of a passage or paragraph, making sure that the transition words, phrases, or sentences are being used effectively not only to connect information and ideas but also to maintain logical structure.

- While introductions and conclusions focus on the beginning and ending of a passage or paragraph, respectively, transitions are a bit more complicated. It's important to identify what two ideas the transition is linking and how it is doing so. Common types and examples of transitions are listed in the following chart.

Contrast Transitions	Cause-and-Effect Transitions	Continuation Transitions
although	as a result	**Providing an example**
but	because	for example
despite	consequently	for instance
even though	since	**Showing emphasis**
however	so	certainly
in contrast	therefore	in fact
nonetheless	thus	indeed
on the other hand		that is
rather than		**Showing a parallel relationship**
though		also
unlike		furthermore
while		in addition
yet		and
		moreover

> ✔ **Remember**
>
> Organization questions require you not only to improve grammar and style but also to ensure that these elements accurately express the author's logic and reasoning.

Let's look at the following Writing & Language passage and questions. After the passage, there are two columns. The left column contains test-like questions. The column on the right features the strategic thinking a test expert employs when approaching the passage and questions presented.

Product Warnings

1 As if malpractice suits and unnecessary bankruptcies were not enough of a problem, lawyers have chosen to increase the burden that they place on society by engineering an excess of increasingly ridiculous product warnings. Why else would a box of sleeping pills be marketed with the cautionary note that consumers may experience drowsiness? Or a cup of coffee be emblazoned with a notice that "THIS PRODUCT MAY BE HOT"? Anyone with common sense will not need to be warned about these possibilities, and anyone WITHOUT common sense is probably not going to be stopped by a warning label from undertaking a foolish course of action anyway. So honestly, in the long run, the only ones who benefit from these warnings are the lawyers who are paid hundreds of dollars an hour to compose them.

Passages & Questions	Strategic Thinking
1. Which choice most effectively establishes the main topic of the paragraph? A) NO CHANGE B) Each year, effective product warning labels help countless people avoid serious injuries resulting from their use of consumer products. C) In recent years, a coalition of lawyers and consumer safety advocates has successfully campaigned to require companies to include safety warnings on product labels. D) Product safety warnings are necessary to protect consumers who thoughtlessly use products without first thinking about the possible risks involved.	**Step 1: Read the passage and identify the issue** The underlined segment contains the introductory sentence, which introduces the passage's topic of the ridiculousness of product warnings. The author concludes that lawyers are the only people who benefit from product warnings because they are paid to write them. **Step 2: Eliminate answer choices that do not address the issue** Eliminate B because the author does not believe the product warnings are "effective." Eliminate C because the author mentions the lawyers only in a negative light. Eliminate D because the author does not believe product safety warnings are "necessary." **Step 3: Plug in the remaining answer choices and select the most correct, concise, and relevant one** Choice (A) is correct.

Public Schools

[1] It is amazing how little the structure of the American public school system has changed since its inception. [2] Students still change classes according to bells, even though the bell system originated during the days of factories. [3] School is still not in session during the summer, although most students will not use that time to work on farms. [4] Although class and school sizes have varied widely and the curriculum has certainly become varied, the actual system remains surprisingly similar to the way it once was. [5] Despite these idiosyncrasies, however, the American public school system continues to educate the children of this country in a fair and equitable fashion. [6] Without the established structure, the chaotic nature of school would severely inhibit learning. **2**

Passages & Questions	Strategic Thinking
2. To make this paragraph most logical, sentence 4 should be placed A) where it is now. B) before sentence 1. C) after sentence 1. D) after sentence 6.	**Step 1: Read the passage and identify the issue** Sentence 4 is about the fact that even though there have been educational changes over the years, the school system itself has actually not changed that much. It is not properly placed within the paragraph. **Step 2: Eliminate answer choices that do not address the issue** Eliminate A because sentence 4's location is incorrect as is. Eliminate B because sentence 4 is not an appropriate introduction to the paragraph. Eliminate D because sentence 4 is not an appropriate conclusion to the paragraph. **Step 3: Plug in the remaining answer choices and select the most correct, concise, and relevant one** Choice (C) is correct.

First Snowfall

I still remember the magic of walking home under the cold, brittle blue sky, watching the sun strike the glittering blanket laid down by that first snowfall. The world dripped with frosting, and everything was pure and silent. I breathed deeply, enjoying the sting of the icy air in my nostrils, and set off through the trees, listening to the muffled crunch of my footsteps and the chirps of the waking birds. Later, the cars and schoolchildren and mundane lives would turn the wonderland back into dingy slush; the hush would be interrupted by horns and shouts. **3** <u>Indeed</u> for now, the sparkling, cloistered world was mine alone. I smiled, and for a moment, my mind was still.

Passages & Questions	Strategic Thinking
3. A) NO CHANGE B) But C) Consequently D) In fact	**Step 1: Read the passage and identify the issue** The underlined word is a continuation transition showing emphasis. It is incorrect as written because the sentence preceding it discusses what will happen to the snow while this sentence discusses what the snow is like now. A contrast transition would be more appropriate in this context. **Step 2: Eliminate answer choices that do not address the issue** Eliminate C and D because they are not contrast transitions. **Step 3: Plug in the remaining answer choices and select the most correct, concise, and relevant one** Choice (B) is correct.

You have seen the ways in which the SAT tests you on Organization in Writing & Language passages and the way an SAT expert approaches these types of questions.

Use the Kaplan Method for Writing & Language to answer the three questions that accompany the following Writing & Language passage excerpt. Remember to look at the strategic thinking questions that have been laid out for you—some of the answers have been filled in, but you will have to complete the answers to others.

Use your answers to the strategic thinking questions to select the correct answer, just as you will on Test Day.

Questions 4-6 are based on the following passage.

Earthquakes

[1]

The recent devastating earthquakes in China, Haiti, Chile, Mexico, and elsewhere have caused many to wonder if this earthquake activity is unusual.

[2]

"While the number of earthquakes is within the normal range, this does not diminish the fact that there has been extreme devastation and loss of life in heavily populated areas," says USGS Associate Coordinator for Earthquake Hazards, Dr. Michael Blanpied. **4**

[3]

Scientists say 2010 is not showing signs of unusually high earthquake activity. Since 1900, an average of 16 magnitude 7 or greater earthquakes—the size that seismologists define as major—have occurred worldwide each year. Some years have had as few as 6, as in 1986 and 1989, while 1943 had 32, with considerable variability from year to year.

[4]

With six major earthquakes striking in the first four months of this year, 2010 is well within the normal range. From April 15, 2009, to April 14, 2010, there have been 18 major earthquakes, a number also well within the expected variation.

[5]

[1] What will happen next? [2] It is unlikely that any of these aftershocks will be stronger than the earthquakes experienced so far, but structures damaged in the previous events could be further damaged and should be treated with caution. [3] Beyond the ongoing aftershock sequences, earthquakes in recent months have not raised the likelihood of future major earthquakes; that likelihood has not decreased, either. [4] Aftershocks will continue in the regions around each of this year's major earthquakes sites. [5] Large earthquakes will continue to occur just as they have in the past. **5**

[6]

Though the recent earthquakes are not unusual, they are a stark reminder that earthquakes can produce disasters when they strike populated areas, especially areas where the buildings have not been designed to withstand strong shaking. What can be done to prepare? Scientists cannot predict the timing of specific earthquakes. **6** However, families and communities can improve their safety and reduce their losses by taking actions to make their homes, places of work, schools, and businesses as earthquake-safe as possible.

Questions	Strategic Thinking
4. To make the passage most logical, paragraph 2 should be placed A) where it is now. B) after paragraph 3. C) after paragraph 4. D) after paragraph 5.	**Step 1: Read the passage and identify the issue** *What is the issue?* Paragraph 2 is not properly placed within the passage. *What is the content of paragraph 2?* A quotation from a USGS official about how, despite the fact that the number of earthquakes is normal for the area, the loss and devastation suffered in populated regions is still profound. *What two topics does this paragraph connect?* The frequency of earthquakes and the damage caused by earthquakes. **Step 2: Eliminate answer choices that do not address the issue** *What answer choice(s) can you eliminate?* _____ _____ _____ **Step 3: Plug in the remaining answer choices and select the most correct, concise, and relevant one** *What is the correct answer?* _____

Questions	Strategic Thinking
5. To make this paragraph most logical, sentence 4 should be placed A) where it is now. B) before sentence 1. C) before sentence 2. D) after sentence 2.	**Step 1: Read the passage and identify the issue** *What is the issue?* Sentence 4 is not properly placed within the paragraph. *What is the content of sentence 4?* It explains what will happen next in the regions that have suffered earthquakes. *Where in the paragraph does this sentence belong (beginning, middle, end)? Why?* In the beginning, because the sentence discusses the immediate future while the paragraph ends with a reference to the far future. **Step 2: Eliminate answer choices that do not address the issue** *What answer choice(s) can you eliminate?* _____ _____ _____ **Step 3: Plug in the remaining answer choices and select the most correct, concise, and relevant one** *What is the correct answer?* _____

Questions	Strategic Thinking
6. Which choice most effectively concludes the paragraph? A) NO CHANGE B) However, earthquake forecasting employs methods to assess the general earthquake hazard in a particular area. C) However, researchers have studied dogs to determine their ability to sense an impending earthquake. D) However, undersea earthquakes produce low-frequency sound waves that can arrive minutes before the associated tsunami wave.	**Step 1: Read the passage and identify the issue** *What is the issue?* The question is asking whether the underlined sentence is an appropriate conclusion for the paragraph. *What is the content of the paragraph?* Earthquakes are normal, yet unpredictable. *All of the answer choices begin with the transition "however." What does this transition indicate?* _____ _____ **Step 2: Eliminate answer choices that do not address the issue** *What answer choice(s) can you eliminate?* _____ _____ _____ **Step 3: Plug in the remaining answer choices and select the most correct, concise, and relevant one** *What is the correct answer?* _____

Now try a test-like Writing & Language passage on your own. Give yourself 5 minutes to read the passage and answer the questions.

Questions 7-14 are based on the following passage.

The Internet and Conversation

[1]

Internet speak is often maligned as vacuous in its reliance on acronyms and abbreviations, but **7** this is far from universal. On certain discussion boards, you can witness opinions stated and arguments debated with an eloquence that people rarely use when speaking, freely sharing knowledge just for the joy of it. I participate in an online Renaissance music discussion group that has a library of original articles that are the product of a master's thesis. The author gained no monetary reward for the information (which he made available for free) and receives little praise for it outside the community that shares his interest. He posts because he is passionate about the music, and that inspires him to share what he knows with anyone who wants to learn.

[2]

[1] In part, this has to do with my habit of observing the world from my bedroom. [2] As a child, I was frequently ill and forced to stay inside. [3] Although my health is much better now, **8** I still go out much less than most people. [4] After all, I have everything I need inside. [5] Everyone can be everywhere they want when they want, and every social situation feels completely comfortable and natural. [6] From my room,

7. A) NO CHANGE
    B) these are
    C) this reliance is
    D) empty chatter is

8. Which choice provides the best transition within the paragraph?
    A) NO CHANGE
    B) I still remember those long afternoons cooped up inside.
    C) I am still careful to eat well and get plenty of rest.
    D) I regret not being able to play outdoors with other children.

I have access to people all over the world. [7] I can talk about medieval literature with a friend in China and later collaborate on a piece of music with a synthesizer virtuoso in Spain. [8] There is no need for awkward introductions or a graceful exit—people feel free to launch right into what they want to talk about and, when they are done, just sign off with a "g2g," or "got to go." [9] Everything is [9] succinct and to the point. [10]

[3]

For as long as I can remember, conversation [11] had always struck me as a strange chimera, something that is half two minds exchanging sophisticated ideas and [12] at the same time two dogs barking at each other. I do not find the banalities of small talk comforting, but boring and idiotic. [13] When I can dispense with it altogether and proceed right to substantive dialogue, it is almost like flying. I can be talking with the closest of friends or a mere acquaintance with a shared interest. Either way, the kinship is there. I don't feel myself included by smiles, pats on the back, or eye contact so much as by the willingness of a partner to share my ideas or gift me with thoughts of his own. There is nothing more ingratiating than intellectual passion. [14]

9. A) NO CHANGE
   B) succinct
   C) succinctly stated and to the point
   D) succinct, brief, and to the point

10. To make this paragraph most logical, sentence 5 should be placed
    A) where it is now.
    B) before sentence 4.
    C) after sentence 7.
    D) after sentence 8.

11. A) NO CHANGE
    B) has
    C) would have
    D) have

12. A) NO CHANGE
    B) similar to
    C) frequently like
    D) half

13. A) NO CHANGE
    B) Now
    C) Later
    D) Where

14. Which choice places the paragraphs of this passage in the most logical order?
    A) NO CHANGE
    B) 1, 3, 2
    C) 3, 1, 2
    D) 3, 2, 1

Answers & Explanations for this chapter begin on page 896.

EXTRA PRACTICE

The following questions provide an opportunity to practice the concepts and strategic thinking covered in this chapter. While many of the questions pertain to Organization, some touch on other concepts tested on the Writing & Language Test to ensure that your practice is test-like, with a variety of question types per passage.

Questions 1-11 are based on the following passage.

Inside Looking Out: Post-Impressionism

Post-Impressionism was an artistic movement that took place between 1886 and 1892 and **1** produces some of the world's foremost artists. Post-Impressionism emerged as one of the many different artistic styles created in response to the Impressionist movement, which focused on creating realistic representations of human perceptions. **2** Next, Impressionists sought to **3** restate nature in their work. They used small, controlled brush strokes in an effort to capture how the human eye sees light. Post-Impressionism was radically different. Artists of this time focused more on self-discovery than anything else. Instead of looking out on a landscape and **4** attempt to paint exactly what they saw, they turned their eyes inward. They interpreted subjects through their own **5** unique vision, which included their personal experiences and emotions. This change influenced the course of all art created since.

1. A) NO CHANGE
    B) produced
    C) was producing
    D) will produce

2. A) NO CHANGE
    B) For example,
    C) Consequently,
    D) However,

3. A) NO CHANGE
    B) obscure
    C) photocopy
    D) replicate

4. A) NO CHANGE
    B) attempting
    C) was attempted
    D) is attempting

5. A) NO CHANGE
    B) single
    C) cautious
    D) acceptable

[6] Among the Impressionist artists were Claude Monet, Pierre-Auguste Renoir, and Edgar Degas. Paul Cezanne and Georges Seurat used shape and color to describe their worlds rather than mimic them. Their work acted as a bridge between Impressionist art and the more abstract subcategories of Post-Impressionism. Two such subcategories were Cubism and Abstract Expressionism. **[7]** Cubism was created by Spanish painter Pablo Picasso and French painter Georges Braque. It featured geometric shapes used to construct conceptual portraits. Both of these artists rejected traditional views on modeling nature and people, as well as classical techniques. Abstract Expressionism used color instead of geometric figures, and artists like Jackson Pollock and Willem de Kooning covered their canvases with color and indistinct forms. Abstract Expressionists aimed to express deep emotional themes. Paul Gauguin and Vincent van Gogh are also considered Abstract Expressionists, as **[8]** they both prioritized the depiction of their memories and emotions over observations that could be made with the eye. Never before had such an emphasis on individualism

6. Which choice most effectively establishes the central idea of the paragraph?

   A) NO CHANGE

   B) Modern artists are well versed in many different kinds of styles thanks to the many artists of the past.

   C) Artists in the Post-Impressionist era employed a wide range of methods when creating their art.

   D) Prior to the Impressionist and Post-Impressionist eras, artists painted in a much more realistic style.

7. Which choice most effectively combines the sentences at the underlined portion?

   A) NO CHANGE

   B) Created by Spanish painter Pablo Picasso and French painter Georges Braque, Cubism featured geometric shapes.

   C) Cubism was created by Spanish painter Pablo Picasso and French painter Georges Braque so it featured geometric shapes.

   D) Cubism was created by Spanish painter Pablo Picasso and French painter Georges Braque, but it featured geometric shapes.

8. A) NO CHANGE

   B) it

   C) you

   D) we

taken precedence over classical technique, a change that laid the foundation for art in the 20th century and beyond. **9**

[1] These artists worked and created during the same time period and movement. [2] However, they had varying world views and techniques. [3] Today, we can get to know the souls of some of the world's greatest artists by visiting **10** they're Post-Impressionist work in museums around the world. [4] These differences cumulatively succeeded in breaking from the natural guidelines of Impressionism to create something entirely new that dramatically influenced all artists who came after them. [5] In the words of Edvard Munch, another Post-Impressionist painter, "Nature is not only all that is visible to the eye . . . it also includes the inner pictures of the soul." **11**

9. Which choice, if added here, most effectively supports the central idea of the paragraph?

 A) Some Impressionist artists, such as Renoir, painted images of children, flowers, and social gatherings.

 B) Degas often painted ballet dancers at the barre as well as molding sculptures of them.

 C) Art is often viewed as a window into the minds and experiences of artists as they lived their lives.

 D) To transfer their emotions to their canvases, Post-Impressionist artists sometimes used violent gestures to apply paint.

10. A) NO CHANGE

 B) their

 C) they are

 D) there

11. To make this paragraph most logical, sentence 3 should be placed

 A) where it is now.

 B) after sentence 1.

 C) before sentence 5.

 D) after sentence 5.

CHAPTER 21

Development

CHAPTER OBJECTIVES

By the end of this chapter, you will be able to:

1. Evaluate the effectiveness and clarity of a passage's arguments, information, and ideas and determine whether a revision is necessary for the passage to be clear and effective

2. Evaluate information and ideas intended to support claims or points in the passage

3. Identify elements in the passage that are not relevant to the passage's topic and purpose

SMARTPOINTS

Point Value	SmartPoint Category
40 Points	Development

Reading & Writing

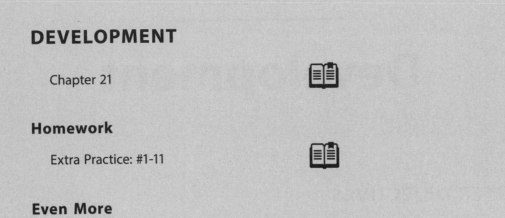

DEVELOPMENT

Chapter 21

Homework

Extra Practice: #1-11

Even More

Writing & Language Quiz 2

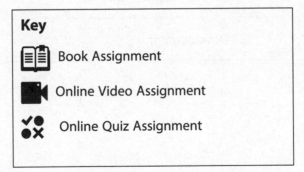

Key

Book Assignment

Online Video Assignment

Online Quiz Assignment

PROPOSITION

Proposition questions ask about how well a writer uses language—arguments, information, and ideas—to express the central purpose of a passage or part of a passage.

You will be asked to add, revise, or retain portions of the passage to communicate key ideas, claims, counterclaims, and topic sentences most clearly and effectively.

To answer Proposition questions, you need to identify the topic and purpose of the passage and focus on the writer's point of view. Ask questions such as:

- What is the central idea of the passage?

- Why did the author write the passage?

- What does the author think about the subject?

- What is the author's tone?

> ✔ **Remember**
>
> The writer's point of view will be consistent throughout the passage. If the writer supports a certain issue, the correct answer choices will reflect this support and how the author effectively communicates it.

SUPPORT

Support questions test issues related to information and ideas presented by the writer. You will be asked to evaluate the effectiveness of the facts and details employed by the writer to support claims made in the passage.

Support questions may ask you to keep, change, or add a detail or example. A Support question could ask about an example used to support a central argument or simply a minor detail used to weaken a point made by the author.

To answer Support questions, look around the underlined portion for a clue indicating what kind of support is required. If the example supports a central idea or claim, ask if the example strengthens the author's central idea. Eliminate answer choices that don't fit the context or have a negative or trivial effect on the central idea.

FOCUS

Focus questions require you to assess whether portions of the passage include only the information and ideas relevant to the author's topic and purpose. You may be asked to add, change, or omit text.

When answering Focus questions, identify whether the text in question fits the topic, scope, and purpose of the entire passage.

> ✔ **Remember**
>
> *Topic* is what the passage is about. *Scope* is the aspect of the broader topic that is the center of the author's focus. *Purpose* is the author's reason for writing.

Let's look at the following Writing & Language passage and questions. After the passage, there are two columns. The left column contains test-like questions. The column on the right features the strategic thinking a test expert employs when approaching the passage and questions presented.

Questions 1-4 are based on the following passage.

Dr. Barry Marshall

For hundreds of years, the medical community and conventional wisdom held that ulcers were caused by stress. Strong gastric juices would sometimes burn sores through the lining of the stomach or intestines, causing widely varied symptoms, including internal bleeding, inflammation, and stomach pain. Doctors reasoned that if patients with ulcers changed their daily habits to reduce the level of tension in their lives, altered their diets to avoid foods that would irritate the stomach, and took medicine to moderate the amount of stomach acid, these ulcers would heal. Although the problem often recurred, no one seriously questioned why. **1** This medical advice remained standard for generations, until Dr. Barry Marshall came along.

Beginning in the 1980s, Marshall, an Australian physician, hypothesized that at least some ulcers were caused by bacteria that often lie dormant in the human stomach. The international medical community scoffed. It was common knowledge, or so Marshall's colleagues believed, that no microbes could survive for long in the highly acidic environment of the stomach. **2** At medical conferences, the veteran, well-known Marshall was regarded as at best, a maverick, and at worst, a quack. Over several years, he and his fellow researcher, Dr. J. Robin Warren, attempted to isolate and identify the bacteria that caused ulcers. As is the case with many medical discoveries, their breakthrough came about partly by accident, when they left a culture growing in the lab overnight. **3**

After this, to further prove his point, Dr. Marshall took a bold step. Although hospitals frown on such potentially dangerous actions, the doctor experimented on himself by deliberately drinking a flask of the bacteria. Over a two-week period, Marshall developed vague, though not disabling, symptoms, and medical tests showed evidence of ulcers and infection. Other researchers' studies later confirmed that Marshall's and Warren's findings apply to about 90% of all ulcers, which can now be cured by a short course of antibiotics instead of being temporarily managed by antacids.

In 2005, Marshall's bold move earned him and Warren the Nobel Prize in Medicine. **4** Dr. Marshall brought his wife to the Nobel Prize ceremony, and she was very proud to witness the public celebration of his work.

Questions	Strategic Thinking
1. A) NO CHANGE B) This medical advice remains the standard today, despite Dr. Barry Marshall's recent efforts. C) This medical advice remained the standard for generations, until Dr. Barry Marshall developed a cure for the stomach ulcer. D) This medical advice remained standard for generations despite a lack of evidence. That is, until Dr. Barry Marshall proved it with scientific experiments.	**Step 1: Read the passage and identify the issue** The underlined portion is the concluding sentence of the first paragraph and should therefore provide a claim central to the passage as a whole. **Step 2: Eliminate answer choices that do not address the issue** Eliminate B because it is untrue according to the rest of the passage. Eliminate C and D because they distort the supporting details provided in the remainder of the passage. **Step 3: Plug in the remaining answer choices and select the most correct, concise, and relevant one** Choice (A) is correct.
2. A) NO CHANGE B) At medical conferences, the young, unknown Marshall was regarded as at best, a maverick, and at worst, a quack. C) At medical conferences, the young, unknown Marshall was regarded as friendly and sociable at after-hours networking events. D) Dr. Marshall mostly avoided medical conferences and symposia.	**Step 1: Read the passage and identify the issue** The underlined sentence provides details about Dr. Marshall's character that you need to make sure fit the tone, scope, and purpose of the passage. **Step 2: Eliminate answer choices that do not address the issue** Eliminate A because the surrounding text does not support that Marshall was "veteran" and "well-known." Eliminate C and D because they are irrelevant to the passage as a whole. **Step 3: Plug in the remaining answer choices and select the most correct, concise, and relevant one** Choice (B) is correct.

Questions	Strategic Thinking
3. Which additional detail is most appropriate to include at this point in the passage? A) Dr. Marshall was a well-organized man and valued a neat workspace; the misplaced petri dish was almost certainly Dr. Warren's fault. B) The following morning, Marshall and Warren found a vibrant culture of a theretofore overlooked bacteria that they soon realized was an important suspect in the formation of ulcers. C) Marshall's and Warren's research was supported by grants, and by that point they were nearing the exhaustion of their funds. D) What Marshall and Warren discovered in their lab the next day brought them closer to finding the link between bacteria, ulcers, and stress.	**Step 1: Read the passage and identify the issue** The question stem asks for the answer choice that includes an "appropriate" detail for this point in the passage. Details should support the passage's central idea. **Step 2: Eliminate answer choices that do not address the issue** The preceding paragraph is about Dr. Marshall's first hypothesis, his career and partnership, and the fact that his and Dr. Warren's breakthrough was an accident. Eliminate A and C because they do not describe the discovery. Eliminate D because it is too general. **Step 3: Plug in the remaining answer choices and select the most correct, concise, and relevant one** Choice (B) is correct.

Questions	Strategic Thinking
4. Which choice most effectively concludes the passage? A) NO CHANGE B) Both of their careers flourished from this point forward, with each earning a tenured, endowed faculty position at a prestigious university. C) Sadly, since 2005, Marshall's and Warren's work has been neglected by the medical and scientific communities, and our understanding of ulcers has not progressed since that time. D) Their important advance, like many other scientific discoveries in history, was a combination of experimentation, persistence, and luck.	**Step 1: Read the passage and identify the issue** The question asks for an effective conclusion for the overall passage. An effective conclusion should contain a summary of the author's central idea and argument. **Step 2: Eliminate answer choices that do not address the issue** Eliminate A and B because they are only details. Eliminate C because it goes beyond the scope of the passage by describing events since 2005 and contradicts the passage's mention of "other researchers' studies." **Step 3: Plug in the remaining answer choices and select the most correct, concise, and relevant one** Choice (D) is correct.

You have seen the ways in which the SAT tests you on Development in Writing & Language passages and the way an SAT expert approaches these types of questions.

Use the Kaplan Method for Writing & Language to answer the four questions that accompany the following Writing & Language passage excerpt. Remember to look at the strategic thinking questions that have been laid out for you—some of the answers have been filled in, but you will have to complete the answers to others.

Use your answers to the strategic thinking questions to select the correct answer, just as you will on Test Day.

Questions 5-8 are based on the following passage.

Human Skin

The skin is the human body's largest organ. An adult's skin comprises between 15 and 20 percent of the total body weight. Each square centimeter has 6 million cells, 5,000 sensory points, 100 sweat glands, and 15 sebaceous glands. The outer layer, the epidermis, consists of rows of cells about 12 to 15 deep and is between .07 and .12 millimeters thick (the thickness of a piece of paper). This top layer **5** <u>has already been studied by countless scientists, and few new discoveries or insights are likely to occur.</u> One square inch of skin contains up to 4.5 m of blood vessels, which regulate body temperature. The skin varies in thickness from .5 mm on the eyelids to 4 mm or more on the palms and the soles.

The skin forms a protective barrier against the action of physical, chemical, and bacterial agents on the deeper tissues and contains the special nerve organs for the various sensations commonly grouped as the sense of touch. The body replaces its skin every month, and because the skin constitutes the first line of defense against dehydration, infection, injuries, and extreme temperatures, **6** <u>the skin detoxifies harmful substances with many of the same enzymatic processes the liver uses.</u>

Skin is constantly being regenerated. A cell is born in the lower layer of the skin, called the dermis, which is supplied with blood vessels and nerve endings. For the next two weeks, the cell migrates upward until it reaches the bottom portion of the epidermis, which is the outermost skin layer. The cell then flattens out and continues moving toward the surface until it dies and is shed.

The most important property of the skin is that it provides our sense of touch. All other senses have a definite key organ that can be studied, but the skin is spread over the entire body and cannot be as easily studied. Receptors located at the ends of nerve fibers are used to detect stimuli and convert them into neural impulses to be sent to the brain through the peripheral and central nervous systems. The sense of touch is actually recorded in the dermis (skin) and passed on to the central nervous system.

The most important job of the skin is to protect the inside of the body; it acts like a "shock absorber." If a body falls, the skin protects all of the internal organs. When the skin is broken, **7** <u>there is an elaborate repair system that relies primarily on blood cells, which clot the breach, fight infection, and initiate healing.</u> The skin also acts as a thermostat to regulate body temperature. **8** <u>It is no exaggeration to say that skin is among the most important organs; without it, a body simply cannot continue living.</u>

Questions	Strategic Thinking
5. A) NO CHANGE B) has already been studied by countless scientists. C) is mainly composed of dead cells and thus is not of great interest to scientists. D) is mainly composed of dead cells and these are constantly being replaced by newer cells.	**Step 1: Read the passage and identify the issue** *What is the issue?* Focus. The underlined portion consists of details in the middle of a paragraph that are unrelated to the main idea. **Step 2: Eliminate answer choices that do not address the issue** *What is this paragraph about?* It introduces the topic of the passage—human skin—and contains many details about said organ. *What answer choice(s) can you eliminate?* _____ _____ _____ **Step 3: Plug in the remaining answer choices and select the most correct, concise, and relevant one** *What is the correct answer?* _____

Reading & Writing

Questions	Strategic Thinking
6. Which choice most effectively concludes the sentence and paragraph? A) NO CHANGE B) the skin detoxifies harmful substances in a way scientists are still trying to understand. C) the skin relies on other organs, such as the liver, to detoxify harmful substances with special enzymatic processes. D) requires careful and upkeep and care.	**Step 1: Read the passage and identify the issue** *What is the issue?* Focus. The underlined portion belongs to the last sentence of a body paragraph, which should tie back into the passage's central idea. **Step 2: Eliminate answer choices that do not address the issue** *What is the central idea of the passage?* _____ _____ _____ *What answer choice(s) can you eliminate?* _____ _____ _____ **Step 3: Plug in the remaining answer choices and select the most correct, concise, and relevant one** *What is the correct answer?* _____

Questions	Strategic Thinking
7. Which choice results in a sentence that best supports the central idea of the paragraph and passage? A) NO CHANGE B) immediate medical attention is necessary to protect the internal organs. C) it has its own defense system that immediately goes into repair mode. D) there is an elaborate repair system that relies primarily on red and white blood cells, which clot the breach, fight infection, and initiate healing.	**Step 1: Read the passage and identify the issue** *What is the issue?* Support. *How do you know?* _____ _____ _____ **Step 2: Eliminate answer choices that do not address the issue** *What is this paragraph about?* _____ _____ _____ *What answer choice(s) can you eliminate?* _____ _____ _____ **Step 3: Plug in the remaining answer choices and select the most correct, concise, and relevant one** *What is the correct answer?* _____

Reading & Writing

Questions	Strategic Thinking
8. Which choice most effectively concludes the passage? A) NO CHANGE B) Since skin covers the body and is easily visible, it is no wonder that its color and decoration have important cultural meanings. C) However, more important organs do indeed exist and likely deserve more scientific attention than the skin. D) Without the skin's properties, most importantly the sense of touch, life would hardly be worth living.	**Step 1: Read the passage and identify the issue** *What is the issue?* _____ *How do you know?* _____ _____ _____ **Step 2: Eliminate answer choices that do not address the issue** *What would effectively conclude the passage?* _____ _____ _____ *What answer choice(s) can you eliminate?* _____ _____ _____ **Step 3: Plug in the remaining answer choices and select the most correct, concise, and relevant one** *What is the correct answer?* _____

Now, try a test-like Writing & Language passage on your own. Give yourself 5 minutes to read the passage and answer the questions.

Questions 9-16 are based on the following passage.

James Polk

For much of his distinguished career, James Knox Polk followed in the footsteps of Andrew Jackson.[1] **9** In fact, "Young Hickory's" policies were very similar to Jackson's: **10** both men favored lower taxes; championed the frontiersmen, farmers, and workers; and neither was afraid to indulge in Tennessee whiskey. Polk, however, did not share Jackson's rather fierce temperament; he was instead known for remaining soft-spoken even as he worked energetically toward his goals. Although history will likely always remember the frontier persona of Andrew Jackson, it was Polk who did much more to shape the course of American history.

9. Which choice, if added here, would provide the most relevant detail?

A) Like the fiery Jackson, Polk was born in North Carolina and moved to Tennessee to begin a political career.

B) Both men were fiery, aggressive personalities who hailed from North Carolina and later moved to Tennessee to begin their political careers.

C) Like the fiery Jackson, Polk was born in North Carolina and moved to Tennessee, but unlike Jackson, he did not fight in the War of 1812.

D) Polk, like Jackson, had antipathy toward the Native Americans of the southeastern United States, and his efforts to remove them defined his career.

10. A) NO CHANGE

B) while they agreed on little regarding taxes or the suffrage of frontiersmen, farmers, and workers, both men were known to indulge in Tennessee whiskey.

C) both men favored lower taxes; championed the frontiersmen, farmers, and workers; and opposed the controversial Bank of the United States.

D) both men favored lower taxes; championed the frontiersmen, farmers, and workers; and yet they could not agree on the controversial Bank of the United States.

11 The Polk family was poor—James's father had emigrated from Scotland and arrived in the U.S. South penniless. From an early age, Polk suffered ill health that would turn out to be a lifelong affliction. Despite his physical shortcomings, he was an able student and graduated from the University of North Carolina with honors in 1818. Two years later, Polk was admitted to the bar to practice law, and in 1823, **12** he married Sarah Childress, the daughter of a prominent planter and merchant from Murfreesboro. From there, he was elected to the U.S. House of Representatives in 1825, serving until 1839. **13** Polk was also Speaker of the House from 1835 to 1839.

11. Which choice most effectively introduces this paragraph?

A) NO CHANGE

B) James Polk's parents tried to discourage the draw of politics and law, instead urging their eldest son to become a farmer.

C) Polk married his wife, Sarah Childress, in 1823.

D) Polk was born in Mecklenburg, North Carolina, in 1795 as the oldest of ten children.

12. Which choice results in a sentence that best supports the point developed in the paragraph and is consistent with the information in the rest of the passage?

A) NO CHANGE

B) he married Sarah Childress.

C) he was elected as governor of Tennessee.

D) he was elected to the Tennessee House of Representatives.

13. Which choice most effectively concludes the paragraph and transitions to the following paragraph?

A) NO CHANGE

B) Polk was also Speaker of the House from 1835 to 1839, an experience that made him wary of wading deeper into national politics.

C) Polk was also Speaker of the House from 1835 to 1839, a post that catapulted him to a position of prominence in politics.

D) Polk was also Speaker of the House from 1835 to 1839, an experience that left his already strained constitution exhausted and forced him into a temporary retirement.

After he left Congress to serve as governor of Tennessee in 1839, it became clear that Polk's political aspirations were high indeed. During the 1844 presidential campaign, **14** a young Abraham Lincoln threw his support behind Whig Henry Clay instead of the Democratic ex-President Martin van Buren. Both men, as part of their platforms, opposed expansionist policies, and neither intended to annex the independent state of Texas or the Oregon Territory. **15** Polk, spurred on by Jackson's advice, recognized that neither candidate had correctly surmised the feelings of the people, so he publicly announced that, as president, he would do his utmost to acquire Texas and Oregon. Polk was the first political "dark horse" in American politics, coming out of nowhere to win the Democratic nomination and the election.

As the eleventh President of the United States, **16** Polk pursued an agenda of diverse issues. First, he reached an agreement with England that divided the Oregon Territory, carving out the present-day states of Washington and Oregon. Polk also quickly annexed Texas and provoked war with Mexico to acquire California and the New Mexico territory. While these triumphs were somewhat diminished by controversy from abolitionists who opposed the spread of slavery into new territories, under Polk's leadership the dream of "manifest destiny" became a reality, and the United States fully extended its borders from the Atlantic to the Pacific.

[1] U.S. President from 1829 to 1837 and War of 1812 hero often referred to as "Old Hickory."

14. Which choice provides the most relevant detail?

   A) NO CHANGE

   B) the leading Democratic candidate was ex-President Martin van Buren and the Whig candidate was Henry Clay.

   C) the issue of slavery's expansion into new territories began its long stint as the most divisive issue to plague national politics.

   D) both the leading Democratic candidate, ex-President Martin van Buren, and the Whig candidate, Henry Clay, sought to campaign under the banner of "Manifest Destiny" and territorial expansion.

15. A) NO CHANGE

   B) Polk, against Jackson's advice, recognized

   C) Polk recognized

   D) Polk, against the wishes of his advisors, recognized

16. Which choice provides the most appropriate introduction to the paragraph?

   A) NO CHANGE

   B) Polk worked tirelessly to expand the borders of the nation.

   C) Polk worked to reign in unchecked expansion of the frontiers.

   D) Polk stopped at nothing short of war to expand the borders of the nation.

Answers & Explanations for this chapter begin on page 899.

EXTRA PRACTICE

Questions 1-11 are based on the following passage and supplementary material.

Reefs at Risk

[1] **1** Coral reefs contain more than one quarter of all marine life and help reduce storm damage to coastal lands. [2] **2** <u>Ultimately,</u> about ten percent of the world's coral reefs have been destroyed and **3** <u>about sixty percent of the remaining reefs are in danger.</u> [3] Many people enjoy snorkeling and fishing near coral reefs. [4] **4** <u>A coral reef is formed by a community of very small plants and animals; these plants and animals are known as algae and polyps.</u> [5] The algae use sunlight to produce their own food for energy and growth. [6] The polyps eat other small animals that come to feed on the algae. [7] They also make a hard substance, called limestone, which eventually builds up to form a reef.

1. Which sentence should be removed in order to improve the focus of this paragraph?
   A) Sentence 1
   B) Sentence 3
   C) Sentence 6
   D) Sentence 7

2. A) NO CHANGE
   B) Unfortunately,
   C) Consequently,
   D) Inevitably,

3. Which choice most accurately represents the information in the pie charts?
   A) NO CHANGE
   B) threats have been made to sixty percent of remaining reefs.
   C) more than 6 in 10 reefs have faced threats of some kind or another.
   D) about sixty percent of the remaining reefs have experienced danger.

4. A) NO CHANGE
   B) Very small plants and animals, known as algae and polyps, make up the community that forms a coral reef.
   C) A coral reef is formed by a community of very small plants and animals called algae and polyps.
   D) Known as algae and polyps, very small plants and animals form a community that is called a coral reef.

The health of a coral reef depends on having clean water and sunlight, but human activities can threaten these **5** basic resources. Oil or chemical spills in the water near the reefs can harm the polyps, and chemical runoff into streams from mines and farms can also destroy the polyps and algae.

6 <u>Fishing and boating are popular sports near coral reefs.</u> People who fish for a living often use explosives to catch the many fish that are attracted to coral reefs, causing significant damage. Boats also destroy reefs with their anchors, and tourists who swim in coral reefs often break coral off to keep as a souvenir.

Development along a coast, such as cutting down trees and building roads or parking lots, **7** <u>increased</u> the amount of dirt and sand that washes into the ocean and settles on the bottom. This covers the coral and blocks sunlight. Without sunlight, the algae cannot grow, and in turn, the polyps lack the energy needed to produce limestone and build up the reef.

5. A) NO CHANGE
   B) elusive
   C) committed
   D) vital

6. Which choice most effectively establishes the paragraph's central idea?
   A) NO CHANGE
   B) People who participate in activities near coral reefs often cause damage.
   C) Boats are dangerous to the health of coral reefs.
   D) Coral reefs are fragile, and people should be careful around them.

7. A) NO CHANGE
   B) increases
   C) increasing
   D) increase

[1] Marine biologists have found that small crabs living in coral reefs can help prevent the damage caused by coastal development. [2] They remove particles of dirt and sand that settle on the coral and **8** stop sunlight. [3] The crabs also eat some of the polyps, which **9** would probably suggest that the crabs might also be a threat to the coral. [4] The crabs help the coral survive **10** but benefit from the relationship as well. [5] The crabs living on the coral have a steady source of food, and the reef provides the crabs with shelter from predators. [6] However, when the biologists removed crabs from sections of coral, less coral survived than in the sections where the crabs remained. **11**

The destruction of coral reefs does not have to continue. Recognizing the part that local animals, such as crabs, can play to reduce the amount of damage will help to slow the loss of coral reefs and may provide better ways to protect them.

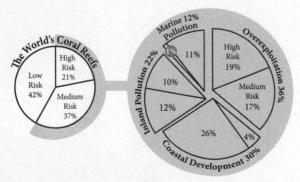

Almost 60% of the world's coral reefs are at high or medium risk of destruction.

Adapted from Wheeling Jesuit University/NASA-supported Classroom of the Future, "Exploring the Environment: Coral Reefs."

8. A) NO CHANGE
    B) hinder
    C) obstruct
    D) cover

9. A) NO CHANGE
    B) would suggest
    C) maybe suggests
    D) almost certainly suggests

10. Which choice results in a sentence that best supports the central idea of the paragraph?
    A) NO CHANGE
    B) but are one of millions of animals that live in coral reefs.
    C) and can be very large or very small in size.
    D) and are found on coral reefs all over the world.

11. To make this paragraph most logical, sentence 6 should be placed
    A) where it is now.
    B) before sentence 1.
    C) after sentence 2.
    D) after sentence 3.

Effective Language Use

CHAPTER OBJECTIVES

By the end of this chapter, you will be able to:

1. Revise the text as needed to improve the exactness or content appropriateness of word choice or eliminate wordiness and redundancy

2. Improve the consistency of style and tone with the passage's purpose as necessary

3. Evaluate the use of sentence structure to accomplish the intended rhetorical purpose of a passage

SMARTPOINTS

Point Value	SmartPoint Category
60 Points	Effective Language Use

Reading & Writing

EFFECTIVE LANGUAGE USE

Chapter 22

Homework

Extra Practice: #1-11

Even More

Writing & Language Quiz 3

Key

 Book Assignment

 Online Video Assignment

 Online Quiz Assignment

PRECISION

On the SAT, precision refers to the exactness and accuracy of the author's choice of words, also known as diction. Precision questions will ask you to revise a text as needed to make a vague word more precise or to change a word or phrase so that it makes sense with the rest of the content.

Word choice is important because being precise in language use allows an author to effectively and clearly convey his or her thoughts, including the thesis and central arguments.

SAT Precision questions mostly test your knowledge of correct word choice in context. Though these questions are similar to the Reading test's Vocab-in-Context questions, Precision questions do not ask about the definition or implication of a word, but about the correctness of it—is it the right word to convey the author's meaning?

CONCISION

Remember the third step of the Kaplan Method for Writing & Language: Plug in the remaining answer choices and select the most clear, *concise*, and relevant one. You must use not only the correct words to convey your ideas but also as few words as possible.

Concision questions will require you to revise text to improve the economy of word choice by eliminating wordiness and redundancy. The SAT tests concision by presenting you with unnecessarily long and complex structures or redundant usage—or sometimes both.

> **✔ On Test Day**
>
> The shortest answer is often but not always the correct one; the portion of the passage in question needs to also be grammatically correct and retain the intended meaning.

Unnecessarily long and complex structure implies that a sentence uses more words than necessary to make its point, even though it may be grammatically correct. Not every long, underlined segment will include a concision issue; sometimes it takes a lot of words to convey meaning. Nevertheless, when a long selection is underlined, you should ask, "Are all of these words necessary? Is there a more concise way to say the same thing?"

Another aspect of concision is redundancy. Redundancy errors occur when two words in the sentence have essentially the same meaning in context or when the meaning of one word is implicit in the meaning of another.

STYLE AND TONE

Elements of an author's style and tone include his or her choices of words, rhetorical devices, and sentence structure. The author might write informally, as if for a friendly, general audience; academically, as if for an expert audience; or forcefully, as if expounding his or her point of view. SAT Style and Tone questions ask you to revise a text to ensure consistency of style and tone or to reflect the author's purpose. You must also confirm that the text's style and tone match the subject and format.

Some Style and Tone questions will have question stems, while others will not. In the case of the latter, you must determine if the underlined segment matches the general tone of the passage or if one of the other choices is more appropriate in context.

> ✔ **Expert Tip**
>
> If you spot a Style and Tone question at the beginning of a passage, read the rest of the passage before answering it so you can first determine the overall tone.

SYNTAX

Syntax refers to the arrangement of words and phrases within a sentence. Questions about syntax will ask you to assess whether different sentence structures accomplish an author's intended rhetorical purpose. In narratives or prose, syntax can enhance the intended meaning and contribute toward tone.

Academic texts, such as the passages you'll see on the SAT, employ varied kinds of syntax. One way in which syntax is categorized is by sentence type. The following table describes four sentence types that are classified by the clauses they contain.

> ✔ **Definition**
>
> A clause is a part of a sentence containing a subject and a predicate verb.

Sentence Type	Description	Example
Simple	Contains a single, independent clause	*I applied for a summer job.*
Compound	Contains two independent clauses that are joined by a coordinating conjunction (e.g., *but, or, and, so*)	*I applied for a summer job, and the human resources manager hired me.*
Complex	Contains an independent clause plus one or more dependent clauses (a dependent clause starts with a coordinating conjunction such as *that, because, while, although, where, if*)	*I applied for a summer job at the local hospital because I am interested in gaining experience in the medical field.*
Compound-Complex	Contains three or more clauses (of which at least two are independent and one is dependent)	*I applied for a summer job at the local hospital, and the human resources manager hired me because I am interested in gaining experience in the medical field.*

Let's look at the following Writing & Language passage and questions. After the passage, there are two columns. The left column contains test-like questions. The column on the right features the strategic thinking a test expert employs when approaching the passage and questions presented.

Questions 1-4 are based on the following passage.

Modern Readers

Judging by the types of novels that typically receive the top rankings on contemporary "best seller" lists, one would be wise to conclude that the modern book consumer does not enjoy reading ancient mythology. Seemingly, such antiquated stories hold little relevance to the concerns of the modern age. It is a literature not for the **1** distracted reader immersed in his "everyday" cares, but for a more imaginative audience with more universal tastes.

To even begin **2** to understand or comprehend this issue, we must understand what it is that most readers seek out in the works they read. What is it in a book—a novel, for example—that causes them to continue turning the pages? The answer can be a bit slippery. Is it the psychological realism of the characters? Is it the drama of the events they encounter? Is it the modern author's consciousness of his position as author and the relationship—distant or intimate, serious or playful—that he develops with his readers?

The obvious answer is that it is all of these things. The defining features of the modern story are its complexity and ambivalence. Narrators are not always reliable. Loyalties are often fleeting, and even a character's central motives may undergo a transformation before the story is done. There is no neat conclusion, no definitive redemption or damnation, and not always even a clear message. In this confusion and dislocation, the modern reader sees his own life reflected, complete with all of its **3** complexity and ambivalence.

In a complex world where the disparate lives of alienated individuals still manage to affect each other on a daily basis, there is a paradoxical credulity extended towards anything murky and unclear. Far from the cosmopolitan savant he would like us to believe he is (to say nothing of the author who writes for him), the modern reader is only able to take comfort in his own confusion. When, for example, George and Jane finish their fairy-tale courtship and suddenly find themselves unable to live together, the contemporary pop intellectual will **4** nod his head sagely, and he will think about the relationships in his own life that he didn't understand either.

What escapes the minds of the masses is that, taken past a certain point, realism is not art. Neither unsatisfying conclusions, nor irritating characters, nor obscure motives are indications of the literary talents of the author. The older, mythic characters may be drawn with a broad brush, and may possess a simplicity and singularity of purpose that finds no parallel in day-to-day life, but that simplicity is not a sign of an author lacking in subtlety. Rather, a purposeful author will have purposeful characters. Whether the story is meant to illustrate moral principles, explore character types, or simply entertain, a quality work of art must have a purpose.

Questions	Strategic Thinking
1. A) NO CHANGE B) prosaic C) voracious D) modern	**Step 1: Read the passage and identify the issue** The underlined word, "distracted," does not directly contrast with the "more imaginative audience with more universal tastes," as indicated by the use of the word "but." A better word choice will describe readers who are less imaginative and more selective in their reading. **Step 2: Eliminate answer choices that do not address the issue** Eliminate A because the underlined word is not precise enough. Eliminate C because a "voracious" reader is one who reads an enormous amount, not a less imaginative reader. Eliminate D because the reader's era has nothing to do with the sentence. **Step 3: Plug in the remaining answer choices and select the most correct, concise, and relevant one** Since "prosaic" means ordinary, (B) is correct.

Reading & Writing

Questions	Strategic Thinking
2. A) NO CHANGE B) to understand or to comprehend C) to understand and comprehend D) to understand	**Step 1: Read the passage and identify the issue** The underlined portion is redundant as written; "understand" and "comprehend" have the same meaning. The underlined portion needs to be more concise. **Step 2: Eliminate answer choices that do not address the issue** Eliminate A because the underlined portion is incorrect as written and needs to be changed. Eliminate B and C because they do not correct the redundancy issue. **Step 3: Plug in the remaining answer choices and select the most correct, concise, and relevant one** Choice (D) is correct.

Questions	Strategic Thinking
3. A) NO CHANGE B) ambivalence C) complexity D) ambivalent complexity	**Step 1: Read the passage and identify the issue** The style and tone of the passage are authoritative and academic. Check to see if the underlined portion reflects this style and tone appropriately. **Step 2: Eliminate answer choices that do not address the issue** The author uses the underlined phrase previously in the second sentence of the paragraph: "The defining features of the modern story are its complexity and ambivalence." Eliminate B and C because they both remove one of the previously used words. Eliminate D because even though it is more concise, it alters the intended meaning. **Step 3: Plug in the remaining answer choices and select the most correct, concise, and relevant one** Choice (A) is correct.

Reading & Writing

Questions	Strategic Thinking
4. Which choice most effectively combines the sentences at the underlined portion? A) NO CHANGE B) nod his head sagely. He will think about C) nod his head sagely, thinking about D) nod his head sagely, be thinking about	**Step 1: Read the passage and identify the issue** Although the two independent clauses are correctly combined with a comma and the conjunction "and," the sentence is wordy as written and unnecessarily repeats the subject "he." The syntax of the sentence needs to be corrected. **Step 2: Eliminate answer choices that do not address the issue** Eliminate A because the sentence is incorrect as written. Eliminate B because it separates the underlined portion into two sentences, which, while grammatically correct, is not the most effective combination; the separated sentences place unnecessary distance between the two parts. Eliminate D because it is grammatically incorrect. **Step 3: Plug in the remaining answer choices and select the most correct, concise, and relevant one** Choice (C) is correct.

You have seen the ways in which the SAT tests you on Effective Language Use in Writing & Language passages and the way an SAT expert approaches these types of questions.

Use the Kaplan Method for Writing & Language to answer the four questions that accompany the following Writing & Language passage excerpt. Remember to look at the strategic thinking questions that have been laid out for you—some of the answers have been filled in, but you will have to complete the answers to others.

Use your answers to the strategic thinking questions to select the correct answer, just as you will on Test Day.

Questions 5-8 are based on the following passage.

Military Nurses

During the American Civil War, Miss Dorothea Dix was in charge of organizing the volunteer nurses who assisted the Union Army. The nurses chosen by Dix were all women, preferably plain ones, and had to dress simply in order to serve. Dorothea Dix's volunteers were the first famous nurses in United States history, but on both the Union and Confederate sides, **5** other health care professionals there that few people knew about were male nurses. As the nineteenth century progressed, nursing became increasingly considered "women's work," until, at the turn of the 20th century, female nurses began to organize, unofficially excluding men. The American Nursing Association was formed in 1917, and men were not officially permitted to join until 1930.

One of the **6** major victories of the female-dominated nursing community was to have men **7** denied admission to and excluded from military nursing. Traditionally, non-volunteer military nurses had been exclusively male, but in 1901, the United States Army Nurse Corps was formed exclusively for women. **8** It is amazing to even think that men couldn't work as military nurses until after the Korean War. Today, depending on the branch of service, anywhere between 35% and 70% of military nurses are men; this is in sharp contrast to the civilian world, where an average of 6% of American nurses are men.

Reading & Writing

Questions	Strategic Thinking
5. A) NO CHANGE B) few people knew there were other health care professionals about: male nurses. C) some health care professionals were male nurses that few people knew about. D) there were other health care professionals that few people knew about: male nurses.	**Step 1: Read the passage and identify the issue** *What is the issue?* Syntax. As written, the sentence is hard to follow due to the placement of the words. **Step 2: Eliminate answer choices that do not address the issue** *What answer choice(s) can you eliminate?* Eliminate A, B, and C because they all contain a syntax error. **Step 3: Plug in the remaining answer choices and select the most correct, concise, and relevant one** *What is the correct answer?* _____

Questions	Strategic Thinking

6. A) NO CHANGE
 	
   B) first triumphs
 	
   C) undisputed wins
 	
   D) finest achievements
	Step 1: Read the passage and identify the issue
	
	What is the issue?
	
	Word choice, or precision.
	
	What does the underlined phrase indicate? Does it fit the context of the passage? Why or why not?
	
	The passage is concerned with the early years of female nursing. The underlined phrase does not make this connection.
	
	Step 2: Eliminate answer choices that do not address the issue
	
	What answer choice(s) can you eliminate?
	
	_____
	
	_____
	
	_____
	
	Step 3: Plug in the remaining answer choices and select the most correct, concise, and relevant one
	
	What is the correct answer? _____

Questions	Strategic Thinking
7. A) NO CHANGE B) denied to and excluded from C) excluded from D) denied and excluded from	**Step 1: Read the passage and identify the issue** *What is the issue?* Redundancy, or concision. *Why is the underlined portion redundant?* _____ _____ **Step 2: Eliminate answer choices that do not address the issue** *What answer choice(s) can you eliminate?* _____ _____ _____ **Step 3: Plug in the remaining answer choices and select the most correct, concise, and relevant one** *What is the correct answer?* _____

Questions	Strategic Thinking
8. A) NO CHANGE B) It was not until after the Korean War that men could once more work as military nurses. C) In this day and age, it is nearly inconceivable that it took until after the Korean War before men could once more exercise their right to work as military nurses. D) Not until after the Korean War could men once more take up the noble calling to serve as military nurses.	**Step 1: Read the passage and identify the issue** *What is the issue?* Style and tone. *What are the style and tone of the passage?* _____ _____ *Does the underlined portion match the style and tone of the passage? Why or why not?* _____ _____ **Step 2: Eliminate answer choices that do not address the issue** *What answer choice(s) can you eliminate?* _____ _____ _____ **Step 3: Plug in the remaining answer choices and select the most correct, concise, and relevant one** *What is the correct answer?* _____

Now try a test-like Writing & Language passage on your own. Give yourself 5 minutes to read the passage and answer the questions.

Questions 9-16 are based on the following passage.

Genetically Modified Organisms

Although biotechnology companies and the chronically naïve 9 imagine that there is no danger to be feared from genetically modified foods, they overlook a plethora of evidence indicating that we may be gambling with our very lives by continuing to 10 interfere and tamper with nature to create these "Frankenfoods." Potential problems range from the relatively minor—increased possibilities of allergic reactions to certain foods, for instance—to the potentially devastating—the complete skewing of the balance of an ecosystem. All of these factors should be carefully considered before 11 we choose to risk so much for the possibility of a better tomato.

For example, the cultivation of insect-resistant plants could lead to the reduction or even destruction of certain insect species that naturally feed on those plants. A change in the insect population could have a disastrous impact on 12 certain bird species. They rely on the affected insects as their food source. Also, alterations in the balance of the bird population could have further-reaching consequences, all the way up the food chain. An ecosystem is a delicate thing, and the ripple created by genetically altering one variety of soybean 13 will translate into a shock wave of unforeseen repercussions in the long term.

9. A) NO CHANGE
    B) insist
    C) hope
    D) think

10. A) NO CHANGE
    B) thoughtlessly interfere and casually tamper
    C) interfere by casually tampering
    D) tamper

11. A) NO CHANGE
    B) we as a society
    C) those of us who comprise society
    D) the citizens making up our population

12. Which choice most effectively combines the sentences at the underlined portion?
    A) NO CHANGE
    B) certain bird species that rely on the affected insects
    C) certain bird species relying on the affected insects
    D) certain bird species, and they rely on the affected insects

13. A) NO CHANGE
    B) must
    C) would
    D) could

14 The actual impact on the genetically modified organisms themselves, and on those who consume foods produced from genetically modified organisms, also remains to be seen. Some studies indicate that certain genetically modified foods have negative effects on the digestive systems and cardiac health of rats that consume those foods in high quantities; although human studies have not been performed, the possibility that tampering with an organism's genetic structure could cause far-reaching health consequences for the people who eat genetically modified foods must be confronted.

Arguments about the potential for genetic engineering to end world hunger by maximizing the quantity and quality of food grown around the world are based on **15** an essential fallacy: people do not starve because there is a lack of food. People starve because it is more profitable to let food go to waste than to distribute it to the world's impoverished and famine-stricken regions. We have plenty of farmland sitting fallow and plenty of food rotting in warehouses. Many of the agribusinesses arguing that genetically modified foods can solve world hunger are the same companies that accept government subsidies now to limit their production of crops in order to avoid flooding the market. These companies are primarily concerned with profit, and whatever lip service they pay to global well-being, the driving force behind genetically modified organisms and foods is profit, not people. **16** In conclusion, the benefits and risks of any new technology must be carefully considered before implementing that technology.

14. A) NO CHANGE
    B) What also remains to be seen, on both the genetically modified organisms themselves and on those who consume foods produced from genetically modified organisms, is the actual impact.
    C) Remaining to be seen is the actual impact on genetically modified organisms themselves and those who consume genetically modified organisms.
    D) The actual impact remains to be seen on genetically modified organisms themselves and those who consume genetically modified organisms.

15. A) NO CHANGE
    B) a harmful delusion:
    C) a fanciful illusion:
    D) a fundamental untruth:

16. Which choice most effectively concludes the paragraph and the passage?
    A) NO CHANGE
    B) It would be nice if we could trust the very companies that could benefit most from the creation of genetically modified organisms.
    C) Unfortunately, those companies affect so many aspects of modern life that we have no choice but to trust them.
    D) Why would we trust our own well-being and that of the planet to companies recklessly pursuing money at the risk of Mother Earth?

Answers & Explanations for this chapter begin on page 902.

Reading & Writing

EXTRA PRACTICE

The following questions provide an opportunity to practice the concepts and strategic thinking covered in this chapter. While many of the questions pertain to Effective Language Use, some touch on other concepts tested on the Writing & Language Test to ensure that your practice is test-like, with a variety of question types per passage.

Questions 1-11 are based on the following passage.

Long History, Short Poem: The Haiku

1 Of the many forms poetry can take, triolet, ballad, ode, and epigram, to name a few, none is quite as briefly beautiful as the Japanese haiku. With a **2** complex history and a challenging structure, the haiku is as popular as it is difficult to master. Composed of only three lines and 17 or fewer syllables, haiku have been written by some of the world's most prominent poets.

1. A) NO CHANGE
    B) Of the many forms poetry can take—triolet, ballad, ode, and epigram, to name a few—none is quite as briefly beautiful as the Japanese haiku.
    C) Of the many forms poetry can take, triolet, ballad, ode and epigram to name a few—none is quite as briefly beautiful as the Japanese haiku.
    D) Of the many forms poetry can take: triolet, ballad, ode, and epigram to name a few, none is quite as briefly beautiful as the Japanese haiku.

2. A) NO CHANGE
    B) controversial
    C) brief
    D) difficult

3 [1] Pre-Buddhist and early Shinto ceremonies included narrative poems called "uta," or songs. [2] These songs were written about common activities like planting and prayer. [3] The most popular "uta" were "waka," or songs featuring 31 syllables broken into five different lines. [4] Later, the "waka" format was distilled into the 5-7-5-7-7 syllables-per-line format that is still used and recognized today. [5] During the same time period, writers played word games. [6] The syllabic 5-7-5-7-7 structure would remain throughout the work, adhering to the guidelines used in ceremonies and royal court proceedings. [7] They would compose lines of poetry, alternating turns, until long strings of text called "renga" were created. [8] It was not until the 15th and 16th centuries that writers of "renga" broke with tradition and shortened the form, writing "hokku," meaning "first verse." [9] **4** This name changed into "haiku" over time. **5**

3. Which choice, if added here, would provide the most appropriate introduction to the topic of the paragraph?

A) Although the format remained unknown to Americans until the 1950s, haiku dates back as early as the seventh century.

B) The art of haiku includes specific rules about how lines are to be structured, but these rules are difficult to pin down.

C) Despite its difficult reputation and the years it takes to master, haiku is highly entertaining.

D) Haiku is a Japanese poetic art form and many poets enjoy the challenge of writing a poem within its rules.

4. A) NO CHANGE

B) Nobody is quite sure when it became known as "haiku."

C) These days, we know this word as "haiku."

D) DELETE the underlined portion.

5. To make this paragraph most logical, sentence 7 should be placed

A) where it is now.

B) after sentence 1.

C) after sentence 5.

D) after sentence 8.

Reading & Writing

6 Previously, hokku master Matsunaga Teitoku began teaching renga in an attempt to ignite a classical renaissance. He founded a writing school where he taught Matsuo Basho, who is now known as one of Japan's most famous writers. Basho traveled throughout Japan writing about nature and his travels.

It is through Basho's many poems that **7** haiku came to be known as being pretty tied up with nature and the seasons. **8** Basho influenced many students of verse over the course of his lifetime and was declared the saint of the haiku in the Shinto religion.

6. A) NO CHANGE
    B) However,
    C) In the next century,
    D) As a result,

7. A) NO CHANGE
    B) haiku transformed into a mode of artistic expression that was irreversibly intertwined with the themes of
    C) haiku became popular because it was seen as having something to do with
    D) haiku developed its common association with

8. Which choice, if added here, would provide the most relevant detail?
    A) However, haiku can be used to communicate many other ideas as well, from love to humor.
    B) His words emphasized contentment and solitary contemplation, ideals linked to Japanese religions.
    C) Basho's poetic influence continues to be felt even now in the work of several modern poets.
    D) For example, a Basho haiku might focus on a frog or on the coming of spring.

It was not until 1827 that hokku was renamed haiku by Masaoka Shiki. [9] Shiki was a poet, and he most famously shrank the structure of the haiku to its current format of 5-7-5. His work [10] helped Western writers like e. e. cummings and Ezra Pound, but haiku did not become the easily recognizable, popular type of poetry that it is today until writers like Allen Ginsberg and Jack Kerouac popularized it.

These writers were taken by [11] the brevity of the form, but it provided them a new, challenging form of expression while enabling them to share full ideas in such a short form. Both Japanese and American poets continue to use the haiku structure to create snapshots of beauty and calm.

9. A) NO CHANGE

   B) Shiki was a poet who also shrank the structure of the haiku to the current 5-7-5 format.

   C) Shiki was the poet who shrank the structure of the haiku to its current 5-7-5 format.

   D) Shiki was the poet who was also known for shrinking the structure of the haiku to its current format of 5-7-5.

10. A) NO CHANGE

    B) inspired

    C) aided

    D) started

11. A) NO CHANGE

    B) the brevity of the form, it

    C) the brevity of the form, and it

    D) the brevity of the form, as it

Reading & Writing

Standard English Conventions

BY THE END OF THIS UNIT, YOU WILL BE ABLE TO:

1. Recognize correct and incorrect instances of conventions of usage and punctuation

2. Identify and correct errors in sentence structure

3. Identify and correct usage errors

CHAPTER 23

Sentence Structure

CHAPTER OBJECTIVES

By the end of this chapter, you will be able to:

1. Recognize and correct grammatically incomplete or substandard sentences

2. Recognize and correct inappropriate grammatical shifts in the construction of verb and pronoun phrases

SMARTPOINTS

Point Value	SmartPoint Category
60 Points	Sentence Formation

Reading & Writing

SENTENCE STRUCTURE

Chapter 23

Homework

Extra Practice: #1-11

Even More

Writing & Language Quiz 4

Key

 Book Assignment

 Online Video Assignment

 Online Quiz Assignment

RUN-ONS AND FRAGMENTS

Run-ons and fragments create grammatically incorrect sentences. The SAT requires that you know the specific rules governing sentence construction.

A complete sentence must have a subject and a predicate verb in an independent clause that expresses a complete thought. If any one of these elements is missing, the sentence is a fragment. You can recognize a fragment because the sentence will not make sense as written. A fragment lacks one of the three components.

- *Seth running down the street.* (The fragment lacks a predicate verb.)

- *Because Michaela led the team in assists.* (The fragment is a dependent clause and does not express a complete thought.)

- *Practiced the piano every day.* (The fragment needs a subject.)

✔ Definition

A **predicate** is the part of the sentence that describes what the **subject** *does* (action), *is* (being), or *has* (condition); the **predicate verb** is the main verb in the sentence.

If a sentence has more than one independent clause, the clauses must be properly joined. Otherwise, the sentence is a run-on.

- *My friends and I usually walk home from school together, we ride the bus if the weather isn't nice.*

To Correct a Run-On	Example
Use a semicolon.	*My friends and I usually walk home from school together**;** we ride the bus if the weather isn't nice.*
Make one clause dependent.	***Although** my friends and I usually walk home from school together, we ride the bus if the weather isn't nice.*
Add a FANBOYS conjunction: *For, And, Nor, But, Or, Yet, So.*	*My friends and I usually walk home from school together, **but** we ride the bus if the weather isn't nice.*

COORDINATION AND SUBORDINATION

Coordination and subordination questions focus on the relationship between clauses. On the SAT, you will be asked to determine the best way to link clauses to most effectively express the writer's intent.

Coordinate Clauses

Coordinate clauses are independent clauses that can stand on their own and express a complete thought. When two or more independent clauses are properly joined, they form a compound sentence.

Two independent clauses are coordinated by using a comma and the conjunction and:

- *The class was interesting, and we prepared thoroughly for each session.* (Equal emphasis on the two ideas suggests that the class would have been interesting whether or not we prepared, and it suggests that we would have prepared whether or not the class was interesting.)

Subordinate Clauses

A subordinate clause cannot stand on its own and still make sense. Combining a subordinate clause with an independent clause by using a connecting word forms a complex sentence in which the independent clause expresses the central idea of the sentence and the subordinate clause provides additional support that modifies or clarifies the central idea.

The central idea of the sentence is changed depending upon which clause is subordinated:

- *Because the class was interesting,* we prepared thoroughly for each session. (The main emphasis is on our preparation. The subordinate clause gives the reason for our thoroughness.)

- The class was interesting *because we prepared thoroughly for each session*. (The main emphasis is on the class. The subordinate clause explains why it was interesting.)

PARALLELISM

Parallelism questions on the SAT test your ability to revise sentences to create parallel structure. Items in a series, list, or compound must be parallel in form. Series, lists, and compounds may contain nouns, adjectives, adverbs, or verb forms.

Check for parallelism if the sentence contains:

Feature	Example	Parallel Form
A list	*Before you leave, you should **charge your phone**, **clean your room**, and **find your bus pass**.*	3 verb phrases
A compound	***Swimming** and **biking** provide aerobic exercise.*	2 gerund verb forms
A correlative	*The debate coach encouraged the students **to listen** carefully and **to speak** clearly.*	2 infinitive verb forms
A comparison	*Your **practice test sessions** are just as important as your **class sessions**.*	2 nouns
Related nouns	***Students** who complete all of their **homework assignments** are more likely to earn **higher test scores**.*	3 related plural nouns

MODIFIERS

A modifier is a word or a group of words that describes, clarifies, or provides additional information about another part of the sentence. Modifier questions on the SAT Writing & Language Test require you to identify the part of a sentence being modified and use the appropriate modifier in the proper place.

> **✔ Expert Tip**
>
> On the SAT, modifiers should be close to the words they modify.

Modifier	Function	Example
Adjective	An adjective is a single word modifier that describes a noun or pronoun.	*Asara bought a **blue** backpack from the **thrift** shop.*
Adverb	An adverb is a single word modifier that describes a verb, an adjective, or another adverb.	*Ian **carefully** walked over the **rapidly** melting ice.*
Modifying phrase	Modifying phrases and clauses must be properly placed to correctly modify another part of the sentence.	***Wanting to do well at the competition**, Sasha devoted extra time to her practice sessions.*

Reading & Writing

Use context clues in the passage to identify the correct placement of a modifier; a misplaced modifier can cause confusion:

- *The restaurant provides carryout meals to its diners **in recyclable containers**.*

Who or what is in the containers? The context of the sentence suggests that the meals are in the containers; however, since modifiers should be placed near what they modify, the sentence can be grammatically interpreted to suggest that the diners are in the containers! When the modifier is correctly placed near what it modifies, the meaning is clarified:

- *The restaurant provides carryout meals **in recyclable containers** to its diners.*

Modifier placement can change the meaning of a sentence:

- *The waiter **just** described the dinner specials.* (The sentence is about **when** the action took place.)

- ***Just** the waiter described the dinner specials.* (The sentence is about **who** completed the action.)

- *The waiter described **just** the dinner specials.* (The sentence is about **what** was acted upon.)

VERB TENSE, MOOD, AND VOICE

On the SAT Writing & Language Test, you will be asked to identify and replace unnecessary shifts in verb tense, mood, and voice. Because these shifts may occur within a single sentence or among different sentences, you will need to read around the underlined portion to identify the error.

In questions about shifts in construction, the underlined segment must logically match the tense, mood, and voice in other parts of the sentence.

Verb tense places the action or state of being described by the verb into a place in time: **present**, **past**, or **future**. Each tense has three forms: **simple**, **progressive**, and **perfect**.

> ✔ **On Test Day**
>
> Shifts in verb tense are grammatically incorrect unless warranted by the context of the sentence or passage.

	Present	Past	Future
Simple: Actions that simply occur at some point in time	*She studies diligently every day.*	*She studied two extra hours before her math test.*	*She will study tomorrow for her French test.*
Progressive: Actions that are ongoing at some point in time	*She is studying today for her math test tomorrow.*	*She was studying yesterday for a French test today.*	*She will be studying tomorrow for her physics test next week.*
Perfect: Actions that are completed at some point in time	*She has studied diligently every day this semester.*	*She had studied two extra hours before her math test yesterday.*	*She will have studied each chapter before her physics test next week.*

Grammatical **moods** are classifications that indicate the attitude of the speaker.

	Description	Example
Indicative Mood	Used to make a statement or ask a question	*Snow **covered** the moonlit field.*
Imperative Mood	Used to give a command or make a request	*Please **drive** carefully in the snow.*
Subjunctive Mood	Used to express hypothetical outcomes	*If I **were** at the library, I could find the book I need.*

The **voice** of a verb describes the relationship between the action expressed by the verb and the subject.

	Description	Example
Active	The subject is the agent or doer of the action.	*The carpenter **hammered** the nail.*
Passive	The subject is the target of the action.	*The nail **was hammered** by the carpenter.*

> ✔ **Expert Tip**
>
> On the SAT, the active voice is preferred over the passive voice.

PRONOUN PERSON AND NUMBER

Pronouns replace nouns in sentences. They must agree with the noun they are replacing in person and number. The SAT will test your ability to recognize and correct inappropriate shifts in pronoun usage. To learn more about pronoun clarity and pronoun-antecedent agreement on the SAT, turn to chapter 24.

Pronoun Person and Number			
Person	**Refers to**	**Singular Pronouns**	**Plural Pronouns**
First person	the person speaking	I, me, my	we, us, our
Second person	the person spoken to	you, your	you, your
Third person	the person or thing spoken about	he, she, it, him, her, his, hers, its	they, them, theirs
Indefinite	a nonspecific person or group	anybody, anyone, each, either, everyone, someone, one	both, few, many, several

Do not shift between "you" and "one" unnecessarily. "You" refers to a specific person or group. "One" refers to an indefinite individual or group.

Let's look at the following Writing & Language passage and questions. After the passage, there are two columns. The left column contains test-like questions. The column on the right features the strategic thinking a test expert employs when approaching the passage and questions presented.

Questions 1-3 are based on the following passage.

SMOM

At 69 Condotti Street in Rome sits what is believed by many to be the smallest country in the world, a country that is not known by many. The Sovereign Military and Hospitaller Order of St. John of Jerusalem of Rhodes and of Malta, or SMOM, is an ancient order of knights well known for its humanitarian activities. The order's headquarters in Rome—a mere 6,000 square meters, or about one acre—is considered an independent state by at least 75 nations. How SMOM got to Rome is a story almost a millennium old, spanning as many places as the order's official name suggests.

SMOM began in 1099, during the First Crusade, as a large-scale military conflict pitting Christian armies against the Muslim rulers of what is now Israel. The order's task was to protect and defend Christian pilgrims traveling to Jerusalem as well as **1** providing a hospital for their care. Though it began as a religious order, SMOM developed into a military knighthood as a result of the volatile political situation.

Because of the ongoing conflict between Muslims and Christians, the order was forced to move a number of times. The Muslims overran Jerusalem in the 1170s, forcing SMOM to relocate first to the Mediterranean island of Cyprus and then to the nearby island of Rhodes. The Ottoman Turks seized Rhodes in 1522, forcing SMOM to move again, this time to Malta. **2** Then Napoleon drives the order from Malta in 1798, and the island fell into British hands soon after. SMOM wandered from city to city in Italy, finally establishing its current headquarters in 1834.

Today, SMOM is a knighthood and a religious order but no longer actively combats Muslims, as it did in the past. Instead, SMOM concentrates on caring for humanitarian needs regardless of **3** creed. Establishing hospitals and charities in all corners of the world. Its many activities include vaccination programs, refugee relief, and philanthropic works to combat deadly diseases, such as leprosy and malnutrition.

Because of the order's dual role, the Vatican, the central governing body of the Catholic Church, has always recognized—and continues to recognize—SMOM as an independent nation and its headquarters in Rome as the sovereignty of SMOM. Seventy-five countries recognize the order as a country, although the United States and Great Britain do not. SMOM coins its own money, mints its own stamps, and issues its own passports. The order is a Permanent Observer in the United Nations and enjoys membership in other international organizations as well. Although not physically important anymore, SMOM continues its more than 90-year mission of helping the sick of every nation from its base in the smallest country on Earth.

Questions	Strategic Thinking
1. A) NO CHANGE B) to provide C) providing them D) ensuring availability of	**Step 1: Read the passage and identify the issue** The underlined verb ("providing") is not parallel to the verbs used earlier in the sentence ("to protect and defend"). **Step 2: Eliminate answer choices that do not address the issue** Eliminate A, C, and D because they do not correct the parallelism error. **Step 3: Plug in the remaining answer choices and select the most correct, concise, and relevant one** Choice (B) is correct.
2. A) NO CHANGE B) Then Napoleon is driving C) Napoleon drove D) Napoleon drives	**Step 1: Read the passage and identify the issue** The verb in the underlined portion is in a different tense from the other verbs in this paragraph. A writer can shift verb tense only when there is a logical reason to do so. In this instance, the writer does not have a reason to switch tenses; the earlier verbs are in the simple past tense, which indicates that the action occurred at some point in the past. **Step 2: Eliminate answer choices that do not address the issue** Eliminate A, B, and D because they are not in the simple past tense. **Step 3: Plug in the remaining answer choices and select the most correct, concise, and relevant one** Choice (C) is correct.

Reading & Writing

Questions	Strategic Thinking

3.   A) NO CHANGE
 	
     B) creed, establishing
 	
     C) creed establishing
 	
     D) creed; establishing
	Step 1: Read the passage and identify the issue
	
	The second sentence in the underlined portion is a fragment because it is missing a predicate verb. Eliminate A.
	
	Step 2: Eliminate answer choices that do not address the issue
	
	Eliminate C because it creates a run-on sentence. Eliminate D because it does not correct the sentence fragment.
	
	Step 3: Plug in the remaining answer choices and select the most correct, concise, and relevant one
	
	Choice (B) is correct.

Reading & Writing

You have seen the ways in which the SAT tests you on Sentence Structure in Writing & Language passages and the way an SAT expert approaches these types of questions.

Use the Kaplan Method for Writing & Language to answer the three questions that accompany the following Writing & Language passage excerpt. Remember to look at the strategic thinking questions that have been laid out for you—some of the answers have been filled in, but you will have to complete the answers to others.

Use your answers to the strategic thinking questions to select the correct answer, just as you will on Test Day.

Questions 4-6 are based on the following passage.

The Sun

It is perhaps impossible to overestimate the impact of the Sun on our planet Earth. Functioning like a great thermonuclear reactor situated roughly 100 million miles away, the Sun provides essentially all of Earth's heat in the form of radiant energy, without which there would be no light, warmth, plants, or animals. In addition, with a core temperature of nearly 30 million degrees Fahrenheit, the Sun affects all of Earth's natural phenomena, including all weather and atmospheric movement. Even the energy sources we use daily to fuel our cars and heat our homes, resources like oil and coal harvested from deep within the Earth's crust, were produced by the power of the Sun acting upon living organisms millions of years ago. Yet, **4** while its ability to provide heat and light can be easily felt by simply lying out on a beach or gazing up into a brilliant blue sky, closer inspection of the Sun's dynamic surface through special telescopes has revealed activity capable of affecting Earth in less obvious ways.

Technically classified by scientists as a yellow dwarf star and thought to be approximately 4 billion years old, the Sun has a constantly changing surface is actually quite stormy, but it is not the visually dramatic gas particle eruptions that constitute the Sun's most volatile surface activity. Instead, **5** they are the seemingly static black spots that pepper the surface, referred to by scientists as sunspots, that are the true storms. At roughly half the Sun's surface temperature of 10,300 degrees Fahrenheit, sunspots are by far the coolest areas of the Sun, which is why they appear darker than the hotter plasma that surrounds them. And, although in telescopic images these spots appear as little more than tiny black specks, they can be more than 19,000 miles across—wide enough to fit two Earths with orbiting moons.

Historical records show that these spots were first viewed by telescope as early as 1610, but scientists today still know relatively little about them. Almost always seen in pairs, sunspots are thought to be **6** powerfully created by magnetic fields that keep heat from flowing up to the Sun's surface. Scientists have also noticed that these spots seem to erupt and fade in 11-year cycles, manifesting incessant change that is thought to affect the Sun's luminosity and, in turn, Earth's climate. In addition, studies have shown that the charged particles released by sunspots can react with Earth's magnetic field and disrupt satellite communications, radio broadcasts, and even cell phone calls. As scientists continue to carefully observe such occurrences, referred to as space weather, they gain a greater understanding of the powerful ability of the Sun to impact our lives.

Questions	Strategic Thinking
4. A) NO CHANGE B) when C) with D) because	**Step 1: Read the passage and identify the issue** *What part of speech is underlined?* A subordinating conjunction. *What does a subordinating conjunction do?* It helps to join an independent clause with a dependent clause. **Step 2: Eliminate answer choices that do not address the issue** *What answer choice(s) can you eliminate?* _____ _____ _____ **Step 3: Plug in the remaining answer choices and select the most correct, concise, and relevant one** *What is the correct answer? _____*

Questions	Strategic Thinking
5. A) NO CHANGE B) they are not C) we are D) it is	**Step 1: Read the passage and identify the issue** *What is the issue?* Pronoun consistency. *What pronoun is used in the sentence before the one to which the underlined portion belongs?* "It." *To what does the underlined pronoun refer?* _____ _____ **Step 2: Eliminate answer choices that do not address the issue** *What answer choice(s) can you eliminate?* _____ _____ _____ **Step 3: Plug in the remaining answer choices and select the most correct, concise, and relevant one** *What is the correct answer?*_____

Questions	Strategic Thinking
6. A) NO CHANGE B) created by powerful magnetic C) powerful created by magnetic D) strongly created by magnetic	**Step 1: Read the passage and identify the issue** *What is the issue?* Modifier placement and form. *What type of modifier is included in the underlined segment?* _____ *What should the adverb ("powerfully") logically modify?* _____ *Based on what the adverb ("powerfully") should logically modify, what part of speech should it be?* _____ **Step 2: Eliminate answer choices that do not address the issue** *What answer choice(s) can you eliminate?* _____ _____ _____ **Step 3: Plug in the remaining answer choices and select the most correct, concise, and relevant one** *What is the correct answer?*_____

Now try a test-like Writing & Language passage on your own. Give yourself 5 minutes to read the passage and answer the questions.

Questions 7-14 are based on the following passage.

Sergei Eisenstein

Considered the father of the montage, a popular cinematic technique that involves a rapid succession of shots, often superimposed, **7** one of the principal architects of the modern movie was the Russian director Sergei Eisenstein. Although his career was not particularly prolific—he completed only seven feature-length films—Eisenstein's work contains a clarity and sharpness of composition that make the depth of his plots and the powerful complexity of his juxtaposed images easily accessible to most **8** viewers, in fact, few filmmakers were more instrumental in pushing the envelope of the established, conservative nineteenth-century Victorian theatre than Eisenstein, whose films helped to usher in a new era of abstract thought and expression in art.

Born in 1898 in what is now the independent nation of Latvia, Eisenstein grew up in affluence as the son of a successful architect. Following in his father's footsteps, he studied at the Institute of Civil Engineering in Petrograd. After the Bolshevik Revolution of 1917, however, Eisenstein was pushed out of academics **9** and into the service of the Red Army as an engineer. When the Russian Civil War ended, Eisenstein sought to leave his work for the new Soviet state behind him. He quickly found employment in show business as a set

7. A) NO CHANGE
   B) Sergei Eisenstein, the Russian director, was one of the principal architects of the modern movie,
   C) the Russian director Sergei Eisenstein was one of the principal architects of the modern movie,
   D) one of the principal architects of the modern movie was Sergei Eisenstein, the Russian director,

8. A) NO CHANGE
   B) viewers. In fact,
   C) viewers—in fact,
   D) viewers in fact,

9. A) NO CHANGE
   B) nor
   C) or
   D) as far as

designer for a prominent Moscow theatre, but the new communist government **10** <u>was likely to remain</u> a heavy influence throughout his career.

It was with **11** <u>Eisenstein's</u> feature debut, a film entitled *Statchka* released in 1924, that Eisenstein introduced moviegoers to the montage. Expanding upon a complex theory of biomechanics, the study of the mechanical forces at work within a particular body or organ, Eisenstein's first montage consisted of a powerful sequence of conflicting images that were able to abbreviate time spans in the film while introducing new metaphors and allusions to the storyline. Essentially, Eisenstein sought to use the montage to create a **12** <u>regressive emotional effect that was greater than the sum of the individual shots.</u> It was with this enormously successful technique that Eisenstein's work caught the eye of the new Communist Party leaders in Moscow, who saw in his cinematic style a film for the **13** <u>"common man." And</u> a chance to use his skills as a propaganda tool for the state.

Eisenstein's second and third films, **14** <u>the enormously famous 1925 hit *Battleship Potemkin* and the 1927 celebration of the October Revolution, *Oktibr*,</u> still widely considered to be masterpieces, were commissioned by party officials in an attempt to use Eisenstein's mass appeal to disseminate Soviet propaganda. As a result, these achievements have been frequently criticized for their lack of artistic integrity. Yet, in the end, regardless of politics, Eisenstein's films continue to have an undeniably significant and lasting impact on filmmakers.

10. A) NO CHANGE
    B) remained
    C) did likely remain
    D) remains

11. A) NO CHANGE
    B) Sergei Eisenstein's
    C) its
    D) his

12. A) NO CHANGE
    B) regressive that was greater than the sum of the individual shots.
    C) detrimental emotional effect that was greater than the sum of the individual shots.
    D) cumulative emotional effect that was greater than the sum of the individual shots.

13. A) NO CHANGE
    B) "common man," and
    C) "common man" and
    D) "common man" and,

14. A) NO CHANGE
    B) the enormously famous 1925 hit and the 1927 celebration of the October Revolution, *Battleship Potemkin* and *Oktibr*,
    C) the famously enormous 1925 hit *Battleship Potemkin* and the 1927 celebration of the October Revolution, *Oktibr*,
    D) the 1925 film *Battleship Potemkin* and the 1927 film *Oktibr*,

Answers & Explanations for this chapter begin on page 906.

EXTRA PRACTICE

The following questions provide an opportunity to practice the concepts and strategic thinking covered in this chapter. While many of the questions pertain to Sentence Structure, some touch on other concepts tested on the Writing & Language Test to ensure that your practice is test-like, with a variety of question types per passage.

Questions 1-11 are based on the following passage.

The Experts of Visual Communication

[1] The digital explosion of the past two decades has resulted in decreased costs of devices for the average consumer. From early cave painters and the intricate craftspeople of ancient worlds to the vast, magnificent artwork that has emerged across countless generations and cultures, art accomplishes fascinating measures of human communication. In today's world, the [2] prominent arena in which art and communication meet is graphic design. The digital age has seen an explosion of media and connectivity. This offers an ever-growing platform for art, through graphic design, to deliver ideas and messages.

Incorporating creativity, communication knowledge, and technological expertise, graphic designers fashion messages for the public eye. Their work is peppered throughout Western life. [3] Business logos; billboard advertisements; website layouts, T-shirt designs; and even the decorated cardboard of cereal boxes and coffee cups feature graphic design. In a culture increasingly wired for visual communication, graphic designers

1. Which choice provides the most appropriate introduction to the passage?
   A) NO CHANGE
   B) Throughout history, visual art has contested verbal communication in its power to convey meaning.
   C) In recent times, cell phone and tablet use have rendered the desktop computer nearly obsolete.
   D) Because of the increasing use of wireless communication, new laws will be needed to regulate usage.

2. A) NO CHANGE
   B) obscure
   C) inconspicuous
   D) distinguished

3. A) NO CHANGE
   B) Business logos, billboard advertisements—website layouts, T-shirt designs, and even the decorated cardboard of cereal boxes and coffee cups feature graphic design.
   C) Business logos and billboard advertisements and website layouts, T-shirt designs, and even the decorated cardboard of cereal boxes and coffee cups feature graphic design.
   D) Business logos, billboard advertisements, website layouts, T-shirt designs, and even the decorated cardboard of cereal boxes and coffee cups feature graphic design.

are the artists of today's media. [4] They create and craft the medium and formats, visual images, and symbols that add vibrancy and color to this world and shape the way information is passed, transmitted, and received.

[1] How do these powerful innovators navigate a career path? [2] Most begin by studying graphic design in a bachelor's degree program. [3] Here they build skills through highly interactive class settings to [5] teach expertise. [4] These programs are heavily project-based, mirroring the sort of experience professional work will entail. [5] Once students have graduated, these portfolios are essential for the job search, revealing an artist's excellence and creative potential. [6] Students gradually compile design portfolios to showcase their best work. [6]

Job competition for graphic designers is rigorous, but graphic design features a variety of professional options. Some work in design studios. [7] There they team with other graphic designers, taking on projects for external clients. Others work "in-house"

4. A) NO CHANGE

B) They create and craft the medium and formats, visual images, and symbols that add color to this world and shape the way information is passed, transmitted, and received.

C) They craft the formats, images, and symbols that color this world and shape the way information is passed and received.

D) They create the formats, visual images, and symbols that add color to this world and shape the way information is passed, transmitted, and received.

5. A) NO CHANGE

B) hone

C) fulfill

D) discipline

6. To make this paragraph most logical, sentence 6 should be placed

A) where it is now.

B) after sentence 2.

C) after sentence 3.

D) after sentence 4.

7. A) NO CHANGE

B) There they team with other graphic designers; taking on projects for external clients.

C) There they team with other graphic designers. Taking on projects for external clients.

D) There they team with other graphic designers—taking on projects for external clients.

for businesses that staff their own graphic designers to create media on a more consistent basis. Those with more entrepreneurial inclinations can work as freelance graphic designers, doing their own networking and contracting. **8**

8. At this point, the writer wants to add information that supports the main topic of the paragraph. Which choice provides the most relevant detail?

A) Often, graphic designers are encouraged by employers to obtain a master's degree.

B) Some graphic designers return to the university to pursue business administration degrees.

C) Increasingly, graphic designers are taking their skills online and transferring them to website and web application design, which is another growing field for tech-minded artists.

D) Graphic designers often earn less as freelancers than their counterparts who are employed by design studios.

[9] <u>Because</u> the demand for graphic designers continues, the highly competitive job market gives some prospective artists pause. The trope of the "struggling artist" holds true, it seems, even in this visually dominant generation. [10] <u>Most graphic designers find their careers not only satisfying, but also one of invigoration.</u> Perhaps, for those brave artists who follow this career path, the thrill and beauty of the work yields enough motivation and inspiration to persevere and succeed. [11]

9. A) NO CHANGE
   B) Although
   C) Since
   D) Consequently,

10. A) NO CHANGE
    B) Most graphic designers find their careers satisfying, in addition to being vigorous.
    C) Most graphic designers find their careers not only satisfying, but also invigorating.
    D) Most graphic designers find their careers to be not only one of satisfaction, but also invigorating.

11. Which choice, if added here, would provide the most relevant detail to this paragraph?
    A) Graphic designers experience creative opportunities not offered by other careers.
    B) This visually dominant generation spends more on entertainment than any previous age group.
    C) Perseverance is vital to a successful career, but luck plays an important factor, too.
    D) Graphic designers, along with physical therapists, experience the most competitive job markets.

Conventions of Usage

CHAPTER OBJECTIVES

By the end of this chapter, you will be able to:

1. Recognize and correct errors in pronoun clarity, grammatical agreement, and logical comparison

2. Distinguish among commonly confused possessive determiners, contractions, and adverbs

3. Recognize and correct incorrectly constructed idioms and frequently misused words

SMARTPOINTS

Point Value	SmartPoint Category
40 Points	Usage

Reading & Writing

CONVENTIONS OF USAGE

Chapter 24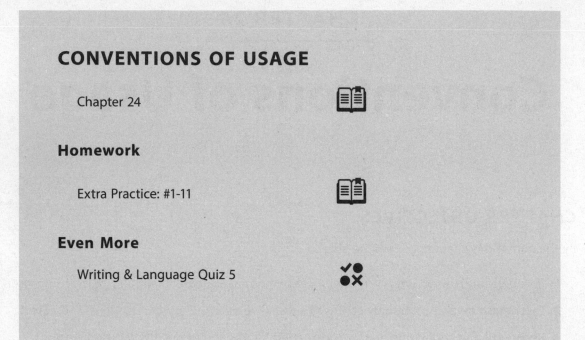

Homework

Extra Practice: #1-11

Even More

Writing & Language Quiz 5

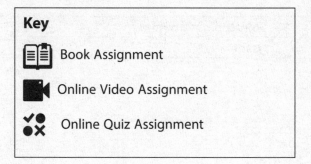

Key

Book Assignment

Online Video Assignment

Online Quiz Assignment

PRONOUNS

A pronoun is ambiguous if the noun to which it refers (its antecedent) is either missing or unclear. On the SAT, you must be able to recognize either situation and make the appropriate correction. When you see an underlined pronoun, make sure you can find the specific noun to which it refers.

Missing Antecedent

- *When the flight arrived, **they** told the passengers to stay seated until the plane reached the gate.* (The pronoun "they" does not have an antecedent in this sentence.)

- *When the flight arrived, **the flight crew** told the passengers to stay seated until the plane reached the gate.* (Replacing the pronoun with a specific noun clarifies the meaning.)

Unclear Antecedent

- *Kayla asked Mia to drive Sree to the airport because **she** was running late.* (The pronoun "she" could refer to any of the three people mentioned in the sentence.)

- *Because Kayla was running late, **she** asked Mia to drive Sree to the airport.* (The pronoun "she" now unambiguously refers to Kayla.)

> ✔ **Definition**
>
> The **antecedent** is the noun that the pronoun replaces or stands in for elsewhere in the sentence. To identify the **antecedent** of a pronoun, check the nouns near the pronoun. Substitute those nouns for the pronoun to see which one makes sense.

AGREEMENT

Pronoun-Antecedent Agreement

Pronouns must agree with their antecedents not only in person and number, but also in gender. Only third-person pronouns make distinctions based on gender.

Gender	Example
Feminine	*Because Yvonne had a question, **she** raised her hand.*
Masculine	*Since **he** had lots of homework, Rico started working right away.*
Neutral	*The rain started slowly, but then **it** became a downpour.*
Unspecified	*If a traveler is lost, **he or she** should ask for directions.*

Pronoun-Case Agreement

There are three pronoun cases:

1. Subjective case: The pronoun is used as the subject

2. Objective case: The pronoun is used as the object of a verb or a preposition

3. Possessive case: The pronoun expresses ownership

Subjective Case	I, you, she, he, it, we, you, they, who
Objective Case	me, you, her, him, it, us, you, them, whom
Possessive Case	my, mine, your, yours, his, her, hers, its, our, ours, their, theirs, whose

✔ **Expert Tip**

When there are two pronouns or a noun and a pronoun in a compound structure, drop the other noun to confirm which pronoun case to use. **For example:** *Leo and me walk into town.* **Would you say, "Me walk into town"? No, you would say, "I walk into town." Therefore, the correct case is subjective and the original sentence should read** *Leo and I walk into town.*

✔ **Remember**

Use "who" when a sentence refers to "she," "he," or "I." (*Quynh was the person* **who** *provided the best answer.*) **Use "whom" when a sentence refers to "her," "him," or "me."** (*With* **whom** *did Aaron attend the event?*)

Subject-Verb Agreement

A verb must agree with its subject in person and number:

- Singular: *The **apple tastes** delicious.*

- Plural: ***Apples taste** delicious.*

The noun closest to a verb may not be its subject: *The **chair** with the cabriole legs **is** an antique.* The noun closest to the verb in this sentence ("is," which is singular) is "legs," which is plural. However, the verb's subject is "chair," so the sentence is correct as written.

Only the conjunction *and* forms a compound subject requiring a plural verb form:

- *Saliyah **and** Taylor **are** in the running club.*

- ***Either** Saliyah **or** Taylor **is** in the running club.*

- ***Neither** Saliyah **nor** Taylor **is** in the running club.*

Noun-Number Agreement

Related nouns must be consistent in number:

- **Students** *applying for college must submit their* **applications** *on time.* (The sentence refers to multiple students, and they all must submit applications.)

FREQUENTLY CONFUSED WORDS

English contains many pairs of words that sound alike but are spelled differently and have different meanings.

ACCEPT/EXCEPT: To *accept* is to take or receive something that is offered: *My neighbor said he would accept my apology for trampling over his rose beds as long as I helped weed them in the spring.* To *except* is to leave out or exclude: *The soldier was excepted from combat duty because he had poor field vision. Except* is usually used as a preposition that signifies "with the exception of, excluding:" *When the receptionist found out that everyone except him had received a raise, he demanded a salary increase as well.*

AFFECT/EFFECT: To *affect* is to have an influence on something: *Eli refused to let the rain affect his plans for a picnic, so he sat under an umbrella and ate his sandwich.* An *affect* is an emotion or behavior: *The guidance counselor noticed that more outdoor time resulted in improved student affect.* To *effect* is to bring something about or cause something to happen: *The young activist received an award for effecting a change in her community.* An *effect* is an influence or a result: *The newspaper article about homeless animals had such an effect on Zarak that he brought home three kittens from the shelter. Affect* is most often used in its verb form, and *effect* is most often used in its noun form.

AFFLICT/INFLICT: To *afflict* is to torment or distress someone or something. It usually appears as a passive verb: *Jeff is afflicted with frequent migraine headaches.* To *inflict* is to impose punishment or suffering on someone or something: *No one dared displease the king, for he was known to inflict severe punishments on those who upset him.*

ALLUSION/ILLUSION: An *allusion* is an indirect reference to something, a hint: *The teacher's comment about the most enigmatic smile in art history was not lost on Sophie; this allusion could only be a reference to Leonardo da Vinci's* Mona Lisa. An *illusion* is a false, misleading, or deceptive appearance: *A magician creates the illusion that something has disappeared by hiding it faster than the eye can follow it.*

EMIGRATE/IMMIGRATE: To *emigrate* is to leave one country for another country. It is usually used with the preposition *from: Many people emigrated from Europe in search of better living conditions.* To *immigrate* is to enter a country to take up permanent residence there. It is usually used with the preposition *to: They immigrated to North America because land was plentiful.*

EMINENT/IMMINENT: Someone who is *eminent* is prominent or outstanding: *The eminent archeologist Dr. Wong has identified the artifact as prehistoric in origin.* Something that is *imminent* is likely to happen soon or is impending: *After being warned that the hurricane's arrival was imminent, beachfront residents left their homes immediately.*

LAY/LIE: To *lay* is to place or put something down and is usually followed by a "something"—a direct object: *Before she begins to paint, Emily lays all of her pencils, brushes, and paints on her worktable to avoid interruptions while she draws and paints.* One form, *laid*, serves as the simple past and the past participle of *lay*: *I laid my necklace on the counter, just where Rebecca had put hers.* To *lie* is to recline, to be in a lying position or at rest. This verb never takes a direct object: you do not lie anything down. The simple past form of *lie* is *lay*; the past participle is *lain*. Notice that the past form of *lie* is identical with the present form of *lay*. This coincidence complicates the task of distinguishing the related meanings of *lay* and *lie*: *Having laid the picnic cloth under the sycamore, they lay in the shady grass all last Sunday afternoon.*

RAISE/RISE: *Raise* means to lift up, or to cause to rise or grow, and it is paired with a direct object: you *raise* weights, roof beams, tomato plants, or children. *Raise* is a regular verb. *The trade tariff on imported leather goods raised the prices of Italian shoes.* To *rise* is to get up, to go up, or to be built up. This verb is never paired with a direct object: you do not *rise* something. The past and past participle forms are irregular; *rose* is the simple past tense, while *risen* is the past participle. *Long-distance commuters must rise early and return home late.*

SET/SIT: The difference between *set* and *sit* is very similar to the difference between *lay* and *lie* and between *raise* and *rise*. To *set* is to put or place, settle or arrange something. However, *set* takes on other specific meanings when it is combined with several different prepositions, so always think carefully about the meaning of the word in the sentence. *Set* is an irregular verb because it has one form that serves as present tense, past tense, and past participle. *Set* usually has a direct object: you *set* a ladder against the fence, a value on family heirlooms, or a date for the family reunion: *The professor set the students' chairs in a semicircle to promote open discussion.* To *sit* is to take a seat or to be in a seated position, to rest somewhere, or to occupy a place. This verb does not usually have a direct object: *The beach house sits on a hill at some distance from the shoreline.* When *sit* doesn't make sense, consider the word *sat*: *The usher sat us in the center seats of the third row from the stage.*

Other pairs of words do not sound alike but have similar meanings that are often confused:

AMONG/BETWEEN: The preposition *among* refers to collective arrangements; use it when referring to three or more people or items. *The soccer team shared dozens of oranges among themselves.* *Between* is also a preposition, but it refers to only two people or items: *Amy and Tonia split the tasks between them.*

AMOUNT/NUMBER: *Amount* is used in reference to mass nouns (also known as uncountable nouns): *The amount of bravery displayed was awe-inspiring.* *Number* is used in reference to countable nouns: *The recipe calls for a specific number of eggs.*

LESS/FEWER: *Less* should be used only with mass nouns, which are grammatically singular: *Diana's yard has less wildlife than mine.* One common misuse of *less* is a sign you probably encounter frequently at the supermarket: The *10 items or less* sign should actually be *10 items or fewer*, because the items are countable. *Fewer* should be used when referring to countable objects and concepts: *Diana's yard has fewer squirrels than mine.*

MUCH/MANY: *Much* modifies things that cannot be counted, often singular nouns: *Jim has much more money than I do. Many*, on the other hand, modifies things that can be counted, such as plural nouns. *Samantha has many awards in her collection.*

The SAT will also test your ability to correctly use and identify possessive pronouns, contractions, and adverbs that sound the same:

ITS/IT'S: *Its* is a possessive pronoun like *his* and *hers*: *The rare book would be worth more if its cover weren't ripped. It's* is a contraction that can mean *it is, it has,* or *it was*: *It's been a long time since I last saw you.*

THEIR/THEY'RE/THERE: *Their* is a possessive form of the pronoun *they*: *The players respected their coach. They're* is a contraction of *they are*: *The students say they're planning to attend college. There* is used to introduce a sentence or indicate a location: *There was plenty of water in the well when we arrived there.*

THEIRS/THERE'S: *Theirs* is the possessive plural form of the pronoun *they*: *The team was ecstatic when it was announced that the prize was theirs. There's* is a contraction of *there is* or *there has*: *There's been a lot of rain this summer.*

WHOSE/WHO'S: *Whose* is a possessive pronoun used to refer to people or things: *Whose phone is ringing? Who's* is a contraction of *who is* or *who has*: *Who's planning to join us for dinner?*

COMPARISONS

The SAT will test your ability to recognize and correct improper comparisons. There are three rules governing correct comparisons:

1. Compare Logical Things

   The **price of tea** has risen sharply, while **coffee** has remained the same.

   This sentence incorrectly compares *the price of tea* to *coffee*. The sentence should read: *The* **price of tea** *has risen sharply, while the* **price of coffee** *has remained the same.*

2. Use Parallel Structure

   On a sunny day, I enjoy **hiking** *and* **to read** *outside.*

   This sentence incorrectly uses the gerund verb form (*hiking*) and then switches to the infinitive verb form (*to read*). To correct the sentence, make sure the verb forms are consistent: *On a sunny day, I enjoy* **hiking** *and* **reading** *outside.*

3. Structure Comparisons Correctly

*Some animals are **better** at endurance running **than** they are at sprinting.*
*Others are **as** good at endurance running **as** they are at sprinting.*
Both of these sentences are correctly structured: the first with the use of *better . . . than,* and the second with the use of *as . . . as.*

When comparing like things, use adjectives that match the number of items being compared. When comparing two items or people, use the comparative form of the adjective. When comparing three or more items or people, use the superlative form.

Comparative	Superlative
Use when comparing two items.	Use when comparing three or more items.
better	best
more	most
newer	newest
older	oldest
shorter	shortest
taller	tallest
worse	worst
younger	youngest

IDIOMS

An **idiom** is a combination of words that must be used together to convey either a figurative or literal meaning. Idioms are tested in four ways on the SAT:

1. Proper Preposition Usage in Context

*The three finalists will compete **for** the grand prize: an all-inclusive cruise to Bali.*
*Roger will compete **against** Rafael in the final round of the tournament.*
*I will compete **with** Deborah in the synchronized swimming competition.*

2. Verb Forms

*The architect likes **to draft** floor plans.*
*The architect enjoys **drafting** floor plans.*

3. Idiomatic Expressions

Idiomatic expressions refer to words or phrases that must be used together to be correct.

*Simone will **either** continue sleeping **or** get up and get ready for school.*
***Neither** the principal **nor** the teachers will tolerate tardiness.*
*This fall, Shari is playing **not only** soccer **but also** field hockey.*

4. Implicit Double Negatives

Some words imply a negative and therefore cannot be paired with an explicit negative.

*Janie **cannot hardly** wait for summer vacation.*

This sentence is incorrect as written. It should read: *Janie **can hardly** wait for summer vacation.*

Frequently Tested Prepositions	Idiomatic Expressions	Words That Can't Be Paired with Negative Words
at	as . . . as	barely
by	between . . . and	hardly
for	both . . . and	scarcely
from	either . . . or	
of	neither . . . nor	
on	just as . . . so too	
to	not only . . . but also	
with	prefer . . . to	

Let's look at the following Writing & Language passage and questions. After the passage, there are two columns. The left column contains test-like questions. The column on the right features the strategic thinking a test expert employs when approaching the passage and questions presented.

Questions 1-4 are based on the following passage.

Akira Kurosawa

What do samurai,[1] cowboys, shogun,[2] gangsters, peasants, and William Shakespeare all have in common? These are just some of the varied influences on the work of Akira Kurosawa (1910–1998), a Japanese film director considered by movie critic Leonard Maltin to be "one of the undisputed giants of cinema." Over his career, Kurosawa's unique blend of Western themes and Eastern settings made him arguably the **1** more important Japanese filmmaker in history.

Kurosawa's style reflects his own experiences. As a young man, he studied Western art and literature, deciding to be a painter. However, World War II led Kurosawa to film; he acted as an assistant director of wartime propaganda films in Tokyo. After Japan's surrender in 1945, he took the lessons he learned in Tokyo and began making his own films— **2** work that took the values and traditions of the West and reinterpreted them with a Japanese sensibility, using distinctly Japanese settings and characters.

The most famous example of Kurosawa's style is his 1954 film *Seven Samurai*. Although the setting is medieval Japan, with peasants and samurai, its story is influenced by Western films: a group of villagers, terrorized by local bandits, turn to seven down-on-their-luck yet good-hearted samurai for their protection. Like movie cowboys, the samurai are romantic heroes, sure of their morals and battling clear forces of evil. This contrasts with the traditional Japanese version of a samurai as a noble and often distant symbol of Japan's imperial heritage. To **3** him, the film's samurai were distinctly human characters, with both a conscience and the will to act to correct the wrongs around them.

Although Kurosawa's films enjoyed—and still enjoy—a lofty reputation in the West, Japanese audiences have regarded his work with suspicion. By using Western ideals and themes—even reinterpreting Western authors such as William Shakespeare and Fyodor Dostoyevsky—Kurosawa is viewed by many critics and moviegoers in his home country as **4** neither original nor particularly Japanese. They see his using Japanese culture as mere "window dressing" applied to what were essentially foreign stories. Ironically, it was Kurosawa's success that opened the door for other, more "Japanese" directors, such as Yasujiro Ozu and Kenji Mizoguchi, to gain a wider audience.

Regardless of the criticism, Kurosawa's effect on Western filmmaking is beyond dispute. Ironically, Kurosawa's films have influenced the very same American movie genres that Kurosawa admired so much. *Seven Samurai* became the basis for the American Western epic *The Magnificent Seven. Yojimbo*, another story of a samurai for hire, strongly influenced the film *A Fistful of Dollars*. Other genres benefited from Kurosawa's work as well; *Rashomon*, a crime story told from different points of view, has influenced almost every crime movie since. Finally, *The Hidden Fortress*, about two peasants escorting a princess during a war, became George Lucas's expressed basis for the science fiction masterpiece *Star Wars*.

[1] samurai: noble warriors of medieval Japan, similar to European knights
[2] shogun: military dictators of Japan from 1603 to 1868

Questions	Strategic Thinking
1. A) NO CHANGE B) important C) most important D) least important	**Step 1: Read the passage and identify the issue** The underlined portion contains the word "more," which is an adjective used to compare two items. In this instance, the author is comparing Kurosawa to all other Japanese filmmakers. **Step 2: Eliminate answer choices that do not address the issue** Eliminate A because more than two items are being compared. Eliminate B because it removes the comparison. Eliminate D because it changes the meaning of the sentence. **Step 3: Plug in the remaining answer choices and select the most correct, concise, and relevant one** Choice (C) is correct.
2. A) NO CHANGE B) works C) working D) idea	**Step 1: Read the passage and identify the issue** The underlined word is used as a synonym for the word that precedes the dash; however, the singular noun, "work," does not match the plural noun, "films." **Step 2: Eliminate answer choices that do not address the issue** Eliminate A because the singular "work" does not agree with the plural "films." Eliminate C because "working" is a verb, not a noun. Eliminate D because it changes the author's meaning. **Step 3: Plug in the remaining answer choices and select the most correct, concise, and relevant one** Choice (B) is correct.

Reading & Writing

Questions	Strategic Thinking
3. A) NO CHANGE B) them C) Kurosawa D) the samurai	**Step 1: Read the passage and identify the issue** The underlined pronoun's antecedent is unclear. **Step 2: Eliminate answer choices that do not address the issue** The most logical antecedent of the underlined pronoun "him" is Akira Kurosawa. Eliminate A because it is ambiguous as written. Eliminate B because it is also ambiguous. Eliminate D because the pronoun does not refer to "the samurai." **Step 3: Plug in the remaining answer choices and select the most correct, concise, and relevant one** Choice (C) is correct.
4. A) NO CHANGE B) either C) never D) both	**Step 1: Read the passage and identify the issue** The underlined word is part of an idiomatic expression. "Neither . . . nor" is a common idiomatic expression; both "neither" and "nor" must be used for the idiom to be used correctly. **Step 2: Eliminate answer choices that do not address the issue** Eliminate B, C, and D because the sentence later uses the word "nor," which means "neither" must precede it. **Step 3: Plug in the remaining answer choices and select the most correct, concise, and relevant one** Choice (A) is correct.

You have seen the ways in which the SAT tests you on Conventions of Usage in Writing & Language passages and the way an SAT expert approaches these types of questions.

Use the Kaplan Method for Writing & Language to answer the four questions that accompany the following Writing & Language passage excerpt. Remember to look at the strategic-thinking questions that have been laid out for you—some of the answers have been filled in, but you will have to complete the answers to others.

Use your answers to the strategic thinking questions to select the correct answer, just as you will on Test Day.

Questions 5-8 are based on the following passage.

Opossum

Commonly seen rooting through the trash or slipping down a sewer grate, the opossum is actually one of North America's **5** best animals. While its rodent-like body seems unremarkable at first glance, the opossum is actually closely related to the kangaroo and is the only marsupial native to this continent. Like all female marsupials, the female opossum has a pouch for carrying and nursing her young. After a 12-day gestation period, thought to be the shortest of any marsupial, between 5 and 25 blind and hairless babies instinctively crawl the two inches from the birth canal to the pouch. Upon arrival, they quickly attach themselves to a nipple, drawing constant nourishment from the mother for more than two months.

The distinctive features of the opossum go beyond its surprising relation to the kangaroo. **6** It boasts an incredible array of 50 razor-sharp teeth, the most of any mammal in the world. The opossum is also among the most primitive of animals, having lived during the time of the dinosaurs. It has survived for millions of years by adapting to diverse habitats—including dense urban areas—and food supplies. Opossums eat beetles and even earthworms as well as tree roots, eggs, vegetables, and fruit. Today, many opossums that live in areas densely populated by humans survive on garbage and small mice. Opossums thrive in fields and woodlands, but they can also survive by digging a nest under a building or deck.

Of course, the opossum does have vulnerabilities. Its average three-year life span is not unusual for its size, typically between two and three feet long. What is unusual is that opossums continue growing throughout their lifetimes. Such a state of constant development is linked with metabolic limitations **7** in the amount of food and energy that can be stored within the opossum's body, requiring that ready food sources be available year-round. In addition, opossums are highly susceptible to the cold, making it rather common to see opossums with frostbitten ears and tails. Nevertheless, opossums have displayed amazing resilience over the years, often surviving attacks from intimidating predators like dogs and even hawks. While the opossum's first reaction when threatened is to begin running to the nearest tree, **8** their primary defense is a nervous system reaction that, when sensing danger, throws the opossum's body into a catatonic state that dramatically slows its heart rate. The opossum will then begin to drool and appear dead, another trait that only adds to the fascinating nature of these animals.

Questions	Strategic Thinking
5. A) NO CHANGE B) most unusual C) better D) abnormal	**Step 1: Read the passage and identify the issue** *What is the issue?* Comparisons. The underlined word is a superlative adjective, used to compare three or more items. **Step 2: Eliminate answer choices that do not address the issue** *What answer choice(s) can you eliminate?* _____ _____ _____ **Step 3: Plug in the remaining answer choices and select the most correct, concise, and relevant one** *What is the correct answer?*_____
6. A) NO CHANGE B) They C) The kangaroo D) The opossum	**Step 1: Read the passage and identify the issue** *What is the issue?* Pronoun clarity. The underlined word is a pronoun that begins a sentence. *To what does the underlined pronoun refer?* _____ _____ **Step 2: Eliminate answer choices that do not address the issue** *What answer choice(s) can you eliminate?* _____ _____ _____ **Step 3: Plug in the remaining answer choices and select the most correct, concise, and relevant one** *What is the correct answer?*_____

Questions	Strategic Thinking

7. A) NO CHANGE
   B) with
   C) on
   D) for
	Step 1: Read the passage and identify the issue
	
	What is the issue?
	Idioms. The underlined word is a preposition, so the question is likely testing proper preposition usage in context.
	
	Step 2: Eliminate answer choices that do not address the issue
	
	What answer choice(s) can you eliminate?
	_____
	_____
	_____
	
	Step 3: Plug in the remaining answer choices and select the most correct, concise, and relevant one
	
	*What is the correct answer?*_____

8. A) NO CHANGE
   B) there
   C) its
   D) his
	Step 1: Read the passage and identify the issue
	
	What is the issue?
	Pronoun-antecedent agreement. The underlined word is a pronoun in the middle of a sentence.
	What is the underlined pronoun's antecedent?
	_____
	_____
	
	Step 2: Eliminate answer choices that do not address the issue
	
	What answer choice(s) can you eliminate?
	_____
	_____
	_____
	
	Step 3: Plug in the remaining answer choices and select the most correct, concise, and relevant one
	
	*What is the correct answer?*_____

Now try a test-like Writing & Language passage on your own. Give yourself 5 minutes to read the passage and answer the questions.

Questions 9-16 are based on the following passage.

The Hindenburg

Today, airships are seen mostly as advertisements hovering in the sky over sporting events. Such companies as Goodyear®, Metropolitan Life®, and Fuji Film® have all made use of "blimps" in this way. But before World War II, [9] airships—as well as other lighter-than-air vehicles—were used as modes of transportation. One in particular, the German airship *Hindenburg*, changed the fate of airships forever. In spectacular fashion, the *Hindenburg* revealed the downside of the use of airships in transportation.

Airships enjoyed many advantages in the early twentieth century, and the *Hindenburg* was considered one of a kind. When the 804-foot *Hindenburg* was launched in 1936, it was the [10] large airship in the world. Like most airships of the period, the *Hindenburg* was built with a solid frame that encased a simple balloon filled with a light gas—in this case, hydrogen. In an age when airplanes could not carry more than 10 passengers at a time, [11] they could initially carry 50 passengers, a capacity that was later upgraded to 72.

Despite these advantages, the *Hindenburg* was hampered by many of the same drawbacks as other airships. Tickets to fly in the *Hindenburg* were not affordable for most people. The massive amount of fuel needed not only to fill the balloon [12] and to power [13] it's propellers

9. A) NO CHANGE
    B) the blimp
    C) the airship
    D) airplanes

10. A) NO CHANGE
    B) largest
    C) big
    D) larger

11. A) NO CHANGE
    B) it
    C) the *Hindenburg*
    D) he

12. A) NO CHANGE
    B) but also
    C) and also
    D) nor

13. A) NO CHANGE
    B) its
    C) it is
    D) their

made this airship very expensive to operate. Even with all of that fuel, the *Hindenburg* flew at a mere 76 miles per hour—a snail's pace considering that it was used for transatlantic passenger service. Because an airship is essentially a balloon with an engine, it is extremely vulnerable to air currents and stormy weather, and the *Hindenburg* was no different.

The *Hindenburg's* fate, however, rested **14** by the most dangerous characteristic of these airships: hydrogen gas is extremely flammable. Any spark or flame that came near the gas could cause a horrific explosion, which is exactly what happened. On May 6, 1937, as the *Hindenburg* was landing in Lakehurst, New Jersey, it suddenly burst into flames, killing 36 of the 97 passengers and crew on board. This explosion, which ultimately destroyed the airship, was believed to have been caused by a discharge of electricity in the air, which reacted with a small leak in the **15** balloons.

However, when the disaster occurred, the airship was already obsolete as a mode of transportation. By the 1940s, commercial airplanes had advanced in development far beyond the airship's capacity. Today, airplanes cost much less to operate and fly at more than seven times the speed of the *Hindenburg*, and airline tickets are far more affordable. The airship thus became outdated as a mode of passenger service and acquired **16** their modern-day role as an advertising platform.

14. A) NO CHANGE
    B) in
    C) on
    D) with

15. A) NO CHANGE
    B) blimps
    C) hydrogen
    D) balloon

16. A) NO CHANGE
    B) its
    C) it's
    D) they're

Answers & Explanations for this chapter begin on page 909.

EXTRA PRACTICE

The following questions provide an opportunity to practice the concepts and strategic thinking covered in this chapter. While many of the questions pertain to Conventions of Usage, some touch on other concepts tested on the Writing & Language Test to ensure that your practice is test-like, with a variety of question types per passage.

Questions 1-11 are based on the following passage and supplementary material.

Batteries Out in the Cold

Many people have trouble starting their cars on a cold winter morning. In a cold car, the engine turns over more slowly, **1** <u>since</u> it sometimes does not turn over at all. Car owners may **2** <u>credit</u> their cold engines, but the real problem is a cold battery.

[1] A motor is generally connected to its circuit through a battery. [2] When a motor is hooked up in a circuit with a battery, electrons move through the circuit, creating a current. [3] Likewise, decreasing the number of electrons moving decreases the current, which then decreases the amount of power available. [4] Increasing the number of electrons moving increases the current, which then increases the amount of power available to the motor. **3**

1. A) NO CHANGE
    B) and
    C) but
    D) yet

2. A) NO CHANGE
    B) criticize
    C) accuse
    D) blame

3. To make this paragraph most logical, sentence 3 should be placed
    A) where it is now.
    B) before sentence 1.
    C) before sentence 2.
    D) after sentence 4.

[4] Electrons move through a battery as a result of two chemical reactions occurring within the battery, one at each pole. **[5]** A typical car battery, uses lead, and sulfuric acid. At the negative pole, lead reacts with sulfate ions in the solution around it to form lead sulfate, giving off electrons. At the positive pole, lead oxide **[6]** would have reacted with sulfate ions, hydrogen ions, and electrons in the same solution to also form lead sulfate, taking in electrons. The electrons produced at the negative pole flow through the **[7]** boundary to the positive pole, providing an electric current in the circuit.

4. Which choice most effectively establishes the main topic of the paragraph?
   A) NO CHANGE
   B) Sulfuric acid can cause burns to the skin, eyes, lungs, and digestive tract, and severe exposure can result in death.
   C) In a direct current circuit, one pole is always negative, the other pole is always positive, and the electrons flow in one direction only.
   D) Lead sulfate is toxic by inhalation, ingestion, and skin contact; repeated exposure may lead to anemia, kidney damage, and other serious health issues.

5. A) NO CHANGE
   B) A typical car battery uses lead, and sulfuric acid.
   C) A typical car battery, uses lead and sulfuric acid.
   D) A typical car battery uses lead and sulfuric acid.

6. A) NO CHANGE
   B) did react
   C) reacts
   D) reacted

7. A) NO CHANGE
   B) cycle
   C) circuit
   D) path

Reading & Writing

A battery charger uses the same reactions, but in reverse. As the current flows in the opposite direction, supplied by house current or a generator, the lead sulfate at the positive pole reacts to change back to lead oxide. **8**

Temperature affects the speed of chemical reactions in two ways. For a chemical reaction to happen, the reactants must collide with enough energy to get the reaction going. As the temperature increases, the motion of the reactants increases. The increased motion of the reactants increases the **9** practicality that they will collide and therefore increases the rate of reaction. The amount of energy in the reactants also increases as temperature increases.

This makes it more likely that any two colliding reactants in a battery will have enough energy to react, and so **10** its rate of reaction increases.

8. At this point, the writer wants to add information that supports the main topic of the paragraph. Which choice most effectively accomplishes this goal?

   A) Lead oxide, sometimes called litharge, is an inorganic compound with a formula including lead and oxygen.

   B) At the same time, the lead sulfate at the negative pole reacts to change back to lead metal.

   C) The difference between a house current and a generator is that the generator converts mechanical energy to electrical energy for use in an external circuit.

   D) Using a battery charger incorrectly can be dangerous since a car battery contains chemicals that produce hydrogen, a potentially volatile gas.

9. A) NO CHANGE

   B) way

   C) question

   D) probability

10. A) NO CHANGE

    B) it's

    C) their

    D) they're

Low temperatures have the opposite effect from high temperatures. The chemicals in the battery react more slowly at low temperatures, due both to fewer collisions and less energetic collisions, so fewer electrons move through the circuit. A cold battery takes longer to charge and often cannot provide enough energy to start a car. A cold car that will not start will need either additional power from another car to get the motor moving or a source of heat to warm up the battery and speed up the chemical reactions. Research conducted by FleetCarma in Waterloo, Ontario, demonstrates that **11** colder temperatures negatively affect the distance electric cars can travel.

Average Range of Electric Cars as a Function of Temperature

Adapted from research published by FleetCarma, Waterloo, Ontario.

11. Which choice most accurately represents the information in the graph?

A) NO CHANGE

B) the number of kilometers an electric car can travel declines as the outside temperature increases.

C) temperatures below 15°C make it extremely difficult to start an electric car.

D) once the electric car's battery has an alternate heat source by which to start, the distance the car can travel is greatly increased.

CHAPTER 25

Conventions
of Punctuation

CHAPTER OBJECTIVES

By the end of this chapter, you will be able to:

1. Recognize and correct inappropriate uses of punctuation within and at the end of sentences

2. Identify and correct inappropriate uses of possessive nouns

3. Recognize and omit unnecessary punctuation

SMARTPOINTS

Point Value	SmartPoint Category
40 Points	Punctuation

Reading & Writing

CONVENTIONS OF PUNCTUATION

Chapter 25

Homework

Extra Practice: #1-11

Even More

Writing & Language Quiz 6

Key

 Book Assignment

 Online Video Assignment

 Online Quiz Assignment

END-OF-SENTENCE AND WITHIN-SENTENCE PUNCTUATION

The SAT Writing & Language Test will require you to identify and correct inappropriate use of ending punctuation that deviates from the intent implied by the context. You will also have to identify and correct inappropriate colons, semicolons, and dashes when used to indicate breaks in thought within a sentence.

You can recognize Punctuation questions because the underlined portion of the text will include a punctuation mark. The answer choices will move that punctuation mark around or replace it with another punctuation mark.

Use **commas** to:

- Separate independent clauses connected by a FANBOYS conjunction (*For, And, Nor, But, Or, Yet, So*)
  Jess finished her homework earlier than expected, so she started on a project that was due the following week.

- Separate an introductory or modifying phrase from the rest of the sentence
  Knowing that soccer practice would be especially strenuous, Tia filled up three water bottles and spent extra time stretching beforehand.

- Set off three or more items in a series or list
  Jeremiah packed a sleeping bag, a raincoat, and a lantern for his upcoming camping trip.

- Separate nonessential information from the rest of the sentence
  Professor Mann, who was the head of the English department, was known for including a wide variety of reading materials in the curriculum.

- Separate an independent and dependent clause
  Tyson arrived at school a few minutes early, which gave him time to clean his locker before class.

> ✔ **Expert Tip**
>
> When you see an underlined comma, ask yourself, "Can the comma be replaced by a period or a semicolon?" If yes, the comma is grammatically incorrect and needs to be changed.

Use **semicolons** to:

- Join two independent clauses that are not connected by a FANBOYS conjunction
  Gaby knew that her term paper would take at least four more hours to write; she got started in study hall and then finished it at home.

- Separate items in a series or list if those items already include commas
  The team needed to bring uniforms, helmets, and gloves; oranges, almonds, and water; and hockey sticks, pucks, and skates.

Reading & Writing

> ✔ **Expert Tip**
>
> When you see an underlined semicolon, ask yourself, "Can the semicolon be replaced by a comma?" If yes, the semicolon is grammatically incorrect and needs to be changed. If the semicolon is separating two independent clauses and can be replaced with a period, it is grammatically correct.

Use **colons** to:

- Introduce and/or emphasize a short phrase, quotation, explanation, example, or list
  Sanjay had two important projects to complete: a science experiment and an expository essay.

Use **dashes** to:

- Indicate a hesitation or a break in thought
  Going to a history museum is a good way to begin researching prehistoric creatures—on second thought, heading to the library will likely be much more efficient.

> ✔ **Expert Tip**
>
> When you see an underlined colon or dash, ask yourself, "Has the author included a new idea by introducing or explaining something, or by breaking his or her thought process?" If yes, the punctuation is often grammatically correct.

Let's look at the following Writing & Language passage and questions. After the passage, there are two columns. The left column contains test-like questions. The column on the right features the strategic thinking a test expert employs when approaching the passage and questions presented.

Questions 1-2 are based on the following passage.

Sir Edmund Hilary

In the late spring of 1953, New Zealand mountaineer Sir Edmund Hillary and Nepalese Sherpa Tenzing Norgay became the first men to walk on the top of the world. After a grueling expedition that spanned several **1** months. They had finally reached the summit of Mount Everest. This was the mountain the Tibetan people called "Mother of the Universe," but despite its maternal nomenclature, it had already claimed the lives of George Mallory and Andrew Irvine before Hillary and Norgay finally conquered its icy peak. The mountain's siren call continues to lure mountaineers to this day. But climbing Mount Everest may be easier than answering the question posed by decades of non-climbers: Why? Perhaps Mallory said it best in 1923 before his ill-fated **2** climb; "Because it is there."

Questions	Strategic Thinking
1. A) NO CHANGE B) months, and they C) months; they D) months, they	**Step 1: Read the passage and identify the issue** The underlined segment includes a period, but the sentence before the period is a fragment. **Step 2: Eliminate answer choices that do not address the issue** Eliminate A because, as written, the sentence before the period is a fragment. Eliminate B because it creates a run-on. Eliminate C because it does not correct the original error. **Step 3: Plug in the remaining answer choices and select the most correct, concise, and relevant one** Choice (D) is correct.

Questions	Strategic Thinking
2. A) NO CHANGE B) climb: "Because it is there." C) climb. "Because it is there." D) climb "Because it is there."	**Step 1: Read the passage and identify the issue** The underlined segment includes a semicolon that is used incorrectly because it neither joins two independent clauses nor separates items containing commas in a series or list. The underlined segment here is intended to provide emphasis. **Step 2: Eliminate answer choices that do not address the issue** Eliminate C because it creates two separate sentences that change the author's intended meaning. Eliminate D because it removes punctuation altogether, creating a new error. **Step 3: Plug in the remaining answer choices and select the most correct, concise, and relevant one** Choice (B) is correct.

POSSESSIVE NOUNS AND PRONOUNS

Possessive nouns and pronouns indicate who or what possesses another noun or pronoun. Each follows different rules, and the SAT will test both. These questions require you to identify both the singular and plural forms.

You can spot errors in possessive noun and pronoun construction by looking for:

- Two nouns in a row

- Context clues

- Pronouns with apostrophes

- Words that sound alike

Possessive Nouns		
Singular	sister's	*My oldest **sister's** soccer game is on Saturday.*
Plural	sisters'	*My two older **sisters'** soccer games are on Saturday.*

Questions about possessive pronouns often require you to watch out for contractions and sound-alike words.

Possessive Pronouns and Words to Watch Out For	
its = possessive	it's = it is
their = possessive	there = location/place
whose = possessive	who's = who is/who has

Let's look at the following Writing & Language passage and questions. After the passage, there are two columns. The left column contains test-like questions. The column on the right features the strategic thinking a test expert employs when approaching the passage and questions presented.

Questions 3-4 are based on the following passage.

Literary Theory

Sometimes, being overeducated about literary theory and criticism can have detrimental effects on one's reading. In some cases, before one even opens a book, one might have certain expectations as to **3** <u>it's</u> literary genre, its cultural and historical significance, its symbolism, its author's life and times, and other matters. One can therefore lose out on the experience of entering a world for the first time, where every **4** <u>sight, sound, and taste</u> is eternally new, where the book is forever in the process of forming itself. When one brings preconceived notions and generalizations to a book, the book is petrified in time and space.

Reading & Writing

Questions	Strategic Thinking
3. A) NO CHANGE B) its C) it is D) the	**Step 1: Read the passage and identify the issue** The underlined apostrophe suggests there is a grammatical issue. "It's" is a contraction meaning "it is," but the sentence requires a possessive pronoun. **Step 2: Eliminate answer choices that do not address the issue** Eliminate A, C, and D because they are not possessive pronouns. **Step 3: Plug in the remaining answer choices and select the most correct, concise, and relevant one** Choice (B) is correct.
4. A) NO CHANGE B) sight, sound, taste C) sight, and sound, and taste D) sight sound and taste	**Step 1: Read the passage and identify the issue** The underlined portion contains a series. Commas should be used to set off three or more items in a series or list. These commas should be placed after every item in the series preceding the "and." A series or list should include the word "and" following the comma before the last item. **Step 2: Eliminate answer choices that do not address the issue** Eliminate B, C, and D because they do not feature proper series or list construction. **Step 3: Plug in the remaining answer choices and select the most correct, concise, and relevant one** Choice (A) is correct.

PARENTHETICAL/NONRESTRICTIVE ELEMENTS AND UNNECESSARY PUNCTUATION

Use **commas**, **dashes**, or **parentheses** to set off parenthetical or nonrestrictive information in a sentence.

> ✔ **Definition**
>
> Parenthetical or nonrestrictive information includes words or phrases that aren't essential to the sentence structure or content. Sometimes, however, this information is explanatory.

The SAT will also ask you to recognize instances of unnecessary punctuation, particularly **commas**.

Do not use a comma to:

- Separate a subject from its predicate
- Separate a verb from its object or its subject, or a preposition from its object
- Set off restrictive elements
- Precede a dependent clause that comes after an independent clause
- Separate adjectives that work together to modify a noun

> ✔ **Expert Tip**
>
> To determine if information is nonessential, read the sentence without the information. If the sentence still makes sense without the omitted words, then those words need to be set off with punctuation.

Let's look at the following Writing & Language passage and questions. After the passage, there are two columns. The left column contains test-like questions. The column on the right features the strategic thinking a test expert employs when approaching the passage and questions presented.

Questions 5-6 are based on the following passage.

Chimpanzees and Language

    Many linguistic researchers are excited about the possibility of humans using language to communicate with chimpanzees, our close cousins in the animal world. Some scientists believe that chimpanzees, and in particular Bonobo chimpanzees, may have the comprehension skills of two-and-a-half-year-old children. With dedicated **5** training, the scientists claim these chimpanzees are able to understand complicated **6** sentences, and to communicate on an advanced level with human beings. In a recent and rather astonishing episode, for example, a Bonobo chimpanzee pressed symbols on a special keyboard in order to tell her trainers about a fight between two chimpanzees in a separate facility.

Reading & Writing

Reading & Writing

Questions	Strategic Thinking
5. A) NO CHANGE B) training, the scientists claim, these C) training the scientists claim these D) training the scientists claim, these	**Step 1: Read the passage and identify the issue** The underlined segment includes a comma that precedes nonessential information that the scientists claim the content of the sentence to be true. The nonessential information ("the scientists claim") is separated from the rest of the sentence by only one comma before "it" rather than one comma before "it" and one after "it." **Step 2: Eliminate answer choices that do not address the issue** Eliminate A because the sentence is incorrect as written. Eliminate C because it removes all punctuation. Eliminate D because it makes the sentence grammatically incorrect. **Step 3: Plug in the remaining answer choices and select the most correct, concise, and relevant one** Choice (B) is correct.
6. A) NO CHANGE B) sentences and to communicate C) sentences: to communicate D) sentences and communicating	**Step 1: Read the passage and identify the issue** The comma used in the underlined portion is incorrect. The phrase "and to communicate" placed after the comma forms a compound with "to understand complicated sentences," which precedes it. No punctuation is necessary when two phrases are joined by "and," thus forming a compound. **Step 2: Eliminate answer choices that do not address the issue** Eliminate A because the sentence is incorrect as written. Eliminate C because it incorrectly replaces the comma with a colon. Eliminate D because it introduces a parallelism error. **Step 3: Plug in the remaining answer choices and select the most correct, concise, and relevant one** Choice (B) is correct.

You have seen the ways in which the SAT tests you on Punctuation in Writing & Language passages and the way an SAT expert approaches these types of questions.

Use the Kaplan Method for Writing & Language to answer the four questions that accompany the following Writing & Language passage excerpt. Remember to look at the strategic thinking questions that have been laid out for you—some of the answers have been filled in, but you will have to complete the answers to others.

Use your answers to the strategic thinking questions to select the correct answer, just as you will on Test Day.

Reading & Writing

Questions 7-10 are based on the following passage.

Bebop Jazz

For a jazz musician in New York City in the early 1940s, the most interesting place to spend the hours between midnight and dawn was probably a Harlem nightclub called Minton's. After finishing their jobs at other clubs, young musicians like **7** Charlie Parker, Dizzy Gillespie, Kenny Clarke, Thelonious Monk would gather at Minton's and have jam sessions, informal performances featuring lengthy group and solo improvisations. The all-night sessions resulted in the birth of modern jazz as these African-American artists together forged a new sound, known as bebop.

Unlike swing, the enormously popular jazz played in the 1930s, bebop was not dance music. It was often blindingly fast, incorporating tricky, irregular rhythms and discordant sounds that jazz audiences had never heard before. Earlier jazz, like practically all of Western music up to that time, used an eight-note scale. Bebop, in contrast, was based on a 12-note **8** scale. Thereby, it opened up vast new harmonic opportunities for musicians.

The musicians who pioneered bebop shared two common elements: a vision of the new music's possibilities and astonishing improvisational skill—the ability to play or compose a musical line on the spur of the moment. After all, **9** improvisation, within the context of a group setting, is the essence of jazz, which has been described as the musical experience of the passing moment. Parker, perhaps the greatest instrumental genius jazz has known, was an especially brilliant improviser. He often played twice as fast as the rest of the band, but his solos were always in rhythm and exquisitely shaped, revealing a harmonic imagination that enthralled his listeners.

Like many revolutions, unfortunately, the bebop movement encountered heavy resistance. Opposition came from older jazz musicians initially, but also, later and more lastingly, from a general public alienated by the **10** music's complexity and sophistication. Furthermore, due to the government ban on recording that was in effect during the early years of World War II (records were made of vinyl, a petroleum product that was essential to the war effort), the creative ferment that first produced bebop remains largely undocumented today.

Questions	Strategic Thinking
7. A) NO CHANGE B) Charlie Parker; Dizzy Gillespie; Kenny Clarke; and Thelonious Monk C) Charlie Parker and Dizzy Gillespie, and Kenny Clarke and Thelonious Monk D) Charlie Parker, Dizzy Gillespie, Kenny Clarke, and Thelonious Monk	**Step 1: Read the passage and identify the issue** *Are there any clues suggesting a grammatical issue?* Yes, the underlined portion contains a series. *What kind of punctuation is used to set off three or more items in a series or list?* Commas. *Where should these punctuation marks be placed?* After every item that precedes the word "and." *Is there anything else a series or list should include? If so, what?* A series or list should include the word "and" following the comma before the last item. **Step 2: Eliminate answer choices that do not address the issue** *What answer choice(s) can you eliminate?* _____ _____ _____ **Step 3: Plug in the remaining answer choices and select the most correct, concise, and relevant one** *What is the correct answer?* _____

Questions	Strategic Thinking
8. A) NO CHANGE B) scale, and thereby opening up C) scale, opening up D) scale, thereby opening up	**Step 1: Read the passage and identify the issue** *What punctuation does the underlined segment include?* A period. *What is the issue?* _____ _____ **Step 2: Eliminate answer choices that do not address the issue** *What answer choice(s) can you eliminate?* _____ _____ _____ **Step 3: Plug in the remaining answer choices and select the most correct, concise, and relevant one** *What is the correct answer?*_____

Reading & Writing

Questions	Strategic Thinking
9. A) NO CHANGE B) improvisation within the context of a group setting is the essence C) improvisation within the context of a group setting, is the essence D) improvisation, within the context of a group setting is the essence	**Step 1: Read the passage and identify the issue** *What punctuation does the underlined segment include?* Two commas surrounding the phrase "within the context of a group setting." *What purpose do two commas surrounding a phrase within a sentence serve?* _____ _____ *Is the information set off by the commas in the underlined portion nonessential? Why or why not?* _____ _____ **Step 2: Eliminate answer choices that do not address the issue** *What answer choice(s) can you eliminate?* _____ _____ _____ **Step 3: Plug in the remaining answer choices and select the most correct, concise, and relevant one** *What is the correct answer?* _____

Questions	Strategic Thinking
10. A) NO CHANGE B) musics C) musics' D) music	**Step 1: Read the passage and identify the issue** *What punctuation does the underlined segment include?* _____ *What is this type of punctuation used for?* _____ _____ **Step 2: Eliminate answer choices that do not address the issue** *What answer choice(s) can you eliminate?* _____ _____ _____ **Step 3: Plug in the remaining answer choices and select the most correct, concise, and relevant one** *What is the correct answer?* _____

Now try a test-like Writing & Language passage on your own. Give yourself 5 minutes to read the passage and answer the questions.

Questions 11-18 are based on the following passage.

Mauritius

[11] Although, most of the products we buy today are made abroad in well-known places like Mexico and China, a quick check of many clothing labels will reveal the name of a country that might not be so [12] familiar. It's Mauritius. Named in honor of Prince Maurice of Nassau by the Dutch who colonized it in 1638, this small island in the Indian Ocean has a complicated history influenced by several international powers. Since gaining independence in 1968, Mauritius has emerged as a stable democracy with one of Africa's highest per capita [13] incomes. Mauritius is considered a significant player in the modern global economy of the Southern Hemisphere.

Yet, Mauritius was not always so conspicuous. The island itself, situated 1,200 miles off the east coast of Africa, covers only about 450 square miles. As recently as the tenth century, it was completely uninhabited by humans, although it was likely known to Arab and Malay sailors of this period. The Portuguese landed in 1511, and with this initial visit, Mauritius gained its first taste of distinction through the discovery of an unlikely creature: the dodo bird. Early Portuguese accounts of encounters with this large, slow-moving bird on the island suggest that the dodo did not recognize humans as [14] predators, making the dodo even easier to catch

11. A) NO CHANGE
    B) Although most
    C) Although; most
    D) Most

12. A) NO CHANGE
    B) familiar, and it's Mauritius.
    C) familiar: Mauritius.
    D) familiar named Mauritius.

13. A) NO CHANGE
    B) incomes; Mauritius is
    C) incomes, and is
    D) incomes and is

14. A) NO CHANGE
    B) predators and made
    C) predators by making
    D) predators making

for food. As a result, by the mid-1600s, the entire dodo population had been wiped out.

Soon after the disappearance of the dodo, the Portuguese presence was replaced by that of the Dutch. Roughly 80 years of Dutch control brought waves of **15** traders, planters, and slaves; indentured laborers, merchants, and artisans, **16** who's collective arrival brought international recognition to Mauritius.

In 1715, the island again changed hands, this time to the French, and in 1810, with a successful invasion during the Napoleonic Wars, the British became the fourth European power to rule the island. Yet it was during this period of changing **17** colonial powers—Mauritius was traded like a commodity, that the demographics of the island began to experience important changes with great political ramifications.

By the time slavery was abolished in 1835, for example, the growing Indian population, the Creoles who could trace their roots back to island's sugarcane plantations, and the Muslim community originating from present-day Pakistan far outnumbered the remaining Franco-Mauritian elites. And with these demographic changes came political change. The first step toward self-rule came with the legislative elections of 1947, and in March of 1968, an official constitution was adopted. Today, Mauritius peacefully balances the diversity of its multicultural society and flourishes in international **18** trade through its advantageous geographic location and large labor force.

15. A) NO CHANGE
    B) traders, planters and slaves, indentured laborers, merchants and artisans,
    C) traders, planters, slaves, indentured laborers, merchants, artisans,
    D) traders, planters, slaves, indentured laborers, merchants, and artisans,

16. A) NO CHANGE
    B) whose collective arrival
    C) their collective arrival
    D) the collective arrival of whom

17. A) NO CHANGE
    B) colonial powers—Mauritius was traded like a commodity that
    C) colonial powers—Mauritius was traded like a commodity—that
    D) colonial powers, Mauritius was traded like a commodity that

18. A) NO CHANGE
    B) trade, through
    C) trade through,
    D) trade; through

Answers & Explanations for this chapter begin on page 912.

EXTRA PRACTICE

The following questions provide an opportunity to practice the concepts and strategic thinking covered in this chapter. While many of the questions pertain to Conventions of Punctuation, some touch on other concepts tested on the Writing & Language Test to ensure that your practice is test-like, with a variety of question types per passage.

Questions 1-11 are based on the following passage and supplementary material.

Feeling the Burn of Lactic Acid

As a person works a muscle excessively or for a long period of time, that person will most likely feel a burning sensation. Coaches and trainers often encourage **1** they're athletes to exercise until they "feel the burn" because that is an indication that the muscle is working hard. Some people **2** bond the burning feeling with "burning" calories, but the burning sensation has nothing to do with the energy released during exercise; **3** first, it is caused by chemicals that form when muscles use more oxygen than they have available.

4 Blood brings the energy muscles need to move in the form of glucose. The muscles cannot use the glucose directly, however; they can use only adenosine triphosphate (ATP), which is a molecule formed when cells break down glucose. First, the muscle cells break the six-carbon glucose into two three-carbon molecules of pyruvic acid. This makes two ATP molecules available for the muscle cells to use. When enough oxygen is available, the cells **5** then continues to break the pyruvic acid down in a series of steps, each of which produces more ATP. The full cycle releases another 34 ATP molecules, as well as carbon dioxide and water, from one molecule of glucose.

When a cell breaks down glucose without oxygen present, however, it can only accomplish the first step. Even

1. A) NO CHANGE
   B) their
   C) it's
   D) its

2. A) NO CHANGE
   B) equate
   C) acquaint
   D) observe

3. A) NO CHANGE
   B) instead,
   C) although,
   D) consequently,

4. Which choice most effectively establishes the central idea of this paragraph?
   A) NO CHANGE
   B) Adenosine triphosphate (ATP) is a molecule that is found in all living cells.
   C) Glucose is a carbohydrate that is absorbed into the blood during digestion.
   D) Muscles are made of soft tissue and require an external energy source to move.

5. A) NO CHANGE
   B) did continue
   C) continue
   D) continued

the first step will halt, unless the cell converts the pyruvic acid formed into lactic acid. The longer we exercise without enough oxygen, the more lactic acid we build up in our muscle tissues. You are probably familiar with the discomfort acetic **6** <u>acid found in vinegar, causes</u> when it comes in contact with a cut; lactic acid **7** <u>annoys</u> muscle tissues in a similar way, causing a burning sensation.

8 [1] Lactic acid does not form during normal daily activities because our muscles have a small store of ATP available, which is easily replenished as it is used. [2] More intense activity, however, quickly uses up that **9** <u>store once the store</u> is used up, and if the level of oxygen needed for the activity is greater than the amount reaching the muscles, lactic acid starts to build up. [3] The buildup of lactic acid occurs most quickly while engaging in so-called power sports, such as sprinting. [4] After we stop exercising, **10** <u>you</u> continue to breathe harder in order to get enough oxygen to convert the lactic acid back to pyruvic acid, to be used in the normal cycle once again. [5] As a result, lactic acid does not return to normal immediately after we stop exercising. **11**

Concentration of Lactic Acid in Blood Before, During, and After Exercise (5-minute fast run)

Based on data from Journal of Sport Sciences, 28(9) pp. 975-982.

6. A) NO CHANGE
   B) acid, found in vinegar, causes
   C) acid found, in vinegar, causes
   D) acid found in vinegar causes

7. A) NO CHANGE
   B) rubs
   C) hurts
   D) irritates

8. Which choice provides the least support for the central idea of this paragraph?
   A) Sentence 1
   B) Sentence 2
   C) Sentence 3
   D) Sentence 4

9. A) NO CHANGE
   B) store once, the store
   C) store; once the store
   D) store: once the store

10. A) NO CHANGE
    B) we
    C) they
    D) them

11. Based on the information in the graph, which choice, if added here, would provide the most effective conclusion to the passage?
    A) Lactic acid concentration peaks at eight minutes then begins to drop.
    B) At 28 minutes, lactic acid concentration is half of what it is during exercise.
    C) We continue to "feel the burn" for about 40 minutes after we stop.
    D) Lactic acid concentration declines steadily when exercise stops.

PART THREE

The Essay

The Essay

BY THE END OF THIS UNIT, YOU WILL BE ABLE TO:

1. Apply the Kaplan Method for the SAT Essay

2. Use the Kaplan Template for the SAT Essay to create an effective outline

The Kaplan Method for the SAT Essay

CHAPTER OBJECTIVES

By the end of this chapter, you will be able to:

1. Apply the Kaplan Method for the SAT Essay to produce a clear analysis of a source text

SMARTPOINTS

Point Value	SmartPoint Category
Point Builder	The Kaplan Method for the SAT Essay

THE KAPLAN METHOD FOR THE SAT ESSAY

Chapter 26

Homework

Extra Practice: Essay Prompt

Even More

The Kaplan Method for Essays

Key

 Book Assignment

 Online Video Assignment

 Online Quiz Assignment

THE SAT ESSAY IS OPTIONAL. SHOULD YOU WRITE IT?

One of the biggest changes for the 2016 SAT is the fact that the SAT Essay is now optional. If you don't want to spend 50 minutes writing an essay, you certainly don't have to. You are free to leave after the final multiple choice section of the test.

However, just because you can leave without completing the SAT Essay doesn't mean that you should. If you can state with 100 percent certainty that the colleges to which you are applying do not require the essay component of the SAT, feel free to omit it on Test Day. However, if you are unsure, or don't yet have a finalized list of colleges, Kaplan recommends you complete the SAT Essay for the following reasons:

First, consider the fact that the SAT is not an exam you can take in bits and pieces. If you want to take the SAT Essay at a later date, you'll have to sit through the entire SAT again. That can translate to a lot of unnecessary stress during your senior year.

Second, if the colleges you apply to don't require you to take the SAT Essay, they won't negatively judge you if you do. There is nothing to lose by completing the essay. You might get a great score and add a few more possibilities to your list of potential schools.

Finally, while the SAT Essay question on the new SAT will be challenging, it is also standardized. That means you can learn how to write a high-scoring essay by putting in some time, effort, and willingness to practice. This chapter is a great place to start.

THE KAPLAN METHOD FOR THE SAT ESSAY

The SAT Essay, while optional, presents you with a challenge: to read and understand a high-quality source text and write an essay analyzing the author's argument in 50 minutes. By using the Kaplan Method for the SAT Essay, you will be able to make the most out of those 50 minutes and produce a high-scoring written response to a previously published, sophisticated source.

The Kaplan Method for the SAT Essay consists of four steps:

Step 1: Read the source text, taking notes on how the author uses:

- Evidence to support claims

- Reasoning to develop ideas and to connect claims and evidence

- Stylistic or persuasive elements to add power to the ideas expressed

Step 2: Use the Kaplan Template to create an outline

Step 3: Write your essay

Step 4: Check your essay for mistakes in grammar, spelling, and clarity

Let's take a closer look at each step.

Step 1: Read the source text, taking notes on how the author uses:

- **Evidence to support claims**
- **Reasoning to develop ideas and to connect claims and evidence**
- **Stylistic or persuasive elements to add power to the ideas expressed**

What is the source text?

The source text for the SAT Essay will consist of a passage that is very similar to the passages you'll see in the Reading Test. It will typically be 500–750 words and will deal with topics of general interest in the arts, sciences, and public life. In many cases, the passages will be biased in favor of the author's argument.

While the source text changes from test to test, the directions and essay prompt remain similar. Spend more time reading and understanding the text—the prompt will likely be very similar to other prompts that you've encountered.

What kinds of notes should I take?

The notes you take while reading the source text are similar to those you would take when creating a Passage Map on the SAT Reading Test (see chapter 13). However, these notes will focus on how the author connects central ideas and important details.

Your notes should focus on:

- Evidence to support claims (e.g., cited data or statistics, or authoritative sources that support the author's argument)
- Reasoning to develop ideas and make connections (e.g., the author explains his logic for using a specific piece of evidence to support a specific claim)
- Stylistic or persuasive elements to add power to the ideas expressed (e.g., using figurative language, irony, metaphor, and other elements to appeal to emotions)

In addition to taking notes in the margins of the passage, it is also helpful to underline and circle the following:

- Central ideas
- Important details
- Facts and opinions
- Textual evidence (quotations, paraphrases, or both)

Your goal is to identify three Features such as juxtaposition, imagery, and symbolism that the author uses to build his or her argument.

> ✔ **Definition**
>
> Features are the key elements of the essay that you marked in your notes. They could include stylistic techniques (such as irony) or data (such as statistics) used to bolster a claim.

You should spend approximately 10 minutes on Step 1.

Step 2: Use the Kaplan Template to create an outline

Why do I need an outline?

Creating an outline before you write your essay is a huge time-saver, which is essential when you have only 50 minutes to complete the SAT Essay. Spending the first part of the allotted time effectively (i.e., reading and taking notes on the source text and creating an outline) will lead to a well-organized, more convincing essay. You'll also find that organizing your thoughts ahead of time will enable you to write much more quickly!

What should I put in my outline?

Kaplan has created an efficient and effective template to outline the SAT Essay. Using the template will prevent you from encountering a writing or thinking block. With the template and the Kaplan Method, you will know what you want to write about the source text and not waste any time.

You should spend approximately 8 minutes on Step 2.

> ✔ **On Test Day**
>
> You will not be able to bring this template with you to Test Day. Therefore, it is important that you memorize the gist and logical flow of the template well before Test Day so that creating an outline is second nature to you when you sit down to write your essay.

Step 3: Write your essay

After you have read and analyzed the source text, your next goal is to write a cohesive essay that demonstrates your use and command of standard written English. To demonstrate your proficiency, you must:

- Provide your own precise central claim
- Use a variety of sentence structures
- Employ precise word choice
- Maintain a constant and appropriate style and tone

You should spend approximately 30 minutes on Step 3.

Step 4: Check your essay for mistakes in grammar, spelling, and clarity

While a few grammar and spelling mistakes won't drastically harm your SAT Essay score, setting aside some time to proofread can help you catch careless errors that you can easily correct, thereby increasing your Writing score on the SAT Essay.

You should spend the remaining 2 minutes on Step 4.

THE SAT ESSAY PROMPT

As mentioned previously in this chapter, the SAT Essay source text will change from administration to administration, but the prompt will remain largely the same in both format and wording.

Become familiar with the idea behind the prompt and assignment as soon as you can so that on Test Day, you will be able to focus on reading, analyzing, and writing, rather than figuring out what the prompt is asking you to accomplish.

The generic SAT Essay prompt is as follows:

As you read the passage below, consider how [the author] uses

- evidence, such as facts or examples, to support claims.

- reasoning to develop ideas and to connect claims and evidence.

- stylistic or persuasive elements, such as word choice or appeals to emotion, to add power to the ideas expressed.

Source Text Will Appear Here

Write an essay in which you explain how [the author] builds an argument to persuade [his/her] audience that [author's claim]. In your essay, analyze how [the author] uses one or more of the features listed above (or features of your own choice) to strengthen the logic and persuasiveness of [his/her] argument. Be sure that your analysis focuses on the most relevant features of the passage.

Your essay should not explain whether you agree with [the author's] claims, but rather explain how [the author] builds an argument to persuade [his/her] audience.

SAT ESSAY SCORING RUBRIC

There are three different scores for the SAT Essay: Reading, Analysis, and Writing. Each category will be scored on a scale of 1 to 4. The scores you receive will range from 2 to 8, as they will be the scores of two raters.

The raters will use the following rubric to determine each area score.

	1	2
Reading	• Demonstrates **little or no comprehension** of the source text • Fails to show an understanding of the text's central idea(s), and may include only details without reference to central idea(s) • May contain numerous errors of fact and/or interpretation with regard to the text • Makes little or no use of textual evidence	• Demonstrates **some comprehension** of the source text • Shows an understanding of the text's central idea(s) but not of important details • May contain errors of fact and/or interpretation with regard to the text • Makes limited and/or haphazard use of textual evidence
Analysis	• Offers **little or no analysis or ineffective analysis** of the source text and demonstrates **little to no understanding** of the analytical task • Identifies without explanation some aspects of the author's use of evidence, reasoning, and/or stylistic and persuasive elements, and/or feature(s) of the student's own choosing • Numerous aspects of analysis are unwarranted based on the text • Contains little or no support for claim(s) or point(s) made, or support is largely irrelevant • May not focus on features of the text that are relevant to addressing the task • Offers no discernible analysis (e.g., is largely or exclusively summary)	• Offers **limited analysis** of the source text and demonstrates only **partial understanding** of the analytical task • Identifies and attempts to describe the author's use of evidence, reasoning, and/or stylistic and persuasive elements, and/or feature(s) of the student's own choosing, but merely asserts rather than explains their importance • One or more aspects of analysis are unwarranted based on the text • Contains little or no support for claim(s) or point(s) made • May lack a clear focus on those features of the text that are most relevant to addressing the task
Writing	• Demonstrates **little or no cohesion** and **inadequate skill** in the use and control of language • May lack a clear central claim or controlling idea • Lacks a recognizable introduction and conclusion; does not have a discernible progression of ideas • Lacks variety in sentence structures; sentence structures may be repetitive; demonstrates general and vague word choice; word choice may be poor or inaccurate; may lack a formal style and objective tone • Shows a weak control of the conventions of standard written English and may contain numerous errors that undermine the quality of writing	• Demonstrates **little or no cohesion** and **limited skill** in the use and control of language • May lack a clear central claim or controlling idea or may deviate from the claim or idea • May include an ineffective introduction and/or conclusion; may demonstrate some progression of ideas within paragraphs but not throughout • Has limited variety in sentence structures; sentence structures may be repetitive; demonstrates general or vague word choice; word choice may be repetitive; may deviate noticeably from a formal style and objective tone • Shows a limited control of the conventions of standard written English and contains errors that detract from the quality of writing and may impede understanding

	3	4
Reading	• Demonstrates **effective comprehension** of the source text • Shows an understanding of the text's central idea(s) and important details • Is free of substantive errors of fact and interpretation with regard to the text • Makes appropriate use of textual evidence	• Demonstrates **thorough comprehension** of the source text • Shows an understanding of the text's central idea(s) and most important details and how they interrelate • Is free of errors of fact or interpretation with regard to the text • Makes skillful use of textual evidence
Analysis	• Offers an **effective analysis** of the source text and demonstrates an **understanding** of the analytical task • Competently evaluates the author's use of evidence, reasoning, and/or stylistic and persuasive elements, and/or feature(s) of the student's own choosing • Contains relevant and sufficient support for claim(s) or point(s) made • Focuses primarily on those features of the text that are most relevant to addressing the task	• Offers an **insightful analysis** of the source text and demonstrates a **sophisticated understanding** of the analytical task • Offers a thorough, well-considered evaluation of the author's use of evidence, reasoning, and/or stylistic and persuasive elements, and/or feature(s) of the student's own choosing • Contains relevant, sufficient, and strategically chosen support for claim(s) or point(s) made • Focuses consistently on those features of the text that are most relevant to addressing the task
Writing	• Is **mostly cohesive** and demonstrates **effective use and control** of language • Includes a central claim or implicit controlling idea • Includes an effective introduction and conclusion; demonstrates a clear progression of ideas both within paragraphs and throughout the essay • Has variety in sentence structures; demonstrates some precise word choice; maintains a formal style and objective tone • Shows a good control of the conventions of standard written English and is free of significant errors that detract from the quality of writing	• Is **cohesive** and demonstrates a **highly effective use and command** of language • Includes a precise central claim • Includes a skillful introduction and conclusion; demonstrates a deliberate and highly effective progression of ideas both within paragraphs and throughout the essay • Has a wide variety of sentence structures; demonstrates a consistent use of precise word choice; maintains a formal style and objective tone • Shows a strong command of the conventions of standard written English and is free or virtually free of errors

THE KAPLAN TEMPLATE FOR THE SAT ESSAY

To maximize your essay score, organize your notes using Kaplan's SAT Essay Template.

¶1: Introductory paragraph

- Introductory statement
- Paraphrase the author's central idea or claim
- Specifically state the Features the author uses to support the central idea or claim

¶2: First body paragraph

- Introduce Feature 1 and provide a quote or paraphrase of the feature
- Specifically state how Feature 1 provides evidence to support the author's reasoning
- Discuss how Feature 1 reflects the author's thinking and the way the author ties his or her claim and evidence together
- Analyze the effect Feature 1 is likely to have on the audience

¶3: Second body paragraph

- Introduce Feature 2 and provide a quote or paraphrase of the feature
- Specifically state how Feature 2 provides evidence to support the author's reasoning
- Discuss how Feature 2 reflects the author's thinking and the way the author ties his or her claim and evidence together
- Analyze the effect Feature 2 is likely to have on the audience

––—**Time valve: If you are running out of time, don't write a 3rd body paragraph. Instead, take the time to write a thorough conclusion paragraph and proofread your essay. —-**

¶4: Third body paragraph

- Introduce Feature 3 and provide a quote or paraphrase of the feature
- Specifically state how Feature 3 provides evidence to support the author's reasoning
- Discuss how Feature 3 reflects the author's thinking and the way the author ties his or her claim and evidence together
- Analyze the effect Feature 3 is likely to have on the audience

¶5: Conclusion paragraph

- Recap author's central idea or claim
- Recap what Features the author used to build his or her argument
- Recap how effective the Features are on the audience

> ✔ **Expert Tip**
>
> Use the time valve option to your advantage. If you are running out of time, focusing on two strong body paragraphs and a complete conclusion is much better than rushing through a third body paragraph or leaving your essay unfinished.

Look at the test-like source text and prompt that follows. Notice what kinds of notes an SAT expert takes in the margins of the passage. Then, look at how the SAT expert creates an outline using the Kaplan template.

As you read the passage below, consider how Tony Blair uses

- evidence, such as facts or examples, to support claims.

- reasoning to develop ideas and to connect claims and evidence.

- stylistic or persuasive elements, such as word choice or appeals to emotion, to add power to the ideas expressed.

Adapted from British Prime Minister Tony Blair's speech to American citizens following 9/11/2001.

1   The only purpose of being in politics is to strive for the values and ideals we believe in: freedom, justice, what we Europeans call solidarity but you might call respect for and help for others. These are the decent democratic values we all avow. But alongside the values we know we need a hard-headed pragmatism— a realpolitik – required to give us any chance of translating those values into the practical world we live in.
     juxt. btwn. Euro & aud. (U.S.)

2   The same tension exists in the two views of international affairs. One is utilitarian: each nation maximizes its own self-interest. The other is utopian: we try to create a better world. Today I want to suggest that more than ever before those two views are merging.
     ev: util. vs utop. views

3   I advocate an enlightened self-interest that puts fighting for our values right at the heart of the policies necessary to protect our nations. Engagement in the world on the basis of these values, not isolationism from it, is the hard-headed pragmatism for the 21st century.

4   Why? In part it is because the countries and people of the world today are more interdependent than ever. In truth, it is very rare today that trouble in one part of the globe remains limited in its effect. Not just in security, but in trade and finance—witness the crisis of 1998 which began in Thailand and ended in Brazil—the world is interlocked.
     rhet. ?
     ev: 1998 crisis

5   <u>This is heightened by mass communications and technology. In Queen Victoria's time, reports of battles came back weeks or months after they were won or lost. Today we see them enacted live on the BBC, Sky or CNN.</u> Their very visibility, immediate and in Technicolor, inflames feelings that can spread worldwide across different ethnic, religious, and cultural communities.

ev: Queen Vic. time's reports vs today's

6   So today, more than ever, ⟨"their"⟩ problem becomes ⟨"our"⟩ problem. Instability is contagious and, again today, more than ever, nations, at least most of them, crave stability. That's for a simple reason. Our people want it, because without it, they can't do business and prosper. What brings nations together—what brought them together post–September 11—is the <u>international recognition</u> that the world needs order. Disorder is the enemy of progress.

quotes → irony

7   The struggle is for stability, for the security within which progress can be made. Of course, countries want to protect their territorial integrity but few are into empire-building. This is especially true of democracies whose people vote for higher living standards and punish governments who don't deliver them. <u>For 2,000 years Europe fought over territory.</u>

ex: 2000 year Eur. fight

8   Today boundaries are virtually fixed. Governments and people know that any territorial ambition threatens stability, and instability threatens prosperity.

9   And of course the <u>surest way to stability</u> is through the very values of <u>freedom, democracy and justice.</u> Where these are strong, the people push for moderation and order. Where they are absent, regimes act unchecked by popular accountability and pose a threat; and the threat spreads.

logic & results

10   So the <u>promotion of these values</u> becomes not just right in itself but <u>part of our long-term security and prosperity.</u> We can't intervene in every case. Not all the wrongs of the world can be put right, but <u>where disorder threatens us all, we should act.</u>

11   Like it or not, whether you are a utilitarian or a utopian, <u>the world is</u> ⟨interdependent.⟩ One consequence of this is that foreign and domestic policy are ever more closely interwoven.

12   It was September 11 that brought these thoughts into sharper focus. Watching the horror unfold, imagining the almost unimaginable suffering of the thousands of innocent victims of the terror and carnage, the dominant emotion after the obvious feelings of revulsion, sympathy, and anger was determination.

what prompted speech
juxt. "imagining… unimaginable"

13   The guts and spirit of the people of New York and America in the aftermath of that terrible day were not just admirable, they were awesome. They were the best riposte to the terrorists that humanity could give and you should be very proud of that. I want you to know too

praising aud.

that the British people were with you from the first moment, and we will always be with you at times like those. We are not half-hearted friends and we never will be. But the determination must be not just to pursue those responsible and bring them to justice but to <u>learn from September 11</u>. There is a real danger we forget the lessons of September 11. Human beings recover from tragedy and the memory becomes less fraught. That is a healthy part of living. But <u>we should learn from our experience</u>.

promises

14   The <u>most obvious lesson is indeed our</u> ⟨interdependence⟩ For a time our world stood still. Quite apart from our security, the shock impacted on economic confidence, on business, on trade, and it is only now, with the terrorist network on the run, that confidence is really returning. <u>Every nation in the world</u> felt the reverberation of that fateful day. And that <u>has been well illustrated</u> by the role which the United Nations—under Kofi Annan's excellent leadership—has played since September 11.

ex: U.N. & Kofi A. global effects of 9/11

15   So if we didn't know it before, we know now: these events and our response to them shape the fate <u>not of one nation but of one world</u>.

For America, it has laid bare the reality. American power affects the world fundamentally. It is there. It is real. It is never irrelevant. It can affect the world for good, or for bad. Stand aside or engage; it never fails to affect.

short sentences

16   You know I want it engaged. Under President Bush, I am confident it will be and for good. But if that's what I and many others want, it comes at a price for us too. It means we don't shirk our responsibility. It means that when America is fighting for those values, then, however tough, we fight with her. No grandstanding, no offering implausible but impractical advice from the comfort of the touchline, no wishing away the hard not the easy choices, but working together, side by side.

personification of America

> Write an essay in which you explain how Tony Blair builds an argument to persuade his audience that imbuing the world with values must be approached pragmatically and universally. In your essay, analyze how Blair uses one or more of the features listed above (or features of your own choice) to strengthen the logic and persuasiveness of his argument. Be sure your analysis focuses on the most relevant features of the passage.
>
> Your essay should not explain whether you agree with Blair's claims, but rather explain how Blair builds an argument to persuade his audience

Now that you've seen what kinds of notes a test expert takes for the SAT Essay source text, look at how he or she does some analysis by using the Kaplan Template to create an outline.

While the following example includes full sentences and quotations from the source text, please know that you should use shorthand and ellipses on Test Day; it's not your outline that's evaluated, but your actual essay.

Essay

¶1: Introductory paragraph

- **Introductory statement:** *In his speech to American citizens after September 11, 2001, British Prime Minister Tony Blair discusses how the world should respond.*

- **Paraphrase the author's central idea or claim:** *All nations must join together to fight for freedom, democracy, and justice.*

- **Specifically state the Features the author uses to support the central idea or claim**

  - *Feature 1: Historical evidence*

  - *Feature 2: Juxtaposition*

  - *Feature 3: Emphatic rhetoric*

¶2: First body paragraph

- **Introduce Feature 1 and provide a quote or paraphrase of the feature**

  - Feature 1: Historical Evidence

    - *¶4: Crisis of 1998, evidence of world's interdependence: ". . . which began in Thailand and ended in Brazil."*

    - *¶15: 9/11: "So if we didn't know it before, we know now: these events and our response to them shape the fate not of one nation but of one world."*

- **Specifically state how Feature 1 provides evidence to support the author's reasoning:** *Provides evidence for author's reasoning by taking his claim from a personal point of view into reality with specific, actual historical events.*

- **Discuss how Feature 1 reflects the author's thinking and the way the author ties his or her claim and evidence together:** *Reflects the author's thinking by providing specific examples to support his claim that the world is interdependent. The evidence and claim are tied together by making a statement and supporting it with historical events.*

- **Analyze the effect Feature 1 is likely to have on the audience:** *Emphasizes and makes the claim concrete by providing examples which are clearly understood by the audience, whose members may well have been affected by 9/11 and the 1998 financial crisis. The intent is to elicit audience agreement with the author.*

Now, look at how these notes translate into the first two paragraphs of a high-scoring student response to the SAT Essay.

In his speech to American citizens after the events of September 11, 2001, British Prime Minister Tony Blair discusses how the interdependent state of the world in the 21st century should influence the way countries respond to this tragedy. Blair emphatically asserts that all nations must band together in the fight for the values of freedom, democracy, and justice. Blair effectively conveys this argument by using historical examples, juxtaposition, and emphatic rhetoric.

Throughout the passage, Blair refers to specific historical events that have changed our perception of the world from separate nations with their own agendas, to a world so interdependent that events in one country echo through all countries. In the fourth paragraph, he reminds the audience of the trade and financial crisis of 1998, stating that it "began in Thailand and ended in Brazil," and uses this example to support his previous sentence that ""In truth, it is very rare today that trouble in one part of the globe remains limited in its effect." The author introduces the events of 9/11 in paragraph 12, stating that "It was September 11 that brought these thoughts into sharper focus," and emphasizing that we should "learn from September 11," and that "the most obvious lesson is indeed our interdependence." The author's blanket statement that "the countries and people of the world today are more interdependent than ever" is strongly supported by these historical examples, which prove that his thesis is not just rhetoric but fact. An audience, faced with the factual events, cannot help but be persuaded of the need for nations to work together toward common goals with common resources.

¶3: Second body paragraph

Introduce Feature 2 and provide a quote or paraphrase of the feature

_____

_____

_____

_____

Specifically state how Feature 2 provides evidence to support the author's reasoning

_____

_____

_____

Discuss how Feature 2 reflects the author's thinking and the way the author ties his or her claim and evidence together

_____

_____

_____

Analyze the effect Feature 2 is likely to have on the audience

_____

_____

_____

You have seen the kinds of notes SAT experts take and the strategic thinking questions they ask while planning their responses to the SAT Essay source text.

Based on the prompt on pages 590-592, use the Kaplan Template to plan an additional body paragraph for the response essay. You may use one of the other two features mentioned on page 593 (Juxtaposition and Emphatic Rhetoric) or come up with one of your own.

Essay

Now, use your ¶3 (the second body paragraph) notes on page 595 to write a full body paragraph on the lines that follow. Give yourself 8 minutes to write the paragraph.

_____
_____
_____
_____
_____
_____
_____
_____
_____
_____
_____
_____
_____
_____
_____
_____
_____
_____
_____
_____
_____
_____
_____
_____
_____
_____
_____
_____
_____
_____

Answers & Explanations for this chapter begin on page 915.

EXTRA PRACTICE

As you read the passage below, consider how Emmeline Pankhurst uses

- evidence, such as facts or examples, to support claims.

- reasoning to develop ideas and to connect claims and evidence.

- stylistic or persuasive elements, such as word choice or appeals to emotion, to add power to the ideas expressed.

Adapted from "Freedom or Death," a speech delivered by Emmeline Pankhurst on November 13, 1913, in Hartford, Connecticut

1   Mrs. Hepburn, ladies, and gentlemen:

2   Tonight I am not here to advocate woman suffrage. American suffragists can do that very well for themselves. I am here as a soldier who has temporarily left the field of battle in order to explain what civil war is like when civil war is waged by women. I am here as a person who, according to the law courts of my country, it has been decided, is of no value to the community at all: and I am adjudged because of my life to be a dangerous person.

3   Now, first of all I want to make you understand the inevitableness of revolution and civil war, even on the part of women, when you reach a certain stage in the development of a community's life. . . It is quite easy for you to understand the desirability of revolution if I were a man. If an Irish revolutionary had addressed this meeting, and many have addressed meetings all over the United States during the last twenty or thirty years, it would not be necessary for that revolutionary to explain the need of revolution beyond saying that the people of his country were denied—and by people, meaning men—were denied the right of self-government. That would explain the whole situation. If I were a man and I said to you, "I come from a country which professes to have representative institutions and yet denies me, a taxpayer, an inhabitant of the country, representative rights," you would at once understand that that human being, being a man, was justified in the adoption of revolutionary methods to get representative institutions. But since I am a woman it is necessary in the twentieth century to explain why women have adopted revolutionary methods in order to win the rights of citizenship.

4   You see, in spite of a good deal that we hear about revolutionary methods not being necessary for American women, we women, in trying to make our case clear, always have to make as part of our argument, and urge upon men in our audience the fact—a very simple fact—that women are human beings. I want to put a few political arguments before you—not arguments

for the suffrage, because I said when I opened, I didn't mean to do that—but arguments for the adoption of militant methods in order to win political rights.

5   Suppose the men of Hartford had a grievance, and they laid that grievance before their legislature, and the legislature obstinately refused to listen to them, or to remove their grievance, what would be the proper and the constitutional and the practical way of getting their grievance removed? Well, it is perfectly obvious at the next general election, when the legislature is elected, the men of Hartford would turn out that legislature and elect a new one: entirely change the personnel of an obstinate legislature.

6   But let the men of Hartford imagine that they were not in the position of being voters at all, that they were governed without their consent being obtained, that the legislature turned an absolutely deaf ear to their demands, what would the men of Hartford do then? They couldn't vote the legislature out. They would have to make a choice of two evils: they would either have to submit indefinitely to an unjust state of affairs, or they would have to rise up and adopt some of the antiquated means by which men in the past got their grievances remedied. We know what happened when your forefathers decided that they must have representation for taxation, many, many years ago. When they felt they couldn't wait any longer, when they laid all the arguments before an obstinate British government that they could think of, and when their arguments were absolutely disregarded, when every other means had failed, they began by the tea party at Boston, and they went on until they had won the independence of the United States of America. That is what happened in the old days.

7   It is perfectly evident to any logical mind that when you have got the vote, you can get out of any legislature whatever you want, or, if you cannot get it, you can send them about their business and choose other people who will be more attentive to your demands. But, it is clear to the meanest intelligence that if you have not got the vote, you must either submit to laws just or unjust, administration just or unjust, or the time inevitably comes when you will revolt against that injustice and use violent means to put an end to it.

> Write an essay in which you explain how Emmeline Pankhurst builds an argument to persuade her audience that violent as well as nonviolent protest tactics are necessary and justifiable to gain political rights for women. In your essay, analyze how Pankhurst uses one or more of the features listed above (or features of your own choice) to strengthen the logic and persuasiveness of her argument. Be sure that your analysis focuses on the most relevant features of the passage.
>
> Your essay should not explain whether you agree with Pankhurst's claims, but rather explain how Pankhurst builds an argument to persuade her audience.

Reading, Analyzing, and Writing the SAT Essay

CHAPTER OBJECTIVES

By the end of this chapter you will be able to:

1. Identify the source text's central ideas and important details and how they interrelate

2. Evaluate the author's use of evidence, reasoning, and/or stylistic and persuasive elements

3. Understand the standards by which the technical aspects of your written response will be evaluated

SMARTPOINTS

Point Value	SmartPoint Category
4 Points	Reading
4 Points	Analysis
4 Points	Writing

Essay

READING, ANALYZING, AND WRITING THE SAY ESSAY

Chapter 27

Homework

Extra Practice: Essay Prompt

Key

 Book Assignment

 Online Video Assignment

 Online Quiz Assignment

THE SAT ESSAY: READING

One of the three scores you'll receive on the SAT Essay is the Reading score. Graded on a scale of 1 to 4 by two different readers for a total score of 2 to 8, the Reading score is based on:

- Your understanding of the source text

- Your comprehension of the source text's central ideas, important details, and their interrelationship

- The accuracy of your interpretation of the source text

- Your use of textual evidence to demonstrate your understanding of the source text

Your ability to achieve a high Reading score depends on how well you accomplish Step 1 of the Kaplan Method for the SAT Essay:

Step 1: Read the source text, taking notes on how the author uses:

- **Evidence to support claims**

- **Reasoning to develop ideas and to connect claims and evidence**

- **Stylistic or persuasive elements to add power to the ideas expressed**

For an in-depth review of the Kaplan Method for the SAT Essay, please read chapter 26.

Central Ideas

The **central idea** of a text is the key point the author wants to make. The central idea is also often referred to as the text's theme or thesis. Here are some questions to help you pinpoint a text's central idea:

- What is the author's central idea or claim?

- Why did the author write this passage?

- What is the tone of the passage?

- What is this passage primarily about?

✔ **Expert Tip**

Do not confuse a text's topic and its central idea. The topic is what the author is writing about, such as ecology, politics, or literary criticism. The central idea is the author's opinion about the topic. The topic can usually be summarized in one sentence; the central idea often requires several sentences to describe the author's point of view and why he or she takes that position.

Essay

Important Details

While a source text will inevitably be full of details, the important details are those that support or explain the author's central idea. Authors often use certain structural clues or keywords to highlight important details. The following chart lists common categories of keywords and examples.

List	to begin with, first, secondly, next, then, finally, most important, also, for instance, in fact, for example, another
Chronology	on (date), not long after, now, as, before, after, when
Compare-and-Contrast	however, but, as well as, on the other hand, not only . . . but also, either . . . or, while, although, unless, similarly, yet, neither . . . nor
Cause-and-Effect	because, since, therefore, consequently, as a result, this led to, so that, nevertheless, accordingly, if . . . then, thus

If you're unsure if a detail is important when reading a source text, it probably isn't. Always ask: "Does this detail support or enhance the author's central idea? How?"

Let's look at the following test-like source text excerpt. Notice what kinds of notes an SAT expert takes in the margins of the passage. After the annotated passage, there is a series of questions and answers an SAT expert would ask to determine the text's central idea and important details.

Adapted from Hayakawa, S.I. Language in *Thought and Action* (Fifth Edition). New York: Harcourt Brace & Company, 1991.

The following passage is excerpted from a book that examines language and its <u>necessity in ensuring survival in society.</u>

central idea: names lead to behavior

1   Names that are "loaded" tend to influence behavior toward those to whom they are applied. Currently, the shop doorways and freeway underpasses of American cities are sheltering tens of thousands of people who have no work and no homes. These people used to be referred to as "bums"—a word that suggests not only a lack of employment but a lack of desire to work, people who are lazy, satisfied with little, and who have no desire to enter the mainstream of the American middle class or subscribe to its values. Thus, to think of these people as "bums" is to think that they are only getting what they deserve. With the search for new names for such people—"street people," "homeless," "displaced persons"—we may find new ways of helping these individuals.

ex. of "bums" connotation

if rename, better help?

2   . . . One other curious fact needs to be recorded about the words we apply to such hotly debated issues as race, religion, political heresy, and economic dissent. Every reader is acquainted with people who, according

to their own flattering descriptions of themselves, ⟨believe in being frank⟩ and like to ⟨tell it like it is.⟩ By "telling it like it is," such people usually mean calling anything or anyone by the term which has the strongest and most disagreeable affective connotations. Why people should pin medals on themselves for "candor" for performing this nasty feat has often puzzled me. Sometimes it is necessary to violate verbal taboos as an aid to clearer thinking, ⟨but⟩ more often, to insist upon "telling it like it is" is to provide our minds with a greased runway down which we may slide back into unexamined and reactive patterns of evaluation and behavior.

"candor" does not = being mean but many think it does

What is the author's central idea or claim? Names or labels, especially those with negative connotations, can lead to negative behavior or beliefs.

Why did the author write this passage? To demonstrate how language, even on the level of word or name choice, can affect society and influence people's attitudes toward others.

What is the tone of this passage? Appalled or indignant.

What is this passage mostly about? How negative names can affect our actions and the excuses people use to continue to be politically incorrect.

What is the most important detail in the first paragraph? The example of the connotations of the word "bums."

How does this detail serve the author's central idea? The example supports the idea that the connotation of a word used to label a group of people can color how most of society views that group and how that view may be skewed.

What is the most important detail in the second paragraph? The author's assertion that when most people "tell it like it is," they call "anything or anyone by the term which has the strongest and most disagreeable affective connotations," thereby allowing society to "slide back into unexamined and reactive patterns of evaluation and behavior."

How does this detail serve the author's central idea? It discusses how the more generalized theory behind why people use derogatory labels causes negative societal behavior.

THE SAT ESSAY: ANALYSIS

One of the three scores you'll receive on the SAT Essay is the Analysis score. Graded on a scale of 1 to 4 by two different readers for a total score of 2 to 8, the Analysis score is based on:

- Your analysis of the source text and understanding of the analytical task
- Your evaluation of the author's use of evidence, reasoning, and/or stylistic and persuasive elements, and/or features of your own choosing
- Your support for the claims or points you make in your response
- Your focus on features of the text that are most relevant to addressing the task

The SAT Essay prompt dictates that you analyze one or more features the author uses to strengthen the logic and persuasiveness of his or her argument. The Kaplan Template for the SAT Essay detailed in chapter 26 suggests that you pick three features to discuss in your response. Because the source text is different for every administration of the SAT, the three features you pick to analyze will depend on the source text.

Commonly Used Features and Styles

Feature	Defintion	Example
Allusion	A literary, historical, religious or mythological reference	*Eli's weakness for sugary drinks is his Achilles' heel.*
Appeals to authority, emotion, and/or logic	Rhetorical arguments in which the speaker claims to be an authority or expert in a field, attempts to play upon the emotions, or appeals to the use of reason	*As the eminent scientist Dr. Carl Sagan suggested, though the world is dependent on science and technology, few understand either. Sound reasoning, then, requires that we expose children to both from their earliest cognitive years.*
Claim	The assertion of something as fact	*It is very clear that the pursuit of riches is the driving force in society today; morality has given way to greed.*
Compare/contrast	A discussion in which two or more things are compared, contrasted, or both	*For years, people have debated the benefits of running for exercise. On one hand, running puts stress on your joints. On the other hand, running can strengthen tissues and tendons if you include moderation, rest, and recovery as part of your approach.*

Essay

Feature	Defintion	Example
Diction	The author's word choice, which often reveals an author's attitude and point of view	*It was quite a surprise when the timid Mr. Patel jumped to his feet, pounded the table, and roared his opposition.*
Hyperbole	Overstatement characterized by exaggerated language, usually to make a point or draw attention	*I told my sister that because she made me wait for an eternity to get a table at her favorite restaurant, I was now dying of hunger.*
Irony	A contrast between what is stated and what is really meant, or between what is expected and what actually happens	*As Petros walked into the classroom and glanced at what his teacher had written on the board, he grimaced and muttered, "A pop quiz in my first class—what a great way to start the day."*
Juxtaposition	Placing two things or ideas together to contrast them	*As Charles Dickens wrote in* A Tale of Two Cities, *"It was the best of times, it was the worst of times, it was the age of wisdom, it was the age of foolishness, it was the epoch of belief, it was the epoch of incredulity . . . "*
Rebuttal/refutation	An argument technique wherein opposing arguments are anticipated and countered	*To formulate a convincing rebuttal to the claim that technology is detrimental to positive social interaction, I compiled information and statistics that show how technology enhances social communication and expression.*
Rhetorical question	A question that is asked simply for the sake of stylistic effect and is not expected to be answered	*Who would not want to have a great satisfying job that allows you to do what you love every day? And what is more satisfying than fulfilling one's dreams?*
Symbolism	Use of a person, place, thing, event, or pattern that figuratively represents or "stands for" something else; often the thing or idea represented is more abstract or general than the symbol, which is concrete	*In William Blake's poem "Ah Sunflower," the sunflower refers to humankind and the sun represents life: "Ah Sunflower, weary of time, Who countest the steps of the sun."*

Essay

You can choose to analyze any of these features in your SAT Essay response; however, make sure to select features that are easily found within the source text and that the author uses to further his or her argument. If you cannot answer the questions posed in the Kaplan Template for the SAT Essay, pick another feature.

Let's look at the following test-like source text excerpt. After the annotated passage, the left column contains the features used in the excerpt. The column on the right describes how those features are used.

Adapted from Jonathan Swift's *A Modest Proposal*, written in 1729.

In the following passage, the narrator is proposing an idea "For Preventing the Children of Poor People From Being a [Burden] to Their Parents."

1   I shall now therefore humbly propose my own thoughts, which I hope will not be liable to the least objection.

2   I have been assured by a very knowing American of my acquaintance in London that a young healthy child well nursed is at a year old a most delicious, nourishing, and wholesome food, whether stewed, roasted, baked, or boiled; and I make no doubt that it will equally serve in a fricassee or a ragout.*

appeal to authority

3   I do therefore humbly offer it to public consideration that of the hundred and twenty thousand children already computed†, twenty thousand may be reserved for breed, whereof only one-fourth part be males; which is more than we allow to sheep, black cattle, or swine; and my reason is that these children are seldom the fruits of marriage, a circumstance not much regarded by our savages; therefore one male will be sufficient to serve four females. That the remaining hundred thousand may, at a year old, be offered in sale to the persons of quality and fortune through the kingdom; always advising the mother to let them suck plentifully in the last month, so as to render them plump and fat for a good table. A child will make two dishes at an entertainment for friends; and when the family dines alone, the fore or hind quarter will make a reasonable dish, and seasoned with a little pepper or salt will be very good boiled on the fourth day, especially in winter.

audience = public

compare boys to livestock

children as food!!

4   I have reckoned upon a medium that a child just born will weigh twelve pounds, and in a solar year, if tolerably nursed, will increase to twenty-eight pounds.

stats/logic/math

5   I grant this food will be somewhat dear, and therefore very proper for landlords, who, as they have already devoured most of the parents, seem to have the best title to the children.

---

* a spicy meat stew
† that is, the number of children annually born to Irish parents who cannot support them

Feature	How It's Used
Appeal to authority	*The author cites his "very knowing American" acquaintance in London who claims that "a young healthy child well nursed is at a year old a most delicious, nourishing, and wholesome food."*
Diction	*The author's repetitive use of the word "humbly" in the first and third paragraphs implies that his proposal is a modest one (thereby reinforcing the title of the essay).*
Irony	*The author presents a completely unacceptable solution to hunger and asks the audience to take seriously a preposterous suggestion.*

THE SAT ESSAY: WRITING

Just as the SAT Writing & Language Test assesses your knowledge of expression of ideas and conformity to the conventions of standard written English grammar, usage, and punctuation by having you revise and edit texts, so too does the SAT Essay Test by having you craft an original response. Therefore, the stronger your mastery of the writing and grammar concepts outlined in Unit 7: Expression of Ideas and Unit 8: Standard English Conventions, the better able you will be to earn a high Writing score on the SAT Essay.

One of the three scores you'll receive on the SAT Essay is the Writing score. Graded on a scale of 1 to 4 by two different readers for a total score of 2 to 8, the Writing score is based on:

- Your use of a central claim

- Your use of effective organization and progression of ideas

- Your use of varied sentence structures

- Your employment of precise word choice

- Your ability to maintain a consistent and appropriate style and tone

- Your command of the conventions of standard written English

Grammar Tips for the SAT Essay

1. **Avoid Sentence Fragments and Run-On Sentences.** Technically, a sentence fragment has no independent clause. A run-on sentence has two or more independent clauses that are improperly connected.

2. **Use Commas Correctly.** When using the comma, follow these guidelines:

- Use commas to separate items in a series. If more than two items are listed in a series, they should be separated by commas.

- Do not place commas before the first element of a series or after the last element.

- Use commas to separate two or more adjectives before a noun; do not use a comma after the last adjective in the series.

- Use commas to set off parenthetical clauses and phrases. A parenthetical expression is one that is not necessary to the central idea of the sentence.

- Use commas after most introductory phrases.

- Use commas to separate independent clauses (clauses that could stand alone as complete sentences) connected by coordinating conjunctions such as *and*, *but*, *not*, and *yet*.

3. **Use Semicolons Correctly.** Follow these guidelines for correct semicolon usage:

- A semicolon may be used instead of a coordinating conjunction such as *and*, *or*, or *but* to link two closely related independent clauses.

- A semicolon may also be used between independent clauses connected by words like *therefore*, *nevertheless*, and *moreover*.

4. **Use Colons Correctly.** When you see a colon, it means "something's coming." Follow these rules for correct colon usage:

- In formal writing, the colon is used only as a means of signaling that what follows is a list, definition, explanation, or concise summary of what has gone before. The colon usually follows an independent clause, and it will frequently be accompanied by a reinforcing expression like *the following*, *as follows*, or *namely*, or by an explicit demonstrative like *this*.

- Be careful not to put a colon between a verb and its direct object.

- Context will occasionally make clear that a second independent clause is closely linked to its predecessor, even without an explicit expression. Here, too, a colon is appropriate, although a period will always be correct too.

5. **Use Apostrophes Correctly.** Follow these guidelines for correct apostrophe usage:

- Use the apostrophe with contracted forms of verbs to indicate that one or more letters have been eliminated in writing. Generally, though, you should try to avoid contractions when writing your SAT Essay response.

- Use the apostrophe to indicate the possessive form of a noun.

- The apostrophe is used to indicate possession only with nouns; in the case of pronouns, there are separate possessives for each person and number, with the exception of the neutral *one*, which forms its possessive by adding an apostrophe and an *s*.

6. **Pay Attention to Subject-Verb Agreement.** Singular subjects and plural subjects take different forms of the verb in the present tense. Usually, the difference lies in the presence or absence of a final *s*, but sometimes the difference is more radical. You can usually trust your ear to give you the correct verb form. However, certain situations may cause difficulty, such as:

- When the subject and verb are separated by a number of words

- When the subject is an indefinite pronoun

- When the subject consists of more than one noun

7. **Use Modifiers Correctly.** In English, the position of a word within a sentence often establishes the word's relationship to other words in the sentence. This is especially true with modifying phrases. Modifiers, like pronouns, are generally connected to the nearest word that agrees with the modifier in person and number. If a modifier is placed too far from the word it modifies (the referent), the meaning may be lost or obscured. Avoid ambiguity by placing modifiers as close as possible to the words they are intended to modify.

8. **Use Pronouns Correctly.** A pronoun is a word that replaces a noun in a sentence. Every time you write a pronoun—*he, him, his, she, her, it, its, they, their, that,* or *which*—be sure there can be absolutely no doubt what its antecedent is. The antecedent is the particular noun a pronoun refers to or stands for. Careless use of pronouns can obscure your intended meaning.

9. **Pay Attention to Parallelism.** Matching constructions must be expressed in parallel form. It is often rhetorically effective to use a particular construction several times in succession in order to provide emphasis. The technique is called parallel construction, and it is effective only when used sparingly. If your sentences are varied, a parallel construction will stand out. If your sentences are already repetitive, a parallel structure will further obscure your meaning.

Style Tips For The SAT Essay

1. **Write succinctly.**

- Do not use several words when one word will do.

- If you have something to say, just say it.

2. **Write assertively.**

- Avoid overuse of qualifiers.

- You don't need to overly clarify your statements.

- Put verbs in the active voice whenever possible.

3. **Write clearly.**

- Try not to begin sentences with *there is, there are, it would be, it could be, it can be,* or *it is.*

- Avoid vague references, indirect language, and general wordiness. Choose specific, descriptive words.

- Avoid clichés, which are overused expressions. Always substitute more specific language for a cliché.

- Limit your use of jargon.

- Avoid using slang and colloquialisms.

Let's look at examples of how to correct common style issues.

The left column contains the issue. The column in the middle features a sample sentence. The column on the right demonstrates how to improve the sample sentence.

Issue	Incorrect	Correct
Needless qualification	This rather serious breach of etiquette may possibly shake the very foundations of the diplomatic community.	This serious breach of etiquette may shake the foundations of the diplomatic community.
Filling up space	Which idea of the author's is more in line with what I believe? This is a very interesting question. . . .	The author's beliefs are similar to mine.
Needless self-reference	I am of the opinion that air pollution is a more serious problem than the government has led us to believe.	Air pollution is a more serious problem than the government has led us to believe.
Weak openings	There are several reasons why Andre and his brother will not share an apartment.	Andre and his brother will not share an apartment for several reasons.
Vagueness	Chantal is highly educated.	Chantal has a master's degree in business administration.

Essay

Remember Step 1 of the Kaplan Method for the SAT Essay: Read the source text, taking notes on how the author uses:

- evidence to support claims

- reasoning to develop ideas and to connect claims and evidence

- stylistic or persuasive elements to add power to the ideas expressed

Read the following test-like source text excerpt and accompanying notes. Then, use the Kaplan Template for the SAT Essay to plan your introduction and first body paragraph.

Adapted from David Foster Wallace's "Tense Present: Democracy, English, and the Wars over Usage." *Harper's Magazine*, April 2001.

The following passage is excerpted from a monthly journal of literature, politics, culture, and the arts.

1   My own humble opinion is that some of the cultural and <u>political</u> <u>realities of American life are themselves racially insensitive and elitist</u> <u>and offensive and unfair</u>, and that tiptoeing around these realities with <u>euphemistic doublespeak</u> is not only hypocritical but toxic to the project of ever actually changing them. Such tiptoeing has of course now achieved the status of a dialect—one powerful enough to have turned the normal politics of the Usage Wars sort of inside out.

varied diction

juxt. of colloquial & academic

some think PCE = joke

2   I refer here to <u>Politically Correct English (PCE).</u> Although it's common to make jokes about PCE, be advised that Politically Correct English's various pre- and proscriptions are <u>taken very seriously *indeed*</u> <u>by colleges and corporations and government agencies,</u> whose own institutional dialects now evolve under the beady scrutiny of a whole new kind of Language Police.

others think PCE = serious

appeal to authority

3   From one perspective, the history of PCE evinces a kind of irony. That is, the same ideological principles that informed the original sixties-era rejections of <u>traditional</u> authority and <u>traditional</u> inequality have now actually produced a far more inflexible <u>tradition</u> or complexity backed by the threat of real-world sanctions (termination, litigation) for those who fail to conform. <u>This is sort of funny in a dark way,</u> <u>maybe,</u> and most criticism of PCE seems to consist in making fun of its trendiness or vapidity. This reviewer's <u>own opinion is that prescriptive</u> <u>PCE is not just silly but confused and dangerous.</u>

explains irony of PCE

use of colloquial makes his opinion clear

4   <u>Usage is always political,</u> of course, but it's complexly political. With respect, for instance, to political change, usage conventions can function in two ways: on the one hand <u>they can be a *reflection* of political</u>

change, and on the other they can be <u>an *instrument* of political change.</u> These two functions are different and have to be kept straight. Confusing them—in particular, mistaking for political efficacy what is really just a ⟨language's political⟩ symbolism—enables the bizarre conviction that America ceases to be elitist or unfair simply because Americans stop using certain vocabulary that is <u>historically associated with elitism and unfairness.</u> This is PCE's central fallacy—that a society's mode of expression is productive of its attitudes rather than a product of those attitudes.

instrument vs reflection of pol. change

central argument

¶1: Introductory paragraph

Introductory statement

_____

_____

Paraphrase the author's central idea or claim

_____

_____

Specifically state the Features the author uses to support the central idea or claim

_____

_____

_____

¶2: First body paragraph

Introduce Feature 1 and provide a quote or paraphrase of the feature

_____

_____

_____

Specifically state how Feature 1 provides evidence to support the author's reasoning

_____

_____

_____

Discuss how Feature 1 reflects the author's thinking and the way the author ties his or her claim and evidence together

_____

_____

_____

Analyze the effect Feature 1 is likely to have on the audience

_____

_____

_____

Essay

Now, use the Kaplan Template notes you wrote on page 614 to complete Steps 3 and 4 of the Kaplan Method for the SAT Essay: Write your essay and check your essay for mistakes in grammar, spelling, and clarity. Give yourself 8 minutes to write the introduction and first body paragraph.

Essay

Answers & Explanations for this chapter begin on page 921.

EXTRA PRACTICE

As you read the passage below, consider how Vice President Agnew uses

- evidence, such as facts or examples, to support claims.

- reasoning to develop ideas and to connect claims and evidence.

- stylistic or persuasive elements, such as word choice or appeals to emotion, to add power to the ideas expressed.

Adapted from Vice President Spiro Agnew's 1969 speech "Television News Coverage."

1 Tonight I want to discuss the importance of the television news medium to the American people. No nation depends more on the intelligent judgment of its citizens. No medium has a more profound influence over public opinion. So, nowhere should there be more conscientious responsibility exercised than by the news media.

2 Monday night a week ago, President Nixon delivered the most important address of his Administration, one of the most important of our decade. His subject was Vietnam. My hope, as his at that time, was to rally the American people to see the conflict through to a lasting and just peace in the Pacific. For 32 minutes, he reasoned with a nation that has suffered almost a third of a million casualties in the longest war in its history.

3 When the President completed his address—an address, incidentally, that he spent weeks in the preparation of—his words and policies were subjected to instant analysis and querulous criticism. The audience of 70 million Americans was inherited by a small band of network commentators and self-appointed analysts, the majority of whom expressed in one way or another their hostility to what he had to say.

4 It was obvious that their minds were made up in advance. Those who recall the fumbling and groping that followed President Johnson's dramatic disclosure of his intention not to seek another term have seen these men in a genuine state of nonpreparedness. This was not it.

5 One commentator twice contradicted the President's statement about the exchange of correspondence with Ho Chi Minh.[1] Another challenged the President's abilities as a politician. A third asserted that the President was following a Pentagon line. Others, by the expressions on their faces, the tone of their questions, and the sarcasm of their responses, made clear their sharp disapproval.

6 To guarantee in advance that the President's plea for national unity would be challenged, one network trotted out Averell Harriman for the occasion.

7 All in all, Mr. Harriman offered a broad range of gratuitous advice challenging and contradicting the policies outlined by the President of the United States. Where the President had issued a call for unity, Mr. Harriman was encouraging the country not to listen to him.

8   Now every American has a right to disagree with the President of the United States and to express publicly that disagreement. But the President of the United States has a right to communicate directly with the people who elected him, and the people of this country have the right to make up their own minds.

9   When Winston Churchill rallied public opinion to stay the course against Hitler's Germany, he didn't have to contend with a gaggle of commentators raising doubts about whether he was reading public opinion right, or whether Britain had the stamina to see the war through. When President Kennedy rallied the nation in the Cuban missile crisis, his address to the people was not chewed over by a roundtable of critics who disparaged the course of action he'd asked America to follow.

10 At least 40 million Americans every night, it's estimated, watch the network news. Seven million of them view ABC, the remainder being divided between NBC and CBS. According to Harris polls and other studies, for millions of Americans the networks are the sole source of national and world news.

11 Now how is this network news determined? A small group of anchormen, commentators, and executive producers settle upon the 20 minutes or so of film and commentary that's to reach the public. This selection is made from the 90 to 180 minutes that may be available. Their powers of choice are broad.

12 They decide what 40 to 50 million Americans will learn of the day's events in the nation and in the world. These men can create national issues overnight. They can make or break by their coverage and commentary a moratorium on the war. They can elevate men from obscurity to national prominence within a week. They can reward some politicians with national exposure and ignore others.

13 The views of the majority of this fraternity do *not*—and I repeat, not—represent the views of America. Not only did the country receive the President's speech more warmly than the networks, but so also did the Congress of the United States.

14 Yesterday, the President was notified that 300 individual Congressmen and 50 Senators of both parties had endorsed his efforts for peace. As with other American institutions, perhaps it is time that the networks were made more responsive to the views of the nation and more responsible to the people they serve.

Write an essay in which you explain how Vice President Agnew builds an argument to persuade his audience that the way in which network news covered a presidential address was inappropriate. In your essay, analyze how Agnew uses one or more of the features listed above (or features of your own choice) to strengthen the logic and persuasiveness of his argument. Be sure that your analysis focuses on the most relevant features of the passage.

Your essay should not explain whether you agree with Agnew's claims, but rather explain how he builds an argument to persuade his audience.

Essay

Essay

Essay

Essay

PART FOUR

Review

CHAPTER 28

Putting It All Together

KAPLAN METHOD FOR MATH

Step 1: Read the question, identifying and organizing important information as you go

Step 2: Choose the best strategy to answer the question

Step 3: Check that you answered the *right* question

Step 1: Read the question, identifying and organizing important information as you go

- **What information am I given?** Take a few seconds to jot down the information you are given and try to group similar items together.

- **Separate the question from the context.** Word problems may include information that is unnecessary to solve the question. Feel free to discard any unnecessary information.

- **How are the answer choices different?** Reading answer choices carefully can help you spot the most efficient way to solve a multiple-choice math question. If the answer choices are decimals, then painstakingly rewriting your final answer as a simplified fraction is a waste of time; you can just use your calculator instead.

- **Should I label or draw a diagram?** If the question describes a shape or figure but doesn't provide one, sketch a diagram so you can see the shape or figure and add notes to it. If a figure is provided, take a few seconds to label it with information from the question.

Step 2: Choose the best strategy to answer the question

- **Look for patterns.** Every SAT math question can be solved in a variety of ways, but not all strategies are created equally. To finish all of the questions, you'll need to solve questions as *efficiently* as possible. If you find yourself about to do time-consuming math, take a moment to look for time-saving shortcuts.

- **Pick numbers or use straightforward math.** While you can always solve an SAT math question with what you've learned in school, doing so won't always be the fastest way. On questions that describe relationships between numbers (such as percentages) but don't actually use numbers, you can often save time on Test Day by using techniques such as Picking Numbers instead of straightforward math.

Step 3: Check that you answered the *right* question

- When you get the final answer, **resist the urge to immediately bubble in the answer.** Take a moment to:

  - Review the question stem.

  - Check units of measurement.

  - Double-check your work.

- The SAT will often ask you for quantities such as $x + 1$ or the product of x and y. **Be careful on these questions!** They often include tempting answer choices that correspond to the values of x or y individually. There's no partial credit on the SAT, so take a moment at the end of every question to make sure you're answering the right question.

KAPLAN METHOD FOR MULTI-PART MATH QUESTIONS

Step 1: Read the first question in the set, looking for clues

Step 2: Identify and organize the information you need

Step 3: Based on what you know, plan your steps to navigate the first question

Step 4: Solve, step-by-step, checking units as you go

Step 5: Did I answer the *right* question?

Step 6: Repeat for remaining questions, incorporating results from the previous question if possible

Step 1: Read the first question in the set, looking for clues

- **Focus all your energy here** instead of diluting it over the whole set of questions; solving a multi-part question in pieces is far simpler than trying to solve all the questions in the set at once. Furthermore, you may be able to use the results from earlier parts to solve subsequent ones. Don't even consider the later parts of the question set until you've solved the first part.

- **Watch for hints** about what information you'll actually need to use to answer the questions. Underlining key quantities is often helpful to separate what's important from extraneous information.

Step 2: Identify and organize the information you need

- **What information am I given?** Jot down key notes, and group-related quantities to develop your strategy.

- **What am I solving for?** This is your target. As you work your way through subsequent steps, keep your target at the front of your mind. This will help you avoid unnecessary work (and subsequent time loss). You'll sometimes need to tackle these problems from both ends, so always keep your goal in mind.

Step 3: Based on what you know, plan your steps to navigate the first question

- **What pieces am I missing?** Many students become frustrated when faced with a roadblock such as missing information, but it's an easy fix. Sometimes you'll need to do an intermediate calculation to reveal the missing piece or pieces of the puzzle.

Step 4: Solve, step-by-step, checking units as you go

- **Work quickly but carefully**, just as you've done on other SAT math questions.

Step 5: Did I answer the *right* question?

- As is the case with the Kaplan Method for Math, **make sure your final answer is the requested answer.**

- Review the first question in the set.

- Double-check your units and your work.

Step 6: Repeat for remaining questions, incorporating results from the previous question if possible

Now take your results from the first question and think critically about whether they fit into the subsequent questions in the set. Previous results won't always be applicable, but when they are, they often lead to huge time savings. But be careful—don't round results from the first question in your calculations for the second question—only the final answer should be rounded.

KAPLAN METHOD FOR READING COMPREHENSION

Step 1: Read actively

Step 2: Examine the question stem

Step 3: Predict and answer

Step 1: Read actively

Active reading means:

- Ask questions and take notes *as* you read the passage. Asking questions about the passage and taking notes are integral parts of your approach to acing the SAT Reading Test.

Some of the questions you might want to ask are:

- Why did the author write this word/detail/sentence/paragraph?

- Is the author taking a side? If so, what side is he or she taking?

- What are the tone and purpose of the passage?

Make sure you remember to:

- Identify the passage type.

- Take notes, circle keywords, and underline key phrases.

Step 2: Examine the question stem

This means you should:

- Identify keywords and line references in the question stem.

- Apply question-type strategies as necessary.

Step 3: Predict and answer

This means you should:

- Predict an answer before looking at the answer choices, also known as "predict before you peek."

- Select the best match.

Predicting before you peek helps you:

- Eliminate the possibility of falling into wrong answer traps.

KAPLAN METHOD FOR INFOGRAPHICS

Step 1: Read the question

Step 2: Examine the infographic

Step 3: Predict and answer

Step 1: Read the question

- Analyze the question stem for information that will help you zero in on the specific parts of the infographic that apply to the question.

Step 2: Examine the infographic

- Circle parts of the infographic that relate directly to the question.

- Identify units of measurement, labels, and titles.

Step 3: Predict and answer

- Do not look at the answer choices until you've used the infographic to make a prediction.

KAPLAN METHOD FOR WRITING & LANGUAGE

Step 1: Read the passage and identify the issue

- If there's an infographic, apply the Kaplan Method for Infographics.

Step 2: Eliminate answer choices that do not address the issue

Step 3: Plug in the remaining answer choices and select the most correct, concise, and relevant one

Step 1: Read the passage and identify the issue

This means:

- Rather than reading the whole passage and then answering all of the questions, you can answer questions as you read because they are mostly embedded in the text itself.

- When you see a number, stop reading and look at the question. If you can answer it with what you've read so far, do so. If you need more information, keep reading for context until you can answer the question.

Step 2: Eliminate answer choices that do not address the issue

Eliminating answer choices that do not address the issue:

- Increases your odds of getting the correct answer by removing obviously incorrect answer choices

Step 3: Plug in the remaining answer choices and select the most correct, concise, and relevant one

Correct, concise, and relevant means that the answer choice you select:

- Makes sense when read with the correction

- Is as short as possible while retaining the information in the text

- Relates well to the passage overall

Answer choices should not:

- Change the intended meaning of the original sentence, paragraph, or passage

- Introduce new grammatical errors

KAPLAN METHOD FOR THE SAT ESSAY

Step 1: Read the source text, taking notes on how the author uses:

- Evidence to support claims
- Reasoning to develop ideas and to connect claims and evidence
- Stylistic or persuasive elements to add power to the ideas expressed

Step 2: Use the Kaplan Template to create an outline

Step 3: Write your essay

Step 4: Check your essay for mistakes in grammar, spelling, and clarity

Step 1: Read the source text, taking notes on how the author uses:

- **Evidence to support claims**
- **Reasoning to develop ideas and to connect claims and evidence**
- **Stylistic or persuasive elements to add power to the ideas expressed**

Your notes should focus on:

- Evidence to support claims (e.g., cited data or statistics, or authoritative sources that support the author's argument)
- Reasoning to develop ideas and make connections (e.g., the author explains his logic for using a specific piece of evidence to support a specific claim)
- Stylistic or persuasive elements to add power to the ideas expressed (e.g., using figurative language, irony, metaphor, and other elements to appeal to emotions)

In addition to taking notes in the margins of the passage, it is also helpful to underline and circle the following:

- Central ideas
- Important details
- Errors of fact or interpretation
- Textual evidence (quotations, paraphrases, or both)

You should spend approximately 10 minutes on Step 1.

Step 2: Use the Kaplan Template to create an outline

Using the Kaplan Template to create an outline before you write your essay is a huge time-saver, which is essential when you have only 50 minutes to complete the SAT Essay Test. Spending the first part of the allotted time effectively (i.e., reading and taking notes on the source text and creating an outline) will lead to a well-organized, more convincing essay. You'll also find that organizing your thoughts ahead of time will enable you to write much more quickly!

You should spend approximately 8 minutes on Step 2.

Step 3: Write your essay

After you have read and analyzed the source text, your next goal is to write a cohesive essay that demonstrates your use and command of standard written English. To demonstrate your proficiency, you must:

- Provide your own precise central claim.
- Use a variety of sentence structures.
- Employ precise word choice.
- Maintain a constant and appropriate style and tone.

You should spend approximately 30 minutes on Step 3.

Step 4: Check your essay for mistakes in grammar, spelling, and clarity

While a few grammar and spelling mistakes won't drastically harm your SAT Essay score, setting aside some time to proofread can help you catch careless errors that you can easily correct, thereby increasing your Writing score on the SAT Essay.

You should spend the remaining 2 minutes on Step 4.

KAPLAN STRATEGY FOR TRANSLATING ENGLISH INTO MATH

- Define any variables, choosing letters that make sense.

- Break sentences into short phrases.

- Translate each phrase into a mathematical expression.

- Put the expressions together to form an equation.

KAPLAN STRATEGY FOR COMMAND OF EVIDENCE QUESTIONS

- When you see a question asking you to choose the best evidence to support your answer to the previous question, review how you selected that answer.

- Avoid answers that provide evidence for incorrect answers to the previous question.

- The correct answer will support why the previous question's answer is correct.

KAPLAN STRATEGY FOR VOCAB-IN-CONTEXT QUESTIONS

- Pretend the word is a blank in the sentence.

- Predict what word could be substituted for the blank.

- Select the answer choice that best matches your prediction.

KAPLAN STRATEGY FOR PAIRED PASSAGES

- Read Passage 1, then answer its questions.

- Read Passage 2, then answer its questions.

- Answer questions about both passages.

COUNTDOWN TO TEST DAY

The Week Before the Test

- Finish up any required homework assignments, including online quizzes.

- Focus your additional practice on the question types and/or subject areas in which you usually score highest. Now is the time to sharpen your best skills, not cram new information.

- Make sure you are registered for the test. Remember, Kaplan cannot register you. If you missed the registration deadlines, you can request Waitlist Status on the test maker's website, collegeboard.org.

- Confirm the location of your test site. Never been there before? Make a practice run to make sure you know exactly how long it will take to get from your home to your test site. Build in extra time in case you hit traffic on the morning of the test.

- Get a great night's sleep the two days before the test.

The Day Before the Test

- Review the Kaplan Methods and Strategies, as well as the ReKap pages.

- Put new batteries in your calculator.

- Pack your backpack or bag for Test Day with the following items:

  - Photo ID
  - Registration slip or printout
  - Directions to your test site location
  - Five or more sharpened no. 2 pencils (no mechanical pencils)
  - Pencil sharpener
  - Eraser
  - Calculator
  - Extra batteries
  - Non-prohibited timepiece
  - Tissues
  - Prepackaged snacks, like granola bars
  - Bottled water, juice, or sports drink
  - Sweatshirt, sweater, or jacket

The Night Before the Test

- No studying!

- Do something relaxing that will take your mind off the test, such as watching a movie or playing video games with friends.

- Set your alarm to wake up early enough so that you won't feel rushed.

- Go to bed early, but not too much earlier than you usually do. You want to fall asleep quickly, not spend hours tossing and turning.

The Morning of the Test

- Dress comfortably and in layers. You need to be prepared for any temperature.

- Eat a filling breakfast, but don't stray too far from your usual routine. If you normally aren't a breakfast eater, don't eat a huge meal, but make sure you have something substantial.

- Read something over breakfast. You need to warm up your brain so you don't go into the test cold. Read a few pages of a newspaper, magazine, or novel.

- Get to your test site early. There is likely to be some confusion about where to go and how to sign in, so allow yourself plenty of time, even if you are taking the test at your own school.

- Leave your cell phone at home or in your car's glovebox. Many test sites do not allow them in the building.

- While you're waiting to sign in or be seated, read more of what you read over breakfast to stay in reading mode.

During the Test

- Be calm and confident. You're ready for this!

- Remember that while the SAT is a three-hour marathon (or four if you opt to do the essay), it is also a series of shorter sections. Focus on the section you're working on at that moment; don't think about previous or upcoming sections.

- Use the Kaplan Methods and Strategies as often as you can.

- Don't linger too long on any one question. Mark it and come back to it later.

- Can't figure out an answer? Try to eliminate some choices and guess strategically. Remember, there is no penalty for an incorrect answer, so even if you can't eliminate any choices, you should take a guess.

- There will be plenty of questions you CAN answer, so spend your time on those first!

- Maintain good posture throughout the test. It will help you stay alert.

- If you find yourself losing concentration, getting frustrated, or stressing about the time, stop for 30 seconds. Close your eyes, put your pencil down, take a few deep breaths, and relax your shoulders. You'll be much more productive after taking a few moments to relax.

- Use your breaks effectively. During the five-minute breaks, go to the restroom, eat your snacks, and get your energy up for the next section.

After the Test

- Congratulate yourself! Also, reward yourself by doing something fun. You've earned it.

- If you got sick during the test or if something else happened that might have negatively affected your score, you can cancel your scores by the Wednesday following your test date. Request a score cancellation form from your test proctor, or visit the test maker's website for more information. If you have questions about whether you should cancel your scores, call 1-800-KAP-TEST.

- Your scores will be available online approximately three to four weeks after your test and will be mailed to you in approximately six weeks.

- Email your instructor or tutor with your SAT scores. We want to hear how you did!

PART FIVE

Practice Tests

HOW TO SCORE YOUR PRACTICE TESTS

For each subject area in the practice test, convert your raw score, or the number of questions you answered correctly, to a scaled score using the table below. To get your raw score for Evidence-Based Reading & Writing, add the total number of Reading questions you answered correctly to the total number of Writing questions you answered correctly; for Math, add the number of questions you answered correctly for the Math—No Calculator and Math—Calculator sections.

Evidence-Based Reading and Writing		Math		Evidence-Based Reading and Writing		Math	
TOTAL Raw Score	Scaled Score	Raw Score	Scaled Score	TOTAL Raw Score	Scaled Score	Raw Score	Scaled Score
0	200	0	200	49	490	49	700
1	200	1	220	50	500	50	710
2	210	2	240	51	500	51	720
3	220	3	260	52	510	52	740
4	240	4	290	53	510	53	750
5	260	5	310	54	520	54	760
6	270	6	320	55	520	55	770
7	270	7	330	56	530	56	780
8	290	8	340	57	530	57	790
9	290	9	360	58	540	58	800
10	300	10	370	59	540		
11	300	11	380	60	550		
12	310	12	390	61	550		
13	320	13	400	62	560		
14	320	14	410	63	560		
15	330	15	420	64	570		
16	330	16	430	65	570		
17	340	17	430	66	580		
18	340	18	440	67	580		
19	350	19	450	68	590		
20	350	20	450	69	590		
21	360	21	460	70	600		
22	360	22	470	71	600		
23	370	23	480	72	610		
24	370	24	490	73	610		
25	370	25	500	74	610		
26	380	26	510	75	620		
27	380	27	520	76	620		
28	380	28	530	77	630		
29	380	29	540	78	630		
30	390	30	540	79	640		
31	390	31	550	80	640		
32	400	32	560	81	660		
33	400	33	560	82	660		
34	410	34	570	83	670		
35	410	35	580	84	680		
36	420	36	590	85	690		
37	430	37	600	86	700		
38	430	38	600	87	700		
39	440	39	610	88	710		
40	440	40	620	89	710		
41	450	41	630	90	730		
42	450	42	640	91	740		
43	460	43	640	92	750		
44	460	44	660	93	760		
45	470	45	670	94	780		
46	480	46	670	95	790		
47	480	47	680	96	800		
48	490	48	690				

SAT DIAGNOSTIC TEST ANSWER SHEET

Remove (or photocopy) this answer sheet and use it to complete the test. See the answer key following the test when finished.

Start with number 1 for each section. If a section has fewer questions than answer spaces, leave the extra spaces blank.

SECTION

1

1. Ⓐ Ⓑ Ⓒ Ⓓ	14. Ⓐ Ⓑ Ⓒ Ⓓ	27. Ⓐ Ⓑ Ⓒ Ⓓ	40. Ⓐ Ⓑ Ⓒ Ⓓ
2. Ⓐ Ⓑ Ⓒ Ⓓ	15. Ⓐ Ⓑ Ⓒ Ⓓ	28. Ⓐ Ⓑ Ⓒ Ⓓ	41. Ⓐ Ⓑ Ⓒ Ⓓ
3. Ⓐ Ⓑ Ⓒ Ⓓ	16. Ⓐ Ⓑ Ⓒ Ⓓ	29. Ⓐ Ⓑ Ⓒ Ⓓ	42. Ⓐ Ⓑ Ⓒ Ⓓ
4. Ⓐ Ⓑ Ⓒ Ⓓ	17. Ⓐ Ⓑ Ⓒ Ⓓ	30. Ⓐ Ⓑ Ⓒ Ⓓ	43. Ⓐ Ⓑ Ⓒ Ⓓ
5. Ⓐ Ⓑ Ⓒ Ⓓ	18. Ⓐ Ⓑ Ⓒ Ⓓ	31. Ⓐ Ⓑ Ⓒ Ⓓ	44. Ⓐ Ⓑ Ⓒ Ⓓ
6. Ⓐ Ⓑ Ⓒ Ⓓ	19. Ⓐ Ⓑ Ⓒ Ⓓ	32. Ⓐ Ⓑ Ⓒ Ⓓ	45. Ⓐ Ⓑ Ⓒ Ⓓ
7. Ⓐ Ⓑ Ⓒ Ⓓ	20. Ⓐ Ⓑ Ⓒ Ⓓ	33. Ⓐ Ⓑ Ⓒ Ⓓ	46. Ⓐ Ⓑ Ⓒ Ⓓ
8. Ⓐ Ⓑ Ⓒ Ⓓ	21. Ⓐ Ⓑ Ⓒ Ⓓ	34. Ⓐ Ⓑ Ⓒ Ⓓ	47. Ⓐ Ⓑ Ⓒ Ⓓ
9. Ⓐ Ⓑ Ⓒ Ⓓ	22. Ⓐ Ⓑ Ⓒ Ⓓ	35. Ⓐ Ⓑ Ⓒ Ⓓ	48. Ⓐ Ⓑ Ⓒ Ⓓ
10. Ⓐ Ⓑ Ⓒ Ⓓ	23. Ⓐ Ⓑ Ⓒ Ⓓ	36. Ⓐ Ⓑ Ⓒ Ⓓ	49. Ⓐ Ⓑ Ⓒ Ⓓ
11. Ⓐ Ⓑ Ⓒ Ⓓ	24. Ⓐ Ⓑ Ⓒ Ⓓ	37. Ⓐ Ⓑ Ⓒ Ⓓ	50. Ⓐ Ⓑ Ⓒ Ⓓ
12. Ⓐ Ⓑ Ⓒ Ⓓ	25. Ⓐ Ⓑ Ⓒ Ⓓ	38. Ⓐ Ⓑ Ⓒ Ⓓ	51. Ⓐ Ⓑ Ⓒ Ⓓ
13. Ⓐ Ⓑ Ⓒ Ⓓ	26. Ⓐ Ⓑ Ⓒ Ⓓ	39. Ⓐ Ⓑ Ⓒ Ⓓ	52. Ⓐ Ⓑ Ⓒ Ⓓ

☐ # correct in Section 1

☐ # incorrect in Section 1

SECTION

2

1. Ⓐ Ⓑ Ⓒ Ⓓ	12. Ⓐ Ⓑ Ⓒ Ⓓ	23. Ⓐ Ⓑ Ⓒ Ⓓ	34. Ⓐ Ⓑ Ⓒ Ⓓ
2. Ⓐ Ⓑ Ⓒ Ⓓ	13. Ⓐ Ⓑ Ⓒ Ⓓ	24. Ⓐ Ⓑ Ⓒ Ⓓ	35. Ⓐ Ⓑ Ⓒ Ⓓ
3. Ⓐ Ⓑ Ⓒ Ⓓ	14. Ⓐ Ⓑ Ⓒ Ⓓ	25. Ⓐ Ⓑ Ⓒ Ⓓ	36. Ⓐ Ⓑ Ⓒ Ⓓ
4. Ⓐ Ⓑ Ⓒ Ⓓ	15. Ⓐ Ⓑ Ⓒ Ⓓ	26. Ⓐ Ⓑ Ⓒ Ⓓ	37. Ⓐ Ⓑ Ⓒ Ⓓ
5. Ⓐ Ⓑ Ⓒ Ⓓ	16. Ⓐ Ⓑ Ⓒ Ⓓ	27. Ⓐ Ⓑ Ⓒ Ⓓ	38. Ⓐ Ⓑ Ⓒ Ⓓ
6. Ⓐ Ⓑ Ⓒ Ⓓ	17. Ⓐ Ⓑ Ⓒ Ⓓ	28. Ⓐ Ⓑ Ⓒ Ⓓ	39. Ⓐ Ⓑ Ⓒ Ⓓ
7. Ⓐ Ⓑ Ⓒ Ⓓ	18. Ⓐ Ⓑ Ⓒ Ⓓ	29. Ⓐ Ⓑ Ⓒ Ⓓ	40. Ⓐ Ⓑ Ⓒ Ⓓ
8. Ⓐ Ⓑ Ⓒ Ⓓ	19. Ⓐ Ⓑ Ⓒ Ⓓ	30. Ⓐ Ⓑ Ⓒ Ⓓ	41. Ⓐ Ⓑ Ⓒ Ⓓ
9. Ⓐ Ⓑ Ⓒ Ⓓ	20. Ⓐ Ⓑ Ⓒ Ⓓ	31. Ⓐ Ⓑ Ⓒ Ⓓ	42. Ⓐ Ⓑ Ⓒ Ⓓ
10. Ⓐ Ⓑ Ⓒ Ⓓ	21. Ⓐ Ⓑ Ⓒ Ⓓ	32. Ⓐ Ⓑ Ⓒ Ⓓ	43. Ⓐ Ⓑ Ⓒ Ⓓ
11. Ⓐ Ⓑ Ⓒ Ⓓ	22. Ⓐ Ⓑ Ⓒ Ⓓ	33. Ⓐ Ⓑ Ⓒ Ⓓ	44. Ⓐ Ⓑ Ⓒ Ⓓ

☐ # correct in Section 2

☐ # incorrect in Section 2

Practice Tests

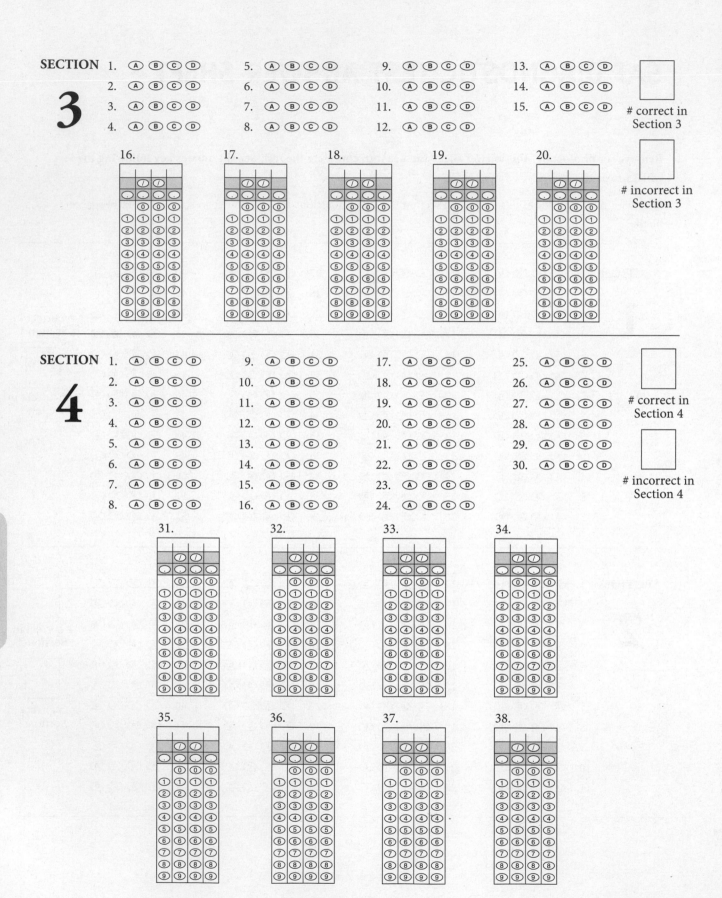

READING TEST

65 Minutes—52 Questions

Turn to Section 1 of your answer sheet to answer the questions in this section.

Directions: Each passage or pair of passages below is followed by a number of questions. After reading each passage or pair, choose the best answer to each question based on what is stated or implied in the passage or passages and in any accompanying graphics (such as a table or graph).

Questions 1-10 are based on the following passage.

The following passage is adapted from Leo Tolstoy's 1873 novel, *Anna Karenina* (translated from the original Russian by Constance Garnett). Prior to this excerpt, one of the major characters, Levin, has realized that he is in love with his longtime friend Kitty Shtcherbatsky.

At four o'clock, conscious of his throbbing heart,
Levin stepped out of a hired sledge at the
Zoological Gardens, and turned along the path
Line to the frozen mounds and the skating ground,
(5) knowing that he would certainly find her there,
as he had seen the Shtcherbatskys' carriage at the
entrance.

It was a bright, frosty day. Rows of carriages,
sledges, drivers, and policemen were standing in the
(10) approach. Crowds of well-dressed people, with hats
bright in the sun, swarmed about the entrance and
along the well-swept little paths between the little
houses adorned with carving in the Russian style.
The old curly birches of the gardens, all their twigs
(15) laden with snow, looked as though freshly decked
in sacred vestments.

He walked along the path towards the skating-
ground, and kept saying to himself—"You mustn't
be excited, you must be calm. What's the matter
(20) with you? What do you want? Be quiet, stupid,"
he conjured his heart. And the more he tried to
compose himself, the more breathless he found
himself. An acquaintance met him and called him
by his name, but Levin did not even recognize
(25) him. He went towards the mounds, whence came
the clank of the chains of sledges as they slipped
down or were dragged up, the rumble of the sliding

sledges, and the sounds of merry voices. He walked
on a few steps, and the skating-ground lay open
(30) before his eyes, and at once, amidst all the skaters,
he knew her.

He knew she was there by the rapture and the
terror that seized on his heart. She was standing
talking to a lady at the opposite end of the ground.
(35) There was apparently nothing striking either in
her dress or her attitude. But for Levin she was as
easy to find in that crowd as a rose among nettles.
Everything was made bright by her. She was the
smile that shed light on all round her. "Is it possible
(40) I can go over there on the ice, go up to her?" he
thought. The place where she stood seemed to
him a holy shrine, unapproachable, and there was
one moment when he was almost retreating, so
overwhelmed was he with terror. He had to make
(45) an effort to master himself, and to remind himself
that people of all sorts were moving about her, and
that he too might come there to skate. He walked
down, for a long while avoiding looking at her
as at the sun, but seeing her, as one does the sun,
(50) without looking.

On that day of the week and at that time of day
people of one set, all acquainted with one another,
used to meet on the ice. There were crack skaters
there, showing off their skill, and learners clinging
(55) to chairs with timid, awkward movements, boys,
and elderly people skating with hygienic motives.
They seemed to Levin an elect band of blissful beings because they were here, near her. All the skaters, it seemed, with perfect self-possession, skated
(60) towards her, skated by her, even spoke to her, and
were happy, quite apart from her, enjoying the capital ice and the fine weather.

GO ON TO THE NEXT PAGE

Practice Tests

Nikolay Shtcherbatsky, Kitty's cousin, in a short jacket and tight trousers, was sitting on a garden seat
(65) with his skates on. Seeing Levin, he shouted to him:
"Ah, the first skater in Russia! Been here long? First-rate ice—do put your skates on."

1. According to the passage, how did Levin first know that Kitty was at the Zoological Gardens?

   A) Kitty's carriage was parked near the entrance.

   B) Nikolay said he had been skating with Kitty earlier.

   C) He saw her talking with another woman near the pond.

   D) Kitty invited him to meet her there at a certain time.

2. As used in line 11, "swarmed" most nearly means

   A) invaded.

   B) gathered.

   C) flew.

   D) obstructed.

3. The passage most strongly suggests that which of the following is true of Levin?

   A) He worries about his appearance.

   B) He wants Kitty to be more enthusiastic.

   C) He is a very passionate person.

   D) He is wary of his surroundings.

4. Which choice provides the best evidence for the answer to the previous question?

   A) Lines 8-13 ("It was a bright, frosty day . . . in the Russian style")

   B) Lines 23-28 ("An acquaintance met him . . . merry voices")

   C) Lines 41-47 ("The place where . . . there to skate")

   D) Lines 51-56 ("On that day . . . hygienic motives")

5. What theme does the passage communicate through the experiences of Levin?

   A) Love is a powerful emotion.

   B) People long to have company.

   C) Life should be filled with joy.

   D) People are meant to work hard.

6. The passage most strongly suggests that which of the following is true of how Levin appears to others?

   A) People think that Levin looks agitated because of the way he is acting.

   B) People think that Levin is sick because he seems to be feverish.

   C) People think that Levin seems normal because he is doing nothing unusual.

   D) People think that Levin is in trouble because he is not protecting himself emotionally.

7. Which choice provides the best evidence for the answer to the previous question?

   A) Lines 1-6 ("At four o'clock . . . at the entrance")

   B) Lines 10-13 ("Crowds . . . the Russian style")

   C) Lines 25-31 ("He went . . . he knew her")

   D) Lines 63-67 ("Nikolay Shtcherbatsky . . . your skates on")

8. As used in line 21, "conjured" most nearly means

   A) begged.

   B) created.

   C) summoned.

   D) tricked.

9. The author's use of the word "throbbing" in line 1 implies that Levin

   A) has cut himself badly.

   B) has a sudden pain in his chest.

   C) is about to collapse.

   D) is in an agitated state.

GO ON TO THE NEXT PAGE ⇨

10. Based on the tone of this passage, what emotion does the author wish the reader to feel about Levin?

   A) Empathy

   B) Cynicism

   C) Hostility

   D) Disgust

Questions 11-20 are based on the following passage.

This passage is adapted from a speech delivered by President Franklin Roosevelt on January 6, 1941, to the United States Congress. In the passage, Roosevelt reveals his intention to preserve and spread American ideals around the world.

The Nation takes great satisfaction and much strength from the things which have been done to make its people conscious of their
Line individual stake in the preservation of democratic
(5) life in America. Those things have toughened the fibre of our people, have renewed their faith and strengthened their devotion to the institutions we make ready to protect.

Certainly this is no time for any of us to stop
(10) thinking about the social and economic problems which are the root cause of the social revolution which is today a supreme factor in the world.

For there is nothing mysterious about the foundations of a healthy and strong democracy.
(15) The basic things expected by our people of their political and economic systems are simple. They are:

• Equality of opportunity for youth and for others.

• Jobs for those who can work.

• Security for those who need it.

(20) • The ending of special privilege for the few.

• The preservation of civil liberties for all.

• The enjoyment of the fruits of scientific progress in a wider and constantly rising standard of living.
These are the simple, basic things that
(25) must never be lost sight of in the turmoil and unbelievable complexity of our modern world. The

inner and abiding strength of our economic and political systems is dependent upon the degree to which they fulfill these expectations.
(30) Many subjects connected with our social economy call for immediate improvement.

As examples:

• We should bring more citizens under the coverage of old-age pensions and unemployment insurance.

(35) • We should widen the opportunities for adequate medical care.

• We should plan a better system by which persons deserving or needing gainful employment may obtain it.

(40) I have called for personal sacrifice. I am assured of the willingness of almost all Americans to respond to that call.

A part of the sacrifice means the payment of more money in taxes. In my Budget Message I
(45) shall recommend that a greater portion of this great defense program be paid for from taxation than we are paying today. No person should try, or be allowed, to get rich out of this program; and the principle of tax payments in accordance with
(50) ability to pay should be constantly before our eyes to guide our legislation.

If the Congress maintains these principles, the voters, putting patriotism ahead of pocketbooks, will give you their applause.

(55) In the future days, which we seek to make secure, we look forward to a world founded upon four essential human freedoms.

The first is freedom of speech and expression—everywhere in the world.

(60) The second is freedom of every person to worship God in his own way—everywhere in the world.

The third is freedom from want—which, translated into world terms, means economic understandings which will secure to every nation
(65) a healthy peacetime life for its inhabitants—everywhere in the world.

The fourth is freedom from fear—which, translated into world terms, means a world-wide reduction of armaments to such a point and in
(70) such a thorough fashion that no nation will be in

GO ON TO THE NEXT PAGE

a position to commit an act of physical aggression against any neighbor—anywhere in the world.

That is no vision of a distant millennium. It is a definite basis for a kind of world attainable in (75) our own time and generation. That kind of world is the very antithesis of the so-called new order of tyranny which the dictators seek to create with the crash of a bomb.

To that new order we oppose the greater (80) conception—the moral order. A good society is able to face schemes of world domination and foreign revolutions alike without fear.

Since the beginning of our American history, we have been engaged in change—in a perpetual (85) peaceful revolution—a revolution which goes on steadily, quietly adjusting itself to changing conditions—without the concentration camp or the quick-lime in the ditch. The world order which we seek is the cooperation of free countries, working (90) together in a friendly, civilized society.

This nation has placed its destiny in the hands and heads and hearts of its millions of free men and women; and its faith in freedom under the guidance of God. Freedom means the supremacy (95) of human rights everywhere. Our support goes to those who struggle to gain those rights or keep them. Our strength is our unity of purpose. To that high concept there can be no end save victory.

11. The primary purpose of President Roosevelt's speech is to

   A) highlight the individuality inherent in patriotism.

   B) define the basic needs of the country.

   C) request money to support worthy causes.

   D) promote support for essential human rights.

12. Which choice provides the best evidence for the answer to the previous question?

   A) Lines 15-16 ("The basic things . . . are simple")

   B) Lines 30-31 ("Many subjects . . . improvement")

   C) Lines 52-54 ("If the Congress . . . applause")

   D) Lines 55-57 ("In the future days . . . freedoms")

13. As used in line 40, "sacrifice" most nearly means

   A) religious offerings to a deity.

   B) service in the military.

   C) losses of limbs in battle.

   D) surrender of interests to a greater good.

14. The passage most strongly suggests a relationship between which of the following?

   A) Protection of human rights abroad and military service

   B) Spread of freedom abroad and defense of democracy at home

   C) Defeat of tyrants abroad and establishment of democratic government at home

   D) Investment in global democracies abroad and strengthening of patriotism at home

15. Which choice provides the best evidence for the answer to the previous question?

   A) Lines 24-29 ("These are . . . expectations")

   B) Lines 52-54 ("If the Congress . . . applause")

   C) Lines 73-78 ("That is no . . . of a bomb")

   D) Lines 94-97 ("Freedom means . . . unity of purpose")

16. In line 53, "pocketbooks" most nearly refers to

   A) local, state, and national taxes.

   B) war debt accumulated by the nation.

   C) citizens' individual monetary interests.

   D) Americans' personal investment in the defense industry.

GO ON TO THE NEXT PAGE

17. In lines 73-75 ("That is no . . . generation"), President Roosevelt is most likely responding to what counterclaim to his own argument?

   A) The spread of global democracy is idealistic and unrealistic.

   B) The defeat of tyrannical dictators in Europe is implausible.

   C) The commitment of the American people to the war effort is limited.

   D) The resources of the United States are insufficient to wage war abroad.

18. Which choice offers evidence that the spread of global democracy is achievable?

   A) Lines 47-48 ("No person . . . this program")

   B) Lines 56-57 ("we look forward . . . human freedoms")

   C) Lines 83-84 ("Since the beginning . . . in change")

   D) Line 97 ("Our strength . . . purpose")

19. In lines 62-66 ("The third is . . . world"), President Roosevelt sets a precedent by which he would most likely support which of the following policies?

   A) Military defense of political borders

   B) Investment in overseas business ventures

   C) Aid to nations struggling due to conflict and other causes

   D) Reduction of domestic services to spur job growth

20. The function of the phrase "the so-called new order of tyranny" in lines 76-77 is to

   A) connect the global conflict for human rights to citizens on a personal level.

   B) demonstrate the power of the global opposition to the United States.

   C) present an alternative vision of the world without democracy.

   D) provide examples of the political and social revolutions underway.

Questions 21-31 are based on the following passage and supplementary material.

The United States Constitution has been amended 27 times since its ratification. Rights such as freedom of speech, religion, and press, for example, are granted by the First Amendment. This passage focuses on the Nineteenth Amendment, which gave women the right to vote.

The American political landscape is constantly shifting on a myriad of issues, but the voting process itself has changed over the years as well. Electronic
Line ballot casting, for example, provides the
(5) public with instantaneous results, and statisticians are more accurate than ever at forecasting our next president. Voting has always been viewed as an intrinsic American right and was one of the major reasons for the nation's secession from Britain's
(10) monarchical rule. Unfortunately, although all men were constitutionally deemed "equal," true equality of the sexes was not extended to the voting booth until 1920.
   The American women's suffrage movement
(15) began in 1848, when Elizabeth Cady Stanton and Lucretia Mott organized the Seneca Falls Convention. The meeting, initially an attempt to have an open dialogue about women's rights, drew a crowd of nearly three hundred women and
(20) included several dozen men. Topics ranged from a woman's role in society to law, but the issue of voting remained a contentious one. A freed slave named Frederick Douglass spoke eloquently about the importance of women in politics and swayed
(25) the opinion of those in attendance. At the end of the convention, one hundred people signed the Seneca Falls Declaration, which demanded "immediate admission to all the rights and privileges which belong to [women] as citizens of the United States."
(30)   Stanton and Mott's first victory came thirty years later when a constitutional amendment allowing women to vote was proposed to Congress in 1878. Unfortunately, election practices were already a controversial issue, as unfair laws that diminished
(35) the African American vote had been passed during

GO ON TO THE NEXT PAGE

Reconstruction. Questionable literacy tests and a "vote tax" levied against the poor kept minority turnout to a minimum. And while several states allowed women to vote, federal consensus was hardly
(40) as equitable. The rest of the world, however, was taking note—and women were ready to act.

In 1893, New Zealand allowed women the right to vote, although women could not run for office in New Zealand. Other countries began reviewing
(45) and ratifying their own laws as well. The United Kingdom took small steps by allowing married women to vote in local elections in 1894. By 1902, all women in Australia could vote in elections, both local and parliamentary.

(50) The suffrage movement in America slowly built momentum throughout the early twentieth century and exploded during World War I. President Woodrow Wilson called the fight abroad a war for democracy, which many suffragettes viewed as
(55) hypocritical. Democracy, after all, was hardly worth fighting for when half of a nation's population was disqualified based on gender. Public acts of civil disobedience, rallies, and marches galvanized pro-women advocates while undermining defenders
(60) of the status quo. Posters read "Kaiser Wilson" and called into question the authenticity of a free country with unjust laws. The cry for equality was impossible to ignore and, in 1919, with the support of President Wilson, Congress passed
(65) the Nineteenth Amendment to the Constitution. It was ratified one year later by three-quarters of the states, effectively changing the Constitution. Only one signatory from the original Seneca Falls Declaration lived long enough to cast her first ballot
(70) in a federal election.

America's election laws were far from equal for all, as tactics to dissuade or prohibit African Americans from effectively voting were still routinely employed. However, the suffrage
(75) movement laid the groundwork for future generations. Laws, like people's minds, could change over time. The civil rights movement in the mid-to late-twentieth century brought an end to segregation and so-called Jim Crow laws that stifled
(80) African American advancement. The Voting Rights Act of 1965 signaled the end of discriminatory

voting laws; what emerged was a free nation guided by elections in which neither skin color nor gender mattered, but only the will of all citizens.

Women's Suffrage in the United States

1848 ➤ Seneca Falls Convention.

1878 ➤ 19th Amendment submitted; not ratified.

1911 ➤ Several states now grant women suffrage.

1914 ➤ Start of World War I.

1917 ➤ Picketing at the White House.

1918 ➤ Amendment passes in the House but fails in the Senate.

1919 ➤ Both the House and Senate pass the amendment.

1920 ➤ 19th Amendment ratified.

21. The stance the author takes in the passage is best described as that of

A) an advocate of women's suffrage proposing a constitutional amendment.

B) a legislator reviewing the arguments for and against women's suffrage.

C) a scholar evaluating the evolution and impact of the women's suffrage movement.

D) a historian summarizing the motivations of women's suffrage leaders.

22. Lines 71-72 ("America's election laws . . . equal for all") most clearly support which claim?

A) The founders of the Constitution did not provide for free and fair elections.

B) The United States still had work to do to secure equal voting rights for some people.

C) Most women in the United States did not want suffrage and equal rights.

D) The women's suffrage movement perpetuated discriminatory voting laws.

GO ON TO THE NEXT PAGE ⟩

23. Which choice provides the best evidence for the answer to the previous question?

    A) Lines 14-15 ("The American . . . in 1848")

    B) Lines 42-43 ("In 1893 . . . to vote")

    C) Lines 64-65 ("Congress . . . the Constitution")

    D) Lines 80-81 ("The Voting Rights Act . . . voting laws")

24. As used in line 58, "galvanized" most nearly means

    A) displaced.

    B) divided.

    C) excited.

    D) organized.

25. The function of lines 76-77 ("Laws, like . . . could change") is to

    A) connect the success of legislative reform with shifts in public sentiment.

    B) dissuade reformers from focusing on grassroots activity rather than political campaigns.

    C) evaluate the effectiveness of judicial rulings based on popular response to public polls.

    D) reject the need for legal actions and court proceedings to attain social change.

26. The passage most strongly suggests that

    A) the American government adapts to the changing needs and ideas of society.

    B) the best-organized reform movements are most likely to achieve their goals.

    C) the nation is more vulnerable to change during the confusion of wartime.

    D) the civil rights movement would not have happened without women suffragists.

27. Which choice provides the best evidence for the answer to the previous question?

    A) Lines 3-7 ("Electronic ballot casting . . . our next president")

    B) Lines 7-10 ("Voting has . . . monarchical rule")

    C) Lines 17-20 ("The meeting . . . dozen men")

    D) Lines 77-80 ("The civil rights . . . advancement")

28. The graphic most clearly illustrates which idea?

    A) The Nineteenth Amendment happened as a result of World War I.

    B) The states slowed reform of national voting rights laws.

    C) Women's suffrage resulted from a slow evolution of events.

    D) Acts of civil disobedience won support for suffrage in Congress.

29. In line 61, the word "authenticity" most nearly means

    A) reliability.

    B) realism.

    C) legitimacy.

    D) truth.

30. The passage suggests that President Wilson contributed to the success of the women's suffrage movement by

    A) circulating government propaganda in support of women's suffrage.

    B) framing the fight in World War I as a fight for democracy and freedom.

    C) engaging in a foreign war to distract the nation from political debate.

    D) working with legislators to write the Nineteenth Amendment.

31. The graphic helps support which statement referred to in the passage?

   A) Early women suffragists did not live to vote in national elections.

   B) The Nineteenth Amendment passed within a few years of its introduction.

   C) A majority of state representatives opposed women's suffrage in 1918.

   D) Many state governments approved suffrage before the federal government did.

Questions 32-42 are based on the following passages and supplementary material.

Passage 1 is about how scientists use radioisotopes to date artifacts and remains. Passage 2 discusses the varying problems with radioactive contaminants.

Passage 1

Archaeologists often rely on measuring the amounts of different atoms present in an item from a site to determine its age. The identity of an atom
Line depends on how many protons it has in its nucleus;
(5) for example, all carbon atoms have 6 protons. Each atom of an element, however, can have a different number of neutrons, so there can be several versions, or isotopes, of each element. Scientists name the isotopes by the total number of protons
(10) plus neutrons. For example, a carbon atom with 6 neutrons is carbon-12 while a carbon atom with 7 neutrons is carbon-13.

Some combinations of protons and neutrons are not stable and will change over time. For example,
(15) carbon-14, which has 6 protons and 8 neutrons, will slowly change into nitrogen-14, with 7 protons and 7 neutrons. Scientists can directly measure the amount of carbon-12 and carbon-14 in a sample or they can use radiation measurements to calcu-
(20) late these amounts. Each atom of carbon-14 that changes to nitrogen-14 emits radiation. Scientists can measure the rate of emission and use that to calculate the total amount of carbon-14 present in a sample.

(25) Carbon-14 atoms are formed in the atmosphere at the same rate at which they decay. Therefore,

the ratio of carbon-12 to carbon-14 atoms in the atmosphere is constant. Living plants and animals have the same ratio of carbon-12 to carbon-14 in
(30) their tissues because they are constantly taking in carbon in the form of food or carbon dioxide. After the plant or animal dies, however, it stops taking in carbon and so the amount of carbon-14 atoms in its tissues starts to decrease at a predictable rate.

(35) By measuring the ratio of carbon-12 to carbon-14 in a bone, for example, a scientist can determine how long the animal the bone came from has been dead. To determine an object's age this way is called "carbon-14 dating." Carbon-14 dating can be
(40) performed on any material made by a living organism, such as wood or paper from trees or bones and skin from animals. Materials with ages up to about 50,000 years old can be dated. By finding the age of several objects found at different depths at an
(45) archeological dig, the archeologists can then make a timeline for the layers of the site. Objects in the same layer will be about the same age. By using carbon dating for a few objects in a layer, archeologists know the age of other objects in that layer, even if
(50) the layer itself cannot be carbon dated.

Passage 2

Radioactive materials contain unstable atoms that decay, releasing energy in the form of radiation. The radiation can be harmful to living tissue because it can penetrate into cells and damage their
(55) DNA. If an explosion or a leak at a nuclear power plant releases large amounts of radioactive materials, the surrounding area could be hazardous until the amount of radioactive material drops back to normal levels. The amount of danger from the
(60) radiation and the amount of time until the areas are safe again depends on how fast the materials emit radiation.

Scientists use the "half-life" of a material to indicate how quickly it decays. The half-life of a
(65) material is the amount of time it takes for half of a sample of that material to decay. A material with a short half-life decays more quickly than a material with a long half-life. For example, io-dine-131 and cesium-137 can both be released as
(70) a result of an accident at a nuclear power plant.

GO ON TO THE NEXT PAGE ▶

Iodine-131 decays rapidly, with a half-life of 8 days. Cesium-137, however, decays more slowly, with a half-life of 30 years.

(75) If an accident releases iodine-131, therefore, it is a short-term concern. The amount of radiation emitted will be high but will drop rapidly. After two months, less than one percent of the original iodine-131 will remain. An accidental release of cesium-137, however, is a long-term concern. The

(80) amount of radiation emitted at first will be low but will drop slowly. It will take about 200 years for the amount of cesium-137 remaining to drop below one percent. The total amount of radiation emitted in both cases will be the same, for the same amount

(85) of initial material. The difference lies in whether the radiation is all released rapidly at high levels in a short time, or is released slowly at low levels, over a long time span.

Decay of Carbon-14

This data is from the *Journal of Research of the National Bureau of Standards*, Vol. 64, No. 4, April 1951, pp. 328 – 333.

32. Based on the information in Passage 1, which of the following could be dated using carbon-14 dating?

   A) An iron pot found in a cave

   B) A rock at the bottom of a quarry

   C) An arrowhead made from bone

   D) The remains of a house made from stone

33. Which choice provides the best evidence for the answer to the previous question?

   A) Lines 10-12 ("For example . . . carbon-13")

   B) Lines 28-31 ("Living plants . . . dioxide")

   C) Lines 31-34 ("After the plant . . . rate")

   D) Lines 39-42 ("Carbon-14 dating . . . animals")

34. As used in line 26, "decay" most nearly means

   A) yield.

   B) deteriorate.

   C) discharge.

   D) circulated.

35. Which statement best describes the relationship between carbon-12 and carbon-14 in living tissue?

   A) There is more carbon-14 than carbon-12.

   B) There is more carbon-12 than carbon-14.

   C) The ratio of carbon-12 to carbon-14 is constant.

   D) The ratio of carbon-12 to carbon-14 fluctuates greatly.

36. Which choice provides the best evidence for the answer to the previous question?

   A) Lines 13-14 ("Some combinations . . . time")

   B) Lines 25-26 ("Carbon-14 atoms . . . decay")

   C) Lines 28-31 ("Living plants . . . carbon dioxide")

   D) Lines 31-34 ("After the plant . . . rate")

Practice Tests

GO ON TO THE NEXT PAGE

37. In Passage 2, the author refers to an accident that results in the release of iodine-131 as a "short-term concern" (line 75) because the initial amount of radiation released is

    A) low but will drop slowly.

    B) high but will drop quickly.

    C) low and will drop quickly.

    D) high and will drop slowly.

38. According to Passage 2, living tissue exposed to radioactive material can

    A) be destroyed by high levels of heat caused by the radiation.

    B) become radioactive itself and damage surrounding tissue.

    C) suffer injury when the cells' components are damaged.

    D) be killed by extra protons released by the radioactive material.

39. As used in line 77, "original" most nearly means

    A) earliest.

    B) unique.

    C) unusual.

    D) critical.

40. According to Passage 2, scientists use the half-life of radioactive material to determine the

    A) amount of danger posed by radiation immediately following a nuclear accident.

    B) likelihood of a nuclear accident involving the release of radioactive material at any given location.

    C) amount of radiation contained in a sample of iodine-131 or cesium-137 used in nuclear reactions.

    D) length of time that must pass until an area is safe after the release of radioactive material.

41. Which generalization about the study of physics is supported by both passages?

    A) The study of atomic and nuclear physics can have many applications in a variety of fields.

    B) The study of physics has helped revolutionize how archaeologists study artifacts.

    C) Scientists use physics to keep people and wildlife safe following a nuclear accident.

    D) Scientists use different concepts to date ancient items and assess danger from nuclear accidents.

42. Based on the graph and the information in the passages, which statement is accurate?

    A) Carbon-14 has a half-life of about 5,400 years.

    B) The half-life of carbon-14 is similar to that of cesium-137.

    C) The half-life of iodine-131 is greater than that of cesium-137.

    D) All radioactive materials have a half-life of 30 to 5,400 years.

Questions 43-52 are based on the following passage and supplementary material.

The following passage is adapted from an essay about the field of biomimicry, which focuses on the design of materials and systems that are based on biological structures.

In 1948, Swiss chemist George de Mestral was impressed with the clinging power of burrs snagged in his dog's fur and on his pant legs after
Line he returned from a hike. While examining the
(5) burrs under a microscope, he observed many hundreds of small fibers that grabbed like hooks. He experimented with replicas of the burrs and eventually invented Velcro®, a synthetic clinging fabric that was first marketed as "the zipperless
(10) zipper." In the 1960s, NASA used de Mestral's invention on space suits, and now, of course, we see it everywhere.

GO ON TO THE NEXT PAGE →

You might say that de Mestral was the father of biomimicry, an increasingly essential field that (15) studies nature, looking for efficiencies in materials and systems, and asks the question "How can our homes, our electronics, and our cities work better?" As one biomimetics company puts it: "Nature is the largest laboratory that ever existed and ever will."

(20) Architecture is one field that is constantly exploring new ways to incorporate biomimicry. Architects have studied everything from beehives to beaver dams to learn how to best use materials, geometry, and physics in buildings. Termite (25) mounds, for example, very efficiently regulate temperature, humidity, and airflow, so architects in Zimbabwe are working to apply what they've learned from termite mounds to human-made structures.

Says Michael Pawlyn, author of *Biomimicry in* (30) *Architecture*, "If you look beyond the nice shapes in nature and understand the principles behind them, you can find some adaptations that can lead to new, innovative solutions that are radically more resource-efficient. It's the direction we need to take (35) in the coming decades."

Designers in various professional fields are drawing on biomimicry; for example, in optics, scientists have examined the surface of insect eyes in hopes of reducing glare on handheld device (40) screens. Engineers in the field of robotics worked to replicate the property found in a gecko's feet that allows adhesion to smooth surfaces.

Sometimes what scientists learn from nature isn't more advanced, but simpler. The abalone (45) shrimp, for example, makes its shell out of calcium carbonate, the same material as soft chalk. It's not a rare or complex substance, but the unique arrangement of the material in the abalone's shell makes it extremely tough. The walls of the shell (50) contain microscopic pieces of calcium carbonate stacked like bricks, which are bound together using proteins just as concrete mortar is used. The result is a shell three thousand times harder than chalk and as tough as Kevlar® (the material used in (55) bullet-proof vests).

Often it is necessary to look at the nanoscale structures of a living material's exceptional properties in order to re-create it synthetically. Andrew Parker, an evolutionary biologist, looked at the skin of the (60) thorny devil (a type of lizard) under a scanning electron microscope, in search of the features that let the animal channel water from its back to its mouth.

Examples like this from the animal world abound. Scientists have learned that colorful birds (65) don't always have pigment in their wings but are sometimes completely brown; it's the layers of keratin in their wings that produce color. Different colors, which have varying wavelengths, reflect differently through keratin. The discovery of this (70) phenomenon can be put to use in creating paints and cosmetics that won't fade or chip. At the same time, paint for outdoor surfaces can be made tougher by copying the structures found in antler bone. Hearing aids are being designed to capture (75) sound as well as the ears of the *Ormia* fly do. And why can't we have a self-healing material like our own skin? Researchers at the Beckman Institute at the University of Illinois are creating just that; they call it an "autonomic materials system." A raptor's (80) feathers, a whale's fluke, a mosquito's proboscis—all have functional features we can learn from.

The driving force behind these innovations, aside from improved performance, is often improved energy efficiency. In a world where (85) nonrenewable energy resources are dwindling and carbon emissions threaten the planet's health, efficiency has never been more important. Pawlyn agrees: "For me, biomimicry is one of the best sources of innovation to get to a world of zero (90) waste because those are the rules under which biological life has had to exist."

Biomimicry is a radical field and one whose practitioners need to be radically optimistic, as Pawlyn is when he says, "We could use natural (95) products such as cellulose, or even harvest carbon from the atmosphere to create bio-rock."

GO ON TO THE NEXT PAGE ➧

Practice Tests

Tiny florets in a sunflower's center are arranged in an interlocking spiral, which inspired engineers in the design of this solar power plant. Mirrors positioned at the same angle as the florets bounce light toward the power plant's central tower.

Adapted from David Ferris, "Innovate: Solar Designs from Nature." © 2014 by Sierra Club.

43. The central focus of the passage is

A) the field of biomimicry, which is the study of materials and systems found in nature and replicated in ways that benefit people.

B) the work of George de Mestral, the Swiss chemist who invented Velcro® after observing burrs under a microscope.

C) the ways in which architects use termite mounds as models for human-made structures in Zimbabwe.

D) how scientists are seeking ways to improve energy efficiency as nonrenewable energy sources decline.

44. Which choice provides the best evidence for the answer to the previous question?

A) Lines 1-6 ("In 1948 . . . hooks")

B) Lines 13-19 ("You might say . . . ever will'")

C) Lines 24-28 ("Termite mounds . . . structures")

D) Lines 82-87 ("The driving . . . more important")

45. The author includes a quote in paragraph 4 in order to

A) explain why architects are looking to biomimicry for solutions in architecture.

B) provide an argument for more scientists to study biomimicry.

C) give an explanation as to why someone might choose a career in architecture.

D) provide a counterargument to the author's central claim.

46. Based on the information in paragraph 6, how does the shell of an abalone shrimp compare with soft chalk?

A) The essential building blocks are arranged in a similar manner, but the material that makes up the shell of an abalone shrimp is harder.

B) Both are made from the same essential building blocks, but the shell of the abalone shrimp is much harder because of the manner in which the materials are arranged.

C) The essential building blocks of both are the same, but the abalone shrimp shell is harder because the soft chalk lacks a protein binding the materials together.

D) They are made from different essential building blocks, but they have a similar hardness because the materials are arranged in a similar manner.

47. In paragraph 9, what is the function of the quote from Pawlyn about efficiency?

   A) To convince readers that Pawlyn is an expert in his field

   B) To prove that great strides are being made in creating products that do not generate waste

   C) To demonstrate the limits of what biomimicry can achieve

   D) To support the statement that energy efficiency "has never been more important"

48. In line 31, "principles" most nearly means

   A) sources.

   B) attitudes.

   C) standards.

   D) concepts.

49. Of the following, the most reasonable inference from the passage is that

   A) more scientists will utilize solutions developed through biomimicry in the future.

   B) the field of biomimicry will eventually decline as more nonrenewable resources are discovered.

   C) scientists will leave the fields they are currently working in and begin research in biomimicry.

   D) doctors will create a self-healing skin called an "autonomic materials system" using methods based in biomimicry.

50. Which choice provides the best evidence for the answer to the previous question?

   A) Lines 36-40 ("Designers . . . screens")

   B) Lines 56-58 ("Often it is . . . synthetically")

   C) Lines 63-67 ("Examples like . . . color")

   D) Lines 92-96 ("Biomimicry . . . bio-rock")

51. As used in line 92, "radical" most nearly means

   A) pervasive.

   B) drastic.

   C) essential.

   D) revolutionary.

52. The graphic and caption that accompany this passage help illustrate how biomimicry can be used to

   A) make a solar plant more attractive.

   B) increase waste generated by energy sources.

   C) improve the efficiency of existing technologies.

   D) replicate a pattern common in nature.

IF YOU FINISH BEFORE TIME IS CALLED, YOU MAY CHECK YOUR WORK ON THIS SECTION ONLY. DO NOT TURN TO ANY OTHER SECTION IN THE TEST. **STOP**

Practice Tests

WRITING AND LANGUAGE TEST

35 Minutes—44 Questions

Turn to Section 2 of your answer sheet to answer the questions in this section.

Directions: Each passage below is accompanied by a number of questions. For some questions, you will consider how the passage might be revised to improve the expression of ideas. For other questions, you will consider how the passage might be edited to correct errors in sentence structure, usage, or punctuation. A passage or a question may be accompanied by one or more graphics (such as a table or graph) that you will consider as you make revising and editing decisions.

Some questions will direct you to an underlined portion of a passage. Other questions will direct you to a location in a passage or ask you to think about the passage as a whole.

After reading each passage, choose the answer to each question that most effectively improves the quality of writing in the passage or that makes the passage conform to the conventions of standard written English. Many questions include a "NO CHANGE" option. Choose that option if you think the best choice is to leave the relevant portion of the passage as it is.

Questions 1-11 are based on the following passage.

The Age of the Librarian

When Kristen Harris **1** is in college, she worked in her university's library and was constantly told, "You really should be studying to be a librarian; this is **2** your home" however Harris was pursuing a bachelor's degree in elementary education at the time. Little did she realize that becoming a school librarian was indeed **3** elective. During the 21st century, the age of information, what could be more necessary than an individual trained to gather, process, and disseminate information? So, after teaching children in the classroom, Harris went back to school to earn her Master of Library Science degree.

1. A) NO CHANGE
   B) has been
   C) was
   D) had been

2. A) NO CHANGE
   B) your home," however Harris
   C) your home."; However Harris
   D) your home." However, Harris

3. A) NO CHANGE
   B) imminent
   C) threatening
   D) optional

GO ON TO THE NEXT PAGE

Practice Tests

Today, Harris is preparing a story time for a group of young students. As it has done with everything else, the technology revolution has elevated the school library to "Library 2.0." Harris's tablet-integrated story time begins when she projects images for *The Very Cranky Bear* onto a projector screen. As a child, Harris got excited whenever a puppet appeared during story time, but now she uses an interactive app (application software) to enhance her own story time and **4** integrate this next generation of children.

As she introduces the children to the problem of cheering up a cranky **5** bear, Harris sees Miguel scouring the library shelves for another book by a popular author. **6** Miguel had said asking Harris for a book two weeks earlier "If you have any funny stories, I like those." "It will always be satisfying," reflects Harris, "to find books for students and have them return to say, 'I really liked that one. Are there any more by that author?'"

7 Harris maintains active profiles on multiple social media networks to connect with her students more effectively. Harris would call herself a media mentor as much as a librarian because she regularly visits her favorite websites for reviews of apps and other digital tools to suggest to students and parents. Librarians have always been an important resource for families in a community, but this importance has grown exponentially because of the advent of technology. Librarians are offering guidance about new media to address the changing information needs in our communities. Furthermore,

4. A) NO CHANGE
    B) enervate
    C) energize
    D) elucidate

5. A) NO CHANGE
    B) bear; Harris sees Miguel
    C) bear: Harris sees Miguel
    D) bear Harris sees Miguel

6. A) NO CHANGE
    B) Miguel had said, "If you have any funny stories, I like those," asking Harris for a book two weeks earlier.
    C) Asking Harris for a book two weeks earlier, Miguel had said, "If you have any funny stories, I like those."
    D) Miguel asked Harris for a book two weeks earlier had said, "If you have any funny stories, I like those."

7. Which sentence would most effectively establish the main idea of the paragraph?
    A) NO CHANGE
    B) In addition to finding books for students, Harris is expected to meet their digital needs.
    C) Librarians still perform many traditional tasks such as putting great literature in the hands of their students.
    D) In the future, many school libraries are unlikely to have books on the shelves because students prefer electronic media.

GO ON TO THE NEXT PAGE ⟶

libraries are becoming increasingly technology driven, for example, [8] enabling access to collections of other libraries, offering remote access to databases, or they house video production studios. [9] Harris sponsors a weekly "Fun Read" book discussion club that is well attended by many of the students at her school. So, in Harris's opinion, librarians must be masters of the digital world.

Harris finishes her story time and heads across the library. A young student stops her and asks, "Ms. Harris, what's new in the library?" [10] She chuckles and thinks about the many collections, services, and programs their school library offers. "Have you seen the Trendy 10

8. A) NO CHANGE
    B) by enabling access to collections of other libraries, offering remote access to databases, or by housing video production studios.
    C) they enable access to collections of other libraries, offering remote access to databases, or they house video production studios.
    D) enabling access to collections of other libraries, offering remote access to databases, or housing video production studios.

9. Which sentence provides evidence that best supports the main idea of the paragraph?
    A) NO CHANGE
    B) Librarians continue to help students and teachers locate the perfect book in the library's collection.
    C) Teachers frequently ask Harris to recommend educational apps to support early literacy for their students.
    D) Many parents are concerned with online safety and digital citizenship due to the proliferation of social media.

10. A) NO CHANGE
    B) He chuckles
    C) Harris chuckles
    D) They chuckle

list? You read the books on the list and blog **11** your ideas about them. I'll set you up with a password and username so you can blog," says Harris. In this library full of information, she's the gatekeeper.

Questions 12-22 are based on the following passage.

Unforeseen Consequences: The Dark Side of the Industrial Revolution

There is no doubt that the Industrial Revolution guided America through the nascent stages of independence **12** and into being a robust economic powerhouse. Inventions like the cotton gin revolutionized the textile industry, and the steam engine ushered in the advent of expeditious cross-country distribution.

The Industrial Revolution marked a shift from an agrarian to an industry-centered society. People eschewed farming in favor of **13** more lucrative enterprises in urban areas which put a strain on existing local resources. Necessary goods such as **14** food crops, vegetables, and meat products also had to be shipped in order to meet the dietary needs of a consolidated population. And because there were fewer people farming, food had to travel farther and in higher quantities to meet demand. Issues like carbon dioxide emissions, therefore, arose not only as byproducts of industrial production but also from the delivery of these products. Moreover, booming metropolises

11. A) NO CHANGE
    B) they're
    C) you're
    D) their

12. A) NO CHANGE
    B) and into the role of a robust economic powerhouse.
    C) and turned into a robust economic powerhouse.
    D) and then became a robust economic powerhouse.

13. A) NO CHANGE
    B) more lucrative enterprises in urban areas, which put a strain on
    C) more lucrative enterprises in urban areas; which put a strain on
    D) more lucrative enterprises in urban areas. Which put a strain on

14. A) NO CHANGE
    B) food
    C) food crops
    D) vegetables and meat products

needed additional lumber, metal, and coal shipped from rural areas to sustain population and industrial growth.

15 [1] The negative effects of such expansion on humans were immediately apparent; improper water sanitization led to cholera outbreaks in big cities. [2] Miners suffered from black lung after spending hours harvesting coal in dark caverns. [3] Combusted fossil fuels **16** released unprecedented amounts of human-made carbon dioxide into the air, resulting in respiratory ailments. [4] The fact remains that smog, now an internationally recognized buzzword, simply did not exist before the factories that produced it.

The critical impact on the environment must also **17** be taken into account. Proper regulations were either not in place or not enforced. Industrial waste was often disposed of in the nearest river or buried in landfills, where it **18** polluted groundwater essential for wildlife to thrive. Deforestation across the United States served the dual purpose of providing inhabitable land and wood, but it also caused animals to migrate or die out completely.

15. To effectively transition from paragraph 2, which sentence should begin paragraph 3?

   A) Sentence 1

   B) Sentence 2

   C) Sentence 3

   D) Sentence 4

16. Which graphic would best support the underlined claim?

   A) A line graph plotting an increase in atmospheric carbon dioxide over time

   B) A pie chart comparing the present percentages of carbon dioxide and other atmospheric gases

   C) A timeline tracking carbon dioxide emissions testing dates

   D) A bar graph showing levels of atmospheric carbon dioxide in different locations

17. Which choice most effectively combines the sentences at the underlined portion?

   A) be taken into account, and proper regulations

   B) be taken into account since without proper regulations

   C) be taken into account because proper regulations

   D) be taken into account; however, proper regulations

18. A) NO CHANGE

   B) disturbed

   C) drained

   D) enhanced

GO ON TO THE NEXT PAGE

Although the Industrial Revolution heralded an age of consumer ease and excess, it also invited a cyclical process of destruction and reduced resources. [19] Greenhouse gases were released into the atmosphere. Numerous health problems caused by [20] depressing working conditions prevented rural emigrants from thriving. And the environment that had cradled humankind since its inception was slowly being [21] degraded. All in the name of progress. [22]

19. Which choice should be added to the end of the underlined sentence to better support the claim in the preceding sentence?

A) NO CHANGE

B) while carbon dioxide-consuming trees were cut down to make way for new living spaces.

C) and caused an increase in global temperatures as well as a rise in coastal sea levels.

D) faster than they could be absorbed by the atmosphere's shrinking ozone layer.

20. A) NO CHANGE

B) urban

C) substandard

D) developing

21. A) NO CHANGE

B) degraded; all

C) degraded! All

D) degraded—all

22. Which choice most effectively states the central idea of the essay?

A) The Industrial Revolution created a new consumer society that replaced the existing farming society.

B) Politicians and historians today disagree about the true consequences of the Industrial Revolution.

C) Although some analysts suggest that industrialization had many problems, its immense benefits outweigh these concerns.

D) Unfortunately, progress came at the expense of environmental and ecological preservation and may well have ruined the future that once looked so bright.

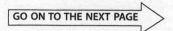

Questions 23-33 are based on the following passage.

Remembering Freud

Psychology has grown momentously over the past century, largely due to the influence of Sigmund Freud, a pioneer of the field. This Austrian-born neurologist founded the practice of psychoanalysis and [23] began scientific study of the unconscious mind. [24] Since his career which ended in the mid-twentieth century, Freud has remained a common cultural and scientific reference point. [25] Even the abiding popularity of terms such as "id," "ego," and talking about a "Freudian slip" serves to indicate how this psychologist lingers powerfully in Western memory.

As neuroscience has progressed, many early practices and theories, including some of Freud's, have been dismissed as outdated, unscientific, or even harmful. Much of Freud's theory, clinical practice, and even lifestyle are now discredited. But when considered in his historical context, alongside the astounding progress catalyzed by his work, Freud's contribution was significant indeed.

[26] Because he is now widely referred to as the Father of Psychoanalysis, Freud was among the first to develop the now-commonplace psychological method of inviting patients to speak freely. For Freud, this was both study and treatment. It helped doctors to understand patients, but more importantly it helped patients to understand themselves. Freud employed the classic (now

23. A) NO CHANGE
    B) continued
    C) spearheaded
    D) led to

24. A) NO CHANGE
    B) Since his career, which ended in the mid-twentieth century, Freud has remained
    C) Since his career ending in the mid-twentieth century; Freud has remained
    D) Since his career (ending in the mid-twentieth century) Freud has remained

25. A) NO CHANGE
    B) Even the abiding popularity of terms such as the "id," "ego," and a "Freudian slip"
    C) Even the abiding popularity of terms such as talking about an "id," "ego," and "Freudian slip"
    D) Even the abiding popularity of terms such as "id," "ego," and "Freudian slip"

26. A) NO CHANGE
    B) Widely remembered as the Father of Psychoanalysis, Freud was among the first to develop the now-commonplace psychological method of inviting patients to speak freely.
    C) Freud was among the first to develop the now-commonplace psychological method of inviting patients to speak freely, which is why he is now widely remembered as the Father of Psychoanalysis.
    D) Although he is widely remembered as the Father of Psychoanalysis, Freud was among the first to develop the now-commonplace psychological method of inviting patients to speak freely.

GO ON TO THE NEXT PAGE

largely outdated) psychiatric style in which the patient lies face-up on a clinical bed, allegedly enabling access to deep **27** parts of the mind. These are better known as the unconscious or subconscious, and they fascinated Freud.

28 He believed that uncovering repressed memories, was necessary for recovery. For Freud, understanding the activity of the innermost mind was essential. **29** In dealing with the conditions of patients, like neurosis or other psychological trauma, he suspected that there was a great deal going on beneath the "surface" of the psyche. He thought it was possible to reunite external, or conscious, thought with the internal, or unconscious. **30** At the same time that Freud practiced, many people were interested in spiritualism. Moreover, the method of inviting patients to speak and process their thoughts aloud remains central to today's psychological practice.

27. A) NO CHANGE
    B) recesses
    C) places
    D) components

28. A) NO CHANGE
    B) He believed that uncovering repressed memories, being necessary for recovery.
    C) He believed that uncovering repressed memories was necessary for recovery.
    D) He believed that uncovering, repressed memories was necessary for recovery.

29. A) NO CHANGE
    B) In dealing with patients' conditions, like neurosis or other psychological trauma, he suspected that
    C) In dealing with patients like neurosis or other psychological trauma conditions he suspected that
    D) He suspected that, in dealing with patients' conditions like neurosis or other psychological trauma,

30. Which sentence provides the best support for the ideas presented in this section?
    A) NO CHANGE
    B) Freud lived and worked mostly in London although he had originally trained in Austria.
    C) While some of Freud's more unusual practices have been criticized or abandoned, his interest in the unconscious altered the trajectory of the field.
    D) Psychologists today employ many theories, not just those developed by Freud.

GO ON TO THE NEXT PAGE ▷

Freud altered the course of twentieth-century medicine by initiating what would become a grand, global conversation about the [31] still vastly mysterious human mind before Freud, medicine had barely scratched the surface in understanding mental health. Patients were met with very few answers, let alone recovery protocols. [32] Through trial and error—scientific method in action—Freud's finding of a method that seemed to work. Since then, decades of ever-sharpening science have used his work as a launching pad. Therefore, as long as occasions arise to celebrate the progress of [33] the field, Sigmund Freud will be remembered for groundbreaking work that enabled countless advances.

31. A) NO CHANGE
    B) still vastly mysterious human mind. Before Freud, medicine
    C) still vastly mysterious human mind, before Freud, medicine
    D) still vastly mysterious human mind before Freud. Medicine

32. A) NO CHANGE
    B) Through trial and error—scientific method in action—Freud's finding a method that seems to work.
    C) Through trial and error—scientific method in action—Freud finds a method that seemed to work.
    D) Through trial and error—scientific method in action—Freud found a method that seemed to work.

33. A) NO CHANGE
    B) the field; Sigmund Freud will be remembered for groundbreaking work that
    C) the field Sigmund Freud will be remembered for groundbreaking work that
    D) the field Sigmund Freud will be remembered for groundbreaking work, and that

Questions 34-44 are based on the following passage and supplementary material.

Success in Montreal

The Montreal Protocol on Substances That Deplete the Ozone Layer is an international treaty that was created to ensure that steps would be taken to reverse damage to Earth's ozone layer and **34** preventing future damage. **35** It was signed in 1987. This document created restrictions on chemicals that were known to be dangerous to the protective barrier that the ozone layer offers Earth. Without the ozone layer, the sun's dangerous UV rays would alter our climate so drastically, life on land and in water would cease to exist.

A hole in Earth's ozone layer was discovered over Antarctica **36** as long as two years prior to the signing of the treaty. The discovery brought the human impact on the environment to the forefront of **37** international conversation, the massive hole was evidence that a global response was necessary and that large-scale action was needed. The Montreal Protocol became effective January 1, 1989, and nearly 100 gases deemed dangerous to the ozone layer have been phased out. As a result, **38** the average size of the ozone hole decreased significantly during the 1990s.

34. A) NO CHANGE
    B) to prevent
    C) prevented
    D) was preventing

35. Which choice most effectively combines the sentences in the underlined portion?
    A) Signed in 1987, this document
    B) Because it was signed in 1987, this document
    C) It was signed in 1987, and this document
    D) It was signed in 1987 so this document

36. A) NO CHANGE
    B) long ago, two years prior.
    C) two years prior.
    D) years prior.

37. A) NO CHANGE
    B) international conversation, yet the massive hole
    C) international conversation. The massive hole
    D) international conversation, so the massive hole

38. Which choice completes the sentence with accurate data based on the graphic?
    A) NO CHANGE
    B) the average size of the ozone hole leveled off beginning in the 1990s.
    C) the average size of the ozone hole decreased beginning in the 2000s.
    D) the average size of the ozone hole increased beginning in the 1980s.

GO ON TO THE NEXT PAGE

Practice Tests

Now that a substantial amount of time has passed since the treaty was put into place, the effects can begin to be [39] <u>looked at</u>. As a part of the treaty, the Montreal Protocol's Scientific Assessment Panel was created to gauge [40] <u>their</u> effect on the hole in the ozone layer. The Panel has since reported the results every four years. The Panel predicts that the ozone layer will return to its former state of health by 2075. [41]

[1] While the treaty is already an obvious success, work continues to ensure that human strides in technology and industry do not reverse the healing process. [2] The Montreal Protocol's Multilateral Fund was established to help developing countries transition away from the consumption and production of harmful chemicals. [3] So far, over $3 billion has been invested by the Fund. [4] The developing countries are referred to as "Article 5 countries." [42]

39. A) NO CHANGE
    B) controlled
    C) measured
    D) governed

40. A) NO CHANGE
    B) its
    C) it's
    D) there

41. Which choice could be added to paragraph 3 to most effectively convey its central idea?

    A) It is the Panel's current estimation that the ozone layer is beginning to heal, but the rate of progress is slow.

    B) The Panel meets once a year to assess the increase or decrease of each gas that has been identified as dangerous.

    C) Of much concern to the Panel was the effect of ultraviolet radiation on the ozone layer.

    D) The Panel has recently updated procedures for the nomination and selection of its membership.

42. Which sentence in paragraph 4 provides the least amount of support for the central idea of the paragraph?

    A) Sentence 1
    B) Sentence 2
    C) Sentence 3
    D) Sentence 4

GO ON TO THE NEXT PAGE

[1] The Montreal Protocol is a living document. [2] A current amendment proposition has been put forth by the United States, Mexico, and Canada jointly. [3] It aims to cut down on harmful gases that were put into use as an alternative to the gases specified in the original Montreal Protocol treaty. [4] It has been amended four times since its inception. [5] Combating the erosion of our ozone layer will take time and flexibility, but the research is clear: If humans stay conscious of what we emit into the atmosphere, we can not only stall the damage we have done in the past, but we can **43** change it. **44**

43. A) NO CHANGE
    B) switch
    C) invert
    D) reverse

44. For the sake of cohesion of this paragraph, sentence 4 should be placed
    A) where it is now.
    B) before sentence 1.
    C) after sentence 1.
    D) after sentence 2.

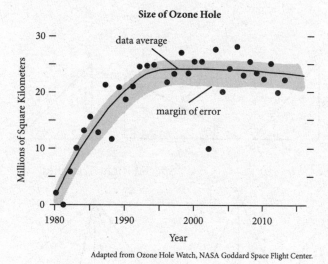

Adapted from Ozone Hole Watch, NASA Goddard Space Flight Center.

IF YOU FINISH BEFORE TIME IS CALLED, YOU MAY CHECK YOUR WORK ON THIS SECTION ONLY. DO NOT TURN TO ANY OTHER SECTION IN THE TEST. **STOP**

MATH TEST

25 Minutes—20 Questions

NO-CALCULATOR SECTION

Turn to Section 3 of your answer sheet to answer the questions in this section.

Directions: For this section, solve each problem and decide which is the best of the choices given. Fill in the corresponding oval on the answer sheet. You may use any available space for scratch work.

Notes:

1. Calculator use is NOT permitted.
2. All numbers used are real numbers.
3. All figures used are necessary to solving the problems that they accompany. All figures are drawn to scale EXCEPT when it is stated that a specific figure is not drawn to scale.
4. Unless stated otherwise, the domain of any function f is assumed to be the set of all real numbers x, for which $f(x)$ is a real number.

Information:

$A = \pi r^2$
$C = 2\pi r$

$A = lw$

$A = \frac{1}{2}bh$

$c^2 = a^2 + b^2$

Special Right Triangles

$V = lwh$

$V = \pi r^2 h$

$V = \frac{4}{3}\pi r^3$

$V = \frac{1}{3}\pi r^2 h$

$V = \frac{1}{3}lwh$

The sum of the degree measures of the angles in a triangle is 180.

The number of degrees of arc in a circle is 360.

The number of radians of arc in a circle is 2π.

GO ON TO THE NEXT PAGE

Number of Games

1. The graph above shows the amount that a new, high-tech video arcade charges its customers. What could the *y*-intercept of this graph represent?

   A) The cost of playing 5 games

   B) The cost per game, which is $5

   C) The entrance fee to enter the arcade

   D) The number of games that are played

$$\frac{3x}{x + 5} \div \frac{6}{4x + 20}$$

2. Which of the following is equivalent to the expression above, given that $x \neq -5$?

   A) $2x$

   B) $\dfrac{x}{2}$

   C) $\dfrac{9x}{2}$

   D) $2x + 4$

$$(x + 3)^2 + (y + 1)^2 = 25$$

3. The graph of the equation above is a circle. What is the area, in square units, of the circle?

   A) 4π

   B) 5π

   C) 16π

   D) 25π

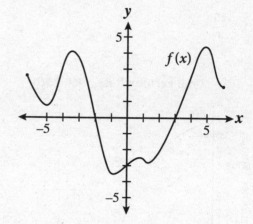

4. The figure above shows the graph of $f(x)$. For which value(s) of *x* does $f(x)$ equal 0 ?

   A) 3 only

   B) −3 only

   C) −2 and 3

   D) −3, −2, and 3

GO ON TO THE NEXT PAGE

Practice Tests

$$\frac{4(d+3)-9}{8} = \frac{10-(2-d)}{6}$$

5. In the equation above, what is the value of d ?

A) $\dfrac{23}{16}$

B) $\dfrac{23}{8}$

C) $\dfrac{25}{8}$

D) $\dfrac{25}{4}$

Total Fertility Rate, 1960-2010

Source: Data from Eurostat.

6. One indicator of a declining economy is a contin-
    ued decline in birth rates. In 2010, birth rates in
    Europe were at an all-time low, with the average
    number of children that a woman has in her life-
    time at well below two. In the figure above, $f(t)$ rep-
    resents birth rates for Portugal between 1960 and
    2010, and $g(t)$ represents birth rates in Slovakia for
    the same time period. For which value(s) of t is
    $f(t) > g(t)$?

A) $1960 < t < 1980$ only

B) $1980 < t < 2000$ only

C) $1960 < t < 1980$ and $1990 < t < 2000$

D) $1960 < t < 1980$ and $2000 < t < 2010$

7. The blue whale is the largest creature in the world
    and has been found in every ocean in the world. A
    marine biologist surveyed the blue whale popula-
    tion in Monterey Bay, off the coast of California,
    every three years between 1995 and 2010. The
    figure above shows her results. If w is the number
    of blue whales present in Monterey Bay and t is
    the number of years since the study began in 1995,
    which of the following equations best represents
    the blue whale population of Monterey Bay?

A) $w = 100 + 2t$

B) $w = 100 + \dfrac{t^2}{4}$

C) $w = 100 \times 2^t$

D) $w = 100 \times 2^{\frac{t}{4}}$

GO ON TO THE NEXT PAGE

Laptop Depreciation

8. The figure above shows the straight-line depreciation of a laptop computer over the first five years of its use. According to the figure, what is the average rate of change in dollars per year of the value of the computer over the five-year period?

A) −1,100

B) −220

C) −100

D) 100

9. What is the coefficient of x^2 when $6x^2 - \dfrac{2}{5}x + 1$ is multiplied by $10x + \dfrac{1}{3}$?

A) −4

B) −2

C) 2

D) 4

10. The graph above could represent which of the following equations?

A) $-6x - 4y = 5$

B) $-6x - 4y = -5$

C) $-6x + 4y = 5$

D) $-6x + 4y = -5$

$$\begin{cases} \dfrac{3}{4}x - \dfrac{1}{2}y = 12 \\ kx - 2y = 22 \end{cases}$$

11. If the system of linear equations above has no solution, and k is a constant, what is the value of k?

A) $-\dfrac{4}{3}$

B) $-\dfrac{3}{4}$

C) 3

D) 4

GO ON TO THE NEXT PAGE

12. In Delray Beach, Florida, you can take a luxury golf cart ride around downtown. The driver charges $4 for the first $\frac{1}{4}$ mile, plus $1.50 for each additional $\frac{1}{2}$ mile. Which inequality represents the number of miles, m, that you could ride and pay no more than $10 ?

A) $3.25 + 1.5m \leq 10$

B) $3.25 + 3m \leq 10$

C) $4 + 1.5m \leq 10$

D) $4 + 3m \leq 10$

13. The graph of $g(x)$ is shown in the figure above. If $h(x) = -g(x) + 1$, which of the following statements is true?

A) The range of $h(x)$ is $-3 \leq y \leq 3$.

B) The minimum value of $h(x)$ is -4.

C) The coordinates of point A on the function $h(x)$ are $(2, 4)$.

D) The graph of $h(x)$ is increasing between $x = -5$ and $x = -2$.

14. If $a + bi$ represents the complex number that results from multiplying $3 + 2i$ times $5 - i$, what is the value of a ?

A) 2

B) 13

C) 15

D) 17

$$\frac{1}{x} + \frac{4}{x} = \frac{1}{72}$$

15. In order to create safe drinking water, cities and towns use water treatment facilities to remove contaminants from surface water and groundwater. Suppose a town has a treatment plant but decides to build a second, more efficient facility. The new treatment plant can filter the water in the reservoir four times as quickly as the older facility. Working together, the two facilities can filter all the water in the reservoir in 72 hours. The equation above represents the scenario. Which of the following describes what the term $\frac{1}{x}$ represents?

A) The portion of the water the older treatment plant can filter in 1 hour

B) The time it takes the older treatment plant to filter the water in the reservoir

C) The time it takes the older treatment plant to filter $\frac{1}{72}$ of the water in the reservoir

D) The portion of the water the new treatment plant can filter in 4 hours

Directions: For questions 16-20, solve the problem and enter your answer in the grid, as described below, on the answer sheet.

1. Although not required, it is suggested that you write your answer in the boxes at the top of the columns to help you fill in the circles accurately. You will receive credit only if the circles are filled in correctly.

2. Mark no more than one circle in any column.

3. No question has a negative answer.

4. Some problems may have more than one correct answer. In such cases, grid only one answer.

5. **Mixed numbers** such as $3\frac{1}{2}$ must be gridded as 3.5 or $\frac{7}{2}$.

    (If $3\frac{1}{2}$ is entered into the grid as [3 1 / 2], it will be interpreted as $\frac{31}{2}$, not $3\frac{1}{2}$.)

6. **Decimal answers:** If you obtain a decimal answer with more digits than the grid can accommodate, it may be either rounded or truncated, but it must fill the entire grid.

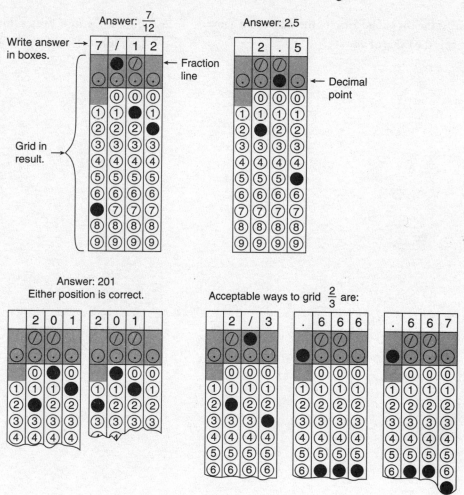

GO ON TO THE NEXT PAGE

16. If $\frac{1}{4}x = 5 - \frac{1}{2}y$, what is the value of $x + 2y$?

$$\begin{cases} x + 3y \le 18 \\ 2x - 3y \le 9 \end{cases}$$

17. If (a, b) is a point in the solution region for the system of inequalities shown above and $a = 6$, what is the minimum possible value for b?

$$\frac{\sqrt{x} \cdot x^{\frac{5}{6}} \cdot x}{\sqrt[3]{x}}$$

18. If x^n is the simplified form of the expression above, what is the value of n?

Note: Figure not drawn to scale.

19. In the figure above, the area of the shaded region is 52 square units. What is the height of the larger triangle?

20. If $y = ax^2 + bx + c$ passes through the points $(-3, 10)$, $(0, 1)$, and $(2, 15)$, what is the value of $a + b + c$?

MATH TEST

55 Minutes—38 Questions

CALCULATOR SECTION

Turn to Section 4 of your answer sheet to answer the questions in this section.

Directions: For this section, solve each problem and decide which is the best of the choices given. Fill in the corresponding oval on the answer sheet. You may use any available space for scratch work.

Notes:

1. Calculator use is permitted.
2. All numbers used are real numbers.
3. All figures used are necessary to solving the problems that they accompany. All figures are drawn to scale EXCEPT when it is stated that a specific figure is not drawn to scale.
4. Unless stated otherwise, the domain of any function f is assumed to be the set of all real numbers x, for which $f(x)$ is a real number.

Information:

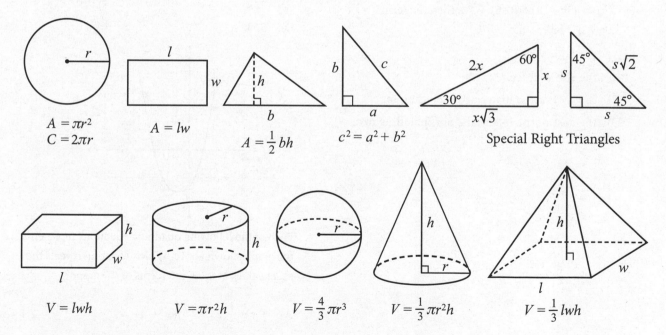

$A = \pi r^2$
$C = 2\pi r$

$A = lw$

$A = \frac{1}{2}bh$

$c^2 = a^2 + b^2$

Special Right Triangles

$V = lwh$

$V = \pi r^2 h$

$V = \frac{4}{3}\pi r^3$

$V = \frac{1}{3}\pi r^2 h$

$V = \frac{1}{3}lwh$

The sum of the degree measures of the angles in a triangle is 180.

The number of degrees of arc in a circle is 360.

The number of radians of arc in a circle is 2π.

GO ON TO THE NEXT PAGE ⟹

1. Oceans, seas, and bays represent about 96.5% of Earth's water, including the water found in our atmosphere. If the volume of the water contained in oceans, seas, and bays is about 321,000,000 cubic miles, which of the following best represents the approximate volume, in cubic miles, of all the world's water?

   A) 308,160,000

   B) 309,765,000

   C) 332,642,000

   D) 334,375,000

2. An electrician charges a one-time site visit fee to evaluate a potential job. If the electrician accepts the job, he charges an hourly rate plus the cost of any materials needed to complete the job. The electrician also charges for tax, but only on the cost of the materials. If the total cost of completing a job that takes h hours is given by the function $C(h) = 45h + 1.06(82.5) + 75$, then the term $1.06(82.5)$ represents

   A) the hourly rate.

   B) the site visit fee.

   C) the cost of the materials, including tax.

   D) the cost of the materials, not including tax.

$$\begin{cases} y > x \\ y \le -\dfrac{3}{7}x + 5 \end{cases}$$

3. The figure above shows the solution set for the system of inequalities. Which of the following is not a solution to the system?

   A) (0, 3)

   B) (1, 2)

   C) (2, 4)

   D) (3, 3)

4. Each of the following quadratic equations represents the graph shown above. Which equation reveals the exact values of the x-intercepts of the graph?

   A) $y = \dfrac{1}{2}(2x - 5)(x + 1)$

   B) $y = x^2 - \dfrac{3}{2}x - \dfrac{5}{2}$

   C) $y + \dfrac{49}{16} = \left(x - \dfrac{3}{4}\right)^2$

   D) $y = \left(x - \dfrac{3}{4}\right)^2 - \dfrac{49}{16}$

GO ON TO THE NEXT PAGE

National Government Concerns

Average Annual Gas Prices

Data from U.S. Energy Information Administration.

5. Margo surveyed all the students in the government classes at her school to see what they thought should be the most important concern of a national government. The results of the survey are shown in the figure above. If the ratio of students who answered "Foreign Policy" to those who answered "Environment" was 5:3, what percentage of the students answered "Environment"?

A) 16%

B) 21%

C) 24%

D) 35%

6. Which of the following best describes the type of association shown in the scatterplot above?

A) Linear, positive

B) Linear, negative

C) Exponential, positive

D) Exponential, negative

7. The figure above shows the average annual gas prices in the United States from 2003 to 2013. Based on the information shown, which of the following conclusions is valid?

A) A gallon of gas cost more in 2008 than in 2013.

B) The price more than doubled between 2003 and 2013.

C) The drop in price from 2008 to 2009 was more than $1.00 per gallon.

D) The overall change in price was greater between 2003 and 2008 than it was between 2008 and 2013.

$$\begin{cases} -2x + 5y = 1 \\ 7x - 10y = -11 \end{cases}$$

8. If (x, y) is a solution to the system of equations above, what is the sum of x and y ?

A) $-\dfrac{137}{30}$

B) -4

C) $-\dfrac{10}{3}$

D) -3

GO ON TO THE NEXT PAGE

Practice Tests

$V_{\text{in}} = 500 \text{ V}$

R_1 $V_{\text{out}} = 330 \text{ V}$

R_2

9. A voltage divider is a simple circuit that converts a large voltage into a smaller one. The figure above shows a voltage divider that consists of two resistors that together have a total resistance of 294 ohms. To produce the desired voltage of 330 volts, R_2 must be 6 ohms less than twice R_1. Solving which of the following systems of equations gives the individual resistances for R_1 and R_2?

A) $\begin{cases} R_2 = 2R_1 - 6 \\ R_1 + R_2 = 294 \end{cases}$

B) $\begin{cases} R_1 = 2R_2 + 6 \\ R_1 + R_2 = 294 \end{cases}$

C) $\begin{cases} R_2 = 2R_1 - 6 \\ R_1 + R_2 = \dfrac{294}{330} \end{cases}$

D) $\begin{cases} R_1 = 2R_2 + 6 \\ R_1 + R_2 = 330(294) \end{cases}$

10. If $\dfrac{2}{5}(5x) + 2(x - 1) = 4(x + 1) - 2$, what is the value of x?

A) $x = -2$

B) $x = 2$

C) There is no value of x for which the equation is true.

D) There are infinitely many values of x for which the equation is true.

11. Crude oil is being transferred from a full rectangular storage container with dimensions 4 meters by 9 meters by 10 meters into a cylindrical transportation container that has a diameter of 6 meters. What is the minimum possible length for a transportation container that will hold all of the oil?

A) 40π

B) $\dfrac{40}{\pi}$

C) 60π

D) $\dfrac{120}{\pi}$

12. The percent increase from 5 to 12 is equal to the percent increase from 12 to what number?

A) 16.8

B) 19.0

C) 26.6

D) 28.8

$$b = \frac{L}{4\pi d^2}$$

13. The brightness of a celestial body, like a star, decreases as you move away from it. In contrast, the luminosity of a celestial body is a constant number that represents its intrinsic brightness. The inverse square law, shown above, is used to find the brightness, b, of a celestial body when you know its luminosity, L, and the distance, d, in meters to the body. Which equation shows the distance to a celestial body, given its brightness and luminosity?

A) $d = \dfrac{1}{2}\sqrt{\dfrac{L}{\pi b}}$

B) $d = \sqrt{\dfrac{L}{2\pi b}}$

C) $d = \dfrac{\sqrt{L}}{2\pi b}$

D) $d = \dfrac{L}{2\sqrt{\pi b}}$

GO ON TO THE NEXT PAGE

Questions 14 and 15 refer to the following information.

Each month, the Bureau of Labor Statistics conducts a survey called the Current Population Survey (CPS) to measure unemployment in the United States. Across the country, about 60,000 households are included in the survey sample. These households are grouped by geographic region. A summary of the January 2014 survey results for male respondents in one geographic region is shown in the table below.

Age Group	Employed	Unemployed	Not in the Labor Force	Total
16 to 19	8	5	10	23
20 to 24	26	7	23	56
25 to 34	142	11	28	157
35 to 44	144	8	32	164
45 to 54	66	6	26	98
Over 54	65	7	36	152
Total	451	44	155	650

14. According to the data in the table, for which age group did the smallest percentage of men report that they were unemployed in January 2014?

A) 20 to 24 years

B) 35 to 44 years

C) 45 to 54 years

D) Over 54 years

15. If one unemployed man from this sample is chosen at random for a follow-up survey, what is the probability that he will be between the ages of 45 and 54?

A) 6.0%

B) 13.6%

C) 15.1%

D) 44.9%

Practice Tests

16. Which of the following are solutions to the quadratic equation $(x - 1)^2 = \dfrac{4}{9}$?

A) $x = -\dfrac{5}{3}, x = \dfrac{5}{3}$

B) $x = \dfrac{1}{3}, x = \dfrac{5}{3}$

C) $x = \dfrac{5}{9}, x = \dfrac{13}{9}$

D) $x = 1 \pm \sqrt{\dfrac{2}{3}}$

17. Damien is throwing darts. He has a total of 6 darts to throw. He gets 5 points for each dart that lands in a blue ring and 10 points for each dart that lands in a red ring. If x of his darts land in a blue ring and the rest land in a red ring, which expression represents his total score?

A) $10x$

B) $10x + 5$

C) $5x + 30$

D) $60 - 5x$

18. Red tide is a form of harmful algae that releases toxins as it breaks down in the environment. A marine biologist is testing a new spray, composed of clay and water, hoping to kill the red tide that almost completely covers a beach in southern Florida. He applies the spray to a representative sample of 200 square feet of the beach. By the end of the week, 184 square feet of the beach is free of the red tide. Based on these results, and assuming the same general conditions, how many square feet of the 10,000-square-foot beach would still be covered by red tide if the spray had been used on the entire area?

A) 800

B) 920

C) 8,000

D) 9,200

$$\begin{cases} y = \dfrac{1}{2}x - 2 \\ y = -x^2 + 1 \end{cases}$$

19. If (a, b) is a solution to the system of equations above, which of the following could be the value of b?

A) -3

B) -2

C) 1

D) 2

20. Given the function $g(x) = \dfrac{2}{3}x + 7$, what domain value corresponds to a range value of 3?

A) -6

B) -2

C) 6

D) 9

21. A landscaper buys a new commercial-grade lawn mower that costs \$2,800. Based on past experience, he expects it to last about 8 years, and then he can sell it for scrap metal with a salvage value of about \$240. Assuming the value of the lawn mower depreciates at a constant rate, which equation could be used to find its approximate value after x years, given that $x < 8$?

A) $y = -8x + 2,560$

B) $y = -240x + 2,800$

C) $y = -320x + 2,800$

D) $y = 240x - 2,560$

GO ON TO THE NEXT PAGE

Practice Tests

22. A microbiologist is studying the effects of a new antibiotic on a culture of 20,000 bacteria. When the antibiotic is added to the culture, the number of bacteria is reduced by half every hour. What kind of function best models the number of bacteria remaining in the culture after the antibiotic is added?

A) A linear function

B) A quadratic function

C) A polynomial function

D) An exponential function

23. An airline company purchased two new airplanes. One can travel at speeds of up to 600 miles per hour and the other at speeds of up to 720 miles per hour. How many more miles can the faster airplane travel in 12 seconds than the slower airplane?

A) $\dfrac{1}{30}$

B) $\dfrac{2}{5}$

C) 2

D) 30

State	Minimum Wage per Hour
Idaho	$7.25
Montana	$7.90
Oregon	$9.10
Washington	$9.32

24. The table above shows the 2014 minimum wages for several states that share a border. Assuming an average workweek of between 35 and 40 hours, which inequality represents how much more a worker who earns minimum wage can earn per week in Oregon than in Idaho?

A) $x \geq 1.85$

B) $7.25 \leq x \leq 9.10$

C) $64.75 \leq x \leq 74$

D) $253.75 \leq x \leq 364$

25. In the United States, the maintenance and construction of airports, transit systems, and major roads is largely funded through a federal excise tax on gasoline. Based on the 2011 statistics given below, how much did the average household pay per year in federal gasoline taxes?

- The federal gasoline tax rate was 18.4 cents per gallon.
- The average motor vehicle was driven approximately 11,340 miles per year.
- The national average fuel economy for noncommercial vehicles was 21.4 miles per gallon.
- The average American household owned 1.75 vehicles.

A) $55.73

B) $68.91

C) $97.52

D) $170.63

GO ON TO THE NEXT PAGE

Practice Tests

Rescued Dolphin Recovery

26. Following the catastrophic oil spill in the Gulf of Mexico in April of 2010, more than 900 bottlenose dolphins were found dead or stranded in the oil spill area. The figure above shows the weight of a rescued dolphin during its recovery. Based on the quadratic model fit to the data shown, which of the following is the closest to the average rate of change in the dolphin's weight between week 2 and week 8 of its recovery?

A) 4 pounds per week

B) 16 pounds per week

C) 20 pounds per week

D) 40 pounds per week

27. As shown in the figure above, a lifeguard sees a struggling swimmer who is 40 feet from the beach. The lifeguard runs 60 feet along the edge of the water at a speed of 12 feet per second. He pauses for 1 second to locate the swimmer again, and then dives into the water and swims along a diagonal path to the swimmer at a speed of 5 feet per second. How many seconds go by between the time the lifeguard sees the struggling swimmer and the time he reaches the swimmer?

A) 16

B) 22

C) 50

D) 56

28. What was the initial amount of gasoline in a fuel trailer, in gallons, if there are now x gallons, y gallons were pumped into a storage tank, and then 50 gallons were added to the trailer?

A) $x + y + 50$

B) $x + y - 50$

C) $y - x + 50$

D) $x - y - 50$

U.S. Foreign Trade, 2014

29. The figure above shows the net change, as a percentage, for U.S. import and export prices from January to July 2014 as reported by the Bureau of Labor Statistics. For example, U.S. import prices declined 0.2 percent in July while export prices remained unchanged for that month. Based on this information, which of the following statements is true for the time period shown in the figure?

A) On average, export prices increased more than import prices.

B) Import prices showed an increase more often than export prices.

C) Import prices showed the greatest change between two consecutive months.

D) From January to July, import prices showed a greater overall decrease than export prices.

$$\frac{3.86}{x} + \frac{180.2}{10x} + \frac{42.2}{5x}$$

30. The Ironman Triathlon originated in Hawaii in 1978. The format of the Ironman has not changed since then: It consists of a 3.86-km swim, a 180.2-km bicycle ride, and a 42.2-km run, all raced in that order and without a break. Suppose an athlete bikes 10 times as fast as he swims and runs 5 times as fast as he swims. The variable x in the expression above represents the rate at which the athlete swims, and the whole expression represents the number of hours that it takes him to complete the race. If it takes him 16.2 hours to complete the race, how many kilometers did he swim in 1 hour?

A) 0.85

B) 1.01

C) 1.17

D) 1.87

Directions: For questions 31-38, solve the problem and enter your answer in the grid, as described below, on the answer sheet.

1. Although not required, it is suggested that you write your answer in the boxes at the top of the columns to help you fill in the circles accurately. You will receive credit only if the circles are filled in correctly.

2. Mark no more than one circle in any column.

3. No question has a negative answer.

4. Some problems may have more than one correct answer. In such cases, grid only one answer.

5. **Mixed numbers** such as $3\frac{1}{2}$ must be gridded as 3.5 or $\frac{7}{2}$.

   (If $3\frac{1}{2}$ is entered into the grid as $\boxed{3\ 1\ /\ 2}$, it will be interpreted as $\frac{31}{2}$, not $3\frac{1}{2}$.)

6. **Decimal answers:** If you obtain a decimal answer with more digits than the grid can accommodate, it may be either rounded or truncated, but it must fill the entire grid.

31. What value of x satisfies the equation
$\frac{2}{3}(5x + 7) = 8x$?

32. Some doctors base the dosage of a drug to be given to a patient on the patient's body surface area (BSA). The most commonly used formula for calculating BSA is $BSA = \sqrt{\frac{wh}{3,600}}$, where w is the patient's weight (in kg), h is the patient's height (in cm), and BSA is measured in square meters. How tall (in cm) is a patient who weighs 150 kg and has a BSA of $2\sqrt{2}$ m² ?

33. A college math professor informs her students that rather than curving final grades, she will replace each student's lowest test score with the next to lowest test score, and then re-average the test grades. If Leeza has test scores of 86, 92, 81, 64, and 83, by how many points does her final test average change based on the professor's policy?

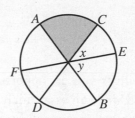

34. In the figure above, $\overline{AB}$, $\overline{CD}$, and $\overline{EF}$ are diameters of the circle. If $y = 2x - 12$, and the shaded area is $\frac{1}{5}$ of the circle, what is the value of x ?

35. If the slope of a line is $-\frac{7}{4}$ and a point on the line is $(4, 7)$, what is the y-intercept of the line?

36. Rory left home and drove straight to the airport at an average speed of 45 miles per hour. He returned home along the same route, but traffic slowed him down and he only averaged 30 miles per hour on the return trip. If his total travel time was 2 hours and 30 minutes, how far is it, in miles, from Rory's house to the airport?

Questions 37 and 38 refer to the following information.

Chemical Makeup of One Mole of Chloroform

Element	Number of Moles	Mass per Mole (grams)
Carbon	1	12.011
Hydrogen	1	1.008
Chlorine	3	35.453

A chemical solvent is a substance that dissolves another to form a solution. For example, water is a solvent for sugar. Unfortunately, many chemical solvents are hazardous to the environment. One eco-friendly chemical solvent is chloroform, also known as trichloromethane ($CHCl_3$). The table above shows the chemical makeup of one mole of chloroform.

37. Carbon makes up what percent of the mass of one mole of chloroform? Round your answer to the nearest whole percent and ignore the percent sign when entering your answer.

38. If a chemist starts with 1,000 grams of chloroform and uses 522.5 grams, how many moles of chlorine are left?

IF YOU FINISH BEFORE TIME IS CALLED, YOU MAY CHECK YOUR WORK ON THIS SECTION ONLY. DO NOT TURN TO ANY OTHER SECTION IN THE TEST. STOP

ESSAY TEST

50 Minutes

The essay gives you an opportunity to show how effectively you can read and comprehend a passage and write an essay analyzing the passage. In your essay, you should demonstrate that you have read the passage carefully, present a clear and logical analysis, and use language precisely.

Your essay must be written on the lines provided in your answer booklet; except for the planning page of the answer booklet, you will receive no other paper on which to write. You will have enough space if you write on every line, avoid wide margins, and keep your handwriting to a reasonable size. Remember that people who are not familiar with your handwriting will read what you write. Try to write or print so that what you are writing is legible to those readers.

You have 50 minutes to read the passage and write an essay in response to the prompt provided inside this booklet.

1. Do not write your essay in this booklet. Only what you write on the lined pages of your answer booklet will be evaluated.
2. An off-topic essay will not be evaluated.

As you read the passage below, consider how Morris uses

- evidence, such as facts or examples, to support claims.

- reasoning to develop ideas and to connect claims and evidence.

- stylistic or persuasive elements, such as word choice or appeals to emotion, to add power to the ideas expressed.

Adapted from Elisabeth Woodbridge Morris's essay "The Tyranny of Things." In this portion, Morris paints a portrait of American consumerism in 1917 and offers a distinct perspective on the joy of freedom from "things, things, things."

1   Two fifteen-year-old girls stood eyeing one another on first acquaintance. Finally one little girl said, "Which do you like best, people or things?" The other little girl said, "Things." They were friends at once.

2   I suppose we all go through a phase when we like things best; and not only like them, but want to possess them under our hand. The passion for accumulation is upon us. We make "collections," we fill our rooms, our walls, our tables, our desks, with things, things, things.

3   Many people never pass out of this phase. They never see a flower without wanting to pick it and put it in a vase, they never enjoy a book without wanting to own it, nor a picture without wanting to hang it on their walls. They keep photographs of all their friends and Kodak albums of all the places they visit, they save all their theater programmes and dinner cards, they bring home all their alpenstocks.* Their houses are filled with an undigested mass of things, like the terminal moraine where a glacier dumps at length everything it has picked up during its progress through the lands.

4   But to some of us a day comes when we begin to grow weary of things. We realize that we do not possess them; they possess us. Our books are a burden to us, our pictures have destroyed every restful wall-space, our china

is a care, our photographs drive us mad, our programmes and alpenstocks fill us with loathing. We feel stifled with the sense of things, and our problem becomes, not how much we can accumulate, but how much we can do without. We send our books to the village library, and our pictures to the college settlement. Such things as we cannot give away, and have not the courage to destroy, we stack in the garret, where they lie huddled in dim and dusty heaps, removed from our sight, to be sure, yet still faintly importunate.

5   Then, as we breathe more freely in the clear space that we have made for ourselves, we grow aware that we must not relax our vigilance, or we shall be once more overwhelmed....

6   It extends to all our doings. For every event there is a "souvenir." We cannot go to luncheon and meet our friends but we must receive a token to carry away. Even our children cannot have a birthday party, and play games, and eat good things, and be happy. The host must receive gifts from every little guest, and provide in return some little remembrance for each to take home. Truly, on all sides we are beset, and we go lumbering along through life like a ship encrusted with barnacles, which can never cut the waves clean and sure and swift until she has been scraped bare again. And there seems little hope for us this side our last port.

7   And to think that there was a time when folk had not even that hope! When a man's possessions were burned with him, so that he might, forsooth, have them all about him in the next world! Suffocating thought! To think one could not even then be clear of things, and make at least a fresh start! That must, indeed, have been in the childhood of the race.

8   Once upon a time, when I was very tired, I chanced to go away to a little house by the sea.... There was nothing in the house to demand care, to claim attention, to cumber my consciousness with its insistent, unchanging companionship. There was nothing but a shelter, and outside, the fields and marshes, the shore and the sea. These did not have to be taken down and put up and arranged and dusted and cared for. They were not things at all, they were powers, presences....

9   If we could but free ourselves once for all, how simple life might become! One of my friends, who, with six young children and only one servant, keeps a spotless house and a soul serene, told me once how she did it. "My dear, once a month I give away every single thing in the house that we do not imperatively need. It sounds wasteful, but I don't believe it really is...."

Write an essay in which you explain how Morris builds an argument to persuade her audience that possessions are oppressive. In your essay, analyze how Morris uses one or more of the features listed in the box that precedes the passage (or features of your own choice) to strengthen the logic and persuasiveness of her argument. Be sure that your analysis focuses on the most relevant features of the passage.

Your essay should not explain whether you agree with Morris's claims, but rather explain how Morris builds an argument to persuade her audience.

ANSWER KEY
READING TEST

1. A	14. B	27. D	40. D
2. B	15. D	28. C	41. A
3. C	16. C	29. C	42. A
4. C	17. A	30. B	43. A
5. A	18. D	31. D	44. B
6. C	19. C	32. C	45. A
7. D	20. C	33. D	46. B
8. A	21. C	34. B	47. D
9. D	22. B	35. C	48. D
10. A	23. D	36. C	49. A
11. D	24. C	37. B	50. C
12. D	25. A	38. C	51. D
13. D	26. A	39. A	52. C

WRITING AND LANGUAGE TEST

1. C	12. B	23. C	34. B
2. D	13. B	24. B	35. A
3. B	14. B	25. D	36. C
4. C	15. A	26. B	37. C
5. A	16. A	27. B	38. B
6. C	17. C	28. C	39. C
7. B	18. A	29. B	40. B
8. D	19. B	30. C	41. A
9. C	20. C	31. B	42. D
10. C	21. D	32. D	43. D
11. A	22. D	33. A	44. C

MATH—NO CALCULATOR TEST

1. C	6. D	11. C	16. 20
2. A	7. D	12. B	17. 1
3. D	8. B	13. A	18. 2
4. C	9. B	14. D	19. 14
5. B	10. A	15. A	20. 6

MATH—CALCULATOR TEST

1. C	11. B	21. C	31. 1
2. C	12. D	22. D	32. 192
3. D	13. A	23. B	33. 3.4
4. A	14. D	24. C	34. 40
5. B	15. B	25. D	35. 14
6. C	16. B	26. C	36. 45
7. D	17. D	27. A	37. 10
8. B	18. A	28. B	38. 12
9. A	19. A	29. B	
10. C	20. A	30. D	

ANSWERS AND EXPLANATIONS

READING TEST

Anna Karenina

Suggested Passage Map notes:

¶1: Levin goes to skating rink to find Kitty

¶2: description of day, people

¶3: walks to skating area; nervous, sees K skating

¶4: knows her right away, still nervous

¶5: lots of happy people skating

¶6: cousin greets him

1. A.   **Difficulty:** Easy

Category: Detail

Getting to the Answer: Make sure to read the passage closely so events are clearly understood. The first paragraph explicitly states how Levin knew that Kitty was there: he saw her family's carriage. Choice (A) matches the information stated in the passage.

2. B   **Difficulty:** Medium

Category: Vocab-in-Context

Getting to the Answer: Use context clues to help you distinguish the shades of meaning each word has. Two of the answer choices have a somewhat negative connotation. The author is not describing the scene in a negative way. In this passage, the word "swarmed" means "gathered." Therefore, (B) is the correct answer. The other words' connotations do not fit with the context of the sentence.

3. C   **Difficulty:** Hard

Category: Inference

Getting to the Answer: Look for clues in the text that suggest what Levin is like. Emotionally charged phrases, such as "the rapture and the terror that seized on his heart," help reveal Levin's personality. Choice (C) reflects the depiction of Levin as a passionate person.

4. C   **Difficulty:** Hard

Category: Command of Evidence

Getting to the Answer: Eliminate answer choices that don't include a description of Levin. Because the excerpt focuses on Levin's feelings toward Kitty, evidence of the kind of person he is will probably reflect this. Choice (C) provides the best evidence.

5. A   **Difficulty:** Medium

Category: Global

Getting to the Answer: The central theme of a passage is the insight about life that the author is trying to get across to the reader. Eliminate any themes that are not revealed by the experiences of Levin. Though you may personally agree with more than one of the themes presented, (A) is the only answer choice that is supported by details in the passage. Levin's feelings and actions support this theme.

6. C   **Difficulty:** Medium

Category: Inference

Getting to the Answer: Examine the passage to see what other characters do in response to Levin. The other skaters go about their business. Most take little notice of Levin. Therefore, (C) is the correct answer.

7. D   **Difficulty:** Medium

Category: Command of Evidence

Getting to the Answer: Reread each quote in the context of the passage. This will help you decide the correct answer. Of all the answer choices, Nikolay's way of greeting Levin is the strongest evidence that people think Levin seems normal. Choice (D) is the correct answer.

8. A   **Difficulty:** Medium

Category: Vocab-in-Context

Getting to the Answer: The context of the passage can help reveal the meaning of the word. Insert each choice in the sentence to see which one makes the most sense. Levin speaks directly to his heart, asking it to behave. Choice (A), "begged," comes closest to meaning the same thing as "conjured" in this context.

9. D   **Difficulty:** Medium

Category: Rhetoric

Getting to the Answer: Think about the entire scene described in the passage and decide why the author chose to describe Levin's heart as "throbbing." Choice (D) is the correct answer. The author chose this word to capture Levin's agitated state.

10. A   **Difficulty:** Hard

Category: Rhetoric

Getting to the Answer: Eliminate answer choices that are clearly not representative of the author's feelings or attitude about Levin. The author presents Levin's situation as one that is painful. The passage's tone suggests that Levin is worthy of the reader's empathy. Choice (A) fits this tone.

Franklin Delano Roosevelt Speech

Suggested Passage Map notes:

    ¶1: US devoted to democracy
    ¶2: must think about soc. & eco problems which → soc. revol.
    ¶3: list of basics of dem.
    ¶4: must maintain basics
    ¶5: list of what should be improved
    ¶6: Americans will personally sacrifice for them
    ¶7: explain tax changes
    ¶8: people will be ok with them
    ¶9: four essential human freedoms
    ¶10: freedom speech and expression
    ¶11: freedom of religion
    ¶12: freedom from want

    ¶13: freedom from fear
    ¶14: are attainable now; against new order of tyranny
    ¶15: moral order
    ¶16: change can made done peacefully
    ¶17: US supports human rights everywhere and will win

11. D   **Difficulty:** Hard

Category: Rhetoric

Getting to the Answer: The introduction to the passage states that President Roosevelt intends to preserve and spread democracy. Choice (D) makes clear that the president wants to promote human rights, which can be achieved by spreading "American ideals around the world."

12. D   **Difficulty:** Hard

Category: Command of Evidence

Getting to the Answer: Be careful of choices that do not provide direct evidence to support the president's purpose. The correct answer will relate specifically to the stated purpose, or intent, of the passage. President Roosevelt makes clear that his intention is to provide support for global efforts to end tyranny and spread democracy and to garner the support of the American people for these goals. In the previous question, his stated purpose is "to make its people conscious of their individual stake in the preservation of democratic life in America." Only (D) provides direct evidence for the previous question.

13. D   **Difficulty:** Easy

Category: Vocab-in-Context

Getting to the Answer: All answer choices are alternate meanings of the word "sacrifice." The correct answer will relate directly to the context of the passage. Despite the fact that Roosevelt gave the speech on the eve of America's involvement in World War II, neither B nor C is the meaning he's after. Choice (D), "surrender of interests to a greater good," is the correct answer.

14. B   Difficulty: Hard

Category: Connections

Getting to the Answer: Keep in mind that you're looking for a relationship that is suggested, not stated. To reach the correct answer, you must infer, or make a logical guess, based on information in the passage. The correct answer will provide support for the stated purpose of the passage while demonstrating a logical relationship. Choice (B) provides support for the stated goal of winning support among U.S. citizens for the spread of democracy abroad. It does so by suggesting that the security of U.S. democracy depends on the advancement of human rights and freedoms globally.

15. D   Difficulty: Medium

Category: Command of Evidence

Getting to the Answer: Avoid answers that provide evidence for incorrect answers to the previous question. The correct answer will use language reflective of the correct answer above to demonstrate a relationship. Principles and ideas such as democracy, freedom, and protection of human rights are used interchangeably throughout Roosevelt's speech. The lines in (D) draw the connection between freedom at home and freedom everywhere.

16. C   Difficulty: Easy

Category: Vocab-in-Context

Getting to the Answer: Substitute each answer choice for the word in question and decide which one fits the context provided in the passage. In the context of the passage, (C) works best. It draws a distinction between individual citizens' monetary interests, or their pocketbooks, and the cause of patriotism, or the greater good.

17. A   Difficulty: Medium

Category: Rhetoric

Getting to the Answer: Keep in mind that the correct answer will relate directly to the meaning of the elements in the identified lines. President Roosevelt is arguing against those who would oppose the overarching goal of his speech, namely to garner support for the spread of democracy overseas. Choice (A) fits best; Roosevelt asserts that his goals are realistic and attainable, not just idealistic visions, as his opponents might claim.

18. D   Difficulty: Medium

Category: Rhetoric

Getting to the Answer: Be wary of answers like A and B that seem to offer specific advice or state specific goals relevant to the purpose of the passage without suggesting how those goals might be achieved. The correct answer will offer a tool, a condition, or another asset for achieving the passage's claim—in this case, the spread of democracy. The previous question identifies that President Roosevelt considers the spread of global democracy achievable. This question asks you to identify how the president envisions achieving that purpose. Choice (D) matches the intent. In this line, President Roosevelt identifies "our unity of purpose" as an asset that will help achieve his goal.

19. C   Difficulty: Hard

Category: Inference

Getting to the Answer: Be careful of answers that cite other policies that the president might support that are not related to the lines quoted. The correct answer will relate directly to the specific lines in question. In this speech, Roosevelt identifies four freedoms that he views the United States as obligated to defend. The freedom from want signifies a commitment to helping struggling populations at home and abroad. Choice (C) fits. The president urges economic understandings among nations to help those in need.

20. C   Difficulty: Medium

Category: Rhetoric

Getting to the Answer: Be careful of answers like

A that offer other viable uses of rhetoric within the larger passage. The correct answer will relate specifically to the text cited in the question. Roosevelt suggests that the preservation of American freedoms cannot exist without the preservation of human rights on a global scale. To cement this connection, he contrasts democratic movements with tyrannical movements occurring in the world. Choice (C) is the correct answer. President Roosevelt references "the so-called new order of tyranny" in order to show what might happen should the United States and the American people not support other nations in their fight against such tyranny.

Women's Suffrage

Suggested Passage Map notes:

¶1: Changes in Am. voting process

¶2: women's voting history; Seneca Falls declaration

¶3: 1878 – amendment proposed, federal gov't not ready

¶4: women voting in New Zealand, Australia, United Kingdom

¶5: WWI → female activism; 19th Amendment passed in 1919, ratified 1920

¶6: elections still not equal b/c Af. Americans often disenfranchised; 1965 Voting Rights Act → voting equality for all

21. C   Difficulty: Medium

Category: Rhetoric

Getting to the Answer: Keep in mind that the "stance" of an author refers to his or her perspective or attitude toward the topic. The passage is written by a scholar or a historian who is looking back on the events that led to the adoption of the Nineteenth Amendment. It is not written by a primary source, such as a legislator or an advocate in the midst of the movement's events. For this reason, (C) is the correct answer. The author of the passage is clearly a scholar

evaluating not just the motivation of women's suffrage leaders but the key events and impact of the movement as a whole.

22. B   Difficulty: Hard

Category: Rhetoric

Getting to the Answer: Avoid answers like A that refer to related issues not relevant to the passage's purpose and answers like D that go too far. The correct answer will identify a claim that is supported by the quotation. In the quote, the author notes that election laws following passage of the Nineteenth Amendment did not secure equal voting rights for all. From this statement, it becomes clear that other groups of people still needed support for their voting rights. Answer (B) is correct.

23. D   Difficulty: Medium

Category: Command of Evidence

Getting to the Answer: Reread the line quoted in the previous question and notice that it occurs in the passage after ratification of the Nineteenth Amendment. Therefore, the evidence you're looking for will refer to an event that came later. The author suggests that the Nineteenth Amendment did not win equal voting rights for all citizens but that it did serve as an important step on the way to free and fair elections. Choice (D) demonstrates that a later event expanded voting rights further, to citizens regardless not only of gender but also of race.

24. C   Difficulty: Easy

Category: Vocab-in-Context

Getting to the Answer: Consider the events that are being described in the paragraph in which the word appears. This will help you choose the best answer. It's clear in this paragraph that the women's suffrage movement was gaining momentum at this time. Events and tactics excited those who supported the movement and attracted more supporters. Therefore, (C) reflects the correct meaning of "galvanized."

25. A   Difficulty: Hard

Category: Rhetoric

Getting to the Answer: Carefully review the paragraph in which the line appears before choosing the best answer. Choice (A) demonstrates the connection between successfully changing one element (people's minds) in order to change the other (laws).

26. A   Difficulty: Hard

Category: Inference

Getting to the Answer: Be wary of answers like D that go too far in asserting unsubstantiated causal relationships. The correct answer will reference an idea or a relationship that is supported by the content of the passage. Choice (A) expresses the idea implicit in the passage that the American government responds, sometimes slowly, to the changing needs and sentiments of the American people.

27. D   Difficulty: Hard

Category: Command of Evidence

Getting to the Answer: Watch for answers like A and C that cite specific changes or examples but do not provide direct support. The correct answer to the previous question states the idea implicit in the passage that the government responds and adapts to changes in U.S. society. This suggests a gradual change. Choice (D) demonstrates the idea that both society and the government have changed over time as the civil rights movement of the late twentieth century overcame social and legal inequalities inherited from earlier in the nation's history.

28. C   Difficulty: Medium

Category: Synthesis

Getting to the Answer: Be careful of answers that aren't backed by sufficient evidence in the graphic. The graphic shows proof that women's suffrage unfolded through a series of events over a long period of time. Choice (C) is the correct answer.

29. C   Difficulty: Medium

Category: Vocab-in-Context

Getting to the Answer: Read the sentence in which the word appears. The correct answer should be interchangeable with the word. The passage states that "Posters . . . called into question the authenticity of a free country with unjust laws." Choice (C) is the correct answer, as "legitimacy" refers to something that is in accordance with established principles.

30. B   Difficulty: Medium

Category: Inference

Getting to the Answer: Be cautious about answers that present accurate facts but that do not directly relate to the content of the question. Choice (B) is the correct answer. Wilson's framing of the conflict abroad as a fight for democracy and freedom helped women suffragists draw attention to the fact that the U.S. government was fighting for justice abroad while denying justice at home.

31. D   Difficulty: Medium

Category: Synthesis

Getting to the Answer: A question like this is asking you to compare information provided in the graphic with information provided in the passage text. Consider each answer choice as you make your comparison. Choice (D) is the correct answer. Both the graphic and the passage indicate that women's suffrage gained early victories in several states quite a few years before becoming law at the federal level through passage of the Nineteenth Amendment.

Paired Passages—Radioisotopes

Suggested Passage Map notes:
   Passage 1

   ¶1: (central idea): use atoms to date things; isotopes def. & exs.

   ¶2: isotopes unstable; measure C-14

¶3: C-14 decay = predictable

¶4: C-14 dating; materials; timeline based on layers

Passage 2

¶1: def. radioactive; why dangerous; danger = radiation rate

¶2: half-life def. = decay rate; exs.

¶3: long half-life = long problem

32. C   Difficulty: Hard

Category: Inference

Getting to the Answer: Use your Passage Map to locate the paragraph that explains carbon-14 dating. This paragraph will contain the description of what materials can be dated using this method. In paragraph 4, the author states that carbon-14 dating can be used on materials made by a living organism. An arrowhead made from a bone is constructed of such material, choice (C).

33. D   Difficulty: Hard

Category: Command of Evidence

Getting to the Answer: Locate each of the answer choices in the passage. The correct answer should provide direct support for the answer to the previous question: the bone arrowhead can be dated using carbon-14 dating. In paragraph 4, the author describes the process for carbon-14 dating. Choice (D) is correct because this sentence provides a direct description of the materials that can be dated using carbon-14 dating.

34. B   Difficulty: Medium

Category: Vocab-in-Context

Getting to the Answer: Pretend that the word "decay" is a blank. Reread around the cited word to predict a word that could substitute for "decay" in context. The previous paragraph discusses how scientists measure the rate of emission to calculate the amount of carbon-14 in a sample. "Emission" means release; therefore, the amount of carbon-14 is be-

coming smaller if the atoms are releasing it. In this sentence, therefore, predict "decay" means to *decrease*, which matches "deteriorate," choice (B).

35. C   Difficulty: Easy

Category: Connections

Getting to the Answer: Look at your notes for paragraph 3. Summarize the ratio of carbon-12 to carbon-14 in living tissue in your own words. Look for the answer choice that most closely matches your prediction. In paragraph 3, the author explains that the ratio of carbon-12 to carbon-14 for living things is the same as the ratio in the atmosphere: constant. Choice (C) is correct.

36. C   Difficulty: Medium

Category: Command of Evidence

Getting to the Answer: Review what part of the passage you used to predict an answer for the previous question: the ratio is constant for living things. Of the answer choices, only lines 28-31 explain the ratio of carbon-12 to carbon-14 in living things. Choice (C) is correct.

37. B   Difficulty: Medium

Category: Detail

Getting to the Answer: Read around the cited lines. The author directly states why a release of iodine-131 is not cause for long-term concern. In paragraph 3, the author explains that the initial release of radiation from an accident involving iodine-131 will be high, but the level of radiation will drop quickly (lines 75–76). Choice (B) is correct.

38. C   Difficulty: Medium

Category: Detail

Getting to the Answer: Use your Passage Map to find the information about why exposure to radiation is dangerous.

Getting to the Answer: In paragraph 1, lines 53-55, the author explains that radiation is harmful to living tissue because it can cause damage to the cells'

DNA, which matches choice (C).

39. A   Difficulty: Easy

Category: Vocab-in-Context

Getting to the Answer: Pretend that the word "original" is a blank. Reread around the cited word to predict a word that could substitute for "original" in context. The previous paragraph explains how scientists use "half-life" to determine how quickly material decays. If the material is decaying, then predict "original" refers to the *first* material. Choice (A) matches your prediction.

40. D   Difficulty: Medium

Category: Detail

Getting to the Answer: Review your notes for Passage 2. Try to put into your own words how scientists use half-life calculations of radioactive materials. Look for the answer that most closely matches your idea. In paragraph 1, the author explains that the level of danger posed by radiation released during a nuclear accident depends on how quickly radiation is released (lines 59-62). In paragraph 2, the author discusses how the half-life of radioactive material is used to determine how long a material will emit radiation. Paragraph 3 then explains how different half-lives translate into short-term or long-term radiation concerns. Choice (D) is correct because it most clearly paraphrases the information in the passage about how scientists use half-life calculations.

41. A   Difficulty: Hard

Category: Synthesis

Getting to the Answer: The central idea will be supported by all of the evidence presented in both passages. Review the central idea you identified for each passage in your Passage Maps. Passage 1 discusses the application of atomic and nuclear physics in archaeology while Passage 2 details how scientists apply atomic and nuclear physics to studies of radioactivity in nuclear power plant accidents. Choice (A) is correct.

42. A   Difficulty: Hard

Category: Synthesis

Getting to the Answer: Analyze the graph to see that it describes the decay of carbon-14 over time. Think about how this data relates to the texts. The graph portrays the decay of carbon-14 as described in Passage 1. The definition of "half-life" is given in Passage 2. The half-life of a material is the amount of time it takes for half of that material to decay. The graph shows that about 50 percent of carbon-14 remains after 5,400 years. Choice (A) is correct.

Biomimicry Passage

Suggested Passage Map notes:

¶1: George de Mestral – invented velcro

¶2: biomimicry – study nature to improve people's homes, cities, etc.

¶3: used in architecture

¶4: Michael Pawlyn - adapt principles behind natural shapes → innovative solutions

¶5: used in optics and robotics

¶6: some natural stuff not advanced but simple: abalone shell

¶7: nanoscale features; Andrew Parker – skin of thorny devil

¶8: can learn from animal features

¶9: improve energy efficiency

¶10: radical, optimistic field

43. A   Difficulty: Medium

Category: Global

Getting to the Answer: Look for the answer choice that describes an idea supported throughout the passage rather than a specific detail. The passage cites several examples of biomimicry, the study of how materials and systems found in nature can be replicated to benefit humans. Therefore, (A) is the best summary of the central idea of the passage.

44. B   **Difficulty:** Medium

Category: Command of Evidence

Getting to the Answer: Think back to why you chose your answer to the previous question. This will help you pick the correct quote as evidence. Choice (B) is the correct answer because it provides evidence for the central idea that the author presents about the field of biomimicry.

45. A   **Difficulty:** Hard

Category: Rhetoric

Getting to the Answer: Think about the primary purpose of the quote. Eliminate any answer choices that don't support this purpose. The quote, which is from a book on architecture, explains why architects turn to biomimicry for solutions in their work. Choice (A) is the correct answer.

46. B   **Difficulty:** Medium

Category: Connections

Getting to the Answer: Reread the paragraph that the question is asking about. Look for specific details about the abalone shrimp shell and soft chalk. The passage clearly states that the abalone shrimp shell is harder than soft chalk because of the way the basic material composing each is arranged, so (B) is the correct answer.

47. D   **Difficulty:** Medium

Category: Rhetoric

Getting to the Answer: In order to understand why an author includes a quote from another person, examine the surrounding sentences. This often makes clear the author's reason for including the quotation. The author includes the quote from Pawlyn to support and strengthen his or her own view that energy efficiency "has never been more important." Therefore, (D) is the correct answer.

48. D   **Difficulty:** Easy

Category: Vocab-in-Context

Getting to the Answer: Replace the word in question with each of the answer choices. This will help you eliminate the ones that don't make sense in the context. Choice (D), "concepts," is the only answer choice that makes sense in this context because it reflects the foundational reasons behind the structures.

49. A   **Difficulty:** Medium

Category: Inference

Getting to the Answer: Keep in mind that you're being asked to make an inference, a logical guess based on information in the passage. Therefore, the correct answer is not stated in the passage. The variety of examples of biomimicry mentioned in the passage make it reasonable to infer that more scientists will utilize solutions developed through biomimicry in the future. Choice (A) is the correct answer.

50. C   **Difficulty:** Medium

Category: Command of Evidence

Getting to the Answer: Reread each quotation in the context of the passage. Consider which one is the best evidence to support the inference made in the previous question. The examples cited in (C) provide strong evidence for the inference that more scientists will probably make use of biomimicry in years to come.

51. D   **Difficulty:** Medium

Category: Vocab-in-Context

Getting to the Answer: Eliminate answer choices that are synonyms for the word in question but do not work in the context of the sentence. Because biomimicry is such an innovative approach, it makes sense that the meaning of "radical" in this context is closest to (D), "revolutionary."

52. C   **Difficulty:** Hard

Category: Synthesis

Getting to the Answer: Remember that a graphic might not refer to something explicitly stated in the passage. Instead, it often provides a visual example of how an important concept discussed in the passage works. The graphic and its caption help illustrate an example of biomimicry not mentioned in the passage: that of a solar power plant designed to mimic the arrangement of petals in a sunflower. This directs more energy toward the power plant's central tower and improves the efficiency of the power plant. Choice (C) is the correct answer.

WRITING AND LANGUAGE TEST

The Age of the Librarian

1. C   **Difficulty:** Easy

Category: Usage

Getting to the Answer: Examine the verb tense in the rest of the sentence. This will help you find the correct answer. As written, the sentence switches verb tense mid-sentence. Other verbs in the sentence, "worked" and "was," indicate that the events happened in the past. Choice (C) is the correct choice because it correctly uses the past tense of the target verb.

2. D   **Difficulty:** Medium

Category: Punctuation

Getting to the Answer: Pay attention to the quotation marks. Reading through the sentence and the answer choices shows that two issues might need correcting. The sentence inside the quotation marks is a complete sentence. The correct answer needs to punctuate that sentence before closing the quote. Additionally, "however" is being used as a connector or transition word and needs to be followed by a comma after beginning the new sentence. Choice (D) appropriately uses a period prior to the end quotes and correctly inserts a comma after the transition word "However."

3. B   **Difficulty:** Medium

Category: Effective Language Use

Getting to the Answer: Watch out for choices that distort the tone of the passage. The passage suggests that people expected or anticipated that Harris would become a librarian. Evidence for this idea is found in the statement that she was "constantly told" that she "should be studying to be a librarian." Harris was certainly aware that people anticipated this course of study for her, but the presence of the phrase "Little did she realize" tells you that she didn't expect to become one. The correct choice is (B), "imminent," meaning that becoming a librarian was about to occur despite her own expectations.

4. C   **Difficulty:** Hard

Category: Effective Language Use

Getting to the Answer: Read the sentence carefully for context clues. Also, think about the tone of what is being described. This will help you choose the best answer. Given the phrasing of the sentence, the answer must be close in meaning to "excited," which is used earlier in the sentence. Therefore, (C) is the correct answer.

5. A   **Difficulty:** Medium

Category: Punctuation

Getting to the Answer: Determine whether a clause is dependent or independent to decide between a comma and a semicolon. Choice (A) is the correct answer. The sentence is correctly punctuated as written because it uses a comma at the end of the introductory dependent clause.

6. C   **Difficulty:** Medium

Category: Sentence Formation

Getting to the Answer: Read the sentence carefully. The sentence sounds clunky and awkward. Look for an answer choice that makes the sentence clear and easy to understand. Notice that the word "asking" is part of a participial phrase that modifies "Miguel." A participial phrase should be placed as close as possible to the noun it modifies. When a participial phrase begins a sentence, it should be set off with a comma. Choice (C) is correct. The placement of commas and modifiers makes the content easy to understand, and the sentence is free of grammatical or punctuation errors.

7. B   Difficulty: Medium

Category: Development

Getting to the Answer: Read the entire paragraph carefully and predict the main idea. Then look for a close match with your prediction. The paragraph discusses how the role of librarian has changed due to an increased use of technology. Choice (B) is the correct answer, as it explicitly addresses the changing role of the librarian.

8. D   Difficulty: Medium

Category: Sentence Formation

Getting to the Answer: Read the sentence and note the series of examples. A series should have parallel structure. The sentence is not correct as written. The items in the series switch forms from participial phrases beginning with "enabling" and "offering" to "they house." All of the items need to fit the same pattern or form. Choice (D) is correct because it appropriately begins each item in the series with a participle.

9. C   Difficulty: Hard

Category: Development

Getting to the Answer: Don't be fooled by answer choices that are true statements but do not directly support the main idea of the paragraph. The paragraph concerns how the role of the librarian has changed due to an increased use of technology. The correct answer needs to support the idea that librarians work with technology in new ways. Choice (C) works best. It offers a specific example of how teachers look to the librarian to be a "media mentor" and illustrates this new role for school librarians.

10. C   Difficulty: Easy

Category: Usage

Getting to the Answer: Read the sentence prior to the pronoun and determine whom the pronoun is referencing. Pronouns should not be ambiguous, and they must match the verb in number. The sentence is ambiguous as written. "She" would presumably refer back to the "young student," but it seems unlikely that the student would be laughing and thinking about the collections in the library after asking the librarian a question. Choice (C) is the best choice. It clearly indicates the subject of the sentence (Harris) and avoids ambiguity.

11. A   Difficulty: Medium

Category: Usage

Getting to the Answer: Figure out whom the pronoun refers to and make sure it matches the antecedent in number. Watch out for confusing contractions and possessives. The pronoun in the sentence needs to indicate who will have the ideas. Harris is talking to a single student, so the sentence will need a singular possessive pronoun. Choice (A) is correct. As it is, the sentence correctly uses a singular possessive pronoun.

Unforeseen Consequences: The Dark Side of the Industrial Revolution

12. B   Difficulty: Medium

Category: Sentence Formation

Getting to the Answer: Be careful of answers that sound correct when they stand alone but do not conform to the structure of the sentence as a whole. The existing text is incorrect, as it does not maintain parallel structure. Choice (B) is the correct answer, as it maintains the parallel structure of preposition ("into") + noun ("the role").

13. B   Difficulty: Easy

Category: Punctuation

Getting to the Answer: Eliminate answers that confuse the usage of commas and semicolons. Choice (B) is correct. Without the comma, the following clause modifies "urban areas" when it should modify the entire preceding clause.

14. B   Difficulty: Medium

Category: Effective Language Use

Getting to the Answer: Avoid choices that are redundant and imprecise. The correct answer will use the clearest, most concise terminology to communicate the idea. Choice (B) is correct. It is the most concise—and clearest—word choice because all of the items listed in the original sentence are simply types of food. The other choices use more words than necessary to convey meaning.

15. A   Difficulty: Medium

Category: Organization

Getting to the Answer: The first sentence should function as a transition between ideas in the previous paragraph and ideas in the current paragraph. Choice (A) makes sense. This choice connects ideas from the previous paragraph with the content of paragraph 3. The sentences that follow provide details to support that introductory idea.

16. A   Difficulty: Hard

Category: Quantitative

Getting to the Answer: Eliminate answers like B that fail to support the cited sentence directly. The underlined sentence references "unprecedented amounts of human-made carbon dioxide into the air." This suggests an increase in the amount of carbon dioxide in the atmosphere over time. Therefore, (A) is the correct answer.

17. C   Difficulty: Medium

Category: Effective Language Use

Getting to the Answer: Choose the answer that presents the correct relationship between ideas. Choice (C) is correct. It shows the causal relationship without adding verbiage.

18. A   Difficulty: Easy

Category: Effective Language Use

Getting to the Answer: Plug in the answer choices and select the one that reflects a specific meaning relevant to the sentence. The paragraph focuses on the negative effects of industrialization and waste production. Therefore, (A) is the correct answer.

19. B   Difficulty: Hard

Category: Development

Getting to the Answer: Be careful of choices that relate to the underlined portion of the text without showing clearly how the underlined portion supports the full implications of the preceding sentence. The paragraph explains that industrialization resulted in the destruction of resources. The correct answer, (B), serves as clear evidence of the "process of destruction and reduced resources."

20. C   Difficulty: Medium

Category: Effective Language Use

Getting to the Answer: Be careful of answers that make sense but do not fully support the meaning of the content. The correct answer will not only flow logically but will also reflect the precise purpose and meaning of the larger sentence and paragraph. Choice (C) is the correct answer. "Substandard" communicates clearly that the working conditions were the cause of the health problems.

21. D   Difficulty: Medium

Category: Sentence Formation

Getting to the Answer: Eliminate choices that result in sentence fragments or fragmented clauses. The correct answer will maintain appropriate syntax without misusing punctuation. Choice (D) is correct.

It sets off the dependent clause without using incorrect punctuation to signal a hard break before an independent clause or second complete sentence.

22. D   Difficulty: Hard

Category: Development

Getting to the Answer: Avoid answers that draw on similar ideas but combine those ideas in a way that communicates a proposition not supported by the essay as a whole. The correct answer will make sense within the larger context of the essay. The central idea of the entire essay is that industrialization and progress came at a cost that made the promise of a bright future difficult to fulfill. Choice (D) is the correct answer.

Remembering Freud

23. C   Difficulty: Hard

Category: Effective Language Use

Getting to the Answer: Consider the fact that there may be a choice that helps make the meaning of the sentence very precise. Choice (C) most accurately indicates that Freud led a whole movement.

24. B   Difficulty: Medium

Category: Punctuation

Getting to the Answer: Plug in each answer choice and select the one that seems most correct. Choice (B) makes it clear to the reader that this is extra information modifying the word "career."

25. D   Difficulty: Medium

Category: Sentence Formation

Getting to the Answer: Remember that in a list, all things listed should be presented with the same grammatical structure. "Id," "ego," and "Freudian slip" are all nouns. Choice (D) is the correct answer because it uses a parallel structure for all three nouns.

26. B   Difficulty: Hard

Category: Development

Getting to the Answer: Notice that the underlined sentence is the first sentence in the paragraph. Think about which choice would make the best topic sentence, given the content of the rest of the paragraph. Choice (B) correctly makes the free-speaking technique the focus of the paragraph's topic sentence, while suggesting that the technique was radical enough to earn Freud his title.

27. B   Difficulty: Medium

Category: Effective Language Use

Getting to the Answer: Eliminate any choices that don't seem as precise as others. Choice (B) is correct. The word "recesses" is more precise; it connotes smaller parts of the brain and a sense of being hidden.

28. C   Difficulty: Easy

Category: Punctuation

Getting to the Answer: Think about how the sentence sounds when read aloud. This often helps you get a good sense of whether or not a comma is needed. Choice (C) would fit here. The sentence eliminates the unneeded comma.

29. B   Difficulty: Hard

Category: Sentence Formation

Getting to the Answer: Remember that a modifier should be adjacent to the noun it is modifying and set off by punctuation. Choice (B) is correct. The modifier "like neurosis or other psychological trauma" should come directly after "conditions."

30. C   Difficulty: Hard

Category: Development

Getting to the Answer: Consider how this sentence relates to the one before it and the one that follows it. Does it offer strong support of the connecting ideas? This section discussed the development and lasting influence of Freud's ideas. The best supporting sentence will provide details connecting these concepts. Choice (C) is correct. It emphasizes that Freud developed new ideas that have had a lasting influence on psychological practices.

31. B   Difficulty: Medium

Category: Sentence Formation

Getting to the Answer: Notice that you are dealing with a run-on sentence. Identify the point in the run-on where it appears two sentences have been fused together. Choice (B) is correct. This choice splits the run-on sentence into two separate, grammatically correct sentences.

32. D   Difficulty: Easy

Category: Sentence Formation

Getting to the Answer: Eliminate answer choices that are not complete sentences or do not maintain the correct verb tense. Choice (D) correctly changes the phrase "Freud's finding of a method" to "Freud found a method," making the sentence complete. It also corrects the verb tense.

33. A   Difficulty: Hard

Category: Sentence Formation

Getting to the Answer: Recall that when a dependent clause precedes an independent clause, it should be set off with a comma. Choice (A) is the best choice. Although lengthy, the dependent clause in the sentence ("as long as occasions arise . . .") is correctly combined with its independent clause ("Sigmund Freud will be remembered . . .") by use of a comma.

Success in Montreal

34. B   Difficulty: Easy

Category: Sentence Formation

Getting to the Answer: Always check whether two

or more verbs that serve the same function have a parallel structure. Choice (B) is correct. "To prevent" is in the infinitive form like the earlier verb in the sentence, "to reverse."

35. A   Difficulty: Hard

Category: Effective Language Use

Getting to the Answer: Look for the choice that most concisely and correctly joins the two sentences. Choice (A) is the best fit. This option joins the sentences concisely and correctly.

36. C   Difficulty: Medium

Category: Effective Language Use

Getting to the Answer: Remember that the best answer is the most concise and effective way of stating the information while ensuring that the information is complete. Choice (C) works best here. It uses the fewest necessary words to convey the complete information.

37. C   Difficulty: Medium

Category: Sentence Formation

Getting to the Answer: Eliminate any choices that use transition words inappropriately. Two complete thoughts should be separated into two different sentences. Therefore, (C) is the best choice.

38. B   Difficulty: Hard

Category: Quantitative

Getting to the Answer: Examine the graphic for details that suggest which answer is correct. Choice (B) accurately reflects the information in the graphic. Beginning in the 1990s, the size of the ozone hole began to level off.

39. C   Difficulty: Medium

Category: Effective Language Use

Getting to the Answer: Check each word to see how it fits with the context of the sentence. While all of the words have similar meanings, only one fits the context of the paragraph. Choice (C), "measured," has a connotation that corresponds to "gauge" in the following sentence.

40. B   **Difficulty:** Easy

Category: Usage

Getting to the Answer: Remember that the possessive form must agree with its antecedent. The correct answer will reflect the gender and number of its antecedent; in this case, the word "treaty." Therefore, (B) is correct.

41. A   **Difficulty:** Hard

Category: Development

Getting to the Answer: To find the central idea of a paragraph, identify important details and then summarize them in a sentence or two. Then find the choice that is the closest to your summary. Choice (A) most clearly states the paragraph's central idea, that the ozone layer is beginning to return to normal.

42. D   **Difficulty:** Medium

Category: Development

Getting to the Answer: To find the correct answer, first determine the central idea of the paragraph. Choice (D) is the least essential sentence in the paragraph, so it is the correct answer.

43. D   **Difficulty:** Medium

Category: Effective Language Use

Getting to the Answer: Context clues indicate which word is appropriate in the sentence. Check to see which word fits best in the sentence. The word "reverse," (D), fits with the context of the sentence and connotes a more precise action than does "change."

44. C   **Difficulty:** Hard

Category: Organization

Getting to the Answer: Examine the entire paragraph. Decide whether the sentence provides more information about a topic mentioned in one of the other sentences. This sentence provides more information related to sentence 1, "The Montreal Protocol is a living document"; it describes how the document is "living." Choice (C) is the correct answer.

MATH—NO CALCULATOR TEST

1. C   **Difficulty:** Easy

Category: Heart of Algebra / Linear Equations

Getting to the Answer: To determine what the y-intercept could mean in the context of a word problem, examine the labels on the graph and note what each axis represents. According to the labels, the y-axis represents cost, and the x-axis represents the number of games played. The y-intercept, $(0, 5)$, has an x-value of 0, which means 0 games were played, yet there is still a cost of $5. The cost must represent a flat fee that is charged before any games are played, such as an entrance fee to enter the arcade, (C).

2. A   **Difficulty:** Easy

Category: Passport to Advanced Math / Exponents

Getting to the Answer: To divide one rational expression by another, multiply the first expression by the reciprocal (the flip) of the second expression. Rewrite the division as multiplication, factor any factorable expressions, and then simplify if possible.

$$\frac{3x}{x+5} \div \frac{6}{4x+20} = \frac{3x}{x+5} \cdot \frac{4x+20}{6}$$
$$= \frac{3x}{x+5} \cdot \frac{4(x+5)}{6}$$
$$= \frac{12x}{6}$$
$$= 2x$$

Note that the question also states that $x \neq -5$. This doesn't affect your answer—it is simply stated because the denominators of rational expressions cannot equal 0. Choice (A) is correct.

3. D **Difficulty:** Easy

Category: Additional Topics in Math / Geometry

Getting to the Answer: When the equation of a circle is written in the form $(x - h)^2 + (y - k)^2 = r^2$, the point (h, k) represents the center of the circle on a coordinate plane, and r represents the length of the radius. To find the area of a circle, use the formula, $A = \pi r^2$. In the equation given in the question, r^2 is the constant on the right-hand side (25)—you don't even need to solve for r because the area , formula involves r^2, not r. So, the area is $\pi(25)$ or 25π, (D).

4. C **Difficulty:** Easy

Category: Passport to Advanced Math / Functions

Getting to the Answer: When using function notation, $f(x)$ is simply another way of saying y, so this question is asking you to find the values of x for which $y = 0$, or in other words, where the graph crosses the x-axis. The graph crosses the x-axis at the points $(-2, 0)$ and $(3, 0)$, so the values of x for which $f(x) = 0$ are -2 and 3, (C).

5. B **Difficulty:** Medium

Category: Heart of Algebra / Linear Equations

Getting to the Answer: Choose the best strategy to answer the question. You could start by cross-multiplying to get rid of the denominators, but simplifying the numerators first will make the calculations easier.

$$\frac{4(d + 3) - 9}{8} = \frac{10 - (2 - d)}{6}$$

$$\frac{4d + 12 - 9}{8} = \frac{10 - 2 + d}{6}$$

$$\frac{4d + 3}{8} = \frac{8 + d}{6}$$

$$6(4d + 3) = 8(8 + d)$$

$$24d + 18 = 64 + 8d$$

$$16d = 46$$

$$d = \frac{46}{16} = \frac{23}{8}$$

Choice (B) is correct.

6. D **Difficulty:** Medium

Category: Passport to Advanced Math / Functions

Getting to the Answer: This is a crossover question, so quickly skim the first couple of sentences. Then look for the relevant information in the last couple of sentences. It may also help to circle the portions of the graph that meet the given requirement.

Because *greater* means *higher* on a graph, the statement $f(t) > g(t)$ translates to "Where is $f(t)$ above $g(t)$?" The solid curve represents f and the dashed curve represents g, so $f > g$ between the years 1960 and 1980 and again between the years 2000 and 2010. Look for these time intervals in the answer choices: $1960 < t < 1980$ and $2000 < t < 2010$. This matches (D).

7. D **Difficulty:** Medium

Category: Passport to Advanced Math / Scatterplots

Getting to the Answer: Use the shape of the data to predict the type of equation that might be used as a model. Then, use specific values from the graph to choose the correct equation. According to the graph, the population of the whales grew slowly at first and then more quickly. This means that an exponential model is probably the best fit, so you can eliminate A (linear) and B (quadratic). The remaining equations are both exponential, so choose a data point and see which equation is the closest fit. Be careful—the vertical axis represents *hundreds* of whales, and the question states that t represents the number of years since the study began, so $t = 0$ for 1995, $t = 3$ for 1998, and so on. If you use the data for 1995, which is the point $(0, 100)$, the results are the same for both equations, so choose a different point. Using the data for 2007, $t = 2007 - 1995 = 12$, and the number of whales was 800. Substitute these values into C and D to see which one is true. Choice C is not true because $800 \neq 100 \times 2^{12}$. Choice (D) is correct because:

$$800 = 100 \times 2^{\frac{12}{4}} = 100 \times 2^3 = 100 \times 8$$

8. B   **Difficulty:** Medium

Category: Heart of Algebra / Linear Equations

Getting to the Answer: To find the average rate of change over the 5-year period, find the slope between the starting point (0, 1,200) and the ending point (5, 100).

$$m = \frac{y_2 - y_1}{x_2 - x_1} = \frac{100 - 1{,}200}{5 - 0} = \frac{-1{,}100}{5} = -220$$

Choice (B) is correct. (The average rate of change is negative because the laptop decreases in value over time.)

Note: Because the question involves *straight-line* depreciation, you could have used any two points on the graph to find the slope. As a general rule, however, you should use the endpoints of the given time interval.

9. B   **Difficulty:** Medium

Category: Passport to Advanced Math / Exponents

Getting to the Answer: When multiplying polynomials, carefully multiply each term in the first factor by each term in the second factor. This question doesn't ask for the entire product, so check to make sure you answered the right question (the coefficient of x^2).

$$\left(6x^2 - \frac{2}{5}x + 1\right)\left(10x + \frac{1}{3}\right)$$

$$= 6x^2\left(10x + \frac{1}{3}\right) - \frac{2}{5}x\left(10x + \frac{1}{3}\right) + 1\left(10x + \frac{1}{3}\right)$$

$$= 60x^3 + \underline{2x^2} \quad \underline{4x^2} - \frac{2}{15}x + 10x + \frac{1}{3}$$

The coefficient of x^2 is $2 + (-4) = -2$, which is (B).

10. A   **Difficulty:** Medium

Category: Heart of Algebra / Linear Equations

Getting to the Answer: The line is decreasing, so the slope (m) is negative. The line crosses the y-axis below 0, so the y-intercept (b) is also negative. Put each answer choice in slope-intercept form, one at a

time, and examine the signs of m and b. Begin with (A):

$$-6x - 4y = 5$$
$$-4y = 6x + 5$$
$$y = \frac{6x}{-4} + \frac{5}{-4}$$
$$y = -\frac{3}{2}x - \frac{5}{4}$$

You don't need to check any of the other equations. Choice (A) has a negative slope and a negative y-intercept, so it is the correct equation.

11. C   **Difficulty:** Hard

Category: Heart of Algebra / Systems of Linear Equations

Getting to the Answer: Graphically, a system of linear equations that has no solution indicates two parallel lines or, in other words, two lines that have the same slope. So, write each of the equations in slope-intercept form ($y = mx + b$) and set their slopes (m) equal to each other to solve for k. Before finding the slopes, multiply the top equation by 4 to make it easier to manipulate.

$$4\left(\frac{3}{4}x - \frac{1}{2}y = 12\right) \rightarrow 3x - 2y = 48 \rightarrow y = \frac{3}{2}x - 24$$

$$kx - 2y = 22 \rightarrow -2y = -kx + 22 \rightarrow y = \frac{k}{2}x - 11$$

The slope of the first line is $\frac{3}{2}$, and the slope of the second line is $\frac{k}{2}$. Set them equal and solve for k.

$$\frac{3}{2} = \frac{k}{2}$$
$$2(3) = 2(k)$$
$$6 = 2k$$
$$3 = k$$

Choice (C) is correct.

12. B   **Difficulty:** Hard

Category: Heart of Algebra / Inequalities

Getting to the Answer: Before you write the inequality, you need to find the per-mile rate for the remaining miles. The driver charges $4.00 for the first $\frac{1}{4}$ mile, which is a flat fee, so write 4. The additional charge is $1.50 per $\frac{1}{2}$ mile, or 1.50 times 2 = $3.00 per mile. The number of miles after the first $\frac{1}{4}$ mile is $m - \frac{1}{4}$, so the cost of the trip, not including the first $\frac{1}{4}$ mile, is $3\left(m - \frac{1}{4}\right)$. This means the cost of the whole trip is $4 + 3\left(m - \frac{1}{4}\right)$. The clue "no more than $10" means that much or less, so use the symbol $\leq$. The inequality is $4 + 3\left(m - \frac{1}{4}\right) \leq 10$, which simplifies to $3.25 + 3m \leq 10$. This matches (B).

13. A   Difficulty: Hard

Category: Passport to Advanced Math / Functions

Getting to the Answer: Based on the equation, the graph of $h(x) = -g(x) + 1$ is a vertical reflection of $g(x)$, over the x-axis, that is then shifted up 1 unit. The graph looks like the dashed line in the following graph:

Now, compare the dashed line to each of the answer choices: The range of $h(x)$ is the set of y-values from lowest to highest (based on the dashed line). The lowest point occurs at point B' and has a y-value of -3; the highest value occurs at both ends of the

graph and is 3, so the range is $-3 \leq y \leq 3$. This means (A) is correct and you can move on to the next question. Don't waste valuable time checking the other answer choices unless you are not sure about the range. (Choice B: The minimum value of $h(x)$ is -3, not -4. Choice C: The coordinates of point A on $h(x)$ are $(-2, -2)$, not $(2, 4)$. Choice D: the graph of $h(x)$ is decreasing, not increasing, between $x = -5$ and $x = -2$.)

14. D   Difficulty: Medium

Category: Additional Topics in Math / Imaginary Numbers

Getting to the Answer: Multiply the two complex numbers just as you would two binomials (using FOIL). Then, combine like terms and use the definition $i^2 = -1$ to simplify the result.

$$
\begin{aligned}
(3 + 2i)(5 - i) &= 3(5 - i) + 2i(5 - i) \\
&= 15 - 3i + 10i - 2i^2 \\
&= 15 + 7i - 2(-1) \\
&= 15 + 7i + 2 \\
&= 17 + 7i
\end{aligned}
$$

The question asks for a in $a + bi$, so the correct answer is 17, (D).

15. A   Difficulty: Hard

Category: Passport to Advanced Math / Exponents

Getting to the Answer: Think of the rate given in the question in terms of the constant term you see on the right-hand side of the equation. Working together, the two treatment plants can filter the water in 72 hours. This is equivalent to saying that they can filter $\frac{1}{72}$ of the water in 1 hour. If $\frac{1}{72}$ is the portion of the water the two treatment plants can filter *together*, then each term on the left side of the equation represents the portion that each plant can filter *individually* in 1 hour. Because the new facility is 4 times as fast as the older facility, $\frac{4}{x}$ represents the portion of the water the new plant can filter in

1 hour, and $\dfrac{1}{x}$ represents the portion of the water the older plant can filter in 1 hour. This matches (A).

16. 20   **Difficulty:** Medium

Category: Heart of Algebra / Linear Equations

Getting to the Answer: Only one equation is given, and it has two variables. This means that you don't have enough information to solve for either variable. Instead, look for the relationship between the variable terms in the equation and those in the expression that you are trying to find, $x + 2y$. First, move the y-term to the left side of the equation to make it look more like the expression you are trying to find. The expression doesn't have fractions, so clear the fractions in the equation by multiplying both sides by 4. This yields the expression that you are looking for, $x + 2y$, so no further work is required—just read the value on the right-hand side of the equation. The answer is 20.

$$\frac{1}{4}x = 5 - \frac{1}{2}y$$

$$\frac{1}{4}x + y\frac{1}{2} = 5$$

$$4\left(\frac{1}{4}x + \frac{1}{2}y\right) = 4(5)$$

$$x + 2y = 20$$

17. 1   **Difficulty:** Medium

Category: Heart of Algebra / Inequalities

Getting to the Answer: This question is extremely difficult to answer unless you draw a sketch. It doesn't have to be perfect—you just need to get an idea of where the solution region is. Don't forget to flip the inequality symbol when you graph the second equation.

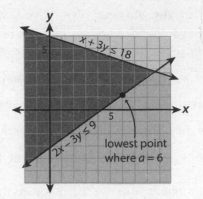

If (a, b) is a solution to the system, then a is the x-coordinate of any point in the darkest shaded region and b is the corresponding y-coordinate. When $a = 6$, the minimum possible value for b lies on the lower boundary line, $2x - 3y \le 9$. It looks like the y-coordinate is 1, but to be sure, substitute $x = 6$ into the equation and solve for y. You can use $=$ in the equation, instead of the inequality symbol, because you are finding a point on the boundary line.

$$2x - 3y = 9$$
$$2(6) - 3y = 9$$
$$12 - 3y = 9$$
$$-3y = -3$$
$$y = 1$$

18. 2   **Difficulty:** Hard

Category: Passport to Advanced Math / Exponents

Getting to the Answer: Write each factor in the expression in exponential form: $\sqrt{x} = x^{\frac{1}{2}}$ and $\sqrt[3]{x} = x^{\frac{1}{3}}$. Then use the rules of exponents to simplify the expression. Add the exponents of the factors that are being multiplied and subtract the exponent of the factor that is being divided:

$$\frac{\sqrt{x} \cdot x^{\frac{5}{6}} \cdot x}{\sqrt[3]{x}} = \frac{x^{\frac{1}{2}} \cdot x^{\frac{5}{6}} \cdot x^{1}}{x^{\frac{1}{3}}}$$

$$= x^{\frac{1}{2} + \frac{5}{6} + \frac{1}{1} - \frac{1}{3}}$$

$$= x^{\frac{3}{6} + \frac{5}{6} + \frac{6}{6} - \frac{2}{6}}$$

$$= x^{\frac{12}{6}} = x^2$$

Because n is the power of x, the value of n is 2.

19. 14   Difficulty: Hard

Category: Additional Topics in Math / Geometry

Getting to the Answer: The shaded region is the area of the larger triangle minus the area of the smaller triangle. Set up and solve an equation using the information from the figure. You don't know the height of the smaller triangle, so call it h. You do know the area of the shaded region—it's 52 square units.

Larger triangle: base = 12; height = $h + 3 + 3$

Smaller triangle: base = 8; height = h

Shaded area = large area − small area

$$52 = \left[\left(\frac{1}{2}\right)(12)(h + 6)\right] - \left[\left(\frac{1}{2}\right)(8)(h)\right]$$
$$52 = 6(h + 6) - 4h$$
$$52 = 6h + 36 - 4h$$
$$52 = 2h + 36$$
$$16 = 2h$$
$$8 = h$$

The question asks for the height of the *larger* triangle, so the correct answer is 8 + 3 + 3 = 14.

20. 6   Difficulty: Hard

Category: Passport to Advanced Math / Quadratics

Getting to the Answer: The highest power of x in the equation is 2, so the function is quadratic. Writing quadratic equations can be tricky and time-consuming. If you know the roots, you can use factors to write the equation. If you don't know the roots, you need to create a system of equations to find the coefficients of the variable terms. You don't know the roots of this equation, so start with the point that has the easiest values to work with, (0, 1), and substitute them into the equation $y = ax^2 + bx + c$.

$$1 = a(0)^2 + b(0) + c$$
$$1 = c$$

Now your equation looks like $y = ax^2 + bx + 1$. Next, use the other two points to create a system of two equations in two variables.

$$(-3, 10) \rightarrow 10 = a(-3)^2 + b(-3) + 1 \rightarrow 9 = 9a - 3b$$
$$(2, 15) \rightarrow 15 = a(2)^2 + b(2) + 1 \rightarrow 14 = 4a + 2b$$

You now have a system of equations to solve. None of the variables has a coefficient of 1, so use elimination to solve the system. If you multiply the top equation by 2 and the bottom equation by 3, the b terms will eliminate each other.

$$2[9a - 3b = 9] \quad \rightarrow \quad 18a - 6b = 18$$
$$3[4a + 2b = 14] \quad \rightarrow \quad \underline{12a + 6b = 42}$$
$$30a = 60$$
$$a = 2$$

Now, find b by substituting $a = 2$ into either of the original equations. Using the top equation, you get:

$$9(2) - 3b = 9$$
$$18 - 3b = 9$$
$$-3b = -9$$
$$b = 3$$

The value of $a + b + c$ is 2 + 3 + 1 = 6.

MATH—CALCULATOR TEST

1. C   Difficulty: Easy

Category: Problem Solving and Data Analysis / Rates, Ratios, Proportions, and Percentages

Getting to the Answer: You can use the formula $\text{Percent} = \frac{\text{part}}{\text{whole}} \times 100\%$ whenever you know two out of the three quantities. The clue "all" tells you that the "whole" is what you don't know. The percent is 96.5, and the part is 321,000,000.

$$96.5 = \frac{321{,}000{,}000}{w} \times 100\%$$

$$96.5w = 32{,}100{,}000{,}000$$

$$w = \frac{32{,}100{,}000{,}000}{96.5}$$

$$w = 332{,}642{,}487$$

The answer choices are rounded to the nearest thousand, so the answer is 332,642,000, (C).

2. C   Difficulty: Easy

Category: Heart of Algebra / Linear Equations

Getting to the Answer: The total cost consists of the one-time site visit fee (a constant), an hourly cost (which depends on the number of hours), and the cost of the materials (which are taxed). The constant in the equation is 75 and is therefore the site visit fee; 45 is being multiplied by h (the number of hours), so $45 must be the hourly rate. That leaves the remaining term, 1.06(82.5), which must be the cost of the materials ($82.50) plus a 6% tax. This matches (C).

3. D   Difficulty: Easy

Category: Heart of Algebra / Inequalities

Getting to the Answer: The intersection (overlap) of the two shaded regions is the solution to the system of inequalities. Check each point to see whether it lies in the region with the darkest shading. Don't forget to check that you answered the right question—you are looking for the point that is *not* a solution to the system. Each of the first three points clearly lies in the overlap. The point (3, 3) looks like it lies on the dashed line, which means it is *not* included in the solution. To check this, plug (3, 3) into the easier inequality: $3 \not> 3$ (3 is equal to itself, not greater than itself), so (D) is correct.

4. A   Difficulty: Easy

Category: Passport to Advanced Math / Quadratics

Getting to the Answer: Quadratic equations can be written in several forms, each of which reveals something special about the graph. The factored

form of a quadratic equation reveals the solutions to the equation, which graphically represent the x-intercepts. Choice (A) is the only equation written in this form and therefore must be correct. You can set each factor equal to 0 and solve to find that the x-intercepts of the graph are $x = \frac{5}{2}$ and $x = -1$.

5. B   Difficulty: Easy

Category: Problem Solving and Data Analysis / Rates, Ratios, Proportions, and Percentages

Getting to the Answer: Break the question into steps. Before you can use the ratio, you need to find the percent of the students who answered either "Foreign Policy" or "Environment." The ratio given in the question is 5:3, so write this as 5 parts "Foreign Policy" and 3 parts "Environment." You don't know how big a *part* is, so call it x. This means that 5x + 3x equals the percent of the students who answered either "Foreign Policy" or "Environment," which is 100% minus all the other answers:

$$100 - (16 + 14 + 9 + 5) = 100 - 44 = 56$$

$$5x + 3x = 56$$

$$8x = 56$$

$$x = 7$$

Each part has a value of 7, and 3 parts answered "Environment," so the correct percentage is 3(7) = 21%, (B).

6. C   Difficulty: Easy

Category: Problem Solving and Data Analysis / Scatterplots

Getting to the Answer: A data set that has a linear association follows the path of a straight line; a data set that is exponential follows a path that is similar to linear data, but with a curve to it because the rate of increase (or decrease) changes over time. This data set has a curve to it, so "exponential" describes the association better than "linear." This means you can eliminate A and B. A positive association between two variables is one in which higher values of one variable correspond to higher values of the other variable, and vice versa. In other words, as the *x*-values of the data points go up, so do the *y*-values. This is indeed the case for this data set, so (C) is correct.

7. D   **Difficulty:** Easy

Category: Problem Solving and Data Analysis / Statistics and Probability

Getting to the Answer: Your only choice for this question is to compare each statement to the figure. Don't waste time trying to figure out the exact value for each bar—an estimate is good enough to determine whether each statement is true. Choice A is incorrect because the price in 2008 was slightly less (not more) than $3.50, while the price in 2013 was right around $3.50. Choice B is incorrect because the price in 2003 was more than $2.00, and the price in 2013 was not more than twice that ($4.00). Choice C is incorrect because the price in 2008 was about $3.25 and the price in 2009 was about $2.75—this is not a difference of more than $1.00. This means (D) must be correct. You don't have to check it—just move on. (Between 2003 and 2008, the change in price was about $3.40 − $2.30 = $1.10; between 2008 and 2013, the change in price was only about $3.50 − $3.40 = $0.10; the change in price was greater between 2003 and 2008.)

8. B   **Difficulty:** Medium

Category: Heart of Algebra / Systems of Linear Equations

Getting to the Answer: Because none of the variable terms has a coefficient of 1, solve the system of equations using elimination (combining the equations). Before you choose an answer, check that you answered the right question (the sum of *x* and *y*). Multiply the top equation by 2 to eliminate the terms that have *y*'s in them.

$$2[-2x + 5y = 1] \rightarrow -4x + 10y = 2$$
$$7x - 10y = -11 \rightarrow \underline{7x - 10y = -11}$$
$$3x = -9$$
$$x = -3$$

Now, substitute the result into either of the original equations and simplify to find *y*:

$$-2x + 5y = 1$$
$$-2(-3) + 5y = 1$$
$$6 + 5y = 1$$
$$5y = -5$$
$$y = -1$$

The question asks for the *sum*, so add *x* and *y* to get −3 + (−1) = −4, which is (B).

9. A   **Difficulty:** Medium

Category: Heart of Algebra / Systems of Linear Equations

Getting to the Answer: Take a quick peek at the answers just to see what variables are being used, but don't study the equations. Instead, write your own system using the same variables as given in the answer choices. One of the equations in the system needs to represent the sum of the two resistors $(R_1 + R_2)$, which is equal to 294. This means you can eliminate C and D. The second equation needs to satisfy the condition that R_2 is 6 less than twice R_1, or $R_2 = 2R_1 - 6$. This means (A) is correct.

10. C   **Difficulty:** Medium

Category: Heart of Algebra / Linear Equations

Getting to the Answer: Use the distributive property to simplify each of the terms that contains parentheses. Then use inverse operations to solve for *x*.

$$\frac{2}{3}(3x) + 2(x - 1) = 4(x + 1) - 2$$
$$2x + 2x - 2 = 4x + 4 - 2$$
$$4x - 2 = 4x + 2$$
$$-2 \neq 2$$

All of the variable terms cancel out, and the resulting numerical statement is false (because negative 2 does not equal positive 2), so there is no solution to the equation. Put another way, there is no value of *x* for which the equation is true, (C).

11. B   Difficulty: Medium

Category: Additional Topics in Math / Geometry

Getting to the Answer: Think about this question logically before you start writing things down—after it's transferred, the volume of the oil in the cylindrical container will be the same volume as the rectangular container, so you need to set the two volumes equal and solve for h. The volume of the rectangular container is $4 \times 9 \times 10$, or 360 cubic meters. The volume of a cylinder equals the area of its base times its height, or $\pi r^2 h$. Because the diameter is 6 meters, the radius, r, is half that, or 3 meters. Now we're ready to set up an equation and solve for h (which is the height of the cylinder or, in this case, the length of the transportation container):

$$\text{Volume of oil} = \text{Volume of rectangular container}$$
$$\pi(3)^2 h = 360$$
$$9\pi h = 360$$
$$h = \frac{360}{9\pi} = \frac{40}{\pi}$$

Choice (B) is correct.

12. D   Difficulty: Medium

Category: Problem Solving and Data Analysis / Rates, Ratios, Proportions, and Percentages

Getting to the Answer: Even though this question uses the word *percent*, you are never asked to find the actual percent itself. Set this question up as a proportion to get the answer more quickly. Remember, percent change equals amount of change divided by the original amount.

$$\frac{12 - 5}{5} = \frac{x - 12}{12}$$
$$\frac{7}{5} = \frac{x - 12}{12}$$
$$12(7) = 5(x - 12)$$
$$84 = 5x - 60$$
$$144 = 5x$$
$$28.8 = x$$

Choice (D) is correct.

13. A   Difficulty: Medium

Category: Passport to Advanced Math / Exponents

Getting to the Answer: Focus on the question at the very end—it's just asking you to solve the equation for d. First, cross-multiply to get rid of the denominator. Then, divide both sides of the equation by $4\pi b$ to isolate d^2. Finally, take the square root of both sides to find d.

$$b(4\pi d^2) = L$$
$$\frac{b(4\pi d^2)}{4\pi b} = \frac{L}{4\pi b}$$
$$d^2 = \frac{L}{4\pi b}$$
$$\sqrt{d^2} = \sqrt{\frac{L}{4\pi b}}$$
$$d = \sqrt{\frac{L}{4\pi b}}$$

Unfortunately, this is not one of the answer choices, so you'll need to simplify further. You can take the square root of 4 (it's 2), but be careful—it's in the denominator of the fraction, so it comes out of the square root as $\frac{1}{2}$. The simplified equation is $d = \frac{1}{2}\sqrt{\frac{L}{\pi b}}$. This matches (A).

14. D   Difficulty: Easy

Category: Problem Solving and Data Analysis / Statistics and Probability

Getting to the Answer: To calculate the percentage of men in each age group who reported being unemployed in January 2014, divide the number in *that* age group who were unemployed by the total number in *that* age group. There are six age groups but only four answer choices, so don't waste time on the age groups that aren't represented. Choice (D) is correct because $7 \div 152 \approx 0.046 = 4.6\%$, which is a lower percentage than that for any other age group (20 to 24 = 12.5%; 35 to 44 = 4.9%; 45 to 54 = 6.1%).

15. B   **Difficulty:** Medium

Category: Problem Solving and Data Analysis / Statistics and Probability

Getting to the Answer: The follow-up survey targets only those respondents who said they were unemployed, so focus on that column in the table. There were 6 respondents out of 44 unemployed males who were between the ages of 45 and 54, so the probability is $\frac{6}{44} = 0.1\overline{36}$, or about 13.6%, (B).

16. B   **Difficulty:** Medium

Category: Passport to Advanced Math / Quadratics

Getting to the Answer: Taking the square root is the inverse operation of squaring, and both sides of the equation are already perfect squares, so take their square roots. Then solve the resulting equations. Remember, there will be two equations to solve.

$$(x - 1)^2 = \frac{4}{9}$$

$$\sqrt{(x - 1)^2} = \sqrt{\frac{4}{9}}$$

$$x - 1 = \pm\frac{\sqrt{4}}{\sqrt{9}}$$

$$x = 1 \pm \frac{2}{3}$$

Now, simplify each equation: $x = 1 + \frac{2}{3} = \frac{3}{3} + \frac{2}{3} = \frac{5}{3}$ and $x = 1 - \frac{2}{3} = \frac{3}{3} - \frac{2}{3} = \frac{1}{3}$. Choice (B) is correct.

17. D   **Difficulty:** Medium

Category: Heart of Algebra / Linear Equations

Getting to the Answer: Write the expression in words first: points per blue ring (5) times number of darts in blue ring (x), plus points per red ring (10) times number of darts in red ring ($6 - x$). Now, translate the words into numbers, variables, and operations: $5x + 10(6 - x)$. This is not one of the answer choices, so simplify the expression by distributing the 10 and then combining like terms: $5x + 10(6 - x) = 5x + 60 - 10x = 60 - 5x$. This matches (D).

18. A   **Difficulty:** Medium

Category: Problem Solving and Data Analysis / Statistics and Probability

Getting to the Answer: This is a science crossover question. Read the first two sentences quickly—they are simply describing the context of the question. The last two sentences pose the question, so read those more carefully. In the sample, 184 out of 200 square feet were free of red tide after applying the spray. This is $\frac{184}{200} = 0.92 = 92\%$ of the area. For the whole beach, 0.92(10,000) = 9,200 square feet should be free of the red tide. Be careful—this is *not* the answer. The question asks how much of the beach would still be covered by red tide, so subtract to get 10,000 − 9,200 = 800 square feet, (A).

19. A   **Difficulty:** Medium

Category: Passport to Advanced Math / Quadratics

Getting to the Answer: The solution to a system of equations is the point(s) where their graphs intersect. You can solve the system algebraically by setting the equations equal to each other, or you can solve it graphically using your calculator. Both equations are given in calculator-friendly format ($y = \dots$), so graphing them is probably the more efficient approach. The graph looks like:

The solution point in the question is given as (a, b), so b represents the y-coordinate of the solution. The y-coordinates of the points of intersection are −3 and −1.25, so choice (A) is correct.

20. A   **Difficulty:** Medium

Category: Passport to Advanced Math / Functions

Getting to the Answer: The given range value is an output value, so substitute 3 for $g(x)$ and use inverse operations to solve for x, which is the corresponding domain value.

$$g(x) = \frac{2}{3}x + 7$$

$$3 = \frac{2}{3}x + 7$$

$$-4 = \frac{2}{3}x$$

$$-12 = 2x$$

$$-6 = x$$

Choice (A) is correct. Note that you could also graph the function and find the value of x (the domain value) for which the value of y (the range value) is 3. The point on the graph is $(-6, 3)$.

21. C   Difficulty: Medium

Category: Heart of Algebra / Linear Equations

Getting to the Answer: Write your own equation using the initial cost and the rate of change in the value of the lawn mower. Remember—when something changes at a constant rate, it can be represented by a linear equation. When a linear equation in the form $y = mx + b$ is used to model a real-world scenario, m represents the constant rate of change, and b represents the starting amount. Here, the starting amount is easy—it's the purchase price, $2,800. To find the rate of change, think of the initial cost as the value at 0 years, or the point $(0, 2,800)$, and the salvage amount as the value at 8 years, or the point $(8, 240)$. Substitute these points into the slope formula:

$$m = \frac{y_2 - y_1}{x_2 - x_1} = \frac{240 - 2,800}{8 - 0} = \frac{-2,560}{8} = -320$$

The correct equation is $y = -320x + 2,800$. This matches (C).

22. D   Difficulty: Medium

Category: Problem Solving and Data Analysis / Functions

Getting to the Answer: Determine whether the change in the number of bacteria is a common difference (linear function) or a common ratio (exponential function) or if the number of bacteria changes direction (quadratic or polynomial function). The question tells you that the number of bacteria is reduced by half every hour after the antibiotic is applied. The microbiologist started with 20,000, so after one hour, there are 10,000 left, or $20,000 \times \frac{1}{2}$.

After 2 hours, there are 5,000 left, or $20,000 \times \frac{1}{2} \times \frac{1}{2}$, and so on. The change in the number of bacteria is a common ratio $\left(\frac{1}{2}\right)$, so the best model is an exponential function, (D), of the form $y = a\left(\frac{1}{2}\right)^x$. In this scenario, a is 20,000.

23. B   Difficulty: Medium

Category: Problem Solving and Data Analysis / Rates, Ratios, Proportions, and Percentages

Getting to the Answer: Let the units in this question guide you to the solution. The speeds of the airplanes are given in miles per hour, but the question asks about the number of miles each airplane can travel in 12 seconds, so convert miles per hour to miles per second and multiply by 12 seconds.

Slower airplane:

$$\frac{600 \text{ mi}}{\text{hr}} \times \frac{1 \text{ hr}}{60 \text{ min}} \times \frac{1 \text{ min}}{60 \text{ sec}} \times 12 \text{ sec} = 2 \text{ mi}$$

Faster airplane:

$$\frac{720 \text{ mi}}{\text{hr}} \times \frac{1 \text{ hr}}{60 \text{ min}} \times \frac{1 \text{ min}}{60 \text{ sec}} \times 12 \text{ sec} = 2.4 \text{ mi}$$

The faster plane can travel $2.4 - 2 = 0.4$ miles farther, which is the same as $\frac{2}{5}$ miles, (B).

24. C   Difficulty: Medium

Category: Heart of Algebra / Inequalities

Getting to the Answer: Based on the data in the

table, a worker would earn $9.10 − $7.25 = $1.85 more for one hour of work in Oregon than in Idaho. If he worked 35 hours per week, he would earn 35(1.85) = $64.75 more. If he worked 40 hours per week, he would earn 40(1.85) = $74 more. So, the worker would earn somewhere between $64.75 and $74 more per week, which can be expressed as the compound inequality $64.75 \leq x \leq 74$. This matches (C).

25. D   Difficulty: Medium

Category: Problem Solving and Data Analysis / Rates, Ratios, Proportions, and Percentages

Getting to the Answer: This is another question where the units can help you find the answer. Use the number of vehicles owned to find the total number of miles driven to find the total number of gallons of gas used to find the total tax paid. Phew!

$$1.75 \ \text{vehicles} \times \frac{11,340 \ \text{miles}}{\text{vehicle}} = 19,845 \ \text{miles}$$

$$19,845 \ \text{miles} \times \frac{1 \ \text{gallon of gas}}{21.4 \ \text{miles}} = 927.336 \ \text{gallons}$$

$$927.336 \ \text{gallons} \times \frac{\$0.184}{\text{gallon}} = \$170.63$$

Choice (D) is correct.

26. C   Difficulty: Medium

Category: Problem Solving and Data Analysis / Scatterplots

Getting to the Answer: The average rate of change of a function over a given interval, from a to b, compares the change in the outputs, $f(b) - f(a)$, to the change in the inputs, $b - a$. In other words, it is the slope of the line that connects the endpoints of the interval, so you can use the slope formula. Look at the quadratic model, not the data points, to find that the endpoints of the given interval, week 2 to week 8, are (2, 280) and (8, 400). The average rate of change is $\frac{400 - 280}{8 - 2} = \frac{120}{6} = 20$, so the dolphin's weight increased by about 20 pounds per week, (C).

27. A   Difficulty: Hard

Category: Additional Topics in Math / Geometry

Getting to the Answer: In this question, information is given in both the diagram and the text. You need to relate the text to the diagram, one piece of information at a time, to calculate how long the lifeguard ran along the beach and how long he swam. Before you find the swim time, you need to know how *far* he swam. Whenever you see a right triangle symbol in a diagram, you should think Pythagorean theorem or, in this question, special right triangles. All multiples of 3-4-5 triangles are right triangles, so the length of the lifeguard's swim is the hypotenuse of a 30-40-50 triangle, or 50 feet. Add this number to the diagram. Now calculate the times using the distances and the speeds given. Don't forget the 1 second that the lifeguard paused.

$$\text{Run time} = 60 \ \text{ft} \times \frac{1 \ \text{sec}}{12 \ \text{ft}} = \frac{60}{12} = 5 \ \text{sec}$$

Pause time = 1 second

$$\text{Swim time} = 50 \ \text{ft} \times \frac{1 \ \text{sec}}{5 \ \text{ft}} = \frac{50}{5} = 10 \ \text{sec}$$

Total time = 5 + 1 + 10 = 16 seconds, (A).

28. B   Difficulty: Hard

Category: Heart of Algebra / Linear Equations

Getting to the Answer: Call the initial amount A. After you've written your equation, solve for A.

Amount now (x) = Initial amount (A) minus y, plus 50

$$x = A - y + 50$$
$$x + y - 50 = A$$

The initial amount was $x + y - 50$ gallons, (B). Note that you could also use Picking Numbers to answer this question.

29. B   Difficulty: Hard

Category: Problem Solving and Data Analysis / Statistics and Probability

Getting to the Answer: When a question involves

reading data from a graph, it is sometimes better to skip an answer choice if it involves long calculations. Skim the answer choices for this question—A involves finding two averages, each of which is composed of 7 data values. Skip this choice for now. Start with (B). Be careful—you are not looking for places where the line segments are increasing. The y-axis already represents the change in prices, so you are simply counting the number of positive values for the imports (5) and for the exports (4). There are more for the imports, so (B) is correct and you don't need to check any of the other statements. Move on to the next question.

30. D **Difficulty:** Hard

Category: Passport to Advanced Math / Exponents

Getting to the Answer: The key to answering this question is deciding what you're trying to find. The question tells you that x represents the athlete's swim rate, and you are looking for the number of kilometers he swam in one hour—these are the same thing. If you find x (in kilometers per hour), you will know how many kilometers he swam in one hour. Set the equation equal to the total time, 16.2, and solve for x. To do this, write the variable terms over a common denominator, $10x$, and combine them into a single term. Then cross-multiply and go from there.

$$16.2 = \frac{10}{10}\left(\frac{3.86}{x}\right) + \frac{180.2}{10x} + \frac{2}{2}\left(\frac{42.2}{5x}\right)$$

$$16.2 = \frac{38.6}{10x} + \frac{180.2}{10x} + \frac{84.4}{10x}$$

$$16.2 = \frac{303.2}{10x}$$

$$10x(16.2) = 303.2$$

$$162x = 303.2$$

$$x = \frac{303.2}{162} \approx 1.87$$

Choice (D) is correct.

31. 1 **Difficulty:** Easy

Category: Heart of Algebra / Linear Equations

Getting to the Answer: Choose the best strategy to answer the question. If you distribute the $\frac{2}{3}$, it creates messy calculations. Instead, clear the fraction by multiplying both sides of the equation by 3. Then use the distributive property and inverse operations to solve for x.

$$\frac{2}{3}(5x + 7) = 8x$$

$$\cancel{3} \cdot \frac{2}{\cancel{3}}(5x + 7) = 3 \cdot 8x$$

$$2(5x + 7) = 24x$$

$$10x + 14 = 24x$$

$$14 = 14x$$

$$1 = x$$

32. 192 **Difficulty:** Medium

Category: Passport to Advanced Math / Exponents

Getting to the Answer: Before you start substituting values, quickly check that the units given match the units required to use the equation—they do, so proceed. The patient's weight (w) is 150 and the patient's BSA is $2\sqrt{2}$, so the equation becomes $2\sqrt{2} = \sqrt{\dfrac{150h}{3,600}}$. The only variable left in the equation is h, and you are trying to find the patient's height, so you're ready to solve the equation. To do this, square both sides of the equation and then continue using inverse operations. Be careful when you square the left side—you must square both the 2 and the root 2.

$$2\sqrt{2} = \sqrt{\frac{150h}{3,600}}$$

$$\left(2\sqrt{2}\right)^2 = \left(\sqrt{\frac{150h}{3,600}}\right)^2$$

$$2^2\left(\sqrt{2}\right)^2 = \frac{150h}{3,600}$$

$$4(2) = \frac{150h}{3,600}$$

$$28,800 = 150h$$

$$192 = h$$

33. 3.4   Difficulty: Medium

Category: Problem Solving and Data Analysis / Statistics and Probability

Getting to the Answer: The test average is the same as the mean of the data. The *mean* is the sum of all the values divided by the number of values. Break the question into short steps to keep your calculations organized. Before gridding in your answer, make sure you answered the right question (how much the final test average changes).

Step 1: Find the original test average:

$$\frac{86 + 92 + 81 + 64 + 83}{5} = \frac{406}{5} = 81.2$$

Step 2: Find the average of the tests after replacing the lowest score (64) with the next to lowest score (81):

$$\frac{86 + 92 + 81 + 81 + 83}{5} = \frac{423}{5} = 84.6$$

Step 3: Subtract the original average from the new average: 84.6 − 81.2 = 3.4.

34. 40   Difficulty: Hard

Category: Additional Topics in Math / Geometry

Getting to the Answer: Because $\overline{AB}$, $\overline{CD}$, and $\overline{EF}$ are diameters, the sum of x, y, and the interior angle of the shaded region is 180 degrees. The question tells you that the shaded region is $\frac{1}{5}$ of the circle, so the interior angle must equal $\frac{1}{5}$ of the degrees in the whole circle, or $\frac{1}{5}$ of 360. Use what you know about y (that it is equal to $2x - 12$) and what you know about the shaded region (that it is $\frac{1}{5}$ of 360 degrees) to write and solve an equation.

$$x + y + \frac{1}{5}(360) = 180$$
$$x + (2x - 12) + 72 = 180$$
$$3x + 60 = 180$$
$$3x = 120$$
$$x = 40$$

35. 14   Difficulty: Hard

Category: Heart of Algebra / Linear Equations

Getting to the Answer: When you know the slope and one point on a line, you can use $y = mx + b$ to write the equation. The slope is given as $-\frac{7}{4}$, so substitute this for m. The point is given as (4, 7), so $x = 4$ and $y = 7$. Now, find b:

$$y = mx + b$$
$$7 = -\frac{7}{4}(4) + b$$
$$7 = -7 + b$$
$$14 = b$$

The y-intercept of the line is 14.

You could also very carefully graph the line using the given point and the slope. Start at (4, 7) and move toward the y-axis by rising 7 and running *to the left* 4 (because the slope is negative). You should land at the point (0, 14).

36. 45   Difficulty: Hard

Category: Problem Solving and Data Analysis / Rates, Ratios, Proportions, and Percentages

Getting to the Answer: Make a chart that represents rate, time, and distance and fill in what you know.

	Rate	Time	Distance
To airport	45 mph	t	d
Back to home	30 mph	$2.5 - t$	d

Now use the formula $d = r \times t$ for both parts of the trip: $d = 45t$ and $d = 30(2.5 - t)$. Because both are equal to d, you can set them equal to each other and solve for t:

$$45t = 30(2.5 - t)$$
$$45t = 75 - 30t$$
$$75t = 75$$
$$t = 1$$

Now plug the value of t back in to solve for d:

$$d = 45t$$
$$d = 45(1)$$
$$d = 45$$

37. 10   Difficulty: Medium

Category: Problem Solving and Data Analysis / Rates, Ratios, Proportions, and Percentages

Getting to the Answer: You don't need to know chemistry to answer this question. All the information you need is in the table. Use the formula Percent $= \dfrac{\text{part}}{\text{whole}} \times 100\%$. To use the formula, find the part of the mass represented by the carbon; there is 1 mole of carbon, and it has a mass of 12.011 grams. Next, find the whole mass of the mole of chloroform: 1 mole carbon (12.011 g) + 1 mole hydrogen (1.008 g) + 3 moles chlorine (3 × 35.453 = 106.359 g) = 12.011 + 1.008 + 106.359 = 119.378. Now use the formula:

$$\text{Percent} = \frac{12.011}{119.378} \times 100\%$$
$$= 0.10053 \times 100\%$$
$$= 10.053\%$$

Before you grid in your answer, make sure you follow the directions—round to the nearest whole percent, which is 10.

38. 12   Difficulty: Hard

Category: Problem Solving and Data Analysis / Rates, Ratios, Proportions, and Percentages

Getting to the Answer: Think about the units given in the question and how you can use what you know to find what you need. Start with grams of chloro-

form; the chemist starts with 1,000 and uses 522.5, so there are 1,000 − 522.5 = 477.5 grams left. From the previous question, you know that 1 mole of chloroform has a mass of 119.378 grams, so there are 477.5 ÷ 119.378 = 3.999, or about 4 moles of chloroform left. Be careful—you're not finished yet. The question asks for the number of moles of *chlorine*, not chloroform. According to the table, each mole of chloroform contains 3 moles of chlorine, so there are 4 × 3 = 12 moles of chlorine left.

ESSAY TEST RUBRIC

The Essay Demonstrates...

4—Advanced	• **(Reading)** A strong ability to comprehend the source text, including its central ideas and important details and how they interrelate; and effectively use evidence (quotations, paraphrases, or both) from the source text. • **(Analysis)** A strong ability to evaluate the author's use of evidence, reasoning, and/or stylistic and persuasive elements, and/or other features of the student's own choosing; make good use of relevant, sufficient, and strategically chosen support for the claims or points made in the student's essay; and focus consistently on features of the source text that are most relevant to addressing the task. • **(Writing)** A strong ability to provide a precise central claim; create an effective organization that includes an introduction and conclusion, as well as a clear progression of ideas; successfully employ a variety of sentence structures; use precise word choice; maintain a formal style and objective tone; and show command of the conventions of standard written English so that the essay is free of errors.
3—Proficient	• **(Reading)** Satisfactory ability to comprehend the source text, including its central ideas and important details and how they interrelate; and use evidence (quotations, paraphrases, or both) from the source text. • **(Analysis)** Satisfactory ability to evaluate the author's use of evidence, reasoning, and/or stylistic and persuasive elements, and/or other features of the student's own choosing; make use of relevant and sufficient support for the claims or points made in the student's essay; and focus primarily on features of the source text that are most relevant to addressing the task. • **(Writing)** Satisfactory ability to provide a central claim; create an organization that includes an introduction and conclusion, as well as a clear progression of ideas; employ a variety of sentence structures; use precise word choice; maintain an appropriate formal style and objective tone; and show control of the conventions of standard written English so that the essay is free of significant errors.
2—Partial	• **(Reading)** Limited ability to comprehend the source text, including its central ideas and important details and how they interrelate; and use evidence (quotations, paraphrases, or both) from the source text. • **(Analysis)** Limited ability to evaluate the author's use of evidence, reasoning, and/or stylistic and persuasive elements, and/or other features of the student's own choosing; make use of support for the claims or points made in the student's essay; and focus on relevant features of the source text. • **(Writing)** Limited ability to provide a central claim; create an effective organization for ideas; employ a variety of sentence structures; use precise word choice; maintain an appropriate style and tone; or show control of the conventions of standard written English, resulting in certain errors that detract from the quality of the writing.

1—Inadequate	• **(Reading)** Little or no ability to comprehend the source text or use evidence from the source text. • **(Analysis)** Little or no ability to evaluate the author's use of evidence, reasoning, and/or stylistic and persuasive elements; choose support for claims or points; or focus on relevant features of the source text. • **(Writing)** Little or no ability to provide a central claim, organization, or progression of ideas; employ a variety of sentence structures; use precise word choice; maintain an appropriate style and tone; or show control of the conventions of standard written English, resulting in numerous errors that undermine the quality of the writing.

SAMPLE ESSAY RESPONSE #1 (ADVANCED SCORE)

As anyone knows who has had to help their family move house, find a textbook in a cluttered room, or even just clean a crowded apartment, possessions can have a huge amount of power over people. Far from being simply objects that we enjoy or that bring us pleasure, it can sometimes feel that our possessions oppress us. This is the point Morris eloquently makes in her essay "The Tyranny of Things." By using anecdotes, examples, reasoning, and powerful imagery, Morris argues that the very things we cherish are nearly crushing the life out of us.

The author begins by relating an anecdote about two teenagers becoming fast friends over their love of things. It is a touching moment, one to which readers can easily relate; even Morris herself says that we all probably go through this phase. This helps establish her credibility with readers, because her examples make sense to them. Gradually, however, Morris makes it clear that this touching moment has a sinister side—the love of things will only result in resentment.

Morris reasons that while it's natural to go through a phase of wanting objects, it is unhealthy to remain in this state. "Many people never pass out of this phase," she writes ominously. "They never see a flower without wanting to pick it … they bring home all their alpenstocks." It begins to sound obsessive, this need to control things. Morris goes on to develop her argument by suggesting that possessions are metaphorically suffocating us. She makes the idea of too many possessions sound repulsive by describing them as "an undigested mass of things." The things almost take on a kind of life force, according to Morris: "they possess us." They "have destroyed" our empty spaces and we feel "stifled."

Another way Morris supports her argument is by giving examples of the unnecessary "tokens" associated with social occasions. She describes how at events, luncheons, and parties, gifts are given and received. She then uses powerful negative imagery to describe the effects of these gifts, comparing the recipient to a "ship encrusted with barnacles" that needs to be "scraped bare again." This language suggests that the gifts are burdensome and even harmful.

By contrast, the imagery Morris uses to describe a simple life filled with fewer things is imagery of ease and relaxation. "We breathe more freely in the clear space that we have made for ourselves," she writes. It is not just that we have literally regained control from our possessions and are now acting rather than being acted upon; it is that we are physically more at ease.

In her conclusion, Morris longs for a day when we can live more simply, with fewer possessions. She describes a "house by the sea" that was simple and empty; it did not "demand care" or "claim attention" or otherwise act upon her. Her wish is that "we could but free ourselves" from the tyranny of things that she feels is draining us of our freedom. And at this point, it is likely the reader's wish, too.

SAMPLE ESSAY RESPONSE #2 (PROFICIENT SCORE)

Although as people we like to think of ourselves as owners of things, in fact it can sometimes feel like the things we own end up owning us. At least this is what Morris argues in her essay "The Tyranny of Things." Through her use of evidence, reasoning, and word choice, she makes a strong argument that we should own fewer things if we ever want to be truly happy.

Morris tells a story about two teenage girls who instantly know they will be friends because they both like things. They are not happy just to be. They have to own things. It's like their own experiences aren't enough for them. But Morris says that this is bad for people, because they will end up feeling like their possessions own them.

Morris's reasoning is that we can basically get control back over our own lives if we stop needing things so much. If we have too many things, "they possess us." So we have to get rid of things, and then we can feel better. At least these days we aren't buried with our things anymore, like they were in the olden days.

The word choices in the essay are interesting. She talks about the way things become a problem for us: "our books are a burden to us, our pictures have destroyed every restful wall-space, our china is a care." By using a lot of repetition, it shows how powerful things are.

Morris's essay encourages people to free themselves from their things. If they do so, they will be happier. Through her personal anecdotes, reasoning, and repetitive word choices, she makes her essay very powerful.

SAT PRACTICE TEST 1 ANSWER SHEET

Remove (or photocopy) this answer sheet and use it to complete the test. See the answer key following the test when finished.

Start with number 1 for each section. If a section has fewer questions than answer spaces, leave the extra spaces blank.

SECTION

1

1. Ⓐ Ⓑ Ⓒ Ⓓ	14. Ⓐ Ⓑ Ⓒ Ⓓ	27. Ⓐ Ⓑ Ⓒ Ⓓ	40. Ⓐ Ⓑ Ⓒ Ⓓ
2. Ⓐ Ⓑ Ⓒ Ⓓ	15. Ⓐ Ⓑ Ⓒ Ⓓ	28. Ⓐ Ⓑ Ⓒ Ⓓ	41. Ⓐ Ⓑ Ⓒ Ⓓ
3. Ⓐ Ⓑ Ⓒ Ⓓ	16. Ⓐ Ⓑ Ⓒ Ⓓ	29. Ⓐ Ⓑ Ⓒ Ⓓ	42. Ⓐ Ⓑ Ⓒ Ⓓ
4. Ⓐ Ⓑ Ⓒ Ⓓ	17. Ⓐ Ⓑ Ⓒ Ⓓ	30. Ⓐ Ⓑ Ⓒ Ⓓ	43. Ⓐ Ⓑ Ⓒ Ⓓ
5. Ⓐ Ⓑ Ⓒ Ⓓ	18. Ⓐ Ⓑ Ⓒ Ⓓ	31. Ⓐ Ⓑ Ⓒ Ⓓ	44. Ⓐ Ⓑ Ⓒ Ⓓ
6. Ⓐ Ⓑ Ⓒ Ⓓ	19. Ⓐ Ⓑ Ⓒ Ⓓ	32. Ⓐ Ⓑ Ⓒ Ⓓ	45. Ⓐ Ⓑ Ⓒ Ⓓ
7. Ⓐ Ⓑ Ⓒ Ⓓ	20. Ⓐ Ⓑ Ⓒ Ⓓ	33. Ⓐ Ⓑ Ⓒ Ⓓ	46. Ⓐ Ⓑ Ⓒ Ⓓ
8. Ⓐ Ⓑ Ⓒ Ⓓ	21. Ⓐ Ⓑ Ⓒ Ⓓ	34. Ⓐ Ⓑ Ⓒ Ⓓ	47. Ⓐ Ⓑ Ⓒ Ⓓ
9. Ⓐ Ⓑ Ⓒ Ⓓ	22. Ⓐ Ⓑ Ⓒ Ⓓ	35. Ⓐ Ⓑ Ⓒ Ⓓ	48. Ⓐ Ⓑ Ⓒ Ⓓ
10. Ⓐ Ⓑ Ⓒ Ⓓ	23. Ⓐ Ⓑ Ⓒ Ⓓ	36. Ⓐ Ⓑ Ⓒ Ⓓ	49. Ⓐ Ⓑ Ⓒ Ⓓ
11. Ⓐ Ⓑ Ⓒ Ⓓ	24. Ⓐ Ⓑ Ⓒ Ⓓ	37. Ⓐ Ⓑ Ⓒ Ⓓ	50. Ⓐ Ⓑ Ⓒ Ⓓ
12. Ⓐ Ⓑ Ⓒ Ⓓ	25. Ⓐ Ⓑ Ⓒ Ⓓ	38. Ⓐ Ⓑ Ⓒ Ⓓ	51. Ⓐ Ⓑ Ⓒ Ⓓ
13. Ⓐ Ⓑ Ⓒ Ⓓ	26. Ⓐ Ⓑ Ⓒ Ⓓ	39. Ⓐ Ⓑ Ⓒ Ⓓ	52. Ⓐ Ⓑ Ⓒ Ⓓ

☐ # correct in Section 1

☐ # incorrect in Section 1

SECTION

2

1. Ⓐ Ⓑ Ⓒ Ⓓ	12. Ⓐ Ⓑ Ⓒ Ⓓ	23. Ⓐ Ⓑ Ⓒ Ⓓ	34. Ⓐ Ⓑ Ⓒ Ⓓ
2. Ⓐ Ⓑ Ⓒ Ⓓ	13. Ⓐ Ⓑ Ⓒ Ⓓ	24. Ⓐ Ⓑ Ⓒ Ⓓ	35. Ⓐ Ⓑ Ⓒ Ⓓ
3. Ⓐ Ⓑ Ⓒ Ⓓ	14. Ⓐ Ⓑ Ⓒ Ⓓ	25. Ⓐ Ⓑ Ⓒ Ⓓ	36. Ⓐ Ⓑ Ⓒ Ⓓ
4. Ⓐ Ⓑ Ⓒ Ⓓ	15. Ⓐ Ⓑ Ⓒ Ⓓ	26. Ⓐ Ⓑ Ⓒ Ⓓ	37. Ⓐ Ⓑ Ⓒ Ⓓ
5. Ⓐ Ⓑ Ⓒ Ⓓ	16. Ⓐ Ⓑ Ⓒ Ⓓ	27. Ⓐ Ⓑ Ⓒ Ⓓ	38. Ⓐ Ⓑ Ⓒ Ⓓ
6. Ⓐ Ⓑ Ⓒ Ⓓ	17. Ⓐ Ⓑ Ⓒ Ⓓ	28. Ⓐ Ⓑ Ⓒ Ⓓ	39. Ⓐ Ⓑ Ⓒ Ⓓ
7. Ⓐ Ⓑ Ⓒ Ⓓ	18. Ⓐ Ⓑ Ⓒ Ⓓ	29. Ⓐ Ⓑ Ⓒ Ⓓ	40. Ⓐ Ⓑ Ⓒ Ⓓ
8. Ⓐ Ⓑ Ⓒ Ⓓ	19. Ⓐ Ⓑ Ⓒ Ⓓ	30. Ⓐ Ⓑ Ⓒ Ⓓ	41. Ⓐ Ⓑ Ⓒ Ⓓ
9. Ⓐ Ⓑ Ⓒ Ⓓ	20. Ⓐ Ⓑ Ⓒ Ⓓ	31. Ⓐ Ⓑ Ⓒ Ⓓ	42. Ⓐ Ⓑ Ⓒ Ⓓ
10. Ⓐ Ⓑ Ⓒ Ⓓ	21. Ⓐ Ⓑ Ⓒ Ⓓ	32. Ⓐ Ⓑ Ⓒ Ⓓ	43. Ⓐ Ⓑ Ⓒ Ⓓ
11. Ⓐ Ⓑ Ⓒ Ⓓ	22. Ⓐ Ⓑ Ⓒ Ⓓ	33. Ⓐ Ⓑ Ⓒ Ⓓ	44. Ⓐ Ⓑ Ⓒ Ⓓ

☐ # correct in Section 2

☐ # incorrect in Section 2

Practice Tests

SECTION

3

1. Ⓐ Ⓑ Ⓒ Ⓓ
2. Ⓐ Ⓑ Ⓒ Ⓓ
3. Ⓐ Ⓑ Ⓒ Ⓓ
4. Ⓐ Ⓑ Ⓒ Ⓓ

5. Ⓐ Ⓑ Ⓒ Ⓓ
6. Ⓐ Ⓑ Ⓒ Ⓓ
7. Ⓐ Ⓑ Ⓒ Ⓓ
8. Ⓐ Ⓑ Ⓒ Ⓓ

9. Ⓐ Ⓑ Ⓒ Ⓓ
10. Ⓐ Ⓑ Ⓒ Ⓓ
11. Ⓐ Ⓑ Ⓒ Ⓓ
12. Ⓐ Ⓑ Ⓒ Ⓓ

13. Ⓐ Ⓑ Ⓒ Ⓓ
14. Ⓐ Ⓑ Ⓒ Ⓓ
15. Ⓐ Ⓑ Ⓒ Ⓓ

correct in
Section 3

incorrect in
Section 3

16. 17. 18. 19. 20.

SECTION

4

1. Ⓐ Ⓑ Ⓒ Ⓓ
2. Ⓐ Ⓑ Ⓒ Ⓓ
3. Ⓐ Ⓑ Ⓒ Ⓓ
4. Ⓐ Ⓑ Ⓒ Ⓓ
5. Ⓐ Ⓑ Ⓒ Ⓓ
6. Ⓐ Ⓑ Ⓒ Ⓓ
7. Ⓐ Ⓑ Ⓒ Ⓓ
8. Ⓐ Ⓑ Ⓒ Ⓓ

9. Ⓐ Ⓑ Ⓒ Ⓓ
10. Ⓐ Ⓑ Ⓒ Ⓓ
11. Ⓐ Ⓑ Ⓒ Ⓓ
12. Ⓐ Ⓑ Ⓒ Ⓓ
13. Ⓐ Ⓑ Ⓒ Ⓓ
14. Ⓐ Ⓑ Ⓒ Ⓓ
15. Ⓐ Ⓑ Ⓒ Ⓓ
16. Ⓐ Ⓑ Ⓒ Ⓓ

17. Ⓐ Ⓑ Ⓒ Ⓓ
18. Ⓐ Ⓑ Ⓒ Ⓓ
19. Ⓐ Ⓑ Ⓒ Ⓓ
20. Ⓐ Ⓑ Ⓒ Ⓓ
21. Ⓐ Ⓑ Ⓒ Ⓓ
22. Ⓐ Ⓑ Ⓒ Ⓓ
23. Ⓐ Ⓑ Ⓒ Ⓓ
24. Ⓐ Ⓑ Ⓒ Ⓓ

25. Ⓐ Ⓑ Ⓒ Ⓓ
26. Ⓐ Ⓑ Ⓒ Ⓓ
27. Ⓐ Ⓑ Ⓒ Ⓓ
28. Ⓐ Ⓑ Ⓒ Ⓓ
29. Ⓐ Ⓑ Ⓒ Ⓓ
30. Ⓐ Ⓑ Ⓒ Ⓓ

correct in
Section 4

incorrect in
Section 4

31. 32. 33. 34.

35. 36. 37. 38.

Practice Tests

READING TEST

65 Minutes—52 Questions

Turn to Section 1 of your answer sheet to answer the questions in this section.

Directions: Each passage or pair of passages below is followed by a number of questions. After reading each passage or pair, choose the best answer to each question based on what is stated or implied in the passage or passages and in any accompanying graphics (such as a table or graph).

Questions 1-10 are based on the following passage.

This passage is adapted from *A Study in Scarlet*, Sir Arthur Conan Doyle's first story in his acclaimed Sherlock Holmes series. In this excerpt the narrator, Dr. Watson, observes Mr. Holmes, with whom he has recently entered into a shared housing arrangement, although he knows very little about this new room-mate as of yet.

As the weeks went by, my interest in him and my curiosity as to his aims in life gradually deepened and increased. His very person and appearance
Line were such as to strike the attention of the most
(5) casual observer. In height he was rather over six feet, and so excessively lean that he seemed to be considerably taller. His eyes were sharp and piercing, save during those intervals of torpor to which I have alluded; and his thin, hawk-like nose gave his
(10) whole expression an air of alertness and decision. His chin, too, had the prominence and squareness which mark the man of determination. His hands were invariably blotted with ink and stained with chemicals, yet he was possessed of extraordinary
(15) delicacy of touch, as I frequently had occasion to observe when I watched him manipulating his fragile philosophical instruments. . . .

He was not studying medicine. He had himself, in reply to a question, confirmed Stamford's[1]
(20) opinion upon that point. Neither did he appear to have pursued any course of reading which might fit him for a degree in science or any other recognized

portal which would give him an entrance into the learned world. Yet his zeal for certain studies
(25) was remarkable, and within eccentric limits his knowledge was so extraordinarily ample and minute that his observations have fairly astounded me. Surely no man would work so hard or attain such precise information unless he had some
(30) definite end in view. Desultory readers are seldom remarkable for the exactness of their learning. No man burdens his mind with small matters unless he has some very good reason for doing so.

His ignorance was as remarkable as his knowledge.
(35) Of contemporary literature, philosophy and politics he appeared to know next to nothing. Upon my quoting Thomas Carlyle,[2] he inquired in the naïvest way who he might be and what he had done. My surprise reached a climax, however, when I found
(40) incidentally that he was ignorant of the Copernican Theory and of the composition of the solar system. That any civilized human being in this nineteenth century should not be aware that the earth travelled round the sun appeared to be to me such an
(45) extraordinary fact that I could hardly realize it.

"You appear to be astonished," he said, smiling at my expression of surprise. "Now that I do know it I shall do my best to forget it."

"To forget it!"

(50) "You see," he explained, "I consider that a man's brain originally is like a little empty attic, and you have to stock it with such furniture as you choose. A fool takes in all the lumber of every sort that he comes across, so that the knowledge which might

---

[1]Stamford is the mutual acquaintance who introduced Dr. Watson to Mr. Holmes. In a previous scene he told Watson that Holmes was not a medical student.

[2]Thomas Carlyle was an influential writer and philosopher whose work was well known at the time of this novel's publication.

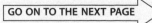
GO ON TO THE NEXT PAGE

Practice Tests

(55) be useful to him gets crowded out, or at best is jumbled up with a lot of other things so that he has a difficulty in laying his hands upon it. Now the skillful workman is very careful indeed as to what he takes into his brain-attic. He will have

(60) nothing but the tools which may help him in doing his work, but of these he has a large assortment, and all in the most perfect order. It is a mistake to think that that little room has elastic walls and can distend to any extent. Depend upon it there comes

(65) a time when for every addition of knowledge you forget something that you knew before. It is of the highest importance, therefore, not to have useless facts elbowing out the useful ones."

"But the solar system!" I protested.

(70) "What the deuce is it to me?"

1. According to the passage, as time passes, Watson finds Holmes

   A) increasingly intriguing.

   B) frequently irritating.

   C) somewhat snobby.

   D) occasionally generous.

2. As used in line 5, "casual" most nearly means

   A) impulsive.

   B) comfortable.

   C) relaxed.

   D) occasional.

3. As presented in the passage, Sherlock Holmes is best described as

   A) very secretive and hard to understand.

   B) an excellent companion to Watson.

   C) highly regarded by his peers.

   D) an unusual and extraordinary man.

4. As used in line 8, "torpor" most nearly means

   A) agitation.

   B) sluggishness.

   C) alertness.

   D) illness.

5. The passage most strongly suggests that which of the following is true of Holmes?

   A) He tried, but failed, to become a doctor.

   B) He was an excellent student at the university.

   C) He studies things he is passionate about.

   D) He is considered an expert in philosophy.

6. Which choice provides the best evidence for the answer to the previous question?

   A) Lines 12-17 ("His hands were . . . instruments")

   B) Lines 18-20 ("He was not . . . that point")

   C) Lines 24-28 ("Yet his . . . astounded me")

   D) Lines 28-30 ("Surely no man . . . in view")

7. The passage most strongly suggests that Holmes believes which of the following about learning?

   A) People should study broadly to know something about everything.

   B) Philosophy is not a valid field of study to pursue.

   C) The brain is limited in capacity, so you should prioritize what you learn.

   D) The Copernican Theory is unfounded and therefore should not be studied.

8. Which choice provides the best evidence for the answer to the previous question?

   A) Line 34 ("His ignorance . . . his knowledge")

   B) Lines 35-36 ("Of contemporary . . . nothing")

   C) Lines 42-45 ("That any . . . realize it")

   D) Lines 66-68 ("It is of the . . . ones")

GO ON TO THE NEXT PAGE ⟹

9. The comparison of the brain to an attic mainly serves to

   A) demonstrate Holmes's unique views on how a person should make use of knowledge.

   B) illustrate Watson's combative nature.

   C) provide an alternate explanation for why Holmes doesn't know about Copernicus.

   D) resolve the conflict between Watson and Holmes.

10. The decision to tell the story from Watson's point of view suggests that the author

    A) wants the reader to dislike Holmes.

    B) needed a sympathetic narrator.

    C) will focus the rest of the story on Watson's actions.

    D) hopes the reader will share Watson's curiosity about Holmes.

Questions 11-20 are based on the following passage.

This passage is adapted from a speech given by President Woodrow Wilson to Congress on January 8, 1918. Here Wilson proposes a 14-point program for world peace. These 14 points became the basis for peace negotiations at the end of World War I.

It will be our wish and purpose that the processes of peace, when they are begun, shall be absolutely open and that they shall involve and
Line permit henceforth no secret understandings of any
(5) kind. The day of conquest and aggrandizement is gone by; so is also the day of secret covenants entered into in the interest of particular governments and likely at some unlooked-for moment to upset the peace of the world. It is this happy fact,
(10) now clear to the view of every public man whose thoughts do not still linger in an age that is dead and gone, which makes it possible for every nation whose purposes are consistent with justice and the peace of the world to avow now or at any other
(15) time the objects it has in view.

We entered this war because violations of right had occurred which touched us to the quick and made the life of our own people impossible unless they were corrected. . . . What we demand in this
(20) war, therefore, is nothing peculiar to ourselves. It is that the world be made fit and safe to live in; and particularly that it be made safe for every peace-loving nation which, like our own, wishes to live its own life, determine its own institutions, be assured
(25) of justice and fair dealing by the other peoples of the world. . . . The programme of the world's peace, therefore, is our programme; and that programme, the only possible programme, as we see it, is this:

   I. Open covenants of peace . . . with no private
(30)   international understandings of any kind but diplomacy shall proceed always frankly and in the public view.

   II. Absolute freedom of navigation upon the seas . . . alike in peace and in war, except as
(35)   the seas may be closed in whole or in part by international action for the enforcement of international covenants.

   III. The removal, so far as possible, of all economic barriers and the establishment of
(40)   an equality of trade conditions among all the nations consenting. . . .

   IV. Adequate guarantees given and taken that national armaments will be reduced to the lowest point consistent with domestic safety.
(45)   V. A free, open-minded, and absolutely impartial adjustment of all colonial claims. . . .

   VI. The evacuation of all Russian territory and such a settlement of all questions affecting Russia as will secure the best and freest
(50)   cooperation of the other nations of the world.

   VII. Belgium . . . must be evacuated and restored, without any attempt to limit the sovereignty which she enjoys in common with all other free nations. . . .

(55)   VIII. All French territory should be freed and the invaded portions restored. . . .

   IX. A readjustment of the frontiers of Italy should be effected along clearly recognizable lines of nationality.

GO ON TO THE NEXT PAGE →

(60) X. The peoples of Austria-Hungary . . . should be accorded the freest opportunity to autonomous development.

XI. Rumania, Serbia, and Montenegro should be evacuated; occupied territories restored;
(65) and Serbia accorded free and secure access to the sea. . . .

XII. The Turkish portion of the present Ottoman Empire should be assured a secure sovereignty, but the other nationalities
(70) which are now under Turkish rule should be assured an undoubted security of life. . . .

XIII. An independent Polish state should be erected which should include the territories inhabited by indisputably Polish populations
(75) . . . . [The state] should be assured a free and secure access to the sea. . . .

XIV. A general association of nations must be formed under specific covenants for the purpose of affording mutual guarantees
(80) of political independence and territorial integrity to great and small states alike.

11. Based on the first two paragraphs, which choice best identifies Wilson's purpose in making this speech?

A) To build an international military and political alliance

B) To declare the sovereignty and independence of the United States

C) To outline ways to maintain peaceful relations in the world

D) To reform governments in aggressor nations bent on conquest

12. Which choice provides the best evidence for the answer to the previous question?

A) Lines 1-5 ("It will be . . . of any kind")

B) Lines 5-6 ("The day of . . . is gone by")

C) Lines 16-17 ("We entered . . . occurred")

D) Lines 26-27 ("The programme . . . is our programme")

13. As used in line 31, "frankly" most nearly means

A) in an honest manner.

B) in a blunt manner.

C) in an abrupt manner.

D) in an outspoken manner.

14. Based on the information in the passage, it can reasonably be inferred that in the past,

A) the United States avoided alliances.

B) some nations formed private pacts with one another.

C) wars usually involved only two nations.

D) the borders of France and Italy were not well-defined.

15. Which choice provides the best evidence for the answer to the previous question?

A) Lines 1-5 ("It will be . . . of any kind")

B) Lines 16-19 ("We entered . . . corrected")

C) Lines 55-59 ("All French . . . of nationality")

D) Lines 77-81 ("A general . . . states alike")

16. As used in line 44, "consistent" most nearly means

A) dependable.

B) continuing.

C) agreeable.

D) rigid.

17. In lines 45-46 ("A free . . . colonial claims"), Wilson argues that to preserve peace, nations must

A) engage in free, open, and fair trade with colonies.

B) give up all aspirations for territorial and economic expansion.

C) provide constitutional protections for colonies.

D) work to resolve conflicts originating from imperial conquests.

 GO ON TO THE NEXT PAGE

18. Points VI through VIII serve as evidence to support which claim made by Wilson throughout the speech?

    A) Democratic nations ought to sign pacts of economic and political cooperation.

    B) During the war, aggressors damaged property that they should be required to repair.

    C) In the past, nations violated one another's territorial sovereignty.

    D) Current colonies are entitled to establish free and democratic governments.

19. Which of the following approaches to international relations is most similar to Wilson's approach?

    A) Economic sanctions against ideological enemies

    B) Joint efforts to mediate conflict among nations

    C) Nongovernmental organizations to regulate trade

    D) Unilateral military action against unfriendly regimes

20. Which choice best describes the developmental pattern of Wilson's argument?

    A) A statement and restatement of the argument

    B) A statement of the argument followed by specific examples

    C) Initial claims followed by counterclaims

    D) Specific examples leading to a concluding argument

Questions 21-31 are based on the following passages and supplementary material.

The following passages are concerned with meditation, particularly the practice of mindfulness. Passage 1 provides an overview of meditation, while Passage 2 focuses on a particular practitioner, Congressmen Tim Ryan.

Passage 1

Meditation has been around for thousands of years, starting as a religious practice. Hindu scripture from around 1500 BCE describes meditating on
Line the divine, and art from this time period shows
(5) people sitting cross-legged and solitary in a garden. In China and India around the fifth century BCE, other forms of meditation developed. Several religions, including Taoism, Buddhism, Islam, and Christianity, have meditative rites. In 20th-century
(10) Europe and America, secular forms of meditation arrived from India. Rather than focusing on spiritual growth, secular meditation emphasizes stress reduction, relaxation, and self-improvement.

Although it still isn't exactly mainstream,
(15) many people practice meditation. Mindfulness meditation, in particular, has become more popular in recent years. The practice involves sitting comfortably, focusing on one's breathing, and bringing the mind's attention to the present.
(20) Concerns about the past or future are let go of. An individual can picture worries popping like a bubble or flitting away like a butterfly.

Mindfulness is about increasing awareness and practicing acceptance. To be present is to
(25) have sharpened attention, or to be in a state of heightened consciousness. Practitioners of mindfulness report having a better quality of experience, deeper engagement, and greater measure of fulfillment.

(30) There are also health benefits. According to the Mayo Clinic, "Meditation can give you a sense of calm, peace and balance that benefits your emotional well-being." Among the emotional benefits are reducing negative emotions, increased
(35) self-awareness, and stress management skills.

GO ON TO THE NEXT PAGE ⟹

Practice Tests

Asthma, depression, and sleep disorders are all conditions worsened by stress. Several studies have shown that patients with these conditions benefit from meditation.

(40) Dr. Robert Schneider, director of the Institute for Natural Medicine and Prevention, says, "I have been researching effects of meditation on health for thirty years and have found it has compelling benefits. The benefits of meditation are coming to

(45) be widely accepted by health professionals, business leaders, and the media. It is now time for the medical profession to catch up."

Passage 2

In 2008, hoping to relax from his stressful job, Congressman Tim Ryan took a weekend retreat

(50) where he first practiced mindfulness meditation. "I came out of it," he says, "with a whole new way of relating with what was going on in the world." Now Ryan is an advocate for the benefits of meditation on health, performance, and social aware-

(55) ness. In the busy and aggressive world of Washington politics, he's a voice for calm consideration.

Every week Ryan, a Democrat representing the 13th congressional district of Ohio, hosts a meditation session for his staff and any other

(60) members of Congress who want to join. Despite the fact that Republicans and Democrats are considered politically opposed, Ryan believes that the benefits of meditation ought to appeal to members of both parties. Meditation promotes self-reliance

(65) and fiscal conservation because it's a health practice that can be self-sustained and doesn't require costly memberships or equipment.

In 2010, Ryan wrote the book *A Mindful Nation: How a Simple Practice Can Help Us Reduce Stress,*

(70) *Improve Performance, and Recapture the American Spirit,* in which he advocates increased mindfulness in many disciplines and professions. After its publication, kindergarten classes in his Ohio district started using deep-breathing techniques;

(75) now teachers rave about their students' improved behavior. "Mental discipline, focus, self-reliance, deep listening—these are fundamental skills that are essential to kids' education," Ryan says. "We yell at kids to pay attention, but we never teach them

(80) *how* to pay attention."

Word seems to be spreading around Capitol Hill. "I've had members of Congress approach me and say, 'I want to learn more about this,'" Ryan says. "Between the fundraising, being away from fam-

(85) ily, (and) the environment of hyperpartisanship, Washington is really stressing people out."

Ryan supports legislation that puts meditation to good use for everyone. Among other bills, he has sponsored one to increase the holistic-medicine

(90) offerings of the Department of Veterans Affairs. "And I haven't met anyone in the country that isn't feeling a high level of anxiety right now, given the economy and what's going on in the world. So mindfulness is for everyone."

(95) Mr. Ryan is quick to point out that mindfulness is not a religious practice, but rather a secular mental technique that can be effective regardless of spiritual beliefs. He compares it to his grandparents praying and to athletes working out until they feel

(100) "in the zone."

"Your mind and body sync up into a flow state, without a lot of mental chatter," Mr. Ryan says.

**Improvements After
Employee Meditation Program**

After the third year of its employee meditation program, a Detroit chemical plant reported these improvements.

21. The central idea of Passage 1 is that meditation and mindfulness

A) were first practiced as religious rites.

B) are becoming more accepted because of their benefits.

C) are valuable tools for psychologists.

D) help practitioners focus on their inner lives.

22. Passage 1 most strongly suggests that which of the following is true?

A) Individuals who practice mediation are less likely to develop illness.

B) Meditation helps people advance in their careers.

C) Not many studies have been done on the results of daily meditation.

D) Many medical professionals embrace the benefits of meditation.

23. Which choice provides the best evidence for the answer to the previous question?

A) Lines 2-5 ("Hindu scripture . . . in a garden")

B) Lines 15-17 ("Mindfulness meditation . . . in recent years")

C) Lines 24-26 ("To be present . . . consciousness")

D) Lines 30-33 ("According to . . . well-being")

24. As used in line 43, "compelling" most nearly means

A) creative.

B) judicial.

C) persuasive.

D) adaptable.

25. In Passage 2, what can be inferred about the author's point of view on meditation?

A) The author is uncertain about its value.

B) The author likes it but acknowledges its limits.

C) The author appreciates its value.

D) The author is devoted to it.

26. Passage 2 most strongly suggests that which of the following is true of Mr. Ryan?

A) He acts on his beliefs.

B) He is afraid to try new things.

C) He likes to try new things.

D) He is concerned about bipartisanship.

27. Which choice provides the best evidence for the answer to the previous question?

A) Lines 48-50 ("In 2008 . . . mindfulness meditation")

B) Lines 64-67 ("Meditation promotes . . . or equipment")

C) Lines 88-90 ("Among other bills . . . Affairs")

D) Lines 95-98 ("Mr. Ryan . . . spiritual beliefs")

28. As used in line 96, "secular" most nearly means

A) nonreligious.

B) serious.

C) impersonal.

D) pristine.

GO ON TO THE NEXT PAGE

Practice Tests

29. In Passage 2, the author's use of the word "chatter" (line 102) implies that

    A) having an inner dialogue is a useful tool.

    B) people enjoy imagining themselves in various situations.

    C) meditation supporters talk about its surprises.

    D) much of what people think is relatively unimportant.

30. Both passages support which generalization about mindfulness meditation?

    A) It has become an acceptable way to show spirituality.

    B) It is making inroads into U.S. culture.

    C) It should be utilized in public institutions.

    D) It will soon be embraced by the American public.

31. Data in the graph provide most direct support for which claim from the passages?

    A) Meditation improves a person's focus and discipline.

    B) Children benefit from learning deep-breathing techniques.

    C) Meditation makes a person more generous.

    D) Health professionals are open to the idea of meditation being healthful.

Questions 32-42 are based on the following passage.

The following passage describes possible causes and impacts of colony collapse disorder, the mysterious disappearance of honey bee colonies.

Colony collapse disorder, sometimes referred to as CCD, is a phenomenon that has garnered much attention over the past few years from both the scientific community and the media alike. The
Line
(5) disorder, which causes entire honey bee colonies to mysteriously disappear, is a major threat to both the environment and the economy. Honey bees are the world's natural pollinators, and are responsible for the production of about one-third of everything
(10) we eat. Without honey bees, produce that we're used to having in our diets, like apples, blueberries, strawberries, and nuts, would no longer be available. Honey bees also have an effect on the meat industry in the United States. They pollinate
(15) the various types of feed used by beef and dairy farmers. The services of the honey bee population are invaluable, and the survival of many different species depends on their well-being.

When colony collapse disorder was first
(20) recognized, beekeepers and scientists assumed that a pathogen was to blame. For example, there are several known viruses and pests that can kill off entire hives of honey bees quickly and be extremely hard to prevent. Mites, fungus, and bacterial
(25) infections are all common killers. Because of how often they're seen in hives, farmers assumed that these common plights were responsible for colony collapse disorder. However, as time passed and the disorder was studied, researchers noticed some-
(30) thing odd. In many cases, there were simply no dead bees to discover. While common killers of the honey bee left telltale signs, colony collapse disor-der left nothing behind but empty hives.

Scientists attributed the rapid disappearance of
(35) the bees to a form of altruistic behavior. When a bee gets sick, it flies away from the hive so as not to spread its illness to the other bees. It naturally prioritizes the overall health of the hive over its own. Although this behavior explained the bees'
(40) disappearing act, the cause of the disorder is yet to be understood and the list of possible explanations just keeps getting longer.

One team of researchers hypothesized that fluctuations in the earth's magnetic field might
(45) be doing damage to the magnetoreceptors, or built-in homing devices, that bees use to find their way home to their hives after flying all day. Honey bees, as well as birds and fish, use the earth's magnetic field to identify their location. Sunspots,

GO ON TO THE NEXT PAGE ⇨

(50) which cause the strength of the earth's magnetic field to fluctuate, might be damaging the honey bee's biological tools.

While solar activity is outside the control of humans, another theory about the cause of colony (55) collapse disorder points to the human invention of pesticides. Pesticides, which are chemicals used to prevent pest infestation of crops on a large scale around the world, are often picked up by honey bees during their foraging and pollination flights. (60) Scientists have found that more than one pesticide can be found in the honey of one hive. They are currently studying the interaction of two or more pesticides, which travel into the hives and are stored by the bees in the pollen they use for protein.

(65) While the presence of one pesticide in a hive would certainly limit the life spans of bees and impair their navigational skills, it could be that it is the interaction of two or more pesticides that cause the entire colony to collapse. There are many ingredi- (70) ents in pesticides that are not regulated by world governments, and this leaves a lot of ground for bee scientists to cover when doing their research.

Research over time usually helps to narrow down the field of possible causes of a disorder, but in the (75) case of colony collapse disorder, scientists feel farther away than ever from finding the root cause and a cure. Many people around the world are taking up the cause of keeping honey bees alive by keeping bees in their backyards or on their roofs. Some (80) cities and towns have relaxed regulations on beekeeping in response to the honey bee population crisis. Hopefully, community initiatives and research can both help to save the world's honey bee population.

32. The primary purpose of the passage is to

A) show that honey bees require certain conditions in order to live.

B) instruct the reader on how to increase the number of honey bees.

C) explain the relationship between sunspots and colony collapse disorder.

D) alert the reader to the impending crisis of decreasing numbers of honey bees.

33. The author's point of view is most similar to

A) an advocate for honey bee survival.

B) an environmentalist concerned about toxic materials.

C) a naturalist who researches changes in animal populations.

D) a concerned citizen who hopes to raise honey bees.

34. The author uses the word "mysteriously" (line 6) to emphasize

A) that fluctuations of the earth's magnetic field are uncontrollable.

B) how little is known about why colony collapse occurs.

C) that the reason a bee leaves its hive when it is sick is unknown.

D) why researchers are studying the effect of pesticides on honey bees.

35. As used in line 27, "plights" most nearly means

A) causes.

B) promises.

C) intentions.

D) troubles.

36. The author uses the fact that no bees are found in a hive after a colony collapses to

A) examine the extent of damage to the honey bee population that has occurred.

B) emphasize the ways in which honey bees relate to human beings.

C) refute the possibility that pathogens are the reason for the collapse.

D) show that pesticides are not to blame for the decrease in the honey bee population.

37. Which choice provides the best evidence for the answer to the previous question?

    A) Lines 4-7 ("The disorder . . . the economy")

    B) Lines 21-24 ("For example . . . to prevent")

    C) Lines 31-33 ("While common . . . empty hives")

    D) Lines 37-39 ("It naturally . . . its own")

38. As used in line 59, "foraging" most nearly means

    A) rejecting.

    B) offering.

    C) watching.

    D) searching.

39. The passage most strongly suggests that

    A) the author is cautiously optimistic about the future existence of the honey bee.

    B) the author thinks that scientists have not tried hard enough to find the reason for colony collapse.

    C) one team of scientists believes that they will have an answer to the problem of colony collapse very soon.

    D) scientists have ruled out the theory that pesticides are at fault for colony collapse.

40. Which choice provides the best evidence for the answer to the previous question?

    A) Lines 7-10 ("Honey bees . . . eat")

    B) Lines 25-28 ("Because of how . . . disorder")

    C) Lines 53-56 ("While solar . . . pesticides")

    D) Lines 82-83 ("Hopefully . . . population")

41. According to the passage, which of the following events has occurred in response to colony collapse disorder?

    A) Concerned citizens have fought to ban certain pesticides.

    B) Some towns have relaxed their regulations on beekeeping.

    C) Farmers have resorted to other means of pollinating their feed.

    D) Scientists are working to control the use of electromagnetic devices.

42. Based on information in the passage, which statement best describes the relationship between honey bees and human beings?

    A) Human beings depend on honey bees to keep the environment and economy healthy.

    B) Human beings depend on honey bees to keep the effects of sunspots to a minimum.

    C) Honey bees depend on human beings to provide them with food.

    D) Honey bees depend on human beings to protect them from solar flares.

Questions 43-52 are based on the following passage and supplementary materials.

The following passage describes the potential problems caused by debris that humans have left behind in space.

In the first days of space exploration, one concern was the possibility that astronauts or spacecraft might be hit by meteoroids. Scientists
Line calculated that this possibility was extremely
(5) small because meteoroids are rare. Astronauts and spacecraft, on the other hand, would almost certainly encounter micrometeorites, which are about the size of grains of dust and much more common.

However, in the 60 years since the beginning of
(10) space exploration, large quantities of human-made

orbital debris have accumulated. Much of the debris consists of satellites that have stopped functioning or rocket booster sections that separated from the main spacecraft during a mission. Some of (15) the debris consists of items lost by astronauts, such as tools or space suit parts. Still more of the debris is the result of collisions, such as when one satellite collides with another or with a large piece of debris.

NASA estimates there are millions of debris (20) particles that are too small to be tracked. These circle Earth at speeds up to 17,500 miles per hour, making even the smallest particles dangerous. One scientist calculated that a chip of paint hitting the window of a spacecraft at orbital speeds will hit (25) with the same amount of force as a bowling ball traveling at 60 mph. Such an impact occurred on the space shuttle *Challenger*'s second flight, chipping the windows and causing minor damage to the protective tiles on the spacecraft. While the damage (30) was not immediately dangerous, it led to the fear that any craft in orbit for long periods of time could accumulate enough damage to cease functioning.

Larger objects are even more dangerous, but they can be monitored and avoided. NASA tracks (35) about 500,000 pieces of debris larger than a marble, about 20,000 of which are larger than a softball. When NASA was still flying shuttle missions, it would often have to direct the shuttle to maneuver to avoid collisions with the larger debris. This could (40) usually be planned and accomplished in a few hours, but moving the International Space Station to avoid a collision takes up to 30 hours of advance notice.

Many satellites have the ability to adjust their (45) course slightly and can be remotely directed to avoid collisions with larger objects that would damage or destroy the satellites. NASA and the European Space Agency (ESA) have departments of scientists and engineers dedicated to cataloging, (50) modeling, and predicting the movements of space debris.

Some debris falls back to Earth, and most of it is burned up in the atmosphere. However, a large piece will survive long enough to get through (55) the atmosphere and crash. In 1979, the obsolete Skylab fell out of orbit, and much of it withstood

the trip through the atmosphere, crashing in the Australian outback. Space agencies also monitor debris to predict if and when any particular piece (60) might fall. Although they can issue warnings, there is currently nothing that can be done about pieces that might get through the atmosphere.

To avoid adding to the aggregation of debris, future satellites may need to be able to take (65) themselves out of orbit as their usefulness comes to an end. Until a way to remove these remains is implemented, however, those 500,000 pieces of large fragments, along with the millions of smaller pieces, will continue to orbit Earth.

Debris in Space

Adapted from NASA: U.S. Satellite Catalog.

43. The passage is primarily concerned with the

A) unintended consequences of space exploration.

B) composition of the space debris that orbits Earth.

C) dangers posed by space debris created by humans.

D) causes and consequences of collisions in space.

GO ON TO THE NEXT PAGE

Practice Tests

44. Which choice provides the best evidence for the answer to the previous question?

    A) Lines 3-8 ("Scientists calculated . . . common")

    B) Lines 20-22 ("These circle . . . dangerous")

    C) Lines 33-34 ("Larger objects . . . avoided")

    D) Lines 44-47 ("Many satellites . . . satellites")

45. The second paragraph helps support the central idea of the passage by providing

    A) an explanation of why space debris left by humans is more dangerous than meteors.

    B) a summary of problems caused by old satellites and discarded equipment.

    C) a description of the types of human-made space debris that are causing problems.

    D) an argument for better tracking of the space debris that is orbiting Earth.

46. According to the passage, why does space debris created by humans pose a greater threat than meteoroids?

    A) Meteoroids are rare, while there are large quantities of space debris.

    B) Meteoroids are much smaller than most pieces of space debris.

    C) Space debris cannot be tracked and monitored, but meteoroids can.

    D) Space debris is only found in a narrow band around Earth.

47. Which of the following pieces of evidence most strengthens the author's central claim?

    A) An explanation of early concerns about space collisions in paragraph 1

    B) Information about how space debris is tracked in paragraph 5

    C) An example of space debris falling to Earth in paragraph 6

    D) The suggestion that obsolete satellites take themselves out of orbit in paragraph 7

48. As used in line 55, "obsolete" most nearly means

    A) displaced.

    B) redundant.

    C) excessive.

    D) outdated.

49. Based on information in the passage, which conclusion can reasonably be inferred?

    A) One way to prevent space debris from causing injuries on Earth is to warn people to avoid the predicted impact site.

    B) The smallest pieces of space debris can be removed by astronauts while they are working in space.

    C) Most space debris is not dangerous to space travelers because of its small size and relatively low speed.

    D) Pieces of space debris will become more of a problem as spacecraft travel farther into outer space.

GO ON TO THE NEXT PAGE ⇨

50. Which choice provides the best evidence for the answer to the previous question?

    A) Lines 19-22 ("NASA estimates . . . dangerous")

    B) Lines 33-34 ("Larger objects . . . avoided")

    C) Lines 34-36 ("NASA tracks . . . softball")

    D) Lines 60-62 ("Although . . . atmosphere")

51. As used in line 67, "implemented" most nearly means

    A) employed.

    B) investigated.

    C) prevented.

    D) appointed.

52. Based on the passage and the graphic, if NASA were to place a new satellite into orbit, which altitude range would pose the greatest danger?

    A) 500-700 kilometers

    B) 700-900 kilometers

    C) 1,400-1,600 kilometers

    D) 1,800-2,000 kilometers

IF YOU FINISH BEFORE TIME IS CALLED, YOU MAY CHECK YOUR WORK ON THIS SECTION ONLY. DO NOT TURN TO ANY OTHER SECTION IN THE TEST. **STOP**

Practice Tests

WRITING AND LANGUAGE TEST

35 Minutes—44 Questions

Turn to Section 2 of your answer sheet to answer the questions in this section.

Directions: Each passage below is accompanied by a number of questions. For some questions, you will consider how the passage might be revised to improve the expression of ideas. For other questions, you will consider how the passage might be edited to correct errors in sentence structure, usage, or punctuation. A passage or a question may be accompanied by one or more graphics (such as a table or graph) that you will consider as you make revising and editing decisions.

Some questions will direct you to an underlined portion of a passage. Other questions will direct you to a location in a passage or ask you to think about the passage as a whole.

After reading each passage, choose the answer to each question that most effectively improves the quality of writing in the passage or that makes the passage conform to the conventions of standard written English. Many questions include a "NO CHANGE" option. Choose that option if you think the best choice is to leave the relevant portion of the passage as it is.

Questions 1-11 are based on the following passage.

A Sweet Discovery

[1] Like most chemists, a laboratory was where Constantin Fahlberg worked on his research. However, the discovery for which he is famous occurred not in the laboratory, but at supper.

1. A) NO CHANGE
   B) Like most chemists, Constantin Fahlberg worked on his research in a laboratory.
   C) Constantin Fahlberg worked on his research, like most chemists, in a laboratory.
   D) A laboratory, like most chemists, is where Constantin Fahlberg worked on his research.

2 Chemical compounds are derived from coal tar, which is what Fahlberg began working on as a research chemist in a laboratory at Johns Hopkins University in early 1878. Coal tar was a by-product of steel manufacturing, and compounds derived **3** from them had been used as medicines and in dye formulations. Fahlberg, and others in the laboratory, were studying ways to add different chemicals to molecules found in coal tar to see if the new compounds formed had other useful properties.

One night in June, Fahlberg finished a long day of work; he had been so **4** demanding in his research that he forgot to eat lunch, so he hurried to his supper without stopping to wash his hands. He might have

2. A) NO CHANGE
   B) Johns Hopkins University is where Fahlberg began working as a research chemist in a laboratory, making chemical compounds derived from coal tar in early 1878.
   C) Coal tar creates chemical compounds. This is what Fahlberg began working on as a research chemist in a laboratory at Johns Hopkins University in early 1878.
   D) In early 1878, Fahlberg began working as a research chemist in a laboratory at Johns Hopkins University, making chemical compounds derived from coal tar.

3. A) NO CHANGE
   B) from it
   C) from these
   D) from him

4. A) NO CHANGE
   B) delayed
   C) engrossed
   D) excited

GO ON TO THE NEXT PAGE

Practice Tests

considered hand washing unnecessary because he had not handled any toxic chemicals that day, or he might have just been so hungry he did not think about it. [5]

The bread tasted so sweet that Fahlberg thought he might have picked up some cake by mistake. He rinsed out his mouth with water and then patted his mustache dry with a napkin. He was surprised to find that the napkin tasted sweet as well. He took another sip of water and realized that the water now tasted sweet. [6] <u>The bread, napkin, and glass of water had something in common.</u> He then tasted his thumb, and it tasted sweeter than any candy he had ever had.

5. At this point, the writer wants to create an ideal transition to the next paragraph. Which choice most effectively accomplishes this goal?

   A) Later, hand washing would become a critical protocol in the laboratory.

   B) Thankfully, he didn't, or he never would have discovered what came next.

   C) Fahlberg had not eaten any cake, or indeed anything sweet, that day.

   D) Either way, he picked up his bread in his unwashed hands and took a bite.

6. A) NO CHANGE

   B) Was there something that the bread, napkin, and glass of water had in common, he wondered?

   C) In fact, everything Fahlberg touched seemed to taste sweeter than usual, which intrigued his scientific mind.

   D) Fahlberg quickly realized that the one thing the bread, napkin, and glass of water had in common was that they had all touched his fingers.

Practice Tests

[1] Fahlberg rushed back into the lab and began to taste the contents of every beaker he had used that day. [2] Fortunately, he had not worked with anything poisonous or corrosive, or the story [7] <u>may have</u> a different ending. [3] [8] <u>He had discovered saccharin, which he named for its intense sweetness.</u> [4] He found a sweet-tasting mixture of chemicals and worked for weeks to isolate the sweet substance from the rest and to determine its chemical composition. [5] Although it is many times more sweet tasting than sugar, it cannot be used for energy by the body and therefore does not contribute to calories consumed or energy use. [6] Soon after Fahlberg started [9] <u>making</u> saccharin commercially in 1886, it became popular with people who needed to lose weight and with diabetic patients who needed to avoid sugar. [10] [11]

7. A) NO CHANGE
    B) would have had
    C) might have
    D) could have had

8. Which choice most clearly and effectively conveys the central idea of the paragraph?

    A) NO CHANGE
    B) The substance was saccharin, and it became known as an artificial sweetener.
    C) Instead, the substance was a harmless sweetener called saccharin.
    D) Interestingly, the substance was extremely sweet and would later be known as saccharin.

9. A) NO CHANGE
    B) inventing
    C) creating
    D) producing

10. To make this paragraph most logical, sentence 4 should be placed

    A) Where it is now
    B) Before sentence 1
    C) Before sentence 3
    D) Before sentence 6

Practice Tests

GO ON TO THE NEXT PAGE

11. Which of the following sentences would provide the best conclusion for the passage?

A) Clearly, Constantin Fahlberg's legacy of research, along with his accidental discovery, continues to have lasting effects on society even today.

B) If Fahlberg had stopped to wash his hands that day, he might have continued his experiments on coal tar derivatives, never knowing that an important substance sat at the bottom of one of his laboratory beakers.

C) In addition to his discovery of saccharin, his work on coal tar proved that Constantin Fahlberg was a talented scientist whose work has applications in the present day, even though a number of new artificial sweeteners have been developed.

D) Fahlberg's discovery of saccharin is just one of the many examples of times when science was advanced through what some might call "a happy accident."

Questions 12-22 are based on the following passage.

René Descartes: The Father of Modern Philosophy

Throughout history, philosophy has shaped culture in pivotal ways. From the ancients to the postmoderns, great philosophers have spoken powerfully within [12] there respective contexts. For modern Western culture, one philosopher's formative impact surpassed his contemporaries: France's René Descartes. Called "the father of modern philosophy," Descartes crucially influenced Western perspectives on knowledge and rationality.

This 17th-century philosopher ushered Western thought through an era of great public doubt and upheaval and into the age of self-reliant rationalism. Political and religious tradition and authority—the [13] obvious premodern sources of truth and knowledge—were being questioned and rejected as new ideas identified potential inconsistencies. [14] Because foundations of truth seemed to be crumbling, Descartes's writings proposed an alternative foundation: individual reason.

12. A) NO CHANGE
    B) their
    C) its
    D) it's

13. A) NO CHANGE
    B) makeshift
    C) innovative
    D) reigning

14. A) NO CHANGE
    B) In a time when foundations of truth seemed to be crumbling, Descartes's writings proposed an alternative foundation: individual reason.
    C) Despite the fact that foundations of truth seemed to be crumbling, Descartes's writings proposed an alternative foundation: individual reason.
    D) Although foundations of truth seemed to be crumbling, Descartes's writings proposed an alternative foundation: individual reason.

Practice Tests

[15] <u>An expert in many fields, Descartes's work</u> would on many levels serve to establish foundations for modern culture and science. [16] This emphasis on reason, as opposed to traditional or authoritative bases for certainty, would become the modern mechanism for determining truth and knowledge.

[17] Modern culture would come to cherish this as an intellectual ideal. In his most famous project, Descartes sought certainty by mentally stripping away every layer of knowledge that was remotely possible to

15. A) NO CHANGE

    B) Expertise in many fields, Descartes created work that

    C) An expert in many fields, Descartes would create work that

    D) With his expertise in many fields, Descartes's work

16. At this point, the writer wants to add specific information that supports the central claim of the paragraph. Which choice provides the strongest support?

    A) Even so, his most impressive contribution was his advocacy for the individual's rationality.

    B) Unlike Descartes, other philosophers argued that reason alone could not provide the basis for knowledge.

    C) The idea known as "Cartesian dualism" posited that in the world there exists only mind and matter.

    D) His work on philosophy has proven to have more importance than his ideas about anatomy, many of which have since been disproven.

17. Which sentence should be added in front of sentence 1 to clarify the topic of the paragraph?

    A) Descartes's contributions to philosophy were seen as threatening to religion.

    B) Descartes focused his work on the pursuit of fact-based certainty.

    C) The foundation for the ideas of many other philosophers is Descartes's work.

    D) Descartes's ideas were rooted in his Jesuit training.

GO ON TO THE NEXT PAGE ⇨

doubt. Descartes arrived at his memorable [18] <u>conclusion, "I think, therefore I am," he could only be certain of the fact that he was thinking.</u> [19] Building from there, he could work toward rational certainty in other areas of knowledge.

Emphasizing the importance of building knowledge on certain evidence, Descartes modeled a reversal of the reigning scientific processes (which typically worked backward from observation to explanation). Descartes founded the modern scientific method, in which research and study could be reliably conducted based on certain evidence. Scientific method, and the emphasis on human reason, would become standard elements of modern thought. Though reimagined by ensuing culture and philosophy, [20] <u>these changes propelled by</u> Descartes's initial contributions to that conversation.

18. A) NO CHANGE
    B) conclusion "I think, therefore I am" he could only be certain of the fact that he was thinking.
    C) conclusion, "I think, therefore I am" he could only be certain of the fact that he was thinking.
    D) conclusion, "I think, therefore I am." He could only be certain of the fact that he was thinking.

19. Which choice most logically follows the previous sentence and sets up the information that follows?
    A) This revelation came as a shock to many people.
    B) However, he believed that this certainty offered evidence to confirm his existence.
    C) Still, it was a place to start.
    D) This was a radical new way to think about thinking.

20. A) NO CHANGE
    B) these changes being propelled by
    C) these changes having been propelled by
    D) these changes were propelled by

[21] Some people may argue that it is impossible to separate what Descartes accomplished from the things his contemporaries did. Certainly, most scientists and philosophers influence and build from each other's work. But Descartes was the crucial voice in early modern dialogue. His expertise drew trusted readership, and his well-read ideas pointed culture down the road to modern understanding—a road paved with reason, modernism's great intellectual virtue. Shifts [22] begun by Descartes's work would influence the very structure of ideas and systems in the modern world, from research methods to public processes like government and health systems.

21. A) NO CHANGE
   B) Some may argue that it is impossible to separate Descartes's accomplishments from those of his contemporaries.
   C) Some people may argue that it is impossible to separate Descartes from his contemporaries.
   D) Some may argue that what Descartes accomplished is no different from what his contemporaries did.

22. A) NO CHANGE
   B) foreseen
   C) initiated
   D) evolved

Questions 23-33 are based on the following passage.

The Novel: Introspection to Escapism

Art is never [23] immovable, nor is it meant to be. A poem written today looks and sounds vastly different from a poem by Shakespeare, and a modern symphony no longer resembles one by Beethoven. So it is with the novel, that still relatively young member of the literary family (many consider *Don Quixote*, published in 1605, to be the first). The novel is evolving to reflect the [24] changing world; for better or for worse.

23. A) NO CHANGE
   B) sluggish
   C) static
   D) stationary

24. A) NO CHANGE
   B) changing world—for better
   C) changing world: for better
   D) changing world for better

[25] The novel, while well regarded, would never match the poem as the ideal form for conveying the struggles of humanity. A few quotations from acclaimed novelists of the past illustrate how [26] loftily the form was once regarded. G. K. Chesterton said, "A good novel tells us the truth about its hero; but a bad novel tells us the truth about its author." English writer Ford Madox Ford believed the novelist played an important role as a recorder of history. [27] Ford said of his friend Joseph Conrad, "We agreed that the novel is absolutely the only vehicle for the thought of our day."

It's not that over centuries writers of novels have shed these ambitions; novels today still address complexities and intricate social dynamics. [28] However, in recent decades, popular novels and their film adaptations have driven the novel market in a broader direction.

25. Which choice most effectively establishes the main topic of the paragraph?

A) NO CHANGE

B) The novel was once sacred ground, meant to capture and reveal universal truths, to depict society and all its ills, to explore and expound upon the human condition.

C) Both poetry and novels enjoyed a resurgence of popularity in the early 1900s due to the notoriety of many of the prominent authors of the day.

D) By the early 1900s, novels had evolved into something entirely different from the form Cervantes pioneered with *Don Quixote*.

26. A) NO CHANGE

B) broadly

C) haughtily

D) pretentiously

27. Which choice best improves the sentence?

A) Ford said of his friend, the novelist Joseph Conrad,

B) Ford said of his great friend, Joseph Conrad,

C) Ford said of Joseph Conrad,

D) Ford said of his friend, Joseph Conrad, a Pole who moved to Britain,

28. A) NO CHANGE

B) However: in recent decades,

C) However in recent decades,

D) In recent decades however;

GO ON TO THE NEXT PAGE

[29] Novels are considered just another entertainment medium, which are now available on digital devices, one that ought to enthrall its passive reader and relieve him or her of the stress and tedium of life. The difficulties, challenges, and triumphs of real life are [30] less often the subject of popular novels; instead, escapist tales of fantastical lands and escapades are more popular. [31]

29. A) NO CHANGE
    B) Novels, which are now available on digital devices, are considered just another entertainment medium,
    C) Novels are considered just another entertainment medium, now available on digital devices,
    D) Novels, just another entertainment medium which are now available on digital devices

30. A) NO CHANGE
    B) less often the subject of popular novels instead, escapist tales of fantastical lands and escapades are more popular.
    C) less often the subject of popular novels, instead, escapist tales of fantastical lands and escapades are more popular.
    D) less often the subject of popular novels: instead, escapist tales of fantastical lands and escapades, are more popular.

31. At this point, the writer wants to add specific information that supports the ideas presented in the paragraph. Which choice provides the most relevant detail?

    A) Novels exploring deep social issues remain the most heavily decorated books come literary award season.
    B) Director James Cameron remarked recently about the "inherent difficulty" of adapting novels with fantasy themes.
    C) Writing in the *New Yorker* magazine in 2014, critic James Woods stated that readers now want novels that, like popcorn, are "easy to consume."
    D) The "slice of life" novel remains tremendously popular among books targeting younger readers.

GO ON TO THE NEXT PAGE

It is rare today for a novelist to attempt to ask, "What does it mean?" Instead, [32] we strive to provide the reader with an answer to the question, "What happens next?"

"Publishers, readers, booksellers, even critics," critic James Woods wrote, "acclaim the novel that one can deliciously sink into, forget oneself in, the novel that returns us to the innocence of childhood or the dream of the cartoon, the novel of a thousand confections and no unwanted significance. What becomes harder to find, and lonelier to defend, is the idea of [33] the novel as—in Ford Madox Ford's words—a 'medium of profoundly serious investigation into the human case.'"

Questions 34-44 are based on the following passage and supplementary material.

Interning: A Bridge Between Classes and Careers

Kelli Blake, a chemical engineering major, recently [34] excepted a summer internship with BP, an international energy company, to gain career experience. Some argue against the value of internships, claiming they pay very little and can involve performing [35] boring tasks, yet Kelli feels her internship is critical to helping her discover whether engineering is right for her.

Kelli wants a real-world perspective on information she has gained in her classes. Her internship with a corporate leader is affording her the opportunity to apply her conceptual knowledge to tasks inside a major

32. A) NO CHANGE
    B) they strive
    C) it strives
    D) he or she strives

33. A) NO CHANGE
    B) the novel as, in Ford Madox Ford's words—a 'medium of profoundly serious investigation into the human case.'"
    C) the novel as, in Ford Madox Ford's words: a 'medium of profoundly serious investigation into the human case.'"
    D) the novel as, in Ford Madox Ford's words; a 'medium of profoundly serious investigation into the human case.'"

34. A) NO CHANGE
    B) accepted
    C) adopted
    D) adapted

35. A) NO CHANGE
    B) skilled
    C) menial
    D) challenging

Practice Tests

oil company. [36] <u>During this internship, for example, Kelli is working on a glycol dehydration project; she will be using the classroom skills she learned from thermodynamics, organic chemistry, and more.</u> She can later add this project to her résumé and portfolio, giving her an edge over other college graduates.

[37] <u>Offshore engineers have many rules and regulations.</u> Helicopter underwater egress safety training is required of employees traveling to offshore facilities, so she will [38] <u>stand out</u> from other applicants by already being safety certified. "I have a new appreciation for the protocols followed by engineers at refineries," she states. Kelli believes that gaining new skills and showing she can apply her classroom knowledge to real situations will give her an advantage over her competition should she decide to join BP.

36. Which choice best supports the central idea of the paragraph?

A) NO CHANGE

B) Kelli can use the materials from her internship in a professional-quality presentation; she can then deliver the presentation to her classmates when she returns to college after her internship.

C) In addition, Kelli is designing the next internship proposal for her classmates after she completes her own and graduates.

D) Kelli is hoping to formulate her project results as a professional published document to sell to BP.

37. Which choice provides the most appropriate introduction to the paragraph?

A) NO CHANGE

B) Kelli admires the engineers who administer the safety training.

C) The skills Kelli acquires can be applied to existing knowledge.

D) Kelli will also earn an underwater safety training certificate.

38. A) NO CHANGE

B) stand down

C) stand up

D) stand alone

GO ON TO THE NEXT PAGE ⟩

Everyone has **39** their own reason for wanting to become an intern. Kelli has several other reasons behind her decision. **40** For example, Kelli wants to meet people to learn about the variety of careers available, from entry level to senior engineer. She will accomplish all of her intern goals **41** by working on technical projects, attend "lunch and learn" meetings, watching webinars, and shadow coworkers.

39. A) NO CHANGE
    B) your
    C) its
    D) his or her

40. A) NO CHANGE
    B) For example; Kelli wants to meet people to learn about the variety of careers available, from entry level to senior engineer.
    C) For example, Kelli wants to meet people—to learn about the variety of careers available, from entry level, to senior engineer.
    D) For example, Kelli wants to meet people to learn about the variety of careers available; from entry level to senior engineer.

41. A) NO CHANGE
    B) by working on technical projects, attending "lunch and learn" meetings, watching webinars, and shadowing coworkers.
    C) by working on technical projects, attend "lunch and learn" meetings, watch webinars, and shadow coworkers.
    D) by working on technical projects, attending "lunch and learn" meetings, watch webinars, and shadowing coworkers.

Practice Tests

GO ON TO THE NEXT PAGE ▷

What are some further benefits of internships? Besides gaining exposure in the field, Kelli is networking. The most important person to her now is her mentor, Dan, a senior engineer who can help her grow professionally by answering her questions. Gaining valuable contacts and [42] good role model. These are other reasons she has pursued this internship.

Kelli is now an acting member of a corporate team. She realizes she will be learning a lot about the industry and will benefit from adopting an entirely new vocabulary. She views her internship as an adventure, one in which engineering teams worldwide must work collaboratively and efficiently. [43] It is worth it to give up her summer, Kelli argues, because though she is losing her summer she is doing the job of an actual engineer through her internship. Moreover, she views the experience as one of the best ways to learn about her field and industry, which typically offers around [44] 35 internships per 1,000 hires.

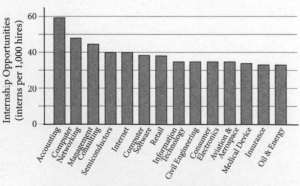

Internship Opportunities (interns per 1,000 hires)

Industries Likely to Hire Their Interns

Adapted from Kurt Wagner, "Which Internships Really Pay Off?" ©2014 by Revere Digital LLC.

42. A) NO CHANGE
    B) a good role model, these are other reasons
    C) a good role model; are other reasons
    D) a good role model are other reasons

43. A) NO CHANGE
    B) It is worth giving up, Kelli argues, because though she is losing her summer, she is doing the job of an actual engineer through her internship.
    C) It is worth it to give up her summer, Kelli argues, because she is doing the job of an actual engineer through her internship.
    D) It is worth it to Kelli to give up her summer, because though summers are usually a time to relax, she argues, she is doing the job of an actual engineer through her internship.

44. Which choice most accurately and effectively represents the information in the graph and the passage?
    A) NO CHANGE
    B) 32 internships per 1,000 hires.
    C) 35 internships per 60 hires.
    D) 32 internships per 60 hires.

MATH TEST

25 Minutes—20 Questions

NO-CALCULATOR SECTION

Turn to Section 3 of your answer sheet to answer the questions in this section.

Directions: For this section, solve each problem and decide which is the best of the choices given. Fill in the corresponding oval on the answer sheet. You may use any available space for scratch work.

Notes:

1. Calculator use is NOT permitted.
2. All numbers used are real numbers.
3. All figures used are necessary to solving the problems that they accompany. All figures are drawn to scale EXCEPT when it is stated that a specific figure is not drawn to scale.
4. Unless stated otherwise, the domain of any function f is assumed to be the set of all real numbers x, for which $f(x)$ is a real number.

Information:

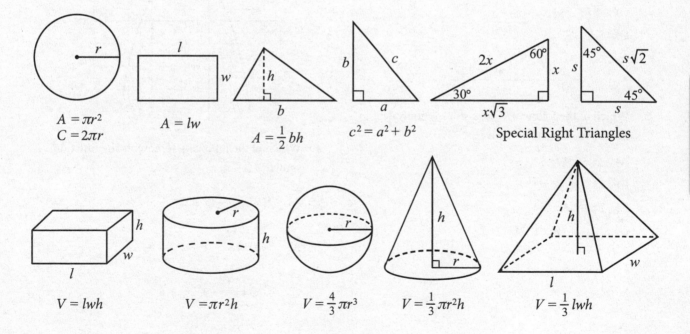

$A = \pi r^2$
$C = 2\pi r$

$A = lw$

$A = \frac{1}{2}bh$

$c^2 = a^2 + b^2$

Special Right Triangles

$V = lwh$

$V = \pi r^2 h$

$V = \frac{4}{3}\pi r^3$

$V = \frac{1}{3}\pi r^2 h$

$V = \frac{1}{3}lwh$

The sum of the degree measures of the angles in a triangle is 180.

The number of degrees of arc in a circle is 360.

The number of radians of arc in a circle is 2π.

GO ON TO THE NEXT PAGE

Fence Installation

1. The graph shows the cost of installing a vinyl privacy fence. The company charges a flat installation fee plus a cost per linear foot of fencing. Based on the graph, how much does one linear foot of this particular vinyl fence cost?

   A) $5

   B) $15

   C) $75

   D) $150

$$\frac{24x^4 + 36x^3 - 12x^2}{12x^2}$$

2. Which of the following expressions is equivalent to the expression shown above?

   A) $2x^2 + 3x$

   B) $24x^4 + 36x^3$

   C) $2x^2 + 3x - 1$

   D) $24x^4 + 36x^3 - 1$

Note: Figure not drawn to scale.

3. In the figure shown, $\triangle ABC \sim \triangle DBE$. What is the length of $\overline{BE}$?

   A) 3.5

   B) 3.75

   C) 4

   D) 4.5

4. Which of the following represents the function shown?

   A) $f(x) = -\dfrac{1}{3}(x - 2)^2 + 5$

   B) $f(x) = -\dfrac{1}{3}(x + 2)^2 + 5$

   C) $f(x) = \dfrac{1}{3}(x + 2)^2 + 5$

   D) $f(x) = 3(x - 2)^2 + 5$

GO ON TO THE NEXT PAGE

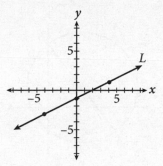

5. If line L shown here is reflected over the x-axis, what is the slope of the new line?

    A) -2

    B) $-\dfrac{1}{2}$

    C) $\dfrac{1}{2}$

    D) 2

6. If $p = 4x^3 + x - 2$, $q = x^2 - 1$, and $r = 3x - 5$, then what is $2p - (q + r)$?

    A) $7x^3 - x + 2$

    B) $8x^3 - x^2 - x + 2$

    C) $8x^3 - x^2 - x - 10$

    D) $8x^3 - x^2 + 5x - 8$

7. Which of the following are the roots of the equation $2x^2 + 4x - 3 = 0$?

    A) $\dfrac{-2 \pm \sqrt{10}}{2}$

    B) $-2 \pm \sqrt{5}$

    C) $-1 \pm \sqrt{10}$

    D) $-1 \pm 2\sqrt{10}$

8. If $g(x) = 3x - 5$ and $h(x) = \dfrac{7x + 10}{4}$, at what point does the graph of $g(x)$ intersect the graph of $h(x)$?

    A) $(-2, -11)$

    B) $(-2, 1)$

    C) $(3, 4)$

    D) $(6, 13)$

9. If $x = k^{-\frac{1}{3}}$, where $x > 0$ and $k > 0$, which of the following equations gives k in terms of x ?

    A) $k = \dfrac{1}{x^3}$

    B) $k = \dfrac{1}{\sqrt[3]{x}}$

    C) $k = -\sqrt[3]{x}$

    D) $k = -x^3$

$$4x - (10 - 2x) = c(3x - 5)$$

10. If the equation shown has infinitely many solutions, and c is a constant, what is the value of c ?

    A) -2

    B) $-\dfrac{2}{3}$

    C) $\dfrac{2}{3}$

    D) 2

11. If $0 < 1 - \dfrac{a}{3} \le \dfrac{1}{2}$, which of the following is not a possible value of a ?

    A) 1.5

    B) 2

    C) 2.5

    D) 3

GO ON TO THE NEXT PAGE

$$\begin{cases} y - \dfrac{2}{k}x \le 0 \\ \dfrac{1}{k}x - \dfrac{1}{2}y \le -1 \end{cases}$$

12. If the system of inequalities shown has no solution, what is the value of k?

A) 1

B) 2

C) There is no value of k that results in no solution.

D) There are infinitely many values of k that result in no solution.

$$\dfrac{4x}{x-7} + \dfrac{2x}{2x-14} = \dfrac{70}{2(x-7)}$$

13. What value(s) of x satisfy the equation above?

A) 0

B) 7

C) No solution

D) Any value such that $x \ne 7$

14. The circle shown is given by the equation $x^2 + y^2 + 6x - 4y = 12$. What is the shortest distance from A to B?

A)   5

B)   10

C) $4\sqrt{3}$

D)   24

15. If g is a function defined over the set of all real numbers and $g(x - 1) = 3x^2 + 5x - 7$, then which of the following defines $g(x)$?

A) $g(x) = 3x^2 - x - 9$

B) $g(x) = 3x^2 + 5x + 1$

C) $g(x) = 3x^2 + 11x + 1$

D) $g(x) = 3x^2 + 11x - 6$

Directions: For questions 16-20, solve the problem and enter your answer in the grid, as described below, on the answer sheet.

1. Although not required, it is suggested that you write your answer in the boxes at the top of the columns to help you fill in the circles accurately. You will receive credit only if the circles are filled in correctly.

2. Mark no more than one circle in any column.

3. No question has a negative answer.

4. Some problems may have more than one correct answer. In such cases, grid only one answer.

5. **Mixed numbers** such as $3\frac{1}{2}$ must be gridded as 3.5 or $\frac{7}{2}$.

    (If $3\frac{1}{2}$ is entered into the grid as $\boxed{\begin{array}{|c|c|c|c|} 3 & 1 & / & 2 \\ \hline & & / & \bullet \end{array}}$, it will be interpreted as $\frac{31}{2}$, not $3\frac{1}{2}$.)

6. **Decimal answers:** If you obtain a decimal answer with more digits than the grid can accommodate, it may be either rounded or truncated, but it must fill the entire grid.

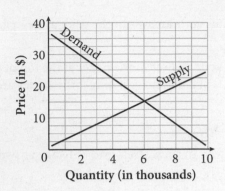

16. Retail businesses strive to price their products so that they sell as many as possible without losing money. Economic equilibrium is the price point at which the supply for a product is equal to the demand for that product. The graph above models this scenario. According to the graph, at what price in dollars will supply equal demand for this particular product?

17. Once an insect reaches its larval stage, its mass increases linearly for a short period of time and then slows down as it prepares to enter pupation. Suppose the larva of a certain species has an initial mass of 10 grams and grows linearly from $t = 0$ to $t = 48$ hours of its larval stage. If after 48 hours, the mass of the larva is 14 grams, what was its mass in grams at $t = 6$ hours ?

x	$f(x)$
−1	−2
0	0
1	2
2	4
3	6

x	$g(x)$
−2	3
−1	2
0	1
1	−1
2	−2

18. Several values for the functions $f(x)$ and $g(x)$ are shown in the tables. What is the value of $f(g(-1))$?

19. If $(4 + 3i)(1 - 2i) = a + bi$, then what is the value of a ? (Note that $i = \sqrt{-1}$.)

20. The maximum value of the data shown in the scatterplot occurs at $x = 56.25$. If the data is modeled using a quadratic regression and the model is an exact fit, then what is the y-value when $x = 90$?

MATH TEST

55 Minutes—38 Questions

CALCULATOR SECTION

Turn to Section 4 of your answer sheet to answer the questions in this section.

Directions: For this section, solve each problem and decide which is the best of the choices given. Fill in the corresponding oval on the answer sheet. You may use any available space for scratch work.

Notes:

1. Calculator use is permitted.
2. All numbers used are real numbers.
3. All figures used are necessary to solving the problems that they accompany. All figures are drawn to scale EXCEPT when it is stated that a specific figure is not drawn to scale.
4. Unless stated otherwise, the domain of any function f is assumed to be the set of all real numbers x, for which $f(x)$ is a real number.

Information:

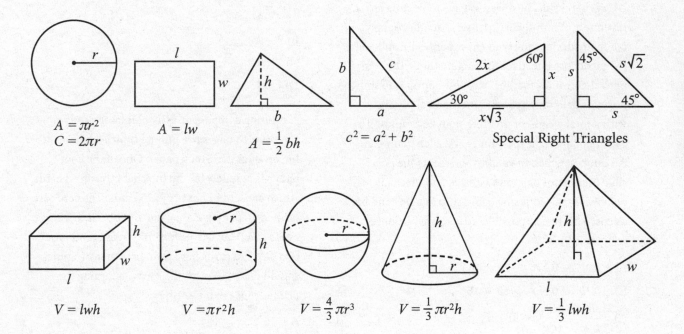

$A = \pi r^2$
$C = 2\pi r$

$A = lw$

$A = \frac{1}{2}bh$

$c^2 = a^2 + b^2$

Special Right Triangles

$V = lwh$

$V = \pi r^2 h$

$V = \frac{4}{3}\pi r^3$

$V = \frac{1}{3}\pi r^2 h$

$V = \frac{1}{3}lwh$

The sum of the degree measures of the angles in a triangle is 180.

The number of degrees of arc in a circle is 360.

The number of radians of arc in a circle is 2π.

GO ON TO THE NEXT PAGE ⟹

1. The U.S. Centers for Disease Control recommends that adults engage in 2.5 hours per week of vigorous exercise. A local health society conducts a survey to see if people are meeting this goal. They ask 100 people with gym memberships how many minutes of exercise they engage in per week. After analyzing the data, the health society finds that the average respondent exercises 142 minutes per week, but the margin of error was approximately 36 minutes. The society wants to lower this margin of error. Using which of the following samples instead would do so?

   A) 50 people with gym memberships

   B) 50 people randomly selected from the entire adult population

   C) 100 people with gym memberships, but from a variety of gyms

   D) 200 people randomly selected from the entire adult population

2. As a general rule, businesses strive to maximize revenue and minimize expenses. An office supply company decides to try to cut expenses by utilizing the most cost-effective shipping method. The company determines that the cheapest option is to ship boxes of ballpoint pens and mechanical pencils with a total weight of no more than 20 pounds. If each pencil weighs 0.2 ounces and each pen weighs 0.3 ounces, which inequality represents the possible number of ballpoint pens, b, and mechanical pencils, m, the company could ship in a box and be as cost-effective as possible? (There are 16 ounces in 1 pound.)

   A) $0.3b + 0.2m < 20 \times 16$

   B) $0.3b + 0.2m \leq 20 \times 16$

   C) $\dfrac{b}{0.3} + \dfrac{m}{0.2} < 20 \times 16$

   D) $\dfrac{b}{0.3} + \dfrac{m}{0.2} \leq 20 \times 16$

3. Where will line Q shown in the graph intersect the x-axis?

   A) 13

   B) 14

   C) 15

   D) 16

4. The function $f(x)$ is defined as $f(x) = 2g(x)$, where $g(x) = x + 5$. What is the value of $f(3)$?

   A) -4

   B) 6

   C) 8

   D) 16

5. A printing company uses a color laser printer that can print 18 pages per minute (ppm) when printing on thick cardstock paper. One of the company's best sellers on the Internet is business cards, which are sold in boxes of 225 cards. The cards are printed 10 per page, then cut and boxed. If a real estate company has 12 full-time agents and orders two boxes of cards per agent, how many minutes should it take to print the cards, assuming the printer runs continuously?

   A) 15

   B) 20

   C) 30

   D) 45

6. If $0.002 \leq x \leq 0.2$ and $5 \leq y \leq 25$, what is the maximum value of $\dfrac{x}{y}$?

   A) 0.04

   B) 0.4

   C) 4

   D) 40

7. Following a study of children in the United States under three years old, the American Academy of Pediatrics stated that there is a positive correlation between the amount of time spent watching television and the likelihood of developing an attention deficit disorder. Which of the following is an appropriate conclusion to draw from this statement?

   A) There is an association between television time and attention disorders for American children under three years old.

   B) There is an association between television time and attention disorders for all children under three years old.

   C) An increase in attention disorders is caused by an increase in television time for American children under three years old.

   D) An increase in attention disorders is caused by an increase in television time for all children under three years old.

8. A bicyclist is training for the Liège-Bastogne-Liège, one of Europe's oldest road bicycle races. The line graph above shows the number of miles she biked each week for eight weeks. According to the graph, what was the greatest change (in absolute value) in the weekly number of miles she biked between two consecutive weeks?

   A) 7

   B) 8

   C) 9

   D) 10

9. If a line that passes through the coordinates $(a - 1, 2a)$ and $(a, 6)$ has a slope of 5, what is the value of a?

   A) -2

   B) $-\dfrac{1}{2}$

   C) $\dfrac{1}{2}$

   D) 2

GO ON TO THE NEXT PAGE

Practice Tests

10. An occupational health organization published a study showing an increase in the number of injuries that resulted from elderly people falling in the bathtub. In response to this increase, a medical supply company decided to drop its price on bathtub lifts from $450 to $375, hoping to still break even on the lifts. The company breaks even when its total revenue (income from selling n bathtub lifts) is equal to its total cost of producing the lifts. If the cost C, in dollars, of producing the lifts is $C = 225n + 3{,}150$, how many more of the lifts does the company need to sell at the new price to break even than at the old price?

A) 7

B) 12

C) 14

D) 21

Questions 11 and 12 refer to the following information.

A zoo is building a penguin exhibit. It will consist of an underwater area and a land area. The land area is made of thick sheets of ice. An outline of the total space covered by the ice is shown below. A pipe 2 feet in diameter runs the full length of the exhibit under the ice. A substance known as ice-cold glycol continuously runs through the pipe to keep the ice frozen.

11. About how many cubic feet of water are needed to create the ice portion of the exhibit?

A) 1,850

B) 2,150

C) 2,450

D) 3,100

12. The zoo is planning to hire a company to fill the space with water. The company plans to use two 4-inch hoses that can each pump 60 gallons of water per minute. About how long should it take to fill the space? (There are 7.48 gallons of water in 1 cubic foot of ice.)

A) 1 hour

B) 1 hour, 30 minutes

C) 1 hour, 55 minutes

D) 2 hours, 15 minutes

GO ON TO THE NEXT PAGE

13. Which of the following quadratic equations has no solution?

    A) $0 = -2(x - 5)^2 + 3$

    B) $0 = -2(x - 5)(x + 3)$

    C) $0 = 2(x - 5)^2 + 3$

    D) $0 = 2(x + 5)(x + 3)$

Questions 14 and 15 refer to the following information.

Three airplanes depart from three different airports at 8:30 AM, all travelling to Chicago O'Hare International Airport (ORD). The distances the planes must travel are recorded in the following table.

From	Distance to Chicago (ORD)
Kansas City (MCI)	402
Boston (BOS)	864
Miami (MIA)	1,200

14. The plane traveling from Boston traveled at an average speed of 360 mph. The plane traveling from Kansas City arrived at 10:34 AM. How many minutes before the plane from Boston arrived did the plane from Kansas City arrive?

    A) 20

    B) 28

    C) 42

    D) 144

15. For the first $\frac{1}{4}$ of the trip, the plane from Miami flew through heavy winds and dense cloud cover at an average speed of 200 mph. For the remaining portion of the trip, the weather was ideal, and the plane flew at an average speed of 450 mph. Due to a backlog of planes at ORD, it was forced to circle overhead in a holding pattern for 25 minutes before landing. At what time did the plane from Miami land in Chicago?

    A) 12:00 PM

    B) 12:25 PM

    C) 12:50 PM

    D) 1:15 PM

16. If $h(t) = \sqrt{t^2 + 9}$ for all real values of t, which of the following is not in the range of $h(t)$?

    A) 1

    B) 3

    C) 9

    D) 10

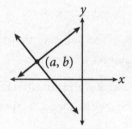

17. If (a, b) represents the solution to the system of equations shown in the graph and $a = -3b$, then which of the following could be the value of $a + b$?

    A) -9

    B) 0

    C) 3

    D) 6

GO ON TO THE NEXT PAGE

Practice Tests

Thermostat A

Thermostat B

18. A car manufacturer tested two types of thermostats to determine which one it wanted to use in a new model of car. The more consistently the thermostat engages the engine's cooling fan, the better the cooling system performs over the long run. The double dot plot above shows the test results, given the following conditions:

   • Zero indicates that the cooling fan engaged at exactly the temperature at which the thermostat was set (the target temperature).

   • Negative numbers indicate that the fan engaged below the target temperature.

   • Positive numbers indicate that the fan engaged above the target temperature.

   • The safe range for the fan to engage is 10 degrees above or below the target temperature.

   Which of the following best states which thermostat the car manufacturer is likely to choose and why?

   A) Thermostat A because the median of the data is 0, and the range is greater than that of Thermostat B

   B) Thermostat B because the median of the data is 0, and the range is less than that of Thermostat A

   C) Thermostat A because the mode of the data is 0, which indicates a more consistent thermostat

   D) Thermostat B because the data is bimodal (has two modes), which indicates a more consistent thermostat

19. If p and q represent the zeros of a quadratic function and $p + q = -3$, which of the following could be the factored form of the function?

   A) $f(x) = (x - 3)(x + 3)$

   B) $f(x) = (x - 4)(x + 1)$

   C) $f(x) = (x - 1)(x + 4)$

   D) $f(x) = (x - 6)(x + 3)$

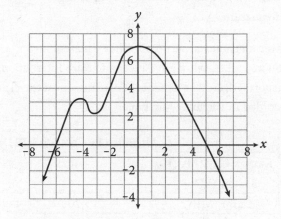

20. The figure above shows the graph of $p(x) - 4$. What is the value of $p(0)$?

   A) 3

   B) 4

   C) 7

   D) 11

GO ON TO THE NEXT PAGE

1.5 in.   3.5 in.

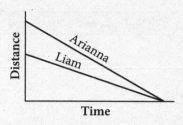

21. Geraldine is making a simple AC electric generator for a science project using copper wire, cardboard, a nail, and magnets. The first step in building the generator is wrapping the wire around and around a rectangular prism made from the cardboard and connecting it to a small lightbulb, as shown in the figure. If Geraldine has 18 feet of wire and needs to leave 3 inches on each end to connect to the lightbulb, how many times can she wrap the wire around the cardboard prism?

A) 21

B) 28

C) 35

D) 42

Organic Vegetable Harvest

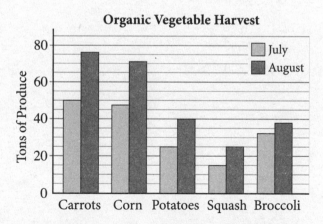

22. The bar graph above shows the vegetable harvest, in tons, at an organic produce farm during July and August. Of the following, which best approximates the percent increase in the harvest of squash at this farm from July to August?

A) 67%

B) 60%

C) 53%

D) 40%

23. Arianna and her brother Liam both walk home from school each day, but they go to different schools. The figure shows their trip home on Monday. Based on the graph, which of the following statements is true?

A) It took Liam longer to walk home because his school is farther away.

B) It took Arianna longer to walk home because her school is farther away.

C) Arianna and Liam walked home at the same rate.

D) Arianna walked home at a faster rate than Liam.

24. If line L passes through the points $(-4, -8)$ and $(8, 1)$, which of the following points does line L not pass through?

A) $(0, -5)$

B) $(4, -1)$

C) $(12, 4)$

D) $(16, 7)$

Practice Tests

	Unemployed	Employed	Totals
Female Degree	12	188	200
Female No Degree	44	156	200
Male Degree	23	177	200
Male No Degree	41	159	200
Totals	120	680	800

25. The table above shows the results of a sociological study identifying the number of males and females with and without college degrees who were unemployed or employed at the time of the study. If one person from the study is chosen at random, what is the probability that that person is an employed person with a college degree?

A) $\dfrac{73}{160}$

B) $\dfrac{10}{17}$

C) $\dfrac{17}{20}$

D) $\dfrac{73}{80}$

Infected Patient

26. Typically, when people contract an infectious disease, their immune system immediately begins to produce extra white blood cells to fight the disease. The scatterplot shows the white blood cells reproducing in an infected patient, along with several values found when modeling the data using a graphing calculator. According to this model, how many white blood cells per microliter of blood did the patient have before he contracted the disease?

A) 3,400

B) 8,500

C) 10,000

D) 13,600

GO ON TO THE NEXT PAGE

Practice Tests

27. A rodeo is building a circular arena. The arena will have a total area of 64π square yards and can either be left open for rodeo competitions or divided into 12 equal sections through the center for auctions. When holding auctions, the rodeo has an average of 4 bulls and 8 horses for sale. A bull cannot be placed in a section directly beside another section containing a bull, and all edges of these sections must be reinforced with strong steel to keep the bulls from getting out. Which of the following represents how much steel in yards the rodeo will need to reinforce the four bull sections?

A) 32π

B) 64π

C) $32 + \dfrac{16\pi}{3}$

D) $64 + \dfrac{16\pi}{3}$

28. Lena bought a saltwater fish tank that holds 400 gallons of water. She started filling the tank on Friday, but then stopped after putting only 70 gallons of water in the tank. On Saturday, she bought a bigger hose and began filling the tank again. It took her 1 hour and 50 minutes on Saturday to completely fill the tank. Which equation represents the number of gallons of water in the fish tank on Saturday, given the amount of time in minutes that Lena spent filling the tank?

A) $y = 3x + 70$

B) $y = 3x + 330$

C) $y = 70x + 330$

D) $y = 110x + 70$

29. A self-storage company has three sizes of storage units. The ratio of small to medium units is 3:5. The ratio of medium to large units is 3:2. The company analyzes its business model and current consumer demand and determines that it can benefit from utilizing larger economies of scale. In other words, it decides to grow its business based on current economic conditions and plans to build a second, larger self-storage building. The company's research indicates that the new market would benefit from having only two sizes of storage units, small and large, in the same ratio as its current facility. What ratio of small to large units should it use?

A) 1:1

B) 3:2

C) 5:3

D) 9:10

$$\frac{1}{x} + \frac{3}{x} = \frac{1}{7}$$

30. The equation shown above represents the following scenario: A chemical laboratory uses two air purifiers to clean the air of contaminants emitted while working with hazardous materials. One is an older model, and the other is a new model that is considerably more energy efficient. The new model can clean the air of contaminants three times as quickly as the older model. Working together, the two air purifiers can clean the air in the lab in 7 hours. Which of the following describes what the term $\dfrac{1}{x}$ in the equation represents?

A) The portion of the air the older model can clean in 1 hour

B) The portion of the air the new model can clean in 1 hour

C) The time it takes the older model to clean the air by itself

D) The time it takes the older model to clean $\dfrac{1}{7}$ of the air by itself

GO ON TO THE NEXT PAGE

Directions: For questions 31-38, solve the problem and enter your answer in the grid, as described below, on the answer sheet.

1. Although not required, it is suggested that you write your answer in the boxes at the top of the columns to help you fill in the circles accurately. You will receive credit only if the circles are filled in correctly.

2. Mark no more than one circle in any column.

3. No question has a negative answer.

4. Some problems may have more than one correct answer. In such cases, grid only one answer.

5. **Mixed numbers** such as $3\frac{1}{2}$ must be gridded as 3.5 or $\frac{7}{2}$.

    (If $3\frac{1}{2}$ is entered into the grid as $\boxed{3\,1\,/\,2}$, it will be interpreted as $\frac{31}{2}$, not $3\frac{1}{2}$.)

6. **Decimal answers:** If you obtain a decimal answer with more digits than the grid can accommodate, it may be either rounded or truncated, but it must fill the entire grid.

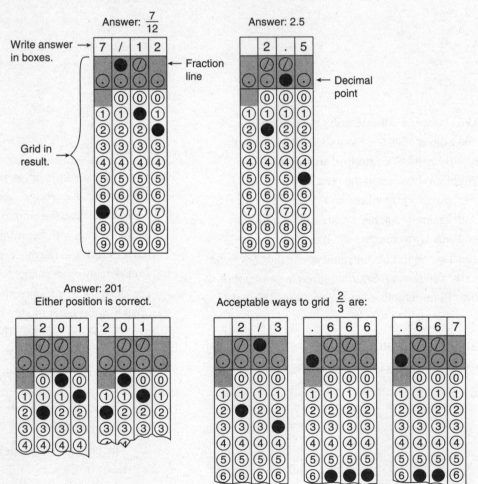

$$\frac{1}{3}(90x - 12) = \frac{1}{2}(8x + 10)$$

31. What is the solution to the equation shown?

32. If $n^{\frac{5}{2}} = 32$, what is the value of n?

33. When a thrift store gets used furniture in good condition to sell, it researches the original price and then marks the used piece down by 40% of that price. On the first day of each of the following months, the price is marked down an additional 15% until it is sold or it reaches 30% of its original price. Suppose the store gets a piece of used furniture on January 15th. If the piece of furniture costs $1,848 new, and it is sold on March 10th of the same year, what is the final selling price, not including tax? Round your answer to the nearest whole dollar.

Note: Figure not drawn to scale.

34. Many sailboat manufacturers sell kits that include instructions and all the materials needed to build a simple sailboat. The figure shows the finished dimensions of a sailboat from such a kit. The instructions indicate that $\cos x° = b$, but do not give the value of b. What is the value of b?

35. In the figure shown, line B (not shown) is parallel to $\overline{CD}$ and passes through the point $(0, -1)$. If line B also passes through the point $(2, y)$, what is the value of y?

36. Recycling of certain metals has been a common practice dating back to preindustrial times. For example, there is evidence of scrap bronze and silver being collected and melted down for reuse in a number of European countries. Today, there are recycling companies and even curbside collection bins for recycling. As a general rule, recycling companies pay for metals by weight. Suppose a person brings in 3 pounds of copper and receives $8.64, and 24 ounces of nickel and receives $10.08. If another person brings in equal weights of copper and nickel, what fractional portion of the money would he receive from the copper? (There are 16 ounces in 1 pound.)

Practice Tests

Questions 37 and 38 refer to the following information.

Body mass index, or BMI, is one of several measures used by doctors to determine a person's health as indicated by weight and height. Low-density lipoprotein, or LDL cholesterol, known as the "bad" cholesterol, is another health indicator and consists of fat proteins that clog arteries. Following are the results of a study showing the relationship between BMI and LDL for 12 individuals and the line of best fit for the data.

37. How many of the 12 people have an actual LDL that differs by 10 or more mg/dL from the LDL predicted by the line of best fit?

38. According to the line of best fit, what is the closest whole number BMI approximation for a person that has an estimated LDL level of 140 mg/dL ?

ESSAY TEST

50 Minutes

The essay gives you an opportunity to show how effectively you can read and comprehend a passage and write an essay analyzing the passage. In your essay, you should demonstrate that you have read the passage carefully, present a clear and logical analysis, and use language precisely.

Your essay must be written on the lines provided in your answer booklet; except for the planning page of the answer booklet, you will receive no other paper on which to write. You will have enough space if you write on every line, avoid wide margins, and keep your handwriting to a reasonable size. Remember that people who are not familiar with your handwriting will read what you write. Try to write or print so that what you are writing is legible to those readers.

You have 50 minutes to read the passage and write an essay in response to the prompt provided inside this booklet.

1. Do not write your essay in this booklet. Only what you write on the lined pages of your answer booklet will be evaluated.

2. An off-topic essay will not be evaluated.

As you read the passage below, consider how the author uses

- evidence, such as facts or examples, to support claims.

- reasoning to develop ideas and to connect claims and evidence.

- stylistic or persuasive elements, such as word choice or appeals to emotion, to add power to the ideas expressed.

This passage deals with the issue of compensation for college athletes.

1   In the world of college sports, there is growing debate about whether student athletes should be awarded monetary compensation for their contribution to teams that garner millions of dollars for universities. Presently, the National Collegiate Athletics Association (NCAA), the governing body of college sports, doesn't allow it. Some hold this law as sacrosanct, saying it keeps college sports from becoming commercial and corrupting the experience of student athletes, who are in school, after all, for an education. But the reality is that we are past that point: college sports are big business, and the system that caps student salaries at zero is tantamount to wage fixing and collusion. If such practices happened in the investment market, universities would be fined by the FTC. In a labor market, they'd be shut down. Student athletes are being defrauded and taken advantage of.

2   So how much money is at stake? Basketball and football are the two main sports in question. Every year, the month of March becomes synonymous with a weeks-long basketball bracket that winnows down 64 teams to the single best. In football, a season of stadium-filling regular season games culminates in half a dozen lucrative "bowl games" sponsored by some of the biggest corporations in the world: FedEx, AT&T, and Mobil Oil.

3   For television networks, advertisers, universities, and local businesses where the events are held, these games are every bit as big as the NFL's Super Bowl and the NBA playoffs. In 2011, ESPN and Fox signed television rights deals worth $3 billion to the Pacific-12 conference. *Forbes* magazine reported that CBS and Turner Broadcasting

GO ON TO THE NEXT PAGE ⟶

make more than one billion dollars off the March Madness broadcasts, "thanks in part to a $700,000 advertising rate for a 30-second spot during the Final Four." One study put the value of a Texas A&M home game at $86 million for businesses in Brazos County, where A&M is located.

4   The dollar figures are indeed vast, and universities get their share. Here are two examples from schools with top football teams. According to the most recent federal data, the University of Texas football team netted a profit of $77.9 million in 2011-2012. Michigan made $61.6 million from football and $85.2 million in revenue.

5   Coaches, too, are a big part of the equation. Average salaries for major college football coaches have jumped more than 70 percent since 2006, to $1.64 million, according to *USA Today*. Nick Saban, head coach for Alabama, makes $7.3 million a year.

6   And yet, players take home no money. None. How can this be? Because, like unscrupulous tycoons from a Dickens novel, college presidents, athletic directors, and conference commissioners set their players' wages as low as they can get them—zero.

7   According to a recent study, if college football operated under the same revenue-sharing model as the NFL, each player on the Texas A&M squad would see a paycheck of about $225,000 per year.

8   All this talk of money might have you thinking that we should go back to square one and take the money out of college sports. But money is in college sports' DNA. It was conceived that way. It all grew out of the Morrill Land-Grant College Act of 1862. "As large public institutions spread into sparsely populated states, the competition for students grew fierce," says Allen Sack, a business professor at the University of New Haven. Football happened to be invented around that time, and schools took it up as a tool to draw students, and spectators, to campuses. The 1894 Harvard-Yale football game, for example, generated $119,000, according to the *New York Times*. That's nearly $3 million in today's dollars.

9   The historic justification for not paying players is that they are amateur student-athletes, and the value of their scholarships is payment enough. But the NCAA's own study shows that its scholarship limit leaves so-called "full" scholarship athletes with $3,000 to $5,000 in out-of-pocket expenses each year. The average shortfall is $3,200. Furthermore, most scholarships are revocable, so if an athlete doesn't perform well on the field, or is injured, he can, in a sense, lose that compensation. A student athlete devotes 40 hours a week on average towards sport; that's equivalent to a full-time job. Zero pay and immediate termination with no recourse? Those are labor conditions that any sensible workforce would unionize to change. But students are powerless to change. They are up against the NCAA, the Big 10 commission, university boards, and the almighty corporate dollar. Someone needs to become their advocate and get student athletes the compensation they deserve.

> Write an essay in which you explain how the author builds an argument to persuade his audience that student athletes deserve fair compensation. In your essay, analyze how the author uses one or more of the features listed in the box that precedes the passage (or features of your own choice) to strengthen the logic and persuasiveness of his argument. Be sure that your analysis focuses on the most relevant features of the passage.
>
> Your essay should not explain whether you agree with the author's claims, but rather explain how the author builds an argument to persuade his audience.

ANSWER KEY
READING TEST

1. A	14. B	27. C	40. D
2. D	15. A	28. A	41. B
3. D	16. C	29. D	42. A
4. B	17. D	30. B	43. C
5. C	18. C	31. A	44. B
6. C	19. B	32. D	45. C
7. C	20. B	33. A	46. A
8. D	21. B	34. B	47. C
9. A	22. D	35. D	48. D
10. D	23. D	36. C	49. A
11. C	24. C	37. C	50. D
12. D	25. C	38. D	51. A
13. A	26. A	39. A	52. B

WRITING AND LANGUAGE TEST

1. B	12. B	23. C	34. B
2. D	13. D	24. B	35. C
3. B	14. B	25. B	36. A
4. C	15. C	26. A	37. D
5. D	16. A	27. A	38. A
6. D	17. B	28. A	39. D
7. B	18. D	29. B	40. A
8. A	19. B	30. A	41. B
9. D	20. D	31. C	42. D
10. C	21. B	32. D	43. C
11. B	22. C	33. A	44. B

MATH—NO CALCULATOR TEST

1. B	6. B	11. D	16. 15
2. C	7. A	12. D	17. 10.5 or 21/2
3. C	8. D	13. C	18. 4
4. A	9. A	14. B	19. 10
5. B	10. D	15. C	20. 50.5

MATH—CALCULATOR TEST

1. D	11. B	21. A	31. 9/26 or .346
2. B	12. D	22. A	32. 4
3. C	13. C	23. D	33. 801
4. D	14. A	24. B	34. 2/3 or .666 or .667
5. C	15. B	25. A	35. 3.5 or 7/2
6. A	16. A	26. B	36. 3/10
7. A	17. A	27. D	37. 3
8. D	18. B	28. A	38. 24
9. C	19. C	29. D	
10. A	20. D	30. A	

ANSWERS AND EXPLANATIONS

READING TEST

A Study in Scarlet

Suggested Passage Map notes:

¶1: W describes H

¶2: W stunned by H's deep knowledge of some subjects

¶3: W astonished by what H doesn't know

¶4: H: brain has only so much room, isn't interested in "useless facts"

1. A   Difficulty: Easy

Category: Detail

Getting to the Answer: Eliminate answers that go against your understanding of the characters in the passage. The first paragraph explicitly states that Watson's curiosity about Holmes "gradually deepened and increased" (lines 2-3). Choice (A) is the correct answer.

2. D   Difficulty: Medium

Category: Vocab-in-Context

Getting to the Answer: Predict a word that could be substituted for "casual" in context. Watson is explaining that Holmes' appearance is noticeable even to someone who hasn't seen him very often; therefore, (D) is correct.

3. D   Difficulty: Easy

Category: Global

Getting to the Answer: The central idea in this passage should reflect the overall picture the author paints of Sherlock Holmes. The passage develops Holmes as an unusual and eccentric character. Watson marvels at Holmes' failure to pursue a typical path for an intelligent person, for example, and describes in detail how Holmes' behavior and knowledge deviate from the ordinary. Choice (D) is the only answer choice that is directly supported by details in the passage.

4. B   Difficulty: Medium

Category: Vocab-in-Context

Getting to the Answer: Use context clues to help you predict the meaning of the word as it is used in the sentence. In this sentence, the context clues provide a contrast to the target word. Watson says Holmes is usually "sharp" and "hawk-like" with great "alertness" except when he is in a period of "torpor" (lines 7-10). You can predict that the meaning of "torpor" will be something close to *the opposite of sharp and alert.* Choice (B) is the correct answer.

5. C   Difficulty: Easy

Category: Inference

Getting to the Answer: Look for clues in the passage about how and why Holmes studies and learns. Watson notes that Holmes has not studied anything "which might fit him for a degree" (lines 21-22). This suggests that his learning is not motivated by something external, like a degree, but by his personal interests. Likewise, he has a "zeal" for particular subjects (line 24). Choice (C) reflects Holmes's motives for studying.

6. C   Difficulty: Medium

Category: Command of Evidence

Getting to the Answer: Eliminate answer choices that don't explain why Holmes studies. A correct answer will allow you to make a logical guess as to Holmes's motives for studying. Choice (C) provides the best evidence by illustrating that Holmes pursues topics that he is passionate about rather than studying for external motivations.

7. C   Difficulty: Medium

Category: Inference

Getting to the Answer: Closely read Holmes's own statements for clues about his views. Holmes clearly suggests that the brain can only hold a limited amount of information, so one should prioritize the things that are most important. Therefore, (C) is the correct answer.

8. D   Difficulty: Easy

Category: Command of Evidence

Getting to the Answer: Reread each quote in the context of the passage. Find the one that supports the previous answer by giving evidence of Holmes' own ideas about learning. Of all the answer choices, Holmes' own statement about the necessity of prioritizing useful facts most directly supports the previous answer. Choice (D) is the correct answer.

9. A   Difficulty: Medium

Category: Rhetoric

Getting to the Answer: Consider what this figurative use of "attic" helps reveal about the character of Holmes. The author has Holmes compare the human brain to an attic to help illustrate Holmes's beliefs about useful facts versus those not worth learning. Choice (A) is the correct answer.

10. D   Difficulty: Medium

Category: Rhetoric

Getting to the Answer: Think about what insights the reader gains by having Watson narrate the story. The author is able to establish Holmes as an intriguing character by showing Watson's thoughts and reactions to Holmes. Presumably, readers will want to find out more about Holmes because the narrator depicts him as a fascinating person. Choice (D) fits this situation.

Woodrow Wilson Speech

Suggested Passage Map notes:

¶1: should be no secrets in peace process

¶2: war fought for justice; 14 pts for world peace

¶3: no secrets

¶4: freedom on the seas

¶5: equal trade

¶6: Americans will personally sacrifice for them

¶7: explain tax changes

¶8: people will be ok with them

¶9: four essential human freedoms

¶10: freedom speech and expression

¶11: freedom of religion

¶12: freedom from want

¶13: freedom from fear

¶14: are attainable now, against new order of tyranny

¶15: moral order

¶16: change can made done peacefully

11. C   Difficulty: Easy

Category: Rhetoric

Getting to the Answer: Examine the first two paragraphs. Try to paraphrase the reason Wilson gives for making the speech. In the first two paragraphs, Wilson anticipates the end of the war and alludes to the "processes of peace" (line 2). Although he refers to national sovereignty and conquest, he states that his purpose is to lay out a program for peace in the world, making (C) the correct answer.

12. D   Difficulty: Medium

Category: Command of Evidence

Getting to the Answer: Remember that the correct answer will provide information that directly relates to the answer to the previous question. The correct answer to the previous question concerns Wilson's plan to maintain peaceful relations in the world. Lines 26-27 read, "The programme of the world's peace, therefore, is our programme," making (D) the correct answer.

13. A   Difficulty: Medium

Category: Vocab-in-Context

Getting to the Answer: Predict a word that could substitute for "frankly" in context. In the list of points he presents, Wilson is defining actions and policies that will promote peace and open communication among nations. In this context, "frankly" suggests honesty, which makes (A) the correct answer.

14. B   Difficulty: Medium

Category: Inference

Getting to the Answer: Eliminate answer choices that cannot be inferred by the information provided in the passage. Calling for an end to "private international understandings" is one of Wilson's 14 points (lines 29-30). Therefore, it can be inferred that in the past, certain nations did indeed form "secret covenants" (line 6), or pacts, with one another. Choice (B) is correct.

15. A   Difficulty: Medium

Category: Command of Evidence

Getting to the Answer: The correct answer will reference a detail that provides evidence for the answer to the previous question. In the first paragraph of his speech, Wilson refers to "secret understandings" that cannot exist anymore if there is to be peace among nations. Therefore, (A) is correct.

16. C   Difficulty: Medium

Category: Vocab-in-Context

Getting to the Answer: Pretend the word is a blank in the sentence. Then predict what word could be substituted for the blank. The sentence states that "national armaments will be reduced to the lowest

point consistent with domestic safety" (lines 43–44). In this sense, Wilson aims to assure nations that they will still be able to protect themselves. Predict that armaments will be reduced to an extent agreeable with maintaining their own safety. (C) is the correct choice.

17. D   Difficulty: Hard

Category: Rhetoric

Getting to the Answer: Though the question is asking you about a specific line, it makes sense to choose an answer that is compatible with the broader context of the passage. In the excerpted line, Wilson identifies the "adjustment of all colonial claims" (line 46) as an item in his program for world peace. If his goal is to safeguard world peace, this must mean he believes conflicts resulting from colonization, itself an imperial pursuit, must be addressed. Choice (D) is correct.

18. C   Difficulty: Hard

Category: Rhetoric

Getting to the Answer: Locate the three points to which the question refers. Do not confuse them with other numbered points in the speech. Points VI through VIII refer to territorial sovereignty, evacuation of occupied lands, and restoration of lands. These points align with the claim that nations have violated one another's territorial sovereignty through invasion and occupation. This makes (C) the correct answer.

19. B   Difficulty: Hard

Category: Connections

Getting to the Answer: Be sure that the answer you choose reflects the ideology and positions expressed by Wilson in his speech. In the passage, Wilson expresses that he is in favor of international cooperation to promote and sustain global peace. Choice (B) is the correct answer because it describes an approach to international relations that is analogous to Wilson's.

Practice Tests

20. B **Difficulty:** Medium

Category: Rhetoric

Getting to the Answer: When asked a question involving the structure of a passage, consider the text as a whole. Often, the structure is visually noticeable. Wilson begins by stating his argument that countries must work together toward peace. He then follows up with specific examples (the 14 points) of how his ideas should be carried out. Choice (B) is the correct answer.

Paired Passages—Meditation

Suggested Passage Map notes:

Passage 1

¶1: history of meditation; secular meditation

¶2: describe mindfulness meditation

¶3: mindfulness → more fulfillment

¶4: health benefits

¶5: Dr. S – meditation good, drs should use it

Passage 2

¶1: Ryan uses mindfulness and sees many benefits

¶2: holds weekly bi-partisan meditation sessions

¶3: wrote book on mindfulness; improved attention

¶4: members of Congress getting interested

¶5: R supports legislation encouraging meditation

¶6: Ryan – not religious but secular

21. B **Difficulty:** Medium

Category: Global

Getting to the Answer: Focus on the big picture rather than supporting details. Choice (B) correctly identifies the central idea in the passage. The other choices are based on misinformation or are details.

22. D **Difficulty:** Hard

Category: Inference

Getting to the Answer: Keep the central idea of the passage in mind as you look for information in the passage about each of the choices. Determine which one can be inferred as true. The last two paragraphs of Passage 1 discuss "health benefits" of meditation (line 30), studies showing positive results of meditation, and a quote from a professional about meditation's advantages. This matches choice (D).

23. D **Difficulty:** Medium

Category: Command of Evidence

Getting to the Answer: Avoid choices that do not provide direct evidence to support your answer to the previous question. Choice (D) supports the inference that some medical professionals accept meditation as beneficial.

24. C **Difficulty:** Easy

Category: Vocab-in-Context

Getting to the Answer: Predict a word that could substitute for "compelling" in context. The context of the sentence suggests that meditation has great or convincing benefits. Therefore, (C) is correct.

25. C **Difficulty:** Easy

Category: Inference

Getting to the Answer: Remember that you're analyzing the author's point of view on meditation, not Tim Ryan's view. Since the author makes statements such as calling Ryan a "voice for calm consideration," (line 56), the author must hold a positive view of meditation. However, there is little evidence that the author is devoted to meditation. Choice (C) correctly reflects the author's point of view.

26. A **Difficulty:** Easy

Category: Inference

Getting to the Answer: Determine what can be inferred about Ryan's personality from what is stated in the passage. The passage contains numerous examples of Ryan putting his belief in the value of mindfulness into action. For instance, he hosts meditation sessions for his staff and supports legislation promoting meditation. Choice (A) is the correct answer.

27. C   Difficulty: Medium

Category: Command of Evidence

Getting to the Answer: Be careful of choices that do not provide direct evidence to support the inference about Ryan from the previous question. Choice (C) is correct. Mr. Ryan shows that he acts on what he believes by supporting legislation that encourages meditation, such as the bill supporting the increase in holistic medicine offered by the Department of Veterans Affairs.

28. A   Difficulty: Easy

Category: Vocab-in-Context

Getting to the Answer: Predict a word that is a synonym for "secular" in context. In the context of the sentence, "but rather" indicates that "secular" means the opposite of "religious," so (A) is the correct answer.

29. D   Difficulty: Easy

Category: Rhetoric

Getting to the Answer: Reread the sentence to determine what connotative meaning the author suggests through the use of "chatter." Since "chatter" in this sentence is contrasted with the "mind and body" syncing together, the word has a negative connotation that suggests background noise or frequent talk. Only (D) fits with this meaning.

30. B   Difficulty: Medium

Category: Synthesis

Getting to the Answer: Look for an answer that fits with the purposes of both passages. Avoid choices that are suggested by only one of the passages. Both passages discuss changing attitudes regarding the

efficacy of mindfulness meditation: Passage 1 states it is becoming "more popular" (lines 16–17) and "widely accepted by health professionals" (line 45), while Passage 2 describes the impact of a politician who is promoting meditation. Only (B) reflects this.

31. A   Difficulty: Medium

Category: Synthesis

Getting to the Answer: Examine the graphic and the two passages to figure out which answer choice is supported by all three. The passages both discussed benefits of meditation. The graphic shows that workers were more productive and had fewer injuries after being in a meditation program. Choice (A) is the only one that relates to the information in the graphic.

Colony Collapse Disorder Passage

Suggested Passage Map notes:

¶1: CCD – all bees disappear; bees perform invaluable services

¶2: pathogens aren't the cause

¶3: altruism explains the disappearance but doesn't explain the cause

¶4: may be caused by fluctuation in earth's magnetic field

¶5: may be caused by pesticides

¶7: may be cause by pesticide combos

¶7: need more research; encourage more beekeeping, relax city rules

32. D   Difficulty: Hard

Category: Global

Getting to the Answer: Think of what the author wants the reader to learn about bees. This will help you figure out the passage's purpose. Choice (D) is the primary purpose of the passage. The author most wants the reader to know about colony collapse disorder.

33. A **Difficulty:** Hard

Category: Connections

Getting to the Answer: Think back to the author's purpose that you explored in question 32. Consider what this purpose suggests about the author's point of view. The author seems knowledgeable about honey bees and very concerned about their loss. The author points out the many losses humans would have if bees were to disappear. Therefore, (A) is the correct answer.

34. B **Difficulty:** Hard

Category: Rhetoric

Getting to the Answer: Notice that the word "mysteriously" appears toward the beginning of the passage, when the author is first introducing the topic. As the author introduces the topic of colony collapse disorder in the first paragraph, the word "mysterious" helps emphasize how puzzling the disorder truly is. Choice (B) is the correct answer.

35. D **Difficulty:** Medium

Category: Vocab-in-Context

Getting to the Answer: Predict a word that is a synonym for "plights" in context. In the sentence, "common plights" refers to pests such as mites, fungus, and bacteria, which farmers commonly see in beehives. Predict a negative word. In this context, (D), "troubles" is the correct answer.

36. C **Difficulty:** Hard

Category: Rhetoric

Getting to the Answer: Examine the part of the passage that discusses the lack of bees after a collapse. The author wants to stress the fact that research has shown that pathogens are not the reason for colony collapse. Choice (C) is the correct answer.

37. C **Difficulty:** Medium

Category: Command of Evidence

Getting to the Answer: Be careful of choices that do not directly support your answer to the previous question. In the context of its paragraph, lines 31-33 provide evidence to support the inference that the cause of colony collapse is not pathogens, since "common killers" such as pathogens would leave "telltale signs." Choice (C) is the correct answer.

38. D **Difficulty:** Easy

Category: Vocab-in-Context

Getting to the Answer: Predict a word that could substitute for "foraging" in context. Predict an action that bees might perform during their "pollination flights," such as searching for flowers. The context of the sentence rules out all but (D), the correct answer.

39. A **Difficulty:** Hard

Category: Inference

Getting to the Answer: Review your passage map and use the passage's central idea as a general prediction. Choice (A) is correct. Though the author laments the disappearance of honey bees and says how challenging it is to solve the problem, the last paragraph ends the passage on a cautiously optimistic note, particularly with the use of the word "hopefully" (line 82).

40. D **Difficulty:** Medium

Category: Command of Evidence

Getting to the Answer: Be careful of choices that might support an incorrect answer in the previous question. Choice (D) is evidence that the author is cautiously optimistic about the future of the honey bee.

41. B **Difficulty:** Medium

Category: Detail

Getting to the Answer: Watch out for answer choices that might sound plausible but are not explicitly stated in the passage. Choice (B) is correct; the last paragraph states that some towns and cities are relaxing their regulations about beekeeping "in response to the honey bee population crisis" (line 81).

42. A **Difficulty:** Medium

Category: Connections

Getting to the Answer: Look for information in the passage that tells what honey bees and human beings do for each other. Paragraph 1 states that if honey bees disappear, people will not have certain foods; even the beef industry will be affected. Therefore, humans depend on the bees to keep the environment and economy healthy. Choice (A) is correct.

Space Debris Passage

Suggested Passage Map notes:

¶1: concern that spacecraft could be hit by micrometeorites

¶2: human-made debris in space; more likely than meteorites to hit spacecraft

¶3: small pieces are dangerous

¶4: larger pieces dangerous, but can be avoided

¶5: satellites can adjust course to avoid collision

¶6: some debris falls to earth; sci. can't stop it

¶7: in future, maybe spacecraft leave orbit when not used anymore

43. C **Difficulty:** Medium

Category: Global

Getting to the Answer: Think about the idea that is developed throughout the passage. Avoid answers that refer only to supporting details. Choice (C) is the correct answer because all the information in the passage relates to the dangers posed by space debris created by humans.

44. B **Difficulty:** Medium

Category: Command of Evidence

Getting to the Answer: Look at each quote from the passage and decide which most clearly supports the central idea. In paragraph 3, the author describes how space debris created by humans is dangerous to spacecraft and the people inside of them. Choice (B) is the correct answer.

45. C **Difficulty:** Medium

Category: Rhetoric

Getting to the Answer: Consider the central idea that you identified in question 43. Identify the central idea of paragraph 2. The passage is mostly about the dangers associated with human-made space debris. Paragraph 2 contains details about the types of human-made space debris orbiting Earth, thus providing support for the central idea. Choice (C) is the correct answer.

46. A **Difficulty:** Medium

Category: Detail

Getting to the Answer: Reread the information about meteoroids at the beginning of the passage. Think about how this compares with the descriptions of space debris in the following paragraphs. The author states that although there were concerns about meteoroids in the early days of space travel, scientists concluded that the risk was small because meteoroids were rare. The author goes on to explain that space debris created by humans is a greater concern because it is so plentiful. Choice (A) is the correct answer.

47. C **Difficulty:** Hard

Category: Rhetoric

Getting to the Answer: The author's central claim in the passage is that space debris left by humans is dangerous. Think about which of the answer choices most directly supports that claim. In paragraph 6, the author describes how Skylab fell to Earth. This example strengthens the claim, illustrating that the debris left in space can be dangerous even on Earth. Therefore, (C) is the correct answer.

48. D **Difficulty:** Medium

Category: Vocab-in-Context

Getting to the Answer: Eliminate answers that are synonyms for "obsolete" but do not make sense in context. Since it was debris that fell out of space, Skylab was no longer in use. In this context, "obsolete" means "outdated," so (D) is the correct answer.

49. A   Difficulty: Hard

Category: Inference

Getting to the Answer: Eliminate answer choices that cannot be supported with information found in the passage. In paragraph 6, the author describes how space debris can be dangerous on Earth if a large enough piece gets through the atmosphere without burning up. It is logical, then, that (A) is the correct answer; warnings could help people avoid areas where impacts are predicted, thereby decreasing the chance of injury. The author explicitly states that agencies monitor debris to make predictions and issue warnings (lines 58–62).

50. D   Difficulty: Medium

Category: Command of Evidence

Getting to the Answer: Avoid answer choices that provide evidence for incorrect answers to the previous question. Choice (D) is the correct answer, because in lines 60–62, the author states that there is nothing to be done about space debris falling to Earth except to issue warnings.

51. A   Difficulty: Medium

Category: Vocab-in-Context

Getting to the Answer: Predict a word that is a synonym for "implemented" in context. Since the debris will remain in space unless a method of removal is "implemented," predict the word means employed. In this context, (A) is the correct answer.

52. B   Difficulty: Hard

Category: Synthesis

Getting to the Answer: Make sure you understand the units and labels in the graphic before choosing an answer. The graphic shows that the highest

density of space debris occurs at an altitude just under 800 kilometers, posing the greatest risk of the dangers discussed in the passage. It is reasonable to conclude, therefore, that if NASA were to place a new satellite into orbit, the agency should choose to avoid the altitude range of 700–900 kilometers. Choice (B) is the correct answer.

WRITING AND LANGUAGE TEST

A Sweet Discovery

1. B   Difficulty: Medium

Category: Sentence Formation

Getting to the Answer: Determine the noun to which the modifier in this sentence is referring. Then check the noun's placement to make sure it is as close as possible to the modifier. The modifier is "like most chemists." Therefore, the noun it modifies should be a person. Choice (B) correctly rearranges the sentence so that "chemists" clearly refers to "Constantin Fahlberg."

2. D   Difficulty: Medium

Category: Development

Getting to the Answer: This is the topic sentence of the paragraph. Make sure that it focuses on the correct subject. The purpose of this sentence is to discuss Fahlberg and the circumstances in which he was working. Choice (D) correctly focuses the sentence on Fahlberg and flows well into the next sentence, which discusses the specifics of coal tar.

3. B   Difficulty: Easy

Category: Usage

Getting to the Answer: The pronoun should agree with the noun to which it refers. Identify this noun to determine the correct pronoun. The antecedent of the pronoun here is "coal tar," a singular, impersonal noun. Choice (B), "from it," is therefore the correct answer.

4. C   **Difficulty:** Easy

Category: Effective Language Use

Getting to the Answer: Predict what meaning the correct word should convey before choosing an answer. The sentence suggests that while working, Fahlberg was so "___" that he forgot to eat lunch. A word that means *focused on* or *preoccupied with* would be most appropriate. Choice (C), "engrossed," conveys this meaning successfully.

5. D   **Difficulty:** Hard

Category: Organization

Getting to the Answer: The passage is telling a story. Choose the answer that most effectively makes the transition between the paragraphs while maintaining a consistent tone with the rest of the story. The correct answer will relate to the sentences both before and after it. While answer B may intrigue readers, its tone is out of place when compared with that of the rest of the passage. Choice (D) is the correct answer. It provides a transition from the previous sentence and tells the next logical step in the story.

6. D   **Difficulty:** Hard

Category: Development

Getting to the Answer: The correct answer will clearly present the central idea of the paragraph. Identify the answer choice that presents the most important point about the scene being described. To be effective as a central idea, the sentence needs to sum up the supporting details in the paragraph and convey their meaning. Only (D) both explains what happened and describes why it was significant, which is the central idea of the paragraph.

7. B   **Difficulty:** Hard

Category: Usage

Getting to the Answer: Examine the context of the sentence. Notice that it's describing a potentially disastrous outcome if conditions have been different. Fortunately, he had not worked with anything poisonous or corrosive, or the story would have had a different ending. If Fahlberg had been working with poisonous or corrosive materials, there is no doubt that "the story" would have had a different—and terrible—ending. The word "might" is too conditional for this situation; therefore, (B), which includes the word "would," is the correct answer.

8. A   **Difficulty:** Hard

Category: Development

Getting to the Answer: Determine which option clearly states the most important information in this paragraph. The most important fact in this paragraph is that Fahlberg discovered a new substance accidentally. The rest of this paragraph provides details about this discovery. Therefore, the correct answer choice will state that Fahlberg made a discovery. Choice (A) makes this idea clear.

9. D   **Difficulty:** Easy

Category: Effective Language Use

Getting to the Answer: Look for clues in the rest of the sentence to determine which verb fits with the exact meaning of the sentence. The sentence states that Fahlberg is making the saccharin "commercially," or as part of a business. Choice (D), "producing," is correct, as it emphasizes the business nature of his work.

10. C   **Difficulty:** Medium

Category: Organization

Getting to the Answer: Try out each answer choice. What information seems confusing when not presented in the right order? Logically, Fahlberg should find the mixture of chemicals and work to isolate it before he names it and understands its significance. Therefore, (C) is the most logical place for sentence 4 and is the correct answer.

11. B   **Difficulty:** Hard

Category: Organization

Getting to the Answer: Specifically state in your own words what the passage is about. Then read the answer choices to see what fits best. The passage focuses on the specific moment of Fahlberg's discovery, including the significance of the discovery itself and its applications. Only (B) convincingly ties the sentence to the main ideas of the passage.

René Descartes: The Father of Modern Philosophy

12. B   **Difficulty:** Easy

Category: Usage

Getting to the Answer: A modifier should match its antecedent in number and gender. Also, be wary of words that sound alike but have different meanings and uses. As it stands, the sentence incorrectly uses the adverb "there." Since it refers to "great philosophers," the correct word is the possessive pronoun "their," which is often confused with "there." Choice (B) is the correct answer.

13. D   **Difficulty:** Hard

Category: Effective Language Use

Getting to the Answer: Read carefully to identify the context of the underlined word. Then, choose the word that best fits the context of the sentence. The underlined word modifies "premodern sources of truth and knowledge," which in turn refers to "political and religious tradition and authority." The context of the sentence indicates that these were powerful ideas that were being challenged by newer ideas. Choice (D), "reigning," conveys the idea that "political and religious tradition and authority" had monarch-like, or ruling, levels of power in people's lives.

14. B   **Difficulty:** Easy

Category: Effective Language Use

Getting to the Answer: Determine the relationship between the two parts of the underlined sentence, and then think about which answer choice best conveys this relationship. The sentence states that "foundations of truth seemed to be crumbling," and "Descartes's writings proposed an alternative foundation." The two ideas are connected to each other: Descartes's writings were a response to this "crumbling." Choice (B) is the answer that identifies this relationship.

15. C   **Difficulty:** Hard

Category: Sentence Formation

Getting to the Answer: Determine whether the modifying phrase in this sentence references the correct noun. If the modifier in this sentence is describing a person, then the noun that is described by the modifier should also be a person. Choice (C) correctly matches the modifier (beginning with "an expert") to the noun "Descartes," rather than the noun "work."

16. A   **Difficulty:** Hard

Category: Development

Getting to the Answer: Determine the central claim in the paragraph and then come back to the question. The central claim of the paragraph is that Descartes's work established the foundation for many modern ideas. The statement found in (A) provides information that best supports this claim and logically transitions to the following sentence. Choice (A) is correct.

17. B   **Difficulty:** Medium

Category: Development

Getting to the Answer: In your own words, identify what idea ties together the ideas presented in the rest of the paragraph. Sentence 1 states that "modern culture would come to cherish this." The question is, what is "this"? The rest of the paragraph goes into detail about Descartes's philosophical methods. Choice (B) identifies Descartes's general philosophical focus and is, therefore, the correct answer.

18. D   Difficulty: Medium

Category: Punctuation

Getting to the Answer: Identify whether the sentence consists of two independent clauses or an independent and a dependent clause. This will provide guidance for punctuating it. The sentence consists of two independent clauses ("Descartes arrived . . ." and "he could only be . . . "). Separating the independent clauses into two sentences is the best way to punctuate them. Choice (D) is the correct answer.

19. B   Difficulty: Hard

Category: Development

Getting to the Answer: Look for the answer choice that most clearly helps to develop the ideas in the surrounding sentences. The inserted sentence comes after a discussion of Descartes's only certainty—that he was thinking. The sentence that follows it explains that from this, he could build additional knowledge. The correct answer will develop the idea of certainty and how it can be used to acquire more knowledge. Choice (B) best conveys this information and therefore is the correct choice.

20. D   Difficulty: Medium

Category: Usage

Getting to the Answer: A grammatically correct sentence will include a verb whose form makes the sentence an independent clause. "Propelled by" needs the addition of an auxiliary verb for this sentence to stand alone. Inserting "were" before this phrase makes the sentence grammatically complete. Choice (D) is the correct answer.

21. B   Difficulty: Medium

Category: Effective Language Use

Getting to the Answer: Determine whether there is a way to make the sentence less wordy without changing its intended meaning. The sentence, especially in the context of the paragraph, seems to be saying that it's difficult to determine exactly what Descartes did versus what other people at the time did. Both answer choices C and D change the meaning of the sentence slightly to say either that Descartes himself could not be separated from his contemporaries or that what they did was identical. Choice (B) is correct, because it eliminates the wordiness of the sentence while maintaining its meaning.

22. C   Difficulty: Medium

Category: Effective Language Use

Getting to the Answer: Determine what role this verb has in the sentence. What is the precise nature of the action it is describing? The sentence is about how Descartes's work brought about shifts in thinking that critically influenced other developments. However, the word "begun," A, does not precisely convey the power with which this occurred. Choice (C), "initiated," conveys this meaning and is the correct answer.

The Novel: Introspection to Escapism

23. C   Difficulty: Medium

Category: Effective Language Use

Getting to the Answer: Reread the surrounding sentences to look for context clues. Then review the answer choices, paying attention to the meaning and nuance of each word. The passage tells us that art is constantly evolving and changing. The correct answer will represent the opposite of this meaning. The word "static" means that something does not change, so (C) is the correct answer.

24. B   Difficulty: Medium

Category: Punctuation

Getting to the Answer: Read the sentence and determine whether the parts of the sentence on either side of the semicolon are independent clauses. If they are not, identify their function and choose the appropriate punctuation. "For better or worse" is not an independent clause; rather, it is a parenthetical element that adds an opinion to the main thrust of the sentence. Choice (B) is correct. It uses a dash to set off this additional information in the sentence.

25. B **Difficulty:** Medium

Category: Development

Getting to the Answer: To determine the main topic of a paragraph, identify important details and then summarize them in a sentence or two. Find a choice that matches your prediction. Avoid choices like A and C, which include details about poetry that are not in the paragraph. The details in this paragraph are about how the writers of the past viewed the novel as a vital way to record and comment on the human experience. Choice (B) captures this main topic.

26. A **Difficulty:** Medium

Category: Effective Language Use

Getting to the Answer: Read the surrounding sentences to get a sense of what the underlined word is meant to convey. Then review the answer choices to find the one that is closest to this meaning. The passage suggests that the novel was held in high regard. The correct answer needs to indicate high regard with a positive connotation. The word "loftily," (A), connotes both high regard and a positive view of the novel as a literary form.

27. A **Difficulty:** Medium

Category: Development

Getting to the Answer: Look for the answer choice that improves the sentence by adding important, relevant information. The paragraph is about the opinions of acclaimed novelists. Choice (A) adds the information that Joseph Conrad was also a novelist.

28. A **Difficulty:** Medium

Category: Punctuation

Getting to the Answer: Identify the role of the underlined phrase; then use this information to determine the necessary punctuation. "However" is an introductory adverbial element that modifies the rest of the sentence. It should be followed by a comma. Choice (A) is correct.

29. B **Difficulty:** Medium

Category: Sentence Formation

Getting to the Answer: Check the placement of dependent clauses set off by commas. A dependent clause that modifies a noun in a sentence should be adjacent or as close as possible to the noun it is modifying. The dependent clause "which are now available on digital devices" modifies "novels," not "entertainment medium." It should be as close as possible to "novels," making (B) the correct answer.

30. A **Difficulty:** Medium

Category: Sentence Formation

Getting to the Answer: A compound sentence should be combined with a semicolon or a comma with a conjunction. Choice (A) is correct. This keeps the semicolon, which appropriately separates two related independent clauses.

31. C **Difficulty:** Hard

Category: Development

Getting to the Answer: Evaluate the paragraph for the central idea. Then review the answer choices to find the one that directly supports that idea. This paragraph discusses the change from novels that tackle serious social issues to books that are meant as light entertainment for mass consumption. Choice (C) is correct. It emphasizes that readers want novels to be "fun," providing a means of escape from their lives.

32. D   Difficulty: Medium

Category: Usage

Getting to the Answer: A pronoun needs to match its antecedent. Locate the antecedent of the pronoun and then predict an answer. The correct answer will match the antecedent in gender and number. The antecedent is "novelist," so the answer must be singular. Choice (D) is correct, as it matches the antecedent in number and appropriately identifies both gender options, since the antecedent did not specify gender.

33. A   Difficulty: Hard

Category: Punctuation

Getting to the Answer: Remember that dashes and parentheses act in similar ways. If the phrase is offering additional information before you get back to the main thrust of the sentence, then a dash is appropriate. A dash is an appropriate way to punctuate the phrase, so (A) is the correct choice.

Interning: A Bridge Between Classes and Careers

34. B   Difficulty: Easy

Category: Usage

Getting to the Answer: Read the entire paragraph to understand the context in which the underlined word appears. Be careful to distinguish between commonly confused words. The paragraph makes it clear that Kelli has started working at BP as a summer intern. The correct answer will convey this meaning. Choice A, "excepted," meaning "excluded from a group," is a word that is commonly confused with "accepted," which means "to have taken or received something." In this case, Kelli has taken the job offer with BP, making (B) the correct choice.

35. C   Difficulty: Medium

Category: Effective Language Use

Getting to the Answer: Read the entire sentence to

determine the context of the underlined word. The context implies that the tasks assigned to interns are low level and meaningless. Choices B, "skilled," and D, "challenging," suggest that the tasks are important, which does not match the context. Only (C) fits the tone and context of the paragraph and is more precise than "boring."

36. A   Difficulty: Hard

Category: Development

Getting to the Answer: Identify the central idea and then review the answer choices to find the one that best supports it. The paragraph is about the importance of gaining a real-world perspective on classroom knowledge. Choice (A) supports this central idea by showing how Kelli's internship will allow her to apply her classroom knowledge to the real world.

37. D   Difficulty: Hard

Category: Development

Getting to the Answer: Skim the paragraph to determine what content the sentences have in common. The paragraph discusses the safety training Kelli is required to complete and explains how this training will offer her an advantage over other job applicants. Choice (D) most effectively establishes the main topic of the paragraph; it introduces the type of certification Kelli will earn.

38. A   Difficulty: Medium

Category: Effective Language Use

Getting to the Answer: Analyze the sentence to determine which phrase best fits the context. Choice (A) is the correct answer. "Stand out" means that Kelli will clearly be noticed when compared with other applicants.

39. D   Difficulty: Medium

Category: Usage

Getting to the Answer: Examine the structure of the sentence and identify the pronoun or pronouns that match the antecedent. Use the word "everyone" in a simple sentence to determine if it's singular or plural: for example, "Everyone goes." "Everyone" is a singular pronoun referring to a person, so it requires a singular possessive pronoun. Using the plural "their" is accepted only in informal usage. Choice (D) is the correct answer because it correctly matches the antecedent in number and appropriately identifies both gender options, since the antecedent did not specify a gender.

40. A   Difficulty: Medium

Category: Punctuation

Getting to the Answer: Determine the need for punctuation within the sentence. "For" and "from" are both prepositions, a clue that both phrases are correctly set off with commas. Because both phrases are dependent on the remainder of the sentence, they are correctly connected with commas. Choice (A) is correct.

41. B   Difficulty: Easy

Category: Sentence Formation

Getting to the Answer: In a sentence with a series of actions, make sure all verbs or verb forms are parallel. Focusing on the action verbs, it becomes clear that they should all end in "-ing." Inconsistencies in this pattern result in a lack of parallel structure. Choice (B) is correct, as it uses the gerund form (nouns formed by adding "-ing" to verbs) of all four action verbs.

42. D   Difficulty: Medium

Category: Sentence Formation

Getting to the Answer: Identify the subject and predicate of each sentence to determine if it is a complete sentence or a fragment. As the sentences are written in A, the first one is an incomplete sentence, or fragment. Only (D) correctly and concisely combines the two to eliminate the fragment.

43. C   Difficulty: Medium

Category: Effective Language Use

Getting to the Answer: Often, when a sentence is long, it's a good idea to see if there are ways to edit out certain words or phrases to make the sentence more concise. Choice (C) is correct. By leaving out the phrase "though she is losing her summer," this answer choice conveys the intended meaning of the sentence with logical and concise language.

44. B   Difficulty: Medium

Category: Quantitative

Getting to the Answer: Make sure you understand the information conveyed by the graphic's labels before you attempt to choose the correct answer. The passage informs you that Kelli's chosen field is oil and energy, represented by the bar on the far right of the graphic. Choice (B) is the correct answer, as it matches the number of oil and energy interns per 1,000 hires noted on the y-axis.

MATH—NO CALCULATOR TEST

1. B   Difficulty: Easy

Category: Heart of Algebra / Linear Equations

Getting to the Answer: In a real-world scenario, the slope of a line represents a unit rate and the y-intercept represents a flat fee or a starting amount. The cost of one linear foot is the same as the unit rate (the cost per linear foot), which is represented by the slope of the line. Use the grid-lines and the axis labels to count the rise and the run from the y-intercept of the line (0, 150) to the next point that hits an intersection of two grid-lines. Pay careful attention to how the grid-lines are marked (by 5s on the x-axis and by 25s on the y-axis). The line rises 75 units and runs 5 units, so the slope is $\frac{75}{5} = 15$ dollars per linear foot of fence, which is (B). Note that you could also use the slope formula and two points from the graph to find the unit rate.

2. C   **Difficulty:** Easy

Category: Passport to Advanced Math / Exponents

Getting to the Answer: Don't be tempted—you can't simply cancel one term when a polynomial is divided by a monomial. Instead, find the greatest common factor of *both* the numerator and the denominator. Factor out the GCF from the numerator and from the denominator, and then you can cancel it. The GCF is $12x^2$.

$$\frac{24x^4 + 36x^3 - 12x^2}{12x^2}$$

$$= \frac{\cancel{12x^2}(2x^2 + 3x - 1)}{\cancel{12x^2}}$$

$$= 2x^2 + 3x - 1$$

This matches (C).

3. C   **Difficulty:** Easy

Category: Additional Topics in Math / Geometry

Getting to the Answer: Corresponding sides of similar triangles are proportional, so write a proportion (paying careful attention to the order of the sides) using the sides that you know and the side that you're looking for. Then, solve the proportion for the missing side.

Call the missing side x. Write a proportion using words first, and then fill in the lengths of the sides that you know:

$$\frac{\text{right side small}\triangle}{\text{base of small}\triangle} = \frac{\text{right side large}\triangle}{\text{base of large}\triangle}$$

$$\frac{x}{4} = \frac{2 + x}{6}$$

$$6x = 4(2 + x)$$

$$6x = 8 + 4x$$

$$2x = 8$$

$$x = 4$$

The length of $\overline{BE}$ is 4, so (C) is correct.

4. A   **Difficulty:** Easy

Category: Passport to Advanced Math / Quadratics

Getting to the Answer: Recognizing the different forms of a quadratic equation can save valuable time on Test Day. Each of the answer choices is given in vertex form, so start by matching the vertex of the parabola in the graph to the correct equation.

When a quadratic equation is written in vertex form, $y = a(x - h)^2 + k$, the vertex is (h, k). The vertex of the parabola in the graph is (2, 5); therefore, the equation should look like $y = a(x - 2)^2 + 5$. This means you can eliminate B and C. To choose between (A) and D, consider the value of a. The parabola in the graph opens downward, so a must be negative. This means (A) is correct.

5. B   **Difficulty:** Medium

Category: Heart of Algebra / Linear Equations

Getting to the Answer: You can approach this question conceptually or concretely. Drawing a quick sketch is most likely the safest approach. Line L shown in the graph rises from left to right, so it has a positive slope. Once reflected over the x-axis, it will fall from left to right, so the new line will have a negative slope. This means you can eliminate C and D. Now, draw a quick sketch of the reflected line on the coordinate plane in your test booklet and count the rise (or fall) and the run from one point to the next.

The reflected line falls 2 units and runs 4 units, so the slope is $-\frac{2}{4}$, which reduces to $-\frac{1}{2}$, making (B) the correct choice.

6. B   **Difficulty:** Medium

Category: Passport to Advanced Math / Exponents

Getting to the Answer: To answer this question, you need to combine like terms, being careful to distribute negative signs where appropriate. Break the calculation into steps: Find $2p$, find $q + r$, and then subtract the results. Arranging the terms in descending order will help keep them organized.

$$2p = 2(4x^3 + x - 2) = 8x^3 + 2x - 4$$
$$q + r = x^2 - 1 + 3x - 5 = x^2 + 3x - 6$$
$$2p - (q + r) = 8x^3 + 2x - 4 - (x^2 + 3x - 6)$$
$$= 8x^3 + 2x - 4 - x^2 - 3x + 6$$
$$= 8x^3 - x^2 + 2x - 3x - 4 + 6$$
$$= 8x^3 - x^2 - x + 2$$

This matches (B).

7. A   **Difficulty:** Medium

Category: Passport to Advanced Math / Quadratics

Getting to the Answer: The roots of an equation are the same as its solutions. The answer choices contain radicals, which tells you that the equation can't be factored. Instead, either complete the square or solve the equation using the quadratic formula, whichever you are most comfortable using. The equation is already written in the form $y = ax^2 + bx + c$ and the coefficients are fairly small, so using the quadratic formula is probably the quickest method. Jot down the values that you'll need: $a = 2$, $b = 4$, and $c = -3$. Then, substitute these values into the quadratic formula and simplify:

$$x = \frac{-b \pm \sqrt{b^2 - 4ac}}{2a}$$
$$= \frac{-(4) \pm \sqrt{(4)^2 - 4(2)(-3)}}{2(2)}$$
$$= \frac{-4 \pm \sqrt{16 + 24}}{4}$$
$$= \frac{-4 \pm \sqrt{40}}{4}$$

This is not one of the answer choices, so simplify the radical. To do this, look for a perfect square that divides into 40 and take its square root.

$$x = \frac{-4 \pm \sqrt{4 \times 10}}{4}$$
$$= \frac{-4 \pm 2\sqrt{10}}{4}$$
$$= \frac{-2 \pm \sqrt{10}}{2}$$

Be careful—you can't simplify the answer any further because you cannot divide the square root of 10 by 2, so (A) is correct.

8. D   **Difficulty:** Medium

Category: Heart of Algebra / Systems of Linear Equations

Getting to the Answer: Although this question asks where the *graphs* of the functions intersect, it is not necessary to actually graph them. Two graphs intersect at the point where they have the same x-value and the same y-value. The notations $g(x)$ and $h(x)$ can both be interpreted as "the y-value at a given value of x," so set $g(x)$ equal to $h(x)$ and solve for x. Then, if needed, plug this value into either function to find the corresponding y-value. Don't let the fraction intimidate you—you can write $g(x)$ as a fraction over 1 and use cross-multiplication.

$$\frac{3x-5}{1} = \frac{7x+10}{4}$$
$$4(3x-5) = 7x+10$$
$$12x-20 = 7x+10$$
$$5x = 30$$
$$x = 6$$

There is only one answer choice for which the x-coordinate is 6, (D), so the graphs of the functions will intersect at (6, 13).

9. A   Difficulty: Medium

Category: Passport to Advanced Math / Exponents

Getting to the Answer: When you write an equation *in terms of* a specific variable, you are simply solving the equation for that variable. In this question, you'll need to relate fractional exponents to radicals and understand how to use negative exponents. Be careful—you're not just rewriting the equation, you're solving it for k.

Raising a quantity to the one-third power is the same as taking its cube root. Applying a negative exponent to a quantity is the same as writing its reciprocal. Rewrite the equation using these properties and then solve for k using inverse operations. Note that the inverse of taking a cube root of a quantity is cubing the quantity.

$$x = k^{-\frac{1}{3}}$$
$$x = \frac{1}{\sqrt[3]{k}}$$
$$(x)^3 = \left(\frac{1}{\sqrt[3]{k}}\right)^3$$
$$x^3 = \frac{1}{k}$$
$$kx^3 = 1$$
$$k = \frac{1}{x^3}$$

Choice (A) is correct.

10. D   Difficulty: Medium

Category: Heart of Algebra / Linear Equations

Getting to the Answer: There are two variables and only one equation, so you can't actually solve the equation for c. Instead, recall that an equation has infinitely many solutions when the left side is identical to the right side. When this happens, everything cancels out and you get the equation 0 = 0, which is always true.

Start by simplifying the left side of the equation. Don't forget to distribute the negative sign to both terms inside the parentheses.

$$4x - (10-2x) = c(3x-5)$$
$$4x - 10 + 2x = c(3x-5)$$
$$6x - 10 = c(3x-5)$$

Next, quickly compare the left side of the equation to the right side. Rather than distributing the c, notice that if c were 2, then both sides of the equation would equal 6x − 10, and it would have infinitely many solutions. Therefore, c is 2, which is (D).

11. D   Difficulty: Medium

Category: Heart of Algebra / Inequalities

Getting to the Answer: You don't need to separate this compound inequality into pieces. Just remember, whatever you do to one piece, you must do to all three pieces. Don't forget to flip the inequality symbols if you multiply or divide by a negative number. Here, the fractions make it look more complicated than it really is, so start by clearing the fractions by multiplying everything by the least common denominator, 6.

$$0 < 1 - \frac{a}{3} \le \frac{1}{2}$$
$$6(0) < 6\left(1-\frac{a}{3}\right) \le 6\left(\frac{1}{2}\right)$$
$$0 < 6 - 2a \le 3$$
$$-6 < -2a \le -3$$
$$3 > a \ge \frac{3}{2}$$
$$1.5 \le a < 3$$

Now, read the inequality symbols carefully. The value of a is between 1.5 and 3, including 1.5, but *not* including 3, so (D) is the correct answer.

12. D Difficulty: Hard

Category: Heart of Algebra / Inequalities

Getting to the Answer: The only way a system of inequalities can have no solution is if the graph consists of two parallel lines with shading in opposite directions so that there is no overlap.

Start by writing each equation in slope-intercept form to help you envision what the graphs will look like. You'll need to multiply the second equation by -2, so don't forget to flip the inequality symbol.

$$y - \frac{2}{k}x \leq 0 \rightarrow y \leq \frac{2}{k}x$$

$$\frac{1}{k}x - \frac{1}{2}y \leq -1 \rightarrow -\frac{1}{2}y \leq -\frac{1}{k}x - 1$$

$$\rightarrow y \geq \frac{2}{k}x + 2$$

Now, think about the graphs. The first equation has a slope of $\frac{2}{k}$, a y-intercept of 0, and is shaded below the line. The second equation also has a slope of $\frac{2}{k}$, but it has a y-intercept of 2 and is shaded above the line. This means that no matter what value of k is used (other than 0), the two lines are parallel and shaded in opposite directions, and thus there are infinitely many values of k that result in a system with no solution, (D).

13. C Difficulty: Hard

Category: Passport to Advanced Math / Exponents

Getting to the Answer: When solving a rational equation, start by getting a common denominator. Then, you can set the numerators equal and solve for the variable. Don't forget, however: If the answer produces zero in any denominator, then it is not a valid answer. The denominators are almost the same

already; you just need to multiply the top and bottom of the first term by 2, factor the denominator of the second term, and you'll be ready to solve the equation.

$$\frac{2}{2}\left(\frac{4x}{x - 7}\right) + \frac{2x}{2x - 14} = \frac{70}{2(x - 7)}$$

$$\frac{8x}{2(x - 7)} + \frac{2x}{2(x - 7)} = \frac{70}{2(x - 7)}$$

Now that the denominators are all the same, you can solve the equation represented by the numerators.

$$8x + 2x = 70$$
$$10x = 70$$
$$x = 7$$

Be careful—this isn't the correct answer. Because there are variables in the denominator, you must check the solution to make sure it isn't extraneous, or in other words, doesn't cause a 0 in the denominator of any term. Here, if $x = 7$, then all of the denominators are zero (and division by zero is not possible), so the equation has no solution, (C).

14. B Difficulty: Hard

Category: Additional Topics in Math / Geometry

Getting to the Answer: The shortest distance from A to B is through the center of the circle, along the diameter, which is twice the radius. When the equation of a circle is written in the form $(x - h)^2 + (y - k)^2 = r^2$, you can easily find the center and the radius of the circle. To find r, complete the square for the x terms and for the y terms. Start by reordering the terms. Then, take the coefficient of the x term and divide it by 2, square it, and add the result to the two terms with x variables. Do the same with the y term. Remember, you must also add these amounts to the other side of the equation. This creates a perfect square of x terms and y terms, and the equation will look more like a circle.

$$x^2 + y^2 + 6x - 4y = 12$$
$$x^2 + 6x + y^2 - 4y = 12$$
$$\left(x^2 + 6x + 9\right) + \left(y^2 - 4y + 4\right) = 12 + 9 + 4$$
$$(x + 3)^2 - (y - 2)^2 = 25$$

This means that the radius of the circle is $\sqrt{25} = 5$, so the diameter is 10, which is also the distance from A to B, making (B) correct. Note that you can do a quick check of your work by looking at the center; according to the equation, the center is $(-3, 2)$, which appears to match the location of the center on the graph.

15. C   Difficulty: Hard

Category: Passport to Advanced Math / Functions

Getting to the Answer: The key to answering this question is in having a conceptual understanding of function notation. Here, the input $(x - 1)$ has already been substituted and simplified in the given function. Your job is to determine what the function would have looked like had x been the input.

To keep things organized, let $u = x - 1$, the old input. This means $x = u + 1$. Substitute this into g and simplify:

$$g(x - 1) = 3x^2 + 5x - 7$$
$$g(u) = 3(u + 1)^2 + 5(u + 1) - 7$$
$$= 3(u^2 + 2u + 1) + 5u + 5 - 7$$
$$= 3u^2 + 6u + 3 + 5u + 5 - 7$$
$$= 3u^2 + 11u + 1$$

This means $g(u) = 3u^2 + 11u + 1$. When working with function notation, you evaluate the function by substituting a given input value for the variable in the parentheses. Here, if the input value is x, then $g(x) = 3x^2 + 11x + 1$, which matches (C).

16. 15   Difficulty: Easy

Category: Heart of Algebra / Systems of Linear Equations

Getting to the Answer: The equilibrium price occurs when the supply and demand are equal. Graphically, this means where the two lines intersect. The lines intersect at the point (6, 15). You can see from the axis labels that price is plotted along the y-axis, so the equilibrium price is \$15.

17. 10.5 or 21/2   Difficulty: Medium

Category: Heart of Algebra / Linear Equations

Getting to the Answer: The key word in this question is *linear*. In a real-world scenario that involves a constant rate of change, you almost always need to find the slope and the initial amount so you can write an equation. The question states that the initial mass of the larva was 10 grams, so all you need to do is find the slope.

Write the information given in the question as ordered pairs (time, mass) so you can find the slope. At $t = 0$, the larva has a mass of 10 grams, so one pair is (0, 10). After 48 hours, the larva has a mass of 14 grams, so a second pair is (48, 14). Now, use the slope formula:

$$m = \frac{y_2 - y_1}{x_2 - x_1}$$
$$= \frac{14 - 10}{48 - 0}$$
$$= \frac{4}{48} = \frac{1}{12}$$

The equation is $y = \dfrac{1}{12}x + 10$, where y represents the mass of the larva after x hours. Substitute 6 for x to find the mass after 6 hours:
$$\frac{1}{12}(6) + 10 = \frac{6}{12} + 10 = 10.5 \text{ grams.}$$

Practice Tests

18. 4   **Difficulty:** Medium

Category: Passport to Advanced Math / Functions

Getting to the Answer: The notation $f(g(x))$ indicates a composition of two functions which is read "f of g of x." It means that the output when x is substituted in $g(x)$ becomes the input for $f(x)$. Use the second table to find that $g(-1)$ is 2. This is your new input. Now, use the first table to find $f(2)$, which is 4.

19. 10   **Difficulty:** Medium

Category: Additional Topics in Math / Imaginary Numbers

Getting to the Answer: Multiply the two complex numbers just as you would two binomials (using FOIL). Then, combine like terms. The question tells you that $i = \sqrt{-1}$. If you square both sides of the equation, this is the same as $i^2 = -1$, which is a more useful fact.

$$(4 + 3i)(1 - 2i) = 4(1 - 2i) + 3i(1 - 2i)$$
$$= 4 - 8i + 3i - 6i^2$$
$$= 4 - 5i - 6(-1)$$
$$= 4 - 5i + 6$$
$$= 10 - 5i$$

The question asks for a in $a + bi$, so the correct answer is 10.

20. 50.5 Difficulty: Hard

Category: Passport to Advanced Math / Scatterplots

Getting to the Answer: This question requires a conceptual understanding of modeling data and properties of quadratic functions. Because the regression model fits the data exactly, you can use what you know about quadratic functions to answer the question.

The graph of a quadratic function is symmetric with respect to its axis of symmetry. The axis of symmetry occurs at the x-value of the vertex, which also happens to be where the maximum (or minimum) of

the function occurs. The question tells you this value—it's $x = 56.25$. Because $x = 90$ is 33.75 (because $90 - 56.25 = 33.75$) units to the right of the axis of symmetry, you know that the y-value will be the same as the point that is 33.75 units to the left of the axis of symmetry. This occurs at $x = 56.25 - 33.75 = 22.5$. Read the y-value from the graphing calculator screenshot to find the answer, which is 50.5.

MATH—CALCULATOR TEST

1. D   **Difficulty:** Easy

Category: Problem Solving and Data Analysis / Statistics and Probability

Getting to the Answer: To reduce the margin of error, the society should use a larger sample size selected from a better representation of the population. The target population is *all* adults, not just those that have gym memberships. Using only adults with gym memberships is likely to skew the results because these respondents probably exercise considerably more than people who do not have gym memberships. This means (D) is correct.

2. B   **Difficulty:** Easy

Category: Heart of Algebra / Inequalities

Getting to the Answer: Think about this question conceptually. If the box cannot weigh *more than* 20 pounds (or 20×16 ounces), this means it can weigh *that much or less*, so the right half of the inequality you are looking for is $\leq 20 \times 16$. This means you can eliminate A and C based on the inequality symbol. A box is made up of ballpoint pens, b, and mechanical pencils, m. Each pen weighs 0.3 ounces, and each pencil weighs 0.2 ounces. The total weight of the box would be the number of pens, b, multiplied by their weight, 0.3, added to the number of pencils, m, multiplied by their weight, 0.2. So the inequality is $0.3b + 0.2m \leq 20 \times 16$, which matches (B).

3. C **Difficulty:** Easy

Category: Heart of Algebra / Linear Equations

Getting to the Answer: Finding an *x*-intercept is easy when you know the equation of the line—it's the value of *x* when *y* is 0. Everything you need to write the equation is shown on the graph. The *y*-intercept is 5 and the line falls 1 unit and runs 3 units from one point to the next, so the slope is $-\frac{1}{3}$. This means the equation of the line, in slope-intercept form, is $y = -\frac{1}{3}x + 5$. Now, set the equation equal to zero and solve for *x*:

$$0 = -\frac{1}{3}x + 5$$

$$\frac{1}{3}x = 5$$

$$x = 15$$

Line *Q* will intercept the *x*-axis at 15, which is (C).

4. D **Difficulty:** Easy

Category: Passport to Advanced Math / Functions

Getting to the Answer: When you see an expression such as *f*(*x*), it means to substitute the given value for *x* in the function's equation. When there is more than one function involved, pay careful attention to which function should be evaluated first. You are looking for the value of *f*(*x*) at *x* = 3. Because *f*(*x*) is defined in terms of *g*(*x*), evaluate *g*(3) first by substituting 3 for *x* in the expression *x* + 5.

$$g(3) = 3 + 5 = 8$$
$$f(3) = 2g(3) = 2(8) = 16$$

Choice (D) is correct.

5. C **Difficulty:** Easy

Category: Problem Solving and Data Analysis / Rates, Ratios, Proportions, and Percentages

Getting to the Answer: Pay careful attention to the units. As you read the question, decide how and when you will need to convert units. In this problem,

work backward—you need to know how many pages of cards will be printed. To find this number, you first need to know how many cards will be printed. So, start with the number of agents (which tells you the number of boxes) and multiply by the number of cards per box:

$$12 \text{ agents} \times \frac{2 \text{ boxes}}{1 \text{ agent}} \times \frac{225 \text{ cards}}{1 \text{ box}} = 5{,}400 \text{ cards}$$

Next, use the information about *pages* to finish the calculations:

$$5{,}400 \text{ cards} \times \frac{1 \text{ page}}{10 \text{ cards}} \times \frac{1 \text{ minute}}{18 \text{ pages}} = 30 \text{ minutes}$$

This means (C) is correct.

6. A **Difficulty:** Medium

Category: Heart of Algebra / Inequalities

Getting to the Answer: The question is asking about $\frac{x}{y}$, so think about how fractions work. Larger numerators result in larger values $\left(\frac{3}{2}\right.$, for example, is greater than $\left.\frac{1}{2}\right)$, and smaller denominators result in larger values $\left(\frac{1}{2}\right.$, for example, is greater than $\left.\frac{1}{4}\right)$. The largest possible value of $\frac{x}{y}$ is found by choosing the largest possible value for *x* and the smallest possible value for *y* which gives $\frac{0.2}{5} = 0.04$, or (A).

7. A **Difficulty:** Medium

Category: Problem Solving and Data Analysis / Statistics and Probability

Getting to the Answer: Results from a study can only be generalized to the population from which the sample was taken. Also, keep in mind that positive correlations do not prove causation. The study was conducted by the American Academy of Pediatrics on children in the United States under three, so the sample is American children under three, which means conclusions can only be drawn about *this* population. Also, because correlations do not prove causation, the only conclusion that can be drawn is that there is an association between television time and attention disorders for American children under three years old, (A).

8. D   Difficulty: Medium

Category: Problem Solving and Data Analysis / Statistics and Probability

Getting to the Answer: The greatest change (in absolute value) in miles ridden per week could be an increase or a decrease. You don't have to worry about whether the change is positive or negative, so to keep things simple, always subtract the smaller number from the larger number. Make a list to show the changes in miles ridden per week between each pair of consecutive weeks. Save yourself some time by skipping weeks that clearly have smaller changes, such as between weeks 1 and 2 and between weeks 3 and 4.

Weeks 2-3: $72 - 64 = 8$

Weeks 4-5: $78 - 70 = 8$

Weeks 5-6: $85 - 78 = 7$

Weeks 6-7: $85 - 75 = 10$

Weeks 7-8: $82 - 75 = 7$

Of the differences, the greatest is from week 6 to week 7, which is a change of 10 miles, making (D) correct.

9. C   Difficulty: Medium

Category: Heart of Algebra / Linear Equations

Getting to the Answer: Given two points (even when the coordinates are variables), the slope of the line is $\frac{y_2 - y_1}{x_2 - x_1}$. You are given a numerical value for the slope and a pair of coordinate points with variables. To find the value of a, plug the points into the slope formula, and then solve for a:

$$\text{Slope} = \frac{y_2 - y_1}{x_2 - x_1}$$

$$5 = \frac{6 - 2a}{a - (a - 1)}$$

$$5 = \frac{6 - 2a}{1}$$

$$5 = 6 - 2a$$

$$-1 = -2a$$

$$\frac{1}{2} = a$$

Choice (C) is correct.

10. A   Difficulty: Hard

Category: Heart of Algebra / Systems of Linear Equations

Getting to the Answer: Questions about breaking even usually involve creating a system of equations (one for cost and one for revenue), setting the equations equal to each other, and solving for the variable. Create a system of equations at each price point using n for the number of bathtub lifts. Then solve each system. Note that the cost equation will be the same for both systems, and it is already given to you in the question.

$$\text{Old Price: } C = 225n + 3{,}150; R = 450n$$
$$C = R$$
$$225n + 3{,}150 = 450n$$
$$3{,}150 = 225n$$
$$14 = n$$

$$\text{New Price: } C = 225n + 3{,}150; R = 375n$$
$$C = R$$
$$225n + 3{,}150 = 375n$$
$$3{,}150 = 150n$$
$$21 = n$$

At the old price, the company needed to sell 14 lifts to break even. At the new price, it needs to sell 21 lifts, so it needs to sell $21 - 14 = 7$ more lifts at the new price to break even, which is (A).

11. B   **Difficulty:** Medium

Category: Additional Topics in Math / Geometry

Getting to the Answer: The amount of water needed to create the ice portion of the exhibit is another way of saying the *volume* of the ice. So, you need to find the volume of the entire space and then subtract the volume of the cylinder that runs through the ice. The volume of a rectangular prism is given by $V = l \times w \times h$, and the volume of a cylinder equals the area of its base times its height, or $\pi r^2 h$. To determine the volume of the ice, start by decomposing the figure into two rectangular prisms and adding their volumes. You can decompose the figure left to right or front to back. Front to back, it looks like the following figure:

The prism in the back has a volume of $32 \times 11 \times 4 = 1,408$ cubic feet. The prism in the front has a length of 15 feet and a height of 4 feet, but the width is missing. Find the missing width by subtracting 11 from 25, which is 14 feet. So, the volume of the prism in the front is $15 \times 14 \times 4 = 840$ cubic feet. The total volume of the prisms is $1,408 + 840 = 2,248$ cubic feet. Be careful—that's not the answer. You still need to find the amount of space taken up by the glycol pipe and subtract it. The diameter of the pipe is 2 feet, so its radius is 1 foot, and the height (or the length in this question) is 32 feet, so the volume is $\pi(1)^2(32) \approx 100.53$ cubic feet. This means the amount of ice needed is $2,248 - 100.53 = 2,147.47$, or about 2,150 cubic feet, (B).

12. D   **Difficulty:** Medium

Category: Problem Solving and Data Analysis / Rates, Ratios, Proportions, and Percentages

Getting to the Answer: Let the units in this question guide you to the answer. You'll also need to use the answer you found in the previous question. The company will use two hoses, each of which pumps at a rate of 60 gallons per minute, so the rate is actually 120 gallons per minute. Convert the volume you found earlier from cubic feet to gallons, and then use the rate to find the time.

$$2{,}150 \; \cancel{ft^3} \times \frac{7.48 \; \cancel{gal}}{1 \; \cancel{ft^3}} \times \frac{1 \; min}{120 \; \cancel{gal}} = 134 \; \text{minutes}$$

The answers are given in hours and minutes, so write 134 minutes as 2 hours and 14 minutes, or about 2 hours and 15 minutes, which is (D).

13. C   **Difficulty:** Medium

Category: Passport to Advanced Math / Quadratics

Getting to the Answer: The graph of every quadratic equation is a parabola, which may or may not cross the *x*-axis, depending on where its vertex is and which way it opens. Don't forget—if the equation is written in vertex form, $y = a(x - h)^2 + k$, then the vertex is (h, k), and the value of *a* tells you which way the parabola opens. The graph of an equation that has *no solution* does not cross the *x*-axis, so try to envision the graph of each of the answer choices. When a quadratic is written in factored form, the factors tell you the *x*-intercepts, which means every quadratic equation that can be written in factored form (over the set of real numbers) must have solutions. This means you can eliminate B and D. Now, imagine the graph of the equation in A: The vertex is (5, 3) and *a* is negative, so the parabola opens downward and consequently must cross the *x*-axis. This means you can eliminate A, and (C) must be correct. The graph of the equation in (C) has a vertex of (5, 3) and opens *up*, so it does not cross the *x*-axis and, therefore, has no solution.

You could also graph each of the answer choices in

your graphing calculator, but this is not the most time-efficient way to answer the question.

14. A   **Difficulty:** Medium

Category: Problem Solving and Data Analysis / Rates, Ratios, Proportions, and Percentages

Getting to the Answer: Questions that involve distance, rate, and time can almost always be solved using the formula Distance = rate × time. Use the speed, or rate, of the plane from Boston, 360 mph, and its distance from Chicago, 864 mi, to determine when it arrived. You don't know the time, so call it t.

$$\text{Distance} = \text{rate} \times \text{time}$$
$$864 = 360t$$
$$2.4 = t$$

This means it took 2.4 hours for the plane to arrive. This is more than 2 full hours, so multiply 2.4 by 60 to find the number of minutes it took: $60 \times 2.4 = 144$ minutes. Now determine how long it took the plane from Kansas City. It left at 8:30 AM and arrived at 10:34 AM, so it took 2 hours and 4 minutes, or 124 minutes. This means the plane from Kansas City arrived $144 - 124 = 20$ minutes before the plane from Boston, (A).

15. B   **Difficulty:** Hard

Category: Problem Solving and Data Analysis / Rates, Ratios, Proportions, and Percentages

Getting to the Answer: Break the question into short steps (first part of trip, second part of trip, circling overhead). To get started, you'll need to find the distance for each part of the trip—the question only tells you the total distance. Then, use the formula Distance = rate × time to find how long the plane flew at 200 mph and then how long it flew at 450 mph.

First part of trip: $\dfrac{1}{4} \times 1,200 = 300$ mi

$$300 = 200t$$
$$t = \frac{300}{200} = 1.5 \text{ hours}$$
$$1.5 \times 60 = 90 \text{ minutes}$$

Second part of trip: $\dfrac{3}{4} \times 1,200 = 900$ mi

$$900 = 450t$$
$$t = \frac{900}{450} = 2 \text{ hours}$$
$$2 \times 60 = 120 \text{ minutes}$$

This means the plane flew for a total of $90 + 120 = 210$ minutes. Next, add the time the plane circled overhead: $210 + 25 = 235$ minutes. The total trip took 235 minutes (3 hours and 55 minutes), which means the plane landed at 8:30 + 3 hours = 11:30 + 55 minutes = 12:25 PM, (B).

16. A   **Difficulty:** Medium

Category: Passport to Advanced Math / Functions

Getting to the Answer: The range of a function is the set of possible outputs, or y-values on a graph. For all real values of any number t, the value of t^2 cannot be negative. This means the smallest possible value of t^2 is 0 and, consequently, the smallest possible value of $h(t)$ is $h(0) = \sqrt{0^2 + 9} = \sqrt{9} = 3$. Thus, the number 1 is not in the range of the function, making (A) correct.

You could also graph the function in your graphing calculator and examine the possible y-values. The graph follows here:

Notice that the lowest point on the graph is (0, 3), which tells you that the range of the function is $h(t) \geq 3$.

17. A   Difficulty: Medium

Category: Heart of Algebra / Systems of Linear Equations

Getting to the Answer: Graphically, the solution to a system of equations is the point or points where the graphs intersect. Whenever a graph with no grid-lines or axis labels is shown, you are usually interested primarily in the sign of the coordinates of a point, not the actual values. The graphs intersect in Quadrant 2 of the coordinate plane, so the x-value of the point of intersection (or a) is negative, and the y-value (or b) is positive. The question states that $a = -3b$, so you can eliminate B right away—the coordinates would have to be equal if their sum was 0. Now try Picking Numbers. Let $b = 1$, which means $a = -3$ and the sum of $a + b$ is -2, which is not one of the answer choices. Try another pair: If $b = 2$, then $a = -6$, and the sum is -4. This is still not one of the answer choices, but you should see a pattern—the x-coordinate will always overpower the y-coordinate, resulting in a negative sum, so the correct answer must be (A).

18. B   Difficulty: Medium

Category: Problem Solving and Data Analysis / Statistics and Probability

Getting to the Answer: When comparing two data sets for consistency, consider both the data center (mean or median) and the spread (standard deviation or range). Each set of data has a median of 0, and Thermostat A also has a mode of 0. Both of these measures indicate good test results. However, Thermostat A has a greater range of data. If the company chooses this thermostat, the cooling fan is likely to engage anywhere from –9 degrees below the target temperature to 10 degrees above the target temperature. Although this is within the safe temperature

range, it is not as consistent as Thermostat B, which engaged the fan within 6 degrees on either side of the target temperature. This means (B) is correct.

19. C   Difficulty: Medium

Category: Passport to Advanced Math / Quadratics

Getting to the Answer: When a quadratic function is written in factored form, you can find its zeros by setting each factor equal to 0 and solving for the variable. Each of the answer choices is written in factored form, so mentally solve each one by asking yourself what number would make each factor equal to 0. Then find the sum of the results:

Choice A: $3 + (-3) \neq -3$. Eliminate.

Choice B: $4 + (-1) \neq -3$. Eliminate.

Choice (C): $1 + (-4) = -3$, so (C) is correct.

Choice D: $6 + (-3) \neq -3$. Eliminate.

20. D   Difficulty: Hard

Category: Passport to Advanced Math / Functions

Getting to the Answer: A constant added or subtracted inside a function will shift the function left or right, while a constant added or subtracted from the outside will shift the function up or down. You're looking for the value of $p(0)$, but the graph shows $p(x) - 4$, which means the original graph has been shifted down 4 units. You'll need to find the y-value of the graph when $x = 0$, then add 4 to get back up to the original function. The graph passes through the point (0, 7), so $p(0) - 4 = 7$. Add 4 to both sides of the equation to get $p(0) = 7 + 4 = 11$, which is (D).

21. A   Difficulty: Medium

Category: Heart of Algebra / Linear Equations

Getting to the Answer: Sometimes writing an equation is the quickest route to answering a question. Assign a variable to the unknown, write the equation in words, and then translate from English into math. The unknown in this question is the number of times Geraldine can wrap the wire around the prism. Call this *n*. Now, write an equation in words: Total amount of wire equals distance around the prism times the number of wraps plus the extra on the ends. To fill in the numbers, you'll need to make a few calculations. Because the dimensions of the prism are given in inches, convert the amount of wire to inches as well: 18 ft = 18 × 12 = 216 inches. Next, figure out the distance around the prism using the picture. Don't forget, you have to go all the way around: 1.5 + 3.5 + 1.5 + 3.5 = 10 inches. Finally, read the question again to determine that the *extra on the ends* is 3 + 3 = 6 inches. Now you're ready to translate from English into math to write your equation, and then solve it.

$$216 = 10n + 6$$
$$210 = 10n$$
$$21 = n$$

Geraldine can wrap the wire around the prism 21 times, (A).

22. A Difficulty: Medium

Category: Problem Solving and Data Analysis / Statistics and Probability

Getting to the Answer: To find a percent change (increase or decrease), use the percent change formula:

$$\text{Percent change} = \frac{\text{new amount} - \text{original amount}}{\text{original amount}}$$

The question asks about the increase from July to August, so the original amount is the July harvest of squash and the new amount is the August harvest. Read the graph's key and the axis labels carefully. Each grid-line represents 5 tons, so the July squash harvest was 15 tons and the August harvest was 25 tons. Substitute these numbers into the percent change formula and simplify:

$$\text{Percent change} = \frac{\text{new amount} - \text{original amount}}{\text{original amount}}$$
$$= \frac{25 - 15}{15}$$
$$= \frac{10}{15} \approx 0.667$$

This is equal to an increase of about 67%, which is (A).

23. D Difficulty: Medium

Category: Problem Solving and Data Analysis / Rates, Ratios, Proportions, and Percentages

Getting to the Answer: Add reasonable numbers to the graph to help you answer the question. An example follows:

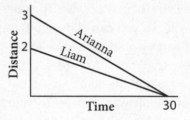

Use the numbers to help you evaluate each statement. It took Liam and Arianna each 30 minutes to walk home, so A and B are incorrect. Arianna walked 3 miles in 30 minutes, while Liam only walked 2 miles in 30 minutes; their rates are not the same, so C is also incorrect. This means (D) must be true. Arianna started out farther away than Liam, so she must have walked at a faster rate to arrive at home in the same amount of time.

24. B Difficulty: Medium

Category: Heart of Algebra / Linear Equations

Getting to the Answer: The slopes between sets of points that lie on the same line are equal. You can find the slope between points using the slope formula or by looking for patterns. Before immediately jumping to the slope formula, take a peek at the answer choices—all the *x*-coordinates of the points are multiples of 4, so looking for a pattern is the quickest way to answer this question. It may help to put all the points in a table (including those given in the question stem), with the *x*-coordinates arranged from smallest to largest, and then see which point doesn't fit the pattern.

x	y
−4	−8
0	−5
4	−1
8	1
12	4
16	7

Notice that all the *x*-coordinates increase by 4, while most of the *y*-coordinates increase by 3. For the slope between each pair of points to be equal, the *y*-coordinate at *x* = 4 would need to be −2, not −1, so the point given in (B) does not lie on the line.

25. A   Difficulty: Medium

Category: Problem Solving and Data Analysis / Statistics and Probability

Getting to the Answer: Identify which pieces of information from the table you need. The question asks for the probability that a randomly chosen person from the study is employed and has a college degree, so you need the total of both females and males with college degrees who are employed compared to all the participants in the study. There are 188 employed females with a college degree and 177 employed males with a college degree for a total of 365 employed people with a college degree out of 800 participants, so the probability is $\frac{365}{800}$, which reduces to $\frac{73}{160}$, (A).

26. B   Difficulty: Medium

Category: Problem Solving and Data Analysis / Scatterplots

Getting to the Answer: Translate from English into math: The number of cells in the original sample means the value of the function at 0 hours, or *f*(0). The first *x*-value on the graph is 4, not 0, so

you'll need to use the values shown in the calculator screenshot to write an equation for the model. Notice that the *y*-values in the calculator screenshot double as the *x*-values increase by 1. This means that the model is an exponential growth function of the form $f(x) = f(0) \cdot 2^x$. Choose a point from the calculator screenshot such as (4, 136), substitute the values into the function, and solve for *f*(0):

$$136 = f(0) \cdot (2)^4$$
$$136 = f(0) \cdot 16$$
$$\frac{136}{16} = f(0)$$
$$8.5 = f(0)$$

The *y*-axis title tells you that the numbers are given in thousands, so there were 8,500 white blood cells per microliter in the original sample, (B).

You could also work backward from the calculator screenshot by dividing by 2 four times (from 4 hours to 3 hours, 3 hours to 2 hours, 2 hours to 1 hour, and 1 hour to before the patient contracted the disease). The result is $136 \div 2^4 = 136 \div 16 = 8.5$, which in thousands is 8,500, (B).

27. D   Difficulty: Hard

Category: Additional Topics in Math / Geometry

Getting to the Answer: Drawing a sketch is the key to answering this question. Your sketch might look like the one below.

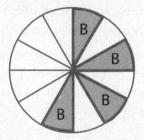

Notice that two radii and an arc form each section, so the amount of steel needed for one section is the length of the radius times 2, plus the length of the outer arc. Once you know this, you can simply multiply by 4.

You are given the total area, which means you can find the radius by substituting 64π for A in the area formula, $A = \pi r^2$.

$$64\pi = \pi r^2$$
$$64 = r^2$$
$$8 = r$$

For auctions, the arena is divided into 12 equal sections through the center, so divide 360 by 12 to find that the central angle measure for each section is $30°$. Now use the arc length formula:

$$\frac{n°}{360°} \times 2\pi r = \frac{30°}{360°} \times 2\pi(8)$$
$$= \frac{1}{12} \times 16\pi$$
$$= \frac{4\pi}{3}$$

The amount of steel needed for one section is $8 + 8 + \frac{4\pi}{3} = 16 + \frac{4\pi}{3}$, so the amount needed for all four sections is $4\left(16 + \frac{4\pi}{3}\right) = 64 + \frac{16\pi}{3}$, which is (D).

28. A   Difficulty: Hard

Category: Heart of Algebra / Linear Equations

Getting to the Answer: To write the equation of a line, you need two things—the starting amount (y-intercept) and the rate of change (slope). Substitute these values into slope-intercept form of a line ($y = mx + b$), and you have your equation.

The initial amount of water in the tank on Saturday is 70 gallons, so you already know b. To find m, you'll need to use the information given in the question to write two data points.

The amount of water in the tank *depends* on how long Lena has been filling it, so the number of gallons is the dependent variable and time is the independent variable. This tells you that the data points should be written in the form (time, gallons). At time = 0 on Saturday, the number of gallons is 70, so the data point is (0, 70). After 1 hour and 50 min-

utes, which is $60 + 50 = 110$ minutes, the tank is full (400 gallons), so another data point is (110, 400).

Now, use the slope formula to find that the rate of change is $\frac{400 - 70}{110 - 0} = \frac{330}{110} = 3$ gallons per minute. Substituting m and b into slope-intercept form results in the equation $y = 3x + 70$, so (A) is correct.

29. D   Difficulty: Hard

Category: Problem Solving and Data Analysis / Rates, Ratios, Proportions, and Percentages

Getting to the Answer: You need to find the ratio of small units to large units. You're given two ratios: small to medium and medium to large. Both of the given ratios contain medium size units, but the medium amounts (5 and 3) are not identical. To directly compare them, find a common multiple (15). Multiply each ratio by the factor that will make the number of medium units equal to 15.

small to medium: $(3:5) \times (3:3) = 9:15$

medium to large: $(3:2) \times (5:5) = 15:10$

Now that the number of medium units needed is the same in both ratios, you can merge the two ratios to compare small to large directly: 9:15:10. Therefore, the proper ratio of small units to large units is 9:10, which is (D).

30. A   Difficulty: Hard

Category: Passport to Advanced Math / Exponents

Getting to the Answer: Think of the rate given in the question in terms of the constant term you see on the right-hand side of the equation. Working together, the two air purifiers can clean the air in 7 hours. This is equivalent to saying that they can clean $\frac{1}{7}$ of the air in 1 hour. If $\frac{1}{7}$ is the portion of the air the two purifiers can clean *together* in 1 hour, then each term on the left side of the equation represents the portion that each purifier can clean *individually* in 1 hour. Because the new model is 3 times as fast as the older model, $\frac{3}{x}$ represents the portion of the air the new model can clean in 1 hour, and $\frac{1}{x}$ represents the portion of the air the older model can clean in 1 hour, which is (A).

31. 9/26 or .346   Difficulty: Easy

Category: Heart of Algebra / Linear Equations

Getting to the Answer: Distribute the fractions because the numbers inside each set of parentheses are evenly divisible by the denominators of the fractions by which they are being multiplied.

$$\frac{1}{3}(90x - 12) = \frac{1}{2}(8x + 10)$$
$$30x - 4 = 4x + 5$$
$$26x = 9$$
$$x = \frac{9}{26}$$

32. 4   Difficulty: Medium

Category: Passport to Advanced Math / Exponents

Getting to the Answer: When solving any type of equation, you should always think of inverse operations. The inverse of raising a quantity to the $\frac{5}{2}$ power is raising it to the $\frac{2}{5}$ power. Eliminate the exponent using inverse operations and then go from there.

$$n^{\frac{5}{2}} = 32$$
$$\left(n^{\frac{5}{2}}\right)^{\frac{2}{5}} = (32)^{\frac{2}{5}}$$
$$n = 32^{\frac{2}{5}}$$

Now, you have two choices—you can enter this value into your calculator as 32^(2/5) or you can evaluate the number using rules of exponents:

$$32^{\frac{2}{5}} = (\sqrt[5]{32})^2 = 2^2 = 4$$

33. 801   Difficulty: Hard

Category: Problem Solving and Data Analysis / Rates, Ratios, Proportions, and Percentages

Getting to the Answer: Draw a chart or diagram detailing the various price reductions for each 30-day period. You'll need to make several calculations, so don't round until the final answer.

Date	% of Most Recent Price	Resulting Price
Jan. 15	100 – 40% = 60%	$1,848 × 0.6 = $1,108.80
Feb. 1	100 – 15% = 85%	$1,108.80 × 0.85 = $942.48
March 1	100 – 15% = 85%	$942.48 × 0.85 = $801.108

You can stop here because the item was sold on March 10th. Before gridding in your answer, check that $801 is not less than 30% of the original price: 0.30 × $1,848 = $554.40. It's not, so the final selling price, rounded to the nearest whole dollar, was $801.

34. 2/3 or .666 or .667   Difficulty: Hard

Category: Additional Topics in Math / Trigonometry

Getting to the Answer: Two angles of the triangle have equal measures, so the triangle is isosceles, which means that drawing an altitude from the top to the base will bisect the base, resulting in two smaller right triangles as shown here:

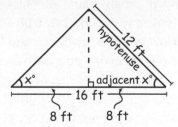

Now, use $\cos x° = \dfrac{\text{adjacent}}{\text{hypotenuse}}$ to find that $b = \dfrac{8}{12}$, which can be simplified to $\dfrac{2}{3}$.

35. 3.5 or **7/2**   **Difficulty:** Hard

Category: Heart of Algebra / Linear Equations

Getting to the Answer: Remember that parallel lines have the same slope. Use the slope formula $m = \dfrac{y_2 - y_1}{x_2 - x_1}$ to find the slope of $\overline{CD}$. Because $\overline{CD}$ passes through the points (0, 0) and (2, 4.5), its slope is $\dfrac{4.5 - 0}{2 - 0} = 2.25$. Line B has the same slope and passes through (0, −1), so you can use the slope formula again to find the y-coordinate of the given point, (2, y).

$$2.25 = \frac{y - (-1)}{2 - 0}$$
$$2.25 = \frac{y + 1}{2}$$
$$4.5 = y + 1$$
$$3.5 = y$$

The y-coordinate of the point is 3.5.

36. 3/10   **Difficulty:** Hard

Category: Problem Solving and Data Analysis / Rates, Ratios, Proportions, and Percentages

Getting to the Answer: Whenever rates are given in different units, start by converting to the same units. In most cases, converting to the smaller unit avoids fractions and decimals. Start with nickel because the weight is already in ounces: $10.08 ÷ 24 = $0.42 per ounce. Now find the per-ounce rate for copper. There are 16 ounces in one pound, so three pounds is 48 ounces: $8.64 ÷ 48 = $0.18 per ounce. So, if a person were to bring in equal amounts of each, he would receive $0.18 per ounce of copper and $0.42 per ounce of nickel. To find the fractional portion he would receive from the copper, set up a comparison between the amount received for copper and the total amount received, $0.18 + $0.42 = $0.60. The portion of the total amount he receives from copper would be $\dfrac{0.18}{0.60}$, which reduces to $\dfrac{3}{10}$.

37. 3   **Difficulty:** Easy

Category: Problem Solving and Data Analysis / Scatterplots

Getting to the Answer: Each grid-line along the vertical axis represents 5 units, so look for points that are at least two grid-lines away from the line of best fit. The people who have BMIs of 20, 25, and 28 have LDLs that are 10 or more mg/dL greater than the LDLs predicted by the line of best fit. This represents 3 people.

38. 24   **Difficulty:** Medium

Category: Problem Solving and Data Analysis / Scatterplots

Getting to the Answer: A line of best fit serves as an approximation of data from which you can estimate an output for a given input (or vice versa). The key is in reading the axis labels carefully. To determine the requested BMI, find the LDL level of 140 (which is already reported in mg/dL) on the vertical axis. The question says "Based on the line of best fit," so trace over to the line (*not* to the closest data point) and then down to the corresponding value on the horizontal axis, which represents BMI. You should end up just slightly to the right of the 24 line. Be sure to follow directions. The closest whole number approximation is 24.

ESSAY TEST RUBRIC

The Essay Demonstrates ...

4—Advanced	• **(Reading)** A strong ability to comprehend the source text, including its central ideas and important details and how they interrelate; and effectively use evidence (quotations, paraphrases, or both) from the source text.
	• **(Analysis)** A strong ability to evaluate the author's use of evidence, reasoning, and/or stylistic and persuasive elements, and/or other features of the student's own choosing; make good use of relevant, sufficient, and strategically chosen support for the claims or points made in the student's essay; and focus consistently on features of the source text that are most relevant to addressing the task.
	• **(Writing)** A strong ability to provide a precise central claim; create an effective organization that includes an introduction and conclusion, as well as a clear progression of ideas; successfully employ a variety of sentence structures; use precise word choice; maintain a formal style and objective tone; and show command of the conventions of standard written English so that the essay is free of errors.
3—Proficient	• **(Reading)** Satisfactory ability to comprehend the source text, including its central ideas and important details and how they interrelate; and use evidence (quotations, paraphrases, or both) from the source text.
	• **(Analysis)** Satisfactory ability to evaluate the author's use of evidence, reasoning, and/or stylistic and persuasive elements, and/or other features of the student's own choosing; make use of relevant and sufficient support for the claims or points made in the student's essay; and focus primarily on features of the source text that are most relevant to addressing the task.
	• **(Writing)** Satisfactory ability to provide a central claim; create an organization that includes an introduction and conclusion, as well as a clear progression of ideas; employ a variety of sentence structures; use precise word choice; maintain an appropriate formal style and objective tone; and show control of the conventions of standard written English so that the essay is free of significant errors.

2—Partial	• **(Reading)** Limited ability to comprehend the source text, including its central ideas and important details and how they interrelate; and use evidence (quotations, paraphrases, or both) from the source text.
	• **(Analysis)** Limited ability to evaluate the author's use of evidence, reasoning, and/or stylistic and persuasive elements, and/or other features of the student's own choosing; make use of support for the claims or points made in the student's essay; and focus on relevant features of the source text.
	• **(Writing)** Limited ability to provide a central claim; create an effective organization for ideas; employ a variety of sentence structures; use precise word choice; maintain an appropriate style and tone; or show control of the conventions of standard written English, resulting in certain errors that detract from the quality of the writing.
1—Inadequate	• **(Reading)** Little or no ability to comprehend the source text or use evidence from the source text.
	• **(Analysis)** Little or no ability to evaluate the author's use of evidence, reasoning, and/or stylistic and persuasive elements; choose support for claims or points; or focus on relevant features of the source text.
	• **(Writing)** Little or no ability to provide a central claim, organization, or progression of ideas; employ a variety of sentence structures; use precise word choice; maintain an appropriate style and tone; or show control of the conventions of standard written English, resulting in numerous errors that undermine the quality of the writing.

SAMPLE ESSAY RESPONSE #1 (ADVANCED SCORE)

Anyone who watches NFL football every Sunday is most likely aware that the athletes on the field make a significant amount of money for their efforts. The NFL generates a lot of income from television contracts, corporate sponsors, and advertisers, and the teams themselves benefit from ticket and merchandise sales. The players in turn are paid market-appropriate salaries. Anyone who watches college football games on Saturday will see similar, if slightly younger athletes, yet how much are those players making? The author of this article correctly notes these players don't earn a salary, and that's something he would like to correct. His argument? College athletes deserve compensation for their work just like any other employee.

The author begins by detailing how much money corporations, athletic conferences, and universities make from advertising and sponsor revenue. The Pacific-12 conference, for example, "signed television rights deals worth $3 billion." Speaking of television, CBS and Turner Broadcasting made a lot of money as well—thirty seconds of commercial advertising during the Final Four cost $700,000. Schools with successful programs also do well. The article points out that the University of Texas football program netted $77.9 million in 2011–2012.

The author uses this evidence to portray corporations, athletic conferences, and universities as the "unscrupulous tycoons from a Dickens novel." Those familiar with Dickens can picture more than one wealthy character who doesn't care for the working poor left eking out miserable lives in relative poverty. And who are these working poor? Student athletes, of course! The author uses the Dickens metaphor to convince the reader that corporations, athletic conferences, and universities do not have the student athletes' interests at heart. He then pivots to how much the athletes make for their efforts on behalf of the "unscrupulous tycoons"—absolutely nothing.

How much is the average student scholarship worth? According to the author, most leave a few thousand dollars in yearly out-of-pocket expenses to the student in spite of an average "forty hours a week" dedicated to their sport. And if an athlete is unable to play due to injury, even that scholarship money can be revoked. The author uses this information to compare a student athlete with an employee who benefits from federal and state labor laws. The comparison is painfully clear and made even more so when the author points out that student athletes do not have the right to unionize.

Throughout his essay, the author has effectively painted a Dickensian picture in which student athletes literally sweat, strain, and toil under the watchful eye of their universities, while those in power rake in millions of dollars. The evidence presented convincingly leads the reader to one conclusion: that student athletes deserve to be compensated.

SAMPLE ESSAY RESPONSE #2 (PROFICIENT SCORE)

Anyone who watches NFL football Sunday knows that those players make a lot of money. They make so much money because the teams and the league make money from television and advertising. But what about college football players or other college athletes? They don't make any money at all. The author thinks that isn't right. He argues that student athletes should get paid for their work just like anyone else.

The author talks about how much money schools, conferences, and corporations make off of college sports. It's a lot of money. For example, a television deal was worth $3 billion for the Pacific-12 conference, and it cost $700,000 for a television commercial during the Final Four basketball tournament. The author includes this to make the point that other people make a lot of money, but student athletes don't. This helps the reader feel some sympathy for the players and supports the author's argument that they should be paid.

The author then turns to a comparison of student athletes and employees. Student athletes don't earn salaries. They do get a scholarship, but that still leaves many of them short of money to pay the bills. They work forty hours a week. If they are hurt, then they may lose their scholarship because they can't play. The author talks about this to compare how student athletes earn money with how typical employees earn money. Employees have legal rights, but student athletes don't really have any. This is a good comparison, and it makes the reader believe that student athletes should be paid like employees, which is the author's concluding point.

PART SIX

Answers & Explanations

CHAPTER 2

PRACTICE

8. D **Difficulty:** Hard
Category: Heart of Algebra / Linear Equations

Getting to the Answer: Pay attention to the order in which the changes to the graph occur. The question states that the downward shift of 2 units occurs first, making the new y-intercept $-\frac{3}{2}$. A reflection over the x-axis follows, which changes the y-intercept to $\frac{3}{2}$ and makes the slope $\frac{7}{4}$. The only graph that correctly depicts these changes is (D). Beware of C; this results from a reflection over the y-axis, not the x-axis. The graphs below visualize each change.

1)

2)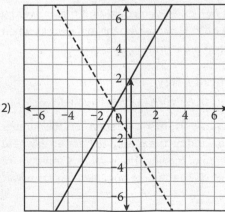

9. C **Difficulty:** Medium
Category: Heart of Algebra / Linear Equations

Getting to the Answer: Look closely; buried in the text are two sets of coordinates you can use. The question states that admission was $2 when the admission charge was first implemented and increased to $2.50 after 3 years, making your coordinates $(0, 2)$ and $(3, 2.5)$. The slope of the line passing through these is $m = \dfrac{2.5 - 2}{3 - 0} = \dfrac{0.5}{3} = \dfrac{1}{6}$. Eliminate A and D. Because the admission fee started at $2, 2 is the y-intercept, so the full equation is $y = \dfrac{c}{6} + 2$. Choice (C) is correct.

Because the question says "three years ago," it may be tempting to use $(-3, 2)$ and $(0, 2.5)$ as your coordinates. Think about what that would mean: The first admission charge would be $2.50, as it's impossible to have a negative year. This contradicts the question stem, so B is incorrect.

PERFORM

10. A **Difficulty:** Easy
Category: Heart of Algebra / Linear Equations

Getting to the Answer: Think about what happens to the slope of a line if you're merely moving the line around the coordinate plane. Any shift of a line, whether it's up, down, left, right, or some combination of these, will not change the line's slope. The slope of the given line is -5 (the coefficient of x), and the slope does not change, so (A) is correct.

11. 36 **Difficulty:** Medium
Category: Heart of Algebra / Linear Equations

Getting to the Answer: That you're asked to find an expression rather than a variable value means there's likely a shortcut. Start by eliminating the fractions. A common multiple of 4 and 3 is 12, so multiply both sides of the equation by that. Once the fractions are gone, move both variable terms to the left side and try to make it look like the desired expression.

$$12\left(\frac{3}{4}y = 6 - \frac{1}{3}c\right)$$
$$9y = 72 - 4c$$
$$4c + 9y = 72$$
$$2c + \frac{9}{2}y = 36$$

The expression on the left side is precisely what you're looking for, so grid in 36.

12. A   **Difficulty:** Hard

Category: Heart of Algebra / Linear Equations

Getting to the Answer: Don't panic over the presence of m. Just solve for y, then think about what kind of graph it can have. Start by distributing m on the right, then move all terms to the left:

$$x - y = m(2x + y)$$
$$x - y = 2mx + my$$
$$x - 2mx - y - my = 0$$

Continue by factoring out x and y, then move any terms without y back to the right:

$$x(1 - 2m) + y(-1 - m) = 0$$
$$y(-1 - m) = -x(1 - 2m)$$

Divide by $(-1 - m)$, then factor out -1 from the denominator and cancel:

$$y = \frac{-x(1 - 2m)}{(-1 - m)} = \frac{-x(1 - 2m)}{-(1 + m)} = \frac{1 - 2m}{1 + m}x$$

Don't worry about how messy the right side looks yet; for now, you just need to realize that it's merely x multiplied by a complicated coefficient. Because the equation is now solved for y, you have an equation of a line. The messy coefficient is the slope, and because there's no added (or subtracted) constant, the y-intercept is 0. You can eliminate B (not a line) and D ($b \neq 0$) based on this.

Examine the remaining choices more closely: They only differ by the sign of their slope. To determine which is correct, pick a value for m between 0 and $\frac{1}{2}$ (but not 0 or $\frac{1}{2}$ themselves), and plug it into the slope expression.

If $m = \frac{1}{4}$, for instance, then the slope would be:

$$\frac{\left(1 - 2 \times \frac{1}{4}\right)}{\left(1 + \frac{1}{4}\right)} = \frac{\left(1 - \frac{1}{2}\right)}{\frac{5}{4}} = \frac{1}{2} \times \frac{4}{5} = \frac{2}{5}$$

Because the slope of this line is positive, (A), which is the only remaining choice with a positive slope, is correct.

EXTRA PRACTICE

1. C   **Difficulty:** Easy

Category: Heart of Algebra / Linear Equations

Getting to the Answer: Don't let this fairly simple question fool you. Just because 5 and −5 are opposites, this does not mean the value on the right-hand side of the equal sign will be the opposite of 11. Solve for x, then substitute that value into the second equation for x and simplify.

$$2x + 5 = 11$$
$$2x = 6$$
$$x = 3$$

$$2x - 5 = 2(3) - 5$$
$$= 6 - 5$$
$$= 1$$

Therefore, (C) is correct.

A quicker approach would be to recognize that $2x - 5$ is 10 less than $2x + 5$, so you could find the answer by subtracting 10 from 11. However, this only works when the variable terms are identical.

2. B   **Difficulty:** Easy

Category: Heart of Algebra / Linear Equations

Getting to the Answer: The x-axis represents the number of lightbulbs, so find 1 on the x-axis and trace up to where it meets the graph of the line. The y-value is somewhere between \$1 and \$2, so the only possible correct answer choice is \$1.80.

You could also find the unit rate by calculating the slope of the line using two of the points shown on the graph: The graph rises 9 units and runs 5 units from one point to the next, so the slope is $\frac{9}{5}$, or 1.80, which means (B) is correct.

3. D **Difficulty:** Medium

Category: Heart of Algebra / Linear Equations

Getting to the Answer: Use the information in the question to write your own expression, and then look for the answer choice that matches. Simplify your expression only if you don't find a match. If a couple earns $50 *per half-hour* that they dance, then they earn $50 \times 2 = $100 *per hour*. Multiply this amount times the number of hours (not including the first 3 hours). This can be expressed as $100(h - 3)$. This is not one of the answer choices, so simplify by distributing to get $100h - 300$, which is (D).

If you're struggling with the algebra, try Picking Numbers. Pick a number of hours a couple might dance, like 5. They don't earn anything for the first 3 hours, but they earn $50 per half-hour for the last 2 hours, which is 50 times 4 half-hours, or $200. Now, find the expression that gives you an answer of $200 when $h = 5$ hours: $100(5) - 300 = 500 - 300 = 200$.

4. D **Difficulty:** Medium

Category: Heart of Algebra / Linear Equations

Getting to the Answer: Take a quick peek at the answer choices. The equations are given in slope-intercept form, so start by finding the slope. Substitute two pairs of values from the table (try to pick easy ones if possible) into the slope formula, $m = \dfrac{y_2 - y_1}{x_2 - x_1}$. Keep in mind that the projected number of pounds sold *depends* on the price, so the price is the independent variable (x) and the projected number is the dependent variable (y). Using the points (1.2, 15,000) and (2, 5,000), the slope is:

$$m = \frac{5{,}000 - 15{,}000}{2 - 1.20}$$
$$m = \frac{-10{,}000}{0.8}$$
$$m = -12{,}500$$

This means you can eliminate A and B because the slope is not correct. Don't let B fool you—the projected number of pounds sold goes *down* as the price goes *up*, so there is an inverse relationship, which means the slope must be negative. To choose between C and (D), you could find the *y*-intercept of the line, but this is a fairly time-intensive

process. Instead, choose the easiest pair of values from the table, (2, 5,000), and substitute into C and (D) only. Choice (D) is correct because $5{,}000 = -12{,}500(2) + 30{,}000$ is a true statement.

5. D **Difficulty:** Hard

Category: Heart of Algebra / Linear Equations

Getting to the Answer: If a linear equation has infinitely many solutions, the variable terms will cancel out, leaving a number that is equal to itself (which is always true). Start by simplifying both sides of the equation using the distributive property.

$$2\left(x - \frac{5}{2}\right) = c\left(\frac{4}{5}x - 2\right)$$
$$2x - 5 = \frac{4c}{5}x - 2c$$

Because the constant terms must be equal, set $-5 = -2c$ and solve for c to get $c = \dfrac{5}{2}$, which means (D) is correct.

Note that you could also set the variable terms equal to each other and solve for c, but the manipulations would be more difficult.

6. B **Difficulty:** Hard

Category: Heart of Algebra / Linear Equations

Getting to the Answer: As written, the equation doesn't tell you a lot about the graph, but you should notice that there are no exponents on the variables, which means the exponents are all equal to 1. This means the equation is linear and the graph must be a line, so you can eliminate D right away (it is an absolute value equation, not a linear equation). To choose the correct line, rearrange the equation so that it is in slope-intercept form, $y = mx + b$. To do this, first collect the *y*-terms on the left side of the equation. Rearranging the equation results in the following:

$$y = ay + ax + x + 1$$
$$y - ay = ax + x + 1$$
$$y(1 - a) = x(a + 1) + 1$$
$$y = \frac{a + 1}{1 - a}x + \frac{1}{1 - a}$$

This manipulation reveals a linear equation with a slope of $\dfrac{a + 1}{1 - a}$ and a *y*-intercept of $\dfrac{1}{1 - a}$. It is given in the question that $a > 1$, so the quantity $a + 1$ is positive, and $1 - a$ is negative, resulting in a negative slope and a negative y-intercept. Of the choices given, only the graph in (B) satisfies these conditions.

7. 18   Difficulty: Easy
Category: Heart of Algebra / Linear Equations

Getting to the Answer: Clear the fractions first by multiplying both sides of the equation by 8. Then solve for x using inverse operations:

$$\frac{7}{8}(n - 6) = \frac{21}{2}$$
$$8\left[\frac{7}{8}(n - 6)\right] = 8\left[\frac{21}{2}\right]$$
$$7(n - 6) = 4(21)$$
$$7n - 42 = 84$$
$$7n = 126$$
$$n = 18$$

8. 70   Difficulty: Hard
Category: Heart of Algebra / Linear Equations

Getting to the Answer: Because 40 pounds is not shown on the graph, you need more information. In a real-world scenario, the y-intercept of a graph usually represents a flat fee or a starting amount. The slope of the line represents a unit rate, such as the cost per pound to airmail the box.

The y-intercept of the graph is 10, so the flat fee is $10. To find the cost per pound (the unit rate), substitute two points from the graph into the slope formula. Using the points (0, 10) and (4, 16), the cost per pound is $\frac{16 - 10}{4 - 0} = \frac{6}{4} = 1.5$, which means it costs $1.50 per pound to airmail a box. The total cost to airmail a 40-pound box is $10 + 1.50(40) = $10 + $60 = $70. Grid in 70.

9. C   Difficulty: Easy
Category: Heart of Algebra / Linear Equations

Getting to the Answer: Try to picture in your head what "increase in property values starts to slow down" would look like. It doesn't say the values start to decrease, but rather that the increase is not as fast.

An increasing line (one with a positive slope) indicates increasing property values. The steepness of the line (the actual *value* of the slope) indicates how fast the values

are increasing. The second line segment in the graph (between $t = 8$ and $t = 16$) still shows a positive slope, but one that is less steep than the first segment, so the increase in property values starts to slow down at $t = 8$, which is the year $2014 + 8 = 2022$, (C).

10. B   Difficulty: Easy
Category: Heart of Algebra / Linear Equations

Getting to the Answer: Read the axis labels carefully. The y-intercept is the point at which $x = 0$, which means the number of songs purchased is 0. The y-intercept is (0, 20), so the cost is $20 before buying any songs, and therefore most likely represents a flat membership fee for joining the service. Choice (B) is correct.

11. C   Difficulty: Easy
Category: Heart of Algebra / Linear Equations

Getting to the Answer: When writing a linear equation to represent a real-world scenario, a flat rate is a constant while a unit rate is always multiplied by the independent variable. You can identify the unit rate by looking for words like *per* or *for each*.

Because the amount Andrew gets paid daily, $120, is a flat rate that doesn't depend on the number of cruises he books, 120 should be the constant in the equation. This means you can eliminate B and D. The clue "for each cruise" tells you to multiply $25 by the number of cruises he books (c), so the equation is $d = 25c + 120$, making (C) correct.

12. A   Difficulty: Medium
Category: Heart of Algebra / Linear Equations

Getting to the Answer: This question has multiple fractions, so clear the $\frac{8}{5}$ by multiplying both sides of the equation by its reciprocal, $\frac{5}{8}$. Then, because the answers are given in decimal form, change the other fraction to a decimal by dividing the numerator by the denominator.

$$\frac{8}{5}\left(x + \frac{33}{12}\right) = 16$$
$$\frac{5}{8} \times \left[\frac{8}{5}\left(x + \frac{33}{12}\right)\right] = \frac{5}{8} \times 16$$
$$x + 2.75 = 10$$
$$x = 7.25$$

Choice (A) is correct.

13. C   Difficulty: Medium

Category: Heart of Algebra / Linear Equations

Getting to the Answer: Because the equation represents the balance if Henry deposits his paycheck for x weeks, then his paycheck amount must be multiplied by the number of weeks he works. The only two factors in the equation being multiplied are 360 and x, so 360 must be the amount of his paycheck. This means you can eliminate A and D. The other number in the equation, -126.13, is a constant, which represents a starting amount. Because the constant is negative, Henry must have had a negative balance in his account before setting up the direct deposit, which means he had overdrawn the account. Thus, (C) is correct.

14. C   Difficulty: Medium

Category: Heart of Algebra / Linear Equations

Getting to the Answer: Use the graph to identify the y-intercept and the slope of the line, and then write an equation in slope-intercept form, $y = mx + b$. Once you have your equation, look for the answer choice that matches. The line crosses the y-axis at $(0, -4)$ so the y-intercept (b) is -4. The line rises 1 unit for every 3 units that it runs to the right, so the slope (m) is $\frac{1}{3}$. The equation of the line is $y = \frac{1}{3}x - 4$, which matches (C).

You could also graph each of the answer choices in your calculator to see which one matches the given graph, but this is not the most time-efficient strategy. You also have to be very careful when entering fractions—to graph (C), for example, you would enter $(1/3)x - 4$.

15. A   Difficulty: Hard

Category: Heart of Algebra / Linear Equations

Getting to the Answer: The question tells you that the functions are all linear, so start by finding the rate of change (the slope, m) using any two pairs of values from the table and the slope formula. Next, substitute the slope and any pair of values from the table, such as $(10, 34)$, into the equation $f(x) = mx + b$, and solve for b. Finally, use the value of m and b to write the function.

$$m = \frac{y_2 - y_1}{x_2 - x_1} = \frac{64 - 34}{30 - 10} = \frac{30}{20} = 1.5$$

You can stop right there! Only Choice (A) has a slope of 1.5, so it must be the correct answer.

16. C   Difficulty: Hard

Category: Heart of Algebra / Linear Equations

Getting to the Answer: Let v represent the number of visits. The question asks when the two memberships will cost the same, so write an equation that sets the total membership costs equal to each other. The first membership type costs $325 for unlimited visits, so write 325 on one side of the equal sign. The second type costs $8 per visit (not including the first 5 visits), or $8(v - 5)$, plus a flat $125 enrollment fee, so write $8(v - 5) + 125$ on the other side of the equal sign. Solve for v:

$$325 = 8(v - 5) + 125$$
$$325 = 8v - 40 + 125$$
$$240 = 8v$$
$$30 = v$$

Choice (C) is correct.

17. D   Difficulty: Hard

Category: Heart of Algebra / Linear Equations

Getting to the Answer: If a linear equation has no solution, the variable terms will cancel out, leaving a false statement that consists of two numbers that are not equal to each other. First, check to see if the variables cancel out. In A and B, they don't, so eliminate these choices. To decide between C and (D), check the constant after both sides of the equation have been simplified. If the constants are equal, then the equation has an infinite number of solutions (because a number is always equal to itself). If they are not equal, then the equation has no solution. Choice (D) is correct because:

$$6\left(\frac{2}{3}x + 5\right) = 4x + 5$$
$$4x + 30 = 4x + 5$$
$$30 \neq 5$$

18. B   Difficulty: Hard

Category: Heart of Algebra / Linear Equations

Getting to the Answer: The key to answering this question is determining how many jumps land across each line. If Vera gets 7 jumps total and x jumps land over the farther line, the rest, or $7 - x$, must land over the closer line. Now, write the expression in words: points per farther line (10) times number of jumps landing over the farther line (x), plus points per closer line (5) times number of jumps landing over the closer line $(7 - x)$. Next, translate the words into numbers, variables, and operations: $10x + 5(7 - x)$. This is not one of the answer choices, so simplify the expression by distributing the 5 and then combining like terms: $10x + 5(7 - x) = 10x + 35 - 5x = 5x + 35$, so the function is $f(x) = 5x + 35$, making (B) correct.

19. D   Difficulty: Medium

Category: Heart of Algebra / Linear Equations

Getting to the Answer: Consider each choice systematically, using the numbers on the figure to help you evaluate each statement.

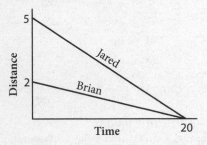

It took Brian and Jared each 20 minutes to bike home so A and B are false. Jared biked 5 miles in 20 minutes, while Brian only biked 2 miles in 20 minutes; their rates are not the same, so C is false. This means (D) must be true. Jared starts out farther away than Brian, so Jared must have biked at a faster rate to arrive home in the same amount of time.

20. B   Difficulty: Hard

Category: Heart of Algebra / Linear Equations

Getting to the Answer: You aren't given any numbers in this question, so make some up. Sketch a quick graph of any simple linear equation that has a positive y-intercept (because it is given that $b > 0$). Then, change the sign of the y-intercept and sketch the new graph on the same coordinate plane. Pick a simple equation that you can sketch quickly, such as $y = x + 3$, and then change the sign of b. The new equation is $y = x - 3$. Sketch both graphs. The second line is shifted down 3 units, twice, or $b \times 2$ units. The graph that follows illustrates this.

If you're not convinced, try another pair of equations. Choice (B) is correct.

CHAPTER 3

PRACTICE

7. A   **Difficulty:** Medium

Category: Heart of Algebra / Systems of Linear Equations

Getting to the Answer: Use the Kaplan Strategy for Translating English into Math to make sense of the situation. First, define your variables: w for wooden and c for crystal are good choices. Breaking apart the question, you know the jewelry artist bought 127 beads total. You're also told each wooden bead costs \$0.20 ($0.2w$) and each crystal bead costs \$0.50 ($0.5c$), as well as the fact that she spent \$41 total. You'll have two equations: one relating the number of wooden beads and crystal beads, and a second relating the costs associated with each.

$$w + c = 127$$
$$0.2w + 0.5c = 41$$

Either combination or substitution is a good choice for solving this system. Both are shown here:

Combination:

$$-0.5(w + c = 127) \rightarrow -0.5w - 0.5c = -63.5$$

$$\begin{array}{r} -0.5w - 0.5c = -63.5 \\ +\ \ 0.2w + 0.5c = 41 \\ \hline -0.3w = -22.5 \\ w = 75 \end{array}$$

Substitution:

$$w + c = 127 \rightarrow c = 127 - w$$

$$0.2w + 0.5(127 - w) = 41$$
$$0.2w + 63.5 - 0.5w = 41$$
$$-0.3w = -22.5$$
$$w = 75$$

$$75 + c = 127 \rightarrow c = 52$$

Be careful here: The question asks for the difference in the amount spent on each type of bead, not the difference in the quantity of each type. Multiply the bead counts by the correct pricing to get \$15 for the wooden beads and \$26 for the crystal beads. Take the difference to get \$11, which is (A).

8. 59   **Difficulty:** Medium

Category: Heart of Algebra / Systems of Linear Equations

Getting to the Answer: You're asked for the value of an expression rather than the value of one of the variables, so there must be a shortcut. Start by rearranging the two equations so that variables and constants are aligned:

$$x + y = -15$$
$$\frac{x}{2} + \frac{5y}{2} = 37$$

Clear the fractions in the second equation, and then add the equations:

$$2\left(\frac{x}{2} + \frac{5y}{2} = 37\right) \rightarrow x + 5y = 74$$

$$\begin{array}{r} x + y = -15 \\ +\ \ x + 5y = 74 \\ \hline 2x + 6y = 59 \end{array}$$

This is precisely what the question asks for, so you're done! Grid in 59 and move on.

PERFORM

9. B   **Difficulty:** Hard

Category: Heart of Algebra / Systems of Linear Equations

Getting to the Answer: A system of equations that has infinitely many solutions describes a single line. Therefore, the equations are dependent, and correct manipulation of one will yield the other. Because q is the coefficient of x in the second equation, look for a way to make the coefficient of y equal to that in the first equation. This can be done by multiplying the second equation by -9:

$$-9\left(qx - \frac{y}{3} = -2\right) \rightarrow -9qx + 3y = 18$$

The y terms and constants in the second equation now match those in the first; all that's left is to set the coefficients of x equal to each other and solve for q:

$$-9q = 6 \rightarrow q = -\frac{6}{9} = -\frac{2}{3}.$$ Choice (B) is correct.

10. 3/17 **Difficulty:** Medium

Category: Heart of Algebra / Systems of Linear Equations

Getting to the Answer: None of the coefficients in either equation is 1, so using combination is the best strategy here.

Answers & Explanations

Examine the coefficients of x: They don't share any factors, so multiply each equation by the coefficient from the other equation, remembering to make one of them negative:

$$-5(12x + 15y = 249) \rightarrow -60x - 75y = -1{,}245$$
$$12(5x + 13y = 124) \rightarrow 60x + 156y = 1{,}488$$

Add the resulting equations:

$$\begin{array}{r} -60x - 75y = -1{,}245 \\ + \ 60x + 156y = 1{,}488 \\ \hline 81y = 243 \\ y = 3 \end{array}$$

Don't stop yet; you need x so you can determine the value of $\dfrac{y}{x}$. Substitute 3 for y in one of the original equations:

$$5x + 13(3) = 124$$
$$5x + 39 = 124$$
$$5x = 85$$
$$x = 17$$

Plug your x- and y-values into $\dfrac{y}{x}$ to get $\dfrac{3}{17}$. Grid in 3/17.

11. C   Difficulty: Hard
Category: Heart of Algebra / Systems of Linear Equations

Getting to the Answer: Write equations to represent the profit generated by selling each type of pizza. You're told The Works sells for $17 each and that its ingredients cost the pizzeria $450 per week. This means weekly profit generated by this pizza's sales can be represented by the equation $y = 17x - 450$. Do the same for The Hawaiian: Each one sells for $13, but the pizzeria loses $310 to pay for ingredients each week. Therefore, weekly profits from this pizza can be represented by $y = 13x - 310$. To determine the point at which profits from one pizza overtake the other, set the two equations equal to each other and solve:

$$17x - 450 = 13x - 310$$
$$4x = 140$$
$$x = 35$$

Although ingredients for The Works cost more, the pizza's higher price tag means its profits will eventually surpass those of The Hawaiian. This will occur after the pizzeria sells 35 of each, making (C) correct. Be careful of D; 145 is the y-value when $x = 35$.

1. A   Difficulty: Easy
Category: Heart of Algebra / Systems of Linear Equations

Getting to the Answer: The solution to a system of equations shown graphically is the point of intersection. Read the axis labels carefully. Each grid-line represents 2 units. The two lines intersect at the point $(-6, -6)$, so $A + B = -6 + (-6) = -12$, which means (A) is correct.

2. C   Difficulty: Medium
Category: Heart of Algebra / Systems of Linear Equations

Getting to the Answer: Because x has a coefficient of 1 in the second equation, solve the system using substitution. Before you select your answer, make sure you found the right quantity (the difference of x and y).

First, solve the second equation for x:

$$x - 5y = 2$$
$$x = 2 + 5y$$
$$4(2 + 5y) + 3y = 14 - y$$
$$8 + 20y + 3y = 14 - y$$
$$8 + 23y = 14 - y$$
$$24y = 6$$
$$y = \frac{6}{24} = \frac{1}{4}$$

Next, substitute this value back into $x = 2 + 5y$ and simplify:

$$x = 2 + 5\left(\frac{1}{4}\right)$$
$$x = \frac{8}{4} + \frac{5}{4}$$
$$x = \frac{13}{4}$$

Finally, subtract $x - y$ to find the difference:

$$\frac{13}{4} - \frac{1}{4} = \frac{12}{4} = 3, \text{ (C)}$$

3. C   Difficulty: Medium
Category: Heart of Algebra / Systems of Linear Equations

Getting to the Answer: Graphically, a system of linear equations that has no solution consists of two parallel lines that will never intersect. They have the same slope but different *y*-intercepts. A system of linear equations that has infinite solutions is actually the same line, just represented in different ways. Graphically, one line would sit on top of the other, intersecting itself an infinite number of times. These lines would have the same slope *and* the same *y*-intercept. Without additional information, it is not possible to determine whether the system that Charlie graphed has no solutions or an infinite number of solutions. Therefore, the solution to Charlie's system of equations depends on the *y*-intercepts of the lines and (C) is correct.

4. C   **Difficulty:** Medium

Category: Heart of Algebra / Systems of Linear Equations

Getting to the Answer: If the graphs intersect at $(-3, 1)$, then the solution to the system is $x = -3$ and $y = 1$. This means you can substitute these values into both equations and go from there.

$$hx - 4y = -10$$
$$h(-3) - 4(1) = -10$$
$$-3h - 4 - -10$$
$$-3h = -6$$
$$h = 2$$

$$kx + 3y = -15$$
$$k(-3) + 3(1) = -15$$
$$-3k + 3 = -15$$
$$-3k = -18$$
$$k = 6$$

So, $\dfrac{k}{h} = \dfrac{6}{2} = 3$, making (C) correct.

5. C   **Difficulty:** Medium

Category: Heart of Algebra / Systems of Linear Equations

Getting to the Answer: Write a system of equations with $c =$ the cost of the chair in dollars and $s =$ the cost of the sofa in dollars. A sofa costs $50 less than three times the cost of the chair, or $s = 3c - 50$; together, a sofa and a chair cost $650, so $s + c = 650$.

The system is:

$$\begin{cases} s = 3c - 50 \\ s + c = 650 \end{cases}$$

The top equation is already solved for *s*, so substitute $3c - 50$ into the bottom equation for *s* and solve for *c*:

$$3c - 50 + c = 650$$
$$4c - 50 = 650$$
$$4c = 700$$
$$c = 175$$

Be careful—that's not the answer! The chair costs $175 so the sofa costs $3(175) - 50 = 525 - 50 = \$475$. This means the sofa costs $\$475 - \$175 = \$300$ more than the chair. Therefore, (C) is correct.

6. D   **Difficulty:** Hard

Category: Heart of Algebra / Systems of Linear Equations

Getting to the Answer: The easiest way to answer this question is to think about how the graphs of the equations would look. Graphically, a system of linear equations that has no solution indicates two parallel lines, or in other words, two lines that have the same slope but different *y*-intercepts.

To have the same slope, the *x*- and *y*-coefficients must be the same. The two *y*-coefficients are $-\dfrac{2}{3}$ and -8. To make $-\dfrac{2}{3}$ equal -8, multiply by 12. Multiplying $\dfrac{1}{2}x$ by 12 as well gives 6*x*. Because the other *x*-coefficient is *a*, it must be that $a = 6$. Note that you could also write each equation in slope-intercept form and set the slopes equal to each other to solve for *a*.

7. C   **Difficulty:** Hard

Category: Heart of Algebra / Systems of Linear Equations

Getting to the Answer: Create a system of linear equations where *e* represents the number of packs with 8 plates and *t* represents the number of packs with 12 plates.

The first equation should represent the total number of *packs*, each with 8 or 12 plates, or $e + t = 54$. The second equation should represent the total number of *plates*. Because *e* represents packs with 8 plates and *t* represents packs with 12 plates, the second equation is $8e + 12t = 496$. Now solve the system using substitution (or combination if it's faster for you). Solve the first equation for either variable and substitute the result into the second equation:

$$e + t = 546$$
$$e = 54 - t$$
$$8(54 - t) + 12t = 496$$
$$432 - 8t + 12t = 496$$
$$432 + 4t = 496$$
$$4t = 64$$
$$t = 16$$

Answers & Explanations

So, 16 packs have 12 plates. The question asks about packs of 12, so you don't need to find the value of e. But you are not done yet. The problem asks how many *plates* a customer would buy if he or she buys all of the packs of 12 the store has, not just the *number of packs*. The customer would buy $16 \times 12 = 192$ plates, which is (C).

8. D   Difficulty: Hard
Category: Heart of Algebra / Systems of Linear Equations

Getting to the Answer: A system of linear equations has infinitely many solutions if both lines in the system have the same slope and the same y-intercept (in other words, they are the same line).

To have the same slope, the x- and y-coefficients of the two equations must be the same. Use the x-coefficients here: To turn $\frac{1}{2}$ into 3, multiply by 6. So c becomes 6c, and $6c = -6$, or $c = -1$, (D).

Note that you could also write each equation in slope-intercept form and set the y-intercepts equal to each other to solve for c.

9. B   Difficulty: Easy
Category: Heart of Algebra / Systems of Linear Equations

Getting to the Answer: The solution to a system of linear equations represented graphically is the point of intersection. If the lines do not intersect, the system has no solution.

According to the graph, the lines intersect, or cross each other, at (6, 3). The question asks for the y-coordinate of the solution, which is 3, making (B) correct.

10. D   Difficulty: Easy
Category: Heart of Algebra / Systems of Linear Equations

Getting to the Answer: The word "and" in this question tells you that you're dealing with a system of equations. Whenever a question involves a system, quickly compare the two equations. Sometimes, writing the equations vertically gives you a clue about how to solve it.

$$\begin{cases} 2x - 3y = 14 \\ 5x + 3y = 21 \end{cases}$$

This system is already set up perfectly to solve using combination because the y terms ($-3y$ and $3y$) are opposites.

Add the two equations to cancel $-3y$ and $3y$. Then solve the resulting equation for x. Remember, the question only asks for the value of x, so you don't need to substitute x back into the equation and solve for y.

$$\begin{array}{r} 2x - 3y = 14 \\ + 5x + 3y = 21 \\ \hline 7x = 35 \\ x = 5 \end{array}$$

Choice (D) is correct.

11. A   Difficulty: Hard
Category: Heart of Algebra / Systems of Linear Equations

Getting to the Answer: Create a system of equations where x represents the number of rows with 20 seats and y represents the number of rows with 24 seats. The first equation should represent the total *number of rows*, each with 20 or 24 seats, or $x + y = 16$. The second equation should represent the total *number of seats*. Because x represents rows with 20 seats and y represents rows with 24 seats, the second equation in the system should be $20x + 24y = 348$. Now solve the system using substitution. Solve the first equation for either variable and substitute the result into the second equation:

$$\begin{aligned} x + y &= 16 \\ x &= 16 - y \\ 20(16 - y) + 24y &= 348 \\ 320 - 20y + 24y &= 348 \\ 320 + 4y &= 348 \\ 4y &= 28 \\ y &= 7 \end{aligned}$$

So 7 rows have 24 seats, which means (A) is correct. This is all the question asks for, so you don't need to find the value of x.

12. 8 **Difficulty:** Medium

Category: Heart of Algebra / Systems of Linear Equations

Getting to the Answer: The solution to the system is the point that both tables will have in common, but the tables, as given, do not share any points. You could use the data to write the equation of each line and then solve the system, but this will use up valuable time on Test Day. Instead, look for patterns that can be extended.

In the table on the left, the *x*-values increase by 2 each time and the *y*-values decrease by 2. In the table on the right, the *x*-values increase by 4 each time and the *y*-values increase by 1. Use these patterns to continue the tables.

Equation 1		Equation 2	
x	y	x	y
−2	6	−8	−8
0	4	−4	−7
2	2	0	−6
4	0	4	−5
6	−2	**8**	**−4**
8	**−4**	12	−3

The point (8, −4) satisfies both equations, so the *x*-coordinate of the solution to the system is 8.

CHAPTER 4

PRACTICE

5. A **Difficulty:** Medium
Category: Heart of Algebra / Inequalities

Getting to the Answer: Use the Kaplan Strategy for Translating English into Math to piece together an inequality. The question states that n represents the number of overnight stays. The cost of hotel accommodations for a trip without the discount card is $180 per night, or $180n$. If a customer purchases the discount card, accommodations would equal the cost of the card plus $120 per night, or $720 + 120n$. Combine these in an inequality, remembering which way the inequality symbol should be oriented. You want the cost with the discount card to be less than the cost without the card, so the inequality is $720 + 120n < 180n$. Solving for n gives $n > 12$; a traveler must stay in hotels in the network more than 12 days for the discount card to be a better deal. Choice (A) is the correct answer.

PERFORM

6. Any value between 0 and 3.5, including 0
Difficulty: Hard

Category: Heart of Algebra / Inequalities

Getting to the Answer: Resist autopilot! Instead of solving two inequalities separately, look for a series of quick manipulations to convert $\frac{4}{3}h + \frac{1}{6}$ to $12h - 4$. Start by multiplying the entire inequality by 9 to yield $-27 < 12h + \frac{3}{2} < 9$. Next, subtract $\frac{3}{2}$ and then 4 more (to get the desired -4) from all parts of the inequality (converting the fraction component to a decimal will make this step easier), which will become $-32.5 < 12h - 4 < 3.5$. Because grid-in answers cannot be negative, pick any value that is greater than or equal to 0 but less than 3.5.

Note that you could also solve the inequality for h and then manipulate the answer so that it looks like the expression in the question, but this strategy is likely to take longer.

7. C **Difficulty:** Medium
Category: Heart of Algebra / Inequalities

Getting to the Answer: Use the Kaplan Strategy for Translating English into Math to assemble a system of inequalities. The question has defined the variables for you (t_s and p_s, t_z and p_z). You know that tops and pants cost $35 and $60 each, respectively. In addition, the question states that Sarah and Zena must sell an average of 75 items each (which means that together they must sell at least 150 items, regardless of who sells more) and that their total sales must be at least $6,000. The sum of the four item counts must meet or exceed 150, so the first inequality is $t_s + p_s + t_z + p_z \geq 150$. Revenue from the sale of tops is $35(t_s + t_z)$, and revenue from the sale of pants is $60(p_s + p_z)$. The minimum revenue required to earn the bonus is $6,000, so the second inequality is $35(t_s + t_z) + 60(p_s + p_z) \geq 6,000$. Choice (C) is the only choice that contains both inequalities.

EXTRA PRACTICE

1. A **Difficulty:** Easy
Category: Heart of Algebra / Inequalities

Getting to the Answer: You solve an inequality just like an equation. The only difference is that if you multiply or divide both sides by a negative number (usually in the last step of the solution), you must reverse (flip) the inequality symbol. Take a second to study the inequality. Distributing the fraction will yield messy calculations. Instead, multiply both sides of the inequality by 5 to clear the fraction. Then, use inverse operations to isolate the variable:

$$\cancel{5} \times \left[\frac{1}{\cancel{5}}(7 - 3b) \right] > 5 \times 2$$
$$7 - 3b > 10$$
$$-3b > 3$$
$$b < -1$$

Notice that the inequality symbol was reversed because the last step in the solution required dividing by -3. The correct answer is (A).

2. B   Difficulty: Easy

Category: Heart of Algebra / Inequalities

Getting to the Answer: There is only one variable here, so solve each inequality for n and then eliminate incorrect choices.

First inequality: $n - 3 > 8$ so $n > 11$. This means you can eliminate A because 11 is not greater than itself.

Second inequality: $n + 1 < 14$ so $n < 13$. This means you can eliminate C and D because neither 13 nor 14 is less than 13. The number 12 is the only answer choice that is both greater than 11 and less than 13, so (B) is correct.

3. D   Difficulty: Medium

Category: Heart of Algebra / Inequalities

Getting to the Answer: You don't have time to try each symbol in the equation. Instead, look at the dot (open or solid?) and the direction of the shading (left or right?). There is a solid dot at 6, which means the sign must be $\geq$ or $\leq$, so you can eliminate A and B. Next, look at the shading. The graph is shaded to the left of the dot. This means the graph shows $x \leq 6$, but be careful—there is a negative coefficient (-1) in front of the x term, so the inequality will be reversed at some point in the solution. This means the original inequality sign, before you reverse it, should be $\geq$, which is (D). You can check your answer by solving the inequality using the sign you chose. If you chose correctly, your answer should match the graph.

4. C   Difficulty: Medium

Category: Heart of Algebra / Inequalities

Getting to the Answer: The best way to answer this question is to pretend you are the person paying for your power. How much less would you pay for *one* kWh of power at Company D than at Company B? If you used 530 kWh, how much would this be? If you used 730 kWh, how much would this be?

Based on the data in the table, a consumer would pay $17.4 - 14.8 = 2.6$ cents (or 0.026) less for one kWh of power at Company D than at Company B. If she used 530 kWh per month, she would pay $530(0.026) = \$13.78$ less at Company D. If she used 730 kWh, she would pay $730(0.026) = \$18.98$ less. So, the consumer would pay somewhere between \$13.78 and \$18.98 less per month, which can be expressed as the compound inequality $13.78 \leq x \leq 18.98$, which matches (C).

5. C   Difficulty: Medium

Category: Heart of Algebra / Inequalities

Getting to the Answer: Use the Kaplan Method for Translating English into Math. The clue "holds a maximum" means it can hold exactly that much or less, so use the symbol $\leq$ throughout. The cargo container can hold a maximum of 50 microwaves, so the first inequality is $m \leq 50$. This means you can eliminate A. The container can hold a maximum of 15 refrigerators, so the second inequality is $r \leq 15$. The third inequality deals with the size of each appliance. The cargo container can hold m microwaves multiplied by the size of the microwave, 6 cubic feet; it can hold r refrigerators multiplied by the size of the refrigerator, 20 cubic feet; and it can hold a maximum of 300 cubic feet total. Put these together to write the final inequality: $6m + 20r \leq 300$, which is (C).

6. D   Difficulty: Hard

Category: Heart of Algebra / Inequalities

Getting to the Answer: Before immediately trying to solve for k, notice that $-6k + 8$ is simply $3k - 4$ multiplied by -2. So, multiply each of the other parts of the inequality by -2 also. Don't forget to flip the inequality symbols because you are multiplying by a negative number.

$$-2\left[-\frac{2}{5} < 3k - 4 < \frac{6}{7}\right]$$

$$\frac{4}{5} > -6k + 8 > -\frac{12}{7}$$

Now, you don't need to solve for k because the question is asking about $-6k + 8$, but it does help to rewrite the inequality from smallest to largest:

$-\frac{12}{7} < -6k + 8 < \frac{4}{5}$. So, any value greater than $-\frac{12}{7}$ but less than $\frac{4}{5}$ is a possible value, but be careful—you are looking for the number that is *not* a possible value. This means you are looking for a number that is *less* than $-\frac{12}{7}$ or *greater* than $\frac{4}{5}$. Choice (D) is correct because $\frac{4}{3} > \frac{4}{5}$.

7. D   Difficulty: Hard

Category: Heart of Algebra / Inequalities

Getting to the Answer: The solution to a system of inequalities is where the shading overlaps. The first inequality is ready to graph, but the second is not, so start by rewriting the second inequality in slope intercept form ($y = mx + b$). Don't forget to reverse the inequality symbol when you divide by -3:

$$2x - 3y \geq 12$$
$$-3y \geq -2x + 12$$
$$y \leq \frac{2}{3}x - 4$$

Now, compare the lines. Because the slopes are the same $\left(\frac{2}{3}\right)$ and the y-intercepts are different (1 and -4), the boundary lines are parallel and never intersect. Don't answer too quickly—the answer is *not* "no solution"! The solution set revolves around the shading, not the boundary lines, so draw a quick sketch of the system.

The region between the two boundary lines is shaded in both directions, so (D) is correct.

8. 8   Difficulty: Medium

Category: Heart of Algebra / Inequalities

Getting to the Answer: Translate from English into math to create an inequality where h represents the number of hours of overtime Marco must work. Marco gets paid a daily wage plus an hourly rate for overtime, so his weekly pay is his daily rate ($80) times 5 days, plus the number of hours of overtime he works (h) times his overtime rate ($15). If he wants to make *at least* $520, which means that

much or more, the inequality is $(80 \times 5) + 15h \geq 520$. Solve for h:

$$400 + 15h \geq 520$$
$$15h \geq 120$$
$$h \geq 8$$

Marco must work at least 8 hours of overtime to make $520 or more this week.

9. C   Difficulty: Easy

Category: Heart of Algebra / Inequalities

Getting to the Answer: Solve the inequality by first distributing the 2 and then using inverse operations.

$$2(4x - 1) > 5x + 13$$
$$8x - 2 > 5x + 13$$
$$8x > 5x + 15$$
$$3x > 15$$
$$x > 5$$

Now, find the number line that matches. Because x is greater than (but *not* equal to) 5, the dot should be open, and the graph should be shaded to the right of 5. This is called a *strict* inequality because the numbers in the solution are strictly greater than 5. This means (C) is correct.

10. B   Difficulty: Medium

Category: Heart of Algebra / Inequalities

Getting to the Answer: Quickly skim the first answer choice to see that you'll need to decide whether the boundary line is dashed or solid, whether it rises or falls from left to right, and which half-plane should be shaded. The inequality symbol tells you two of these—the symbol does not have an equal sign, so the line should be dashed; the symbol represents *less than*, so the half-plane *below* the line should be shaded. This means either A or B must be correct. To decide which one, recall that when a line is written in the form $y = mx + b$, the variable m represents the slope of the line. Here, $m = -2$, so the line is decreasing, which means it falls from left to right, making (B) correct.

11. B   **Difficulty:** Medium

Category: Heart of Algebra / Inequalities

Getting to the Answer: The intersection (overlap) of the two shaded regions is the solution to the system of inequalities. Check each point to see whether it lies in the region where the shading overlaps. Be careful—you are looking for the point that is *not* a solution to the system. Choices A and C clearly lie in the overlap so you can eliminate them. Choice D, which is the point (6, −3), lies on a boundary line, and because the line is solid, the point *is* included in the solution region. The only point that does not lie within the overlap is (B). To check this, plug (1, −1) into the first inequality:

$$y < \frac{3}{5}x - 2$$

$$-1 < \frac{3}{5}(1) - 2$$

$$-1 \not< -\frac{7}{5}$$

Choice (B) is correct because −1 is not less than $-\frac{7}{5}$.

12. C   **Difficulty:** Medium

Category: Heart of Algebra / Inequalities

Getting to the Answer: A question like this is purely conceptual. The only time a system of inequalities has *no solution* (no overlap at all) is when the boundary lines are parallel and the shading is in opposite directions (above the upper boundary line and below the lower boundary line). For the boundary lines to be parallel, the slope of the second line must be equal to the slope of the first line, which is 2. This means you can eliminate A and B. The inequality symbol < (in the first inequality) tells you that the half-plane *below* the boundary line is shaded, which means the half-plane *above* the second boundary line must be shaded. Therefore, the correct symbol is greater than (>). Choice (C) is correct.

13. 2   **Difficulty:** Medium

Category: Heart of Algebra / Inequalities

Getting to the Answer: If (a, b) is a solution to the system, then a is the x-coordinate of any point in the region where the shading overlaps, and b is the corresponding y-coordinate. When $a = 0$ (or $x = 0$), the maximum possible value for b lies on the upper boundary line, $y < 2x + 3$. It looks like the y-coordinate is 3, but to be sure, substitute $x = 0$ into the equation and simplify. You can use = in the equation, instead of the inequality symbol, because you are finding a point on the boundary line.

$$y = 2(0) + 3$$

$$y = 3$$

The point on the boundary line is (0, 3). The boundary line is dashed (because the inequality is strictly less than), so (0, 3) is *not* a solution to the system. This means 2 is the greatest possible *integer* value for b when $a = 0$.

CHAPTER 5

PRACTICE

8. C **Difficulty**: Medium
Category: Problem Solving and Data Analysis / Rates, Ratios, Proportions, and Percentages

Getting to the Answer: You have a couple rates, but you need to manipulate them slightly before using them in the DIRT equation. Start by changing the given rates to unit rates. For the 5-second interval, $r_5 = 1$ car per 5 s $= 0.2$ cars/s. The 8-second interval becomes $r_8 = 1$ car per 8 s $= 0.125$ cars/s. Next, convert the time window into seconds to match your rates: $3\,h \times \dfrac{60\,min}{1\,h} \times \dfrac{60\,h}{1\,min} = 10{,}800$ s.

Now you can use the DIRT equation to find the number of cars allowed through at each interval.

5 seconds: $d_5 = 0.2$ cars/s $\times 10{,}800$ s $= 2{,}160$ cars

8 seconds: $d_8 = 0.125$ cars/s $\times 10{,}800$ s $= 1{,}350$ cars

Subtracting these gives $2{,}160 - 1{,}350 = 810$ more cars, which is (C).

9. D **Difficulty**: Hard
Category: Problem Solving and Data Analysis / Rates, Ratios, Proportions, and Percentages

Getting to the Answer: Murray starts with $75,400 per year. The first deduction is the 20% 401(k) contribution. Using the three-part percent formula, you'll find Murray has $0.8 \times \$75{,}400 = \$60{,}320$ left. He pays $150 per month for insurance, which is $1,800 per year. This leaves $58,520 pre-tax. Taxes are trickier, so work carefully. State taxes are easy; just take 4.5% of the pre-tax total: $0.045 \times \$58{,}520 = \$2{,}633.40$. Federal taxes involve three separate calculations as follows:

10% bracket: $0.1 \times \$9{,}225 = \$922.50$
15% bracket: $0.15 \times (\$37{,}450 - \$9{,}225) = \$4{,}233.75$
25% bracket: $0.25 \times (\$58{,}520 - \$37{,}450) = \$5{,}267.50$

Adding up all of Murray's tax liability gives $13,057.15. Subtract this from his pre-tax total to get $45,462.85. Don't stop yet! The question asks for Murray's biweekly pay. Divide $45,462.85 by 26, the number of pay periods in one year, to get $1,748.57, which is (D).

10. 7/16 **Difficulty**: Hard
Category: Problem Solving and Data Analysis / Rates, Ratios, Proportions, and Percentages

Getting to the Answer: The question asks for a fraction, a relative quantity, so don't panic about not having exact dimensions for the squares. Pick your own instead. Start by labeling each square for clarity.

Pick a side length for square 1; 1 inch is an excellent choice. This means its area is 1 square inch. If the square edges are 0.5 inches apart, that means square 2 has a side length of $1 + 0.5 + 0.5 = 2$ inches, square 3 has a side length of $2 + 0.5 + 0.5 = 3$ inches, and so on. This translates to areas of 1, 4, 9, 16, 25, 36, 49, and 64 (all in square inches). But don't forget that you need to subtract the square within each to get the true areas! You'll get the following:

$$\text{sq. 1 (gray)} = 1 \text{ in.}^2$$
$$\text{sq. 2 (black)} = 2^2 - 1 = 3 \text{ in.}^2$$
$$\text{sq. 3 (gray)} = 3^2 - 4 = 5 \text{ in.}^2$$
$$\text{sq. 4 (black)} = 4^2 - 9 = 7 \text{ in.}^2$$
$$\text{sq. 5 (gray)} = 5^2 - 16 = 9 \text{ in.}^2$$
$$\text{sq. 6 (black)} = 6^2 - 25 = 11 \text{ in.}^2$$
$$\text{sq. 7 (gray)} = 7^2 - 36 = 13 \text{ in.}^2$$
$$\text{sq. 8 (black)} = 8^2 - 49 = 15 \text{ in.}^2$$

After a few calculations you might start to see a pattern; if so, great! You can shave off a few seconds of number crunching. Now add up the gray squares to get 28, then divide by the area of the whole plate (64) to get $\dfrac{28}{64} = \dfrac{7}{16}$. Grid in 7/16, then move on to the next question in the set.

11. 10/9 Difficulty: Medium

Category: Problem Solving and Data Analysis / Rates, Ratios, Proportions, and Percentages

Getting to the Answer: You've already done most of the work for this part; look closely at your work for the first question to see what you can reuse. Finding the large plate black fraction is easy; just subtract the large plate gray fraction from 1 to get $\frac{9}{16}$. Because the small plate is just a smaller version of the large plate with only four squares, you can use your calculations for squares 1-4 from the first question here. Squares 1 and 3 (gray) comprise 6 square inches, and squares 2 and 4 (black) comprise 10 square inches. This means the small plate black fraction is $\frac{10}{16} = \frac{5}{8}$. To find how many times more black glaze is on the small plate, divide the small plate black fraction by its large plate counterpart: $\frac{5}{8} \div \frac{9}{16} = \frac{5}{8} \times \frac{16}{9} = \frac{10}{9}$. Grid in 10/9, and you're done!

PERFORM

12. A Difficulty: Easy

Category: Problem Solving and Data Analysis / Rates, Ratios, Proportions, and Percentages

Getting to the Answer: Convert all four rates into the same units before comparing. You might think you should convert each price into cost per banana, but a closer look reveals that all but one price already uses weight. Save time by converting the units into cost per pound; the order will be no different than if you did cost per banana. Use the banana-pound relationship to convert each price into cost per pound. FoodCo's price is already per pound, so no work is needed there. Bob's charges $0.29 per banana, which becomes $\frac{\$0.29}{1\,\text{banana}} \times \frac{1\,\text{banana}}{\frac{1}{3}\,\text{lb}} = \frac{\$0.87}{1\,\text{lb}}$.

Acme's price is $1.50 for 2 pounds or $0.75 per pound. The deal at Stu's means you pay $1.95 for 4 pounds, which is $0.4875 per pound. Therefore, the correct order is Bob's, Acme, FoodCo, Stu's. This matches (A).

13. 18.2 Difficulty: Easy

Category: Problem Solving and Data Analysis / Rates, Ratios, Proportions, and Percentages

Getting to the Answer: Start by drawing a diagram to make sense of the situation. Each zipline is the hypotenuse of a right triangle. Because the two zipline setups are proportional, the triangles are similar.

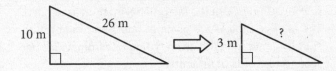

You can use a proportion to solve for the length of the kids' zipline: $\frac{10}{26} = \frac{3}{x}$. Solving for x gives 7.8 meters. But you're not done yet! The question asks for the difference in zipline length, so subtract 7.8 from 26 to get 18.2.

14. 166 Difficulty: Medium

Category: Problem Solving and Data Analysis / Rates, Ratios, Proportions, and Percentages

Getting to the Answer: Identify the units of the start and end quantities, then string together the proper conversion factors. You know Mark will drive 960 miles over the course of his trip, and you need to determine what he should budget for fuel. The full conversion is as follows:

$$960\,\text{mi} \times \frac{1\,\text{gal}}{40\,\text{mi}} \times \frac{3.785\,\text{L}}{1\,\text{gal}} \times \frac{1.20\,\text{GBP}}{1\,\text{L}} \times \frac{1.52\,\text{USD}}{1\,\text{GBP}} =$$

165.69 USD. Round to 166 per the question instructions.

15. 17 Difficulty: Hard

Category: Problem Solving and Data Analysis / Rates, Ratios, Proportions, and Percentages

Getting to the Answer: Determine Mark's fuel cost with the offer, then compare it to the original. If you stopped your calculations in the previous question after the gallon-to-liter conversion, you would find that Mark will use 90.84 L of fuel. At the new fuel price, Mark would pay $90.84 \times 0.75 = 68.13$ GBP for fuel. Add the 30 GBP cost for the rate reduction to get 98.13 GBP. Use the GBP-USD conversion to get 149.15 USD. Subtracting this from 166 gives 16.85, which is rounded to 17.

EXTRA PRACTICE

1. A   **Difficulty**: Medium

Category: Problem Solving and Data Analysis / Rates, Ratios, Proportions, and Percentages

Getting to the Answer: Whenever multiple rates are given, pay very careful attention to the units. As you read the question, decide how and when you will need to convert units. Use the factor-label method as needed. The answer choices are given in hours and minutes, so start by converting the given typing rate from words per second to words per minute:

$$\frac{3.75 \text{ words}}{1 \text{ second}} \times \frac{60 \text{ seconds}}{1 \text{ minute}} = \frac{225 \text{ words}}{1 \text{ minute}}$$

Next, find the number of words in the 25-page transcript:

$$\frac{675 \text{ words}}{1 \text{ page}} \times 25 \text{ pages} = 16{,}875 \text{ words}$$

Finally, let m be the number of minutes it takes the court reporter to type the whole transcript. Set up a proportion and solve for m:

$$\frac{225 \text{ words}}{1 \text{ minute}} = \frac{16{,}875 \text{ words}}{m \text{ minutes}}$$
$$225m = 16{,}875$$
$$m = 75$$

Because 75 minutes is not an answer choice, convert it to hours and minutes: 75 minutes = 1 hour, 15 minutes, making (A) the correct answer.

2. C   **Difficulty**: Medium

Category: Problem Solving and Data Analysis / Rates, Ratios, Proportions, and Percentages

Getting to the Answer: Don't let the three-way ratio scare you. You can solve this problem just like any other ratio question. Set up an equation using *parts*: 35 parts of the vote were for Taft, 41 parts were for Roosevelt, and 63 parts were for Wilson. You don't know how big a part is, so call it x. Now, write and solve an equation:

$$35x + 41x + 63x = 208{,}500$$
$$139x = 208{,}500$$
$$x = 1{,}500$$

Look back at the ratio—35 parts of the vote were for Taft, so the number of votes cast for Taft was $35(1{,}500) = 52{,}500$, which matches (C).

3. D   **Difficulty**: Medium

Category: Problem Solving and Data Analysis / Rates, Ratios, Proportions, and Percentages

Getting to the Answer: Use a variation of the three-part percent formula: Whole × percent = part.

First, find the number of people at each location who responded favorably using the formula. Start with the first location: $125 \times 0.224 = 28$. Move on to the second location: $272 \times 0.375 = 102$. Next, find the total number of people that were surveyed at both locations, which was $125 + 272 = 397$, and the total number who responded favorably, $28 + 102 = 130$. Finally, find the percent of people who responded favorably by using the formula one more time:

$$397 \times \text{percent} = 130 \times 100\%$$
$$\text{percent} = \frac{130}{397} \times 100\%$$
$$= 0.3274 \times 100\%$$
$$= 32.7\%$$

Of all the people surveyed, about 32.7% responded favorably, making (D) the correct answer.

4. A   **Difficulty**: Medium

Category: Problem Solving and Data Analysis / Rates, Ratios, Proportions, and Percentages

Getting to the Answer: Let the units in this question guide you to the solution. The cooking rates of the ovens are given in pounds per hour, but the question asks about the number of ounces each oven can cook in 10 minutes, so use the factor-label method to convert pounds per hour to ounces per minute.

Start by converting pounds to ounces. You are given that 1 pound = 16 ounces, so 3 pounds is 48 ounces and 4.5 pounds is 72 ounces. Now convert the hours to minutes:

Oven at 350°:

$$\frac{48 \text{ oz}}{1 \text{ hr}} \times \frac{1 \text{ hr}}{60 \text{ min}} \times 10 \text{ min} = 8 \text{ oz}$$

Oven at 450°:

$$\frac{72 \text{ oz}}{1 \text{ hr}} \times \frac{1 \text{ hr}}{60 \text{ min}} \times 10 \text{ min} = 12 \text{ oz}$$

In 10 minutes, the oven at 450° can cook $12 - 8 = 4$ ounces more than the oven at 350°, making (A) the correct answer.

5. B   Difficulty: Medium
Category: Problem Solving and Data Analysis / Rates, Ratios, Proportions, and Percentages

Getting to the Answer: Don't let all the technical words in this question overwhelm you. Solve it step-by-step examining the units as you go. Use the factor-label method to help you stay organized.

Step 1: Determine the number of megabytes the company can upload in 1 evening (4 hours):

$$\frac{12 \text{ MB}}{1 \text{ sec}} \times \frac{60 \text{ sec}}{1 \text{ min}} \times \frac{60 \text{ min}}{1 \text{ hr}} \times \frac{4 \text{ hr}}{1 \text{ evening}} = \frac{172,800 \text{ MB}}{1 \text{ evening}}$$

Step 2: Convert this amount to gigabytes (because the information about the scans is given in gigabytes, not megabytes):

$$172,800 \text{ MB} \times \frac{1 \text{ GB}}{1,024 \text{ MB}} = 168.75 \text{ GB}$$

Step 3: Each video file is about 4.5 gigabytes, so divide by 4.5 to determine how many videos the company can upload to the cloud using its internet service provider: $168.75 \div 4.5 = 37.5$ videos. Remember, you should round this number down to 37, because the question asks for the maximum number the company can upload and it cannot complete the 38th video upload in the time allowed. The correct answer is (B).

6. B   Difficulty: Medium
Category: Problem Solving and Data Analysis / Rates, Ratios, Proportions, and Percentages

Getting to the Answer: Pay careful attention to the units. You need to convert all of the dimensions to inches, and then find the scale factor. You'll have to start with the skull because it's the only part of the T-rex for which you know both the actual length and the model length.

There are 12 inches in one foot, so Sue's skull length was $12 \times 5 = 60$ inches and the model skull is $3 \times 12 = 36 + 1.5 = 37.5$ inches. Find the scale factor by writing

this as a fraction. Multiply both numbers by 10 to get rid of the decimal and then simplify the ratio to get $\frac{37.5}{60} = \frac{375}{600} = \frac{5}{8}$.

This means the scale factor is $\frac{5}{8}$. You might be tempted to now find the scale model's length and height by multiplying 40 and 13 by $\frac{5}{8}$, but this would waste valuable time. Because the model is a $\frac{5}{8}$-scale model, the difference between the model's length and height will be exactly $\frac{5}{8}$ of the difference between Sue's actual length and height, which is $40 - 13 = 27$ feet. Multiply 27 by $\frac{5}{8}$ to find that the difference between the length and height of the model should be 16.875 feet, or 16 feet, 10.5 inches, which matches (B).

7. 660   Difficulty: Easy
Category: Problem Solving and Data Analysis / Rates, Ratios, Proportions, and Percentages

Getting to the Answer: Break this question into short steps. Find the amount of the hostess share for one evening. Multiply this by the number of evenings per week, 5, and then the number of weeks, 4. Do this for each restaurant, and then subtract to find the difference.

Restaurant A:	*Restaurant B:*
$0.07 \times \$1,100 = \$77$	$0.04 \times \$1,100 = \$44$
$\$77 \times 5 = 385$	$\$44 \times 5 = \$220$
$\$385 \times 4 = \$1,540$	$\$220 \times 4 = \$880$

Mia would make $\$1,540 - \$880 = \$660$ more at Restaurant A.

8. 75   Difficulty: Hard
Category: Problem Solving and Data Analysis / Rates, Ratios, Proportions, and Percentages

Getting to the Answer: This question requires multiple steps and multiple formulas, so make a plan before you dive in. The formula for percent increase is:

$$\text{Percent increase} = \frac{\text{final amount} - \text{original amount}}{\text{original amount}}$$

This tells you that you need the final amount in tips that Restaurant B needs to bring in to be equal to Restaurant A, which will depend on the amount in tips Restaurant

A brings in. You'll need to use the percent formula (Percent × whole = part) to determine what amount would be required at 4% for the hostess share to be equal.

The hostess tip share for one evening at Restaurant A is $1,100 × 0.07 = $77. Use this amount to find the final amount of tips, t, Restaurant B needs:

$$0.04 \times t = 77$$
$$0.04t = 77$$
$$t = \$1,925$$

Now use the percent increase formula:

$$\text{Percent increase} = \frac{1,925 - 1,100}{1,100}$$
$$= \frac{825}{1,100}$$
$$= 0.75$$

The percent increase needed is 75%. Per the question's instructions, enter this as 75 (not .75).

9. D   Difficulty: Easy
Category: Problem Solving and Data Analysis / Rates, Ratios, Proportions, and Percentages

Getting to the Answer: To answer a question that says "directly proportional," set two ratios equal to each other and solve for the missing amount. Don't forget—match the units in the numerators and in the denominators on both sides of the proportion.

Because the first rate is given in minutes, write 1 hour as 60 minutes. Let t equal the number of topics the teacher can cover in a 60-minute period. Set up a proportion and solve for t:

$$\frac{9 \text{ topics}}{45 \text{ minutes}} = \frac{t \text{ topics}}{60 \text{ minutes}}$$
$$9(60) = 45(t)$$
$$540 = 45t$$
$$12 = t$$

Choice (D) is correct.

10. C   Difficulty: Easy
Category: Problem Solving and Data Analysis / Rates, Ratios, Proportions, and Percentages

Getting to the Answer: It can be confusing to decide which operation to perform when dealing with conversions, especially when the conversions involve decimals. Think about how your answer should look first. A person weighs *less* on the moon, so he or she should weigh *more* on Earth. This means your answer must be greater than 29, so you can eliminate A right away.

The easiest way to convert the units and keep them straight is to set up a proportion.

$$\frac{0.166 \text{ lb on moon}}{1 \text{ lb on Earth}} = \frac{29 \text{ lb on moon}}{p \text{ lb on Earth}}$$
$$29(1) = 0.166p$$
$$174.7 \approx p$$

The man weighs about 175 pounds on Earth. Choice (C) is correct.

11. C   Difficulty: Easy
Category: Problem Solving and Data Analysis / Rates, Ratios, Proportions, and Percentages

Getting to the Answer: According to the pie graph, 25% of the customers are totally dissatisfied and 15% are somewhat dissatisfied. So, 100% − 25% − 15% = 60% of the customers are totally or somewhat satisfied. Thus, the *number* of customers that are totally or somewhat satisfied is 60% of 240, or 0.6 × 240 = 144 customers, making (C) correct.

12. B   Difficulty: Medium
Category: Problem Solving and Data Analysis / Rates, Ratios, Proportions, and Percentages

Getting to the Answer: This is a typical proportion question. Use words first to write the proportion. Then translate from English into math. Let n equal the number of people tested. Set up a proportion and solve for n. Be sure to match the units in the numerators and in the denominators on both sides of the proportion.

$$\frac{\text{false positives}}{\text{number tested}} = \frac{\text{false positives}}{\text{number tested}}$$
$$\frac{6}{3,500} = \frac{27}{n}$$
$$6n = 27(3,500)$$
$$6n = 94,500$$
$$n = 15,750$$

This means (B) is correct.

13. C   **Difficulty**: Medium

Category: Problem Solving and Data Analysis / Rates, Ratios, Proportions, and Percentages

Getting to the Answer: Start with the hours. The client received 25 hours of tutoring, of which 1 hour was free. So, the client paid for 24 hours of tutoring. The first 10 hours were at a different rate than the discounted rate, so subtract these to find that the client paid the discounted rate for 24 − 10 = 14 hours. Now look at the money: The first 10 hours the client was actually billed for cost $30 per hour for a total of $300, so subtract this from the total amount paid to get $664 − $300 = $364. This is the amount charged for the 14 discounted hours. Divide this amount by the number of hours billed at the discounted rate to get $364 ÷ 14 = $26 per hour, making (C) the correct choice.

14. C   **Difficulty**: Medium

Category: Problem Solving and Data Analysis / Rates, Ratios, Proportions, and Percentages

Getting to the Answer: You are given a lot of numbers in this question. Break the question into short steps. Before you move on, check that you answered the right question (the number of LED bulbs that were *not* defective).

Step 1: Find the number of LED bulbs produced. A total of 12,500 of both kinds of bulbs were produced. The ratio of LED to CFL is 2:3, so two parts LED plus three parts CFL equals 12,500. Write this as $2x + 3x = 12,500$. Simplify and solve this equation to find that $x = 2,500$. Multiply this amount by 2 (because two parts were LED bulbs): $2,500 \times 2 = 5,000$.

Step 2: Use that number to find the number of LED bulbs that were defective: 3% of 5,000 or $0.03 \times 5,000 = 150$ defective LEDs.

Step 3: Find the number of LED bulbs that were *not* defective: $5,000 − 150 = 4,850$. Choice (C) is correct.

15. B   **Difficulty**: Medium

Category: Problem Solving and Data Analysis / Rates, Ratios, Proportions, and Percentages

Getting to the Answer: Find the percent increase using this formula: % increase $= \dfrac{\text{amount of increase}}{\text{original amount}}$.

Then apply the same percent increase to the animal population in 2000. The amount of increase is $7,200 − 6,400 = 800$, so the percent increase is $\dfrac{800}{6,400} = 0.125 = 12.5\%$ between 1950 and 2000. If the total percent increase over the next 50 years is the same, the animal population should be about $7,200 \times 1.125 = 8,100$. Choose (B) and move on to the next question.

16. 14   **Difficulty:** Easy

Category: Problem Solving and Data Analysis / Rates, Ratios, Proportions, and Percentages

Getting to the Answer: You know the length of Betsy's book and the rate at which she reads. You need to know how many minutes she reads.

$$116 \text{ pg} \times \frac{1.5 \text{ min}}{1 \text{ pg}} = 174 \text{ min}$$

It takes Betsy 174 minutes to read her book. You know Raymond starts reading at 8:30 AM and reads until 11:38 AM, which is $11:38 − 8:30 = 3$ hours, 8 minutes, or 188 minutes. It takes Raymond $188 − 174 = 14$ minutes longer to read his book.

17. 50   **Difficulty**: Medium

Category: Problem Solving and Data Analysis / Rates, Ratios, Proportions, and Percentages

Getting to the Answer: Break this problem into short steps.

Step one: Find the total number of drips needed by multiplying the amount of medication prescribed, 800 mL, by the number of drips needed to deliver 1 mL: $800 \times 30 = 24,000$ drips.

Step two: Divide this number by 8 to find how many drips per hour are needed: $24,000 \div 8 = 3,000$ drips per hour.

Step three: Divide this by 60 (because there are 60 minutes in one hour) to convert drips per hour to drips per minute: $3,000 \div 60 = 50$ drips per minute.

18. 40 Difficulty: Hard

Category: Problem Solving and Data Analysis / Rates, Ratios, Proportions, and Percentages

Getting to the Answer: Start by determining what the question is asking. You need to find the net change in the power allocated to Grid 1 over the course of a day. To do this, you need to know how much the grid was allocated at the beginning of the day and how much at the end.

You aren't given a concrete starting point (or units of power), so simply pick a starting number. The best number to use when dealing with percents is 100. First, find how much power the grid was allocated after the first 20% increase: $100 \times 1.2 = 120$. Next, find the amount after the 10% decrease: $120 \times 0.9 = 108$. Finally, find the amount after the last 30% increase: $108 \times 1.3 = 140.4$, which is $140.4 - 100 = 40.4$ more than it started the day with. To find the percent change, use the formula Percent change $= \dfrac{\text{amount of change}}{\text{original amount}}$ to get $\dfrac{40.4}{100} = 0.404$. Rounded to the nearest whole percent, this is 40 percent.

19. 10.5 Difficulty: Medium

Category: Problem Solving and Data Analysis / Rates, Ratios, Proportions, and Percentages

Getting to the Answer: For each of the three friends, you know how long they traveled and their rate. Use the DIRT formula to find the distance for each one. But be careful—the rates are given in miles per hour, which means you must use hours, not minutes, for the times.

Andrea:

30 minutes $= 0.5$ hours

Distance $= 3 \times 0.5 = 1.5$ miles

Kellan:

45 minutes $= 0.75$ hours

Distance $= 14 \times 0.75 = 10.5$ miles

Joelle:

15 minutes $= 0.25$ hours

Distance $= 35 \times 0.25 = 8.75$ miles

Kellan lives the farthest away at 10.5 miles. An important note here—the question did not tell you to round and the entire answer fits in the grid, so you MUST grid the answer in as 10.5. However, had you gotten an answer like 10.57 (which wouldn't fit in the grid), then you could either round to 10.6 or truncate (cut off) the answer at 10.5 because it would still fill the entire grid.

20. 731 Difficulty: Hard

Category: Problem Solving and Data Analysis / Rates, Ratios, Proportions, and Percentages

Getting to the Answer: When answering question sets that share information, you can often save some time by using amounts you found in the first question to answer the second one.

In the previous question, you found that Andrea's house is 1.5 miles from the restaurant. Use the DIRT formula to determine how long Kellan walked with Andrea:

$$1.5 = 2.5 \times \text{time}$$
$$1.5 = 2.5t$$
$$0.6 = t$$

They walked for 0.6 hours, or $60 \times 0.6 = 36$ minutes. Now calculate how long Kellan biked. Again, you have the distance and the rate, so you need to use the formula to find the time:

$$12 = 15 \times \text{time}$$
$$12 = 15t$$
$$0.8 = t$$

Kellan biked for 0.8 hours, or $60 \times 0.8 = 48$ minutes. So Kellan traveled for a total of $36 + 48 = 84$ minutes, or 1 hour, 24 minutes. Don't forget that they arrived 5 minutes early, or at 8:55. So Kellan must have left his house at $8:55 - 1$ hour $= 7:55 - 24$ minutes which is 7:31 AM. Enter this as 731.

CHAPTER 6

PRACTICE

4. C   **Difficulty:** Easy
Category: Problem Solving and Data Analysis / Scatterplots

Getting to the Answer: Examine the equation to determine the type of plot it will produce. When the exponent in an equation is a variable, the graph of the equation is exponential, so eliminate choices A and B. To distinguish between the remaining choices, pick an easy-to-use value to plug into the given equation for x (e.g., 0). You'll see that when $x = 0$, y should equal 5, which matches the graph in (C).

5. 2   **Difficulty:** Medium
Category: Problem Solving and Data Analysis / Scatterplots

Getting to the Answer: You're asked for a rate; this means finding the slope of the line of best fit. Start by picking a pair of points, preferably where the line of best fit passes through a grid-line intersection to minimize error. The points (50, 20) and (100, 40) are good choices. Determine the slope:

$$m = \frac{y_2 - y_1}{x_2 - x_1} = \frac{40 - 20}{100 - 50} = \frac{20}{50} = \frac{2}{5}$$

Don't grid in $\frac{2}{5}$, though. Remember what you're being asked: You need the road clearing duration increase for a 5% increase in snowpack water content, not 1%. Multiply $\frac{2}{5}$ by 5, which yields 2.

6. 99.2   **Difficulty:** Medium
Category: Problem Solving and Data Analysis / Scatterplots

Getting to the Answer: The slope you found in the previous question will save you some time here. The line of best fit on the scatterplot intersects the y-axis at (0, 0). Therefore, the equation of the line of best fit is $y = \frac{2}{5}x$. Plug 248 in for x and simplify:

$$y = \frac{2}{5} \times 248 = \frac{496}{5} = 99.2$$

PERFORM

7. A   **Difficulty:** Easy
Category: Problem Solving and Data Analysis / Scatterplots

Getting to the Answer: The question asks for a rate of change, which means you'll need the slope of the line of best fit. Pick a pair of points to use in the slope formula, such as (1998, 20) and (2012, 90):

$$m = \frac{y_2 - y_1}{x_2 - x_1} = \frac{90 - 20}{2012 - 1998} = \frac{70}{14} = 5$$

Choice (A) is correct.

8. A   **Difficulty:** Easy
Category: Problem Solving and Data Analysis / Scatterplots

Getting to the Answer: Identify the type of change described in the question to narrow down your choices. If the number of smartphone users increases by 35% each year, then the amount of the increase is variable (because it's 35% of a bigger number each time), indicating nonlinear (exponential) growth. Eliminate C and D. Recall that when assembling an exponential growth model, r (the rate) must be in decimal form. Therefore, the number raised to the power of x should be $1 + 0.35$ or 1.35. Choice (A) is the only one that fits these criteria.

9. D   **Difficulty:** Medium
Category: Problem Solving and Data Analysis / Scatterplots

Getting to the Answer: Compare each statement to the infographic one at a time, eliminating true statements as you work. Start with A: It is impossible to tell from the graph which strain has the higher reading at 20 hours, so you cannot say the statement is NOT true. Eliminate A. Choice B states that Strain 2's growth rate (slope) overtook Strain 1's at hour 50, which is consistent with the infographic; eliminate it. Choice C requires math, so skip it for now. Choice (D) states that Strain 1's growth rate was greater than Strain 2's over the entire period. Although Strain 1's growth rate was greater for part of the monitored period, it is not greater for the entire period (because the slope of Strain 1's curve is not steeper than that of Strain 2's curve for every line segment on the graph), which makes (D) false and, therefore, correct.

EXTRA PRACTICE

1. C   Difficulty: Easy
Category: Problem Solving and Data Analysis / Scatterplots

Getting to the Answer: A regression equation is the equation of the line (or curve) that best fits the data. A *linear* regression is used to model data that follows the path of a straight line. In the equation given, *a* represents the slope of the linear regression (the line of best fit), so you are looking for data that is linear (looks like a line) and is decreasing, or falling from left to right ($a < 0$ means a is negative). You can eliminate A and D because the data is not linear (A is quadratic and D is exponential). You can also eliminate B because the data is increasing (rising from left to right). This means (C) is correct.

2. A   Difficulty: Easy
Category: Problem Solving and Data Analysis / Scatterplots

Getting to the Answer: When an exponential equation is written in the form $y = x_0(1 + r)^x$, the value of x_0 gives the y-intercept of the equation's graph. To answer this question, you need to think about what the y-intercept would represent in the context described.

Whenever time is involved in a relationship that is modeled by an equation or a graph, it is always the independent variable and therefore graphed on the x-axis. Therefore, for this question, population would be graphed on the y-axis, so x_0 most likely represents the population when the time elapsed was zero, or in other words, in the year that Adriana was born, making (A) correct.

3. D   Difficulty: Medium
Category: Problem Solving and Data Analysis / Scatterplots

Getting to the Answer: A line that "represents the trend of the data" is another way of saying line of best fit. The trend of the data is clearly linear because the path of the dots does not turn around or curve, so draw a line

of best fit on the graph. Remember, about half of the points should be above the line and half below.

If you draw the line all the way to the y-axis, you'll save a step by finding the y-intercept just by looking at the scatterplot. For this graph, it's about 25. This means you can eliminate B and C. To choose between A and (D), find the approximate slope using two points that lie on (or very close to) the line of best fit. You can use the y-intercept, (0, 25), as one of the points to save time and estimate the second, such as (21, 80). Use the slope formula to find the slope:

$$m = \frac{y_2 - y_1}{x_2 - x_1} = \frac{80 - 25}{21 - 0} = \frac{55}{21} = 2.62$$

The result is very close to the slope in (D), making it the correct answer.

4. A   Difficulty: Medium
Category: Problem Solving and Data Analysis / Scatterplots

Getting to the Answer: Examine the graph, paying careful attention to units and labels. The average rate of change is the same as the slope of the line of best fit. The data is decreasing (going down from left to right) so you can immediately eliminate C and D. To choose between (A) and B, find the slope of the line of best fit using the slope formula, $m = \frac{y_2 - y_1}{x_2 - x_1}$, and any two points that lie on (or very close to) the line. Using the two points

(5, 14) and (10, 8), the average rate of change is about $\frac{8-14}{10-5} = \frac{-6}{5} = -1.2$, which matches (A).

5. A   **Difficulty:** Medium

Category: Problem Solving and Data Analysis / Scatterplots

Getting to the Answer: Determine whether the predicted change in the interest rate is a common difference (linear function) or a common ratio (exponential function), or if it changes direction (quadratic or polynomial function).

The company predicts that every six months, the Federal Reserve will *raise* rates by 0.25 percentage points. Interest rates are already expressed as percentages, so raising the rates by 0.25 percentage points means *adding* a quarter of a percent every six months. It does not mean it will increase *by* 0.25% every six months. The function therefore involves a common difference, so the best model would be a linear function, which is (A).

6. B   **Difficulty:** Hard

Category: Problem Solving and Data Analysis / Scatterplots

Getting to the Answer: When presented with a "series" of data, making a chart helps. In this question, the chart should include the number of bounces and the height after the bounce. You can then look for patterns that may tell you which function to pick, or at the very least, which functions to eliminate.

Bounce Number (b)	Height After Bounce (H(b))
1	80
2	40
3	20
4	10

Look for a pattern: the heights are decreasing by a common ratio each time $\left(\frac{1}{2}\right)$, so an exponential function will be the best match. This means you can eliminate C and D (which are linear functions). To choose between A and (B), evaluate each function at $b = 1$ and see what happens.

Choice A: $H(1) = \frac{80}{2^1} = \frac{80}{2} = 40$. The height should be 80 after the first bounce, so eliminate this choice.

Choice B: $H(1) = \frac{80}{2^{1-1}} = \frac{80}{2^0} = \frac{80}{1} = 80$. Choice (B) is correct.

If you're not convinced (or if both results had been 80), move on to $b = 2$ and evaluate each function again, until you are able to eliminate one of them.

7. 2   **Difficulty:** Easy

Category: Problem Solving and Data Analysis / Scatterplots

Getting to the Answer: Examine the graph, including the axis labels and numbering. Each vertical grid-line represents 5 eggs, so look to see how many data points are more than a complete grid space away from the line of best fit. Only 2 are more than 5 away—the first data point and the one between 30 and 35 weeks, making 2 the correct answer.

8. 57   **Difficulty:** Hard

Category: Problem Solving and Data Analysis / Scatterplots

Getting to the Answer: This is a Grid-in question, so you can't just use the graph to estimate the y-value when $x = 36$. Instead, you need to find the equation of the line of best fit, and then substitute 36 for x and simplify. Start with the slope—you could pick two points on the line and use the slope formula, or you could count the rise and the run. The latter is easier in this question. Beginning at the point (0, 75), the line falls 5 units and runs 10 units to the first point on the line, so the slope is $\frac{-5}{10} = -\frac{1}{2}$.

This means that the equation looks like $y = -\frac{1}{2}x + b$. Next, find the y-intercept. You can see clearly from the graph that it is approximately 75.

The equation is $y = -\frac{1}{2}x + 75$. Now, substitute 36 for x and simplify to find y:

$$y = -\frac{1}{2}(36) + 75$$
$$y = -18 + 75$$
$$y = 57$$

The correct answer is 57.

9. C   **Difficulty:** Easy

Category: Problem Solving and Data Analysis / Scatterplots

Getting to the Answer: Correlation means that there is a discernible relationship between two or more variables. A positive correlation means that as one variable increases, so does the other variable. A negative correlation means that as one variable increases, the other decreases. The closer the relationship is, the stronger the correlation.

Take a quick peek at the answer choices and picture or draw a sketch of each one. *Linear* indicates that the data follows the path of a straight line. *Positive* means rising from left to right. Finally, *strong* means the relationship is a close one, but not perfect, so the data points should be fairly close to, but not exactly on, the line; choice (C) is correct.

10. A   **Difficulty:** Easy

Category: Problem Solving and Data Analysis / Scatterplots

Getting to the Answer: A line with a downward slant has a negative slope, so you can immediately eliminate C and D. To choose between (A) and B, recall that slope is a ratio that compares vertical change (rise) to horizontal change (run). Mark the bordered area using equal measures and then estimate the slope of a line drawn through the center of the points as shown.

The line appears to fall 3 units and run 1 unit, so a good estimate for the slope is −3, making (A) correct. Note that you could also use what you know about slope to answer the question—lines that have fractional slopes, between −1 and 1, are not steep lines, which means B can't be correct.

11. D   **Difficulty:** Easy

Category: Problem Solving and Data Analysis / Scatterplots

Getting to the Answer: Knowing where the *y*-intercept of the line of best fits falls will help you eliminate answer choices.

The line of best fit intercepts the *y*-axis below the *x*-axis, and is therefore negative, so you can eliminate B and C (the *y*-intercept is +1 for each of those lines). Now, look at the slope. The line rises along the *y*-axis slightly faster than it runs along the *x*-axis, so the slope must be slightly greater than 1, making (D) correct. If you have trouble choosing between A and (D), you could also graph each equation in your calculator to see which one is a better match for the line. Use a viewing window that is approximately the same as in the graph. Here, the viewing window would be $-2 \le x \le 5$ and $-2 \le y \le 7$.

12. C   **Difficulty:** Medium

Category: Problem Solving and Data Analysis / Scatterplots

Getting to the Answer: "Correlation" simply means relationship. The word "weak" refers to the strength of the relationship (how close the data lies to the line of best fit), which has no effect on slope. Be careful not to confuse slope and strength. The fact that a data set shows a weak correlation does not give you any information about the magnitude of the slope. This means you can eliminate A and B. Also, keep in mind that the terms "weak" and "negative" are not related, but rather are two independent descriptors of the correlation. So the fact that the rate of change is negative has nothing to do with the strength of the correlation. In a weak correlation, the data points will loosely follow the line of best fit, making (C) the correct answer.

13. B   Difficulty: Medium
Category: Problem Solving and Data Analysis / Scatterplots

Getting to the Answer: There are two things to keep in mind for a question like this: Correlation does not prove causation, and as a general rule, conclusions can only be drawn about the population studied, not about all populations. The data points are scattered and do not form any discernible pattern. This means there is no correlation, which is another way of saying the two variables aren't related, so you can eliminate D. You can also eliminate C because the HR representative *is* able to draw a conclusion—that there is no relationship. To choose between A and (B), recall that when you analyze data from a given population (the employees at that particular company), you can only draw conclusions about that population, not about employee populations in general. Therefore, (B) is correct.

14. D   Difficulty: Medium
Category: Problem Solving and Data Analysis / Scatterplots

Getting to the Answer: The fact that the two variables are strongly correlated, whether it be negatively or positively, only shows that there is a relationship between the variables. It does not indicate whether the change in one variable caused the change in the other. For example, Population A might thrive in wet climates, while Population B does not, and in the years studied, rainfall may have increased, which caused the changes in the populations. This means (D) is the correct answer.

15. D   Difficulty: Medium
Category: Problem Solving and Data Analysis / Scatterplots

Getting to the Answer: Try drawing a quick graph (or at least visualizing a graph) that matches the description in the question (decreases quickly at first and then at a much slower rate). The shape and direction of the curve should tell you which type of model to choose.

The question doesn't say anything about the data points changing direction at any time, so you can eliminate A and B—they are both quadratic functions, which always turn around at their vertex. To choose between C and (D), skim through the question again. The data is decreasing, or getting smaller. In an exponential function, when the rate

(*r*) is greater than 0, as in C, the function is an exponential growth model, which increases, not decreases, and therefore cannot be correct. This means (D) is correct. When the rate (*r*) is less than 0, the function is an exponential decay model, which matches the description of the data.

16. D   Difficulty: Medium
Category: Problem Solving and Data Analysis / Scatterplots

Getting to the Answer: According to the question, the amount of milk a typical baby needs starts at 0 ounces and increases until it peaks at about 6 months of age. Then the amount of milk needed decreases until one year of age, when it becomes 0 ounces again. This means the shape of the data would look like an upside down parabola, which would match a negative quadratic model, making (D) correct. (Note: a negative absolute value model could also be used, depending on whether the rates of increase and decrease are constant, but that is not one of the answer choices.)

17. B   Difficulty: Medium
Category: Problem Solving and Data Analysis / Scatterplots

Getting to the Answer: Think logically about what happens to the data points and the line of best fit. The amount of snowfall is recorded on the *y*-axis, so the *y*-values of the data points stay the same. The *x*-values of the points all shift to the right 10 units (because Genji adds 10 degrees to each of the temperature readings). This means that all the data points stay in the same place vertically, but shift horizontally, resulting in the same rate of change, so you can eliminate C and D. The line of best fit would also still look the same, just shifted to the right. This means the strength of correlation does not change, as the points will still be the same distance away from the (now moved) line of best fit, making (B) correct.

18. D   Difficulty: Hard
Category: Problem Solving and Data Analysis / Scatterplots

Getting to the Answer: When a regression model has a correlation coefficient of 1.0, it means that the model exactly fits the data. This tells you that you can use what you know about quadratic functions to answer the question.

The graph of a quadratic function is symmetric with respect to its axis of symmetry. The axis of symmetry passes through the x-value of the vertex, which also happens to be where the maximum (or minimum) of the function occurs. The question tells you this value—it's $x = 25$. Because 35 is $35 - 25 = 10$ units to the right of the axis of symmetry, you know that the y-value will be the same as the point that is 10 units to the left of the axis of symmetry. This occurs at $x = 25 - 10 = 15$. Read the y-value from the graphing calculator screenshot to find the answer, which is 27. Therefore, (D) is correct.

19. 3   Difficulty: Medium
Category: Problem Solving and Data Analysis / Scatterplots

Getting to the Answer: Percent error gives the deviation of an actual value from an expected value. Graphically, this is determined by how far from the line of best fit the data point is. You don't need to find the percent error of every point (or even a single point) to answer this question. Instead, you just need to understand that the point with the greatest percent error from the mean of the data is the point that is farthest from the line of best fit. Use the grid-lines on the graph to find the point. The point (9, 3) is 4 full grid-lines away from the line of best fit, which is farther than any other data point. The question asks for the y-value of this point, so the correct answer is 3.

20. 18   Difficulty: Medium
Category: Problem Solving and Data Analysis / Scatterplots

Getting to the Answer: Because the y-value of the graph when $x = 3,400$ is not shown, this question requires a mathematical solution; extending the line of best fit will not provide an accurate enough answer. The equation of the model is given as $y = -\dfrac{1}{200}x + 35$. Miles over recommended servicing are graphed along the x-axis, so substitute 3,400 for x to find the answer:

$$y = -\frac{1}{200}(3,400) + 35 = -17 + 35 = 18$$

CHAPTER 7

PRACTICE

8. B Difficulty: Medium

Category: Problem Solving and Data Analysis / Statistics and Probability

Getting to the Answer: The professor starts with a normal distribution; when the new data are added, the distribution changes:

Added more data here.

The new distribution is skewed to the left (in the direction of the graph's tail, not in the direction of its biggest bump), and the median has increased. Although the range of the new data alone might be smaller than the original set, when all data are combined, the range will not have changed from the original data. The correct answer is (B).

9. 28.7 Difficulty: Easy

Category: Problem Solving and Data Analysis / Statistics and Probability

Getting to the Answer: To be considered "bad," a game must have a rating of 1 or 2. Begin by counting the number of "bad" games. There are $5 + 3 + 3 = 11$ games with a rating of 1 and $17 + 12 + 10 = 39$ games with a rating of 2. That's a total of $11 + 39 = 50$ games. Divide this by the total number of games and multiply by 100: $\frac{50}{61 + 54 + 59} \times 100 = 28.7\%$. Grid in 28.7.

10. 11.9 Difficulty: Medium

Category: Problem Solving and Data Analysis / Statistics and Probability

Getting to the Answer: You know from the previous question that 50 games are "bad." Reducing this number by 50% is the same as halving it, meaning there will be 25 remaining "bad" games after the removal. Subtract this from the original total game count ($61 + 54 + 59 = 174$) to get the new total, which is 149. Divide the new "bad" count by this total, and then multiply by 100 as you did before: $\frac{25}{149} \times 100 = 16.8\%$. Subtract the new percentage from the old one gives $28.7\% - 16.8\% = 11.9\%$. Grid in 11.9.

PERFORM

11. D Difficulty: Medium

Category: Problem Solving and Data Analysis / Statistics and Probability

Getting to the Answer: Consider finding the probability of *not* selecting one of the puzzles specified, as there will be fewer dots to count. You can then subtract that probability from 1. There are only three puzzles that *didn't* take Randolph fewer than 100 seconds to solve. Of these, 2 do *not* have fewer than 6 clues. Therefore, the probability that the conditions *won't* be met is $\frac{2}{20} = 0.1$. This isn't what you're asked to find, so don't stop yet. Subtract 0.1 from 1 to get 0.9. Multiply this by 100 to get 90%; (D) is correct.

12. B Difficulty: Easy

Category: Problem Solving and Data Analysis / Statistics and Probability

Getting to the Answer: Consider the difference between mean and standard deviation: Mean is a measure of center, while standard deviation is a measure of spread. The four answers all involve consistency, which means the explanation should involve standard deviation. Based on this, you can eliminate A and D. Higher consistency means lower standard deviation (and vice versa); the only choice that reflects this—and correctly represents the data in the table—is (B).

13. 594 Difficulty: Medium

Category: Problem Solving and Data Analysis / Statistics and Probability

Getting to the Answer: Identify Wilhelmina and Alexandra's hat contributions from the table, and then extrapolate to find how many solid-colored hats they should knit for Spirit Week. According to the table, Wilhelmina will be responsible for $\frac{24}{60}$ of the hats, and Alexandra will knit $\frac{9}{60}$ of them. The knitting club needs to knit 1,800 hats total, 60% of which should be solid-colored per the survey results, so $0.6 \times 1,080 = 1,080$ hats should be solid-colored. Add together the fractions for Wilhelmina and Alexandra to get $\frac{33}{60}$. Multiplying this by the total number of solid-colored hats will yield the number that Wilhelmina and Alexandra will knit: $\frac{33}{60} \times 1,080 = 594$.

14. 282   Difficulty: Medium
Category: Problem Solving and Data Analysis / Statistics and Probability

Getting to the Answer: Work through this one step at a time. Read carefully; you're asked about the two other club members' Spirit Week production here, and the question is not limited to solid-colored hats. Start with the number of prizes: 20% of 1,800 hats = 360 hats with emblems and therefore 360 prize scarves. The two boys make $\frac{27}{60}$ of the 360 hats = 162 hats. The two boys make $\frac{11}{33} = \frac{1}{3}$ of the 360 scarves = 120 scarves. They are responsible for $162 + 120 = 282$ of these items.

EXTRA PRACTICE

1. D   Difficulty: Easy
Category: Problem Solving and Data Analysis / Statistics and Probability

Getting to the Answer: Look carefully at the infographic's axes. Look at the vertical axis—the frequency tells you the number of contestants who named each number of states: 1 contestant named only 1 state, 1 contestant named 2 states, 5 contestants named 3 states, and so on. To answer the question, add all the frequencies to find the total number of contestants: $1 + 1 + 5 + 6 + 4 + 0 + 2 + 1 = 20$, which is (D).

2. C   Difficulty: Medium
Category: Problem Solving and Data Analysis / Statistics and Probability

Getting to the Answer: Not everyone who shops at an electronics store owns a tablet. Customers who bought other items, such as laptops, TVs, or MP3 players are likely to make up at least a portion of the surveys distributed with customers' purchases. This means that, despite being randomly selected, the sample is unlikely to be a good representative sample because there is no way to verify whether the responders to the survey actually own a tablet. Therefore, (C) is correct.

3. D   Difficulty: Medium
Category: Problem Solving and Data Analysis / Statistics and Probability

Getting to the Answer: Understanding how averages and sums are connected is the key to answering a question like this. If the average of 14 numbers is 6, then the sum of the 14 numbers must be 84 (because $84 \div 14 = 6$). Use the dot plot to find the total number of appliances the salesman has already sold. Then, subtract this amount from 84. The salesman has already sold $3(2) + 4(3) + 5 + 6(3) + 7 + 8 + 10(2) = 76$ appliances, so he needs to sell $84 - 76 = 8$ appliances on the 14th day to reach his goal. This means (D) is correct.

4. B   Difficulty: Medium
Category: Problem Solving and Data Analysis / Statistics and Probability

Getting to the Answer: According to the sample survey, $\frac{40}{300}$ *say* they would join the gym. But the gym estimates that only 30% of these respondents would *actually* join, so multiply 40 by 30% to find that the gym can expect $\frac{12}{300} = 0.04 = 4\%$ of the respondents to join. Multiply this by the total number of residents: $12,600 \times 0.04 = 504$ residents, so (B) is correct.

5. D   Difficulty: Hard
Category: Problem Solving and Data Analysis / Statistics and Probability

Getting to the Answer: The probability that one randomly selected salmon from those that were tested would have a dangerous level of mercury is equal to the number of salmon that had dangerous mercury levels divided by the total number of salmon that were tested. This means you only need two numbers to answer this question. One of those numbers is in the table—6 salmon had dangerous mercury levels. Finding the other number is the tricky part. Use information from the question stem and the pie graph. The biologist tested 5% of the total number of each breed of fish, or 5% of 25% of 6,000 fish. Multiply to find that $0.05 \times 0.25 \times 6,000 = 75$ salmon were tested. This means the probability is $\frac{6}{75} = 0.08$, which matches (D).

6. 627   Difficulty: Medium
Category: Problem Solving and Data Analysis / Statistics and Probability

Getting to the Answer: When making inferences about populations based on sample data, find the percent of the sample data that matches the given criteria and multiply by the number in the population. Of the 250 writers in the sample, $250 - 74 - 22 - 30 - 29 = 95$ writers said they would like sandwiches for lunch. This represents $\frac{95}{250} = 0.38$, or 38%. Multiply $0.38 \times 1,650$ to arrive at 627 writers that want sandwiches for lunch.

7. B   Difficulty: Medium
Category: Problem Solving and Data Analysis / Statistics and Probability

Getting to the Answer: To calculate the percentage of people in each age group with a healthy blood sugar level (< 100), divide the number of people in *that* age group with a healthy blood sugar level by the total number of participants in *that* age group. Choice (B) is correct because $16 \div 98 \approx 0.1633 = 16.33\%$, which is a lower percentage than in the other age groups (18-25 = 18.75%, 36-45 = 20.21%, and Older than 45 = 20%).

8. D   Difficulty: Medium
Category: Problem Solving and Data Analysis / Statistics and Probability

Getting to the Answer: This question requires careful reading of the table. The first criterion is fairly straight-forward—you're looking for a participant with a blood sugar level in the 100-125 range, so focus on that column in the table. The second criterion is a bit trickier—*at least 36 years old* means 36 years old or older, so you'll need

to use the values in the rows for 36-45, and Older than 45. There were 35 in the 36-45 age group who were considered at risk, and 27 in the Older than 45 age group, resulting in a total of $35 + 27 = 62$ out of 300 participants. The probability of randomly selecting one participant from either of these two groups is $\frac{62}{300}$, which reduces to $\frac{31}{150}$, or (D).

9. C   Difficulty: Easy
Category: Problem Solving and Data Analysis / Statistics and Probability

Getting to the Answer: The question states that the data was collected in California about jackrabbits, so any conclusion drawn can only be generalized to that particular geographic region and to that breed of rabbit. California is in the Northern Hemisphere, so its spring months are March, April, and May. According to the data, the California jackrabbit gives birth mostly during those months, so (C) is correct.

10. B   Difficulty: Medium
Category: Problem Solving and Data Analysis / Statistics and Probability

Getting to the Answer: The table is not complete, so your first step is to fill in the missing values. Start with what you know and work from there. It may not be necessary to complete the entire table, but rather only what you need to answer the question.

You know there are 186 cookies total and that 104 are without nuts, which means $186 - 104 = 82$ have nuts. Because you already know that 40 of those cookies are oatmeal raisin, this mean $82 - 40 = 42$ are chocolate chip. You also know that $\frac{2}{3}$ of the total number of cookies are chocolate chip, which means there are $\frac{2}{3} \times 186 = 124$ chocolate chips cookies, total, so you can fill this number in the "Total" row of that column. You do not need to fill in any more of the table because the question only asks about chocolate chip cookies with nuts. There are 124 chocolate chip cookies total and 42 of them have nuts, so the probability of randomly choosing one with nuts is $\frac{42}{124}$, or $\frac{21}{62}$, which matches (B).

11. A   Difficulty: Medium

Category: Problem Solving and Data Analysis / Statistics and Probability

Getting to the Answer: As long as a sample is both representative and without bias, inferences can be drawn from the sample data to the population from which the sample was taken. In this example, if the mean number of bottles of water consumed per person each day was 2.5, then it can be assumed that the average number consumed in the general population is also 2.5, so the means are equal, and (A) is the correct answer.

12. D   Difficulty: Medium

Category: Problem Solving and Data Analysis / Statistics and Probability

Getting to the Answer: The wording in this question implies that the population for the study includes all nutrients. However, the study only tests for nitrogen and potassium, so the sample was limited. You can eliminate A and B because all nutrients were not included in the sample, so you can't say anything about them, one way or the other. The compounds may or may not help the soil retain other types of nutrients, and you certainly don't know which of the five would produce the best results. You can eliminate C because the question doesn't tell you anything about the data collection methods, so you can't determine whether or not the study was biased. This means that choice (D) is correct—the study will only be able to produce results concerning the effects of the compounds on the soil retaining nitrogen and potassium.

13. B   Difficulty: Medium

Category: Problem Solving and Data Analysis / Statistics and Probability

Getting to the Answer: The median is the middle number in a series of numbers. Arrange the number of history majors from least to greatest, making sure that 225 is in the middle. Use s to balance out the number of history majors on either side of 225. Because there are already two numbers above the median (240 and 287), there must be two numbers below the median, 162 and s:

s, 162, 225, 240, 287

or

162, s, 225, 240, 287

Because s could be on either side of 162, it could be anything less than or equal to 225. Its greatest possible value is therefore 225, which is (B).

14. 2/5 or .4   Difficulty: Medium

Category: Problem Solving and Data Analysis / Statistics and Probability

Getting to the Answer: Take a second to think about the quickest way to answer the question—you're not asked to find the popularity rating of each performer and then compare them. Based on the host's definition, you can pick the most popular performer by simply looking at the numbers in the table. More people attended on Day 3, so you only need to find the popularity rating for Entertainer C: 1,600 people attended on that day out of a total of $1,280 + 1,120 + 1,600 = 4,000$ festival goers, so Entertainer C's popularity rating is $\frac{1,600}{4,000} = \frac{2}{5}$, or .4.

15. B   Difficulty: Easy

Category: Problem Solving and Data Analysis / Statistics and Probability

Getting to the Answer: The question only asks about participants who were outside a healthy weight range, so focus on this row: 38 out of the 74 participants who were outside a healthy weight range ate breakfast one or fewer times per week. This represents $\frac{38}{74} = 0.51351$, or 51.35%, which matches (B).

16. D   Difficulty: Medium

Category: Problem Solving and Data Analysis / Statistics and Probability

Getting to the Answer: The question asks about employees who eat breakfast every weekday, so focus on the "5-7 times per week" column in the table. Assuming the participants in the study were a good representative sample, 36 out of 45, or 80%, of the 3,000 employees are likely to be within a healthy weight range. Multiply $0.8 \times 3,000$ to arrive at 2,400, which is (D).

17. 300   Difficulty: Easy

Category: Problem Solving and Data Analysis / Statistics and Probability

Getting to the Answer: Read the graph carefully, including the key at the bottom indicating that each bar represents 15 minutes. The question states that only stage 3 is considered *deep* sleep, and the question asks how much time was spent in *light* sleep. You could count all of the bars that don't represent stage 3, but it would be faster to count the bars that do and subtract. There are 12 bars that represent stage 3, which means the person spent $12 \times 15 = 180$ minutes in deep sleep. The study was for 8 hours, or 480 minutes, so the person spent $480 - 180 = 300$ minutes in light sleep.

18. 3/8 or .375   Difficulty: Medium
Category: Problem Solving and Data Analysis / Statistics and Probability

Getting to the Answer: Probability compares the number of desired outcomes (here, the number of 15-minute periods with a sleep stage of 3) with the total number of possible outcomes (here, the total number of 15-minute periods over the course of the 8 hours). The opening paragraph tells you that the total amount of sleep over the course of the study is 8 hours. In the previous question, you calculated that 180 minutes, or 3 hours are spent in deep sleep. Therefore, the probability would be $\frac{3}{8}$.

19. 15   Difficulty: Medium
Category: Problem Solving and Data Analysis / Statistics and Probability

Getting to the Answer: The question asks *on average* how many more cents consumers are willing to pay, so you will need to find a weighted average for each version of the product. Start with the store brand. Multiply each dollar amount by the height of the corresponding bar:

$$5 \times 68 = 340$$
$$6 \times 56 = 336$$
$$7 \times 48 = 336$$
$$8 \times 32 = 256$$
$$9 \times 30 = 270$$
$$10 \times 14 = 140$$

Next, add them all together: $1,678. Now, divide this number by the total number of respondents ($68 + 56 + 48 + 32 + 30 + 14 = 248$): $1,678 \div 248 = 6.766$, which means *on average* consumers are willing to pay $6.77 for the store brand version of the product. Repeat this process for the brand name version.

$$5 \times 85 = 425$$
$$6 \times 79 = 474$$
$$7 \times 64 = 448$$
$$8 \times 55 = 440$$
$$9 \times 42 = 378$$
$$10 \times 27 = 270$$

Add them all together to get 2,435, and divide by the number of respondents ($85 + 79 + 64 + 55 + 42 + 27 = 352$) to arrive at $2,435 \div 352 = 6.917$, or $6.92. *On average*, consumers are willing to pay $6.92 - $6.77 = $0.15, or 15 more cents for the brand name version than the store brand version.

20. 1/3 or .333   Difficulty: Hard
Category: Problem Solving and Data Analysis / Statistics and Probability

Getting to the Answer: First, find the number of respondents willing to pay at least $8 (which means $8 or more). Be careful—the question doesn't specify store brand or brand name, so use both versions of the product:

$$32 + 55 + 30 + 42 + 14 + 27 = 200$$

Now, find the total number of people in the survey. Again, the question doesn't specify store brand or brand name. You know from the previous question that 248 people responded to the store brand survey and 352 responded to the name brand survey, for a total of 600 respondents. This means the probability that a randomly chosen respondent is willing to pay at least $8 is $\frac{200}{600}$, or $\frac{1}{3}$.

CHAPTER 8

PRACTICE

8. D **Difficulty:** Hard

Category: Passport to Advanced Math / Exponents

Getting to the Answer: Relative velocity is represented by v, so that's the variable you need to isolate. The manipulation sequence is shown here.

$$\gamma = \frac{1}{\sqrt{1 - \dfrac{v^2}{c^2}}}$$

$$\gamma\sqrt{1 - \frac{v^2}{c^2}} = 1$$

$$\sqrt{1 - \frac{v^2}{c^2}} = \frac{1}{\gamma}$$

$$1 - \frac{v^2}{c^2} = \frac{1}{\gamma^2}$$

$$-\frac{v^2}{c^2} = \frac{1}{\gamma^2} - 1$$

$$v^2 = -c^2\left(\frac{1}{\gamma^2} - 1\right)$$

$$v = c\sqrt{1 - \frac{1}{\gamma^2}}$$

The correct answer is (D).

9. B **Difficulty:** Medium

Category: Passport to Advanced Math / Exponents

Getting to the Answer: The GCF of the two expressions under the radical is g^4h^3; factoring this out yields $\sqrt[3]{g^4h^3(g^2 - 27)}$. You can now pull a g and an h out from under the radical to obtain $gh\sqrt[3]{g(g^2 - 27)}$, which cannot be further simplified except for redistribution of g, which yields $gh\sqrt[3]{g^3 - 27g}$, making (B) correct. Note that $\sqrt[3]{g^3 - 27g}$ *does not* become $g - 3\sqrt[3]{g}$, as you cannot split the expression into two radicals.

10. D **Difficulty:** Medium

Category: Passport to Advanced Math / Exponents

Getting to the Answer: Start by setting up a ratio that compares RBC count to total blood cell count. Manipulate the quantities to make all the exponents the same (to convert 7.5×10^3 to a product of 10^6 and another number, move the decimal point in 7.5 three places to the left and write "$\times 10^6$" after it), factor out 10^6, and then add the quantities in parentheses together. Once there, you can use exponent rules to simplify your equation. Divide through and multiply by 100 to get the RBC component as a percentage. Work is shown here:

$$\begin{aligned}
\text{RBC} &= \frac{5.4 \times 10^6}{5.4 \times 10^6 + 7.5 \times 10^3 + 3.5 \times 10^5} \\
&= \frac{5.4 \times 10^6}{5.4 \times 10^6 + 0.0075 \times 10^6 + 0.35 \times 10^6} \\
&= \frac{5.4 \times 10^6}{10^6(5.4 + 0.0075 + 0.35)} \\
&= \frac{5.4}{5.7575}
\end{aligned}$$

Note that the answer choices are, for the most part, far apart. Because 5.4 is relatively close to 5.7575, you can conclude with confidence that the correct answer is likely close to 100%. Therefore, (D) is the correct answer. If this question is in the calculator section, you can plug the numbers into your calculator to check:

$$\% \text{ RBC} = \frac{5.4}{5.7575} \times 100 \approx 93.79\%$$

Choice (D) is still correct.

11. A **Difficulty:** Medium

Category: Passport to Advanced Math / Exponents

Getting to the Answer: Start by arranging the pumps in order of increasing drain speed; you get P3 < P1 < P2. You're told that the second pump is twice as fast as the first and that the first is three times as fast as the third. You can turn the words into a ratio: If the portion of the draining completed by pump 3 in 1 hour is $\frac{1}{x}$, then the portion completed by pump 1 is $\frac{1}{x} \times 3 = \frac{3}{x}$, and the portion completed by pump 2 is $\frac{3}{x} \times 2 = \frac{6}{x}$. The term $\frac{6}{x}$ matches (A).

PERFORM

12. C   Difficulty: Medium

Category: Passport to Advanced Math / Exponents

Getting to the Answer: Begin by moving all terms that don't contain an a to one side of the equation. Once there, multiply both sides by 2 to eliminate the fraction, and then divide by t^2 to isolate a. The manipulation sequence is shown here.

$$h = \frac{1}{2}at^2 + v_0t + h_0$$

$$h - v_0t - h_0 = \frac{1}{2}at^2$$

$$at^2 = 2(h - v_0t - h_0)$$

$$a = \frac{2(h - v_0t - h_0)}{t^2}$$

Choice (C) is the correct answer.

13. A   Difficulty: Hard

Category: Passport to Advanced Math / Exponents

Getting to the Answer: Start by simplifying the radicals: 72 is the product of 2 and 36, so $\sqrt{72} = 6\sqrt{2}$. You can then factor 3 out of the numerator and denominator to yield $\frac{3(1 + 2\sqrt{2})}{3(1 - 2\sqrt{2})}$. Cancel the 3s, and you're left with $\frac{1 + 2\sqrt{2}}{1 - 2\sqrt{2}}$. You can't leave a radical in the denominator, so you'll need to rationalize it. The conjugate of the denominator is $1 + 2\sqrt{2}$, so multiply the entire expression by $\frac{1 + 2\sqrt{2}}{1 + 2\sqrt{2}}$, and then simplify as usual (think FOIL):

$$\frac{1 + 2\sqrt{2}}{1 - 2\sqrt{2}} \times \frac{1 + 2\sqrt{2}}{1 + 2\sqrt{2}}$$

$$= \frac{1 + 2\sqrt{2} + 2\sqrt{2} + 8}{1 + 2\sqrt{2} - 2\sqrt{2} - 8}$$

$$= \frac{1 + 2\sqrt{2} + 2\sqrt{2} + 8}{1 - 8}$$

$$= \frac{9 + 4\sqrt{2}}{-7}$$

This expression matches (A).

14. 41   Difficulty: Hard

Category: Passport to Advanced Math / Exponents

Getting to the Answer: In this question, you're given all the variables you need and an equation that relates them. All you need to do is plug the given values into the correct locations ($m = 200$, $r = \frac{0.015}{12}$, $N = 60$) and solve for what's missing (P in this case). Decimals are truncated for brevity here, but no rounding was done until the final step.

$$m = \frac{Pr}{1 - (1 + r)^{-N}}$$

$$200 = \frac{P \times \frac{0.015}{12}}{1 - \left(1 + \frac{0.015}{12}\right)^{-60}}$$

$$200 = \frac{0.00125P}{1 - (1 + 0.00125)^{-60}}$$

$$200 = \frac{0.00125P}{1 - (1.00125)^{-60}}$$

$$200 = \frac{0.00125P}{1 - 0.9278}$$

$$14.4426 = 0.00125P$$

$$P = 11,554.0987$$

Subtract P from the total price (19,560) to obtain Teri's down payment. Divide this by 19,560 and multiply by 100 to arrive at 40.93%. Rounded properly, the correct answer is 41.

EXTRA PRACTICE

1. A   Difficulty: Easy

Category: Passport to Advanced Math / Exponents

Getting to the Answer: Carefully multiply each term in the first factor by each term in the second factor. Then find the x terms and add their coefficients. To save time, you do not need to simplify the other terms in the expression.

$$(-2x^2 + 5x - 8)(4x - 9)$$
$$= -2x^2(4x - 9) + 5x(4x - 9) - 8(4x - 9)$$
$$= -8x^3 + 18x^2 + 20x^2 - \underline{45x - 32x} + 72$$

The coefficient of x in the product is $-45 - 32 = -77$, which means (A) is correct.

2. D   Difficulty: Medium

Category: Passport to Advanced Math / Exponents

Getting to the Answer: A *double zero* occurs in a polynomial when a factor is repeated, or in other words, squared. For example, the factor $(x - a)$ produces a simple zero at $x = a$, while $(x - b)^2$ produces a double zero at $x = b$. The polynomial has a simple zero at $x = -3$, which corresponds to a factor of $(x + 3)$. The double zero at $x = \frac{5}{4}$ results from a repeated (squared) factor, so you can eliminate A and C. To choose between B and (D), set each factor equal to 0, and then solve for x (mentally if possible). Choice (D) is correct because:

$$4x - 5 = 0$$
$$4x = 5$$
$$x = \frac{5}{4}$$

3. B   Difficulty: Medium

Category: Passport to Advanced Math / Exponents

Getting to the Answer: The goal here is to solve the equation for T. Start by getting T out of the denominator of the fraction. To do this, multiply both sides of the equation by T, and then divide both sides by v:

$$v = \frac{2\pi r}{T}$$
$$T \times v = \frac{2\pi r}{T} \times T$$
$$Tv = 2\pi r$$
$$T = \frac{2\pi r}{v}$$

Choice (B) is the correct answer.

4. C   Difficulty: Medium

Category: Passport to Advanced Math / Exponents

Getting to the Answer: Because the denominators are the same (just written in different forms), multiplying both sides of the equation by $3x - 15$ will immediately clear all the fractions, the result of which is a much easier equation to solve:

$$8x + 2x = 50$$
$$10x = 50$$
$$x = 5$$

Because there are variables in the denominator, you must check the solution to make sure it is not extraneous. When $x = 5$, each of the denominators is equal to 0, and division by 0 is not possible. Therefore, there is no solution to the equation, making (C) the correct answer.

5. A   Difficulty: Medium

Category: Passport to Advanced Math / Exponents

Getting to the Answer: There are two variables and only one equation, but because you're asked to solve for one of them *in terms of* the other, you solve it the same way you would any other equation. Because there is only one term on each side of the equal sign, cross-multiplying is probably the quickest route to the solution. Don't forget—you want to get x by itself on one side of the equation.

$$\frac{6}{x} = \frac{3}{k + 2}$$
$$6(k + 2) = 3x$$
$$6k + 12 = 3x$$
$$\frac{6k}{3} + \frac{12}{3} = \frac{3x}{3}$$
$$2k + 4 = x$$

Switch x to the left side of the equation and the result matches (A).

6. D   Difficulty: Medium

Category: Passport to Advanced Math / Exponents

Getting to the Answer: Multiply each term in the first expression by $\frac{3}{2}$ and each term in the second expression by -2. Then add the two polynomials by writing them vertically and combining like terms.

$$\frac{3}{2}A = \frac{3}{2}(4x^2 + 7x - 1) = 6x^2 + \frac{21}{2}x - \frac{3}{2}$$
$$-2B = -2(-x^2 - 5x + 3) = 2x^2 + 10x - 6$$

$$
\begin{array}{r}
6x^2 + \dfrac{21}{2}x - \dfrac{3}{2} \\[2mm]
+\ 2x^2 + \dfrac{20}{2}x - \dfrac{12}{2} \\[1mm]
\hline
8x^2 + \dfrac{41}{2}x - \dfrac{15}{2}
\end{array}
$$

This means (D) is correct.

7. 10/3   Difficulty: Hard

Category: Passport to Advanced Math / Exponents

Getting to the Answer: Write each factor in the expression in exponential form (using fractional exponents for the radicals). Then use exponent rules to simplify the expression. Add the exponents of the factors that are being multiplied and subtract the exponent of the factor that is being divided:

$$\frac{\sqrt[3]{x} \cdot x^{\frac{5}{2}} \cdot x}{\sqrt{x}} = \frac{x^{\frac{1}{3}} \cdot x^{\frac{5}{2}} \cdot x^1}{x^{\frac{1}{2}}}$$
$$= x^{\frac{1}{3} + \frac{5}{2} + \frac{1}{1} - \frac{1}{2}} = x^{\frac{2}{6} + \frac{15}{6} + \frac{6}{6} - \frac{3}{6}}$$
$$= x^{\frac{20}{6}} = x^{\frac{10}{3}}$$

The question states that n is the power of x, so the value of n is $\frac{10}{3}$.

8. B   Difficulty: Hard

Category: Passport to Advanced Math / Exponents

Getting to the Answer: Because the question states that the expressions are equivalent, set up the equation $\frac{16}{7x + 4} + A = \frac{49x^2}{7x + 4}$ and solve for A. Start by subtracting the first term from both sides of the equation to isolate A. Then, simplify if possible (usually by cancelling common factors). The denominators of the rational terms are the same, so they can be combined.

$$\frac{16}{7x + 4} + A = \frac{49x^2}{7x + 4}$$
$$A = \frac{49x^2}{7x + 4} - \frac{16}{7x + 4}$$
$$A = \frac{49x^2 - 16}{7x + 4}$$
$$A = \frac{(7x + 4)(7x - 4)}{7x + 4}$$
$$A = 7x - 4$$

The correct answer is (B).

9. C   Difficulty: Easy

Category: Passport to Advanced Math / Exponents

Getting to the Answer: Follow the standard order of operations—deal with the exponent first, and then attach the negative sign (because a negative in front of an expression means multiplication by -1). The variable x is being raised to the $\frac{1}{4}$ power, so rewrite the term as a radical expression with 4 as the degree of the root and 1 as the power to which the radicand, x, is being raised.

$$x^{\frac{1}{4}} = \sqrt[4]{x^1} = \sqrt[4]{x}$$

Now attach the negative to arrive at the correct answer, $-\sqrt[4]{x}$, which is (C).

10. C   Difficulty: Easy

Category: Passport to Advanced Math / Exponents

Getting to the Answer: First, write the question as a subtraction problem. Pay careful attention to which expression is being subtracted.

$$\frac{8x - 5}{x - 1} - \frac{3x + 7}{x - 1}$$

The terms in the expression have the same denominator, $x - 1$, so their numerators can be subtracted. Simply combine like terms and keep the denominator the same. Don't forget to distribute the negative to both $3x$ and 7.

$$\frac{8x - 5}{x - 1} - \frac{3x + 7}{x - 1} = \frac{8x - 5 - 3x - 7}{x - 1} = \frac{5x - 12}{x - 1}$$

The reduced expression matches (C).

11. A   **Difficulty:** Easy

Category: Passport to Advanced Math / Exponents

Getting to the Answer: Add polynomial expressions by combining like terms. Be careful of the signs of each term. It may help to write the sum vertically (like you would with big numbers), lining up the like terms.

$$6a^2 - 17a - 9$$
$$+ -5a^2 + 8a - 2$$
$$\overline{a^2 - 9a - 11}$$

The correct answer is (A).

12. A   **Difficulty:** Easy

Category: Passport to Advanced Math / Exponents

Getting to the Answer: Find the greatest common factor of both the numerator and the denominator, which in this question happens to be the denominator. Factor out the GCF, $9x^2$, from the numerator and denominator and then cancel what you can.

$$\frac{18x^4 + 27x^3 - 36x^2}{9x^2} = \frac{9x^2(2x^2 + 3x - 4)}{9x^2}$$
$$= 2x^2 + 3x - 4$$

This matches (A). As an alternate method, you could split the expression up and reduce each term, one at a time.

$$\frac{18x^4 + 27x^3 - 36x^2}{9x^2} = \frac{18x^4}{9x^2} + \frac{27x^3}{9x^2} - \frac{36x^2}{9x^2}$$
$$= 2x^2 + 3x - 4$$

13. A   **Difficulty:** Medium

Category: Passport to Advanced Math / Exponents

Getting to the Answer: Solve equations containing radical expressions the same way you solve any other equation: Isolate the variable using inverse operations. Start by subtracting 8 from both sides of the equation, and then multiply by 3. Then, square both sides to remove the radical.

$$8 + \frac{\sqrt{2x + 29}}{3} = 9$$
$$\frac{\sqrt{2x + 29}}{3} = 1$$
$$\sqrt{2x + 29} = 3$$
$$2x + 29 = 9$$

Now you have a simple linear equation that you can solve using more inverse operations: Subtract 29 and divide by 2 to find that $x = -10$. Be careful—just because the equation started with a radical and the answer is negative, does not mean that *No solution* is the correct answer. If you plug -10 into the expression under the radical, the result is a positive number, which means -10 is a perfectly valid solution. Therefore, (A) is correct.

14. C   **Difficulty:** Medium

Category: Passport to Advanced Math / Exponents

Getting to the Answer: A fraction is the same as division, so you can use polynomial long division to simplify the expression.

$$\begin{array}{r} 3x + 2 \\ 2x + 5 \overline{) 6x^2 + 19x + 10} \\ -(6x^2 + 15x) \\ \hline 4x + 10 \\ -(4x + 10) \\ \hline 0 \end{array}$$

The simplified expression is $3x + 2$, so $a + b = 3 + 2 = 5$, which is (C). As an alternate method, you could factor the numerator of the expression, and cancel common factors:

$$\frac{6x^2 + 19x + 10}{2x + 5} = \frac{(2x + 5)(3x + 2)}{(2x + 5)} = 3x + 2$$

Use whichever method gets you to the correct answer in the shortest amount of time.

15. D   **Difficulty:** Medium

Category: Passport to Advanced Math / Exponents

Getting to the Answer: Notice that each term is a perfect square and there is a minus sign between the terms, which means you can use the difference of squares rule,

$a^2 - b^2 = (a - b)(a + b)$, to rewrite the expression. If you can't mentally determine what a and b are, write each term as the square of something:

$$25x^2y^4 - 1 = (5xy^2)^2 - 1^2$$
$$= (5xy^2 - 1)(5xy^2 + 1)$$

This matches (D).

16. C   Difficulty: Medium

Category: Passport to Advanced Math / Exponents

Getting to the Answer: Whenever a binomial is squared (or raised to any power), you should rewrite it as repeated multiplication and expand it. Do this for both binomials and combine like terms to find the sum.

$$(a - b)^2 + (a + b)^2$$
$$= [(a - b)(a - b)] + [(a + b)(a + b)]$$
$$= (a^2 - ab - ba + b^2) + (a^2 + ab + ba + b^2)$$
$$= (a^2 - 2ab + b^2) + (a^2 + 2ab + b^2)$$
$$= 2a^2 + 2b^2$$

This matches (C).

17. B   Difficulty: Medium

Category: Passport to Advanced Math / Exponents

Getting to the Answer: The question asks you to solve the equation for L. Use inverse operations to accomplish the task: Divide both sides of the equation by 2π and then square both sides. You'll need to apply the exponent to all the terms on the left side of the equation, including the π:

$$T = 2\pi\sqrt{\frac{L}{g}}$$

$$\frac{T}{2\pi} = \sqrt{\frac{L}{g}}$$

$$\left(\frac{T}{2\pi}\right)^2 = \left(\sqrt{\frac{L}{g}}\right)^2$$

$$\frac{T^2}{4\pi^2} = \frac{L}{g}$$

Finally, multiply both sides by g to remove g from the denominator and isolate L.

$$L = \frac{gT^2}{4\pi^2}$$

The correct answer is (B).

18. B   Difficulty: Hard

Category: Passport to Advanced Math / Exponents

Getting to the Answer: You can solve almost every *work* problem using the formula $W = rt$ or some manipulation of this formula, such as $r = \dfrac{W}{t}$ or $t = \dfrac{W}{r}$. If two or more machines (or people) are working together, start by finding their combined rate and go from there. (Note: W is often 1 because many questions ask about completing *a job*, which is the same as *one job*.)

The first pill counter can complete one batch in 1 hour, so its rate is $r = \dfrac{1}{1} = 1$ batch per hour. The second pill counter can complete one batch in 40 minutes (which is $\dfrac{40}{60} = \dfrac{2}{3}$ hours), so its rate is $r = \dfrac{1}{\frac{2}{3}} = \dfrac{3}{2}$ batches per hour. Working together, the combined rate is $1 + \dfrac{3}{2} = \dfrac{2}{2} + \dfrac{3}{2} = \dfrac{5}{2}$ batches per hour. Use this combined rate in the formula for time to arrive at $t_{combined} = \dfrac{W}{r_{combined}} = \dfrac{1}{\frac{5}{2}} = \dfrac{2}{5}$ hours, which is equivalent to $\dfrac{2}{\cancel{5}} \times \cancel{60}^{12} = 24$ minutes. This means (B) is correct.

19. 16   Difficulty: Hard

Category: Passport to Advanced Math / Exponents

Getting to the Answer: Because this is a no-calculator question, you need to rewrite the exponent in a way that makes it easier to evaluate: Use exponent rules to rewrite $\dfrac{4}{3}$ as a unit fraction raised to a power. Then write the expression in radical form and simplify.

$$8^{\frac{4}{3}} = \left(8^{\frac{1}{3}}\right)^4$$
$$= \left(\sqrt[3]{8}\right)^4$$
$$= 2^4$$
$$= 2 \times 2 \times 2 \times 2$$
$$= 16$$

20. 8   **Difficulty:** Medium

Category: Passport to Advanced Math / Exponents

Getting to the Answer: A fraction bar indicates division, so use polynomial long division and your reasoning skills.

$$
\begin{array}{r}
2x^3 + 8x^2 + 2x + 2 \\
x+4\overline{\smash{\big)}\,2x^4 + 16x^3 + 34x^2 + 10x + k} \\
\underline{-(2x^4 + 8x^3)} \\
8x^3 + 34x^2 + 10x + k \\
\underline{-(8x^3 + 32x^2)} \\
2x^2 + 10x + k \\
\underline{-(2x^2 + 8x)} \\
2x + k \\
\underline{-(2x + 8)} \\
k - 8
\end{array}
$$

For there to be no remainder (i.e., a remainder of 0), k must be 8.

CHAPTER 9

PRACTICE

8. C**Difficulty:** Medium
Category: Passport to Advanced Math / Functions

Getting to the Answer: You're told the honeybee population decreases 35% each month; this means exponential decay is occurring, so use $y = x_0(1 + r)^x$ as your function template. Set p as the honeybee population and t as the time in months; watch the sign of r. Your function should be $p(t) = (4.23 \times 10^8)(0.65)^t$. Now plug in the time in months:

$$p(12) = (4.23 \times 10^8)(0.65)^{12} \approx 2,406,028$$

The correct answer is (C).

9. C**Difficulty:** Hard
Category: Passport to Advanced Math / Functions

Getting to the Answer: Translate the composition notation: $(b \circ a)(x)$ means $b(a(x))$ or b of $a(x)$. This tells you to use $a(x)$ as the input for $b(x)$. You can rewrite this as $\dfrac{1}{a(x)}$, which is the reciprocal of $a(x)$. This new function will be undefined anywhere that $a(x) = 0$. Looking at the graph, you can see that $a(x)$ crosses the x-axis four times, making (C) correct.

PERFORM

10. B**Difficulty:** Hard
Category: Passport to Advanced Math / Functions

Getting to the Answer: Don't panic about this involving a trigonometric function; the question is only testing your ability to apply multiple transformations to a graph. The easiest transformation to identify is the −4 downward shift. Eliminate C and D, as neither contains this shift. Both A and (B) contain a vertical expansion, but the difference is subtle, so hone in on the transformed function's horizontal compression effected by the 2 in parentheses. Choice (B) has a compressed sine graph, so it is correct.

11. A**Difficulty:** Medium
Category: Passport to Advanced Math / Functions

Getting to the Answer: Use the two given rates to determine Briana's typing rate in pages per minute. She types 45 words per minute, which becomes:

$$\frac{45 \text{ words}}{1 \text{ min}} \times \frac{1 \text{ page}}{500 \text{ words}} = \frac{45 \text{ pages}}{500 \text{ min}} = \frac{9 \text{ pages}}{100 \text{ min}}$$

Multiplying this rate by m gets you the number of pages typed after m minutes, which can then be subtracted from the starting page count (60) to get the number of pages Briana has left to type. The function should read $p(m) = 60 - \dfrac{9m}{100}$, which matches (A).

12. D**Difficulty:** Medium
Category: Passport to Advanced Math / Functions

Getting to the Answer: Examine the graph. A peak in fuel economy at 50 mph is obvious, but what else can be said? A closer look at the increase below 50 mph (to the left of 50 on the horizontal axis) and the decrease above 50 mph (to the right of 50) reveals a critical detail: The decreasing part of the graph is steeper than the increasing part. This means the rate of decrease is faster than the rate of increase. This corresponds to (D).

EXTRA PRACTICE

1. A**Difficulty:** Easy
Category: Passport to Advanced Math / Functions

Getting to the Answer: The notation $k(4)$ means the output value of the function when 4 is substituted for the input (x), and $k(1)$ means the output value of the function when 1 is substituted for the input (x). Substitute 4 and 1 into the function, one at a time, and then subtract the results.

$$k(4) = 5(4) + 2 = 20 + 2 = 22$$
$$k(1) = 5(1) + 2 = 5 + 2 = 7$$
$$k(4) - k(1) = 22 - 7 = 15$$

Choice (A) is correct. Caution—this is not the same as subtracting $4 - 1$ and then substituting 3 into the function.

2. C   **Difficulty:** Easy

Category: Passport to Advanced Math / Functions

Getting to the Answer: The function graphed is the absolute value function, and you can see that all values in its range (the *y*-values) are positive. That makes the negative value in (C) impossible. Because you're looking for the statement that is NOT true, you can safely conclude that (C) is correct.

3. D   **Difficulty:** Medium

Category: Passport to Advanced Math / Functions

Getting to the Answer: Compare each answer choice to the graph, eliminating false statements as you go.

Choice A: Carmel went to the library first, so the library (not the grocery store) is about 5 miles from his home. Eliminate this choice.

Choice B: Carmel traveled 7 miles away from his home (between $t = 0$ minutes and $t = 30$ minutes), but then also traveled 7 miles back (between $t = 45$ minutes and $t = 60$ minutes), so he traveled a total of 14 miles. Eliminate this choice.

Choice C: When Carmel reached the library, he was 5 miles from home; when he reached the grocery store, he was 7 miles from home. This means the grocery store must be $7 - 5 = 2$ miles farther away. Eliminate this choice.

Choice (D) must be correct. Carmel is the same distance from home (5 miles) between $t = 15$ minutes and $t = 25$ minutes, so he spent 10 minutes at the library. He is stopped once again (at the grocery store) between $t = 30$ minutes and $t = 45$ minutes, so he spent 15 minutes at the grocery store.

4. C   **Difficulty:** Medium

Category: Passport to Advanced Math / Functions

Getting to the Answer: Transformations that are grouped with the *x* in a function shift the graph horizontally and therefore affect the *x*-coordinates of points on the graph. Transformations that are not grouped with the *x* shift the graph vertically and therefore affect the *y*-coordinates of points on the graph. Remember, horizontal shifts are always the reverse of what they look like. When working with multiple transformations, follow the same order of operations as always—parentheses first, then multiply and divide, then add and subtract.

Start with the parentheses: $(x - 2)$. This shifts the graph right 2 units, so add 2 to the *x*-coordinate of the given point: $(5, 3) \rightarrow (5 + 2, 3) = (7, 3)$. Next, apply the negative in front of *g* because it represents multiplication. The negative is not grouped with the *x*, so multiply the *y*-coordinate by -1 to get $(7, 3(-1)) \rightarrow (7, -3)$. Finally, the $+ 8$ is not grouped with *x*, so add 8 to the *y*-coordinate: $(7, -3) \rightarrow (7, -3 + 8) = (7, 5)$, which matches (C).

You could also plot the point on a coordinate plane, perform the transformations (right 2, reflect vertically over the *x*-axis, and then up 8), to find the new point. The result will be the same.

5. A   **Difficulty:** Medium

Category: Passport to Advanced Math / Functions

Getting to the Answer: The notation $g(h(x))$ indicates a composition of two functions which can be read "*g* of *h* of *x*." It means that the output when *x* is substituted in $h(x)$ becomes the input for $g(x)$. First, use the table on the right to find that $h(3)$ is 0. This is your new input. Now, use the table on the left to find $g(0)$, which is -1, making (A) the correct answer.

6. B   **Difficulty:** Hard

Category: Passport to Advanced Math / Functions

Getting to the Answer: The key to answering this question is to have a conceptual understanding of function notation. Here, the input $(x + 2)$ has already been substituted and simplified in the given function. Your job is to determine what the function would have looked like had *x* been the input instead. To keep things organized, let $u = x + 2$, the old input. This means $x = u - 2$. Substitute this into *p* and simplify:

$$p(x + 2) = 3x^2 + 4x + 1$$

$$\begin{aligned} p(u) &= 3(u - 2)^2 + 4(u - 2) + 1 \\ &= 3(u^2 - 4u + 4) + 4u - 8 + 1 \\ &= 3u^2 - 12u + 12 + 4u - 8 + 1 \\ &= 3u^2 - 8u + 5 \end{aligned}$$

When working with function notation, you evaluate the function by substituting a given input value for the variable in the parentheses. Here, if the input value is *x*, then $p(x) = 3x^2 - 8x + 5$, which means (B) is correct.

7. **3.5** or **3.50** **Difficulty:** Medium

Category: Passport to Advanced Math / Functions

Getting to the Answer: Start by evaluating the function at $x = 25$ and at $x = 20$. Make sure you follow the correct order of operations as you simplify.

$$P(25) = 150(25) - (25)^2$$
$$= 3,750 - 625$$
$$= 3,125$$
$$P(20) = 150(20) - (20)^2$$
$$= 3,000 - 400$$
$$= 2,600$$

The question asks how much more profit *per unit* the company makes, so find the difference in the amounts of profit and divide by the number of units (150) to get

$$\frac{3,125 - 2,600}{150} = \frac{525}{150} = \$3.50\overline{4}, \text{ or } 3.5.$$

8. **305** **Difficulty:** Medium

Category: Passport to Advanced Math / Functions

Getting to the Answer: Always pay careful attention to what the variable in a function represents, especially in questions that deal with real-world scenarios. In this question, t does *not* represent the time, so don't find $C(5)$. Rather, you need to start by finding the number of hours that pass between 7 AM and 5 PM. Because there are 10 hours between 7 AM and 5 PM, evaluate the function at $t = 10$. Make sure you follow the correct order of operations as you simplify.

$$C(t) = -0.0814t^4 + t^3 + 12t$$
$$C(10) = -0.0815(10)^4 + 10^3 + 12(10)$$
$$= -0.0815(10,000) + 1,000 + 120$$
$$= -815 + 1,000 + 120$$
$$= 305$$

9. **A** **Difficulty:** Easy

Category: Passport to Advanced Math / Functions

Getting to the Answer: The notation $g(-2)$ means the value of the function when $x = -2$, so substitute -2 for x and simplify. Don't forget to use the correct order of operations as you work:

$$g(-2) = -2(-2)^2 + 7(-2) - 3$$
$$= -2(4) + (-14) - 3$$
$$= -8 - 14 - 3$$
$$= -25$$

Choice (A) is correct.

10. **C** **Difficulty:** Easy

Category: Passport to Advanced Math / Functions

Getting to the Answer: A function, by definition, only has one output for every input. When you're given graphs to consider, use the vertical line test to see if the graph represents a function. If a vertical line intersects a graph more than one time, then the graph has more than one output for a given input and is therefore *not* a function. The graph in (C) fails the test, so it is not a function.

11. **D** **Difficulty:** Easy

Category: Passport to Advanced Math / Functions

Getting to the Answer: The domain of a function represents the possible values of x, or the input values. In this function, x is represented by p, which is the number of seeds germinated by the plants over a given period of time. Because there cannot be a negative number of seeds germinated, or a fraction of a seed germinated, the list in (D) is the only one that could represent a portion of the function's domain.

12. **D** **Difficulty:** Medium

Category: Passport to Advanced Math / Functions

Getting to the Answer: To determine the domain, look at the x-values. To determine the range, look at the y-values. For the domain, the graph is continuous (no holes or gaps in the graph) and has arrows on both sides, so the domain is all real numbers. This means you can eliminate A and B. For the range, the function's maximum (the vertex) is located at (−3, 4), which means the highest possible y-value of f(x) is 4. The graph is continuous and opens downward, so the range of the function is y ≤ 4, which is the same as f(x) ≤ 4, making (D) correct.

13. D   Difficulty: Medium

Category: Passport to Advanced Math / Functions

Getting to the Answer: Draw a quick sketch of the equation (or graph it in your graphing calculator).

Based on the equation, the graph is a parabola that opens upward with a vertex of (2, −5). A parabola changes direction at the x-coordinate of its vertex. This is all the information you need to answer the question. You can immediately eliminate A and B. To choose between C and (D), take a closer look at the sketch. To the left of 2 (or x < 2), the parabola is decreasing, and to the right of 2 (or x > 2), it is increasing. This makes (D) correct.

14. B   Difficulty: Medium

Category: Passport to Advanced Math / Functions

Getting to the Answer: In this question, you are given a range value (14), which means f(x) = 14, and you are asked for the corresponding domain value (x-value). This means you are solving for x, not substituting for x. Set the function equal to 14 and solve using inverse operations:

$$14 = \frac{x^2}{4} - 11$$

$$25 = \frac{x^2}{4}$$

$$100 = x^2$$

$$\pm 10 = x$$

Negative 10 is not one of the answer choices, so (B) is correct.

15. C   Difficulty: Medium

Category: Passport to Advanced Math / Functions

Getting to the Answer: Piecewise functions look intimidating, but they are usually very simple functions—they're just written in pieces. The right-hand side of each piece of the function tells you what part of the domain (which x-values) goes with that particular expression. In this function, only values of x that are less than or equal to 0 go with the top expression, values of x greater than 0 and less than or equal to 3 go with the middle expression, and values of x that are greater than 3 go with the bottom expression. Because −3 is less than 0, plug it into the top expression and simplify:

$$f(-3) = (-3)^2 + 1$$

$$= 9 + 1$$

$$= 10$$

This matches (C).

16. C   Difficulty: Medium

Category: Passport to Advanced Math / Functions

Getting to the Answer: Graphically, the notation f(−2) means the y-value when x is −2. Pay careful attention to which graph is which. It may help to draw dots on the graph. Find x = −2 along the horizontal axis, trace up to the graph of f(x), and draw a dot on the graph. Do the same for g(2), as shown here:

Now, read the y-coordinates from the graph and subtract: f(−2) is 6 and g(2) is −3, so f(−2) + g(2) = 6 + (−3) = 3, which is (C).

17. D   Difficulty: Hard

Category: Passport to Advanced Math / Functions

Getting to the Answer: When working with a composition, the range of the inner function becomes the domain of the outer function, which in turn produces the range of the composition. In the composition $f(g(x))$, the function $g(x) = \dfrac{x^2}{2}$ is the inner function. Every value of x, when substituted into this function, will result in a nonnegative value (because the result of squaring a number is always a positive number). This means the smallest possible range value of $g(x)$ is 0. Now look at $f(x)$. Substituting large positive values of x in the function will result in large negative numbers. Consequently, substituting the smallest value from the range of g, which is 0, results in the largest range value for the composition, which is $3 - 0 = 3$. Because $4 > 3$, it is not in the range of $f(g(x))$. Therefore, (D) is correct.

18. D   Difficulty: Hard

Category: Passport to Advanced Math / Functions

Getting to the Answer: Graphing piecewise functions can be tricky. Try describing the graph in words first, and then find the matching function. Use words such as "to the left of" (which translates as *less than*) and "to the right of" (which translates as *greater than*).

First notice that there is a hole in the graph at $x = 4$. This means you can eliminate A right away because the inequality symbol in the top piece would include the endpoint at 4. To choose between the remaining answers, think about parent functions and transformations. To the left of $x = 4$, the graph is an absolute value function that has been reflected vertically across the x-axis and then shifted up one unit. This means either C or (D) must be correct. Now look to the right of $x = 4$: The graph is a horizontal line, which means a line that has a slope of 0. The slope of the line in C is negative 3, so it can't be correct. This means (D) is correct. (The equation of a horizontal line always looks like $y = b$, or in this case, $g(x) = -3$.)

CHAPTER 10

PRACTICE

8. D   Difficulty: Hard
Category: Passport to Advanced Math / Quadratics

Getting to the Answer: Find the maximum height of the potato, then find the time it takes the potato to hit the ground. The x-coordinate of the vertex is given by $h = \dfrac{-b}{2a} = \dfrac{-224}{2(-16)} = 7$. Plug this into the function to get the y-coordinate: $f(7) = -16(7)^2 + 224(7) + 240 = 1{,}024$. Next, calculate how long it takes for the potato to hit the ground. This will occur when $f(t) = 0$. Plug in and factor to solve:

$$-16t^2 + 224t + 240 = 0$$
$$-16\left(t^2 - 14t - 15\right) = 0$$
$$t^2 - 14t - 15 = 0$$
$$(t - 15)(t + 1) = 0$$
$$t = 15 \text{ or } t = -1$$

Because time can't be negative, $t = 15$. Don't forget that you were asked for the sum of the height and the time, not for either of the raw values. The sum of 15 and 1,024 is 1,039, choice (D).

9. B   Difficulty: Medium
Category: Passport to Advanced Math / Quadratics

Getting to the Answer: If $ab > 0$, then a and b are either both positive or both negative. In the second inequality, $b^2ac < 0$, you can ignore the b^2 term because it will be positive regardless of the sign of b. This implies that either a or c is positive, and the other is negative. The x-intercepts are b and c. Because b has the same sign as a, while c has the opposite sign as a, it follows that b and c have opposite signs. The correct answer must therefore be a function with one negative root and one positive root. Scan the functions to find the correct one. Ignore the complicated-looking numbers—all that matter are the signs! Choice (B) is correct.

PERFORM

10. A   Difficulty: Hard
Category: Passport to Advanced Math / Quadratics

Getting to the Answer: Technically, this isn't a quadratic equation because the highest power on the variable isn't 2. However, it is a "quadratic-type" equation because the square of the variable part of the middle term is equal to the variable in the leading term. This means you can use factoring techniques you learned for quadratics to answer this question as well. The presence of 4, 9, and 16—all perfect squares—is a big clue. Observe that $4x - 12\sqrt{x} + 9$ is an instance of the quadratic shortcut $(a - b)^2 = a^2 - 2ab + b^2$. Use the shortcut to factor the equation and see where that leads you.

$$4x - 12\sqrt{x} + 9 = 16$$
$$(2\sqrt{x} - 3)^2 = 16$$
$$2\sqrt{x} - 3 = \pm 4$$

Now go back to what you're looking for: $10\sqrt{x} - 15$ is 5 times the quantity on the left side of the last equation above, so multiply the positive result, 4, by 5 to get 20. The correct answer is (A).

11. B   Difficulty: Medium
Category: Passport to Advanced Math / Quadratics

Getting to the Answer: Neither of the functions is presented in standard form, so make this question a little easier by simplifying each one before setting them equal to each other.

$$f(x) = 3(x - 4)^2 + 4 = 3(x^2 - 8x + 16) + 4$$
$$= 3x^2 - 24x + 48 + 4$$
$$= 3x^2 - 24x + 52$$

$$g(x) = (x + 5)^2 + 2x - 135$$
$$= x^2 + 10x + 25 + 2x - 135$$
$$= x^2 + 12x - 110$$

$$f(x) = g(x)$$
$$3x^2 - 24x + 52 = x^2 + 12x - 110$$
$$2x^2 - 36x + 162 = 0$$
$$2(x^2 - 18x + 81) = 0$$
$$x^2 - 18x + 81 = 0$$

Notice that you can now use a quadratic shortcut:

$$x^2 - 18x + 81 = 0$$
$$(x - 9)^2 = 0$$
$$x = 9$$

Note that the question asks how many intersection points there are, *not* what the points are. Since there is only one solution for *x*, there must be only one point of intersection, which is (B). Don't waste time plugging 9 back in.

12. 2   Difficulty: Medium
Category: Passport to Advanced Math / Quadratics

Getting to the Answer: An *x*-intercept of a function is a point at which the *y*-coordinate equals 0. Set the equation equal to zero, simplify, and factor.

$$g(x) = -2.5x^2 + 10x - 7.5$$
$$0 = -2.5x^2 + 10x - 7.5$$
$$0 = -2.5(x^2 - 4x + 3)$$
$$0 = x^2 - 4x + 3$$
$$0 = (x - 1)(x - 3)$$
$$x = 1 \text{ or } x = 3$$

Recall that the question asks for the *difference* between the *x*-intercepts, not for the *x*-intercepts themselves. The difference between 3 and 1 is 2.

13. C   Difficulty: Medium
Category: Passport to Advanced Math / Quadratics

Getting to the Answer: An axis of symmetry splits a parabola in half and travels through the vertex. You have a formula to find *h* instantly. All you have to do is plug and chug to get your answer—just be careful with the fractions and the negatives.

$$x = -\frac{b}{2a}$$
$$= -17 \div 2\left(\frac{-11}{3}\right)$$
$$= -17 \div \frac{-22}{3}$$
$$= -17 \times \frac{-3}{22}$$
$$= \frac{51}{22}$$

The correct answer is (C).

EXTRA PRACTICE

1. B   Difficulty: Easy
Category: Passport to Advanced Math / Quadratics

Getting to the Answer: Using the first equation, set each of the factors equal to 0 and solve for *x* to find that the *x*-intercepts are $-\frac{1}{2}$ and 5. This means you can eliminate A and D. From the standard form of the equation, you can see that the *y*-intercept is −5 (the value of *c*) because $0^2 - 3(0) - 5 = -5$, so (B) is correct.

2. A   Difficulty: Medium
Category: Passport to Advanced Math / Quadratics

Getting to the Answer: The answer choices all look very similar, so think logically to eliminate a couple. A rocket goes *up*, hits a maximum height, and then comes *down*. This tells you that the graph will be an upside-down parabola, which means the equation should have a negative sign in front. Eliminate C and D. To choose between (A) and B, you need to recall what the *vertex form* of a quadratic looks like and what it tells you. When a quadratic equation is written in the form $y = a(x - h)^2 + k$, the vertex of the graph is (*h*, *k*). The *h* tells you *where* the maximum (or minimum) occurs, and the *k* tells you *what* the maximum (or minimum) value is. Here, the maximum height of 34 feet occurs at 3 seconds, so *k* is 34 and *h* is 3. Substitute these values into vertex form to find that the correct equation is $y = -16(x - 3)^2 + 34$. Translate this to function language (*h*(*t*) = *y* and *t* = *x*) to arrive at the answer: $h(t) = -16(t - 3)^2 + 34$, which is (A).

3. A   Difficulty: Medium
Category: Passport to Advanced Math / Quadratics

Getting to the Answer: When finding solutions to a quadratic equation, always start by rewriting the equation to make it equal 0 (unless both sides of the equation are already perfect squares). To make the equation equal 0, subtract 30 from both sides to get $x^2 - 7x - 30 = 0$. The answer choices are all integers, so factor the equation. Look for two numbers whose product is −30 and whose sum is −7. The two numbers are −10 and 3, so the factors are (x − 10) and (x + 3). Set each factor equal to 0 and solve to find that x = 10 and x = −3. The question states that x > 0, so x must equal 10. Before selecting an answer, don't forget to check that you answered the right question—the

Answers & Explanations

question asks for the value of $x - 5$, not just x, so the correct answer is $10 - 5 = 5$, which means (A) is correct.

4. C Difficulty: Medium

Category: Passport to Advanced Math / Quadratics

Getting to the Answer: Understanding that in algebra "divides evenly" means "is a factor" is the key to answering this question. You could use polynomial long division, but in most cases, factoring is quicker. The leading coefficient of the equation is not 1, so you'll need to use the *AC method* and grouping to factor the equation. Multiply *a* times *c* (6×-20) and then look for two factors of that product whose sum is equal to the coefficient of the middle term. Break the middle term ($7x$) into two terms using the numbers you found, and then factor by grouping. The product is -120 and the two factors of -120 that add up to 7 are 15 and -8.

$$\begin{aligned} 6x^2 + 7x - 20 &= 6x^2 + 15x - 8x - 20 \\ &= (6x^2 + 15x) - (8x + 20) \\ &= 3x(2x + 5) - 4(2x + 5) \\ &= (2x + 5)(3x - 4) \end{aligned}$$

So, $3x - 4$ divides evenly into the expression, making (C) correct.

5. A Difficulty: Medium

Category: Passport to Advanced Math / Quadratics

Getting to the Answer: Even though one of the equations in this system isn't linear, you can still solve the system using substitution. You already know that y is equal to $2x$, so substitute $2x$ for y in the second equation. Don't forget that when you square $2x$, you must square both the coefficient and the variable. Also, be careful—there are a lot of 2s floating around, so pay careful attention as you plug in values.

$$2x^2 + 2y^2 = 240$$
$$x^2 + y^2 = 120$$

$$x^2 + (2x)^2 = 120$$
$$x^2 + 4x^2 = 120$$
$$5x^2 = 120$$
$$x^2 = 24$$

The question asks for the value of x^2, not x, so there is no need to take the square root of 24 to find the value of x. Choice (A) is correct.

6. B Difficulty: Hard

Category: Passport to Advanced Math / Quadratics

Getting to the Answer: The maximum value shown in the graph is about 56 or 57 feet. When a quadratic equation is written in vertex form, $y = a(x - h)^2 + k$, the maximum value is given by k, so check C and D first because they will be the easiest to compare to the graph. In C, k is 48, which is not greater than 56 or 57 and therefore not correct. In D, k is 52, which is also not greater than 56 or 57. This means either A or (B) must be correct. You now have two options—you could expand the equation in each answer choice and then complete the square to find the vertex, or you could expand the equations, find the x-coordinate of the vertex using the formula $x = \dfrac{-b}{2a}$, and then plug in the result to find the y-value. Completing the square usually takes a bit of time, so the second option is probably the quicker route to take. Expanding A, you get $h = -16t^2 + 48t$ with $a = -16$ and $b = 48$. The x-coordinate of the vertex is $\dfrac{-48}{2(-16)} = \dfrac{-48}{-32} = 1.5$. Substituting this back into the equation, the y-value of the vertex (which is the maximum value of the function) is $-16(1.5)^2 + 48(1.5) = 36$, which is not greater than 56 or 57, so (B) must be correct. Don't waste valuable time checking, but if you use the same strategy, you'll find that the maximum height of the equation in (B) is 81 feet.

7. 5 Difficulty: Medium

Category: Passport to Advanced Math / Quadratics

Getting to the Answer: Before you plug -5 in for x, which creates messy numbers, factor the given equation.

$$x^2 + 2xk + k^2 = 0$$
$$(x + k)(x + k) = 0$$
$$(x + k)^2 = 0$$

Now plug in -5 for x and solve for k:

$$(-5 + k)^2 = 0$$
$$\sqrt[2]{(-5 + k)^2} = \pm\sqrt{0}$$
$$-5 + k = 0$$
$$k = 5$$

8. 6.5 or **13/2**   **Difficulty:** Hard

Category: Passport to Advanced Math / Quadratics

Getting to the Answer: This is a tough question with no real shortcuts. The highest power of x in the equation is 2, so the equation is quadratic. Writing quadratic equations can be tricky and time-consuming. If you know the roots, you can use factors to write the equation. You don't know the roots of this equation, so start with the point that has the nicest values (0, 2) and substitute them into the equation, $y = ax^2 + bx + c$.

$$2 = a(0)^2 + b(0) + c$$
$$2 = c$$

Now your equation looks like $y = ax^2 + bx + 2$. Next, use the other two points to create a system of two equations in two variables.

$$(-2, -10) \rightarrow -10 = a(-2)^2 + b(-2) + 2 \rightarrow -12 = 4a - 2b$$

$$(4, 14) \rightarrow 14 = a(4)^2 + b(4) + 2 \rightarrow 12 = 16a + 4b$$

You now have a system of equations to solve. None of the variables has a coefficient of 1, so use combination to solve the system. If you multiply the top equation by 2, the b terms will eliminate each other.

$$2[4a - 2b = -12] \rightarrow 8a - 4b = -24$$
$$16a + 4b = 12 \rightarrow \underline{16a + 4b = 12}$$
$$24a = -12$$
$$a = -\frac{1}{2}$$

Now, find b by substituting the value of a into either of the original equations. Using the bottom equation, you get this:

$$16\left(-\frac{1}{2}\right) + 4b = 12$$
$$-8 + 4b = 12$$
$$4b = 20$$
$$b = 5$$

The value of $a + b + c = -\frac{1}{2} + 5 + 2 = 6\frac{1}{2}$. You can't enter a mixed number, so grid in your answer as the decimal number 6.5 or the improper fraction 13/2.

9. B   Difficulty: Easy

Category: Passport to Advanced Math / Quadratics

Getting to the Answer: To multiply two binomials, distribute each term in the first set of parentheses to each term in the second set. You can also think FOIL. Multiply $2a$ by each term in the second factor and then multiply $5b$ by each term. Combine like terms if possible.

$$(2a + 5b)(a - 3b)$$
$$= 2a(a - 3b) + 5b(a - 3b)$$
$$= 2a(a) + 2a(-3b) + 5b(a) + 5b(-3b)$$
$$= 2a^2 - 6ab + 5ab - 15b^2$$
$$= 2a^2 - ab - 15b^2$$

Choice (B) is correct.

10. A   Difficulty: Easy

Category: Passport to Advanced Math / Quadratics

Getting to the Answer: *Roots* are the same as *solutions* to an equation, so you need to solve the equation for x. Taking the square root of a quantity is the inverse operation of squaring it, and both sides of this equation are already perfect squares, so take their square roots. Then solve the resulting equations. Remember, there will be two equations to solve.

$$(x + 3)^2 = 49$$
$$\sqrt[2]{(x + 3)^2} = \pm\sqrt{49}$$
$$x + 3 = \pm 7$$

Now simplify each equation: $x + 3 = -7$, or $x = -10$; and $x + 3 = 7$, or $x = 4$, so (A) is correct.

If you didn't recognize that you could use square rooting to solve the equation, you could also expand the left side, then subtract 49, factor the resulting equation, and set the factors equal to 0. This is a perfectly fine way to solve the equation, but it takes considerably longer.

11. C   Difficulty: Easy

Category: Passport to Advanced Math / Quadratics

Getting to the Answer: Being able to make connections between equations and graphs is a valuable skill. The pieces of a quadratic equation written in standard form give you lots of information about its graph. For example, finding the value of $\frac{-b}{2a}$ (the quadratic formula without

Answers & Explanations

the radical part) tells you where the axis of symmetry occurs.

This question is asking about c, which is the only constant term in the equation. If you substitute 0 for x, the equation becomes $y = a(0)^2 + b(0) + c$, or just $y = c$. This means the point $(0, c)$ will be on the graph, which is the y-intercept, making (C) correct.

12. D   Difficulty: Easy
Category: Passport to Advanced Math / Quadratics

Getting to the Answer: The graph is a parabola, so you can eliminate A right way (the equation is linear, not quadratic). The x-intercepts of the graph are −2 and 5, so the factors of this quadratic must be $(x + 2)$ and $(x − 5)$. The parabola opens downward, so there should be a negative sign in front of the factors. The correct equation is $y = -(x + 2)(x − 5)$. Don't let C fool you—those factors would produce x-intercepts of +2 and −5. If you're not convinced, set each factor equal to 0 and solve for x. Therefore, (D) is correct.

13. C   Difficulty: Medium
Category: Passport to Advanced Math / Quadratics

Getting to the Answer: Equations that are equivalent have the same solutions, so you are looking for the equation that is simply written in a different form. You could expand each of the equations in the answer choices, but unless you get lucky, this will use up quite a bit of time. The answer choices are written in vertex form, so use the method of completing the square to convert the equation in the question to the same form. First, write the equation in standard form: $y = x^2 + 6x − 40$. Move the 40 to the other side to temporarily get it out of the way. Then, complete the square on the right-hand side, by finding $\left(\frac{b}{2}\right)^2 = \left(\frac{6}{2}\right)^2 = 3^2 = 9$, and adding the result to both sides of the equation.

$$y = x^2 + 6x − 40$$
$$y + 40 = x^2 + 6x$$
$$y + 40 + 9 = x^2 + 6x + 9$$
$$y + 49 = x^2 + 6x + 9$$

Next, factor the right-hand side of the equation (which should be a perfect square trinomial) and rewrite it as a square.

$$y + 49 = (x + 3)(x + 3)$$
$$y + 49 = (x + 3)^2$$

Finally, solve for y to get $y = (x + 3)^2 − 49$, which makes (C) correct.

14. B   Difficulty: Medium
Category: Passport to Advanced Math / Quadratics

Getting to the Answer: Quadratic equations can be written in several different forms, each of which reveals something special about the graph. For example, the vertex form of a quadratic equation ($y = a(x − h)^2 + k$) gives the minimum or maximum value of the function (it's k), while the standard form ($y = ax^2 + bx + c$) reveals the y-intercept (it's c). The factored form of a quadratic equation reveals the solutions to the equation, which graphically represent the x-intercepts. Choice (B) is the only equation written in factored form and therefore must be correct. You can set each factor equal to 0 and quickly solve to find that the x-intercepts of the graph are $x = -\frac{3}{4}$ and $x = 1$, which agree with the graph.

15. A   Difficulty: Hard
Category: Passport to Advanced Math / Quadratics

Getting to the Answer: To answer this question, you need to recall just about everything you've learned about quadratic graphs. Be careful—the equation looks like vertex form, $y = a(x − h)^2 + k$, but it's not quite there because of the 2 inside the parentheses. You could rewrite the equation in vertex form, but this would involve squaring the quantity in parentheses and then completing the square, which will take quite a bit of time. So, skip A for now and compare each of the other answer choices to the equation. Don't forget, you are looking for the statement that is *not* true.

Choice B: Substitute 0 for x and simplify to find that the y-intercept is indeed $(0, −9)$.

Choice C: There is a negative in front of the equation, so the parabola *does* open downward.

Choice D: Look at the equation as a transformation of the parent function $y = x^2$. The parabola has been shifted to the right, moved up 7 units, and flipped upside down. Picture this in your head—it has to cross the x-axis at least one time.

This means (A) must be correct. As it turns out, the vertex is (2, 7), not (4, 7).

16. C   **Difficulty:** Hard

Category: Passport to Advanced Math / Quadratics

Getting to the Answer: You are not expected to solve each system. Instead, think about it graphically. The solution to a system of equations is the point(s) where their graphs intersect, so graph each pair of equations in your graphing calculator and look for the ones that intersect at $x = 3.5$ and $x = 6$, both of which happen to be positive values and would lie to the right of the x-axis. The graphs of the equations in A and B don't intersect at all, so you can eliminate both answers right away. The graphs in (C) *do* intersect, and both points of intersection are to the right of the x-axis, so (C) could be correct, but check D just in case. The graphs don't intersect at all, so (C) is correct.

A note of caution here—just because the solutions were given as 3.5 and 6, that does *not* mean that either number has to appear in one or both of the equations.

17. 0   **Difficulty:** Medium

Category: Passport to Advanced Math / Quadratics

Getting to the Answer: To find the roots of an equation, you need to set it equal to 0, factor it, and then solve. Whenever the leading coefficient is a fraction, factoring becomes very messy. Luckily, you can clear the fraction the same way you do when solving equations (multiply both sides of the equation by the denominator of the fraction).

$$0 = \frac{1}{3}x^2 - 2x + 3$$
$$3(0) = 3\left(\frac{1}{3}x^2 - 2x + 3\right)$$
$$0 = x^2 - 6x + 9$$
$$0 = (x - 3)(x - 3)$$

The equation only has one unique solution ($x = 3$), so the positive difference between the roots is actually 0.

18. 8   **Difficulty:** Easy

Category: Passport to Advanced Math / Quadratics

Getting to the Answer: Whenever you're given the equation for a function, you can evaluate it at any given value by substituting that value for the variable. The variable t

represents the number of seconds after the rockets were fired, so find $h_2(1)$ and $h_1(1)$ and subtract. (Note that the equations are provided in the graphic.) To make the calculations easier, simplify each equation first.

$$h_2(t) = -8t(2t - 7) = -16t^2 + 56t$$
$$h_2(1) = -16(1)^2 + 56(1) = -16 + 56 = 40$$
$$h_1(t) = -16t(t - 3) = -16t^2 + 48t$$
$$h_1(1) = -16(1)^2 + 48(1) = -16 + 48 = 32$$

So, after 1 second the second rocket was $40 - 32 = 8$ feet higher.

19. .25 or 1/4   **Difficulty:** Hard

Category: Passport to Advanced Math / Quadratics

Getting to the Answer: A quadratic function reaches its maximum (or minimum) value at its vertex. Don't do rework—you've already written each equation in standard form, so use the formula $x = \dfrac{-b}{2a}$ to find the x-coordinate of the vertex for each function.

$h_2(t)$: $a = -16$ and $b = 56$, so $x = \dfrac{-56}{2(-16)} = \dfrac{-56}{-32} = \dfrac{7}{4}$. This means the second rocket reaches its maximum height at 1.75 seconds.

$h_1(t)$: $a = -16$ and $b = 48$, so $x = \dfrac{-48}{2(-16)} = \dfrac{-48}{-32} = \dfrac{3}{2}$. This means the first rocket reaches its maximum height at 1.5 seconds.

So, it took the second rocket $1.75 - 1.5 = 0.25$ seconds longer to reach its maximum height.

If you are comfortable using your graphing calculator (which could save quite a bit of time), you could graph each equation and use the "maximum" function on the calculator.

20. 8   **Difficulty:** Medium

Category: Passport to Advanced Math / Quadratics

Getting to the Answer: This question is testing whether you can interpret an equation. If you look carefully, it tells you that the coefficient of the x term from each equation is all you need. Again, don't do rework—you've already written each equation in standard form.

The standard form of the equation for the second rocket is $h_2(t) = -16t^2 + 56t$, so the initial velocity was 56 feet per second. The standard form of the equation for the first rocket is $h_1(t) = -16t^2 + 48t$, so the initial velocity was 48 feet per second. The second rocket's initial velocity was $56 - 48 = 8$ more feet per second than the first rocket's.

CHAPTER 11

PRACTICE

7. C   **Difficulty:** Hard

Category: Additional Topics in Math / Geometry

Getting to the Answer: Look for hidden special right triangles to help you find the answer, and add new information to your diagram as you find it. Start by finding $m\angle ACD$ from the two given angles: $m\angle ACD = 180° - 15° - 30° = 135°$. Because $\angle ACB$ is supplementary to $\angle ACD$, $\angle ACB$ measures 45°. $\triangle ABC$ is a right triangle, so its missing angle ($\angle BAC$) is also 45°, making $\triangle ABC$ a 45-45-90 triangle. This means $\angle BAD$ is 60°; therefore, $\triangle ABD$ is a 30-60-90 triangle.

Knowing that you have two special right triangles will allow you to unlock the unknown side lengths. $\overline{AC}$ is the hypotenuse of the 45-45-90 triangle (side ratio of $x:x:x\sqrt{2}$), so $\overline{AB}$ and $\overline{BC}$ (the two legs) must be $2\sqrt{2}$ (solve the equation $4 = x\sqrt{2}$ to find this). $\overline{AB}$ is also the shorter leg of the 30-60-90 triangle (side ratio of $x:x\sqrt{3}:2x$), so $\overline{BD}$ (longer leg) is $2\sqrt{6}$, and $\overline{AD}$ (hypotenuse) is $4\sqrt{2}$. Don't stop just yet; remember which perimeter you need. Take the difference of $\overline{BD}$ and $\overline{BC}$ to determine $\overline{CD}$, which is $2\sqrt{6} - 2\sqrt{2}$. You now have all three sides of $\triangle ACD$, so add them together to get your answer:

$$P_{\triangle ACD} = 4 + \left(2\sqrt{6} - 2\sqrt{2}\right) + 4\sqrt{2}$$

This simplifies to $4 + 2\sqrt{6} + 2\sqrt{2}$, making (C) correct.

The completed diagram is shown here:

8. 426   **Difficulty:** Medium

Category: Additional Topics in Math / Geometry

Getting to the Answer: The figure contains a pair of similar triangles. Use the ratio within them to determine the requested length. The shadow cast by the flagpole is 50% longer than the flagpole itself; that is, $1.5 \times 40 = 60$ feet. Use this in conjunction with the lengths provided to determine the distance from the building to the end of the flagpole's shadow.

$$\frac{40}{324} = \frac{60}{x}$$
$$\frac{10}{81} = \frac{60}{x}$$
$$10x = 4{,}860$$
$$x = 486$$

Subtract the length of the flagpole's shadow, 60, from 486 to obtain 426, the distance from the building to the flagpole. Grid in 426.

9. B   **Difficulty:** Medium

Category: Additional Topics in Math / Geometry

Getting to the Answer: Start by drawing in $\overline{PR}$ and $\overline{PS}$ as shown here.

Because the angle formed by $\overline{PR}$ and $\overline{PS}$ subtends the same arc as the angle formed by $\overline{QR}$ and $\overline{QS}$, $\angle RPS$ must be twice $\angle RQS$, which is $45° \times 2 = 90°$. In addition to being legs of $\triangle PRS$, $\overline{PR}$ and $\overline{PS}$ are radii, so they are congruent, which makes $\triangle PRS$ a 45-45-90 triangle. Therefore, the radius of circle P is $\dfrac{4}{\sqrt{2}} = 2\sqrt{2}$, and the circumference is $2\pi \times 2\sqrt{2} = 4\pi\sqrt{2}$, which makes (B) correct.

10. B **Difficulty:** Hard

Category: Additional Topics in Math / Geometry

Getting to the Answer: Begin by finding the volume of one beach ball using the volume formula for a sphere, remembering to halve the diameter first:

$$V_{sphere} = \frac{4}{3}\pi r^3 = \frac{4}{3}\pi\left(\frac{66}{2}\right)^3 = 47{,}916\pi \text{ cm}^3$$

Convert to breaths using the relationships given:

$$47{,}916\pi \text{ cm}^3 \times \frac{1\,\text{L}}{1000\,\text{cm}^3} \times \frac{1\,\text{breath}}{6\,\text{L}} \approx 8\pi$$

This is about 25.09, or 25, full breaths. Multiply this by 3 to get 75 full breaths for three beach balls, which is (B).

PERFORM

11. A **Difficulty:** Medium

Category: Additional Topics in Math / Geometry

Getting to the Answer: Draw a diagram of Aundria and Annette's routes to the summit to visualize the situation. After drawing and labeling the diagram with the information given, look for a way to uncover a right triangle by drawing in additional lines. Once complete, use the rectangle you created to fill in the lengths of the new segments. The completed diagram is shown here:

Use the Pythagorean theorem to calculate the distance Annette will travel:

$$c^2 = (5 + 7)^2 + 4^2$$
$$c^2 = 144 + 16$$
$$c^2 = 160$$
$$c = \sqrt{160} = 4\sqrt{10}$$

But you're not done yet! The question asks you to find the total distance the two women will travel. Aundria travels $5 + 6 + 7 + 2 = 20$ miles; together, she and Annette will travel $20 + 4\sqrt{10}$ miles, which is approximately 32.65 miles. Choice (A) is correct.

12. B **Difficulty:** Medium

Category: Additional Topics in Math / Geometry

Getting to the Answer: Given the area of $\triangle ABC$ and the length of the base AB, you can find its height:

$$150 = \frac{1}{2}(20)(BC)$$
$$150 = 10(BC)$$
$$15 = BC$$

Because $\overline{BC} = 15$ and $\overline{AB} = 20$, $\triangle ABC$ is a 3-4-5 triangle with dimensions scaled up by a factor of 5, so the hypotenuse $(\overline{AC})$ must be $5 \times 5 = 25$. Next, turn your attention to the smaller triangle, $\triangle AGH$. You're told that the hypotenuse of this triangle, $\overline{AH}$, is 20. $\triangle ABC$ and $\triangle AGH$ are similar triangles (because they share an angle at vertex A and they each have a right angle), so their corresponding sides must be proportional.

$$\frac{AH}{AC} = \frac{HG}{CB}$$
$$\frac{20}{25} = \frac{HG}{15}$$
$$300 = 25HG$$
$$\overline{HG} = 12$$

Choice (B) is the correct answer.

13. B **Difficulty:** Medium

Category: Additional Topics in Math / Geometry

Getting to the Answer: Read carefully; you're asked for information on the portion that is *not* strawberry rhubarb. The diagram includes the measures of central angles, and you're told that the pie tin has a diameter of 10 inches (which means the radius is 5 inches and the area is 25π square inches). Therefore, you can set up a proportion to determine the area of non–strawberry rhubarb pie (which represents 129.6° out of a full 360° circle):

$$\frac{\text{central angle}}{360°} = \frac{\text{sector area}}{\text{circle area}}$$

$$\frac{360 - 129.6}{360} = \frac{x}{25\pi}$$

$$5{,}760\pi = 360x$$

$$x = 16\pi$$

The portion of leftover pie that is not strawberry rhubarb is 16π square inches, which makes (B) correct.

14. B   Difficulty: Medium

Category: Additional Topics in Math / Geometry

Getting to the Answer: Adding 96 cubic feet of sand will completely fill the sandbox that starts one-third full, so 96 cubic feet is two-thirds of the total volume. Thus, one-third is $\frac{96}{2} = 48$ cubic feet, and the total volume is $3 \times 48 = 144$ cubic feet. The sandbox described is a rectangular solid, so the volume can be found using the formula $V = lwh$. Because the base of the sandbox is a square, you know the length and width are both 24. With the total volume in hand, you can find the depth (or height) of the sandbox: $144 = 24 \times 24 \times h$, which simplifies to $h = 0.25$. A height of 0.25 feet is the same as 3 inches, so (B) is correct.

EXTRA PRACTICE

1. A   Difficulty: Medium

Category: Additional Topics in Math / Geometry

Getting to the Answer: Start by connecting the ranch to the campsite. Then draw in a horizontal line and a vertical line to form a right triangle.

The length of one leg of the triangle is 15 miles, the distance from the watering hole to the barn. The length of the other leg is $6 + 2 = 8$ miles, the distance from the ranch to the watering hole and then from the barn to the campsite. The two legs of the right triangle are 8 and 15. You might recognize the Pythagorean triplet, 8, 15, 17, but if you don't, you can always rely on the Pythagorean theorem:

$$8^2 + 15^2 = c^2$$

$$64 + 225 = c^2$$

$$289 = c^2$$

$$\sqrt{289} = \sqrt{c^2}$$

$$17 = c$$

The actual trail is $6 + 15 + 2 = 23$ miles long. The direct route is 17 miles, so the direct route is $23 - 17 = 6$ miles shorter, making (A) the correct answer.

2. B   Difficulty: Medium

Category: Additional Topics in Math / Geometry

Getting to the Answer: You are told that $\overline{HI}$ is the bisector of $\overline{LO}$ and $\overline{OW}$. This tells you two things: 1) The definition of *bisector* tells you that that $\overline{HI}$ divides both $\overline{LO}$ and $\overline{OW}$ exactly in half, and 2) a straight line connecting the midpoints of two sides of a triangle is parallel to the third side, so $\overline{HI}$ is parallel to $\overline{LW}$.

Because $\overline{HI}$ is parallel to $\overline{LW}$, angles L and H must be congruent (they are corresponding angles), and angles W and I must be congruent (they are also corresponding angles). Angle O is shared by both triangles and is equal to itself by the Reflexive Property. This means the side lengths of the two triangles are different, but the corresponding angles are the same, so the triangles are similar. Side lengths of similar triangles are in proportion to one another. You are given the side lengths of $\overline{LW}$ and $\overline{HI}$. Because I is the midpoint of $\overline{OW}$, $\overline{OI}$ is half as long as $\overline{OW}$. The same is true for the other side. So the sides are in the ratio 1:2. Use this ratio to set up a proportion and solve for x:

$$\frac{1}{2} = \frac{4x - 1}{30}$$

$$30 = 2(4x - 1)$$

$$30 = 8x - 2$$

$$32 = 8x$$

$$4 = x$$

The correct answer is (B).

3. A   **Difficulty:** Medium

Category: Additional Topics in Math / Geometry

Getting to the Answer: Distance around *part* of a circle is the same as arc length, so use the relationship $\frac{\text{arc length}}{\text{circumference}} = \frac{\text{central angle}}{360°}$ to answer the question. The unknown in the relationship is the central angle, so call it a. Before you can fill in the rest of the equation, you need to find the circumference of the circle: $C = 2\pi r = 2\pi(120) = 240\pi$. Now you're ready to solve for a:

$$\frac{\text{arc length}}{\text{circumference}} = \frac{\text{central angle}}{360°}$$

$$\frac{200}{240\pi} = \frac{a}{360}$$

$$\frac{200(360)}{240\pi} = a$$

$$95.5 \approx a$$

Be careful when you enter this expression into your calculator—you need to put 240π in parentheses so that the calculator doesn't divide by 240 and then multiply by π. If entered correctly, the result is about 95.5 degrees, which matches (A).

4. C   **Difficulty:** Medium

Category: Additional Topics in Math / Geometry

Getting to the Answer: First, think logically: After it's poured into the larger glass, the volume of the water in the glass will still be the same as the volume when it was in the smaller glass. Find the volume of the water in the smaller glass. Then, substitute this volume into a second equation where the height is unknown and solve for h. The volume of a cylinder equals the area of its base times its height, or $V = \pi r^2 h$.

$$V = \pi r^2 h$$

$$V = \pi(1.5)^2(6)$$

$$V = \pi(2.25)(6)$$

$$V = 13.5\pi$$

$$13.5\pi = \pi(2)^2 h$$

$$13.5\pi = 4\pi h$$

$$3.375 = h$$

The water will reach 3.375 inches high in the bigger glass, which is (C).

5. B   **Difficulty:** Hard

Category: Additional Topics in Math / Geometry

Getting to the Answer: First, find the measure of the missing angle in the triangle: $180 - 105 - 45 = 30°$. Now, draw the height of the triangle up from B to a point, D, on $\overline{AC}$; this creates two right triangles.

Triangle ABD is a 45-45-90 triangle, so its side lengths are in the ratio $x:x:x\sqrt{2}$. Because $\overline{AB}$ is the hypotenuse, set up an equation using the ratio of the sides:

$$6 = x\sqrt{2}$$

$$\frac{6}{\sqrt{2}} = x$$

$$\frac{6}{\sqrt{2}}\left(\frac{\sqrt{2}}{\sqrt{2}}\right) = x$$

$$\frac{6\sqrt{2}}{2} = x$$

$$3\sqrt{2} = x$$

Triangle BDC is a 30-60-90 triangle, so its side lengths are in the ratio of $x:x\sqrt{3}:2x$. You just found the dimensions of the shorter leg, $3\sqrt{2}$, so multiply it by $\sqrt{3}$ to find the length of the longer leg ($\sqrt{3} \times 3\sqrt{2} = 3\sqrt{6}$). Now, find the length of AC, which is the base of the triangle, by adding $\overline{AD}$ to $\overline{DC}$. The result is $3\sqrt{2} + 3\sqrt{6}$. Finally, use the area formula, $A = \frac{1}{2}bh$, to find the area of the whole triangle:

$$A = \frac{1}{2}\left(3\sqrt{2} + 3\sqrt{6}\right)\left(3\sqrt{2}\right)$$
$$= \frac{1}{2}\left(18 + 9\sqrt{12}\right)$$
$$= \frac{1}{2}\left(18 + 9 \cdot 2\sqrt{3}\right)$$
$$= \frac{1}{2}\left(18 + 18\sqrt{3}\right)$$
$$= 9 + 9\sqrt{3}$$

Choice (B) is correct.

6. B   Difficulty: Hard

Category: Additional Topics in Math / Geometry

Getting to the Answer: When the equation of a circle is in the form $(x - h)^2 + (y - k)^2 = r^2$, the r represents the length of the radius. To get the equation into this form, complete the square. Then you can double r to find the diameter.

You already have an x^2 and a y^2 in the given equation and the coefficients of x and y are even, so completing the square is fairly straightforward—there are just a lot of steps. Start by grouping the x's and y's together. Then, take the coefficient of the x term and divide it by 2, square it, and add it to the two terms with x variables. Do the same with the y term. Don't forget to add these amounts to the other side of the equation as well. This creates a perfect square of x terms and y terms, so take the square root of each.

$$x^2 + y^2 + 8x - 20y = 28$$
$$x^2 + 8x + y^2 - 20y = 28$$
$$(x^2 + 8x + 16) + (y^2 - 20y + 100) = 28 + 16 + 100$$
$$(x + 4)^2 + (y - 10)^2 = 144$$

The equation tells you that r^2 is 144, which means that the radius is 12 and the diameter is twice that, or 24, which is (B).

7. C   Difficulty: Hard

Category: Additional Topics in Math / Geometry

Getting to the Answer: Don't be too quick to answer a question like this. You can't simply find three-fourths of

the volume of the cone because the top is considerably smaller than the bottom. Instead, you'll need to find the volume of the whole cone and subtract the volume of the top piece that is being discarded.

The figure shows a right triangle inside the cone. The height of the cone is the longer leg of the triangle, 16. The hypotenuse is given as 20. You might recognize this as a multiple of a Pythagorean triplet, 3-4-5, or in this case, 12-16-20. This means the radius of the original cone is 12. Substitute this into the formula for volume:

$$V = \frac{1}{3}\pi r^2 h$$
$$V = \frac{1}{3}\pi(12)^2(16)$$
$$V = 768\pi$$

To determine the dimensions of the top piece, use similar triangles.

One quarter of the height is $16 \div 4 = 4$, resulting in a 3-4-5 triangle, making the height 4 and the radius 3.

$$V = \frac{1}{3}\pi(3)^2(4) = 12\pi$$

Thus, the volume of the remaining solid is $768\pi - 12\pi$ $= 756\pi$, which is (C).

8. 9   Difficulty: Hard

Category: Additional Topics in Math / Geometry

Getting to the Answer: Corresponding sides of similar triangles are proportional. Draw a quick sketch to find as many side lengths as you can, find the ratio of the sides between the two triangles, and use that ratio to find the missing vertex.

Plot all the points given in the question, labeling them as you go so you don't get confused (especially because you won't have graph paper). You know that A and B are in the same quadrant, which means the triangles are both oriented the same way. So make your sketch accordingly.

Once you have plotted *ANT* and the base of *BUG*, you can determine that the ratio of the triangles is 1:4 (the base of *ANT* has a length of 4 and the base of *BUG* has a length of 16). To determine where you should put *B*, find the length of side *AN* and then multiply by 4. The length of the vertical side of *BUG* is 12. Because one vertex is at (8, −3), vertex *B* must be 12 vertical units above that point, or (8, 9). The *y*-coordinate of *B* is 9.

9. C   Difficulty: Easy
Category: Additional Topics in Math / Geometry

Getting to the Answer: Line *L* forms a right triangle with the *x*- and *y*-axes, so one of the interior angles of the triangle has a measure of 90°. You know that $q = 140$, and together *p* and *q* form a straight line, which means they are supplementary angles. Thus, *p* must equal $180 - 140 = 40$. One of the interior angles of the triangle is vertical to *p*, so it also equals 40°. Now find the last angle measure inside the triangle by subtracting: $180° - 90° - 40° = 50°$. This angle is supplementary to *r*, so $r = 180 - 50 = 130$. This means that $r - p = 130 - 40 = 90$, making (C) the correct choice.

10. D   Difficulty: Easy
Category: Additional Topics in Math / Geometry

Getting to the Answer: If you're not sure how to start a question with a circle in it, look for the radius. The equation of circle takes the form $(x - h)^2 + (y - k)^2 = r^2$, where (h, k) is the center of the circle and *r* is the length of the radius.

To find the equation of a circle, you need the radius and the *x*- and *y*-coordinates of the center point. Look at the figure—the center has coordinates (−1, 2). From the center, you can count horizontally or vertically to the

edge of the circle to find that its radius is 6. This means the equation is $(x - (-1))^2 + (y - 2)^2 = 6^2$, or $(x + 1)^2 + (y - 2)^2 = 36$, which matches the equation in (D).

11. D   Difficulty: Medium
Category: Additional Topics in Math / Geometry

Getting to the Answer: The sides 3*d*, 5*d*, and *h* form a right triangle, so plug these values into the Pythagorean theorem and then solve for *h*. Be careful—when you square 3*d* and 5*d*, you must square the coefficient and the variable.

$$a^2 + b^2 = c^2$$
$$(3d)^2 + (5d)^2 = h^2$$
$$9d^2 + 25d^2 = h^2$$
$$34d^2 = h^2$$
$$\sqrt{34d^2} = h$$
$$d\sqrt{34} = h$$

Choice (D) is correct.

12. D   Difficulty: Medium
Category: Additional Topics in Math / Geometry

Getting to the Answer: You can eliminate B immediately because corresponding angles of similar triangles are congruent, so they are in a 1:1 ratio. You can also eliminate A, because $\overline{OD}$ would be proportional to $\overline{NW}$, not $\overline{EW}$. Evaluating C might get complicated, so skip it for now. Because the side lengths of the two triangles are proportional, when you find the sum of the side lengths (the perimeter), this number will be in the same proportion. You can check this by assigning numbers that are in the ratio 7:4 and finding the perimeter of each triangle:

$$OL = 7 \text{ and } NE = 4$$
$$LD = 14 \text{ and } EW = 8$$
$$OD = 21 \text{ and } NW = 12$$
$$\text{Perimeter}_{\triangle OLD} = 7 + 14 + 21 = 42$$
$$\text{Perimeter}_{\triangle NEW} = 4 + 8 + 12 = 24$$
$$42{:}24 = 7{:}4$$

This means (D) is correct.

13. A   **Difficulty:** Medium

Category: Additional Topics in Math / Geometry

Getting to the Answer: Use the relationship $\dfrac{\text{area of sector}}{\text{area of circle}} = \dfrac{\text{central angle}}{360°}$ to answer this question. To help remember this relationship, just think $\dfrac{\text{partial area}}{\text{whole area}} = \dfrac{\text{partial angle}}{\text{whole angle}}$.

The unknown in this question is the radius, which you can find by first finding the area of the whole circle and then by using the equation for area of a circle $A = \pi r^2$. You have everything you need to find the area of the circle:

$$\frac{\text{area of sector}}{\text{area of circle}} = \frac{\text{central angle}}{360°}$$

$$\frac{14\pi}{A} = \frac{140}{360}$$

$$5{,}040\pi = 140A$$

$$36\pi = A$$

Now, solve for r using $A = \pi r^2$:

$$36\pi = \pi r^2$$

$$36 = r^2$$

$$\pm 6 = r$$

The radius can't be negative, so the correct answer is 6, which is (A).

14. C   **Difficulty:** Medium

Category: Additional Topics in Math / Geometry

Getting to the Answer: The formula for finding the volume of a pyramid with a rectangular base is $V = \dfrac{1}{3}lwh$. Start by substituting what you know into the formula. You know the volume is represented by $x^3 - x$. You also know the length is $x + 1$ and the width is $3x$.

$$V = \frac{1}{3}lwh$$

$$x^3 - x = \frac{1}{3}(x + 1)(3x)h$$

Multiply both sides of the equation by 3 to clear the fraction, but don't multiply anything else just yet. First, look for a pattern.

$$3x^3 - 3x = (x + 1)(3x)h$$

Notice that if you divide both sides of the equation by the width, $3x$, you'll be left with $x^2 - 1$ on the left side and $(x + 1)$ times h on the right side. The difference of squares rule tells you that the factors of $x^2 - 1$ are $x + 1$ and $x - 1$. This means the height of the pyramid must be represented by $x - 1$. Therefore, (C) is correct.

15. B   **Difficulty:** Medium

Category: Additional Topics in Math / Geometry

Getting to the Answer: Solve this question one step at a time. The volume of sand in one tank (only two inches of the height) will be $V = 24 \times 9 \times 2 = 432$ cubic inches, which means the volume of sand in all 50 tanks will be $50 \times 432 = 21{,}600$ cubic inches. Each cubic inch of sand weighs about 2 ounces, so the weight of all the sand will be $2 \times 21{,}600 = 43{,}200$ ounces. There are 16 ounces in one pound, so the weight of the sand in pounds is $43{,}200 \div 16 = 2{,}700$. Finally, each bag contains 40 pounds of sand, so the pet store needs to buy $2{,}700 \div 40 = 67.5$, or about 68 bags of sand. This means (B) is the correct answer.

16. A   **Difficulty:** Medium

Category: Additional Topics in Math / Geometry

Getting to the Answer: Just like triangles, corresponding sides of similar quadrilaterals are proportional. This means the perimeters of similar quadrilaterals are also proportional and in the same proportion as each pair of corresponding side lengths.

Find the perimeter of rectangle *LION* and compare it to the perimeter of *PUMA*. *LION* has a perimeter of $86 + 86 + 52 + 52 = 276$. Therefore, the ratio of the perimeter of *LION* to the perimeter of *PUMA* is 276 : 69, which reduces to 4 : 1. This tells you that the width of *LION* is 4 times greater than the width of *PUMA*, which means *PUMA*'s width is $52 \div 4 = 13$ units, making (A) correct.

17. C   **Difficulty:** Medium

Category: Additional Topics in Math / Geometry

Getting to the Answer: Because the ratio of the shaded area to the unshaded area is 4 : 5, the ratio of the shaded area to the entire circle is 4 : (4 + 5) = 4 : 9. This ratio is the same as the ratio of the interior angle of the shaded sector to 360°, or x : 360. Set up a proportion using these ratios:

Answers & Explanations

$$\frac{4}{9} = \frac{x}{360}$$
$$360(4) = 9x$$
$$1{,}440 = 9x$$
$$160 = x$$

Choice (C) is correct.

18. D   Difficulty: Hard

Category: Additional Topics in Math / Geometry

Getting to the Answer: In a right triangle, one leg is the base and the other is the height. Use x and $x + 3$ to represent the lengths of these two legs (because the question states that one leg is 3 inches longer than the other). Use the area formula and set the equation equal to the given area:

$$35 = \frac{1}{2}(x)(x + 3)$$
$$2(35) = 2\left[\frac{1}{2}(x)(x + 3)\right]$$
$$70 = (x)(x + 3)$$
$$70 = x^2 + 3x$$

Now, subtract 70 to make the equation equal 0 and then factor it. The factors are $(x + 10)$ and $(x - 7)$, which means $x = -10$ and $x = 7$. Lengths cannot be negative, so the shorter leg must have a length of 7. This means the longer leg has a length of $7 + 3 = 10$. Now use the Pythagorean theorem to find the length of the hypotenuse.

$$a^2 + b^2 = c^2$$
$$7^2 + 10^2 = c^2$$
$$49 + 100 = c^2$$
$$149 = c^2$$
$$\sqrt{149} = \sqrt{c^2}$$
$$\sqrt{149} = c$$

Choice (D) is correct.

19. B   Difficulty: Hard

Category: Additional Topics in Math / Geometry

Getting to the Answer: There are two triangles in this figure, ACE and BCD. Because $\overline{BD}$ is parallel to $\overline{AE}$, angles A and B must be congruent (they are corresponding angles), and angles D and E must be congruent (they are also corresponding angles). Angle C is shared by both

triangles and is equal to itself by the Reflexive Property. This means the side lengths of the two triangles are different, but the angles are the same, so the triangles are similar by AAA. Side lengths of similar triangles are in proportion to one another.

You know the two triangles are similar, so set up a proportion using their side lengths. You'll need to translate from English into math as you go: $AB = 5$ and BC is three times that or 15. This means $AC = 5 + 15 = 20$. CD is 2 more than half AC or $20 \div 2 = 10 + 2 = 12$. Now you know three side lengths, so you can set up and solve a proportion:

$$\frac{BC}{AC} = \frac{DC}{EC}$$
$$\frac{15}{20} = \frac{12}{EC}$$
$$15EC = 240$$
$$EC = 16$$

This is the length of side EC, but the question asks for the length of segment DE, which is $EC - CD$, or $16 - 12 = 4$. This makes (B) the correct choice.

20. B   Difficulty: Hard

Category: Additional Topics in Math / Geometry

Getting to the Answer: Find the volume of the container using the formula for volume of a cylinder, $V = \pi r^2 h$. The question gives you the width, or the diameter of the container, so divide by 2 to get the radius.

$$V = \pi(1.25)^2(4)$$
$$V = \pi(1.5625)(4)$$
$$V = 6.25\pi$$

The factory only fills the cup 80% of the way up, so multiply the container volume by 0.8 to find that the actual volume of the yogurt is $6.25\pi \times 0.8 = 5\pi$, or about 15.708 cubic inches. Divide this by 6 ounces to determine that 1 ounce takes up approximately 2.6 cubic inches of space, which matches (B).

CHAPTER 12

PRACTICE

8. B   **Difficulty:** Hard

Category: Additional Topics in Math / Imaginary Numbers

Getting to the Answer: Substitute $38 + 18j$ for E and $4 + 6j$ for Z. Then rearrange the equation so that I is isolated. Multiply the numerator and denominator by the latter's conjugate and then use FOIL. Combine like terms and reduce fractions as needed. The steps for this sequence are shown below.

$$E = I \times z$$

$$I = \frac{E}{z} = \frac{38 + 18j}{4 + 6j}$$

$$= \frac{38 + 18j}{4 + 6j} \times \frac{4 - 6j}{4 - 6j}$$

$$= \frac{(38 \times 4) + (38 \times -6j) + (18j \times 4) + (18j \times -6j)}{16 - 36j^2}$$

$$= \frac{152 - 228j + 72j - 108j^2}{16 - (-36)}$$

$$= \frac{152 - 156j - (-108)}{52}$$

$$= \frac{260 - 156j}{52}$$

$$= \frac{260}{52} - \frac{156}{52}j$$

$$= 5 - 3j$$

Choice (B) is the correct answer.

9. B   **Difficulty:** Easy

Category: Additional Topics in Math / Trigonometry

Getting to the Answer: Recall that the sum of the acute angles in a right triangle is $180° - 90° = 90°$. Convert this to radians to find the measure of the missing angle. The sum of the acute angles, in radians, is $90° \times \frac{\pi}{180°} = \frac{90\pi}{180} = \frac{\pi}{2}$. Subtract the known angle to find the other angle: $\frac{\pi}{2} - \frac{\pi}{3} = \frac{3\pi}{6} - \frac{2\pi}{6} = \frac{\pi}{6}$. This matches (B).

PERFORM

10. 2338   **Difficulty:** Easy

Category: Additional Topics in Math / Imaginary Numbers

Getting to the Answer: Set your TI-83/84 to $a + bi$ mode (or the equivalent if you have a different calculator) and then compute $(11 + 14i)^3$. The result is $-5{,}137 + 2{,}338i$. The question asks for b, the coefficient of the imaginary component, so grid in 2338. Note that you could also expand the expression by writing it as a product and multiplying it all out.

11. C   **Difficulty:** Medium

Category: Additional Topics in Math / Imaginary Numbers

Getting to the Answer: Factoring the first trinomial yields $(x^2 + 81)(x^2 + 3)$, and factoring the second gives $(x + 9)(x - 4)$. Set each expression equal to 0 and solve for x; you'll find that (C) is the only choice that is not in this list of values, so it is correct.

12. C   **Difficulty:** Medium

Category: Additional Topics in Math / Trigonometry

Getting to the Answer: Dealing with smaller angles usually makes trig questions easier, so start by reducing the given angle so that it is in the first quadrant. To do this, subtract 2π from $\frac{13\pi}{6}$ to get $\frac{13\pi}{6} - 2\pi = \frac{13\pi}{6} - \frac{12\pi}{6} = \frac{\pi}{6}$. The equation in the question stem becomes $\sin x = \cos \frac{\pi}{6}$. Next, think about complementary angles—they have a special relationship relative to trig values—the cosine of an acute angle is equal to the sine of the angle's complement and vice versa. The angle measures are given in radians, so you're looking for an angle that, when added to $\frac{\pi}{6}$, gives $\frac{\pi}{2}$ (because $\frac{\pi}{2} = 90°$). Because $\frac{\pi}{6} + \frac{2\pi}{6} = \frac{3\pi}{6} = \frac{\pi}{2}$, the two angles, $\frac{\pi}{6}$ and $\frac{\pi}{3}$, are complementary angles, which means (C) is correct.

EXTRA PRACTICE

1. D   Difficulty: Easy

Category: Additional Topics in Math / Imaginary Numbers

Getting to the Answer: The definition of i is given as $i = \sqrt{-1}$. If you square both sides of this definition, you arrive at a more useful form: $i^2 = (\sqrt{-1})^2 = -1$. Distribute the $4i$ and then substitute -1 for i^2:

$$4i(5 - 7i) = 4i(5) - 4i(7i)$$
$$= 20i - 28i^2$$
$$= 20i - 28(-1)$$
$$= 20i + 28$$

Switch the terms so that the real part is first $(28 + 20i)$ to find that (D) is correct.

2. A   Difficulty: Medium

Category: Additional Topics in Math / Imaginary Numbers

Getting to the Answer: Because $i = \sqrt{-1}$, it isn't considered "proper" to leave i in the denominator of a fraction (just as you shouldn't leave a radical in the denominator). Use the same strategy you learned for rationalizing the denominator of a radical expression to rationalize a complex number (by multiplying by the conjugate). The conjugate of $3 - i$ is $3 + i$, so multiply the expression by $\dfrac{3 + i}{3 + i}$:

$$\frac{1}{3 - i} \times \frac{3 + i}{3 + i} = \frac{3 + i}{(3 - i)(3 + i)}$$
$$= \frac{3 + i}{9 + 3i - 3i - i^2}$$
$$= \frac{3 + i}{9 - (-1)}$$
$$= \frac{3 + i}{10}$$

This isn't one of the answer choices, so split the number into its real part and its imaginary part by writing each of the terms in the numerator over 10. The result is $\dfrac{3}{10} + \dfrac{1}{10}i$, which matches (A).

3. B   Difficulty: Medium

Category: Additional Topics in Math / Imaginary Numbers

Getting to the Answer: You will not be expected to raise a complex number like the one in this question to the fourth power by hand. That's a clue that you should be able to use your calculator. The definition of i has been programmed into all graphing calculators, so you can perform basic operations on complex numbers using the calculator (in the calculator section of the test). Enter the expression as follows: $(3 + 2i)^4$. On the TI83/84 calculators, you can find i on the button with the decimal point. After you enter the expression, the calculator should return $-119 + 120i$, which is (B).

4. B   Difficulty: Medium

Category: Additional Topics in Math / Imaginary Numbers

Getting to the Answer: A question like this requires an understanding of how the powers of i cycle. Whenever you're evaluating a high power of i, divide the power by 4 and let the remainder point you to the correct answer. Recall the power pattern for i: i, -1, $-i$, 1, and repeat. Divide 14 by 4, which yields 3 with a remainder of 2. This means $i^{14} = (i^4)^3 \times i^2 = 1 \times -1 = -1$. Repeat this process for i^{122} to get $i^{122} = (i^4)^{30} \times i^2 = 1 \times -1 = -1$. The sum is therefore $-1 + -1 = -2$, which means you're looking for an expression that has the same value. Choices B and C should look tempting (because of the 2), so start with them. In (B), you know $i^2 = -1$ and $2(-1) = -2$, so this is the correct answer.

5. B   Difficulty: Hard

Category: Additional Topics in Math / Imaginary Numbers

Getting to the Answer: Take a peek at the answer choices—they're all complex numbers. This means factoring is out of the question, so think quadratic formula. Before you can use the quadratic formula, the equation must equal 0, so move all the terms to the left side of the equal sign; the quadratic (written in standard form) becomes $x^2 - 4x + 13 = 0$. Now, jot down the values you'll need: $a = 1$, $b = -4$, and $c = 13$.

$$x = \frac{-b \pm \sqrt{b^2 - 4ac}}{2a}$$

$$= \frac{-(-4) \pm \sqrt{(-4)^2 - 4(1)(13)}}{2(1)}$$

$$= \frac{4 \pm \sqrt{16 - 52}}{2}$$

$$= \frac{4 \pm \sqrt{-36}}{2}$$

$$= \frac{4 \pm \sqrt{-1 \times 36}}{2}$$

$$= \frac{4 \pm 6i}{2}$$

$$= \frac{\cancel{2}(2 \pm 3i)}{\cancel{2}}$$

The final answer is $2 \pm 3i$, which matches (B).

6. A   **Difficulty:** Hard
Category: Additional Topics in Math / Imaginary Numbers

Getting to the Answer: Each of the factors in this product has two terms, so they behave like binomials. This means you can use FOIL to find the product. To avoid messy numbers, simplify the two radicals first using the definition of i. Write each of the numbers under the radicals as a product of -1 and the number, take the square roots, and then FOIL the resulting expressions.

$$\left(2 + \sqrt{-9}\right)\left(-1 + \sqrt{-4}\right)$$

$$= \left(2 + \sqrt{-1 \times 9}\right)\left(-1 + \sqrt{-1 \times 4}\right)$$

$$= (2 + 3i)(-1 + 2i)$$

$$= -2 + 4i - 3i + 6i^2$$

$$= -2 + i + 6(-1)$$

$$= -8 + i$$

Choice (A) is correct.

7. C   **Difficulty:** Hard
Category: Additional Topics in Math / Imaginary Numbers

Getting to the Answer: Find a common denominator by multiplying the second term by $4 - 2i$. As always, you're given that $\sqrt{-1} = i$, but a more useful fact is that $i^2 = -1$, so be sure to make this substitution as you work. Once you've found the common denominator, you can simply add like terms.

$$\frac{1}{4 - 2i} + (3 + i) = \frac{1}{4 - 2i} + \frac{3 + i}{1}$$

$$= \frac{1}{4 - 2i} + \frac{3 + i}{1}\left(\frac{4 - 2i}{4 - 2i}\right)$$

$$= \frac{1}{4 - 2i} + \frac{12 - 6i + 4i - 2i^2}{4 - 2i}$$

$$= \frac{1}{4 - 2i} + \frac{12 - 2i - 2(-1)}{4 - 2i}$$

$$= \frac{1 + 12 - 2i + 2}{4 - 2i}$$

$$= \frac{15 - 2i}{4 - 2i}$$

This matches (C).

8. 17   **Difficulty:** Medium
Category: Additional Topics in Math / Imaginary Numbers

Getting to the Answer: Don't let this "new" definition intimidate you. All you're asked to do is to find the square root of the sum of a^2 and b^2. You don't even have to involve the i at all.

$$|15 + 8i| = \sqrt{15^2 + 8^2}$$

$$= \sqrt{225 + 64}$$

$$= \sqrt{289}$$

$$= 17$$

There is nothing else to do—the answer is 17.

9. D   **Difficulty:** Easy
Category: Additional Topics in Math / Trigonometry

Getting to the Answer: The answers are given in degrees, and it's easier to add degrees than radians, so convert each angle measure to degrees and then find the sum. Use the conversion $180° = \pi$, with π written in the denominator so that it will cancel.

$$\frac{\cancel{\pi}}{4} \times \frac{180°}{\cancel{\pi}} = 45°$$

$$\frac{7\cancel{\pi}}{\cancel{12}^{2}} \times \frac{{}^{30}\cancel{180}°}{\cancel{\pi}} = \frac{210°}{2} = 105°$$

The measure of $\angle PQR$ is $45° + 105° = 150°$, which matches (D).

10. D   **Difficulty:** Easy

Category: Additional Topics in Math / Trigonometry

Getting to the Answer: Angles that are coterminal (land in the same place when rotated full circle) have the same trigonometric values. To find coterminal angles, subtract 360° (one full circle) from the given angle: 450° − 360° = 90°. The figure below provides a visual representation of this relationship:

A 90° angle has the same trigonometric values as a 450° angle, making (D) correct.

11. B   **Difficulty:** Medium

Category: Additional Topics in Math / Trigonometry

Getting to the Answer: When you're not asked to find a specific value, drawing a quick sketch to determine which quadrant each angle lies in may provide enough information to answer the question. Sketch each angle on a unit circle. It doesn't have to be perfect—you just need to know which quadrant the angle falls in.

Three of the angles (120°, 240°, and −120°) fall to the left of the y-axis (in Quadrants II and III) and therefore have a cosine value that is negative. The angle in (B) falls to the right of the vertical axis (in Quadrant IV) and therefore has a cosine value that is positive. This means (B) is correct because cos(−60°) cannot have the same value as the other three angles.

12. D   **Difficulty:** Medium

Category: Additional Topics in Math / Trigonometry

Getting to the Answer: Fill in the missing parts of the triangle. Use the Pythagorean theorem to find the missing leg length and use properties of triangles to find the missing angle.

Sine and cosine both involve the hypotenuse (13), so you can eliminate A right away because it doesn't have a 13 in it. Next, quickly compare each answer choice to the trig ratios given by SOH CAH TOA. Sine is opposite over hypotenuse; in B, the side opposite the 67.4° angle has length 5 (not 12), so eliminate B. Cosine is adjacent over hypotenuse; in C, the side adjacent to the 22.6° angle has length 12 (not 5), so eliminate C. This means (D) must be correct. The side adjacent to the 67.4° angle has length 5 and the hypotenuse has length 13, so $\cos 67.4° = \dfrac{5}{13}$.

13. C   **Difficulty:** Medium

Category: Additional Topics in Math / Trigonometry

Getting to the Answer: The angle given $\left(\dfrac{\pi}{6}\right)$ is in the first quadrant, so its cosine is positive. The question states that sin x is equal to the cosine of $\dfrac{\pi}{6}$, so x be must an angle for which the sine is positive, which means it must lie in the first or second quadrant (above the x-axis). This means you're looking for the angle that is *not* in one of those quadrants, which is (C): $\dfrac{5\pi}{3}$ is in the fourth quadrant and therefore has a negative sine value. (The angles in A and B meet this criterion because each one is less than π. The angle in D also meets the criterion because $\dfrac{7\pi}{3} - 2\pi = \dfrac{7\pi}{3} - \dfrac{6\pi}{3} = \dfrac{\pi}{3}$, which is in the first quadrant.)

14. A   Difficulty: Medium
Category: Additional Topics in Math / Trigonometry

Getting to the Answer: When the measure of an angle in a triangle is given in radians, convert it to degrees so you'll have a better idea of what you're looking at. Use the relationship $180° = \pi$ to convert the angle: $\dfrac{\cancel{\pi}}{3} \times \dfrac{180°}{\cancel{\pi}} = 60°$.

Now you know the triangle is a 30-60-90 triangle, which has sides that are in the ratio $x : x\sqrt{3} : 2x$. The hypotenuse is $2x = 24$, so $x = 12$ and $x\sqrt{3} = 12\sqrt{3}$. This means the base and height of the triangle are 12 and $12\sqrt{3}$, and the area of the triangle is $\dfrac{1}{2}(12\sqrt{3})(12) = 72\sqrt{3}$, which is (A).

15. 3/5 or .6   Difficulty: Hard
Category: Additional Topics in Math / Trigonometry

Getting to the Answer: Because trig functions typically apply to right triangles, draw in an altitude and label what you know. You know the trough is 24 inches deep and 36 inches across the top. Because the given angles have equal measures ($x°$), the triangle is isosceles and the altitude bisects the top. Your figure should look like this:

You're given that $B = \cos x$, and the cosine of an angle involves the hypotenuse, so you need to find the length of the hypotenuse using the Pythagorean theorem:

$$18^2 + 24^2 = c^2$$
$$324 + 576 = c^2$$
$$900 = c^2$$
$$30 = c$$

Finally, $\cos x = \dfrac{\text{adj}}{\text{hyp}} = \dfrac{18}{30} = \dfrac{3}{5}$. Grid in 3/5 or .6.

16. 12/5 or 2.4   Difficulty: Hard
Category: Additional Topics in Math / Trigonometry

Getting to the Answer: Find the height of the triangle using the information given about the area and add it to the figure.

$$A = \frac{1}{2}bh$$
$$240 = \frac{1}{2}(40)h$$
$$240 = 20h$$
$$12 = h$$

After you find the height, you might recognize the 5-12-13 Pythagorean triplet, which gives you another side of the triangle that contains β.

Note: Figure not drawn to scale.

Now use SOH CAH TOA: $\tan\beta = \dfrac{\text{opp}}{\text{adj}} = \dfrac{12}{5}$. Grid in 12/5 or 2.4.

CHAPTER 13

PRACTICE

Suggested Passage Map notes:

¶1: 4 forces of flight (central idea)

¶2: #1 - thrust

¶2, cont.: #2 - drag, impact on aircraft design

¶3: #3 - gravity

¶3, cont.: #4 - lift

¶3, cont.: Bern. principle = lift

7. B **Difficulty:** Medium

Category: Vocab-in-Context

Getting to the Answer: When you see the phrase "most nearly means" and a cited word or phrase, pretend that word or phrase is blank and predict a synonym for it. Read the sentence without "acts" (line 29) and ask what "lift force" (line 28) does. Predict that it "functions" or "works." Choice (B) is correct.

8. B **Difficulty:** Medium

Category: Inference

Getting to the Answer: Review your Passage Map notes regarding drag. Remember to be wary of answer choices that are outside the scope of the passage. Paragraph 2 provides details about drag, specifically that it is "the air resistance that the plane encounters in flight" (lines 16-17). At the end of the paragraph, the author writes that drag decreases when "there is little friction at the airplane's surface" (lines 23-24). Choice (B) reflects the relationship between drag and friction and is therefore correct. Choice C may be tempting, but it is incorrect because drag doesn't decrease as thrust increases; instead, thrust must be enough to overcome drag force (line 15).

PERFORM

Suggested Passage Map notes:

¶1: AL humble family background (purpose)

¶2: childhood – "wild" region, little ed

¶3: early jobs

¶4: captain in war, politician, lawyer

¶5: personal description

9. D **Difficulty:** Medium

Category: Rhetoric

Getting to the Answer: When a question asks you to identify the author's stance, think about the author's point of view and purpose. The author begins by referring to his parents' families as "undistinguished" (line 3) and keeps the focus of the passage on the simplicity of his life and circumstances. Predict that the author sees himself as an ordinary person who grew up without many advantages. Choice (D) is correct.

10. C **Difficulty:** Medium

Category: Global

Getting to the Answer: To summarize the central purpose of the passage, review the key ideas you noted in your Passage Map. Always identify the author's purpose when mapping History/Social Studies passages. While the author does spend a good deal of the passage discussing education, this is not his reason for writing. The overall purpose of the passage is to provide his own history, which shifts from his modest childhood to his national importance. This is underscored by the phrase "What I have done since then is pretty well known" (lines 61-62). Choice (C) is correct.

11. B **Difficulty:** Medium

Category: Vocab-in-Context

Getting to the Answer: When you see the phrase "most nearly means" and a cited line, pretend the word or phrase is a blank and predict the meaning of the word or phrase in context. Read the lines surrounding the cited phrase. The author states that he has not been to school since his childhood but "picked up" (line 37) the "little advance . . . upon this store of education . . . under the pressure of necessity" (lines 36-38). Predict that the phrase means that he learned when he had to, or when it was necessary. Choice (B) is correct.

12. C **Difficulty:** Hard

Category: Inference

Getting to the Answer: If you are not provided with a line reference, use your Passage Map to locate the part of the passage to which the question stem refers. The question asks about the effect of the Black Hawk War, which is first mentioned in the beginning of paragraph 4. The overall topic of paragraph 4 is the author's campaigns and subsequent elections, suggesting a connection between the war and the author's political career. Choice (C) is correct. The other answer choices may be tempting, but they are all are assumptions that the text itself does not support.

EXTRA PRACTICE

Suggested Passage Map notes:

¶1-2: ML loves girl w/ simple beauty

¶3: ML & girl marry, happy, girl good w/ $

¶4: only 2 faults

¶5: #1 - ML didn't want to go to theater

¶6: #2 - wife wears fake jewelry

¶7-10: ML and wife disagree about jewelry

¶11: wife dies

¶12-14: ML mourns wife

¶15-19: ML is poor, has to sell wife's jewelry

¶20-22: ML is shocked to learn jewelry is real (theme)

1. D   Difficulty: Medium
Category: Vocab-in-Context

Getting to the Answer: Use context clues and tone to help determine the meaning of the word. Create a mental picture of what is being described by using the surrounding text. Finally, make sure the answer choice does not alter the meaning of the sentence when inserted. The paragraph in which the word appears describes the girl as "simple" (line 5) and "pure" (line 8), and as having a "lovely soul" (line 8). Therefore, choice (D) is correct. "Angelic" means "innocent" in this context.

2. C   Difficulty: Medium
Category: Detail

Getting to the Answer: Skim the passage to locate descriptions of Lantin's wife at the beginning of their marriage. Paragraph 3 describes the Lantins' "snug" (line 10) income and attribute their luxurious lifestyle to Lantin's wife's "clever economy" (line 14). Choice (C) is correct. "Frugal" describes someone who is thrifty and economical.

3. A   Difficulty: Medium
Category: Inference

Getting to the Answer: Look for Lantin's thoughts and statements about the jewels. Use this as evidence of his attitude. The Lantins are described as making a "snug" (line 10) salary, and Madame Lantin has to be very economical. Later

in the passage, Lantin mentions that they "cannot afford" (line 35) to buy real jewelry. Choice (A) is correct because Lantin clearly believes they cannot afford real gems.

4. D   Difficulty: Easy
Category: Command of Evidence

Getting to the Answer: Review your answer to the previous question. Decide which lines of text provide evidence that the Lantins did not have enough money to buy large jewels. Choice (D) offers the best support. In these lines, Lantin explicitly states they cannot afford real jewelry.

5. B   Difficulty: Medium
Category: Inference

Getting to the Answer: Reread the text to make a prediction. This section of the passage describes Lantin's intense mourning for his wife, which suggests a deep unhappiness. Choice (B) is correct.

6. B   Difficulty: Medium
Category: Command of Evidence

Getting to the Answer: Review your answer to the previous question. Read each choice and figure out which one provides specific support for that answer. Choice (B) provides the best support. These lines show that Lantin is overcome with grief, as he "wept unceasingly; his heart was broken" (line 47).

7. D   Difficulty: Easy
Category: Vocab-in-Context

Getting to the Answer: Use context clues from the target sentence and surrounding sentences. Predict the meaning of the word and look for a match in the answer choices. Lantin views the jewels as "deceptions" (line 61) and speaks of the irritation her jewels caused him. Looking at the jewels also "spoiled, somewhat" (line 63) the memory of his wife. Choice (D) provides a suitably negative word and makes sense in the context of the rest of the paragraph.

8. C   Difficulty: Medium
Category: Rhetoric

Getting to the Answer: Contrast this sentence with what has already occurred in the passage. Analyze the new information it provides and the response it provokes when you read it. The sentence calls into question the reliability of everything we have learned about Madame

Lantin. Although she and her husband were not wealthy, Madame Lantin has somehow acquired at least one very expensive piece of jewelry. Choice (C) is correct. The author uses this sentence to create an unresolved conflict. Lantin does not know how his wife obtained the jewels, and the sentence suggests the answer might call his wife's virtue into question.

9. D   Difficulty: Hard
Category: Inference

Getting to the Answer: Review the end of the excerpt. Think about what this text might suggest broadly. Don't speculate by choosing an overly specific answer. The correct answer will provide a logical conclusion about Madame Lantin based on what you have learned about her throughout the passage. Her husband idealized her but has discovered that she has been dishonest and hidden things from him. Choice (D) provides a reasonable conclusion that a reader can make about Madame Lantin. Choices A, B, and C are possible reasons that Madame Lantin had the expensive necklace, but they are not directly supported by the passage.

10. A   Difficulty: Hard
Category: Global

Getting to the Answer: Ask yourself what the author's theme is in this passage. The events in the passage show that Lantin judges his wife for her love of costume jewelry. After her death, he finds that her jewels are real. Both the "paste" jewels that turn out to be real and Lantin's realization about his wife's jewel collection after her death support the idea that appearances can be deceiving. Choice (A) best describes the central theme the author develops throughout the excerpt.

CHAPTER 14

PRACTICE

Suggested Passage Map notes:

Passage 1

¶1: author: SC = "miracle cure;" how SC work

¶2: embryonic → adult SCs; help diseases; help research

¶3: author: SC research must go on

Passage 2

¶1: ?s of ethics

¶2: SCs useful, but embryo use moral?

¶3: author: use adult SCs

4. C **Difficulty:** Medium

Category: Synthesis

Getting to the Answer: Synthesis questions ask you to find similarities and differences between paired passages. Use your Passage Map to compare the different points of view, focusing on how the authors agree and disagree. The author of Passage 1 maintains that stem cell research can provide benefits and recommends using stem cells regardless of the source. The author of Passage 2 agrees that stem cell research can provide benefits but argues that using adult stem cells is the course to follow. Both authors agree that stem cell research has benefits. Choice (C) is correct.

5. D **Difficulty:** Hard

Category: Synthesis

Getting to the Answer: To make a strong prediction when faced with a general question, focus on the central idea, topic, and scope of each passage. Harder Synthesis questions will require you to identify not only how the authors agree or disagree but also why they agree or disagree. What these authors disagree on is easy to identify: which type of stem cells should be used in the research. Now, ask why they disagree. The author of Passage 1 thinks that the benefits are defined solely by the physical improvements possible, and the author of Passage 2 thinks that the benefits of stem cell research must be considered in terms of the moral as well as the physical results. Choice (D) is correct.

6. C **Difficulty:** Medium

Category: Synthesis

Getting to the Answer: Look for trends in the data. Evaluate the categories and time frames mentioned in the answer choices. Compare the changes on the graph to the changes described in each answer choice and eliminate answer choices that don't match. When you check the time frame of 2005 to 2007, note that opposition to stem cell research increased one full square, and support for stem cell research decreased about one half of a square. This matches the changes in the data described in choice (C).

PERFORM

Suggested Passage Map notes:

Passage 1

¶1: U could not avoid politics; bond among groups

¶2: causes of unrest

¶3: U peasants joined M; M necessary, reasons

Passage 2

¶1: Bol. vs M; soldier quote = difference in theory (accepted vs debated)

¶2: Bol. controlling; if differ = enemy

¶3: ex: T writings view M as good or bad

¶4: T quote: must be loyal to Red Army

¶5: T/Bol. negatively portrays U/M

7. C **Difficulty:** Medium

Category: Synthesis

Getting to the Answer: To answer Synthesis questions, focus on the similarities and differences between the passages. This question stem asks what the author of Passage 2 thinks about a promise made by the Bolsheviks. Review your Passage Map of Passage 1 to identify the Bolsheviks' promise: "equality and the rule of the proletariat" (lines 16-17). Now use your Passage Map of Passage 2 to locate what author 2 thinks of the Bolsheviks. Paragraph 2 discusses the extreme control the Bolsheviks held in Russia. Predict that the author of Passage 2 would view the Bolsheviks' promise in a negative light. Choice (C) is correct.

Choices A, B, and D may be tempting, but they do not match your prediction. Choice A is incorrect because lines 56–58 explain that the Makhnovists made decisions based on "the needs of the community for food, freedom, and self-defense," not the Bolsheviks' ideological promises. Choice B is incorrect because in lines 50-52 author 2 claims the theories of the Bolsheviks were "never doubted or questioned." Choice D is incorrect because passage 2 uses the Tolstoy quotes to describe his portrayal of the Makhnovists, not to suggest the writings influenced Bolshevik promises.

8. D   Difficulty: Medium
Category: Synthesis

Getting to the Answer: Synthesis questions that ask what the authors agree on require you to identify the similarities in each author's purpose for writing the passage. Since each passage focuses on a different aspect of the Makhnovischina, the correct answer will probably be a general statement about the group. Both describe the Makhnovischina as a group formed to provide mutual aid, intellectual freedom, and military defense (see lines 31-35 in Passage 1 and lines 54-57 in Passage 2). Choice (D) is correct.

Choices A, B, and C may be tempting, but they do not match your prediction. Choice A is incorrect because paragraph 1 of Passage 2 explains the ideological differences between the Bolsheviks and Makhnovischinas. Choice B is incorrect because only Passage 1 even mentions the Austro-Hungarian army, and never claims it was the greatest threat. Choice C is incorrect because it only represents Trotsky's view in Passage 2.

9. A   Difficulty: Hard
Category: Synthesis

Getting to the Answer: Read the question stem closely to identify what it asks you to look for. Because the question stem asks what can be inferred by looking at Passage 2 and the data in the pie chart in tandem, base your interpretation of that data on the negative viewpoint that the author of Passage 2 expresses regarding the Bolsheviks. Your Passage Map shows that paragraph 2 discusses the extent of the Bolsheviks' control in Russia, so you can assume they must have been a powerful group. Analyze the chart to see that the Bolsheviks only composed about a quarter of the government. Predict

that the Bolsheviks were stronger than their proportion of seats on the assembly would suggest. Choice (A) is correct.

EXTRA PRACTICE

Suggested Passage Map notes:
Passage 1

¶1: (purpose): describe SSB origin; War of 1812 = high stakes

¶2: Br. involvement low to high; Br. victories; bomb Ft. McH

¶3: Key on Br. ship

¶4: saw flag; inspired to write

¶5: war turning point; song symbol of patriotism

Passage 2

¶1: poem early popularity

¶2: history of use: military, baseball

¶3: law = official anthem; current uses; words = reminder; (purpose): explain history of poem/anthem

1. C   Difficulty: Medium
Category: Rhetoric

Getting to the Answer: Review your Passage Map for Passage 1. Paraphrase the purpose before reading the answer choices. The author begins by referencing "the story behind 'The Star-Spangled Banner,' America's national anthem" (lines 1–2). Predict that Passage 1's purpose is to describe the origin of the national anthem. The introduction to the passages also could have provided your prediction for the passage's purpose. Never skip these introductions! Choice (C) is correct.

Remember to answer the questions about Passage 1 immediately after reading it. Choice D reflects the purpose of Passage 2, which could be a tempting answer choice if both passages were read together.

2. D   Difficulty: Medium
Category: Rhetoric

Getting to the Answer: Reread around the cited lines and consider their role in the complete paragraph. The reason for including the lines will reflect their role and purpose in relation to the other information. The paragraph introduces the scope of the passage, which is the story behind the national anthem. It then relates the origin of that story in the War of 1812 and provides context for the war. These lines show the significance of the war for the American people and the importance of its outcome, which gives added meaning to the poem that would become the national anthem; however, the lines don't actually "explain" the symbolism as in C. Choice (D) is correct.

3. D   Difficulty: Easy
Category: Vocab-in-Context

Getting to the Answer: Read the complete sentence in which the cited word appears. Predict a definition before reviewing the answer choices. Compare your prediction with the answer choices and select the one that most nearly reflects the meaning you identified. The line states that "America's defenses prevailed" against an attack by the British. In this context, predict the term most nearly means that America's defenses *hung on*, making choice (D) correct.

4. B   Difficulty: Medium
Category: Inference

Getting to the Answer: Review your notes and the cited lines. Then, paraphrase their meaning and significance. Select the answer choice that best reflects why and how Key came to write the national anthem. Paragraph 4 demonstrates that Key expected Fort McHenry to fall to British forces. He was surprised by American perseverance and, as a result, was inspired to write the national anthem in response to the Americans' survival during the nightlong British bombardment. Choice (B) is correct.

5. D   Difficulty: Medium
Category: Command of Evidence

Getting to the Answer: Review your answer to the previous question and your notes on the referenced paragraph. Identify the phrase that most clearly supports the conclusion identified in the previous question: Key wrote to honor the American resistance. Lines 45-46 ("Moved by . . . to write") clearly explain why Key wrote the words that would become the national anthem. In these lines, the author states Key was moved by the "sight." Confirm from the previous sentences that this "sight" is indeed

the American victory he witnessed: "by dawn's light he saw the American flag" (lines 43-44). Choice (D) is correct.

6. B   Difficulty: Hard
Category: Rhetoric

Getting to the Answer: Using your Passage Map, think about the author's overall tone and purpose to predict what point of view he or she might hold about the national anthem and its origins. Compare your conclusion with the answer choices. The passage begins by explaining the national anthem originated during the War of 1812. The first paragraph goes on to state America was defending its "status as a sovereign nation" (line 8). The last lines of the passage (53–55) describe Key's words as a symbol of America's victory. Taken all together, the passage's purpose is to describe the patriotic origins of "The Star-Spangled Banner." This is best reflected in choice (B) as an accurate description of the entire passage.

7. A   Difficulty: Easy
Category: Rhetoric

Getting to the Answer: Reread the cited lines and review your notes for Passage 2. Consider the placement of the lines in relation to the rest of the passage and how the lines prepare you to interpret subsequent content. The cited lines lay the foundation for the rest of the passage, which describes how Francis Scott Key's poem came to be the official national anthem known as "The Star-Spangled Banner." Choice (A) is correct because the cited lines state clearly that Key first wrote his words as a poem, not as a song or an anthem.

8. A   Difficulty: Easy
Category: Vocab-in-Context

Getting to the Answer: Predict a word or phrase that makes sense in context in place of the existing phrase. Lines 73-80 discuss how the national anthem had begun to increase in popularity and appear regularly in sporting events. The implication in the referenced sentence is that the singing of the national anthem has become a "tradition"; predict *very frequent*. Choice (A) is correct.

9. D   Difficulty: Medium
Category: Inference

Getting to the Answer: Consider how the quotation reflects the specific rhetoric and purpose of the complete sentence. The correct answer will relate the words of the quotation to the rest of the sentence. The text explains that these lyrics "remind Americans of the liberty for which the country was established, and the courage of those who fought for it" (lines 97-99). The author draws a parallel between "land of the free" and "the liberty for which the country was established," and between "home of the brave" and "the courage of those who fought for it." Choice (D) is correct.

10. D   **Difficulty:** Medium
Category: Synthesis

Getting to the Answer: Review your notes for both passages. Identify what each passage offers to your understanding of the national anthem. The correct answer will reflect the specific contribution of Passage 2. While both passages describe aspects of the history and symbolism of "The Star-Spangled Banner," only Passage 2 traces the events that led to Key's words being officially adopted as the national anthem in 1931. Choice (D) is correct.

Choices A, B, and C may be tempting, but they do not match your prediction. While it is mentioned in Passage 2, choice A only addresses the first paragraph and not the overall contribution of the passage. Choice B is also incorrect. Although Passage 2 does emphasize the national anthem's "patriotic nature," Passage 1 does so as well, so this is not Passage 2's particular enhancement to Passage 1. Choice C is incorrect because the anthem's origins in the War of 1812 are only described at length in Passage 1.

11. B   **Difficulty:** Medium
Category: Command of Evidence

Getting to the Answer: Predict what type of information would most support your answer to the previous question: something that explains how Key's words became the national anthem. Then, select the answer choice that most closely matches your prediction. Lines 69-73 ("At the time . . . national anthem") demonstrate one way in which the words written by Francis Scott Key gained popularity over time in the United States and even began being thought of as a "national anthem." Choice (B) is correct.

CHAPTER 15

PRACTICE

Suggested Passage Map notes:

¶ 1: oak problems; pests & disease, other trees

¶2: oaks in danger

¶3: research into problems and solutions; various solutions including fire

¶4: ecological restoration

¶5: more human interaction needed

¶6: go back to Native American ways

¶7: human intervention important

4. C   **Difficulty:** Medium
Category: Global

Getting to the Answer: Even when you can't make a specific prediction, summarize the author's central idea by reviewing your Passage Map. The author begins by listing the problems plaguing oak trees and continues by describing possible solutions to each of the problems. Common to each of the solutions is the requirement that humans actively participate in an ongoing process. The author concludes the passage by describing this kind of participation as "ethnobotanical restoration" (line 83). Predict that humans need to participate actively in efforts to restore oaks. Choice (C) matches this prediction.

5. B   **Difficulty:** Medium
Category: Detail

Getting to the Answer: Use your Passage Map to locate cited phrases. Rephrase what each phrase means. The author describes ecological restoration as a process that is completed in a very short time and ethnobotanical restoration as a process that seeks to restore ongoing human interaction with plant communities. Choice (B) is correct.

6. D   **Difficulty:** Easy
Category: Command of Evidence

Getting to the Answer: To answer this question, use the prediction you made to answer the previous question. To answer the previous question, you needed to recognize that the main difference between the two types of restoration is that while ecological restoration

takes place over a short period of time and can be completed, ethnobotanical restoration requires long-term involvement by humans in the natural process of maintaining historic plant communities. Choice (D) is correct.

PERFORM

Suggested Passage Map notes:

¶1: history of newborn screenings; medical advances meant deaths now from rare issues

¶2: link between PKU and mental retardation

¶3: despite risky, use of low phen diet tried

¶4: new test for PKU done earlier

¶5: test not perfect, but successful

7. C   **Difficulty:** Medium
Category: Connections

Getting to the Answer: The phrase "most strongly suggests" and the clue word "prior" indicate that this is a Connections question asking about an explicit relationship. Review your Passage Map to understand how the author connects certain ideas to each other. The word "prior" and the cited lines indicate that the relationship is sequential. First, the low phenylalanine diet, which was implemented despite its risks, proved beneficial. Then, the research initiatives began because of the benefits associated with the diet. Predict that the diet was prescribed in spite of those negative outcomes. Choice (C) matches this prediction.

8. D   **Difficulty:** Medium
Category: Command of Evidence

Getting to the Answer: When answering a Command of Evidence question, find the cited lines that most closely support the prediction you made to answer the previous question. You predicted that the diet was prescribed in spite of the drawbacks. Compare each of the answer choices to your prediction. Only choice (D) describes the drawbacks associated with the special diet.

9. B   **Difficulty:** Medium
Category: Global

Getting to the Answer: Use your Passage Map to quickly summarize the passage. Maintain focus on the general context of each paragraph. Concentrate on the central ideas in each paragraph, not on specific details. The author introduces the passage by discussing the practice of screening newborns and concludes the passage by describing genetic screening as "a permanent part of infant health care" (lines 79–80). Throughout the passage, the author focuses on the process that brought about the use of genetic screening. Choice (B) is correct.

10. D   Difficulty: Easy
Category: Detail

Getting to the Answer: "According to the passage" indicates that this is a Detail question. Use your Passage Map to locate the referenced details. Locate each referenced detail and determine why the author included that detail. Choice A is mentioned as a contributor to the decline in the infant mortality rate and can be eliminated. Eliminate B because Lofenalac was developed to treat PKU. Eliminate C because it discusses problems with the test. Choice (D) is correct because the general success of the test showed the potential of screening tests, as explained in lines 74–77.

11. D   Difficulty: Medium
Category: Command of Evidence

Getting to the Answer: To answer a Command of Evidence question, return to the place in the passage that provided the answer to the previous question. Check to see if one of the answer choices to this question includes the detail you found for the previous question. Choice (D) is correct.

EXTRA PRACTICE

Suggested Passage Map notes:

¶1: history of S warbler, concern for many birds losing habitats

¶2: S warbler declining due to gradual loss of habitats;

¶3: hard for scientists to conserve; birds adapting on their own

¶4: birds using man made pine plantations

¶5: pine plantations good for birds when trees 20 feet high

¶6: lots of space on plantations

¶7: only some plantations useful

¶8: plantations will become new habitat

1. C   Difficulty: Medium
Category: Global

Getting to the Answer: Think about the central idea of the passage. Eliminate answer choices such as A and D that contain supporting details for the central idea. The correct answer will be an idea that is supported by all of the details in the passage. This passage is mostly about how the Swainson's warbler population has begun to recover after its natural habitat was reduced by deforestation. Choice (C) is correct.

2. C   Difficulty: Medium
Category: Rhetoric

Getting to the Answer: Review your notes for the first paragraph. Consider the central idea of the paragraph and how it relates to the central idea of the passage. Select the answer choice that most accurately describes the purpose this sentence serves in the passage. The author mentions these other species of birds to give examples of other animals that are at risk because their habitats have been destroyed, which matches choice (C).

3. C   Difficulty: Medium
Category: Inference

Getting to the Answer: Review your paragraph 3 notes. How did scientists attempt to preserve the population of the Swainson's warbler? The correct answer should paraphrase your own idea. In lines 30–34 of paragraph 3, the author explains that previous attempts at conservation have been unsuccessful because scientists did not understand what the birds need in a habitat. This matches choice (C).

4. C   Difficulty: Medium
Category: Command of Evidence

Getting to the Answer: Locate each of the answer choices in the passage. The correct answer should provide direct support for the answer to the previous question. In paragraph 3, the author describes why previous conservation efforts by scientists have failed. Choice (C) is correct.

5. D   Difficulty: Medium
Category: Vocab-in-Context

Getting to the Answer: When approaching Vocab-in-Context questions, replace the word in question with a blank and predict a possible synonym. In this sentence, *change* can replace "conversion" without changing the overall meaning. Choice (D) is correct.

6. A   Difficulty: Hard
Category: Inference

Getting to the Answer: This type of open-ended question stem can make it difficult to predict the answer. Instead, look for the answer choice that is directly supported by the evidence in the text. Eliminate answer choices that are related to the main topic but go too far, such as D. In paragraph 1, the author discusses the risk of extinction of other birds due to a decrease in their habitats. Choice (A) is correct because it is most directly supported by the evidence in the passage.

7. B   Difficulty: Medium
Category: Command of Evidence

Getting to the Answer: Use your reasoning for answering the previous question to figure out where in the passage the best evidence for that answer will come from. Lines 9-14 in paragraph 1 provide the most direct support for the idea that more birds will become extinct if their habitats continue to disappear. Choice (B) is correct.

8. D   Difficulty: Easy
Category: Global

Getting to the Answer: Consider the central idea of the passage and the message conveyed by the information included. This passage is mostly about how the Swainson's warbler has adapted after losing much of its natural habitat. Select the answer that most closely explains that the author wants to relate this to the reader. The author's purpose is to explain how this happened, choice (D).

9. C   Difficulty: Hard
Category: Inference

Getting to the Answer: Think about the process undertaken in each of the answer choices and compare it to the Swainson's warbler's migrating to a new, man-made habitat. The migration of the Swainson's warbler to pine forests planted by humans is most similar to aquatic animals making new homes from shipwrecks. In both instances, animals have taken something created by humans and made it into a home. Choice (C) is correct.

10. A   Difficulty: Medium
Category: Vocab-in-Context

Getting to the Answer: In this sentence, the author is describing the stage of development that most closely resembles the bird's natural habitat. Predict that "point" most nearly means *stage*. Eliminate answer choices such as B and D that are synonyms for "point" but do not make sense in context. The prediction is an exact match for choice (A).

11. A   Difficulty: Medium
Category: Synthesis

Getting to the Answer: Consider only the information presented in the graph. The correct answer will be directly supported by the data. The graph shows that over the decade, the number of acres of pine plantations has grown steadily while that of natural pine forests has declined. The conclusion that the number of acres of pine plantations could soon surpass that of natural pine forests is supported by the data presented in the graph. Choice (A) is correct.

CHAPTER 16

PRACTICE

Suggested Passage Map notes:

¶1: book is not fiction

¶2: MF conceals name

¶3: MF used modest tone

¶4: MF's story is dark

¶5: author (DD) focuses on MF's repentance

¶6: DD wants readers to focus on moral

¶7: book includes happiness

¶8: readers can learn from MF's life

4. D   Difficulty: Medium

Category: Connections

Getting to the Answer: The phrase "According to the passage" and a relationship clue word indicate that you should ask yourself how items are being related. The clue word "because" suggests that this is a cause-and-effect relationship. Find the reference to the narrator's concern and reread the section. Predict that the recent popularity of novels encourages readers to believe what they read is fictional. This prediction matches choice (D).

5. C   Difficulty: Medium

Category: Connections

Getting to the Answer: Open-ended Connections questions about relationships (explicit or implicit) require you to describe the relationship in your own words and the correct answers can be difficult to predict. Because the question stem is asking about why the narrator wrote the story described in the passage and not the passage itself, focus on what the narrator says about the purpose of the story. By paraphrasing the narrator's intent stated in the final paragraph, you can predict that the narrator thinks readers can learn good things from the story. Choice (C) matches this prediction.

6. B   Difficulty: Medium

Category: Vocab-in-Context

Getting to the Answer: When answering Vocab-in-Context questions, focus on synonyms for the word in question, not on a specific definition. Read the sentence without "usefully applied" and ask what the narrator is trying to convey. Throughout the passage, the narrator

returns to the idea that the story is written not to relate "wicked" tales but to provide readers with an opportunity to learn from the lessons found in the story. Predict that the narrator is reaffirming the purpose for writing such stories. Choice (B) matches your prediction.

PERFORM

Suggested Passage Map notes:

¶1: NDE raises q's about history

¶2: NDE gives date and mine location of coins

¶3: study to compare methods

¶4: scholars disagree about origin

¶5: how problems of corrosion were overcome

¶6: findings contradict previous scholars

¶7: forced scholars to rethink regional politics

¶8: more tests will be done

7. A   Difficulty: Medium

Category: Vocab-in-Context

Getting to the Answer: Remember to avoid common meanings when answering Vocab-in-Context questions. Read the sentence without "struck" and rephrase what the author means. Predict that the author is referring to when the coins were minted. Choice (A) is correct.

8. D   Difficulty: Medium

Category: Connections

Getting to the Answer: To answer Connections questions that are not about specific parts of the passage, find the author's thesis and look for the answer choice that is consistent with it. Use your Passage Map to locate the thesis. The author states in the first sentence that science can help us learn about history. Lead isotope analysis is presented as an example of how science "can inform" (lines 1-2) history. In the first paragraph, the author states that this analysis has raised questions, and in paragraph 6, the author indicates that the analysis answered questions about when the analyzed coins were made. Therefore, choice (D) is correct.

9. D   Difficulty: Medium

Category: Connections

Getting to the Answer: The phrase "according to the passage" and a relationship keyword in the question stem signal a Connections question. The relationship keyword "because" indicates a cause-and-effect relationship, so identify why the researchers chose the coin in question. Predict that if the scientists' technique could help answer historians' questions, then historians would recognize the value of the technique. Choice (D) is correct.

10. A Difficulty: Easy
Category: Vocab-in-Context

Getting to the Answer: The phrase "most nearly means" and a cited line indicate a Vocab-in-Context question. Read the sentence without "establish" and think of a synonym that can replace it. Predict that because scientists wanted to determine facts through their research, they wanted to determine who made the coins. Choice (A) matches your prediction.

EXTRA PRACTICE

Suggested Passage Map notes:
¶1: F's daily routine
¶1, cont: F's friends
¶2-10: recent robbery
¶11: lack of security at bank
¶12: thief not a professional robber
¶13-19: disagree whether thief will be caught

1. D Difficulty: Medium
Category: Vocab-in-Context

Getting to the Answer: Locate context clues to help determine the meaning of the word. Predict a meaning for the word and then match it to the closest answer choice. The sentence describes Fogg arriving at the club and going to his usual table. A good prediction might be *went*. Be careful of answer choices that offer alternate meanings for the target word that don't make sense in context. Look for the nearest match in the answers. Choice (D) fits with the tone and context of the sentence.

2. C Difficulty: Medium
Category: Inference

Getting to the Answer: Review the descriptions of Phileas Fogg and his actions in your Passage Map. Summarize what the beginning of the passage says about Fogg. Paragraph 1 describes Fogg counting out his steps on his way to the club. Upon arriving at the club, Fogg

goes to his "habitual table" (line 7) and performs a routine series of actions. Choice (C) is correct, as the details in paragraph 1 depict a man who likes to keep to a set routine.

3. A Difficulty: Medium
Category: Command of Evidence

Getting to the Answer: Review your answer to the previous question. Locate the answer choice that directly supports the conclusion you drew. Choice (A) is correct. It provides the best support for the idea that Phileas Fogg is a man of habit and routine. The word "habitual" (line 7) and the fact that his table was prepared ahead of time for him suggest that Fogg followed this routine regularly.

4. A Difficulty: Medium
Category: Inference

Getting to the answer: This is a very open-ended question stem, so it can be difficult to predict the answer without reviewing the answer choices first. Be sure to return to the passage before choosing an answer; skim your Passage Map for evidence that would prove the answer correct answer choice. Fogg reads the newspaper at the beginning of the passage. He later chimes in with a comment on the robbery the other men are discussing based on the information he learned in the paper. Therefore, choice (A) is correct.

5. D Difficulty: Easy
Category: Command of Evidence

Getting to the Answer: Review your answer to the previous question. Decide which lines of text show Fogg's knowledge of current events. Choice (D) is correct. In these lines, Fogg interjects with additional information about a crime that is a current event.

6. B Difficulty: Medium
Category: Detail

Getting to the Answer: Locate the portion of the text that discusses the bank. Your Passage Map for paragraph 11 should note a lack of security at the bank. This paragraph describes the lack of security measures at the bank that led to a theft in broad daylight; lines 51-54 reference a lack of guards or protective gratings. Choice (B) is correct.

7. A   **Difficulty:** Easy

Category: Vocab-in-Context

Getting to the Answer: Find context clues in the target sentence. Predict the meaning of the word and look for a match in the answer choices. "Functionary" (line 46) refers back to the "principal cashier" (line 46) mentioned earlier in the sentence. When you see two related answer choices, such as "official" and "servant," pay attention to the tone and specific context clues to help you choose. Choice (A) is correct; it provides a suitably neutral word that could substitute for "principal cashier, while C, servant, implies a hierarchy that is not present in the passage.

8. C   **Difficulty:** Medium

Category: Connections

Getting to the Answer: Find the part of the passage that describes the thief. Locate sentences that focus on a description of the suspect. Summarize the details in a one-sentence description. Lines 69-72 ("On the day . . . crime was committed") describe the suspect as a gentleman. Choice (C) is correct because the passage suggests that the police do not believe the man to be a professional thief due to the description of his appearance and demeanor.

9. B   **Difficulty:** Hard

Category: Rhetoric

Getting to the Answer: Reread the cited line. Concentrate on how the sentence impacts the text surrounding it. Examining the surrounding text shows that this comment occurs during a discussion about the thief being on the run. Fogg has silently listened to the conversation to this point, but now quietly interjects. This suggests that Fogg will have more to say about the topic; choice (B) is correct.

10. C   **Difficulty:** Medium

Category: Rhetoric

Getting to the Answer: Think about the passage as a whole. Use one sentence to predict the purpose of this passage. Make sure the tone of the answer choice matches the tone of the passage. The excerpt provides a brief character sketch of Phileas Fogg and establishes the dynamics of his friendships at the Reform Club. Choice (C) is correct; it accurately identifies the purpose of the excerpt.

CHAPTER 17

PRACTICE

Suggested Passage Map notes:

¶1: impossible to describe Karnak

¶2: details of K temple ruins

¶3: description of the people at L ("savages")

¶4: K peaceful, not scary at night

4. B   **Difficulty:** Easy
Category: Rhetoric

Getting to the Answer: Questions about why an author includes a section in a passage require you to identify how it fits into the passage as a whole. The author concentrates, throughout the passage, on how much Egypt has affected her. The cited section is not so much about the lack of effect Egypt has had on the other people mentioned, but more about the great effect Egypt has had on the author. Choice (B) is correct.

5. C   **Difficulty:** Medium
Category: Rhetoric

Getting to the Answer: Authors often use contrast to make a point or strengthen an argument. Reread around the cited lines and paraphrase the main points the author makes about the ideas being contrasted. To answer this question, you must compare the author's experiences in Karnak and Luxor. The author describes Karnak in lofty, ethereal language filled with references to the eternal. The author expects to find the same thing in Luxor—"I had expected the temples of Thebes to be solemn . . ." (lines 41–42)—but finds something completely different: "but Luxor was fearful" (lines 42–43). Predict that the comparison between the two cities highlights the author's negative reaction to the conditions at Luxor. Choice (C) matches your prediction.

6. A   **Difficulty:** Medium
Category: Rhetoric

Getting to the Answer: Questions concerning the overall structure of a text require you to think about how the author presents the central ideas and builds the main argument. Review your Passage Map and look for patterns in how the author expresses the important ideas in the passage. In the second paragraph, the author shifts between the real and the imagined: "Gigantic shadows spring up on every side; 'the dead are stirred up for thee to meet . . .'" (lines 14–16). This shift between the real and the imagined continues in the third paragraph: "Rows of painted . . . golden clouds" (lines 42–56). Predict that the author mixes real descriptions with imaginative descriptions, which matches choice (A).

PERFORM

Suggested Passage Map notes:

¶1: owls = optimize bio strengths

¶2: maximize vision adv.

¶3: humans map world diff. than owls

¶4: owls = complex sens. detail

7. D   **Difficulty:** Medium
Category: Rhetoric

Getting to the Answer: Use your Passage Map to answer questions concerning the central argument in a passage. Review the first paragraph to determine the author's thesis. Think about what must be true for the claim to be correct. The author begins with the claim that "humans and animals perceive the world in different ways" (lines 1–2). Predict that the assumption must have to do with how our brains work in different ways, which matches choice (D).

8. C   **Difficulty:** Medium
Category: Rhetoric

Getting to the Answer: To answer a Rhetoric question that asks about support for a claim, use your Passage Map to locate the claims the author makes and the support the author provides. Make a general prediction about the claims the author supports and then find the answer choice that matches. The author claims that owls and humans have adapted to their environments in different ways. Since this question asks about owls, focus on the claims the author makes about them. Predict that the author provides support for the claim that owls have effectively adapted to their environment. In the second paragraph, the author provides several examples of ways owls successfully adapted. Choice (C) is correct.

9. D   **Difficulty:** Easy

Category: Rhetoric

Getting to the Answer: When you see the phrase "in order to" and a cited line, identify how the cited detail fits into the overall structure of the passage. Overall, the passage compares the differences between the sensory adaptations of owls and humans. Read around the cited line and paraphrase why the author mentions barn owls. Predict that barn owl hearing is an example of how owls have adapted to improve their ability to hunt. Choice (D) matches your prediction.

10. A   **Difficulty:** Medium

Category: Rhetoric

Getting to the Answer: Review your Passage Map, focusing on how the author presents the information in the passage. In paragraph 1, the author compares human perception to that of other animals, specifically owls. The author then discusses different ways in which owls and humans use their respective sensory apparatuses. Predict that the passage is structured by comparing the differences between how owls and humans perceive the world. Choice (A) is correct.

EXTRA PRACTICE

Suggested Passage Map notes:

¶1: 2 types of univ. = pub. & private

¶2: pub univ. goal = ↑ higher ed opportunity

¶3: 1862 - gov't gave pub. land for univ.

¶4: history of diversity

¶5: major growth

¶6: US univ. part of global conv.

¶7: univ. reflect diversity, liberty, creativity

1. C   **Difficulty:** Hard

Category: Rhetoric

Getting to the Answer: The correct answer will reflect a specific position supported in both the second paragraph and the passage as a whole. Predict that the author is citing political and economic reasons to explain why the government "acknowledged the need" (line 22) for educated citizens. Choice (C) is correct.

2. B   **Difficulty:** Medium

Category: Command of Evidence

Getting to the Answer: Use your support for the previous question to predict the answer. Consider which choice best shows a clear relationship to your answer. In the previous question, line 22 offered support for our answer; Choice (B) is correct because it explicitly states that the government saw the "need for broader higher education opportunities" (lines 22–23).

3. A   **Difficulty:** Medium

Category: Rhetoric

Getting to the Answer: Summarize the paragraph and think about what the author would want the reader to know after reading it. Be sure to review your Passage Map, which should already state important information about the paragraph. Your Passage Map notes that in 1862, the government gave public land for university development; the paragraph states that the Morill Act was an early example of the federal government's desire to increase enrollment at public universities. Predict that the purpose of the paragraph is to explain how the government supported public higher education. Choice (A) is correct.

4. B   **Difficulty:** Medium

Category: Rhetoric

Getting to the Answer: The author's choice of words is deliberate. Read the sentence carefully and think about what the author is suggesting when he uses the word "accessible." The passage notes that public universities received federal and state support, which means the universities could then function at a lower cost and could enable more students to attend. Predict that "accessible" was used to describe how higher education was remodeled to be available to more people, especially those with limited means. Choice (B) is correct.

5. D   **Difficulty:** Easy

Category: Vocab-in-Context

Getting to the Answer: Use context clues to help you predict the meaning of the word as it is used in the sentence. The last sentence in paragraph 3 contrasts the fact that although universities would be operated by states, they would still need to follow, or comply with, federal regulations because they received federal support. Predict that *adhere most nearly* means *follow* or *comply with*. Choice (D) is correct.

6. C   Difficulty: Hard
Category: Rhetoric

Getting to the Answer: It is difficult to predict the exact answer for this type of question, but concisely stating the author's line of reasoning before reviewing the answer choices will help you eliminate the choices that do not strengthen that theme. Throughout the passage, the author discusses how the expansion of public universities has impacted American culture. In paragraph 4, the author describes how public universities have gradually become more diverse, offering educational opportunities to many people who would not have otherwise had them in previous years. This has had a significant impact on American culture. Consider which of these pieces of evidence best supports that theme; choice (C) is correct.

7. C   Difficulty: Medium
Category: Rhetoric

Getting to the Answer: Think about why the author would want to include this fact. The paragraph's central idea is that the student populations of public universities have grown increasingly diverse. Predict that the author is describing an example of how public universities have become more diverse. Look for the answer choice that matches this prediction. Choice (C) is correct.

8. B   Difficulty: Easy
Category: Command of Evidence

Getting to the Answer: There should be a clear relationship between the correct choice and the previous answer. Since you used the fourth paragraph as a whole to predict the last question, look for the choice that offers support for the specific answer to the previous question. Choice (B) clearly states that public universities are diverse today, even though the 1890 land act did not increase diversity when it was passed. This corresponds to the answer to the previous question.

9. D   Difficulty: Easy
Category: Vocab-in-Context

Getting to the Answer: Predict the meaning of the word with context clues from the sentence and paragraph. The second sentence of paragraph 5 states that the public

university system "has evolved," which implies it has done so in response to changes or variations in American culture over time. Predict that "nuances" most nearly means *changes* or *variations*. Always check your answer choice in the sentence to ensure it makes the most sense. Choice (D) is correct.

10. C   Difficulty: Hard
Category: Rhetoric

Getting to the Answer: Consider what the passage is about overall and what the author wants the reader to learn, rather than an idea that is mentioned only in passing or in support of the passage's purpose. Reviewing your whole Passage Map can help you focus on the entirety of the passage. The author has written a brief history of public higher education in the United States; in both the introduction and conclusion, the author connects the evolution of the public university system with the evolution of generally accepted ideals and cultural values, such as diversity and liberty. Predict that the author is discussing the connection between public higher education and generally accepted ideals. Choice (C) is correct.

11. B   Difficulty: Medium
Category: Rhetoric

Getting to the Answer: Consider the central idea of the passage that you identified in a previous question and the central idea in the fifth paragraph. The passage is primarily about the way in which U.S. higher education has reflected American cultural identity. The fifth paragraph summarizes the major growth public higher education has undergone. Predict that as the American culture has grown to value public higher education, public higher education has undergone major growth; the fifth paragraph gives an example that supports the central idea. Choice (B) is correct.

CHAPTER 18

PRACTICE

Suggested Passage Map notes:

¶1: artifacts show how colonists lived

¶2: clues about life

¶3: settlers used woodworking skills

¶4: early structures primitive, focus on survival

¶5: brick processes similar to England

¶6: most hardware from England

¶7: use of glass

¶8: after hardship, gained luxuries

4. C   Difficulty: Easy
Category: Inference

Getting to the Answer: The phrase "the statement . . . suggests" signals that this is an Inference question. Find the relevant details and look for clues indicating how the author connects them. Read around the cited text. In the previous two sentences, the author discusses the hardships the colonists faced in the early years. Focus on the reasons they didn't think about plastering during the early years. Predict that the colonists were too busy trying to stay alive. Choice (C) matches your prediction.

5. D   Difficulty: Easy
Category: Detail

Getting to the Answer: When presented with an EXCEPT question, use your Passage Map to locate the cited details. When you find one of the cited details in the passage, eliminate that answer choice. The third paragraph describes Virginia as a "carpenter's paradise" (line 23) and says the wooden artifacts were skillfully made. Eliminate A. Paragraph 4 describes how the settlers had "a difficult time staying alive" (lines 36-37); eliminate B. In the fourth paragraph, you learn that the colonists made floors from clay, allowing you to eliminate C. The sixth paragraph says that most of the hardware was imported, which directly contradicts choice (D).

6. D   Difficulty: Medium
Category: Inference

Getting to the Answer: The phrase " . . . most comparable to . . . " indicates that this is an Analogical Reasoning Inference question. Identify the relationship between the ideas. The description of the brick industry implies that the colonists made bricks with local materials using techniques they brought with them from England. The relationship is one of local materials formed using imported methods. Choice (D) reflects this relationship.

PERFORM

Suggested Passage Map notes:

¶1: narrator impressed with other's imagination

¶2: secluded life, other character's name revealed: Dupin

¶3: preferred darkness

¶4: narrator admired Dupin's analytic ability

7. C   Difficulty: Medium
Category: Inference

Getting to the Answer: The word "suggests" and the line reference indicate that this is an Inference question. Determine which answer choice can be concluded based on the information in the passage. Read around the cited section. Substituting "because" for "as" clarifies that this is a cause-and-effect relationship. The cause is Dupin's "embarrassed" circumstances (line 18), and the effect is that the narrator paid for everything. Predict that the narrator had more money than Dupin. Choice (C) is correct.

8. D   Difficulty: Hard
Category: Inference

Getting to the Answer: The phrase "closely parallels" is a clue that this is an Analogical Reasoning Inference question. To identify how the ideas are connected, describe the relationship. In the third paragraph, the narrator states that he followed Dupin's lead in everything, indicating that the narrator is subordinate to Dupin. Look for the answer choice that describes a relationship in which one side of the relationship is subordinate to the other. Although C might be tempting, the student acts independently in the second half of the answer choice. Choice (D) is correct.

9. B   Difficulty: Medium
Category: Detail

Getting to the Answer: Because this question does not provide a line reference, use your Passage Map to locate the relevant text. Then, paraphrase the detail. Locate the details about how and where the narrator met Dupin. In the first sentence, the narrator mentions first meeting Dupin in a library while searching for a rare book. Predict that they were looking for the same book. Choice (B) is correct.

10. A   Difficulty: Hard
Category: Inference

Getting to the Answer: "Most likely agree" signals a broad or open-ended Inference question. Summarize the passage to zero in on statements with which the narrator would most likely agree. The passage focuses on the ways the narrator becomes involved with Dupin. The final paragraph discusses Dupin's ability to see into other people's inner thoughts: "windows in their bosoms" (line 62). The passage ends with the narrator's speculating on how Dupin could do so. Choice (A) is correct.

EXTRA PRACTICE

Suggested Passage Map notes:

¶1: U.S. idea of national parks
¶2: parks scope and history
¶3: millions appreciate parks, parks encourage preservation
¶4: JM father of national parks
¶5: JM focus on ecology, natural beauty and worth
¶6: political impact, started Sierra Club
¶7: JM greatest accomplishment importance of nature

1. C   Difficulty: Medium
Category: Vocab-in-Context

Getting to the Answer: Look for context clues to help you determine the meaning of unknown words. Read the rest of the paragraph to get a better idea of the relationship between America's national parks and the rest of the world. The last sentence of the paragraph states that "globally over a thousand parks are now protected

by similar systems" (lines 10-11). The idea that originated in the United States later became popular worldwide. Choice (C), "imitated," is correct.

2. A   Difficulty: Medium
Category: Rhetoric

Getting to the Answer: As you take notes, identify the general idea of each paragraph in the passage in your own words. Compare your notes to each choice to find the correct answer. The second paragraph provides the reader with statistics about the scale of the National Parks System, including the diversity of the parks, the number of employees required to manage the system, and the number of acres the system includes. Choice (A) correctly summarizes the purpose of this paragraph.

3. D   Difficulty: Medium
Category: Inference

Getting to the Answer: Look for specific textual evidence in the passage that may support each answer choice. The correct answer will be concluded directly from the passage. The passage mentions the international influence of the United States National Parks System several times. Other answer choices are not supported by evidence. Only choice (D) is directly found within the passage.

4. D   Difficulty: Medium
Category: Command of Evidence

Getting to the Answer: Review your answer to the previous question. Then, choose the textual evidence that best supports that conclusion. According to the passage, "over a hundred countries now participate" (lines 36-37) in a national parks system. Choice (D) provides direct evidence for the passage's assertion that America's national parks idea has been influential internationally.

5. A   Difficulty: Easy
Category: Vocab-in-Context

Getting to the Answer: Break the word down into its component parts to determine the correct answer. "Wander" suggests travel and "lust" suggests a positive interest. Looking at the context, "his activism and wanderlust also drew him to other picturesque locations" (lines 65-67), an interest in travel is the most logical choice.

Answers & Explanations

6. B **Difficulty:** Hard

Category: Rhetoric

Getting to the Answer: Consider why the word "channeling" is used instead of an alternative word. What meaning does it add that a more general word like "communicating" does not? The context of the sentence suggests that Muir's writings were powerful. They seem to have captured the "marvel" (line 71) of the wilderness and transmitted it directly to readers, making them feel it, too. "Channeling" emphasizes the way the power of his writing took the emotion he felt and communicated it directly and powerfully to readers. Choice (B) successfully captures this idea.

7. A **Difficulty:** Hard

Category: Inference

Getting to the Answer: Consider the passage as a whole. Are there any answers you can immediately eliminate as being obviously incorrect? The passage consistently states that John Muir was hugely influential during his lifetime, so B can be eliminated. It does acknowledge, however, that the preservation of such vast amounts of wilderness did come at an economic cost, though the passage suggests that this cost was worthwhile. Choice (A) is correct.

8. D **Difficulty:** Medium

Category: Command of Evidence

Getting to the Answer: Test each possible answer choice against your selection for the preceding question. Which piece of evidence most directly supports the previous answer choice? The passage states that conserving the wilderness was worthwhile, "even at the expense of short-lived material gains" (lines 90-91). This suggests that there was an economic cost to Muir's preservation goals. Choice (D) is correct, as it directly connects the parks system to ideas of money.

9. A **Difficulty:** Hard

Category: Synthesis

Getting to the Answer: Use your Passage Map to summarize each passage. Then, find the answer choice that best matches your ideas. Passage 1 describes the American National Parks System in general, focusing on its creation, its size, and its parks' diversity. Passage

2 focuses specifically on the importance of John Muir and his influence on conservation. Choice (A) correctly summarizes these differences.

10. A **Difficulty:** Easy

Category: Synthesis

Getting to the Answer: Evaluate how each passage describes the national parks. What do the word choices suggest about the purpose and value of the parks? Both passages use words like "awe" (line 29) and "wonder" (line 70) to discuss the national parks. Clearly, the authors of both passages agree that the main value of national parks is to preserve natural beauty for visitors. Choice (A) correctly reflects this idea.

11. D **Difficulty:** Easy

Category: Synthesis

Getting to the Answer: Carefully study the *x*- and *y*-axes to determine what trends can be inferred from the graph. According to the graph, visits to all five parks have increased from 1930 to 2010. No conclusions can be drawn about why parks have been more or less popular during these periods. However, the graph does show that during each period, the Grand Canyon has received more visitors than has Olympic National Park. Choice (D) is the only answer choice that can be definitely concluded from the chart.

CHAPTER 19

PRACTICE

3. C   **Difficulty:** Medium
Category: Effective Language Use

Getting to the Answer: Consider how you would refer to a number in a different context. Would you say you started school "hundred days" ago? "Hundred" refers to a digit (ones digit, tens digit, hundreds digit, etc.), whereas "one hundred" is an actual number. In order to begin the sentence in an idiomatically correct way, it is necessary to use the full number, "one hundred." Choice (C) matches.

4. C   **Difficulty:** Medium
Category: Sentence Formation

Getting to the Answer: If there is no obvious error in the underlined segment, keep reading until you can identify the issue. The underlined portion is correctly used as the subject of an independent clause. However, because the clause after the comma is also independent, the sentence is a run-on. Since you are not given the option to fix the comma splice, look for the answer choice that makes the first clause dependent without introducing another error. Choice (C) correctly subordinates the first clause by beginning the sentence with "when."

5. B   **Difficulty:** Easy
Category: Usage

Getting to the Answer: Subjects and verbs must agree in person and number. Singular third person subjects need singular third person verbs, and plural third person subjects need plural third person verbs. Keep in mind that the closest noun to an underlined verb may not be its subject. Read around the underlined portion until you can identify the subject of the underlined verb. Remember, a noun that is the object of a preposition cannot be the subject of a sentence. In this sentence, the subject is the plural noun "components" and needs a plural verb. Choice (B) is correct.

PERFORM

6. B   **Difficulty:** Medium
Category: Effective Language Use

Getting to the Answer: Using two words that mean the same thing is redundant. Look for the answer choice that creates the most concise sentence. As written, the sentence uses a compound predicate made up of "fascinated and intrigued." Because both words convey the same idea, namely that scientists found Jupiter to be very interesting, using one is sufficient. Choice (B) concisely conveys the idea.

7. D   **Difficulty:** Medium
Category: Sentence Formation

Getting to the Answer: Read around an underlined period and check to make sure that each clause forms a complete sentence. Because the second clause is a fragment, it needs to be properly connected to the previous sentence with either subordination or punctuation. Choice B provides punctuation that corrects the fragment but does not form an effective sentence. Since the information in the second clause explains why the moons of Jupiter provided evidence for a theory, the second clause needs to be combined with the previous sentence. Choice (D) joins the clause to the sentence.

8. D   **Difficulty:** Easy
Category: Sentence Formation

Getting to the Answer: Compare underlined verbs with related verbs. Related verb forms need to be parallel. The verbs "completed" and "collected" form a compound predicate and need to be parallel in form. As written, the underlined section unnecessarily reintroduces the subject. Join the two verbs without punctuation. Choice (D) is correct.

9. C   **Difficulty:** Easy
Category: Development

Getting to the Answer: If you have the option to omit a sentence, think carefully about the author's topic. If the underlined portion strays from the topic, omit it. The author's topic is Jupiter. The underlined portion adds information about *Pioneer 10* that is irrelevant to the topic. Choice (C) correctly omits the sentence for this reason.

10. B   Difficulty: Medium
Category: Effective Language Use

Getting to the Answer: If an underlined segment does not contain a grammatical error, check for other kinds of errors tested on the SAT. As written, the underlined portion is a complete sentence. Reread that sentence in the context of the following sentence. Together, these two sentences sound choppy and create a wordiness issue. Because the underlined sentence provides information about Jupiter, it can be incorporated into the next sentence. Choice (B) forms a modifying phrase that effectively introduces the subject of the sentence.

11. D   Difficulty: Medium
Category: Usage

Getting to the Answer: Related nouns must be consistent in number. Check other nouns around an underlined noun to make sure they agree. The underlined noun is related to the noun phrase "number of probes." Because there was more than one probe, there was more than one measurement. Choice (D) correctly makes the underlined noun plural.

12. C   Difficulty: Medium
Category: Quantitative

Getting to the Answer: When you see a question with an infographic, remember to use the Kaplan Method for Infographics. The sentence to which the underlined portion belongs is comparing Earth's rotational speed to that of Jupiter's. The relevant information is how much faster Jupiter rotates. Look in the third column of the table for that data. Compare the information you find with the answer choices. Choice (C) provides accurate and relevant information.

13. D   Difficulty: Medium
Category: Usage

Getting to the Answer: A pronoun's antecedent must be clear and unambiguous. Always identify the antecedent of an underlined pronoun. The underlined possessive pronoun could refer to a number of things: our diameter, Earth's diameter, and Earth's rotational speed. Reread the sentence to determine what the author means. The sentence compares the diameter of Jupiter to the diameter of Earth. Look for the answer choice that makes that comparison clear. Choice (D) is correct.

EXTRA PRACTICE

1. B   Difficulty: Medium
Category: Effective Language Use

Getting to the Answer: Read the entire paragraph to determine if a career in physical therapy is rated as a good career choice by the Bureau of Labor Statistics. "Concurrently" means at the same time, and "unusually" means not common. "Finally" implies that physical therapy was not a good career choice in the past. Choice (B) is correct because it means with regularity.

2. D   Difficulty: Medium
Category: Effective Language Use

Getting to the Answer: Read the sentence and determine how it can be more concise. As written, the text begins with a conjunction and uses a dash to indicate an unnecessary break in thought. Choice (D) eliminates both problems, creating a more direct sentence.

3. B   Difficulty: Medium
Category: Development

Getting to the Answer: Read the entire paragraph to identify its focus. Choices A, C, and D each offer only one component of the paragraph. Only choice (B) effectively establishes the main topic of the second paragraph.

4. A   Difficulty: Easy
Category: Punctuation

Getting to the Answer: Read the sentence and determine whether it is grammatically complete. To form a grammatically complete sentence, you must have an independent clause after a semicolon. Choices B, C, and D all have excessive and incorrect punctuation. The sentence is correct as written; choice (A) is correct.

5. B   Difficulty: Hard
Category: Development

Getting to the Answer: Read the entire paragraph to determine the pattern of the evidence. Most sentences include descriptions of the types of patients a PT will encounter. Since (B) is the only sentence that supports the topic sentence, it is the correct answer.

6. B   Difficulty: Medium
Category: Sentence Formation

Getting to the Answer: Read the sentence to determine how to improve its clarity. Consider whether the modifiers are correctly placed near the nouns or verbs they modify. The use of the modifier "minimally" at the end of the sentence is awkward. Choice (B) correctly moves the modifier next to the word it modifies: "interaction." It also removes the conjunction "And" at the beginning of the sentence.

7. D   Difficulty: Medium
Category: Effective Language Use

Getting to the Answer: Read the sentences and determine what words can be eliminated. As written, the text uses short, choppy sentences. Choice (D) combines the two sentences effectively to improve the economy of word choice.

8. B   Difficulty: Hard
Category: Sentence Formation

Getting to the Answer: Read the sentence and examine the order of the details. Reorganize the sentence so that it is clear and smooth. As written, the text contains coordinated ideas without regard to their grammatical form. Choice (B) correctly rearranges the ideas so that the three main ideas are nouns combined with "and" instead of "in addition to."

9. A   Difficulty: Easy
Category: Effective Language Use

Getting to the Answer: Read the sentence and determine the function of the word in the sentence. "Concentrated" means clustered or gathered together, "planned" means to arrange beforehand, and "consolidated" means brought together in a single whole. Only choice (A), "collaborated," means working together intellectually.

10. D   Difficulty: Hard
Category: Organization

Getting to the Answer: Read the paragraph and determine if the sequence of events is logical. For the paragraph to be logical, the examples need to build upon one another. Sentence 7 does not offer a proper conclusion to the paragraph, but sentence 2 gives a good summation.

Choice (D) correctly moves the summative sentence to conclude the paragraph.

11. D   Difficulty: Medium
Category: Development

Getting to the Answer: Closely read the paragraph to find the central idea. Then, determine which sentence does not match the content. The evidence regarding physical therapy assistants does not connect with the main idea of this paragraph, which centers on the benefits of choosing to become a certified physical therapist. Choice (D) is correct.

CHAPTER 20

PRACTICE

4. C   **Difficulty:** Hard
Category: Organization

Getting to the Answer: An effective body paragraph can provide evidence to support the author's central idea or introduce a change in the focus of the passage. This paragraph begins with the transition word "while" and establishes a contrast between the number of recent earthquakes and the damage that those earthquakes can cause. The passage also shifts focus from a discussion of earthquake frequency to one of earthquake damage. Therefore, placing this paragraph between the two discussions in paragraph 4 and paragraph 5 makes the most sense. Choice (C) is correct.

5. C   **Difficulty:** Medium
Category: Organization

Getting to the Answer: When reordering a sentence within a paragraph, identify the information in the sentence and locate where in the paragraph that information is discussed. The topic of sentence 4 is aftershocks. Aftershocks are also discussed in sentence 2. However, in sentence 2 the pronoun "these" indicates that aftershocks have been previously discussed in the paragraph. The logical place for sentence 4 is before sentence 2. Choice (C) is correct.

6. A   **Difficulty:** Easy
Category: Organization

Getting to the Answer: Don't answer questions that ask about the conclusion of a paragraph until you have read the entire paragraph. The paragraph focuses on the damage that earthquakes can cause and ways to improve safety in the event of an earthquake. Although the sentence preceding the concluding sentence mentions earthquake predictions, it does so in the context of how to prepare for these natural disasters. Therefore, the final sentence needs to discuss preparations, not predictions. Choice (A) provides a logical conclusion to the paragraph.

PERFORM

7. D   **Difficulty:** Medium
Category: Usage

Getting to the Answer: A pronoun is ambiguous when its antecedent is either missing or unclear. To find the antecedent for the underlined pronoun, read the previous sentence and think about the focus of the paragraph. The previous sentence has more than one possible antecedent—vacuous "Internet speak," "reliance," or "acronyms and abbreviations." However, in the context of the passage, "empty chatter," or choice (D), is the clearest and most relevant antecedent.

8. A   **Difficulty:** Medium
Category: Organization

Getting to the Answer: To answer questions about effective transitions within a paragraph, identify the focus of the paragraph both before and after the transition. The first part of the paragraph discusses the reasons the narrator stayed in his room as a child—because he was ill. After the transition, the narrator discusses why he still stays in his room—because he has access to the world. The transition needs to show how those ideas are linked. Choice (A) provides a logical transition as written.

9. B   **Difficulty:** Easy
Category: Effective Language Use

Getting to the Answer: When two words or phrases in the sentence have the same meaning, the sentence is redundant and contains a concision error. In this sentence, "succinct" and "to the point" have the same meaning, so the correct answer will eliminate one. Choice (B) is correct.

10. C   **Difficulty:** Hard
Category: Organization

Getting to the Answer: To reorder a sentence within a paragraph, identify the information in the sentence and locate what sentence that information should logically precede or follow. As written, sentence 5 summarizes the freedom people experience when connected by the Internet. However, sentence 6 makes a claim about that freedom, and sentence 7 provides examples of that freedom. The summary in sentence 5 should logically follow both the claim and the examples. Choice (C) is correct.

11. B   Difficulty: Easy
Category: Usage

Getting to the Answer: Unless the context in the passage indicates that the time frame has changed, the verb tense should not change. As written, this verb is in the past perfect tense. However, the context of the passage indicates that the action described by the verb continued up until the present moment. Choice (B) correctly uses the present perfect tense.

12. D   Difficulty: Hard
Category: Sentence Formation

Getting to the Answer: Whenever you see a compound, series, or list, check to make sure that all of the items are in parallel form. The underlined phrase is part of a compound formed by the conjunction "and." Reread the sentence and identify the other part of the compound. In this sentence, "half two minds exchanging sophisticated ideas" forms the first part of the compound. The second part must be parallel. Choice (D) is correct.

13. A   Difficulty: Medium
Category: Organization

Getting to the Answer: Introductory transitions must logically connect the information and ideas in the sentences before and after the transition. In the sentence before the underlined transition, the author describes small talk as boring. In the following sentence, he compares a conversation without small talk to flying. The sentence suggests that small talk can be dispensed with only occasionally. This sentence is correct as written, so choice (A) is correct.

14. D   Difficulty: Medium
Category: Organization

Getting to the Answer: Paragraphs in a well-written passage will flow from the general to the specific. To put paragraphs in the most logical order, begin with the paragraph that introduces the central idea in broad terms. As written, paragraph 1 contains a very specific discussion of a particular form of speech. Paragraph 2 introduces the idea of conversation in general terms and outlines the narrator's thoughts about it. Only choice (D) arranges the paragraphs from the general to the specific.

EXTRA PRACTICE

1. B   Difficulty: Easy
Category: Usage

Getting to the Answer: As currently written, this sentence switches verb tense mid-sentence. The other verb in the sentence, "was," indicates that the events happened in the past. The tense of the underlined verb should match and also be in a correct past tense. Choice (B) is correct because it correctly uses the past tense of "produce."

2. B   Difficulty: Medium
Category: Organization

Getting to the Answer: Look for the relationship between this sentence and the previous one. Choice (B) shows the relationship between the two sentences by giving an example of what kind of art the Post-Impressionists were creating.

3. D   Difficulty: Medium
Category: Effective Language Use

Getting to the Answer: Read the complete passage to learn more about the work of Impressionists. The passage states that Impressionists tried to paint exactly what they saw in nature. Only choice (D) has the correct connotation and fits within the context of the sentence.

4. B   Difficulty: Medium
Category: Sentence Formation

Getting to the Answer: The verbs in a sentence have to be parallel. The correct answer is in the same form as the first verb in the sentence, "looking." That means that the gerund, or -ing verb, "attempting" in choice (B) is correct.

5. A   Difficulty: Easy
Category: Effective Language Use

Getting to the Answer: Check each word for its connotations and pick the answer choice that fits the context of the sentence. This sentence describes how Post-Impressionists focused on self-discovery in art by letting their personal experiences and emotions guide their interpretation of their subjects. Therefore, each artist had his or her own distinct, or "unique," vision. The underlined portion is correct as written, and the answer is therefore choice (A).

6. C   **Difficulty:** Hard
Category: Development

Getting to the Answer: Read the entire paragraph and determine the central idea. The paragraph discusses different ways artists in the Post-Impressionism era painted. Choice (C) reflects this summary.

7. B   **Difficulty:** Hard
Category: Effective Language Use

Getting to the Answer: Choice (B) joins the sentences concisely and correctly by changing the verb tense of the first sentence to make it a dependent clause.

8. A   **Difficulty:** Easy
Category: Usage

Getting to the Answer: Read the sentence prior to the pronoun to determine whom the pronoun is referencing. The pronoun "they" refers to Paul Gauguin and Vincent van Gogh, so the pronoun needs to be plural and in the third person. Choice (A) is correct.

9. D   **Difficulty:** Hard
Category: Development

Getting to the Answer: Read the entire paragraph to identify the central idea. Then find the answer choice that provides evidence about this idea. The paragraph concerns the Post-Impressionist period and what kinds of methods Post-Impressionists used to create their art. Choice (D) addresses the central idea by providing additional information about these methods.

10. B   **Difficulty:** Medium
Category: Usage

Getting to the Answer: "They're" is a contraction meaning "they are," which does not make sense in the context of the sentence. What is needed here is a possessive plural pronoun to match the antecedent "artists." Choice (B) is correct.

11. D   **Difficulty:** Medium
Category: Organization

Getting to the Answer: Try inserting this sentence into all of the possible places to figure out where it makes the most sense. Choice (D) is the most logical position for this sentence because it is a comment based on the quotation in sentence 5.

CHAPTER 21

PRACTICE

5. D   **Difficulty:** Medium
Category: Development

Getting to the Answer: Scrutinize details of densely factual passages to make sure they are on-topic and do not conflict with other details or the central idea. This passage is concerned with the details of human skin and explaining the properties and purposes of skin. Choice (D) abides by the author's scope and purpose for the passage and is therefore correct.

6. A   **Difficulty:** Medium
Category: Development

Getting to the Answer: Pick the answer choice that is in line with the author's central idea and tone. In this passage, the author explains how the skin is essential to life by listing its various properties and processes for keeping the body in healthy operation. The underlined section is in line with the author's overall effort. Choice (A) is correct.

7. C   **Difficulty:** Medium
Category: Development

Getting to the Answer: Make sure details in the underlined section are relevant to the topic. Even if a detail matches the tone of the passage (in this case, strictly fact-based), it might not be relevant to the central idea. Most of the answer choices for this question sound legitimate and even factually correct. However, only choice (C) keeps the focus on the human skin and its characteristics, so it is correct. Remember, the focus of the paragraph is on the defensive functions of the skin, *not* on how those functions work at a cellular level. You also know that immediate medical attention (choice B) is too extreme for every instance of skin breaking (small cuts, etc.).

8. A   **Difficulty:** Medium
Category: Development

Getting to the Answer: Concluding sentences often reassert or summarize the author's central idea; therefore, they cannot fundamentally conflict with the author's assertions. In this passage, the author has made clear that the skin is a very important organ that protects the body from a variety of illnesses and disorders, as well as from physical harm. Choice (A) is correct, as it ties preceding points and details together into a coherent conclusion for the author's argument.

PERFORM

9. A   **Difficulty:** Medium
Category: Development

Getting to the Answer: Scrutinize the answer choices for how they relate to the author's central ideas as well as how they potentially conflict with details that come later in the passage. Choice (A) is correct because—without going off-topic or conflicting with later details—it elaborates on the idea that Polk followed in Jackson's footsteps.

10. C   **Difficulty:** Easy
Category: Development

Getting to the Answer: Pay close attention to long lists of evidence to make sure that each component is in line with the central idea and context of the sentence. Choice (C) is correct because it is the only answer choice that both stays focused on matters of policy (as the first part of the sentence mentions) and supports the thesis that Polk and Jackson were in agreement on most points of public policy.

11. D   **Difficulty:** Easy
Category: Development

Getting to the Answer: The first sentence of a paragraph sets the paragraph's tone and purpose. Pay attention to what the other sentences of the paragraph are describing and pick the answer choice that is the best introduction for those details. This paragraph is concerned with explaining the chronology of Polk's early life. Choice (D) is correct because it states the place and date of Polk's birth, making it a logical introduction to the following sentences.

12. D   **Difficulty:** Medium
Category: Development

Getting to the Answer: Supporting details fit the context of the paragraph and do not contradict details found elsewhere in the passage. Select the answer choice that satisfies these guidelines. This paragraph is narrowly concerned with Polk's origins and early political career. Only choice (D) fits the context and does not contradict later details.

13. C **Difficulty:** Medium
Category: Development

Getting to the Answer: A paragraph's final sentence ideally guides the paragraph's central idea to a conclusion and remains linked to the central idea of the passage. Choice (C) is correct because it is the most effective conclusion for a paragraph tasked with explaining Polk's early political career. Choice (C) also makes a clear connection to the following paragraph, helping the narrative flow.

14. B **Difficulty:** Medium
Category: Development

Getting to the Answer: Remember that supporting evidence needs to focus on and contribute to the central idea. The author's intent is to introduce the two main candidates in the 1844 election, leading to the following sentence that discusses their opinions of expansionism. Choice (B) is correct because it stays focused on the paragraph's topic and contributes to the argument that Polk recognized popular support for expansionism that other candidates overlooked or ignored.

15. A **Difficulty:** Medium
Category: Development

Getting to the Answer: Examine details and parenthetical asides for relevance to the central idea. The goal is to make sure that no contradictions are being introduced into the narrative. No change is necessary because the underlined section touches on two central themes of the passage: Polk's support for expansionist policies and his Jacksonian view of America. Choice (A) is correct.

16. B **Difficulty:** Hard
Category: Development

Getting to the Answer: Pay close attention to a paragraph's first sentence. It should set the stage for details to follow and also be in line with the passage's central idea. As alluded to in the first paragraph and explained clearly in the final paragraph, Polk did much to expand the borders of the United States. He even supported war with Mexico to gain territory. Choice (B) is correct.

EXTRA PRACTICE

1. B **Difficulty:** Medium
Category: Development

Getting to the Answer: Identify the main idea of the paragraph. Eliminate options that do not support the main idea. Although sentence 3 is related to the main topic of the paragraph, coral reefs, the information in this sentence does nothing to support the main idea: coral reefs' function, threatened status, and composition. Choice (B) is correct.

2. B **Difficulty:** Medium
Category: Organization

Getting to the Answer: Read the preceding sentence along with this one and look for a relationship between the ideas in the sentences. The first sentence describes the importance of coral reefs, and this sentence explains how they are in danger of disappearing. "Unfortunately" is the best transition to use here, and choice (B) is the correct answer.

3. A **Difficulty:** Medium
Category: Quantitative

Getting to the Answer: Evaluate the data presented in the infographic that accompanies the passage. Read each answer choice and eliminate those not supported by the data in the graph. Choice (A) is correct. As the pie chart shows and the caption confirms, about sixty percent of living reefs are in danger.

4. B **Difficulty:** Medium
Category: Effective Language Use

Getting to the Answer: As written, the sentence contains redundant language. Look for the answer choice that retains the meaning of the two original sentences but is less wordy and redundant. Choice (B) is the correct answer because it contains the same information as the original sentences but in a more concise manner. While C is similar, it uses passive voice, which you should avoid using on the SAT.

5. D **Difficulty:** Medium
Category: Effective Language Use

Getting to the Answer: Look for the answer that creates the clearest idea within the sentence. The resources referred to in the sentence are clean water and sunlight—things the reef must have to survive. These resources are vital to the coral reefs, so choice (D) is the correct answer.

6. B   Difficulty: Easy
Category: Development

Getting to the Answer: The correct answer will briefly describe the main idea of the paragraph and will be supported by the details in the paragraph. Be careful of answer choices like C that summarize a detail provided in the paragraph rather than the central idea. Choice (B) best describes the main idea of the paragraph. All of the details presented in the paragraph are related to how people engaging in activities near coral reefs often cause damage.

7. B   Difficulty: Easy
Category: Usage

Getting to the Answer: Check the verb tense in the sentences that follow this one. Be sure that the verb tense is consistent. To agree with the sentences in the rest of the paragraph, the verb in this sentence should be written in present tense. Because the noun is singular, choice (B) is the correct answer.

8. C   Difficulty: Medium
Category: Effective Language Use

Getting to the Answer: Look for the answer that creates the clearest idea within the sentence. The word "obstruct" most clearly illustrates how the particles that settle on the coral keep sunlight from reaching the coral. Choice (C) is correct.

9. B   Difficulty: Easy
Category: Effective Language Use

Getting to the Answer: Avoid answers that are grammatically correct but wordy or redundant. The correct answer is the most concise choice. "Would suggest" fits grammatically and is the most concise choice, so choice (B) is the correct answer.

10. A   Difficulty: Medium
Category: Development

Getting to the Answer: Avoid answers that are related to the main topic but do not add relevant details to the paragraph. The paragraph explains how crabs and coral reefs help each other. Choice (A) is the best addition to this paragraph to support the central idea.

11. D   Difficulty: Medium
Category: Organization

Getting to the Answer: Read the paragraph with the sentence moved to the places suggested by the answer choices. Look for relationships between the ideas in the surrounding sentences. This sentence is a continuation of the idea introduced in sentence 3 (crabs might be damaging the coral) and belongs after sentence 3. Choice (D) is the correct answer.

CHAPTER 22

PRACTICE

5. D   **Difficulty:** Hard
Category: Effective Language Use

Getting to the Answer: Make sure the order in which words and phrases are written makes sense logically. As written, this sentence is hard to follow. The author is trying to emphasize the information that men also served as nurses during the Civil War. Choice (D) is correct because it is the only answer choice with grammatically and logically correct syntax.

6. B   **Difficulty:** Medium
Category: Effective Language Use

Getting to the Answer: Even if an underlined word or phrase sounds correct, analyze its meaning—both literal and figurative—to ensure it is appropriate in context. While it is easy to interpret a meaning from the underlined phrase "major victories," that meaning does not convey the author's intention. The phrase "major victories" suggests that of all the accomplishments of this organization, excluding men was one of the most important. Reread the sentences before and after the underlined phrase to understand that what the author means to convey is the idea that this exclusion occurred early in the history of the nurses' organization. Choice (B) corrects this error by explaining that this exclusion was one of the early victories within a series of accomplishments.

7. C   **Difficulty:** Easy
Category: Effective Language Use

Getting to the Answer: Avoid the temptation to use more words than necessary. As written, the underlined segment is redundant: "denied admission to" and "excluded from" have the same meaning. Look for the most succinct way to convey the author's intended meaning. Choice (C) is correct.

8. B   **Difficulty:** Medium
Category: Effective Language Use

Getting to the Answer: Style and tone errors are nuanced—pay attention to the details in the sentences surrounding the underlined word or phrase. As written, the underlined portion does not match the style and tone of the passage because it includes the author's opinion while the rest of the passage offers no judgment on any of the situations discussed. Choice (B) correctly maintains the objective tone of the passage by omitting any subjective viewpoints.

PERFORM

9. B   **Difficulty:** Medium
Category: Effective Language Use

Getting to the Answer: Read the sentence to understand the context in which the underlined word, "imagine," is used. The author uses "imagine" to describe how certain groups portray the risks associated with genetically modified organisms. Because the author views these groups as the opposition, the word needs to convey a stronger sense of resistance to the truth. As written, the sentence is too benign. Choice (B) is correct.

10. D   **Difficulty:** Easy
Category: Effective Language Use

Getting to the Answer: "Interfere" and "tamper" have the same meaning and are used to express a single idea about intentionally changing nature. The correct answer will eliminate one of those words. Choice (D) is correct.

11. B   **Difficulty:** Medium
Category: Effective Language Use

Getting to the Answer: Do not automatically select the shortest answer choice when presented with a Concision question. The correct answer choice must fully convey the author's intended meaning. As written, the underlined segment is the shortest answer choice, but it is difficult to determine exactly which group of people the "we" is referencing. Choice (B) is correct because it specifies the people included in "we" most concisely.

12. B   **Difficulty:** Hard
Category: Effective Language Use

Getting to the Answer: Effective Language Use questions focused on syntax often require you to recognize that grammatically correct sentence structure alone may not produce the most effective writing. Although the sentences are grammatically correct as written, the question stem asks which of the answer choices most effectively combines the two sentences. Because the second sentence provides additional information about "certain bird species" mentioned in the first sentence, use the relative pronoun "that" to indicate which species could be affected by the decline in the insect population. Choice (B) is correct.

13. D   Difficulty: Medium
Category: Effective Language Use

Getting to the Answer: Auxiliary verbs, like the underlined "will," add functional or grammatical meaning like expressing tense, voice, or emphasis to the clause in which they appear. When an auxiliary verb is underlined, make sure it fits the context of the paragraph or passage. Throughout the paragraph, the author uses the auxiliary verb "could" to indicate the possibility that certain things could happen—"could lead" and" could have." Nothing in the paragraph suggests that the author has shifted from conjecture (indicated by "could") to either certainty ("will" and "would") or necessity ("must"). Choice (D) is correct.

14. A   Difficulty: Medium
Category: Effective Language Use

Getting to the Answer: When an entire sentence is underlined, check for a syntax error. This sentence is correct as written. The author arranges the parts of the sentence in the most logical order by introducing the topic ("actual impact"), describing what is being impacted, and drawing a conclusion about the topic. Choice (A) is correct.

15. A   Difficulty: Medium
Category: Effective Language Use

Getting to the Answer: To answer Effective Language Use questions focused on word choice, or precision, reread the sentence containing the underlined word or phrase to determine the author's intended meaning. Determine that the underlined phrase "essential fallacy" provides information about the basis for the argument discussed in this sentence. Rephrase the sentence as: the argument is based on a false idea. However, a false idea is not the same as a lie. Choice (A) is correct.

16. D   Difficulty: Medium
Category: Effective Language Use

Getting to the Answer: When answering a question about style and tone, you will sometimes first need to read the entire passage or paragraph. In the first three paragraphs, the author focuses on the negative aspects of genetically modified organisms. In the fourth paragraph, he dismisses the counter argument raised by advocates for genetically modified organisms. The tone in the final paragraph becomes strident and accusatory. The final sentence must match this tone in order to effectively conclude the paragraph and the passage. Choice (D) is correct because it suggests that the stakes for the planet are enormous and our misplaced trust would have dire consequences.

EXTRA PRACTICE

1. B   Difficulty: Medium
Category: Punctuation

Getting to the Answer: Read the sentence to determine how the list within it should be formatted. If it is more of an aside than a direct part of the sentence's main structure, the list should be set off by punctuation. As the sentence is written, its many commas are confusing. Because there is a list in the sentence, the commas within that list should remain. However, the list of poetic forms is not directly related to the rest of the sentence, so this should be clarified with punctuation. Dashes are the best way to mark this as a separate thought. Choice (B) correctly adds dashes to both the beginning and end of the list.

2. A   Difficulty: Easy
Category: Effective Language Use

Getting to the Answer: Determine what the sentence is saying about the history of the haiku. Is "complex" the most accurate way to describe it? The passage describes the many forms and many centuries that comprise the history of haiku. Choice (A), "complex," perfectly describes the long, rich, and detailed history of the poetic form.

3. A   **Difficulty:** Hard

Category: Development

Getting to the Answer: Consider the purpose of the paragraph, then determine which answer choice makes the most sense as an introduction to the paragraph. The purpose of this paragraph, based on its other sentences, is to explain the history of haiku and how its structure has changed over time. Choice (A) is the only answer choice related to these ideas. While the other answer choices may briefly mention the structure of haiku or its history, they all focus on other aspects of haiku—its entertainment value, the difficulty of understanding its rules, or the challenge of writing it.

4. D   **Difficulty:** Easy

Category: Development

Getting to the Answer: The sentence's placement in the passage is not optimal. The next sentence returns the discussion to the hokku form and readers encounter another explanation of the name "haiku" later, in paragraph 5. Choice (D) is correct because the sentence should be omitted from paragraph 2.

5. C   **Difficulty:** Medium

Category: Organization

Getting to the Answer: Consider the information presented by the rest of the paragraph to determine the meaning of the phrase "alternating turns." Sentence 7 describes the specifics of different word games introduced in sentence 5, so it makes sense that it would follow sentence 5. Choice (C) is correct.

6. C   **Difficulty:** Easy

Category: Organization

Getting to the Answer: Make sure that this sentence clearly and precisely transitions from the topic of the previous paragraph to the topic of this paragraph. As currently written, the first sentence does not make a clear connection to the preceding paragraph. By making the discussion of time more precise, the beginning of this paragraph flows better from the previous one. The reader understands more clearly how the details in each paragraph connect. Choice (C) is correct.

7. D   **Difficulty:** Medium

Category: Effective Language Use

Getting to the Answer: Determine the purpose of sharing this information with readers. The tone of the sentence should be suited to its purpose. The paragraph is a straightforward piece of informative writing. The original segment and C are both too casual for the rest of the passage, while B is too formal and wordy. Choice (D) correctly communicates the information of this sentence with the right level of formality.

8. D   **Difficulty:** Hard

Category: Development

Getting to the Answer: Find the answer choice that clearly supports the topic sentence of the paragraph while elegantly tying into the next sentence. The topic sentence of this paragraph emphasizes the themes in Basho's work and how haiku became associated with nature and the seasons. Choice (D) provides examples of possible subjects of Basho haiku and is therefore correct.

9. C   **Difficulty:** Hard

Category: Effective Language Use

Getting to the Answer: Consider what the sentence is communicating and if it can be made more concise. The sentence uses too many words to communicate its point. By combining ideas and eliminating wordiness, the sentence can flow more smoothly. Choice (C) is correct because it maintains the sentence's meaning while using fewer words.

10. B   **Difficulty:** Medium

Category: Effective Language Use

Getting to the Answer: Consider the precise relationship between Shiki and the other poets mentioned. The correct answer choice will describe his effect on them. It seems clear that Shiki's work influenced cummings and Pound. While "helped" and "aided" both generally suggest that his effect on them was positive, "inspired" is more accurate. Shiki had left his mark, and the other poets learned from him. Choice (B) is correct.

11. D   **Difficulty:** Medium

Category: Effective Language Use

Getting to the Answer: Read the sentence and determine whether its thoughts are joined logically. The two parts of the sentence are directly related; the writers are "taken with the brevity of the form" because of what it provides them. The sentence does not express this relationship as written, so eliminate A. Eliminate B and C because neither choice correctly relates the two parts of the sentence. Choice (D) correctly combines the sentence while maintaining the relationship between the two clauses.

CHAPTER 23

PRACTICE

4. A   **Difficulty:** Medium
Category: Sentence Formation

Getting to the Answer: Words such as *while, when*, and *because* are subordinating conjunctions that work to join independent clauses with dependent clauses. Make sure that the subordinating conjunction fits the context of the sentence and makes the author's intent clear. Here, the author presents a contrast between the aspects of the Sun that are easily identifiable (light, heat) and other phenomena that are less obvious. At the same time, the author admits that all of these aspects of the Sun are always happening simultaneously. The current construction of "Yet, while" most clearly conveys the author's meaning of contrast. Choice (A) is correct.

5. D   **Difficulty:** Hard
Category: Usage

Getting to the Answer: Pronouns need to agree with the noun or noun phrase to which they refer. The noun is often in the same sentence but can sometimes be found in preceding sentences. The noun phrase to which the pronoun refers is found at the end of the previous sentence: "the Sun's most volatile surface activity." Since "activity" is singular, the pronoun must agree with a singular noun. "They" is plural and is thus incorrect. Choice (D) is correct because it matches the singular noun.

6. B   **Difficulty:** Medium
Category: Sentence Formation

Getting to the Answer: Pay close attention to modifier placement. If modifiers are misplaced or incorrectly used, they can change the author's meaning or harm the sentence's clarity. As the sentence is currently written, the modifier "powerful" is misplaced. The author's intent is to explain the power of the magnetic fields to prevent heat from reaching the Sun's surface. Choice (B) is correct because "powerful" is placed before "magnetic fields," thereby correctly modifying the noun.

PERFORM

7. C   **Difficulty:** Medium
Category: Usage

Getting to the Answer: Active voice construction is almost always better than passive voice construction, as it has the subject of the sentence performing the action. This makes a sentence simpler and clearer. Choice (C) is correct because it is an active voice construction and is not interrupted by parentheticals set off by commas.

8. B   **Difficulty:** Easy
Category: Sentence Formation

Getting to the Answer: When the passage presents a long, complex sentence, be sure that it is not a run-on that would be better presented as two or more separate sentences. The underlined section is a juncture within a very long sentence; this is made obvious by the comma and the transitional phrase "in fact." Before this juncture, the sentence discusses the accessibility of Eisenstein's work, and after, it addresses his lasting effect on film. These two ideas are more clearly presented in two separate sentences instead of the current run-on. Choice (B) is correct.

9. A   **Difficulty:** Easy
Category: Sentence Formation

Getting to the Answer: If the underlined section is a coordinating conjunction—a word or phrase that joins two equally important phrases or clauses—pay attention to the appropriateness of the word choice. Keep clarity of the sentence and passage in mind. No change is necessary because "and" clearly demonstrates that Eisenstein was pushed out of one pursuit and into another. The other answer choices would confuse the reader and harm the author's clarity. Choice (A) is correct.

10. B   **Difficulty:** Medium
Category: Sentence Formation

Getting to the Answer: Within complex sentences that contain parallel structure, make sure that verb conjugation, tense, and voice of the sentence are consistent. The underlined section is incorrect because it modifies a past-tense structure that was established earlier in the sentence with the phrase "He quickly found." The current construction blurs the author's clarity and intent. Choice (B) is correct because it is consistent with the past-tense structure already established.

11. D   Difficulty: Medium
Category: Usage

Getting to the Answer: Be aware of improper pronoun use, and keep in mind that not using a pronoun at all can also be incorrect. If the underlined section is a noun, consider whether a pronoun would be better suited for the quality of the narrative. Eisenstein's name is already mentioned in one other part of the sentence, so in this instance it is unnecessary to use it. A possessive pronoun is a better option as it improves the quality of the sentence by not unnecessarily repeating Eisenstein's name. Choice (D) is correct.

12. D   Difficulty: Medium
Category: Sentence Formation

Getting to the Answer: The correct use of modifiers includes vocabulary: making sure the word being used as a modifier has the appropriate definition for the context. Choice (D) is correct because "cumulative" is the correct word for the author's meaning. A montage is inherently cumulative: its meaning grows with the progression of each component shown.

13. C   Difficulty: Hard
Category: Sentence Formation

Getting to the Answer: Sentence fragments—stand-alone sentences that are missing either a subject or a predicate—should always be avoided because they are grammatically incorrect. Pay close attention to sentences that begin with "And," as they often can be combined with their preceding sentences. The sentence that begins with "And" is a sentence fragment because it has no subject. The best way to join this sentence with the previous sentence is to simply remove the period and make "And" lowercase. No other punctuation is needed. Choice (C) is correct.

14. A   Difficulty: Medium
Category: Sentence Formation

Getting to the Answer: Modifiers, while not always grammatically necessary, may be required for the author

to make a point or emphasize a detail. Scrutinize their use to determine which answer choice preserves the author's intent in the sentence and context. Choice (A) is correct because its use of the modifying phrases "enormously famous 1925 hit" and "1927 celebration of the October Revolution" is correct. Their use is also rhetorically effective, as it's clear to which film each refers, giving each movie context for the reader.

EXTRA PRACTICE

1. B   Difficulty: Medium
Category: Development

Getting to the Answer: Identify the common words in all the sentences of the opening paragraph. All the sentences in this paragraph refer to art as a form of communication throughout history, not to the devices required for digital communication; (B) is correct.

2. A   Difficulty: Easy
Category: Effective Language Use

Getting to the Answer: Determine how the word "prominent" is used in the sentence. The opening sentences of the passage describe art as a method of communication and the meeting place as an arena. Choice (A), "prominent," is an adjective meaning "noticeable," so it is the correct answer.

3. D   Difficulty: Easy
Category: Punctuation

Getting to the Answer: Determine whether the list of items is a series needing commas or semicolons. As the sentence is written, its many semicolons are unnecessary; none of the individual items in the list use commas. Since each item in the list is a simple word or phrase, commas are necessary, and choice (D) is correct.

4. C   Difficulty: Medium
Category: Effective Language Use

Getting to the Answer: Eliminate the redundant words from the sentence. Words with similar meanings, such as "create" and "craft," are unnecessary. Using the fewest words, choice (C) correctly conveys the meaning of the sentence.

5. B   **Difficulty:** Medium

Category: Effective Language Use

Getting to the Answer: Examine the sentence in relationship to the rest of the paragraph. The students are learning from the interactive settings, not teaching them. Choice (B), "hone," is the correct verb to describe how to sharpen or improve expertise.

6. D   **Difficulty:** Hard

Category: Organization

Getting to the Answer: Identify how the content of sentence 6 is related to the entire paragraph. The compilation of the portfolio happens as a result of the projects discussed in sentence 4 but before the graduates begin their job searches; (D) is correct.

7. A   **Difficulty:** Easy

Category: Punctuation

Getting to the Answer: Determine whether or not the two parts of the sentence can stand independently. The gerund phrase "taking on projects for external clients" cannot stand on its own because it lacks a subject. Choice (A) is correct.

8. C   **Difficulty:** Hard

Category: Development

Getting to the Answer: Identify the central idea of the paragraph in the topic sentence and the details presented in the support. The central idea is "graphic design features a variety of professional options." Only (C) supports the topic sentence because it identifies an option. All other choices discuss additional education or salary.

9. B   **Difficulty:** Easy

Category: Organization

Getting to the Answer: Determine the relationship between the two sentence parts. The two sentence parts present opposing ideas; (B), the subordinating conjunction "although," is correct.

10. C   **Difficulty:** Medium

Category: Sentence Formation

Getting to the Answer: Identify the two verbs describing how graphic designers feel about their careers. Parallel

ideas must be expressed in the same grammatical form. Correlative constructions require the transitive verb "satisfying" to be paired with the same form: "invigorating." Choice (C) is correct.

11. A   **Difficulty:** Hard

Category: Development

Getting to the Answer: Determine the main idea of the paragraph by closely examining the topic sentence. Choice (A) is the only option that adds relevant information to the rewards experienced by graphic designers in spite of the job competition.

CHAPTER 24

PRACTICE

5. B **Difficulty:** Medium
Category: Usage

Getting to the Answer: Make sure that comparisons use the correct construction that is aligned with the central idea and context of the passage. The author is making a comparison involving all North American animals—definitely a group larger than two. A superlative construction is appropriate, but it also needs to align with the thesis that the opossum is a very unusual animal. Choice (B) is correct because it is grammatically correct and fits the author's central idea.

6. D **Difficulty:** Medium
Category: Usage

Getting to the Answer: When a pronoun is the subject of a sentence, make sure that its antecedent is clear. If it is not clear to which noun the pronoun is referring, replace the pronoun with the appropriate noun. The current construction of the sentence creates an ambiguity: does "It" refer to the opossum or the kangaroo? Since the passage describes the characteristics of the opossum, this sentence should be about that animal as well. Choice (D) is correct because it makes the sentence's subject clear to the reader.

7. C **Difficulty:** Medium
Category: Usage

Getting to the Answer: Make sure that the proper prepositions are being used in the passage. The preposition "in" is incorrect, given the context. The author is describing "limitations *on* the amount of food . . . that can be stored . . ." Choice (C) is correct. If idioms are tricky, think of an analogous situation. A computer's limited warranty has limitations *on* the kinds of things you can do with it. It doesn't have limitations *in* those things.

8. C **Difficulty:** Easy
Category: Usage

Getting to the Answer: Review a pronoun's antecedent to make sure there is agreement throughout the sentence or section. Early in this sentence, the author establishes the singular possessive form ("the opossum's") as the antecedent of the pronoun in the underlined section. Also, except for an earlier section that discusses "the female opossum," the author uses the non-gendered pronoun "it" when referring to the animal. Choice (C) is correct because it is singular, possessive, and non-gendered.

PERFORM

9. A **Difficulty:** Medium
Category: Usage

Getting to the Answer: Read the sentence in its entirety to make sure there is no subject-verb disagreement. The verb in the underlined section, "were," appears after the parenthetical remark set aside by dashes. The current version of the subject, "airships," agrees with the verb. No change is necessary; choice (A) is correct.

10. B **Difficulty:** Medium
Category: Usage

Getting to the Answer: Make sure that comparisons are in the appropriate format—comparative when comparing two things, superlative when comparing three or more things. In the previous sentence, the author states that the *Hindenburg* was "one of a kind." The ship was unique out of all airships, making superlative descriptions appropriate. Given the superlative construction and the author's focus on the ship's dimensions, you can infer that the Hindenberg was the "largest" airship of its time. Choice (B) is correct.

11. C **Difficulty:** Medium
Category: Usage

Getting to the Answer: Complex sentences can often benefit from the use of pronouns, reducing wordiness and repetition. That said, make sure that the use of a pronoun will not introduce ambiguity into the sentence.

In a complicated sentence including multiple nouns, it is often better to avoid pronouns to preserve the clarity of the author's claims. Choice (C) is correct.

12. B   Difficulty: Hard
Category: Usage

Getting to the Answer: Check to see if the underlined section is part of an idiomatic expression, such as *either . . . or*. The sentence contains the first half of the idiomatic combination *not only . . . but also*. The use of "and" in this context is incorrect. Choice (B), "but also," is correct.

13. B   Difficulty: Easy
Category: Usage

Getting to the Answer: Pay attention to commonly confused words, such as *except* and *accept*, to make sure that careless mistakes do not go unaddressed in a passage. "It's" is a contraction of "it is" and is incorrect in this context. The sentence requires the singular possessive pronoun, "its." Choice (B) is correct.

14. C   Difficulty: Medium
Category: Usage

Getting to the Answer: Make sure the underlined section is using the appropriate preposition. If the verb "rest" refers to a direct object, the preposition "on" is required. Choice (C) is correct because it correctly constructs the idiom.

15. D   Difficulty: Easy
Category: Usage

Getting to the Answer: Examine any nouns that are used as synonyms within the same sentence. They should agree in number, and their shared meaning should either be easily understood or previously explained by the author. At this point in the passage, the author has already established that "balloon" is a synonym for "blimp" and "airship." The underlined section is therefore the correct term, but it disagrees in number with the rest of the sentence in which the associated noun ("airship") is singular. Choice (D) is correct because it is in numerical agreement with the previous noun.

16. B   Difficulty: Easy
Category: Usage

Getting to the Answer: Examine the sentence's use of pronouns for agreement with antecedents. The sentence's use of "their" as a possessive pronoun conflicts with the antecedent "the airship," which is singular. Choice (B) is correct because it is a singular possessive pronoun in agreement with its antecedent.

EXTRA PRACTICE

1. B   Difficulty: Medium
Category: Sentence Formation

Getting to the Answer: Compare the two parts of the sentence. Is the second part a subordinate or coordinate clause? "Since" is a conjunction used between subordinating ideas. These two clauses are coordinating and require a coordinating conjunction meaning "in addition to." Choice (B) is correct.

2. D   Difficulty: Medium
Category: Effective Language Use

Getting to the Answer: Analyze how the underlined word is used in the sentence. Test each answer choice to see if it improves the overall clarity of the text. The opening sentences of the passage are about how the cold weather makes starting cars difficult. When used as a verb, "credit" means to acknowledge (someone or something). Choice (D), "blame," means to hold responsible, and is correct.

3. D   Difficulty: Hard
Category: Organization

Getting to the Answer: Review how the content of sentence 3 is related to the entire paragraph. Recall that transitions help the reader understand logical relationships between ideas. What words in sentence 3 signal a transition? Sentence 4 explains what happens when the number of electrons increases. Because sentence 3 further develops the explanation of what happens when the number of electrons decreases, the transition "likewise" is a clue that it should follow sentence 4. Choice (D) is correct.

4. A   **Difficulty:** Hard
Category: Development

Getting to the Answer: Identify the key details in the paragraph. Then, summarize them to find the central idea. All of the sentences in this paragraph describe how a battery is constructed and works. Choice (A) is correct.

5. D   **Difficulty:** Easy
Category: Punctuation

Getting to the Answer: Determine if the items listed need to be treated as a series. Since there are only two items, no commas are needed. Choice (D) is correct.

6. C   **Difficulty:** Easy
Category: Usage

Getting to the Answer: Determine the tense and the number of the subject. Then, predict the verb form that matches. Since "lead oxide" is singular and the paragraph is written in present tense, choice (C) is correct.

7. C   **Difficulty:** Medium
Category: Effective Language Use

Getting to the Answer: Establish how the underlined word is used in the sentence; consider the connotations and denotations of the answer choices. Remember that the correct term should reflect the scientific subject matter. "Boundary" is a term meaning a limitation. "Circuit," a noun, is the scientific term that means circumference or course. Choice (C) is correct.

8. B   **Difficulty:** Hard
Category: Development

Getting to the Answer: Closely examine the topic sentence and the supporting details; identify the central idea of the paragraph. Choice (B) is the only option that adds supporting information about how a current flows through a battery charger.

9. D   **Difficulty:** Medium
Category: Effective Language Use

Getting to the Answer: Look at how the word is used in the sentence and analyze its grammatical function. Use context clues to determine which choice is correct. "Practicality" is an adverb meaning in a practical manner

and doesn't make sense here. "Probability" is a noun meaning likelihood, which is more appropriate. Choice (D) is correct.

10. A   **Difficulty:** Medium
Category: Usage

Getting to the Answer: Look for the antecedent of a pronoun to see if the pronoun agrees. The antecedent of "its" is "a battery," which is singular. The contraction "it's" is short for *it is* and is inappropriate here. Choice (A) is correct.

11. A   **Difficulty:** Hard
Category: Quantitative

Getting to the Answer: Study the graph carefully and consider how its data points connect to the content of the passage. The overall graph trend suggests that battery performance peaks at moderate temperatures, suffers slightly at higher temperatures, and declines greatly at lower ones. Since cold temperatures adversely affect the battery performance of an electric car, choice (A) is correct.

CHAPTER 25

PRACTICE

7. D   Difficulty: Easy
Category: Punctuation

Getting to the Answer: Use commas to separate three or more items forming a series or list. This series contains four items. Separate each item with a comma and use a comma with the conjunction "and" to separate the final item from the rest of the series. Choice (D) is correct.

8. C   Difficulty: Hard
Category: Punctuation

Getting to the Answer: When a period is underlined, make sure it's being used correctly. The period correctly separates two sentences but breaks up the flow of the ideas. The second sentence contributes useful information regarding the results of using the "12-note scale." Make the second sentence a modifying phrase, and connect it to the sentence with a comma. Choice (C) is correct.

9. B   Difficulty: Medium
Category: Punctuation

Getting to the Answer: When you see a phrase set off by commas, always read the sentence without the phrase to determine if the phrase is nonessential. Although the sentence is still grammatically correct without the information that is set off by the commas, an essential part of the meaning is lost. The author is stating that it is the group setting that distinguishes the improvisation found in jazz from the improvisation found in other types of music. Choice (B) properly removes the commas that set off the phrase.

10. A   Difficulty: Easy
Category: Punctuation

Getting to the Answer: When an underlined section features an apostrophe after a noun, check the noun's number. This sentence is correct as written. Although there are many styles of music, the noun "music" is a collective noun and singular. Choice (A) correctly uses the singular possessive.

PERFORM

11. B   Difficulty: Medium
Category: Punctuation

Getting to the Answer: When a comma is underlined, check to see if the parts of the sentence before and after the comma need to be separated. In this sentence, the comma separates the subordinate conjunction "although" from the clause it introduces and breaks the link between the dependent clause and the main clause. Choice (B) correctly eliminates the unnecessary punctuation.

12. C   Difficulty: Hard
Category: Punctuation

Getting to the Answer: Make sure period use is warranted—determine whether or not the sentences should really be separate. Although the second sentence is an independent clause and could stand on its own, the information in the second sentence belongs in the previous sentence. Choice (C) correctly uses a colon to indicate a break in thought to provide additional explanatory information.

13. D   Difficulty: Hard
Category: Punctuation

Getting to the Answer: A period separates independent clauses into sentences and indicates a strong break in thought. Make sure the context of the sentences requires them to be separated. Since both clauses form complete sentences, look at the information they share. Each sentence has Mauritius as its subject and a verb phrase providing information about the island. Combine the two sentences by creating a compound predicate joined by the conjunction "and." Choice (D) is correct.

14. A   Difficulty: Medium
Category: Punctuation

Getting to the Answer: Although a parenthetical or nonrestrictive phrase may appear in the beginning, middle, or end of a sentence, punctuation will always separate it from the rest of the sentence. Read the sentence without the parenthetical information to determine if the sentence still makes sense. This sentence is correct as written. Because the sentence makes logical sense without the phrase beginning with "making the dodo," the comma is necessary to correctly set off the phrase. Choice D may be tempting, but without the comma, the phrase incorrectly modifies "predators," suggesting that the predators themselves, not the dodo's failure to recognize the danger those predators posed, made the dodo easier to catch. Choice (A) is correct.

15. D   Difficulty: Easy
Category: Punctuation

Getting to the Answer: Separate three or more items in a series or list with commas. Separate the last two items with a comma and the conjunction "and." This series contains six distinct items. Separate each item with a comma and use the conjunction "and" with a comma to separate the final item from the rest of the series. Choice (D) is correct.

16. B   Difficulty: Easy
Category: Punctuation

Getting to the Answer: Watch out for easily confused words: keep straight your possessive determiners, contractions, and adverbs. "Who's" is a contraction for "who is" or "who has," which makes no sense in the context of the underlined portion. Choice (B) correctly uses "whose," the possessive form of the relative pronoun "who."

17. C   Difficulty: Medium
Category: Punctuation

Getting to the Answer: If a dash is used to introduce a break in thought, a second dash must be used to end the parenthetical phrase unless a period ends both the phrase and the sentence. Determine if the information after the dash is parenthetical or nonrestrictive by reading the sentence without that information. Although the phrase provides a description of how the "colonial powers" treated Mauritius, the sentence makes logical sense without it. The phrase is therefore parenthetical and must be properly set off. Only choice (C) correctly sets off the phrase with both an opening and closing dash.

18. A   Difficulty: Medium
Category: Punctuation

Getting to the Answer: Avoid using unnecessary punctuation. Reread the sentence to determine how its parts are related. This sentence is correct as written because

no punctuation is required. The phrase "through its advantageous geographic location and large labor force" completes the thought in the sentence by providing information on how Mauritius "balances" and "flourishes." Choice (A) is correct.

EXTRA PRACTICE

1. B   Difficulty: Medium
Category: Usage

Getting to the Answer: Consider the function of the underlined word in the sentence. The underlined word should be a plural possessive pronoun that refers to "coaches and trainers." Choice (B) is correct.

2. B   Difficulty: Medium
Category: Effective Language Use

Getting to the Answer: Think about the overall meaning of the sentence. Consider which answer choice most closely matches the author's intended meaning. The author explains that some people connect, or equate, the exercise-prompted burning feeling with burning calories. "Equate" is the most precise word to convey this meaning. Choice (B) is correct.

3. B   Difficulty: Medium
Category: Organization

Getting to the Answer: Two complete thoughts make up this sentence. Consider the relationship between the thoughts expressed on either side of the semicolon. The author presents contrasting ideas in this sentence. The relationship between these ideas is best expressed by inserting the transition word "instead" to indicate the contrast between the thoughts. Choice (B) is correct.

4. A   Difficulty: Hard
Category: Development

Getting to the Answer: The correct answer will include an idea that ties together all the information in the paragraph. Paraphrase the central idea into your own words. This paragraph is primarily about how muscles use glucose to get the energy they need to move. Choice (A) is correct because it most effectively states the central idea.

5. C   **Difficulty:** Medium
Category: Usage

Getting to the Answer: Identify the noun in the clause. Determine whether the noun is singular or plural and what verb tense is used elsewhere in the sentence. The noun "cells" in this clause is plural, and the rest of the sentence is written in present tense. Choice (C) is correct because it features the plural present tense form of the verb "to continue."

6. B   **Difficulty:** Medium
Category: Punctuation

Getting to the Answer: Determine the function of the phrase "found in vinegar" within the sentence. Remember that nonrestrictive elements must be set off from the rest of the sentence with commas before and after. The phrase "found in vinegar" modifies "acetic acid" and is not essential to the understanding of the sentence. Choice (B) is correct.

7. D   **Difficulty:** Medium
Category: Effective Language Use

Getting to the Answer: Reread the sentence with each of the answer choices in place of the underlined word. All of the answer choices are similar in meaning, so think about the connotation of each one in relation to the overall meaning of the sentence. In this sentence, the connotation of "irritates" most precisely communicates the meaning of what the author is trying to convey to the reader: bothers. While "annoys" is similar to this meaning, it is mostly used when referring to people, not inanimate or biological objects like lactic acid. Choice (D) is correct.

8. C   **Difficulty:** Medium
Category: Development

Getting to the Answer: Identify the central idea of paragraph 4. Think about which sentences are essential to understand the rest of the paragraph. The correct answer could be taken out without changing the meaning or the reader's understanding of the central idea. Although (C) is related to the central idea, the details in this sentence provide the least amount of support because they provide an example of a situation in which lactic acid builds up more quickly. The central idea of the paragraph, however, is the buildup and conversion of lactic acid during exercise. Choice (C) is correct.

9. C   **Difficulty:** Medium
Category: Punctuation

Getting to the Answer: Determine whether two complete thoughts are expressed in this sentence. Two complete sentences, each with a subject and predicate, become a run-on without proper punctuation. As written, this is a run-on sentence. Placing a semicolon between the two complete thoughts makes the sentence grammatically correct. Choice (C) is correct.

10. B   **Difficulty:** Easy
Category: Usage

Getting to the Answer: Read the entire sentence. Make sure that related pronouns agree in number and person. In this sentence, the author is referring to all human beings and uses "we" to do so. The underlined pronoun "you" does not match the use of the third person plural pronoun. Choice (B) is correct.

11. C   **Difficulty:** Hard
Category: Quantitative

Getting to the Answer: The correct answer will both reflect the information presented in the graph and be an appropriate conclusion for the passage. Avoid answers like B that do not strengthen the central idea of the passage. Choice (C) is correct because it contains details presented in the graph that are relevant to the central idea of the passage and because it provides an appropriate conclusion to the passage.

CHAPTER 26

PRACTICE

¶3: Second body paragraph

- **Introduce Feature 2 and provide a quote or paraphrase of the feature**

- Feature 2: Juxtaposition

  - ¶1 and ¶9: Stability vs. disorder: "strive for the values and ideals we believe in: freedom, justice" and "... the surest way to stability is through the very values of freedom, democracy and justice."

  - ¶2: Utilitarian vs. utopian: "more than ever before those two views are merging."

  - ¶4: Delayed vs. immediate information: slow communication of military battles in Queen Victoria's time vs. the immediate news reports of today

  - ¶5: Utilitarian vs. utopian views of international affairs: "So today, more than ever, 'their' problem becomes 'our' problem."

- **Specifically state how Feature 2 provides evidence to support the author's reasoning:** Provides evidence for author's reasoning by showing Blair's audience that the world has changed, and in the long run we must become one in common effort.

- **Discuss how Feature 2 reflects the author's thinking and the way the author ties his or her claim and evidence together:** Blair's repeated juxtapositions bring contrasts into sharp focus, making the alternatives crystal clear to the audience.

- **Analyze the effect Feature 2 is likely to have on the audience:** Emphasizes the need to present a united front, which reflects Blair's theme of world interdependence.

PERFORM

Prime Minister Blair also bolsters his argument by his use of juxtaposition, comparing situations and alternatives to show his audience that the world has changed, and in the long run we must become one in common effort. Blair notes the difference between stability and disorder in both the first and ninth paragraphs of this speech. He ties his discussion in the ninth paragraph with his opening statement by articulating that "the surest way to stability is through the very values of freedom, democracy and justice." In the second paragraph, he contrasts the utilitarian and utopian views of international affairs, not to give the audience a choice between the two but "to suggest that more than ever before those two views are merging." In the fourth paragraph he juxtaposes the slow communication of military battles in Queen Victoria's time with the immediate reports we see today, then follows this up in the fifth paragraph with "So today, more than ever, 'their' problem becomes 'our' problem." Blair puts quotation marks around the words "their" and "our" to emphasize that no one nation exists in isolation and no one problem is limited to one area. His repeated juxtapositions bring contrasts into sharp focus, making the alternatives crystal clear to the audience, while his emphasis on the need to present a united front again returns to his theme of world interdependence.

Answers & Explanations

EXTRA PRACTICE

Adapted from "Freedom or Death," a speech delivered by Emmeline Pankhurst on November 13, 1913, in Hartford, Connecticut

1   Mrs. Hepburn, ladies and gentlemen:

2   Tonight I am not here to advocate woman suffrage. American suffragists can do that very well for themselves. <u>I am here as a soldier who has temporarily left the field of battle in order to explain what civil war is like when civil war is waged by women.</u> I am here as a person who, according to the law courts of my country, it has been decided, is of no value to the community at all: and I am adjudged because of my life to be a dangerous person.

purpose

war metaphor

3   (Now,) first of all I want to make you understand the <u>inevitableness of revolution and civil war, even on the part of women,</u> when you reach a certain stage in the development of a community's life. It is quite easy for you to understand the desirability of revolution <u>if I were a man.</u> If an Irish revolutionary had addressed this meeting, and many have addressed meetings all over the United States during the last twenty or thirty years, it would not be necessary for that revolutionary to explain the need of revolution beyond saying that the people of his country were denied—and by people, meaning men—were denied the right of self-government. That would explain the whole situation. <u>If I were a man</u> and I said to you, "I come from a country which professes to have representative institutions and (yet) denies me, a taxpayer, an inhabitant of the country, representative rights," you would at once understand that that human being, being a man, was justified in the adoption of revolutionary methods to get representative institutions. (But) since I am a woman it is <u>necessary in the twentieth century to explain why women have adopted revolutionary methods in order to win the rights of citizenship.</u>

hypothetical

must do this bc woman

4   You see, (in spite of) a good deal that we hear about revolutionary methods not being necessary for American women, we women, in trying to make our case clear, always have to make as part of our argument, and urge upon men in our audience the fact—a very simple fact—that women are human beings. <u>I want to put a few political arguments before you—not arguments for the suffrage, because I said when I opened, I didn't mean to do that—but arguments for the adoption of militant methods in order to win political rights.</u>

kinds of arguments for ev.

5   (Suppose) the men of Hartford had a grievance, and they laid that grievance before their legislature, and the legislature obstinately refused to listen to them, or to remove their grievance, what would be the

more hypothet.

proper and the constitutional and the practical way of getting their grievance removed? Well, <u>it is perfectly obvious</u> at the next general election, when the legislature is elected, <u>the men of Hartford would turn out that legislature and elect a new one: entirely change the personnel of an obstinate legislature.</u>

6 (But) let the men of Hartford <u>imagine</u> that they were not in the position of being voters at all, that they were governed without their consent being obtained, that the legislature turned an absolutely deaf ear to their demands, what would the men of Hartford do then? They couldn't vote the legislature out. They would have to make a <u>choice of two evils</u>: they would either have to <u>submit indefinitely to an unjust state of affairs</u>, or they would have <u>to rise up and adopt some of the antiquated means by which men in the past got their grievances remedied</u>. We know what happened when <u>your forefathers</u> decided that they must have representation for taxation, many, many years ago. When they felt they couldn't wait any longer, when they laid all the arguments before an obstinate British government that they could think of, and when their arguments were absolutely disregarded, when every other means had failed, they began by the tea party at Boston, and they went on until they had won the independence of the United States of America. <u>That is what happened in the old days</u>.

effects of men not having rights

ex. of Am. Rev.

7 <u>It is perfectly evident to any (logical mind)</u> that when you have got the vote, you can get out of any legislature whatever you want, (or,) if you cannot get it, you can send them about their business and choose other people who will be more attentive to your demands. (But) it is clear to the meanest intelligence that if you have not got the vote, you must either submit to laws just or unjust, administration just or unjust, or <u>the time inevitably comes when you will revolt against that injustice and use violent means to put an end to it</u>.

war = inevitable

Sample Student Response #1

Though Emmeline Pankhurst is a militant suffragist, she has not come to Hartford, Connecticut, to speak about suffrage. No, she makes that clear with the first line of her speech. Pankhurst does not want to explain why woman suffrage is just and necessary; she has come to explain why the way that she and her fellow suffragists fight for suffrage is just and necessary. She has come to justify not her cause but her methods, not her ideas but her strategies, not her goals but her tactics. Pankhurst claims that the government, by denying women the vote to begin with, has left them with only protest and revolt as a means to win political change. With her masterful use of historical examples, comparison, and irony, she positions her speech as a defense of her methods, but in doing so, also affirms her cause.

From the start, Pankhurst use historical examples to support her claim that the fight for woman suffrage is not merely a difference of opinion but a battle, as were the historical battles fought for Independence and Union. She immediately references "civil war," and proclaims herself a soldier who has come away from the battlefield "to explain what civil war is like when civil war is waged by women." Though she does not specify the War Between the States—a war which, being won only 50 years earlier could well be in the experience of her audience—her allusion is clear. She is not a reformer, an activist, or an ideologue. She is a soldier! She further compares the tactics used by women to those of American revolutionaries. Deprived of political representation, they, "began by the tea party at Boston, and . . . went on until they had won the independence of the United States of America." She claims that if she were a male revolutionary (as her audience might have been "in the old days"), no one would deny the right of her methods; it is only because she is a female revolutionary that there is any question. Her historical references are not limited to those of our forefathers but also encompass those of Ireland, claiming that the men of Hartford would immediately understand the need for Irish revolution simply by being told—by a man—that "the people of his country were denied—and by people, meaning men—were denied the right of self-government." Pankhurst emphasizes that revolution has always been a means to redress wrongs, and clearly states that the only reason it is questioned today is because "women have adopted revolutionary methods in order to win the rights of citizenship." By reminding her audience of the legitimacy of revolution, she compels them to ask the question: "if right for men, why not for women?" hoping to begin their reevaluation of women's right to citizenship.

Recognizing that the more she can make men understand the suffragettes' position in light of their own, the more they might understand its cause and correctness, Pankhurst makes several telling comparisons. Not only does she compare the male revolutionaries' rights to militancy to those of women, but she also compares their rights as citizens to women who have no such rights. She speaks of what citizens (men only) may do if they are dissatisfied with the government: "They would have to make a choice of two evils: they would either have to submit indefinitely to an unjust state of affairs, or they would have to rise up and adopt some of the antiquated means by which men in the past got their grievances remedied." Her contention is that women now face the same choice, but barring their ability to "turn out that legislature and elect a new one," they would need to use the same "antiquated" methods. Furthermore, Pankhurst makes the bold and clear comparison between women "of no value to the community at all," and "a very simple fact—that women are human beings." Even her use of the words "your forefathers," rather than "our forefathers," makes a comparison: this country was founded by men, with little regard for women. In making the comparisons between the political wrongs her audience faced and those now faced by women, Pankhurst again appeals to their emotions and sense of logic – other than gender, what is the difference between the rights of men and those of women?

Finally, Pankhurst is masterful in her use of irony throughout her speech. She begins with the irony that legally, she does not exist as a person, but has been judged "a dangerous person" because of her insistence on being heard. She speaks of adopting "antiquated means ... many, many years ago," making militancy sound quaint and out of style, but supports it as a viable means of correcting wrongs. How ironic that the means that procured American independence is now deplored as "antiquated," merely because it is now in the wrong hands: those of women.

She addresses those of even the "meanest intelligence," pointing an imaginary finger at the self-satisfied men in her audience, giving them the benefit of logic which must bring them to the conclusion that, at this point, women have no other way to gain the vote but by revolutionary methods. Indeed, it is ironic that she consistently abjures the label of "suffragette" in favor of "soldier." Her rhetoric conflates the two, for the cause is one and the same. The irony of "us" vs. "them," when in reality all are human beings deserving of the same rights, brings the political divide home to the audience and undermines their ill-conceived and unjust assumptions.

Emmeline Pankhurst is a forceful, intelligent speaker, whose message to the men of Hartford is vigorous and assertive: female submission is not an option; the right to citizenship with its concomitant right to vote is just, and the same means by which men fought for freedom is a legitimate means open to women. She points out the historical acceptance of militancy, the comparisons between the choices American men faced when ill-used by England and those women face when ill-used by their government, and the incongruity between women's logical right to citizenship and the real state of affairs. Each element of her speech supports her primary idea, each one is intended to provoke the audience to rethink their stance either by logic or by inferred reproach, and each one goes beyond Pankhurst's stated reason for the speech to support the "inevitableness of revolution and civil war" to underscore that women will not stop until equality is achieved.

Reading—4: This writer demonstrates thorough comprehension of the source text. The writer clearly identifies Pankhurst's central purpose (*to explain why the way that she and her fellow suffragists fight for suffrage is just and necessary*), identifies important details, and skillfully includes textual evidence.

Analysis—4: This writer demonstrates a comprehensive understanding of the analytical task by developing a critical review of the source text. The writer identifies pieces of evidence Pankhurst uses and explains their importance in regard to the central argument.

Writing—4: This response is cohesive and demonstrates highly developed skill in the use and control of standard written English. The writer includes fully reasoned introduction and conclusion paragraphs that enhance the comprehensiveness of the essay. There is an intentional progression of ideas both within and among paragraphs. The writer includes a variety of sentence structures, demonstrates thoughtful word choice, and sustains a scholarly style and tone throughout the essay.

Sample Student Response #2

Emmeline Pankhurst does appear in Hartford, Connecticut, to speak about suffrage. From the start of her speech, she makes clear that she does not want to explain why woman suffrage is necessary. Rather, she means to explain why the way that she and her fellow suffragists fight for suffrage is necessary. Pankhurst looks at the battle for woman suffrage as a civil war. She calls herself a soldier sent to explain her tactics in the war, not the importance of her side in the war. In her speech, Pankhurst explains that she and the suffragists must use violent means to win change because it is the only means open to them. She asserts that they cannot win reform any other way precisely because suffrage is denied to them. In this way, she uses her defense of her methods to actually justify the underlying cause—suffrage for women.

Pankhurst grabs her audience's attention by calling woman suffrage not just a political debate but a civil war. In the same way, she makes herself more than a reformer or an activist; she declares herself a soldier. In this way, she gets men and woman to listen to what she has to say. Her references to revolution and civil war also call up America's own history, rooted in political revolt. In addition to this comparison, she compares the struggle of suffragists with that of Irish revolutionaries. Not only is the woman suffrage movement a political revolution, she seems to say, but also women (revolutionary and otherwise) are equal with men. If she were a man, she says no one would doubt her right to revolt, but because she's a woman, she and her fellow suffragists have to explain themselves.

Pankhurst also claims that the struggle for suffrage is really a fight for "the rights of citizenship." She implies that by denying women the right to vote, the government is denying them citizenships. In using this rhetoric, she makes the idea that suffrage is something to which women are entitled as citizens clear. This means that to deny woman suffrage is to deny them as citizens. She goes on to say "that women are human beings," making the debate over suffrage also a denial of women's humanity. By doing this, Pankhurst tries to appeal to her audience's emotions and sympathies. She begins by talking about the way she works for political change, but by calling attention to the battle and to women as citizens and humans, she really makes the case for suffrage itself.

Finally, Pankhurst ties it all together in her final paragraph. She even suggests that reason itself is on her side by stating that it's "perfectly evident to any logical mind" and "clear to the meanest intelligence" that if you can vote, you can change government peacefully, while if you can't vote, you have to resort to other means. For this reason, using even violent means of protest and revolt to win suffrage is just. Pankhurst concludes by claiming that her tactics are needed precisely because women can't vote. This argument rests on the assumption that woman suffrage itself is right and necessary, and in a circular kind of way, ends up defending suffrage as well as the tactics to win suffrage.

Reading—2: This writer demonstrates some comprehension of the source text. The writer shortly relates an overview of Pankhurst's central purpose (*she does not want to explain why woman suffrage is necessary*). However, the writer does not go beyond what can be interpreted from Pankhurst's speech and misunderstands some important details. There is very little textual evidence used in the response.

Analysis—2: This writer demonstrates a partial understanding of the analytical task, offering a limited analysis of the source text. The writer is able to identify pieces of evidence Pankhurst uses, but is ineffective in explaining their importance in regard to the central argument. Also, the lack of direct quotations or paraphrases from the text leaves much of the writer's analysis unsubstantiated. There is also a lack of focus on the features of the text most relevant to furthering Pankhurst's central argument.

Writing—2: This response has little cohesion and demonstrates limited skill in the use and control of standard written English. Rather than using the introduction and conclusion as touchstones of the response, the writer merely uses the four paragraphs (including the two body paragraphs) to describe Pankhurst's argument as it unfolds. There is limited progression of ideas within paragraphs but this progression is absent from the overall response. The sentence structures utilized are repetitive and the style and tone are nowhere near as formal and objective as they should be. While there are some careless grammatical and spelling errors, they do not detract from the author's intended meaning.

CHAPTER 27

PRACTICE

¶1: Introductory paragraph

- **Introductory statement:** *David Foster Wallace argues that while language is inherently political, how society expresses itself is a product of preexisting attitudes.*

- **Paraphrase the author's central idea or claim:** *Politically Correct English (PCE) is dangerous because using "politically correct" language doesn't get rid of elitism or unfairness.*

- **Specifically state the Features the author uses to support the central idea or claim**

  - *Feature 1: Diction*

  - *Feature 2: Appeal to authority*

  - *Feature 3: Juxtaposition*

¶2: First body paragraph

- **Introduce Feature 1 and provide a quote or paraphrase of the feature**

  - Feature 1: Diction

    - *¶1: "insensitive and elitist and offensive and unfair"*

    - *¶2: "taken very seriously indeed"*

- **Specifically state how Feature 1 provides evidence to support the author's reasoning:** *Helps him subtly convey his central argument by using both politically correct and incorrect diction to make a point about language itself.*

- **Discuss how Feature 1 reflects the author's thinking and the way the author ties his or her claim and evidence together:** *Using informal and formal language side-by-side reinforces the fact that language itself, whether politically correct or not, is not indicative of societal attitudes.*

- **Analyze the effect Feature 1 is likely to have on the audience:** *By alternating between formal and informal diction, the author keeps the audience interested, which promotes further discussion.*

PERFORM

In his essay on the use of language, David Foster Wallace asserts that it is dangerous to promote strict use of Politically Correct English (PCE) because the use of PCE alone does not automatically make someone politically correct. Wallace effectively conveys the argument that PCE does not reverse instances of elitism or unfairness by using contrasting diction, appeals to authority, and juxtaposition.

Throughout the essay, Wallace uses both informal, colloquial diction and professional, academic diction. The seamless overlap of these two extremes not only forces Wallace's audience to pay attention but also reinforces the central argument that language itself, whether politically correct or not, is not indicative of societal attitudes or beliefs. In the first paragraph, Wallace writes that the "political realities of American life are themselves racially insensitive and elitist and offensive and unfair." The four adjectives Wallace uses to describe American political realities are progressively informal: "insensitive" could be considered PCE, while "unfair" evokes a child's temper tantrum. The use of four words that are similar in meaning but vary in sophistication to describe one concept strengthens Wallace's assertion that a point can be conveyed regardless of the type of language employed. The italicized word "indeed" in the second paragraph ("taken very seriously indeed") serves to emphasize that "prescriptive PCE is . . . silly." By highlighting the word "indeed" through italicization, Wallace underscores that the word itself does not enhance the statement in which it appears, but is merely a construction to enhance political correctness. By using both politically correct and incorrect diction, Wallace subtly enhances his central argument about how politically correct language is "sort of funny in a dark way, maybe."

EXTRA PRACTICE

Adapted from Vice President Spiro Agnew's 1969 speech "Television News Coverage."

1   Tonight I want to discuss the importance of the television news medium to the American people. No nation depends more on the intelligent judgment of its citizens. No medium has a more profound influence over public opinion. So, nowhere should there be more conscientious responsibility exercised than by the news media.

> SA: TV should be responsible

2   Monday night a week ago, President Nixon delivered the <u>most important address</u> of his Administration, one of the <u>most important of our decade.</u> His subject was Vietnam. My hope, as his at that time, was to rally the American people to see the conflict through to a lasting and just peace in the Pacific. For 32 minutes, he reasoned with a nation that has suffered <u>almost a third of a million casualties in the longest war</u> in its history.

> dramatic lang. emphasizes importance

3   When the President completed his address—an address, incidentally, that <u>he spent weeks</u> in the preparation of—his words and policies were subjected to <u>instant analysis and querulous criticism.</u> The audience of 70 million Americans was inherited by a small band of network commentators and self-appointed analysts, the majority of whom expressed in one way or another their hostility to what he had to say.

> imagery = band of commentators

4   (It was obvious) that their minds were made up in advance. Those who recall the fumbling and groping that followed President Johnson's dramatic disclosure of his intention not to seek another term have seen these men in a genuine state of nonpreparedness. This was not it.

> contrast w/ Johnson

5   (One) commentator twice contradicted the President's statement about the exchange of correspondence with Ho Chi Minh.[1] (Another) challenged the President's abilities as a politician. A (third) asserted that the President was following a Pentagon line. (Others) by the expressions on their faces, the tone of their questions, and the sarcasm of their responses, made clear their sharp disapproval.

> supporting data = examples of bias

6   To guarantee in advance that the President's plea for national unity would be challenged, one network <u>trotted out</u> Averell Harriman for the occasion. All in all, Mr. Harriman offered a broad range of gratuitous advice challenging and contradicting the policies outlined by the President of the United States. Where the President had issued a call for unity, Mr. Harriman was encouraging the country not to listen to him.

> AH = evidence of agenda

7   Now every American has a right to disagree with the President of
    the United States and to express publicly that disagreement. (But) the
    President of the United States has a right to communicate directly with
    the people who elected him, and the people of this country have the
    right to make up their own minds.

call to arms

8   When Winston Churchill rallied public opinion to stay the course
    against Hitler's Germany, he didn't have to contend with a gaggle of
    commentators raising doubts about whether he was reading public
    opinion right, or whether Britain had the stamina to see the war
    through. When President Kennedy rallied the nation in the Cuban
    missile crisis, his address to the people was not chewed over by a
    roundtable of critics who disparaged the course of action he'd asked
    America to follow.

*parallel examples: WC
rallying public vs Hitler;
JFK rallying U.S. in crisis*

*media left
them alone*

9   At least 40 million Americans every night, it's estimated, watch the
    network news. Seven million of them view ABC, the remainder being
    divided between NBC and CBS. According to Harris polls and other
    studies, for millions of Americans the networks are the sole source of
    national and world news.

10 Now how is this network news determined? A small group of anchormen,
    commentators, and executive producers settle upon the 20 minutes or
    so of film and commentary that's to reach the public. This selection is
    made from the 90 to 180 minutes that may be available. Their powers of
    choice are broad.

*contrast: small # elites
vs millions*

11 They decide what 40 to 50 million Americans will learn of the day's
    events in the nation and in the world. These men can create national
    issues overnight. They can make or break by their coverage and
    commentary a moratorium on the war. They can elevate men from
    obscurity to national prominence within a week. They can reward some
    politicians with national exposure and ignore others.

*repetition of "they"
& "they can" →
emphasizes media power*

12 The views of the majority of this fraternity do *not*—and I repeat, not—
    represent the views of America. Not only did the country receive the
    President's speech more warmly than the networks, but so also did the
    Congress of the United States.

13 Yesterday, the President was notified that 300 individual Congressmen
    and 50 Senators of both parties had endorsed his efforts for peace. As
    with other American institutions, perhaps it is time that the networks
    were made more responsive to the views of the nation and more
    responsible to the people they serve.

*central idea = media should
reflect how "the nation"
feels but not distort or
persuade them*

[1]Ho Chi Minh—president of North Vietnam, the enemy of the U.S. in the Vietnam War

Sample Student Response #1

While many people today get their news from different online sources, in the 1960s, a majority of Americans got their news from newspapers and television networks. Television in particular was a popular source of news, and presidents like Richard Nixon sometimes used it to communicate policy decisions to the American people. After Nixon gave a televised address about Vietnam, some network news correspondents disagreed with the president's position. Vice President Agnew disagreed with the network's criticism of the president's address. His argument? Network news coverage unduly influenced and did not accurately reflect popular opinion of the president's position on Vietnam.

After giving his implicit support for the president's address, Agnew begins his critique of the networks by explaining their outsize influence relative to the number of Americans who watch the news. He notes that at least 40 million people watch the news, yet what they see on the programs is decided by a relatively small number of people like producers and commentators. Then he explains this outsize influence by writing that they can "create national issues overnight," they can "elevate men from obscurity," and even "reward some politicians with national exposure." This is true today as it was then, but how does Agnew feel about this influence? The reader can see Agnew's opinion in the language he uses. For example, he describes news analysts as "self-appointed," which diminishes the reliability of their opinion in the reader's eyes.

Agnew does not restrict his criticism of network coverage to undue influence. He also argues that the opinion expressed on the networks did not accurately reflect that of Americans as a whole. His evidence for this idea can be seen in the last paragraph where he explains that over 300 congressmen and 50 senators "endorsed his efforts for peace." This implies that the will of Congress is also that of the American people. He also explicitly attacks Averell Harriman by contrasting Harriman's position with the president's, noting that other leaders such as Churchill and Kennedy were not criticized by media pundits. Agnew does this to equate the popular choices these leaders made during World War II and the Cuban Missile Crisis with Nixon's choices about Vietnam. The implication is that Churchill and Kennedy were correct, so Nixon must be too.

Throughout his speech, Agnew portrays the news networks as a minority of people with undue influence who are presenting an outsize opinion of Nixon's speech that does not "represent the views of America." In the end, the reader is left questioning the veracity and reliability of media coverage, something that many Americans continue to do today in the age of the Internet.

Reading—4: The writer demonstrates thorough understanding of the source text as evidenced by use of direct quotations and paraphrases. The writer succinctly and accurately relays Agnew's central idea at the end of the introductory paragraph (*Network news coverage unduly influenced and did not accurately reflect popular opinion of the president's position on Vietnam*). The writer also references and cites many important details of Agnew's speech, making sure to interrelate them to the central idea. For example, at the end of the third paragraph, the writer states, *Agnew does this to equate the popular choices these leaders made during World War II and the Cuban Missile Crisis with Nixon's choices about Vietnam. The implication is that Churchill and Kennedy were correct, so Nixon must be too.* This response demonstrates thorough comprehension of the source text.

Analysis—3: This response offers effective analysis of the source text and demonstrates an understanding of the analytical task. The third paragraph is stronger than the second paragraph in that the writer cites evidence Agnew uses to support a claim and proceeds to explain why this evidence serves to advance Agnew's central argument. However, the second body paragraph is merely a summary of Agnew's speech.

Writing—3: The writer demonstrates effective use and control of standard written English in this mostly cohesive response. The introduction is not as focused as it should be; the writer focuses more on providing background information to Agnew's speech than presenting his or her own central claim. The manner in which the writer introduces his or her interpretation of Agnew's central idea (*His argument?*) is a bit too casual for an SAT Essay. Overall, the writing in this response is proficient. While the response is well written and conforms to standard written English, the fact that the writer does not provide his or her own central claim lowers the Writing score.

Sample Student Response #2

Today people get their news from different places like the Internet and television. But back in the 1960s, it was mainly from newspapers and television. Lots of people watched television news and presidents like Richard Nixon would explain their decisions on television to the American people. Nixon gave a speech about Vietnam and people on network news disagreed with what he said. In response, Vice President Agnew gave his own speech to support President Nixon. Agnew thought that the opinion of many in the network news was wrong because it was different than the opinion of a majority of Americans.

In his speech, we can see Agnew thinks they have too much power to influence opinion. He supports that idea with statements like the networks can "create national issues overnight" and "elevate men from obscurity." He doesn't think a small number of people should be able to do that.

We can also see that Agnew thinks a majority of Americans disagree with the opinion shown on networks. He says that a majority of Congress thinks that Nixon is right about Vietnam, so he probably thinks a lot of Americans must support Nixon's ideas about Vietnam too. He says that people supported Churchill and Kennedy, so they should support Nixon now. This is a good comparison, because he makes the readers think Nixon is a good leader like Kennedy and Churchill.

In conclusion, Agnew supports Nixon and doesn't approve of how the news networks are talking about him. He thinks the president knows what he's talking about when it comes to Vietnam. But now that we have the Internet, people have a choice about where to get their news.

Reading—2: This writer demonstrates some comprehension of the source text. The writer understands the surface function and central idea of Agnew's speech, but does not delve into important details; rather, he or she sticks to sweeping generalizations. Furthermore, the last sentence of the essay (*But now that we have the Internet, people have a choice about where to get their news*) veers from not only the central idea of Agnew's speech but also goes beyond the scope of the SAT Essay task.

Analysis—2: This writer demonstrates a partial understanding of the analytical task, offering a limited analysis of the source text. The writer summarizes Agnew's position and uses the third paragraph to partly discuss a comparison Agnew makes, but instead of accurately explaining how this comparison helps his argument, the writer qualifies it as "good." (*This is a good comparison, because he makes the readers think Nixon is a good leader like Kennedy and Churchill*)

Writing—2: This response has little cohesion and demonstrates limited skill in the use and control of standard written English. The writer never asserts his or her own central claim but merely describes the circumstances surrounding Agnew's speech. The lack of varied sentence structure and overuse of the third person plural (*we*) also contribute to this low Writing score. Overall, the language used is far too casual for an SAT Essay response.